Strategic Portfolio Management

This book provides a powerful insight into strategic portfolio management and its central role in the delivery of organisational strategy, maximisation of value creation, and efficient allocation of resources and capabilities to achieve organisational strategic objectives. The book makes a valuable contribution to the development of thinking on the translation of strategy into actionable work. Whether you are a senior manager building a high-performing strategic portfolio for your organisation or an academic searching for new perspectives on strategy execution through portfolio management, you will find great significance in this book. Twenty-eight chapters in four sections provide multiple perspectives on the topic, with in-depth guidance on organisational design for strategic portfolio management and covering all process, capability, and leadership aspects of strategic portfolio management. The book includes several detailed case studies for the effective deployment of strategic portfolios, bringing together theory and practice for strategic portfolio management. This book is particularly valuable for advanced undergraduate and postgraduate students of project and portfolio management, strategic management, and leadership who are looking to expand their knowledge within the multi-project environment. Highly practical and logical in its structure, it also shows project management professionals how to effectively manage their business portfolios and align this with their business strategy.

Katy Angliss is Associate Professor at the University of Warwick and, as an academic in the discipline of program and project management, has worked with many students and professionals, specialising in the area of multi-project and portfolio management. Prior to joining Warwick, as a chartered engineer, Katy has had over 20 years' experience working in the field of portfolios, programs, and projects.

Pete Harpum is Professeur Affilié de Management des Biotechnologies at Grenoble Ecole de Management, Module Director and External Examiner for Design Management at University College London, and visiting faculty for Portfolio, Program, and Project Management at the University of Warwick. Pete's consultancy work is focused on helping organisations to successfully navigate change in how they deliver strategic objectives.

"Delivering Strategic Portfolios"

Strategic Portfolio Management

In the Multi-Project and Program Organisation

Edited by Katy Angliss and Pete Harpum

Routledge
Taylor & Francis Group
LONDON AND NEW YORK

Designed cover image: © Getty Images

First published 2023
by Routledge
4 Park Square, Milton Park, Abingdon, Oxon OX14 4RN

and by Routledge
605 Third Avenue, New York, NY 10158

Routledge is an imprint of the Taylor & Francis Group, an informa business

British Library Cataloguing-in-Publication Data
A catalogue record for this book is available from the British Library

ISBN: 978-0-367-42505-0 (hbk)
ISBN: 978-0-367-42503-6 (pbk)
ISBN: 978-0-367-85312-9 (ebk)

DOI: 10.4324/9780367853129

Typeset in Bembo
by Apex CoVantage, LLC

Access the Support Material: www.routledge.com/9780367425050

Contents

Foreword

Whether as an entrepreneur, government minister, or business leader, two challenges have remained consistent across the varied leadership roles I have held. Firstly, how to set the right objectives for my organisation, recognising that these will have to change over time. Secondly, how to balance the competing priorities, resource demands, and need for management attention of the various programs and projects set up to achieve those objectives.

The questions these challenges raise will be familiar to any leader. Are we confident we are pursuing the right projects to deliver our strategic goals? Are the objectives and strategies of the programs and projects aligned to organisational strategy and to each other? What combination of projects creates the maximum value to the organisation? Do we understand the resource implications of this set of projects? Are we prioritising the projects to ensure optimal use of finances, people, equipment, space, etc.? What is the risk profile flowing from this set of projects in comparison to the anticipated value they will create?

Katy Angliss and Pete Harpum argue in this book that the answers to these fundamental questions are best provided through effective strategic portfolio management. An approach that, by definition, makes portfolio management strategic, as opposed to being a group of tactical and analytical processes. They position strategic portfolio management firmly in the space of business management, lifting it from the more commonly held view of being the concern primarily of the project management community.

It is rarely the case that a single project or program can deliver the entire objective of an organisation, meaning, that in most organisations, strategic value must be delivered across a portfolio of projects and programs. The first section of the book sets the theoretical definition for this approach, recognising that every portfolio is specific to each organisation and context. By understanding and assessing the aggregated benefits of each part of the portfolio to the overall purposes and needs of the business, portfolio management can ensure that projects and programs within the portfolio are continuously managed against strategic objectives, even as the strategic portfolio is affected by uncertain and complex organisational and external factors demanding change.

Building a reliable, robust, and effective framework to manage the strategic portfolio, whether at the operational, business, or corporate level, is clearly essential to delivering strategic objectives. Section II of the book looks at the core components of strategic portfolio management, from organisational integration through to design of the process, in selecting projects and programs for the portfolio. Following this, Section III takes us through the needed support activities for strategic portfolio management, including resource management, effective governance with data management, and portfolio leadership.

Finally, within Section IV, detailed case study chapters provide an insight into how theory is evident in practice. Comprehensive, real-world examples are discussed and, in the process, demonstrate the value of strategic portfolio management, through the successful delivery of organisational strategic objectives.

By being given both a theoretical perspective on what portfolio management is and practical examples of its effective deployment, the reader of this book gains a powerful insight into how strategic portfolio management contributes to the delivery of organisational strategy, maximises value, and effectively allocates resources and capabilities, whilst balancing capacity, risk, and financial constraints, in achieving the overarching aims of the business moving forward.

Whether you are a senior manager building a high-performing strategic portfolio for your organisation or an academic searching for new perspectives on strategy execution through portfolio management, you should find this book of real significance, gaining a thorough appreciation of strategic portfolio management.

Margot James
Chair, Warwick Manufacturing Group, University of Warwick,
Former Government Minister, and Business Leader

Margot James has had a wide-ranging career in both business and politics. In 1986, Margot co-founded a public relations and medical education business, Shire Health Group, sold in 2004. She is former Minister of Culture, Communications, and Creative Industries for the UK government, has been a member of Parliament for Stourbridge for nearly ten years, and held other government positions, including Assistant Government Whip, Parliamentary Private Secretary, and Parliamentary Under-Secretary of State with the Minister for Small Business, Consumers, and Corporate Responsibility.

Contributors

Katy Angliss is Associate Professor at the University of Warwick and, as an academic in the discipline of Program and Project Management, has worked with many students and professionals, specialising in the area of multi-project and portfolio management. Prior to joining Warwick, as a chartered engineer, Katy has had over 20 years' experience working as a project and program manager, predominantly within telecommunications and utilities, having knowledge of New Product Introduction, working with portfolios of projects, leading large transformation programs, and being involved with several strategic change projects, programs, and portfolios within different industrial sectors. Katy is also a subject reviewer for academic journals, presented at various conferences, and has worked with a range of organisations and individuals in developing portfolio management capabilities.

Paul Clarke has worked for over 25 years in the project management arena, including as Senior Project manager at EDF Energy, as Principal Engineering Manager at EDF Energy Renewables, and currently, as Project Director at Urenco Group. Paul became interested in portfolio management maturity whilst completing his MSc with Distinction at the University of Warwick, in the Warwick Manufacturing Group.

Darren Dalcher is Professor in Strategic Project Management at Lancaster University Management School and Founder and Director of the National Centre for Project Management. He is a Visiting International Scholar at InnoLab, University of Vaasa. Darren has been named by the Association for Project Management (APM) as one of the top ten "movers and shapers" in project management and was voted Project Magazine's "Academic of the Year" for his contribution in "integrating and weaving academic work with practice". Professor Dalcher is Honorary Fellow of the APM and Chartered Fellow of the British Computer Society. He has written over 300 papers and book chapters on project management and software engineering. He is Editor-in-Chief of the *Journal of Software: Evolution and Process*, a leading international software engineering journal, and Editor of two established book series focused on managing projects and change initiatives, published by Routledge. He is the academic advisor, author, and co-editor of the highly influential seventh edition of the *APM Body of Knowledge*.

Adrian Dooley is the lead author of the Praxis framework, a predominantly online free resource for the management of projects, programs, and portfolios, with over 40 years' experience in industry. After being involved with project planning software in the 1980s, Adrian set up his own training and consultancy company, which he led for over 20 years. Adrian was a founding member of *Project Manager Today* magazine and is an honorary fellow of the Association for Project Management, having served on the APM Council. Adrian has published a wide range of newspaper, magazine articles, and journal papers and contributed to other publications on projects, programs, and portfolio management.

David Dunning has been involved with projects, programs, and portfolios for over 20 years and is the founder of the Core P3M Data Club, a voluntary initiative delivering public domain content across business governance, assurance, and data. David is also the founder of Deepteam, a consultancy specialising in "strategy to delivery to objective realisation" with the business integrated governance (BIG) model. David started his career with Westland Helicopters and moved into project management, working with various organisations, before working freelance with customers such as Balfour Beatty and Sainsbury's, forming CPS, a project management solutions and recruitment company in 1995. The company expanded to work with a portfolio of Microsoft technology solutions, with David as the head of professional services and latterly chair. David is an APMG-registered consultant, certified management consultant. He has accreditations in portfolio, program, project management, and P3 offices.

Stuart Forsyth is Honorary Professor at Alliance Manchester Business School (AMBS) and Director, Advanced Sensors, at BAE Systems Air. Prior to his current role, Stuart was Project Management Director for BAE Systems Group and led the introduction of many initiatives aimed at improving the standard of project, program, and portfolio management across the company. This including conceiving and supporting the development with AMBS of a major executive PM development program called LCP3 (Leading Complex Project, Programme and Portfolio Management). He has over 20 years' experience in bidding, establishing, and delivering complex engineering programs within the military aerospace sector, all with international dimensions. These days, Stuart spends a lot of time reviewing such programs as part of the company assurance process. Stuart is also a trustee on the Board of the Association for Project Management (APM).

Carl Gavin is Senior Lecturer in Project Management at Alliance Manchester Business School (AMBS), University of Manchester, and is Director of several bespoke executive education programs for multinational companies delivering complex projects – on project management, project leadership, and project sponsorship. Carl has 35 years' experience in project management, directing and managing large-scale projects for a diverse range of businesses and public-sector organisations, and, prior to joining AMBS, was Managing Director of a projects-based business in the North West of England.

Pete Harpum is *Professeur Affilié de Management des Biotechnologies* at Grenoble Ecole de Management, Module Director and External Examiner for Design Management at University College London, and Visiting Faculty for Portfolio, Program, and Project Management at the University of Warwick. He is Editor of the standard reference text *Portfolio, Program, and Project Management in the Pharmaceutical and Biotechnology Industries* (Wiley) and has contributed to several other reference texts in the project management field. His research areas include managing creative design in project environments, organisational dynamics and leadership development, and portfolio, program, and project management leadership competencies. He has a PhD from the University of Manchester, UK. Pete's work as a partner-level management consultant is focused on helping organisations to successfully navigate major transformational change in how they deliver strategic objectives.

David Hillson, as "The Risk Doctor", is a recognised global authority and author of many publications on project risk management, having worked internationally as a speaker and consultant on the subject of risk management for many years. David has more than eleven books published and over 100 journal articles.

Catherine Killen is the director of the postgraduate project management program at the University of Technology Sydney (UTS). She has a background in mechanical engineering and ten years of industry experience in projects for product development, innovation, and the introduction of new technologies. Catherine has published more than 75 journal articles, book chapters, and conference papers based on her research in project portfolio management. Current research themes explore strategic multi-project management practices in a variety of contexts; the role of visualisations in portfolio decision-making; tools for managing interdependencies between projects; and the establishment of sensemaking capabilities to improve project management practice.

Carol A. Long has a career of more than three decades in professional management, specialising in improving engineering management and governance associated with project portfolios. She has worked in global technology companies, the public sector, smaller enterprises, and not-for-profit organisations as a manager and P3M consultant. She is a visiting fellow at WMG at the University of Warwick and an external associate at Arden University, supporting the development of courses in international project management. She is an external examiner for a leading corporate governance professional body. Carol has 20-plus years' involvement in working groups to develop international professional standards, most recently focusing on AI system design and ethics. She contributed to three editions of the APM Body of Knowledge and other APM publications, including *Directing Change: A Guide to Governance of Project Management.* She has also contributed to the PMI project management body of knowledge and IEEE international standards. Carol holds European Engineer status, is Chartered Fellow of the British Computer Society, Chartered Information Technology Professional, and Chartered Engineer. She is also Fellow of the Royal Society for Arts, Manufacturers and Commerce (FRSA) and a member of the Chartered Management Institute.

Donnie MacNicol is passionate about developing leadership capabilities of individuals, teams, and organisations for strategic delivery success. As an experienced project and program leader, he works with a wide range of organisations, including technology, infrastructure, aerospace, and governments, focusing on the improvement of delivery and leadership capability. Donnie is an associate at several universities, including Warwick, and has presented at over 150 events and conferences. Previously, Donnie has chaired the PMI UK Chapter OPM Forum and APM's People Special Interest Group. Donnie is a published author in this field of P3M leadership, with over 30 articles and publications.

Miia Martinsuo, DSc (Tech.), is Professor of Industrial Management at Tampere University, Department of Industrial Engineering and Management. Her field of research and teaching is project and service business. Her current research interests include project-based organizing, multi-project management, the autonomy and control of projects, managing manufacturing and process innovations, industrial service operations and innovations, and organisational transformation towards service business.

Steve Messenger is an agile and DSDM (dynamic systems development method) trainer, coach, and consultant as CEO of Herald Associates Ltd. Steve started his career in project management and business support with Napp before becoming part of the senior management team for Mundipharma IT services, responsible for portfolio management, resource management, and development of standards and procedures. Steve was Chair of the Agile Business Consortium for nearly ten years and is an international author of various agile methodologies best practice publications.

Aleksandar Nikolov is undertaking a full-time PhD at WMG, University of Warwick. The PhD project is a prime example of applying academic leadership to industry challenges and is a cross-organisational, cross-functional, and cross-learning opportunity. Before joining the project, Aleksander spent nine years in education and industry. After completing an undergraduate degree at Oxford Brookes University, Aleksandar completed an MSc at Cranfield University, specialising in logistics and supply chain management. After graduation, Aleksandar has worked as a consultant and project manager on projects in the oil and gas, infrastructure, and public services sectors in the UK and internationally.

Jayne Redfern recently retired as an associate professor at WMG at the University of Warwick after several successful years introducing leading edge project management postgraduate courses. Jayne previously worked as a consultant in program, portfolio, and project management and, prior to that, was a P3M practitioner involved in many situations, including facilities installation and operation, company rescues, organisational reformatting, training and support activities, working in many sectors, including aviation, automotive, engineering, and other manufacturing operations. Previous to this, Jayne had a succession of directorships of manufacturing companies. Jayne is the author of a number of academic papers published in professional journals. Her academic and practical professional experience is deployed in her role of Academic Lead for a number of WMG's professional programs and association with the APM and as External Associate at Cardiff Metropolitan University.

Dave Reggi is a project manager with experience in strategic and operational projects, delivering short- and long-term R&D solutions. His experience includes strategic planning, portfolio reporting, R&D, clinical development and operations, metrics and analytics, and process improvement. He has provided analytical insights through internal and external data/intelligence sources for effective and optimal planning. Dave has led global initiatives, managing large cross-functional and international teams. His knowledge and experience span across strategic planning, decision analytics, R&D project and portfolio management, clinical development/operations, and regulatory functions, with a focus on functional interdependencies and systems thinking. Dave spent 18 years at Bristol Myers Squibb, 2 years at J&J, and 16 years as a consultant. Prior to entering pharmaceuticals, Dave was a psychologist working in psychometrics and educational research in language development at Educational Testing Service and taught psychology at the College of New Jersey.

Carlos Eduardo Martins Serra is internationally recognised as a subject matter expert with over 20 years' experience in managing projects, programs, portfolios, and PMOs as head of project management at the Church of England and with previous experience of PMO lead roles at various organisations. Carlos is author of several journal articles and books focusing on benefits management, including *Benefits Realization Management* (CRC Press), and founded the online BRM Academy. Carlos is an external associate at the University of Warwick and is a well-respected thought leader, being a reviewer for PMI and IPMA publications, standards, and other academic journals. Carlos was announced as the PMI UK National Project Awards overall winner for the Project Professional of the Year in 2020.

Ranjit Sidhu is a chartered management consultant with a background in project and change management, including communication and people aspects of managing business transformation. As founder and director of ChangeQuest Ltd, Ranjit works closely with a range of clients on global implementations (including the BBC, Dell, Central Bank of Tanzania, States of Guernsey, United Nations, and the UK Government Cabinet Office), helping them make change happen in their organisations for lasting and sustainable transformation, often developing leadership and change management capability across the organisation. Ranjit is also an assessor for the chartered management consultant award, is visiting speaker on change management for postgraduate students at Solent University, and is a published author and speaker on change management. Ranjit has previously been an examiner for the change management practitioner qualification and a trustee board member for the Association of Project Management (APM).

Adam Skinner is business transformation consultancy P2 Consulting's Director of Consulting and a member of their Lead Team with 20 years of successful project, program, and agile delivery experience. His career spans UK Government Treasury, PA Consulting, WS Atkins, and P2 Consulting. He is Co-Chair of the Association of Project Management's Portfolio Management Committee, is RPP (Registered Project Professional), and is co-author of the APM's *Portfolio Management: A Practical Guide*. Following his MSc in Major Programme Management from Oxford University, he has a particular interest in the intersection between academia and industry and how this can support successful transformation. He is a regular blogger and talker on the topics of PMO, scaled agile, and portfolio management.

Paul Taylor is the executive technical director of Program Management at Stantec UK, part of one of the world's largest consulting engineering companies. Paul's role in Stantec UK is to ensure consistency, predictability, and the delivery of measurable benefits and tangible outcomes across the large capital infrastructure programs managed by the company. Prior to his Stantec role, Paul worked for Sellafield, Bechtel, BNFL Fuel Division (now Westinghouse Springfields), Amec (now Jacobs), and MWH Global (now Stantec). Paul has worked in the UK, Europe, United States, Middle East, and India, providing program management to organisations in multiple sectors, including petrochemical, construction, nuclear, telecommunications, industrial, and water. Paul is a member of the Chartered Management Institute and Institution of Engineering and Technology. He is also a chartered manager and an incorporated engineer and has lectured and presented throughout the UK on a range of program management topics.

Geoff Vincent is a writer, lecturer, and practitioner of innovation, is a graduate of the University of Cambridge, and is currently inspiring Warwick University students. Geoff has vast experience of change management, project and program management, and program assurance, working in organisations across a 30-plus-year career, such as with Hitachi consulting, British Gas, and Atkins. As an innovation consultant running his own business, Geoff led the personal computer development group at Acorn Computers (responsible for the microcomputer and ARM processor), as well as leading the development of the world's first personal pocket phone and the Cambridge trials for the interactive TV.

Lauri Vuorinen, DSc (Tech.), works as a postdoctoral research fellow at Tampere University, Department of Industrial Engineering and Management. Dr Vuorinen's field of research is project business. His current research interests include multi-project management, stakeholder management, and value creation in temporary organisations.

Hedley Walls has worked with many different organisations and has vast experience of consultancy in the area of portfolio management, change management, and program management for program and project assurance. Hedley is Group Head of Internal Audit at Admiral Group PLC, after working for over 15 years in several leading consultancy companies, including Deloitte, KPMG, and PA Consulting.

Dave Yazdani, as a chartered engineer, leader, and change agent, has extensive experience of aerospace product development, program management, systems thinking, and business transformation, having worked at Rolls-Royce in various project- and program-related senior roles for over 30 years. Dave is currently the experimental functional lead delivering business transformation benefit in excess of £200m per annum. Dave has spoken at several conferences and presented papers associated with projects, programs, and portfolios, such as at the Major Projects Association.

Permissions

We would like to thank the following for granting permission to reproduce material relating to areas of portfolio management in Sections I–III.

- Permission has been granted from Berrett-Koehler publishers to include within Chapter 17 on portfolio risk management by David Hillson, published as Chapter 18–2 in David's book. See reference given here:

  Reference: Hillson & Simon (2020) *Practical Project Risk Management: The ATOM Methodology*. Third Edition. Berrett-Koehler publishers.

- Chapter 7 is based on the paper by Serra and Kunc (2015) "Benefits realisation management and its influence on project success and on the execution of business strategies", published in the *International Journal of Project Management* 33 (1), 53–56, by Elsevier. This article is published under the terms of the Creative Commons Attribution-NonCommercial-ShareAlike License (CC BY NC SA). See reference given here.

  Reference: Serra & Kunc (2015) Benefits realisation management and its influence on project success and on the execution of business strategies. *International Journal of Project Management* 33 (1), 53–56.

- Permission has been granted to reproduce 16.1 in the chapter visualising data for portfolio decision-making by Mario Arlt from his PhD thesis work.
- A PLSClear Licence (54262) from Informa Ltd has been granted for work reproduced in Chapter 20, enabling adoption of portfolio management.

Thanks also goes to those organisations who have been willing to share their knowledge and experience in providing the rich case studies to enhance the learning in Section IV. These include:

- Thames Water for the case study in Chapter 25, Stantec for the case study in Chapter 26, BAE Systems for the case study as part of Chapter 18, and P2 Consulting for the diagrams and case study as part of Chapter 15.
- The information for Chapter 23 case study is provided by Rolls-Royce in good faith based upon the latest information available to it; no warranty or representation is given, and no contractual or other binding commitment is implied. © 2022 Rolls-Royce.

Figures

Tables

Preface

This book is not intended to answer all the questions about strategic portfolio management or provide a "how to" book for the subject area. It is written to gain traction for the conversation about strategic portfolio management with practitioners, business leaders, portfolio managers, strategists, and students. This book is a mix of academic and non-academic, combining theoretical and practical aspects, including examples of practical application of strategic portfolio management with case study chapters.

The idea for the book arose through working with students, business leaders, and practicing project and program managers. While writing this book, we have also discovered an ever-growing group in the academic field holding similar views to our own on strategic portfolio management, with varying levels of agreement on the scope and logic of the current work in this area.

Despite portfolio management having been used for decades to manage the myriad activities of modern organisations, it is only relatively recently that there has been a formalisation of the concept within the theories and practices of project management. Portfolio management as a means for managing multiple discrete work activities became significantly more visible with the publication of *Portfolio Management for New Products* originally in 1998 (Cooper et al., 2001, 2nd ed.), helped by further contributions from both Dye & Pennypacker (1999) and Pennypacker & Dye (2002). Since then, the connection of project management with the execution of strategy has developed. Alongside this have been conceptualisations about managing portfolios of programs and projects.

The logical next step is to bring together thinking about strategy execution through project portfolio management (which we consider a separate but related topic to strategic portfolio management) and organisational and business perspectives on the management of strategic portfolios. This textbook argues that the main focus of strategic portfolio management is on translating strategy into a set of projects and programs to execute that strategy and the ongoing management of that portfolio through the environmental turbulence. This approach allows for sub-portfolios, such as divisional or operational portfolios, within the overall strategic portfolio.

Speaking over several years with many professional students as well as other practitioners, we realise it is clear that strategic portfolio management is still not widely recognised by organisations and its value is largely underrated. Some organisations may be practising it in some guise, but it is often not recognised as portfolio management. We see two reasons for this: firstly, it is because the word *portfolio* is often associated with investment of financial assets; secondly, perhaps more concerningly, a portfolio of projects and programs is not seen by executive management as the mechanism by which strategic objectives are delivered.

Evidence abounds of the need for organisations to manage change effectively and, in extreme circumstances, pivot their businesses to deliver on significantly revised strategic objectives. This is happening as a result of rapidly changing external environments and increased attention to emergent strategy – often in an effort simply to survive. Effective strategic portfolio management is increasingly being recognised as a critical component of the organisational structure, leadership, and culture needed for continuous delivery of strategic objectives.

The book starts by placing strategic portfolio management in context to set the scene, starting with its history and current thinking. The aim is to make the distinction between project portfolio management (managing multiple projects simultaneously) and strategic portfolio management (ensuring that all work in the organisation is delivering strategic objectives). This first section of the book looks in detail at the underpinning theory. The strategic portfolio management approach is contextualised. The connection to organisational strategy is explored and developed, and an integrated view of organisational value and program and projects' benefits is presented. There is also an interesting discussion, possibly unique in the field, on how strategic portfolio management can support organisational change and transformation.

Section II of the book covers the definition and management of the strategic portfolio, introducing some new thinking and conceptual ideas to move this topic forward. This section of the book looks at the core components of strategic portfolio management, from integration mechanisms, accounting for the organisational environment, through to design of the process to select projects for the portfolio, including financial management. This is followed by the third section, which considers practical perspectives of portfolio management in organisations, including effective governance and assurance, resource and asset management, data management with decision-making, risk management, and leadership approaches. The fourth and final section presents various case studies, showing how strategic portfolio management is embedded and operationalised with real-world examples. The successful delivery of organisational strategic objectives is shown in a range of different contexts and through various perspectives.

The book is not prescriptive about the tools and techniques used for strategic portfolio management. Every organisation has its own unique context, and context is crucial, including, but not limited to, industry sector, organisational size, governance structure, culture and environmental demands, and it is important that the ideas presented are tailored to the specific requirements for the organisation. Although, by its nature, the book has strong connections with project management, the aim is to provide a more far-reaching journey, to raise the profile of the topic in the area where it will have the biggest impact: within the strategic management and organisational design areas of the business. It is worth noting that the term *organisation* is used frequently within the text. It is used in its widest context, to mean any corporation, business, SME (small and medium enterprise), not-for-profit, for-purpose, or other grouping of people that desire to achieve strategic goals and organisational change through the use of a strategic portfolio of projects and programs, at any scale. The spelling of *program* (rather than *programme*) in this book follows the logic set out by Morris (throughout his publications and most recently in 2013, p93).

On a final note, we hope you find this textbook full of insights that ignite your further interest in strategic portfolio management within your own industrial or organisational context. If you have any comments, queries, or contributions for future developments, please make contact with Katy Angliss at k.angliss@warwick.ac.uk.

Editor acknowledgements and dedications

This textbook has benefited hugely from significant academic and practitioner contributions, and we offer sincere thanks to all those contributors who spent much time and effort writing and rewriting the chapters. A heartfelt thanks goes to Jayne Redfern and Carol A. Long for their input and ongoing support. Jayne's contribution to this book has been significant, not just with the chapter on organisational strategy and portfolio management, but with her ongoing support for the book right from the early days. Carol has also contributed chapters, notes, and huge encouragement for this book, again from early on in its development. Much of the book would not exist without the other contributing authors. Thanks are due to all the academics who have shared their thoughts, insights, and intellectual perspectives to help us interpret the developing landscape of strategic portfolio management. We also offer special thanks to those contributors who are practitioners. They have generously shared their experiences of working in various industrial sectors through their range of rich case studies.

Acknowledgements from Katy Angliss

It has been quite a while since the original idea for this book emerged between myself and a very encouraging commissioning editor at Taylor & Francis, and I would very much like to thank the original Routledge team for their ongoing support. I would most notably like to thank my co-author, Professor Pete Harpum. Without Pete's significant support, knowledge of publishing, and great contribution, this book may never have materialised. Thanks also to Jayne Redfern for her much-appreciated support throughout. A special tribute is also needed here for the late, and much respected, Geoff Reiss. I discussed this book on several occasions with Geoff, and as usual, he offered his vast pearls of wisdom, which were gratefully received, especially as the original publisher's deadline approached! I hope that, although he wasn't able to contribute, he would have enjoyed celebrating, and no doubt discussing, this publication with us.

Acknowledgements from Pete Harpum

One of our contributing authors and energetic cheerleaders, Jayne Redfern, asked me in 2018 if I would like to contribute to a textbook on strategic portfolio management and subsequently introduced me to Katy Angliss. Katy and I have argued and parsed each other's views on the subject from that day until this. Our developing editorial relationship has been formative for me in too many ways to list. I am grateful to Katy for her unswerving kindness and patience as I have pedantically dissected thousands of paragraphs for this book. She has been courageous in her editorial decisions and willingness to push boundaries in pursuit of a high-value text for readers. Thank you, Katy. Since we began this book, Professor Peter Morris has died. He was one of the great thinkers and writers in the field of project management. I am very grateful to have known him personally, as a friend, boss, and academic mentor. He was, for me, a compelling and inspirational man, and I dedicate my work in this book to him. "A *pedibus usque ad caput*."

References

Cooper R., Edgett S. & Kleinschmidt E. (2001) *Portfolio Management for New Products*. Second Edition. Basic books.

Dye L. & Pennypacker J. (1999) *Project Portfolio Management: Selecting and Prioritizing Projects for Competitive Advantage*. Centre for Business Practices.

Morris P. (2013) *Reconstructing Project Management.* Wiley-Blackwell, London.
Pennypacker J. & Dye L. (2002) *Managing Multiple Projects: Planning, Scheduling, and Allocating Resources for Competitive Advantage.* Marcel Decker PM Practices.

Preface

Notes on COVID-19 pandemic responses in relation to strategic portfolio management

The need for strategic portfolio management goes far beyond the current moment, or moments of transformation, or crisis more generally. Whatever field we work in, whatever challenges we face, from the potential for digitisation to the need to pivot the business due to the pandemic or to achieve a net-zero economy, a critical question for all businesses is how to successfully move from setting and revising strategic goals to achieving those goals.

The period 2020–2021 was extraordinary for, amongst other things, large-scale strategic portfolio management across national boundaries. Portfolios of activities to combat the COVID-19 pandemic were observable at national, local, and global levels and under rarely seen levels of scrutiny from authorities, media, and commentators. Each organisation and government had their individual initiatives to monitor, minimise, and treat the effects of the virus pandemic on their people in terms of both health and economic measures.

As an example of an emerging national government portfolio, the United Kingdom government response grew initially from a public health concern for those travellers abroad. The portfolio of measures expanded into managing a foreign policy issue, a home territory public health emergency, and a generalised threat to good order and to the economy. By mid-March 2020, the action plans visible to any UK subject suggested the scope of the portfolio of activities included considerable operational changes and funding redirection in public health, the frontline health service, police, fire and rescue service, government support for businesses and employment, emergency support for healthcare workers, changes to school provision, postponement of elections, changes in local government activity, public information campaigns, restrictions on movement, and redirected foreign aid packages. The UK's government by cabinet became especially noticeable in this. In every government department, a minister was assigned duties associated with managing this portfolio.

There was also an extraordinary portfolio of work focused on medical solutions to the virus, initiated by private philanthropy, diverse government funding, and pharmaceutical corporations. At the centre of this was a global partnership called the Coalition for Epidemic Preparedness Innovations (CEPI). This organisation was launched in 2017 and took up the mantle of managing a worldwide response to the novel coronavirus causing COVID-19 in a development portfolio known as COVAX.

This organisation quickly received huge funding from governments to support research work that had started in the not-for-profit and private sectors to address vaccine development for other diseases, including Rift Valley fever and Ebola virus. By coordinating funding for multiple COVID-19 vaccine developments, the commercialisation risks were reduced for the pharmaceutical companies as they were assured of funding of development through clinical trials, data reviews, and approval (when a viable vaccine is found) either as grants or guaranteed purchase of doses.

The process of developing and testing has five distinct steps in America's Federal Drug Administration (FDA, 2020) model (the European model adds a distinct sixth step, post-release monitoring, that is implied in the FDA process). The pipeline of drug development within individual pharmaceutical companies tends to have a major decision point after the discovery and pre-clinical trials are completed. The human effort, governance input, and sheer amount of money needed for clinical trials are only deemed viable when there is some assurance that a commercial product will be profitable. Value-based pricing of a drug (as proposed by Munshaw & Chawla, 2019) may aid profitability, but generally the market for a vaccine is time-bound (use of the vaccine should tail towards eradication) and price-limited (often as part of government-funded initiatives or because of the ethical concerns around profiteering during a national emergency). This financial risk means that some viable technologies are not developed into products that are available for the general population.

Some vaccines in the CEPI COVID-19 portfolio are based on relatively innovative technology that has been in a state of potential use for many months awaiting a viable commercial opportunity (Garde et al., 2020). Both Moderna (mRNA-1273) and Pfizer-BioNTech (BNT162b2) use a relatively new technology called mRNA (messenger RNA) (NASDAQ Trefis Blog, 2020). In a 2018 paper, Pardi et al. noted that "[h]ighly efficient and non-toxic RNA carriers have been developed" and that many of these platforms had varying side effects. However, they conclude that CEPI support and "translation of basic research into clinical testing is also made more expedient by the commercialisation of custom GMP (good manufacturing practice) products".

A key benefit of this centralised portfolio approach was noted by the World Economic Forum (WEF): equidistribution of vaccines and therapeutics for such a pandemic has greater benefits than focusing these treatments on those who can best afford their development and purchase. (WEF research [Masterson, 2020] indicates that there are negative economic and social impacts to wealthier nations of denying less-wealthy regions access to vaccines.)

Reflecting the nature of these developments as a portfolio is particularly instructive when considering projects that are halted as no longer viable. In reviewing one vaccine from the University of Queensland partnership (v451), CEPI funding was discontinued following the identification of an issue in the phase 1 clinical trials (University of Queensland, December 2020). The commercial loss on such developments in other circumstances may have been prohibitive for the development of this vaccine technology to go into clinical trial stages. However, as a part of the strategic portfolio, the phase 1 trial for v451 will not be abandoned but completed, to ensure the collection of useful data for the wider portfolio. This might not have happened if the decision cancelling this phase 1 trial had been made judging the v451 initiative as an individual project with commercial and resource pressures suggesting a faster withdrawal.

Bringing COVID-19 vaccines to the public has been facilitated by an unusual speed of approval of these drugs. The unprecedentedly short approval period is not derived from a lack of vigour in the governance of the process; it is enabled by careful examination of the process steps and searching for overlapping activities that could compress the overall time elapsed. This type of process improvement project is unlikely to make sense in normal business when there is not a significant difference between the priorities on the range of drugs to be approved. However, as part of the UK government's portfolio of support for public health initiatives during the pandemic, there was both political will and the focus of resource to make the review of COVID-19 drugs a priority (United Kingdom Government Website, March & December 2020). This enabled changes in MHRA (Medicines and Healthcare products Regulatory Agency) processes to compress time without compromising rigour, governance, or controls (EMA, 2020). The USA implemented a similar fast-track process in its response to COVID-19, titled "Operation Warp Speed" (U.S. Department of Defense, December 2020). Warp Speed is a public–private partnership integrated supply chain improvement initiative to address the accelerated development, manufacturing, approval, and distribution of COVID-19 vaccines and other countermeasures (U.S. Department of Health & Human Services, December 2020).

Thus, we can see from this pandemic that portfolios can be literally global, across otherwise separated silos, and not contained within one organisation. We can also recognise the advantage of viewing a broad supply chain development as portfolio work and choosing to allocate resources that might, under purely commercial constraints, be considered wasteful or suboptimal to achieving strategic initiatives.

Note

1 With thanks to Carol A. Long for contributing the foundation of this preface addendum.

References

CEPI (2017) Vaccine portfolio. https://cepi.net/research_dev/our-portfolio/

EMA (European Medicines Agency) (2020) From laboratory to patient: The journey of a centrally authorised medicine. *2019 The Netherlands, EMA/103813/2018 Rev. 1.* www.ema.europa.eu/en/documents/other/laboratory-patient-journey-centrally-authorised-medicine_en.pdf

FDA (2020) The drug development process. www.fda.gov/patients/learn-about-drug-and-device-approvals/drug-development-process

Garde D., Saltzman J. & Arsenault M. (2020) The story of mRNA: How a once-dismissed idea became a leading technology in the Covid vaccine race. *StatNews/Boston Globe.* www.statnews.com/2020/11/10/the-story-of-mrna-how-a-once-dismissed-idea-became-a-leading-technology-in-the-covid-vaccine-race/

Masterson V. (2020) Equal access to COVID-19 vaccines could be worth billions. *World Economic Forum.* www.weforum.org/agenda/2020/12/who-covid-vaccines-equitable-access/

Munshaw S. & Chawla A. (2019) Pricing a new drug. In *SAGE Business Cases.* SAGE Publications, SAGE Business Cases Originals.

NASDAQ Trefis Blog (2020) Pfizer and moderna's vaccines could be more profit than you think. www.nasdaq.com/articles/pfizer-and-modernas-vaccines-could-be-more-profitable-than-you-think-2020–12–17

Pardi N., Hogan M., Porter F. & Weissman D. (2018) mRNA vaccines – A new era in vaccinology. *Nature Reviews Drug Discovery* 17, 261–279.

United Kingdom Government Website (March 2020) Press Release: Prime Minister Boris Johnson has announced record funding to find a coronavirus vaccine. www.gov.uk/government/news/pm-announces-record-funding-to-find-a-coronavirus-vaccine

United Kingdom Government Website (December 2020) June coronavirus announcements (date order). www.gov.uk/search/all?level_one_taxon=5b7b9532-a775-4bd2-a3aa-6ce380184b6c&content_purpose_supergroup%5B%5D=news_and_communications&order=updated-oldest

University of Queensland (December 2020) Update on UQ-19 vaccine. www.uq.edu.au/news/article/2020/12/update-uq-covid-19-vaccine

U.S. Department of Defense (December 2020) Coronavirus: Operation warp speed. www.defense.gov/Explore/Spotlight/Coronavirus/Operation-Warp-Speed/

U.S. Department of Health & Human Services (December 2020) Fact sheet: Explaining operation warp speed. www.hhs.gov/coronavirus/explaining-operation-warp-speed/index.html

1 Introduction

Katy Angliss

The term "portfolio" is not new. It can be traced back to the eighteenth century, originating from the Italian word "portafoglio", meaning a case for carrying documents. It became known more specifically as a collection of documents, such as those by an artist or photographer (Merriam-Webster, 2021). This has developed into a wider meaning of *portfolio* as a collection or grouping. The term has been used in various different contexts, most prevalently being associated with the financial industry, where "portfolio" often means a collection of investments. The term *portfolio* can also be found in several other contexts in more recent years, such as in politics with "ministerial portfolios", in education with "teaching portfolios", and also as a term used for individuals who have a "portfolio career". The term *portfolio* is also used in organisational and business contexts, as with a marketing portfolio as a collection of products, services, or brands. Since the late 1990s, with the growing interest in managing the complexity of delivering multiple projects, there has been a recognition that a project portfolio can be defined and managed. With the recognition of the importance of multi-projects and programs in delivering organisational strategy (Morris, 2022), the strategic portfolio is increasingly being understood to be a collection of projects and programs delivering strategic objectives.

This book takes the view that organisational strategy is executed, in most organisations, by a portfolio of programs and projects (and other non-project activities when required). This places strategic portfolio management in the domain of organisational strategic management. The anticipation is, this book will appeal to executive managers in all departmental areas, strategists, portfolio directors, managers, and analysts, as well as program and project managers, and students of all these areas of study.

This introduction looks briefly at the origins of portfolio management in the organisational context, including why the importance of portfolio management may not be fully recognised. It also discusses the significant value brought to organisations by integrating strategic portfolio management (SPM) within the strategic processes and structures. The book does not cover project and program management, except as far as is needed to understand ideas about portfolio management. Annex 1 to this chapter illustrates the differing but connected roles of projects, programs, and portfolios.

Portfolio management within the strategic context

The academic fields of organisational and strategic management have mainly focused on strategy development, with fairly minimal reference to the implementation of the strategy, once it has been developed. Some of the thinking in this field, however, does recognise

DOI: 10.4324/9780367853129-1

the role of portfolios, discussing portfolio matrices and the portfolio manager in the context of the corporate entity. Portfolio managers are defined as having a role to improve performance and extract maximum value through target setting, intervention, and provision or withdrawal of investment (Whittington et al., 2020).

In parallel, the project management–orientated academic literature has started to broaden its interest in executing strategy, from focusing on single-project environments to multi-project environments. This has happened firstly through developing theory about project portfolio management (PPM) and, secondly, conceptualising project, program, and portfolio management (P3M) as an integrated system for delivering strategic objectives. The project management field of research, however, still tends to conceptualise portfolio management as being an extension of project and program management theory.

There are a number of publications on the subject of project portfolio management (PPM), where PPM is concerned with managing a collection of projects. Dye and Pennypacker (1999) identified the current perspective on PPM and its capacity to help achieve competitive advantage. This helped to move project management theory beyond business benefits delivery as the "*raison d'etre*" for projects' existence, towards recognising that, in fact, value creation is the fundamental imperative (Morris, 2013; Pennypacker and Dye, 2002; Pennypacker and Retna, 2009).

Figure 1.1 shows the relationship between the portfolio and the projects and programs that are within the strategic portfolio. The premise of this book is that portfolio management is not a continuation "upwards" from projects and programs; it is the *critical linking structure and framework from strategy formulation to strategy* execution. Strategic portfolio management translates organisational strategy into action. The strategic portfolio is integrated within the organisational environment and incorporates all work needed to achieve strategic objectives. Projects and programs deliver strategically defined business benefits that are then aggregated into strategic value for the organisation (Cooper et al., 2001).

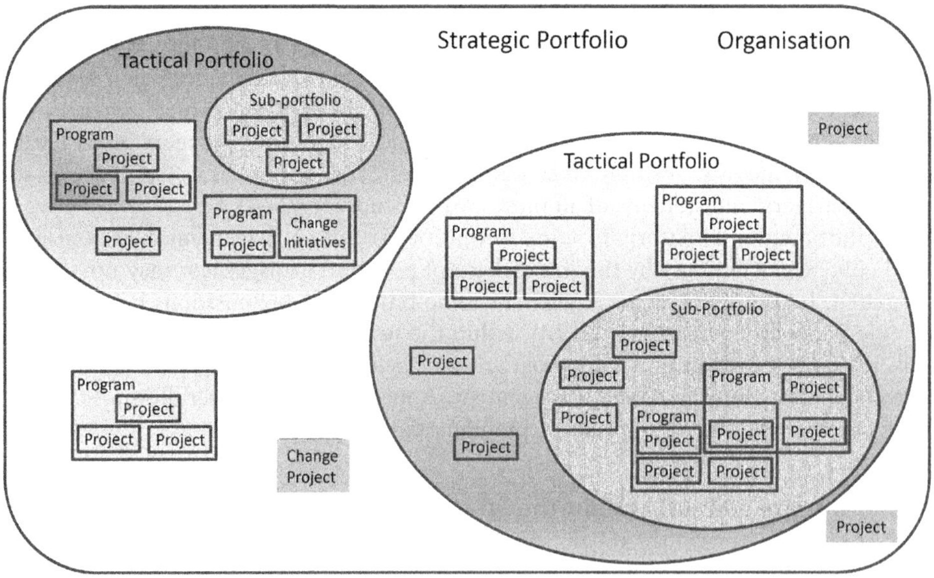

Figure 1.1 The SPM relationship between portfolios, programs, and projects.

Source: Adapted from Lock & Wagner (2016).

Emphasising the criticality of the strategic portfolio and its effective management requires a shift in mindset from much of the established literature on portfolio management. From the viewpoint of those in strategic and executive management, programs and projects must become understood as, crucially, the most effective way to deliver strategic objectives and are therefore of central importance and not "merely" tactically useful entities. From a program and project management viewpoint, the portfolio and its management are not an extension of project management theory and practice; it is a strategic activity that has little relation to project theory, except in the broadest sense. For example, project resource allocation and portfolio resource allocation are connected by general theories of resource allocation, but not by a specific theory of resource allocation as practiced in projects.

Differences of orientation on portfolio management, depending on perspective, can be found in the literature. The framework around which the strategic portfolio is managed, in Lazar (2019), has four pillars: organisational agility, strategy, risk, and resources. From a PPM perspective, we find Moustafaev (2016) has three pillars: projects maximising value, projects selected for a balanced portfolio, and projects strategically aligned with business strategy. In the project management world, the UK government, back in 2011, noted that the time had come to fully recognise portfolio management as a separate discipline – distinct from project and program management (Axelos, 2011). This process is still underway.

Strategic portfolio management focuses on whether the right projects and programs are being delivered, through strategic alignment and integration processes: by *choosing* the right projects to start with, *not* aligning projects to strategy "*post facto*", maximising value to the organisation on a continuous basis, ensuring project and program delivery is effectively achieving strategic objectives, and prioritising resource allocation to support effective execution of strategy.

The strategic portfolio

Whittington et al. (2020) define three levels of strategy as corporate, business, and operational. Following the logic of the preceding section, there is a clear implication that portfolios must exist at each of these three levels, to translate strategic intentions into actionable projects and programs. Figure 1.2 shows the three levels of strategy in relation to portfolio levels and to the themes of strategic alignment, together with the top-down

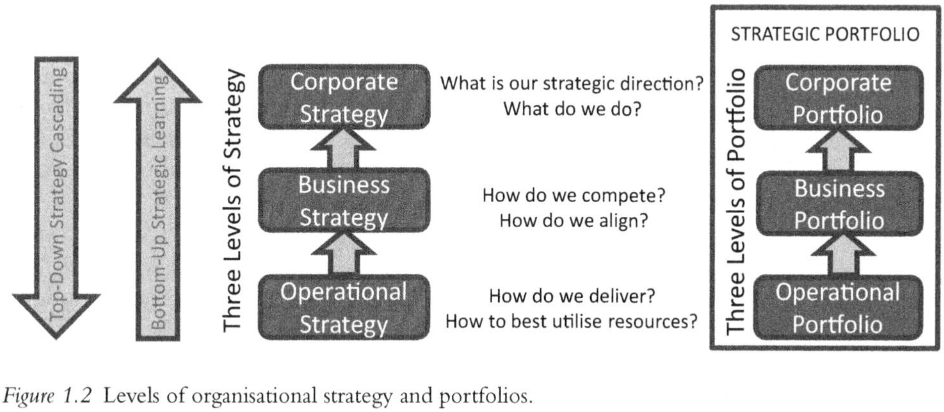

Figure 1.2 Levels of organisational strategy and portfolios.

and bottom-up (or emergent strategy, discussed in detail in Chapter 3). The themes of strategic alignment shown here, with the strategy cascading down through the three levels from a top-down approach, consider firstly the question of assessing and defining the strategic direction at the corporate level, with the business level agreeing how they will align to the corporate direction and their resulting main areas of focus. This flows down to the tactical portfolios and how each operational unit will deliver the strategic objectives they are responsible for, matching this with the required resources and asset management.

Taking the organisational view, that all business activity should be related to moving the organisation toward its strategic objectives, all the activities of the organisation (including all its business units) are contained in the corporate "book of work" (Harpum, 2010) – strategic portfolios should therefore include the whole organisation. Such a viewpoint helps reduce executives' only-human tendency to focus on some strategic projects and not others. Such selective focus easily leads to negative effects on overall performance for short-term gain, fostering fragmentation of strategic effort, and reduces coordination of resources (Martinsuo & Geraldi, 2020).

At the sub-portfolio level, the operational portfolios could be at departmental level, where management of resourcing is a priority. For example, an engineering manager may make decisions about which engineers in the team are allocated to specific projects or programs. Project portfolio management (PPM), as distinct from strategic portfolio management, is relevant here for managing a subset of the overall strategic portfolio, such as business divisional portfolios, departmental portfolios, operational portfolios, tactical portfolios, or a change portfolio. This means the strategic portfolio could include multiple sub-portfolios, programs, projects, and/or non-project (operations) initiatives (see Figure 1.1). In cases where the strategic portfolio is constructed with this range of ways of organising work, it is inevitable that it will have a high level of complexity (Marcondes et al., 2019, Müller et al., 2019) that needs careful, dedicated, and high-quality management.

Strategic portfolios, in this context, are defined as:

> Strategic portfolios define, manage, and deliver all the "organisational work" (including projects, programs, and other change activity) to continuously achieve organisational strategic objectives.

Strategic portfolio management

Unlike projects and programs, portfolios are continuous rather than having a defined life cycle (see Figure 1.3). The portfolio activities are shown as a continuous cycle typically aligned with the business strategic planning cycle, as proposed by much of the literature (for example, Platje et al., 1994). The portfolio is seen to continuously adapt and change with emergent strategy, redefining, reclassifying, reprioritising, and rebalancing as needed, whilst maintaining stability and direction within the organisational environment. A range of processes and capabilities are needed to manage the strategic portfolio.

Garfein (2008) proposed a model that integrates the life cycle aspect and multiple managerial capabilities and processes needed to effectively manage portfolios (Figure 1.4). In this model, there are four areas of focus: portfolio strategic objectives that are unique to the enterprise, portfolio dependencies as the channels through which the portfolio objectives are achieved, portfolio delivery as the heart of the model, and portfolio management capabilities.

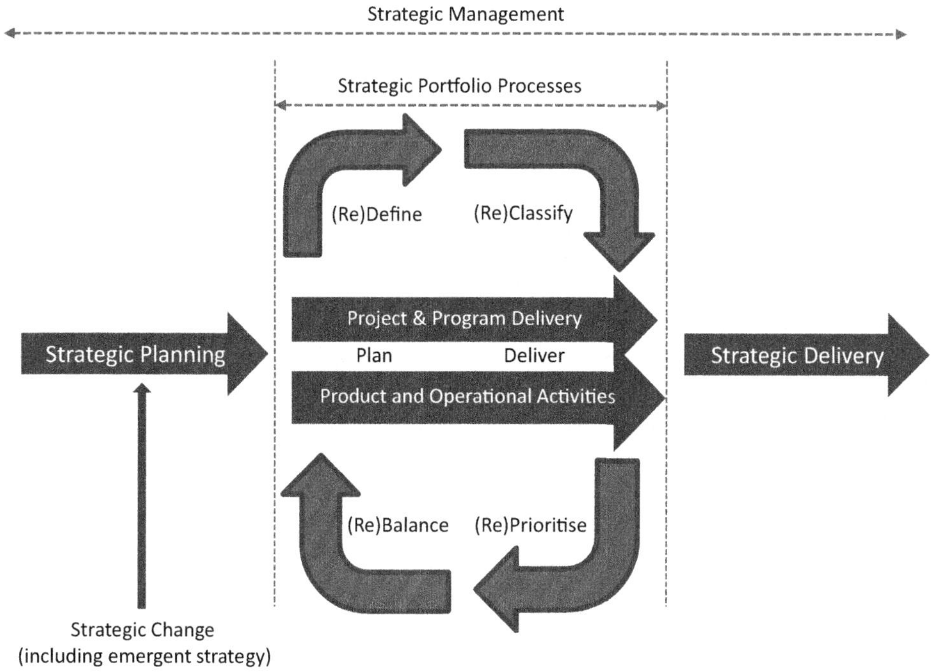

Figure 1.3 Strategic portfolio activities and the strategic planning cycle.

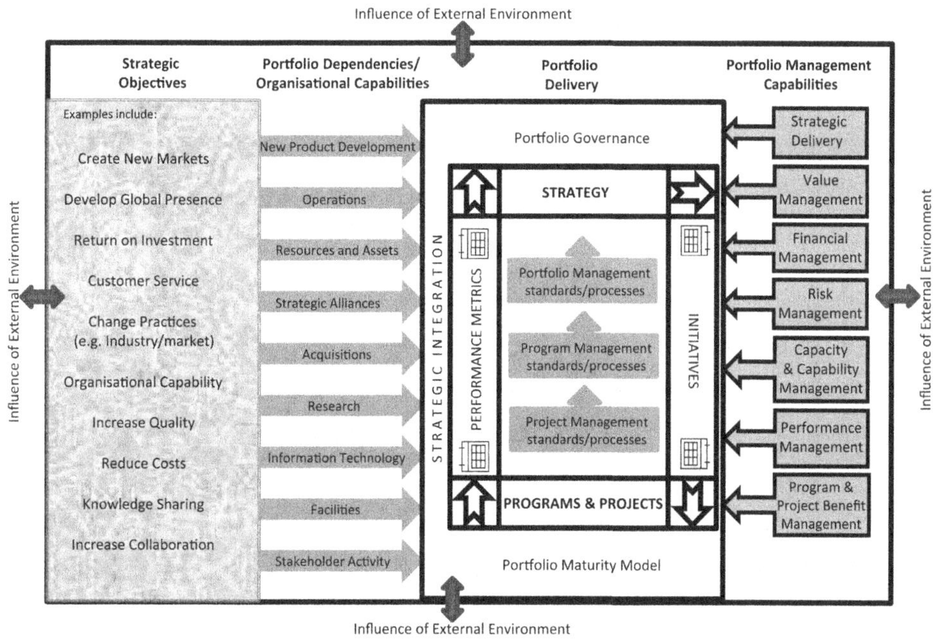

Figure 1.4 Strategic portfolio management model.

Source: Adapted from Garfein (2008).

From Garfein's model, it is clear that delivering organisational strategy means integration is an essential element of SPM. This book takes the view that, in fact, integration, and strategic integration, within and across the strategic portfolio, is not just one of the pillars for success but *is the central pillar*, driving all other aspects of portfolio direction and delivery (see Figure 1.5).

The portfolio environment covers not only projects and programs, although these are important to portfolio success, but also the wider organisational environment. There are four main capabilities for SPM discussed: strategic value optimisation; project, program, and organisational change prioritisation and allocation; portfolio management and organisational capabilities; and integrated governance and assured delivery (Figure 1.5).

The premise of this book, structured around the main themes from Figure 1.5, is that portfolio management is not a continuation "upwards" from projects and programs; it is the *critical linking structure and framework from strategy formulation to strategy* execution. Strategic portfolio management translates organisational strategy into action, and hence, one of the initial chapters in the first section discusses organisational strategy and strategic delivery with portfolio management – "SPM is the strategy for strategic deployment." The latter chapters of the first section expand on how projects, programs, and other change activities deliver strategically defined business benefits that are then aggregated into strategic value for the organisation (Cooper et al., 2001).

The strategic portfolio is introduced in the second section, demonstrating how it is integrated within the organisational environment and incorporates all work needed to achieve the strategic objectives. Again, considering the organisational view, strategic

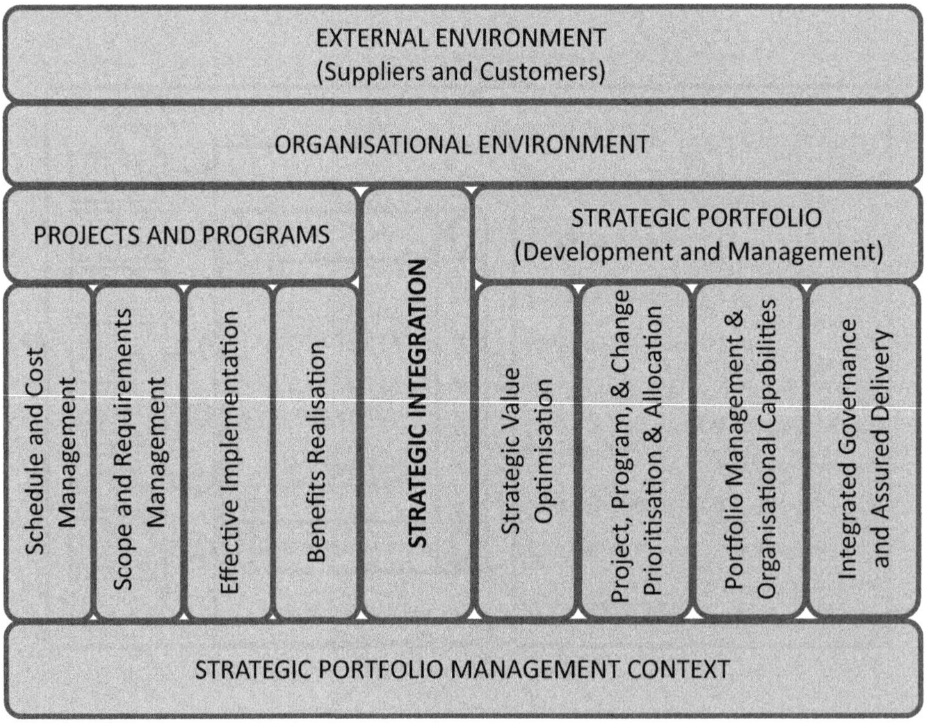

Figure 1.5 The wider portfolio management context with strategic integration.

portfolio management should encompass the capabilities and processes required to ensure and assure the delivery of the strategic portfolio in its entirety. These portfolio and organisational capabilities are discussed in Section III.

Strategic portfolio management in this context is therefore defined as follows:

> *Strategic portfolio management* is the continuous delivery of organisational strategy in creating strategic value through strategic portfolios.

Key themes and structure of the book

This book provides the knowledge, both theoretical and practical, to build and manage such high-performing strategic portfolios, based on the following premise:

- *Strategic portfolio management* is the primary link between organisational strategic planning (at the corporate level or equivalent) and the delivery areas of the organisation, such as projects, programs, and operational activities (the corporate "portfolio of work").
- The primary focus is on *strategic delivery* with *strategic alignment and integration* through portfolio management with strategic portfolios and effective portfolio management capabilities.
- *Strategic value* is primarily delivered at the portfolio level with aggregated benefits from the projects and programs in measuring the delivery of strategic objectives.
- *Projects and programs are fundamental* in delivering the organisational strategy and value within the strategic portfolio.
- *Strategic portfolios* are multi-layered (strategic and tactical) and can mirror the three levels of strategy: operational, business, and corporate.
- The *strategic portfolio should be flexibly aligned (realigned) and fully integrated within its organisational environment*, ensuring capacity and capability of portfolio elements are continuously managed against strategic objectives. The predominant focus of portfolio management is on the uncertain and complex organisational and external environment, with a top-down rather than bottom-up approach where applicable, recognising emergent strategy.

Large organisations often have a vast array of different projects and programs, within several business units, across multiple locations. These projects and programs will be competing for resources. Individual project and program benefits may not be clear. The overall value to be achieved by the strategic portfolio may not be clear (or even defined). Some work may not be aligned to the strategic objectives. Some projects and programs may not have been prioritised correctly and require significant investment of money and/or people. Some projects may be delivering only minimal (or no) strategic value. Those leaders with portfolio management and strategic delivery responsibility might be asking themselves these questions:

- Is the business effectively delivering the organisational strategy?
- Are all projects and programs aligned to business strategy?
- Are projects and programs continuously delivering investment value?
- Are the benefits to the business outstripping the investment in change and improvements (and the overall spend on projects and programs managed collectively)?

- Are all the resources available in the business units to achieve the desired change, being well managed, and not overloaded with change?
- Is the portfolio being managed at the correct level within the organisation, with the portfolio risks sufficiently managed?

High-quality, effectively designed strategic portfolio management provides the answers to these questions, and more. The four sections of this book cover each of these in more detail.

Section I: strategic portfolio management in context

This first section discusses the background to portfolio management in detail and focuses on the key theme of organisational strategy as a main driver for SPM in delivering organisational strategy, developing the argument for an integrated portfolio within the organisational environment. Organisational strategy is discussed where it relates to effective portfolio management, including the more specific topic of scenario planning. This section establishes that the delivery of benefits from projects and programs and other activities to the strategy is fundamental in achieving strategic value and that organisational change activities are also a key part of the portfolio. The section also discusses the challenges in defining strategic value. These aspects are brought together in considering portfolio management success.

Section II: defining and managing the strategic portfolio

This section develops the discussion of the strategic portfolio, covering integration of the portfolio within the organisational environment and strategic portfolio context, followed by discussion of environmental factors, establishing the portfolio as part of an open system, and introducing the portfolio management capabilities for further expansion in Section III. The portfolio processes are used as a framework for discussion of the definition of the portfolio, such as portfolio selection, including portfolio classification, prioritisation, and balancing, and the selection methods themselves (including financial measures for establishing strategic value).

Section III: portfolio management capabilities

This section brings together the aspects of portfolio management and the strategic portfolio discussed in previous sections and looks more specifically at portfolio management capabilities, including asset and resource management, portfolio governance and the portfolio office, data analysis and management, portfolio risk management, portfolio decision-making, and portfolio leadership. The section concludes by considering portfolio management in the context of the supply chain and agile portfolio management for enabled delivery.

Section IV: portfolio management case studies

This section covers case studies from different industrial sectors, focusing on varying aspects of strategic portfolio management, including:

- Engineering of complex systems with portfolio management.
- Developing a portfolio management decision-making tool in the pharmaceutical industry.

- Delivering a multi-billion-pound portfolio in the utilities sector.
- A utilities and construction portfolio focusing on design for manufacture and assembly.
- A case study discussing governance and leadership for portfolios across industrial sectors.
- An example of the development of a portfolio management maturity model.

These case studies provide real-world examples of how effective portfolio management can be beneficial to an organisation, as well as offering insights and advice on the challenges of implementation of SPM.

Questions

Questions to consider when reading through each chapter are presented after the introduction to each section. The material review questions provide signposting for the key takeaway messages for each chapter. A second set of further discussion questions are also included, perhaps for a classroom discussion, or for consideration within an organisation contemplating refining or developing strategic portfolio management.

Conclusion

This chapter has introduced strategic portfolios and strategic portfolio management, starting with the origins of portfolio management, identifying the main topics for SPM, and the key themes discussed throughout the book. This book is not intended to provide a "how-to" manual for portfolio management but to present alternative perspectives in identifying strategic portfolio management as a subject within organisational studies and business research, rather than solely within project management, and to bring insight and practical wisdom to practitioners working in strategy formulation, selection, and strategy execution.

Further reading

Alkhuraiji A., Liu S., Oderanti F.O. & Megicks P. (2016) New structured knowledge network for strategic decision-making in IT innovative and implementable projects. *Journal of Business Research* 69, 1534–1538.

APM (2012/19) *Body of Knowledge*. Sixth and Seventh Edition. Association for Project Management.

Artto K., Kujala J., Dietrich P. & Martinsuo M. (2008) What is project strategy? *International Journal of Project Management* 26(1), 4–12.

Artto K. & Wikstrom K. (2005) What is project business? *International Journal of Project Management* 23(5), 343–353.

BS6079 (2019) *Part 1: Principles and Guidelines for the Management of Projects*. British Standards Institution.

Buttrick R. (2020) *The Programme and Portfolio Workout: Directing Business-Led Programme and Portfolios*. Routledge.

HM Government (2018) *GOVS 002, Project Delivery*. HM Government

ISO (2012) *ISO 21500:2012 Guidance on Project Management*. ISO

ISO (2015) *ISO 21504:2015 Project, Programme and Portfolio Management – Guidance on Portfolio Management*. ISO

ISO (2021) *ISO 37000:2021 Governance of Organisations*. ISO

Jamieson A. & Morris P. (2007) Moving from corporate strategy to project strategy. In *The Wiley Guide to Project, Program and Portfolio Management*. Wiley.

Killen C.P., Jugdev K., Drouin N. & Petit Y. (2012) Advancing project and portfolio management research: Applying strategic management theories. *International Journal of Project Management* 30(5), 525–538.

Kim Y., Sting F. & Loch C. (2014) Top-down, bottom-up, or both? Toward an integrative perspective on operations strategy formation. *Journal of Operations Management* 32(7–8), 462–474.

Lock D. & Wagner R. (2019) *The Handbook of Project Portfolio Management*. Routledge.

Martinsuo M. (2012) Toward strategic value from projects. *International Journal of Project Management* 30(6), 637–638.

Perry R. & Hatcher E. (2008) *Portfolio Management: How to Maximise Value of the Investment in Projects while Minimising Risks*. International Data Corporation (IDC).

PMI (2017) *The Standard for Portfolio Management*. Fourth Edition. Project Management Institute.

Raynor P. & Reiss G. (2012) *Portfolio and Programme Management Demystified: Managing Multiple Projects Successfully*. Routledge.

Sicotte, H., Drouin, N. & Delerue, H. (2014) Innovation portfolio management as a subset of dynamic capabilities: Measurement and impact on innovative performance. *Project Management Journal* 45(6), 58–72.

Teller J., Unger, BN, Kock A. & Gemünden HG. (2012) Formalization of project portfolio management: The moderating role of project portfolio complexity. *International Journal of Project Management* 30, 596–607.

References

Axelos (2011) *Management of Portfolios*. TSO.

Cooper R., Edgett S. & Kleinschmidt E. (2001) *Portfolio Management for New Products*. Second Edition. Basic Books.

Dye L. & Pennypacker J. (1999) *Project Portfolio Management: Selecting and Prioritizing Projects for Competitive Advantage*. Centre for Business Practices.

Garfein S. (2008) Strategic Portfolio Management: The key to the executive suite. Paper presented at PMI Global Congress 2008 (EMEA, St Julian's Malta). Project Management Institute.

Harpum P. (2010) *Portfolio, Program and Project Management in the Pharmaceutical and Biotechnology Industries*. Wiley.

Lazar O. (2019) *The Four Pillars of Portfolio Management: Organisational Agility, Strategy, Risk, and Resources*. CRC Press.

Lock D. & Wagner R. (2016) *Gower Handbook of Program Management*. Routledge.

Marcondes, Barucke; Leme, & Carvalho, (2019) Framework for integrated project portfolio selection and adjustment. *IEEE Transactions on Engineering Management* 66(4), 677–688.

Martinsuo M. & Geraldi J. (2020) Management of project portfolios: Relationships of project portfolios with their contexts. *International Journal of Project Management* 38(6), 441–453.

Merriam-Webster (2021). Merriam-Webster.com dictionary. www.merriam-webster.com/dictionary.

Morris P. (2013) *Reconstructing Project Management*. Wiley-Blackwell.

Morris P. (2022) A working account of the rise of project management. *International Journal of Project Management* 40(2), 91–94.

Moustafaev J. (2016) *Project Portfolio Management in Theory and Practice: Thirty Case Studies from around the World*. CRC Press.

Müller R., Drouin N. & Sankaran S. (2019) Modeling organizational project management. *Project Management Journal* 50(4), 499–513.

Pennypacker J. & Dye L. (2002) *Managing Multiple Projects: Planning, Scheduling, and Allocating Resources for Competitive Advantage*. Marcel Decker PM Practices.

Pennypacker J. & Retna S. (2009) *Project Portfolio Management: A View from the Management Trenches* (The Enterprise portfolio management council). Wiley.

Platje A., Seidel H. & Wadman S. (1994) Project and portfolio planning cycle – project-based management for the multiproject challenge. *International Journal of Project Management* 12(2), 100–106.

Whittington R., Regner P, Angwin D, Johnson G. & Scholes K. (2020) *Exploring Strategy*. Twelfth Edition. Pearson.

Annex

Comparison of portfolios, programs, and projects

To set the context, Table 1.1 provides a comparison of the three organisational constructs of portfolios, programs, and projects. This is predominantly based on the (controversial) viewpoint of a linear hierarchy for portfolios, programs, and projects, shown in Figure 1.6.

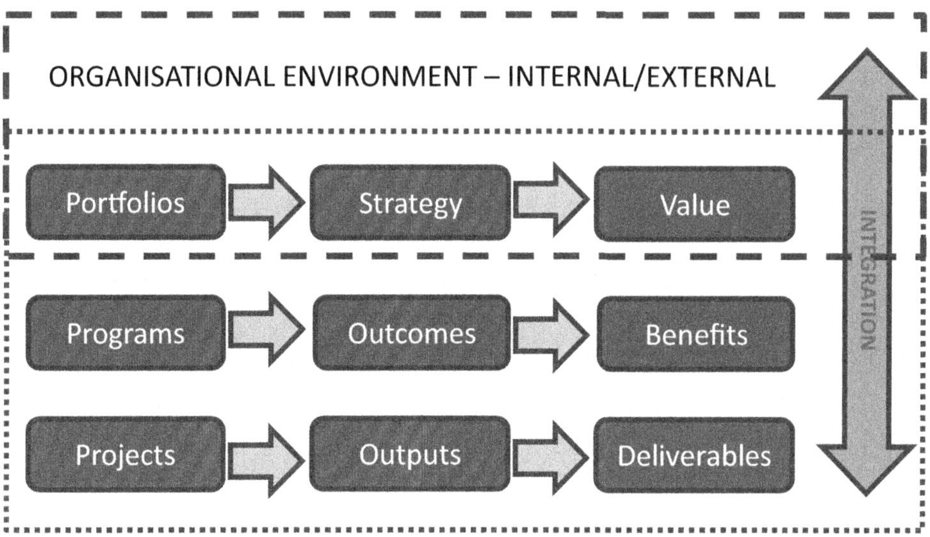

Figure 1.6 The traditional relationship between portfolios, programs, and projects.

Table 1.1 Comparison of projects, programs, and portfolios (adapted from Axelos, 2011)

Area	*Project*	*Program*	*Portfolio*
Life Cycle	Defined, typically five phases	Longer, less defined, includes tranches and islands of stability	Longer term, no defined end date, can be continuous within the strategic planning life cycle
Focus	Management and coordination	Direction and delivery of strategy	Alignment with corporate strategy
Vision and Blueprint	Not applicable for project boundary, focus on project goals	Within program boundary; focus typically on one strategic objective	For the entire organisation at portfolio level or for sub-portfolios

(*Continued*)

Table 1.1 (Continued)

Area	*Project*	*Program*	*Portfolio*
Business Case	Budgeting for output delivery	Benefits vs costs of program and associated projects	May not exist or be conceptual; incremental vs entire business transformation through projects and programs
Success Criteria	Measured by achievement of product cost, quality, and timescales	Benefits realisation and stakeholder perception	Organisational performance and value to investors and stakeholders
Benefits and Value	Fit for purpose outputs to enable benefit realisation	Dominant focus on benefits profiling and realisation	Organisational value, benefits, and goals
Scope	Defined	Benefit focus; transient with desired change	Strategic business objectives and value creation; can change with strategic goals of organisation
Governance	Follow set governance standards	Program-level standards and strategies	Setting organisational standards and policies
Stakeholder Engagement	All levels, mainly inside organisation	All levels, inside and outside organisation	Strategic and external focus
Leadership	Execution orientated; main focus on project team	Relationship building and conflict resolution; focus on program vision	Add value to portfolio decisions; focus on mission and organisational direction
Risk Focus	Cost, quality, and timescales; focus on threats	Project, operation, and strategic; focus on opportunities.	Strategic and business continuity; deviation from expectations (portfolio balance)
Issue Focus	Product and fit for purpose	Inter-project and benefits delivery	Beyond program boundaries and margins
Quality Focus	Fit for purpose outputs to meet requirements	Control of outcomes and improvement.	Portfolio alignment and effectiveness
Planning	Product and activities, outputs and deliverables	Outcomes, interdependencies, tranches	Outcome dependency and conflict resolution
Timescales	Constrained and specific	Loosely defined, focused end point	Vague or undefined, continuous
Schedule	Time to deliver quality product	Combined schedules of project and other program activities	No defined schedules; achieved strategic value through aggregated benefits tracking
Monitoring and Control	Directly monitor and control activities	Program governance mechanism	Monitors aggregated performance of portfolio components and strategic value indicators against external environment

Source: Table for area, project, program, portfolio for comparison of P3M.

Section I

Strategic portfolio management in context

Introduction

This first section of the book introduces the premise of strategic portfolio management in the organisational context. In this foundational part of the book, the chapters look to develop a wide and thorough base of knowledge from which the rest of the book then provides further depth.

Chapter 2 begins with a discussion of how strategy execution is integrated with a portfolio of programs and projects. Here, Harpum takes the approach that strategy execution and the delivery of a portfolio of strategic work are, in fact, synonymous. This initial chapter covers strategy at a fairly high level, which is then developed in more detail in Chapter 3 by Redfern. Chapter 3 also includes an overview of the mechanisms and structures of portfolio, program, and project management.

Chapter 4 is based on the premise that strategic portfolio management plays a significant role in influencing the ability of organisations to successfully navigate organisational change. Sidhu and Harpum have written this chapter to begin what may become the first significant discussion on the intersection of organisational change and portfolio management. In Chapter 5, Long and Harpum develop further the ideas in the previous two chapters, looking at how the strategic activity of scenario futures planning influences strategy from a portfolio perspective.

Chapter 6, again by Harpum and Long, and Chapter 7, by Serra and Harpum, discuss the interrelated areas of defining and delivering strategic value and how benefits realisation management (BRM) for projects and programs fits within this. Chapter 8, by Dalcher, concludes this section, bringing together the key themes from previous chapters when delivering organisational strategy, discussing the key influences on portfolio success.

If you believe you are already well versed in strategy or program and project management or both, feel free to bypass the relevant chapters in this section. However, please be aware that existing conceptualisations of these topics may differ, perhaps noticeably, from those presented in this book. Much of the first two sections of the book challenge normative models espoused by some of the literature, the professional institutions, and how they might be operationalised in organisations.

Chapter questions

Katy Angliss

For each section of the book, there are a set of questions to have in mind when working through the chapters. These are titled the "material review questions" and are designed to prime the approach and thinking when reading through the contents, as well as highlighting key areas of interest throughout the chapter. There is also the option, after reading each section, to return to the questions and test your understanding, perhaps as a learning tool. For each chapter, there are also a second set of questions, entitled "further discussion questions", which can help with envisioning the specific context of your own organisation or for further student learning as appropriate. Where references are included in the following questions, these relate to the references in the relevant chapter.

Chapter 2 Strategic portfolio management in context

Material review questions

2.1 Why is strategy, and the delivery of strategic objectives, such a fundamental part of portfolio management?
2.2 Why should senior roles within portfolio management and the wider organisational community be involved with the development of strategic goals?
2.3 How does strategic portfolio management support strategy execution?
2.4 How and where should the strategic portfolio be managed?

Further discussion questions

2.5 Discuss why Portfolio Management should be considered as important within an organisation.
2.6 Discuss how projects and programs influence the strategic portfolio and how they are aligned to organisational strategy within your organisation.
2.7 Discuss the key roles of a portfolio within an organisation.
2.8 Considering the PPM-to-SPM discussion in this chapter, debate the following:

Some of the P3M literature are called "standards" – implying that a normative model of portfolio, program, and project management is the standard one. This is critiqued not least by Cicmil and Hodgson (2006), suggesting that "the tendency in the field is still to treat the basic framework of 'project management' as compelling . . . with the assumption that such an ideal model objectively exists in the world of practice".

Chapter 3 Organisational strategy and portfolio management

Material review questions

3.1 Which part of the strategic process is the most important aspect where portfolio management can add value: formulation, development, or execution?
3.2 What are some of the key influencing factors to consider for strategy development?
3.3 Is an adaptable, resilient strategy the focus of an emergent or deterministic strategy?
3.4 How does the role of supply chains influence organisational strategy?
3.5 Which level of the portfolio should typically focus on benefits and benefits realisation?

Further discussion questions

3.6 Discuss the challenges of effective strategy execution and the advantages of strategy execution through portfolios.
3.7 Discuss the core elements of successful strategy execution with portfolio management.
3.8 Evaluate whether there should be clear boundaries between strategic planning and strategic implementation.
3.9 Discuss whether portfolios should always contain both projects and programs.
3.10 Discuss whether the management of assets and resources should be within the responsibility of the portfolio.
3.11 What are some of the reasons for portfolio management failure.
3.12 Which is the main strategy formulation approach and strategic delivery approach adopted in your organisation.

Chapter 4 Organisational change and portfolio management

Material review questions

4.1 Compare how planned and emergent strategy can be related to managing change.
4.2 Consider how important the "affect factors" can be for change readiness.
4.3 Establish the role that portfolio managers should engage with for effective organisational change.

Further discussion questions

4.4 Discuss the level of influence people's perceptions, experiences, emotions, and responses have on managing change effectively.
4.5 Discuss the role of strategic portfolios in managing change.
4.6 Determine an example "BART" analysis for a portfolio.

Chapter 5 Scenario planning for strategic portfolios

Material review questions

5.1 How does scenario planning and analysis inform portfolio definition?
5.2 Considering Figure 5.1. in this chapter, what are the main challenges with developing scenarios for defining strategy and portfolio development?

Further discussion questions

5.3 Discuss the three typical approaches to scenario analysis and how effective they may be in different context and within your own particular context.

Chapter 6 Delivering strategic value through the portfolio

Material review questions

6.1 Compare and contrast the different definitions and sources of value.
6.2 Discuss how the definition of strategic value affects strategic delivery of objectives within the portfolio.
6.3 Discuss how strategic value can be measured within the portfolio.
6.4 Consider how business benefits and benefits from projects and programs relate to portfolio value?

Further discussion questions

6.5 Establish the chain of value creation in an (your) organisation.
6.6 Discuss how the business case for projects and programs are developed to realise benefits and strategic value.

Chapter 7 Benefits realisation management (BRM) as a driver for delivering strategic value

Material review questions

7.1 How is BRM related to both project success and the creation of strategic value?
7.2 Suggest ways in which BRM can be measured.
7.3 How important is portfolio governance for a benefits management strategy?

Further discussion questions

7.4 Consider how an organisation might plan to introduce BRM, thinking, for example, about the processes, culture, organisational environment, etc.
7.5 Discuss how your organisation could improve on benefits management for projects and programs.

Chapter 8 Rethinking portfolio success

Material review questions

8.1 Discuss how portfolio management contributes to business success.
8.2 How and why is the success of a project portfolio (as a collection of projects) influenced by its context and culture within the organisation?
8.3 Critique the multidimensional portfolio success criteria considered by Beringer et al. (2013) and Meskendahl (2010), and compare this with the three dimensions of portfolio success advocated by Kopmann (2014)?

Further discussion questions

8.4 Why might it be more effective to measure success at the enterprise (organisational) portfolio level and/or the strategic initiative level?
8.5 Discuss how important agility might be to portfolio success.

2 Strategic portfolio management in context

Pete Harpum

Introduction

A central premise of this book is that a properly integrated and well-managed "portfolio of work" is the most effective approach for delivering organisational strategic objectives, whether this is the delivery of new products, the built environment, business-to-business or business-to-consumer services, new or improved organisational processes, new employee ways of working or cultural changes, other organisational change, cost savings, or a multitude of other strategic imperatives. Another, perhaps secondary, premise of the book is that the delivery of specific strategic objectives – "the work" – is best and most effectively achieved through a well-designed approach to the management of programs and projects in which that work is carried out, properly integrated with each other and with the portfolio(s) within which they exist.

The idea of an integrated *portfolio, program, and project management (P3M)* approach has existed since at least the early 2000s (Cooke-Davies, 2004, Harpum, 2006). The idea that strategy execution and P3M are essentially the same thing was also emerging at the same time (Morris & Pinto, 2004, 2007). However, in the past, adopting only a "management by projects" approach, without a formal or integrated portfolio process, has often been ineffective in meeting the intended needs of P3M: the wrong projects have been run, at the wrong time, creating outcomes that did not contribute to corporate strategic objectives (Cooke-Davies, 2002). Fundamentally, the needs, to be addressed by having greater focus on portfolios in the P3M context and, more specifically, with portfolio management, are to ensure *strategic objectives are delivered* and to *maximise process efficiency*.

Therefore, this chapter is essential in establishing where to place portfolio management in its role within organisations: to correctly translate strategic objectives into the most effective arrangement of work to ensure that strategy is executed. In order to orientate the thinking towards the importance of portfolio management as the vital integration mechanism of strategic objectives, strategy, and strategy execution fundamentally through a combination of programs, projects, and other strategic activities, this chapter will:

1 Introduce the key concepts and elements of strategic management and portfolio management.
2. Discuss the way portfolio management impacts on the strategy process and then delivers strategic objectives.
3 Provide an overview of the processes and techniques used by organisations to execute strategy through the use of portfolio management.

DOI: 10.4324/9780367853129-3

There is insufficient space in this chapter to give anything like a full account of the many techniques and practices used to formulate and implement strategy, and many of these are often disputed by one or another of the schools of strategic thought. See the following discussion and further expansion on organisational strategic aspects in Chapter 3. However, in this chapter a few brief notes will be provided in highlighting the importance of strategy for portfolio management and which is seen to most succinctly identify some of the factors that need to be addressed in the strategic management process, from the prescriptive school of strategic thinking (Mintzberg et al., 2008), remembering that there are many other considerations which may influence strategy formulation and implementation (such as power relationships, corporate culture, logical incrementalism, strategy as imposed by environmental considerations, etc.).

Strategic management

Firms will decide what overall direction they are moving towards in using a process previously called "business policy" but now more often referred to as "strategic management". The definition of *strategy* is as difficult to pin down as can be the definition of a *project*. In the words of Mintzberg (Mintzberg et al., 1998), "the word strategy has long been used in different ways, even if it has been traditionally defined in only one". Explicit recognition of multiple definitions can help people to manoeuvre through this difficult field. Some of the varying opinions as to what strategy means are listed as follows (note that Chapter 3 will further discuss and expand on some of these definitions):

- "Strategic thinking is the art of outdoing an adversary, knowing that the adversary is trying to do the same to you" (Dixit & Nalebuff, 1993).
- "[T]he general direction in which the [companies] objectives are to be pursued" (Cleland & King, 1983).
- "[S]trategy is the handful of decisions that:
    - Drive or shape most of a company's subsequent actions,
    - Are not easily changed once made, and
    - Have the greatest impact on whether the company's strategic objectives are met" (Coyne & Subramaniam, 1996).
- "[S]trategies embrace those patterns of high-leverage decisions (on major goals, policies, and action sequences) which affect the viability and direction of the entire enterprise or determine its competitive posture for an extended period of time" (Quinn, 1978).
- "The long-term direction of an organisation" (Whittington et al., 2020).

There are also numerous multifaceted definitions used when defining *strategic management* and *corporate* or *business strategy*. The following definitions, although useful at this stage, are therefore not absolute:

- *A strategy* is the pattern of decisions, and subsequent plans of activity, that integrates an organisation's vision, major goals, policies, and action sequences into a cohesive whole. A well-formulated strategy helps marshal and allocate an organisation's resources into a unique and viable posture based on its relative internal competencies and shortcomings, anticipated changes in sthe environment, and contingent moves by intelligent opponents.

- *Goals* (or objectives) state what is to be achieved and when results are to be accomplished, but they do not state how the results are to be achieved. All organisations have multiple goals existing in a complex hierarchy: from value objectives, which express the broad value premises toward which the company is to strive; through overall organisational objectives, towards which it should move; to a series of less-permanent goals that define targets for each organisational unit, its sub-units, and finally, all major program activities within each sub-unit. Major goals – those that affect the entity's overall direction and viability – are called strategic goals.
- *Policies* are rules or guidelines that express the limits within which action should occur. These rules often take the form of contingent decisions for resolving conflicts among specific objectives. Like the objectives they support, policies exist in a hierarchy throughout the organisation. Major policies – those that guide the entity's overall direction and posture or determine its viability – are called strategic policies.
- *Strategic programs* specify the step-by-step sequence of actions necessary to achieve major objectives. They express how objectives will be achieved within the limits set by policy. They ensure that resources are committed to achieve goals, and they provide the dynamic track against which progress can be measured. They determine the entity's overall thrust and viability.
- *Strategic decisions* are those that determine the overall direction of an enterprise and its ultimate viability in light of the predictable, the unpredictable, and the unknowable changes that may occur in its most important surrounding environments. They intimately shape the true goals of the enterprise. They help delineate the broad limits within which the enterprise operates. They dictate both the resources the enterprise will have accessible for its tasks and the principal patterns in which these resources will be allocated.

Effective formal strategies contain three essential elements. All three of these elements benefit significantly from input of the senior portfolio community.

1. The most important goals (or objectives) to be achieved.
2. The most significant policies guiding or limiting action.
3. The major action sequences (*programs and, where applicable, projects*) that are to accomplish the defined goals within the limits set.

Since strategy determines the overall direction and action focus of the organisation, its formulation cannot be regarded as the mere generation and alignment of programs (or projects) to meet predetermined goals. Goal development is an integral part of strategy formulation. Portfolio (and program and project) management specialists should have a key role to play in supporting the definition of strategic goals that are likely to be achievable. People in these senior portfolio roles have expertise in "strategising" at each level of the portfolio and are (or at least ought to be) well informed about the organisations' competencies and capabilities to deliver within given environments (Löwstedt et al., 2018).

Understanding the envelope within which action can be taken when implementing strategic action has a direct impact on what goals, and hence actions, are realistic within an organisation. Senior portfolio managers should have experience of managing activities (in portfolios of programs and projects) that push on these policy limits. They know which limits (and/or organisational boundaries) can be broken, be pushed, be bent, or are inviolate. What the organisational policy says on paper is often not the same as how that same policy is in fact enforced or enacted, especially when the policy in question may be hampering the implementation of a strategic imperative.

Effective strategies develop around a few key concepts and thrusts, which give them cohesion, balance, and focus. Understanding this set of strategic actions (programs and projects) as a whole (a portfolio or, indeed, a strategic portfolio of sub-portfolios) is vital to effective strategy implementation (strategy execution). Some thrusts of activity are temporary: others are carried through to the end of the strategy. Some actions cost more per unit gain than others. Yet resources must be allocated in patterns that provide sufficient resources for each thrust to succeed regardless of its relative cost/gain ratio, and organisational units must be coordinated, and actions controlled, to support the intended strategic thrust, or else the total strategy will fail. These aspects are at the heart of the effective management of a strategic portfolio of programs and projects.

Strategy and its execution deal not just with the unpredictable but also with the unknowable outcomes of complex interactions in the environment. For major enterprise strategies, no analyst could predict the precise ways to which all impinging forces could interact with each other, be distorted by nature or human emotions, or be modified by the imaginations and purposeful counteraction of intelligent opponents. Large systems can respond quite counter-intuitively to apparently rational actions by organisations within the system. A seemingly bizarre series of events can conspire to prevent or assist success in the execution of organisational strategy.

Consequently, the essence of strategy is to build a posture that is so strong (and potentially flexible) in selective ways that the organisation can achieve its goals despite the unforeseeable ways external forces (or risks) may actually interact when the time comes. This flexibility is, or should be, built into P3M, particularly at the portfolio and program levels. Projects tend to be less flexible, but when the outputs they are creating are no longer relevant, the project should be stopped, whilst the program of which they are constituent may well continue, after being adjusted to take account of the new environment.

These various ways of thinking about how strategy is formed and implemented can be reduced to a diagram, as shown at Figure 2.1 (Mintzberg et al., 1998). The diagram shows that there are two main sources of strategy – deliberate and emergent – and it is likely that there is a balance at any one time in any single organisation of the deliberate and emergent forms of strategy. It is probable that strategy will be mainly deliberate, during times of relative stability, with few emergent strategies being realised. During times of great uncertainty and turbulence in the business, emergent strategies may predominate as crises are dealt with by people relying on their experience and intuition, due to the lack of time (or leadership) available to create deliberate strategy. The balance will change over time as the organisational context of strategy formulation and implementation changes. It is worth noting that portfolio management can be, when set up well, particularly good at helping emerging strategies to be identified, assessed, and fed into the strategy execution "machine" – that is, the portfolio (or P3M) structure. (Chapter 3 discusses the implications and integration of emergent strategy flowing "back up" from the execution of projects/programs.)

Strategy also occurs in two distinct parts of the organisation – at the corporate level and at the level of the business unit. Corporate strategy is about moving the entire organisation towards long- and short-term goals, to ensure the overall group remains profitable – its survival is of primary importance. Business unit strategy is likely to be more focused

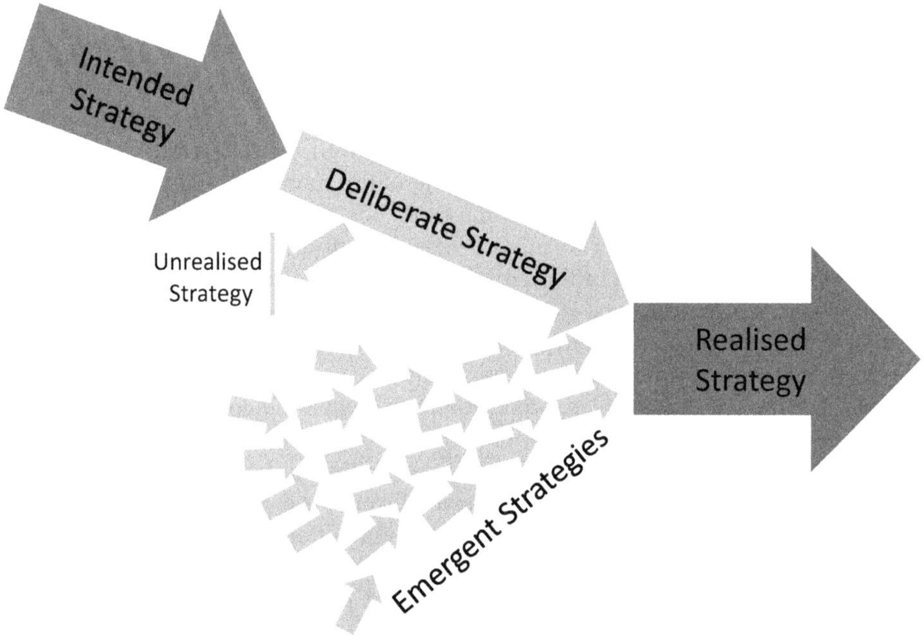

Figure 2.1 Deliberate and emergent strategies.

Source: Adapted from Mintzberg et al. (1998).

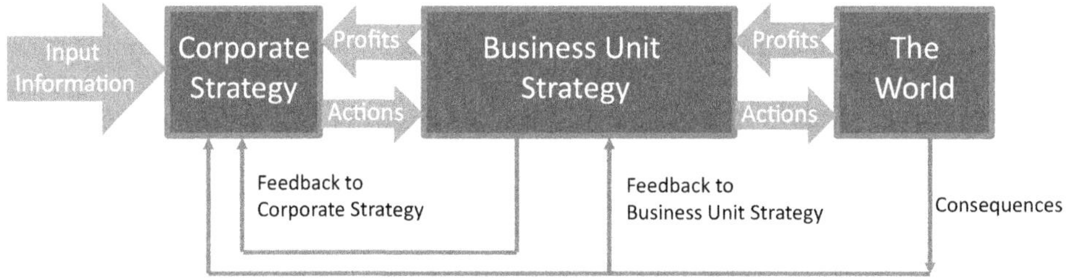

Figure 2.2 Relationship between corporate and business unit strategy.

Source: Adapted from Cleland and King (1983).

on ensuring profitability in its own marketplace, feeding the operating margin back into the corporation. This situation can be represented as in Figure 2.2.

From this diagram, it is clear that portfolio management needs to be a systemic part of the way the organisation operates at various levels to be able to manage and execute strategy, whilst at the corporate level there is a whole company portfolio (strategic portfolio), made up of other portfolios, and perhaps including a few massive strategic programs and/or projects. At successively lower levels, further portfolios of programs and projects then exist (such as tactical or sub-portfolios).

In order for the organisation to get commitment from its employees, there is a need for the strategies at both corporate and business unit level to be fully and clearly articulated and disseminated throughout the organisation. The ease with which this will happen will be dependent on the corporate culture and whether it is considered to be important for the strategy to be kept secret from competitors (meaning, that it is not made explicit within the organisation either). However, when all employees understand what the corporate and business unit strategies are, they are more likely to be motivated towards achieving the intended outcome of the strategies. The issues to be considered when planning corporate strategy will naturally be dependent on which way, or ways, of developing strategy is used (Sierotowicz, 2020).

Contextualising portfolio management

In almost all organisations, there is, *de facto*, a portfolio of work to be done. Even in a theoretical single-project organisation, there is more work to be done than to simply deliver the single project. The organisation must engage with regulatory bodies of some kind or another (at the very least, those national regulators responsible for, say, company formation), people need to be recruited, IT systems need to be put in place, premises are required, etc. This work may, or may not, be carried out as projects – but it falls into the overall "book of work" that has to be accomplished. This book of work is a portfolio, *by definition*.

Thus, the management of portfolios of work has been going on since organisations existed:

> Centuries ago, the Fugger banking family dynasty, which dominated Europe in the 15th and 16th centuries, and the East India Company, the powerful megacorporation that had a near-monopoly on all commerce in India and China between the 17th and 19th centuries, were aware of the need to successfully manage different business activities, such as expanding into new ventures, allocating scarce resources, closing down unprofitable branches, and dealing with dissenting governors. The same is true for large companies that emerged during the industrialization era in the late 19th century, such as General Electric and Siemens.
>
> (Nippa et al., 2010, p. 51)

A brief history of portfolio management

Portfolio management theory is therefore rooted in the collection and management of sets of assets, most frequently financial assets – stocks and shares, bonds, cash, and a multiplicity of other financial instruments. Modern work on effective management of portfolios can be traced to Marschak, Williams, and others in the late 1930s (Rubinstein, 2002), culminating with Markowitz publishing a seminal paper in 1952 distinguishing efficient from inefficient investment portfolios (Markowitz, 1952). Nevertheless, the central importance of careful management of sets of assets goes back centuries and is found in Shakespeare, where Antonio says in *The Merchant of Venice*:

> My ventures are not in one bottom trusted, nor to one place; nor is my whole estate. Upon the fortune of this present year; therefore, my merchandise makes me not sad.
>
> (Shakespeare, 1605, Act 1, Scene 1)

Arising from Markowitz's and others' work, portfolio management became an important driver of corporate strategy, particularly within multi-divisional organisations in the 1970s and 1980s. Divisions within such organisations were managed as a corporate portfolio, with the interactions between the divisions explicitly taken into account, as well as risk/return across the portfolio. Achieving a balanced portfolio was a business-critical management preoccupation (Smith, 2014). That portfolio management–driven strategy led to disappointment with the outcomes achieved by these organisations. This configuration (a reverse configuration – strategy drives portfolio, not the other way around) was dropped by the end of the 1980s, as portfolio management became tasked with the work to translate strategy into projects/programs. The need to understand the corporate portfolio through the lens of an investment portfolio was reinforced by this change in approach, not dismissed (Sanwal, 2007).

A text frequently referenced by writers on portfolio management, from within and outside project management academia and practitioners, is *Portfolio Management for New Products*, by Cooper et al. (2001). Cooper and colleagues undertook research on the management of portfolios of new products in the mid- to late-1990s, and it's worth quoting from the beginning of Chapter 2 of this book, titled "Three Decades of R&D Portfolio Management":

> The concept of portfolio management for new product development is not new. Over the decades, the topic has surfaced under various guises, including "R&D project selection", "R&D resource allocation", "project prioritisation", and "portfolio management". By the early 1970s, dozens of articles had appeared on the topic. . . . The objective was to develop a portfolio of new and existing projects to maximise some objective function (for example, the expected profits), subject to a set of resource constraints.

Clearly, the idea that effectively managing a portfolio of new projects is strategically vital was established in the 1970s and continued into the 1980s, with work ongoing into the best ways to manage multiple projects to ensure delivery of strategy (see, for example, Roetheli & Pesenti, 1986; Petit & Hobbs, 2010; Young et al., 2011). It can also be seen that other aspects of portfolio management precede the 1970s significantly. Cooper et al. did not approach new product portfolio management from the project management theoretical or even practical perspective. They looked at what organisations need to do to meet these requirements (adapted from Cooper et al., 2001):

1. Corporate goals, objectives, and strategies must be the basis for new product (or R&D) portfolio selection.
2. Senior management is the driver of strategy and must be closely involved in new product (or R&D) project selection decisions.
3. Good communication and understanding must exist between senior corporate managers and R&D management.
4. Portfolio methods must mesh with the decision framework for the business.
5. Portfolio methods should be used for information display only and not yield an optimisation decision.
6. The portfolio selection method must accommodate change and the interaction of goals and players.
7. Risk must be accommodated by the selection technique.
8. Organisational structure and appropriate support systems are required.

Whilst acknowledging that the emphasis of these authors was on new products/R&D, the requirements previously listed seem to be somewhat obvious and applicable to all portfolios delivering strategic goals through a portfolio of projects and programs. McFarlan was discussing the importance of understanding IT project risk at the portfolio level in 1981 in the *Harvard*

Business Review (McFarlan, 1981). The need for a wide range of senior managers, including finance and financial engineers, to be involved with decision-making about projects-as-investment-assets in a portfolio became clearer than ever as financial engineering work with risk management emerged in the 1990s and was reported in the project management literature (Farrell, 2002). Indeed, early in the 2000s, the general applicability of these ideas, and the need to make clear the link from strategy to execution through the portfolio, was being taken into a fully general view for project management, applicable to everywhere that multiple projects and programs must be managed in a coordinated manner (Harpum, 2006).

Apart from the significant ongoing research regarding new products in the 1970s and the development of those ideas in the world of projects, the need to make effective decisions about what to allocate capital to, to create and manage the corporate book of work that will deliver strategic objectives, and how to make calculations to support such decisions, was beginning to be formalised in the early 1950s. Dean (1951) makes explicit reference to capital allocation to projects in a portfolio, their prioritisation, and the need to classify them to facilitate adequate allocations to different types of projects, including those that produce no or little direct financial return. Indeed, it is his view that these decisions regarding the "planning and control of capital expenditure is the basic top-management function, since management is originally hired to take control of stockholder's funds and to maximise their earning power." This is clearly supported, in current UK statutory law at least, with the single most important duty of a company director: "to act in good faith to promote the success of the company for the benefit of its members" or shareholders (the UK term for stockholders) (HM Government, 2006). It would therefore not be much of a stretch to say that it is a legal requirement for directors and senior managers of a (commercial) organisation to effectively manage the *corporate book of work* – the strategic portfolio – in order to meet the objectives of the shareholders. (In a non-commercial organisation, the duty is still to members with controlling interests in the organisation.)

During the 1990s, program management developed as a distinct approach. As previously discussed, portfolio management already existed in a number of forms (investment portfolios and the collections of projects delivered by construction and engineering companies to their clients). Most organisations had systems to manage their project work. However, in many companies, these various project-related processes (portfolio, program, where they formally existed, and project) were poorly integrated – and this is often still the case today. One can imagine a football (soccer) team with superb strikers, a powerful midfield, and well-oiled defence who cannot operate as a team up and down the pitch and with a defensive strategy that does not match the striker's strategy.

The business context

Before the concept of "management by projects" was established and change in, and to, organisations was not endemic, most businesses managed their activities as an ongoing *operation* – which often is called "business-as-usual". Some projects did exist but often were not managed as such. (Arguably, here, projectisation may have provided benefits since it helps to view operational and project management as alternative approaches to carrying out work. For example, one can ask, Is a surgical procedure in a hospital "operational" or a "project"? Actually, there is a choice, succinctly expressed by Artto [1999], when questioning as to why every activity or change should not be viewed as a project.) Many parts of today's organisations are still managed operationally, such as manufacturing, customer support, and administration. The basic aim of this approach, that is, incremental improvement of efficiency whilst supporting corporate strategy, is reasonably well understood.

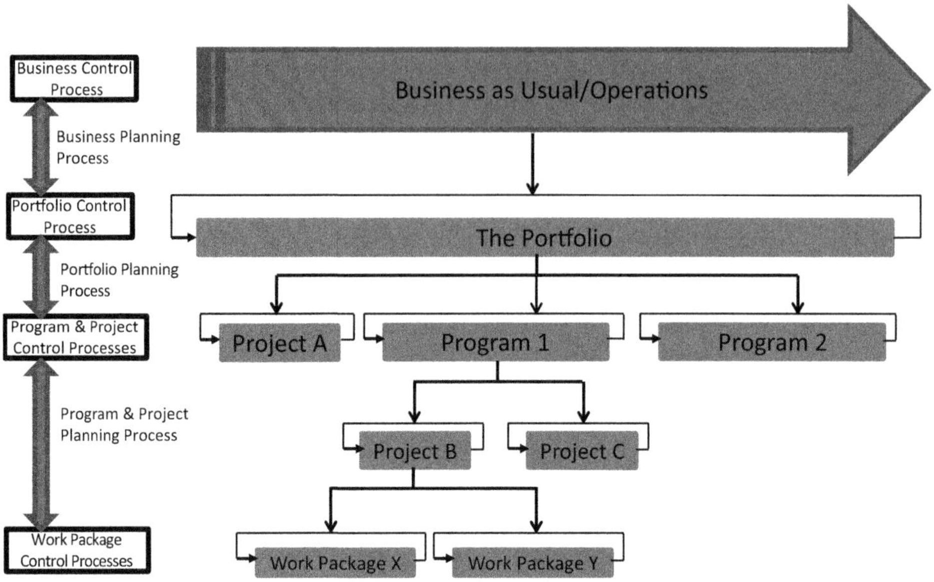

Figure 2.3 Portfolio management and business-as-usual.

Source: Adapted from Harpum (2004).

Against this background, it can be said that portfolio management does not replace, wholesale, general management (or operational) systems, procedures, and processes. It can, however, and should, be the primary or only mechanism through which strategic objectives are delivered (see Figure 2.3). (This argument is developed further in Chapter 6.)

There are enormous variations in the business contexts in which portfolios of programs and projects are run. These differences contribute to the difficulty in agreeing with the meanings of the terms used. Despite this, ensuring strategic linkage and process alignment, from the corporate level through to project management, leads to the maximisation of value creation in a "projectised" organisation, which in modern times means in most organisations.

> The viable organizations will be the ones that master the science and art of organization design to achieve both high differentiation and high integration.
>
> (Lawrence & Lorsch, 1986)

Many organisations are simply not there yet. Managing portfolios, programs, and projects in an integrated way, ensuring that delivery of business value is the overriding objective, is neither fad nor panacea. It is a realistic way forward for applying common sense to "projectised" work in a complex organisational setting.

From project portfolio management (PPM) to strategic portfolio management (SPM)

The idea that program and project management *exists to deliver or execute strategy* is slowly becoming accepted in the relevant literature (for example Lock & Wagner, 2019; Morris, 2009) as well as within industry. The argument, then, is that the portfolio is the mechanism for linking strategy and strategic objectives to the set of work needed to be done to execute the strategy. This implies, by definition, that the portfolio and its management is a top-down structure and process. This view is in contrast to much current project management–orientated literature that frequently theorises from the perspective of project and program management, not strategy execution.

Many sources in the project and program management literature look to begin the discussion and review of portfolios and portfolio management from the bottom-up perspective of aligning and balancing a set of projects and programs (and operations) to the strategy – as though the projects and programs exist independently of strategy and strategic goals.

Project management researchers and professionals have been developing, and have begun to introduce, a "new management approach" to cope with these effects and to account for the growing need for structured and proactive management of the project landscape. Project portfolio management (PPM) can be viewed as a type of "required management innovation" (Hamel, 2006; Jonas, 2010). That is, it is a key competence for companies handling numerous projects simultaneously (Beringer et al., 2012). Rather than simply managing multiple projects, project portfolio management has started to go beyond the boundaries of traditional project management, to "bridging the gap between projects and organisational strategy" (Jiang et al., 2020, p. 101).

This so-called "new management approach" and "required management innovation" has become manifest in "standards" for project professionals and in the writings of established authors in the field (the field of project management, that is), such as the following examples.

> It is the application of portfolio management principles to align the portfolio and its components with the organizational strategy.
>
> (PMI, 2017, p. 5)

PPM [project portfolio management] is the management of the project portfolio so as to maximise the contribution of projects to the overall welfare and success of the enterprise. This means that:

- Projects must be aligned with the firm's strategy and goals.
- Projects must be consistent with the firm's values and culture.
- Projects must not only provide for current contributions to the firm's health but must help position the firm for future success.

(Levine, 2005, p. 23)

> [T]here is a need to understand the latest thinking in PPM [portfolio project management] and how far both the discipline and technology has moved beyond the simple Gantt chart.
>
> (Moore, 2010, p. ix)

> Portfolio management is a coordinated collection of strategic processes and decisions that together enable a more effective balance or organisational change and business as usual.
>
> (Axelos, 2011, p. ix)

This is all, surely, somewhat backwards. For specific projects and programs to exist, they should, before becoming part of the portfolio, be already aligned to strategy, because if they are not, they should not be in the portfolio. Conceptualising (project) portfolio management as an extension of project management theory is to put the cart before the horse. In order to bring a genuinely critical approach to the subject of portfolio management and its role in strategy execution, there is a need to understand the notion of *what a portfolio exists to achieve*; once that is understood, the integration and alignment mechanisms can be understood in light of the objectives these mechanisms are intended to achieve.

Therefore, where we really need to start is the need to be clear on the organisational logic to create a portfolio of strategic work and the specificity of the objectives of managing that portfolio, *and then agree how to set up management mechanisms that link it to program and project management.*

There are three really important reasons to labour the point that it has been known for a very long time that it is important to effectively manage a portfolio of projects (irrespective of whether the modern construct and terminology of portfolio and project was known):

1. Acknowledging this historical fact opens our eyes to research and knowledge flowing from it, which was done before the 1990s, which otherwise we may miss.
2. It reinforces the strategic orientation of portfolio management – it simply is not an extension of project management theory, and to approach it in this way limits the range of ideas available.
3. Overlapping with the second point, it makes absolutely plain that portfolio management is a strategic activity that is of vital importance as the operational link between the development/agreement of strategic objectives and strategic plans and the definition and overall direction of the projects and programs that are created to deliver those strategic objectives.

To reiterate, that projects deliver strategic objectives, managed and mediated through the portfolio, was recognised as far back as the 1970s (Scheinberg & Stretton, 1994; Petit & Hobbs, 2010; Nippa et al., 2010), hinted at strongly by Dean (1951) when presenting theoretical and practical implications of capital budgeting, and reinforced by Markowitz's seminal work on mathematical modelling of portfolios (Markowitz, 1999).

Executing strategy through integrated portfolio management

The critical importance of integrating increasingly differentiated work processes in organisations was identified in the mid-1960s during landmark research most notably by Lawrence and Lorsch (1986). Generally speaking, integrated *horizontal* processes are now common in projectised companies at the project level – project control, the management of uncertainty, value management, etc. However, vertical integration is often missing – the wrong projects at the wrong time! Portfolio management aims specifically to improve vertical integration of "projectised" work. Figure 2.4 shows how measures of strategic alignment (strategic goals, performance indicators, and other targets and measures) are cascaded down the hierarchy.

The three management approaches within P3M – portfolio, program, and project – are quite different in their execution, both strategically and tactically. The central point about managing them in an integrated way is that they should have a strong linkage, through strategy at the very least. Each project in each program in each portfolio must contribute to delivery of the corporate strategy in a measurable way. Corporate strategy should

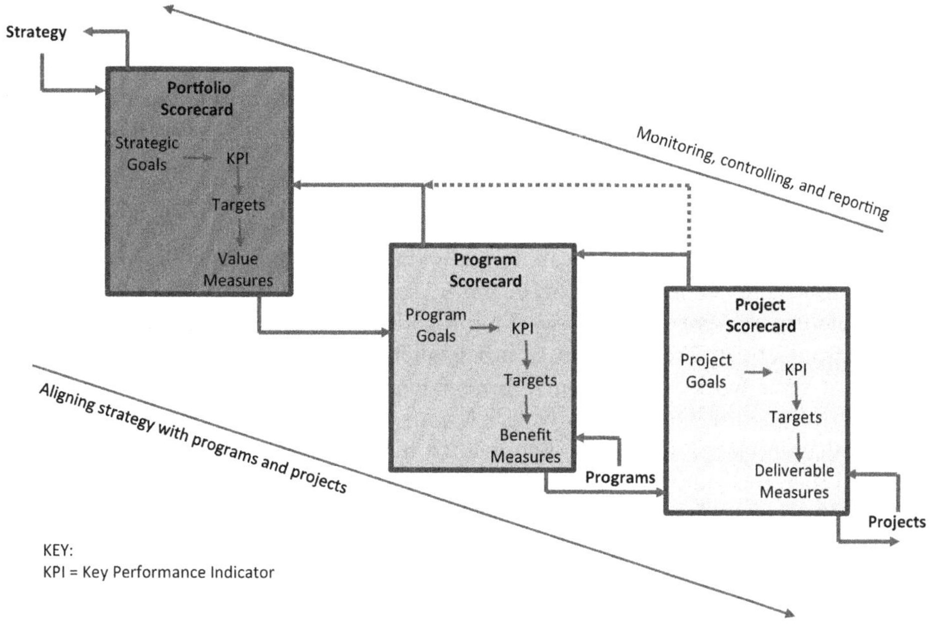

Figure 2.4 Linking strategy and P3M.

Source: Adapted from Lock and Wagner (2016).

define portfolio decision-making rules. The organisation must decide which programs and "stand-alone" projects should be run and in what order of prioritisation they receive resources. The integration between portfolios, programs, and projects is further discussed in Chapter 9.

Program strategy must be aligned to portfolio strategy – the program is delivering key parts of the overall strategy, through creating outcomes or, as commonly called in this context, business "*benefits*" (discussed in Chapter 7). Similarly, project strategy must reflect program strategy, and in some cases for multiple programs. Project scope is determined by project strategy. Without a clear connection to corporate strategy, the project may deliver the "wrong" outcomes. Note that in this context, project outcomes are commonly called products or deliverables, whereas where projects are within programs, the definitional situation becomes confusing. In this case, the current "standards" (such as APM, 2012; Axelos, 2011; HM Government, 2018; BS ISO 21500, 2012) define what a project makes as "outputs" and what a program delivers as "outcomes". It is also clear that to ensure effective integration and control of the portfolio of work, there should be vertical and horizontal (i.e. between projects or programs) process integration of each management approach, tuned to meet the needs of the business and adapted to suit the other business processes that exist. These include:

- Control processes – scope change, resource allocation, schedule, budget, quality, etc.
- Uncertainty management – risk and opportunity.
- Benefits realisation.

- Value management.
- Performance measurement – monitoring and reporting progress, definition of critical success factors and key performance indicators, etc.

Organisations exist for a multiplicity of reasons, and a vast literature exists to explain why people gather themselves into groups to achieve objectives. No matter the theoretical explanations for people to decide to work together in achieving goals, rather than alone, the point is that the group has gathered because a decision is made (consciously or otherwise) that it will be easier to achieve the goal(s) as a group rather than as individuals. Indeed, generally speaking, individuals simply cannot achieve many goals working alone, and this is the crux of the point: a group of people (team or department) have decided to achieve a goal by working together. There is a fundamental requirement in groups to differentiate work into smaller units, to enable each individual to know what their work is and then (re)integrate that work effectively to achieve the group's goals (see, for example, Lawrence & Lorsch, 1986). Work needs to be broken down so that specialist skills can be applied to maximise the efficiency of doing that work, and then the multiple pieces of work need to be integrated to ensure the goal is achieved. Integration is not achieved if the individual elements do not work together.

Strategic objectives are achieved by defining and pursuing organisational strategy. In order to achieve strategic goals, there is a need to define a strategy, and the strategy consists of defining what needs to be done, by whom, to achieve the objectives and how the work will be differentiated to allow specialists to work most efficiently on the work. There is therefore a vertical flow downwards, from strategic objectives to strategy to achieve those objectives to differentiating, or breaking down, the work needed to execute strategy. Table 2.1 is a summary of the connections between the fundamental elements of strategy and how portfolio management, supported by programs and projects, executes or delivers the strategy.

Strategic portfolio management in context

The point of this opening series of arguments is that portfolio management is a strategic business process and structure, not an extension upwards of project and program management theory, practice, and organisation, as seems to be evident in the way much of the project management literature portrays portfolio management (also, as something recent and new). Understanding this, and approaching portfolios and their management from, in principle, a top-down perspective, influences the way in which differentiation and integration mechanisms are designed and implemented in the vertical structure, as shown in Figure 2.5.

Recognising that portfolio management is not a new discipline and is not an extension of project/program management theory allows us to look at portfolio management drawing on theory that has existed for decades. In fact, the theory becomes relatively straightforward (albeit that financial modelling of projects within portfolios is sophisticated and complicated, but straightforward and well known). The portfolio thus has the following roles to accomplish:

1. *Creating a set of projects* (and if necessary, programs and/or other activities) that will deliver the strategic objectives of the organisation, following a strategic approach defined by strategists (and the P3M community) working in the organisation.

Table 2.1 How portfolio management matches strategic management's definition of strategy

Strategy and strategic management	*Portfolio management*
Definitions	
A strategy is the pattern that integrates an organisation's major goals, policies, and action sequences into a cohesive whole.	Portfolio management properly implemented reflects these criteria.
Goals (or objectives) state what is to be achieved and when results are to be accomplished, but they do not state how the results are to be achieved.	Because portfolio management is to do with aligning and implementing strategy, it states how the strategy is to be achieved. Doing this includes showing the way the strategy will be delivered.
Policies are rules or guidelines that express the limits within which action should occur. Major policies – those that guide the entity's overall direction and posture or determine its viability – are called *strategic* policies.	Governance at each level of the portfolio defines the limits of actions by those involved.
Programs specify the step-by-step sequence of actions necessary to achieve major objectives. They express how objectives will be achieved within the limits set by policy. They ensure that resources are committed to achieve goals, and they provide the dynamic track against which progress can be measured. Those major programs that determine the entity's overall thrust and viability are called *strategic programs*.	Through this definition, strategic management accepts that programs are the means of delivering strategy. Programs are an integral part of portfolio management (and P3M).
Criteria for effective strategy	
Clear, decisive objectives: Are all efforts directed toward clearly understood, decisive, and attainable overall goals? Specific goals of subordinate units may change in the heat of the campaigns or competition, but the overriding goals of the strategy for all units must remain clear enough to provide continuity and cohesion for tactical choices during the time horizon of the strategy. All goals need not be written down or numerically precise, but they must be understood and be decisive – that is, if they are achieved, they should ensure the continued viability and vitality of the entity vis-à-vis its opponents.	A distinctive characteristic of portfolio management is clear and decisive objectives at each level. The requirement is also to document the objectives as part of portfolio management.
Concentration: Does the strategy concentrate superior power at the place and time likely to be decisive? Has the strategy defined precisely what will make the enterprise superior in power – that is, "best" in critical dimensions – in relation to its opponents? A distinctive competency yields greater success with fewer resources and is the essential basis for higher gains (or profits) than competitors.	Portfolio management concentrates decisive power and is a core competency in delivering strategy.

(*Continued*)

Table 2.1 (Continued)

Strategy and strategic management	*Portfolio management*
Coordinated and committed leadership: Does the strategy provide responsible, committed leadership for each of its major goals? Leaders must be so chosen and motivated that their own interests and values match the needs of their roles. Successful strategies require commitment, not just acceptance.	Coordinated and committed leadership is pivotal in portfolio management and, through it, delivering strategy.
Surprise: Has the strategy made use of speed, secrecy, and intelligence to strike new or emerging markets, at unexpected times, to exposed or unprepared competitors? With surprise and correct timing, success can be achieved out of all proportion to the energy exerted and can decisively change strategic positions.	Portfolio management is a very effective process for identifying opportunities in the market and enabling them through synergy. This is another example of portfolio management (and P3M) delivering strategy.
Security: Does the strategy secure resource bases and all vital operating points for the enterprise? Does it develop an effective intelligence system sufficient to prevent surprises by opponents? Does it develop the full logistics to support each of its major thrusts? Does it use coalitions effectively to extend the resource base and zones of friendly acceptance for the enterprise?	Identification, acquisition, and timely utilisation of resources is a core competence of portfolio management.

Source: Table with strategy/strategic management and portfolio management as a comparison.

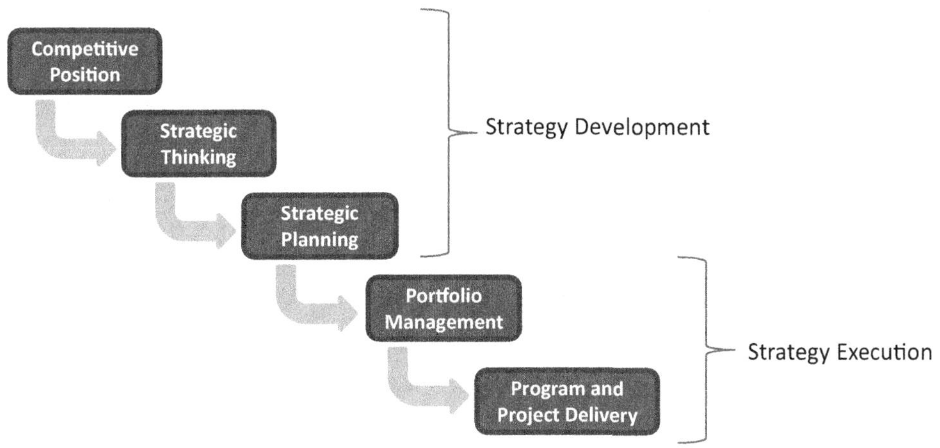

Figure 2.5 Top-down portfolio management.

2. *Optimising the set of projects/programs* to deliver the organisation's strategic objectives (or parts of the objectives) – there are normally multiple different ways work can be turned into projects/programs, and the portfolio needs to define the most effective and efficient ways to differentiate the overall work.
3. *Allocating assets and resources within the organisation most efficiently* to the set of projects/programs (and, where necessary, other activities or business-as-usual).
4. *Responding to changes in organisational strategy* by bringing new work into the portfolio and removing work not needed and reallocating assets to ensure efficiency remains optimised.
5. *Dealing with uncertainty* in the possibility of executing the projects and programs as anticipated (reality impacts on project/program plans and changes what is actually possible compared to what was thought was possible), preparing as far as possible for black swan events, anti-fragile and diversity in the portfolio, that is, managing the risk in the portfolio. (Note, black swan events [Taleb, 2010] are, in principle, impossible to predict and have very significant impacts on the organisation and its ability to execute strategy.)

Portfolio management is therefore less about detailed processes and procedures and accurate scheduling; it is more akin to strategic planning, with long timescales and low levels of detail, good governance, alignment, prioritisation of investment in change, and flexible processes and procedures (Axelos, 2011). It is better to get this right than to look for a portfolio management IT solution. It is importantly also an ongoing organisational activity, as strategic objectives change, the strategy for achieving them is adjusted as reality impacts what is working and what is not, and therefore the set of required projects and programs needed must, by definition, change. Portfolio management can be seen as the "glue" between projects and programs and the organisational direction.

Conclusion

In summary and to reiterate a key theme, this book consciously sets out to offer a perspective on portfolio management that starts from the concept of portfolios being essentially a strategic and business management construct and not the "discovery" of portfolios of projects as a relatively new domain within project management theory. Portfolio management, and the strategic portfolio, is viewed as an entity within the organisational environment, focused on delivering strategic objectives and adapting to its internal and external environment in continuously delivering the "portfolio of work" by ensuring the strategic portfolio is aligned and integrated with the strategic direction of the business.

References

APM (2012) *Body of Knowledge.* Sixth Edition. Association for Project Management, UK.

Artto K. (1999) Management across the business. *International Project Management Journal* 5(1), 4–9.

Axelos (2011) *Management of Portfolios.* The Stationary Office (TSO).

Beringer C., Jonas D. & Gemünden H. (2012) Establishing project portfolio management: An exploratory analysis of the influence of internal stakeholders' interactions. *Project Management Journal* 43(6), 16–32.

BS ISO 21500 (2012) *Guidance on Project Management.* BS ISO.

Cicmil S. & Hodgson D. (2006) *Making Projects Critical.* Palgrave.

Cleland D. & King W. (1983) *Systems Analysis and Project Management* [International edition]. McGraw Hill.

Cooke-Davies T. (2002) The "real" success factors on projects. *International Journal of Project Management* 20(3), 185–190.

Cooke-Davies T. (2004) 'Project Success', in Morris, P. & Pinto, J. *The Wiley Guide to the Management of Projects.* Wiley, pp. 99–122.

Cooper R., Edgett S. & Kleinschmidt E. (2001) *Portfolio Management for New Products.* Second Edition. Basic Books.

Coyne K. & Subramaniam S. (1996) Bringing discipline to strategy. *The McKinsey Quarterly* 4.

Dean J. (1951) *Capital Budgeting: Top-Management Policy on Plant, Equipment, and Product Development.* Columbia University Press.

Dixit A. K. & Nalebuff B. (1993) *Thinking Strategically: The Competitive Edge in Business, Politics, and Everyday Life.* Fourth Edition. Norton & Co.

Farrell M. (2002) Financial engineering in project management. *Project Management Journal* 33(1), 27–36.

Hamel G. (2006) The why, what and how of management innovation. *Harvard Business Review* 1–12.

Harpum, P. (2004) Project control. in Morris, P. & Pinto, J. *The Wiley Guide to the Management of Projects.* Wiley.

Harpum, P. (2006) *Portfolio, Program, and Project Management: Panacea or Fad? (APM Yearbook 2005/06).* Association for Project Management.

HM Government (2006) Companies Act (England) 2006: section 172. www.legislation.gov.uk/ukpga/2006/46/section/172 (link correct at time of print).

HM Government (2018) *GOVS 002, Project Delivery.* HM Government.

Jiang J., Klein G. & Huang W. (2020) *Projects, Programs, and Portfolios in Strategic Organizational Transformation.* Business Expert Press.

Jonas D. (2010) Empowering project portfolio managers: How management involvement impacts project portfolio management performance. *International Journal of Project Management* 28(8), 818–831.

Lawrence P. & Lorsch J. (1986) *Organization and Environment.* Revised Edition. Harvard Business School Press.

Levine H. (2005) *Project Portfolio Management: A Practical Guide to Selecting Projects, Managing Portfolios and Maximizing Benefits.* Jossey Bass, Wiley.

Lock D. & Wagner R. (2016) *Gower Handbook of Program Management.* Routledge.

Lock D. & Wagner R. (2019) *The Handbook of Project Portfolio Management.* Routledge.

Löwstedt M., Raisanen C. & Leiringer R. (2018) Doing strategy in project-based organizations: Actors and patterns of action. *International Journal of Project Management* 36 (2018) 889–898.

Markowitz H. (1952) The utility of wealth. *Journal of Political Economy* 60(2).

Markowitz H. (1999) The early history of portfolio theory 1600–1960. *Financial Analysts Journal* 55(4), 5–16.

McFarlan F. (1981) Portfolio approach to information systems. *Harvard Business Review*.

Mintzberg H., Lampel J. & Ahlstrand B. (2008) *Strategy Safari: A Guided Tour through the Wilds of Strategic Management*. Second Edition. FT Publishing International.

Mintzberg H., Quinn J. & Ghoshal S. (1998) *The Strategy Process*. European Edition. Prentice Europe.

Moore S (2010) *Strategic Project Portfolio Management: Enabling a Productive Organization*. Wiley.

Morris P. (2009) Implementing strategy through project management: The importance of managing the project front-end. in Williams T., Samset K. & Sunnevåg K. *Making Essential Choices with Scant Information*. Palgrave Macmillan.

Morris P. & Pinto J (2004) *The Wiley Guide to the Management of Projects*. Wiley.

Morris P. & Pinto J. (2007) *The Wiley Guide to Project, Program and Portfolio Management*. Wiley.

Nippa M., Pidun U. & Rubner H. (2010) Corporate portfolio management: Appraising four decades of academic research. *Academy of Management Perspectives* 50–66.

Petit Y. & Hobbs B. (2010) Project portfolios in dynamic environments: Sources of uncertainty and sensing mechanisms. *Project Management Journal* 41(4), 46–58.

PMI (2017) *The Standard for Portfolio Management*. Fourth Edition. Project Management Institute.

Quinn J. (1978) Strategic change: Logical incrementalism. *Sloan Management Review* 7–11.

Roetheli R. & Pesenti, P. (1986) Portfolio method: A control tool in the multiproject organization. *International Journal of Project Management* 4(2), 87–90.

Rubinstein M. (2002) Markowitz's "portfolio selection": A fifty-year retrospective. *The Journal of Finance* 57(3), 1041–1045.

Sanwal A. (2007) Get sustained growth by savvy portfolio management. *The Journal of Corporate Accounting and Finance* 19(1), 3–10.

Scheinberg M. & Stretton A. (1994) Multiproject planning: Tuning portfolio indices. *International Journal of Project Management* 12(2), 107–114.

Shakespeare W. (1605) *The Merchant of Venice: Act I, Scene 1*. Simon & Schuster, reprint 2009.

Sierotowicz T. (2020) Scientific foundation of strategies: Towards a model for strategies. *Academy of Strategic Management Journal* 19(2), 1–16.

Smith C. (2014) Portfolio management. in Cooper C. *Wiley Encyclopedia of Management*. Wiley.

Taleb N. (2010) *The Black Swan: The Impact of the Highly Improbable*. Second Edition. Penguin.

Whittington R., Regner P., Angwin D., Johnson G. & Scholes K. (2020) *Exploring Strategy*. Twelfth Edition. Pearson.

Young M., Owen J. & Connor J. (2011) Whole of enterprise portfolio management: A case study of NSW Government and Sydney Water Corporation. *International Journal of Projects in Business* 4(3), 412–435.

3 Organisational strategy and portfolio management

Jayne Redfern

Introduction

This chapter continues the discussion of organisational strategy originated in the previous chapter and looks to develop some of the relevant concepts for strategy *formulation*, *development*, and most importantly, *execution* when considering portfolio management. There are countless texts and many renowned academics who have covered strategy in some significant depth, and this chapter is not intended to comprehensively cover the evolution of organisational strategy and strategic research. The chapter will, however, reference some of these thinkers in discussing strategy at the organisational level, with the aim of enabling understanding of how strategy forms the input to the portfolio, as well as guiding the management of the portfolio.

What is strategy and strategic intent

It is generally accepted that the modern word *strategy* evolved from the Greek "strategos", interpreted as "the art of the general", or "how to win military confrontations" (Hughes, 1993). However, a more modern, practical definition of *strategy* in the organisational context, or for corporate strategy, could be analogous to strategy being "*statements of corporate goals and the high-level view of how to get there*". As such, organisational strategy is concerned with the overall purpose and scope of the organisation in order to meet the expectations of owners/shareholders, boards of trustees, government departments, the clients and customers, and other important stakeholders (Johnson & Scholes, 1993). Strategy is intimately connected to the drive of organisations to add value, and this also often includes different parts of an organisation (business units, government departments, etc.). Thus, strategy is about what the decision-makers in an organisation desire the organisation to be like in the future. Strategy is made in advance of the actions to which it applies, and it is, in most cases, developed consciously and purposefully. (There are approaches to strategy development that are more fluid and reactive to various aspects of the organisation's internal and external environment – Mintzberg and Waters [1985] discuss this with an analysis of different schools of strategy formulation, expanded on later in this chapter.)

There is the question of where strategy ends and tactics take over, and the two terms are frequently misused in business. A useable differentiator could be that whereas strategy is deciding on what to do, tactics is about how to do it. Of key importance are the links to those who need to be motivated to do what is needed, particularly in an increasingly VUCA world (volatile, uncertain, complex, ambiguous). Strategies seek to achieve

DOI: 10.4324/9780367853129-4

significant changes to organisational structures, operational processes, and procedures. Strategies often seek to achieve a big impact on the organisation's resourcing needs. This is particularly so if the strategy is based on extending the organisational capabilities or core competencies and/or if many or all parts of the organisation are going to be involved. Consequently, operational managers need to be both supporters of, and involved in, the strategic planning. This tends to blur the established ideas of the boundary between those who develop strategy in organisations and those expected to implement strategy. This includes functional managers, general managers, and of course, project and program managers.

Realistically, most of what is recognised as strategy is driven by a corporate vision: a desirable position, attainable at some point in the future – "[a] look towards the unknown to define the future which combines current facts, hopes, dreams, threats, and opportunities" (Ozdem, 2011). The vision is most commonly expressed as, "Where are we now, and where do we want to be?" The vision, if it is to be of any use in guiding and motivating those who are to realise it, needs to be coherent, realistic, achievable, and enthusing. Moreover, though it will indicate the principles and tenets of that organisation's strategy, it can only express the essence, and not the detail that the portfolio manager needs to know – which is where the strategic statement is vital. Therefore, if the vision statement is to have any functionality beyond giving all concerned a warm, idealistic feeling, it needs to be translatable into what is intended to actually be done.

Despite these challenges, however, much care and attention are usually given to ascertaining an organisation's strategy, and Drucker's (1993) "uncertain environment" still needs to be contended with in the deployment of the strategy. To be sustainable, strategy must anticipate changes in the environment and competitors' (and others') reactions. Drucker believed that the purpose of business strategy was to enable organisations to attain their ambitions in an uncertain environment or, more pragmatically perhaps, of organisations trying to resolve their complex and chaotic environments into scenarios that they can make sense of (Drucker, 1993). However, he did suggest that, essentially, the organisation should identify certainties about itself, and probabilities about its likely future environment, so that it could be successful in bringing about changes that are necessary for that strategy to result in success.

In general, this approach is traditionally applied as a SWOT (strengths, opportunities, weaknesses, and threats) analysis – a broad consideration of internal and external factors affecting the organisation's situation. Viable corporate strategies often involve finding and exploiting novel opportunities. This usually means the organisation exploiting unique capabilities that may need to be developed. Most authors assert a belief that organisations must be *realistic* about their capabilities and situation and therefore adopt realistic strategies. For this reason, many organisations base their strategy on extending an existing capability.

Briefly returning to the origins of strategy, Helmuth von Moltke (Hughes, 1993) was the chief of staff of the Prussian Army before World War I, in a period when technology was advancing apace. He was classically trained and had studied Napoleonic approaches. Thus, even then, his skill sets were obsolescent, and as he began to recognise this, he stated, "No battle plan survives contact with the enemy." However, that realisation also stimulated him to develop approaches to warfare that went beyond deterministic strategies in favour of adaptable resilient strategies. In modern parlance, we could paraphrase Moltke with "no deliberate business strategy entirely survives first contact with reality", meaning that Drucker's "uncertain environment" (Drucker, 1993) will cause some aspects of our intended strategy to be demonstrably not effective, operable, or viable, and this leads us on to considering alternative "emergent strategies".

The strategy formulation process within organisations

This is a topic about which much has been written. Until recently, most was written about intended or planned strategy. With the recent rapid changes in most sectors, driven by the increasingly VUCA environments, much more attention is now being given to emergent strategies. In most organisational strategy statements, the strategic objective(s) feature boldly, but that is not, itself, strategy; the means to achieving the strategic objective(s) is actually the strategy, and there are two stages, firstly, formulation (or development) and, secondly, execution (or deployment/enactment/implementation).

Approaches to formulating strategy

There are four main approaches to the development of organisational strategy, as observed by Pettigrew et al. (2002):

- *Classical* – usually based on profitability as the goal, and the belief that the organisation needs to find (or make) its own niche. This approach is deliberate and tends to take a longer-term view.
- *Evolutionist* – perceives the organisational environment as less predictable, even volatile, and sees organisations playing a part in the development of markets.
- *Processualist* – also perceives the organisational environment as unpredictable but is less convinced about markets presenting clear opportunities. Opportunities are likely to emerge in an indistinctive, vague form incrementally.
- *Systemic theorist* – this approach acknowledges that, in today's world, to be successful, strategies must be sensitive to sociological considerations.

It would seem that all four perspectives are relevant and valid in some ways. The classical approach provides the starting point of planned strategy, the evolutionist and processualist approaches then acknowledge emergent strategy, and the systemic theorists add the constraints and conditions.

In concise terms, this can also be interpreted as:

- *Doing something new* – finding or creating uncontested new markets; classical/evolutionist.
- *Building on what you already do well* – processualist/systemic theory/competitive response.
- *Reacting opportunistically to emerging possibilities* – processualist.

Recent research continues to adopt similar approaches, considering alternative internal and external factors. Mishra and Mohanty (2020) highlight six approaches to formulating strategy, namely, the planning approach, related to long-term planning; fit approach, matching internal and external strengths, weaknesses, opportunities, and threats; positioning approach, placing the company for maximum competitive advantage; emergent/dynamic adaptation approach, adapting to change; resource-based approach, utilising key resources; and stakeholders' approach, protecting stakeholder interests.

The questions to answer when formulating strategy

Although all organisations pursue concepts of effective management, much management time is devoted to regular activity commonly referred to as business-as-usual (BAU). Strategic management is concerned with elements of BAU, but mainly with planning and enacting irregular new activity to constantly adjust the organisation's capability and competencies to match the strategic aims. (See Chapter 6 for an alternative view on BAU.)

Previously, classical approaches to the creation of planned strategy within organisations included such examples as Henry Mintzberg's "5Ps", as in Figure 3.1, involving:

- Plan – a high-level view of how the organisation thinks *realistically* it may be able to realise its ambitions.
- Ploy – the possibility of deploying a new tactic or technological development, unexpected in the organisation's environment.
- Pattern – consideration of strategies that have been successfully deployed previously, mainly by that organisation, but also from learning by observation of others.

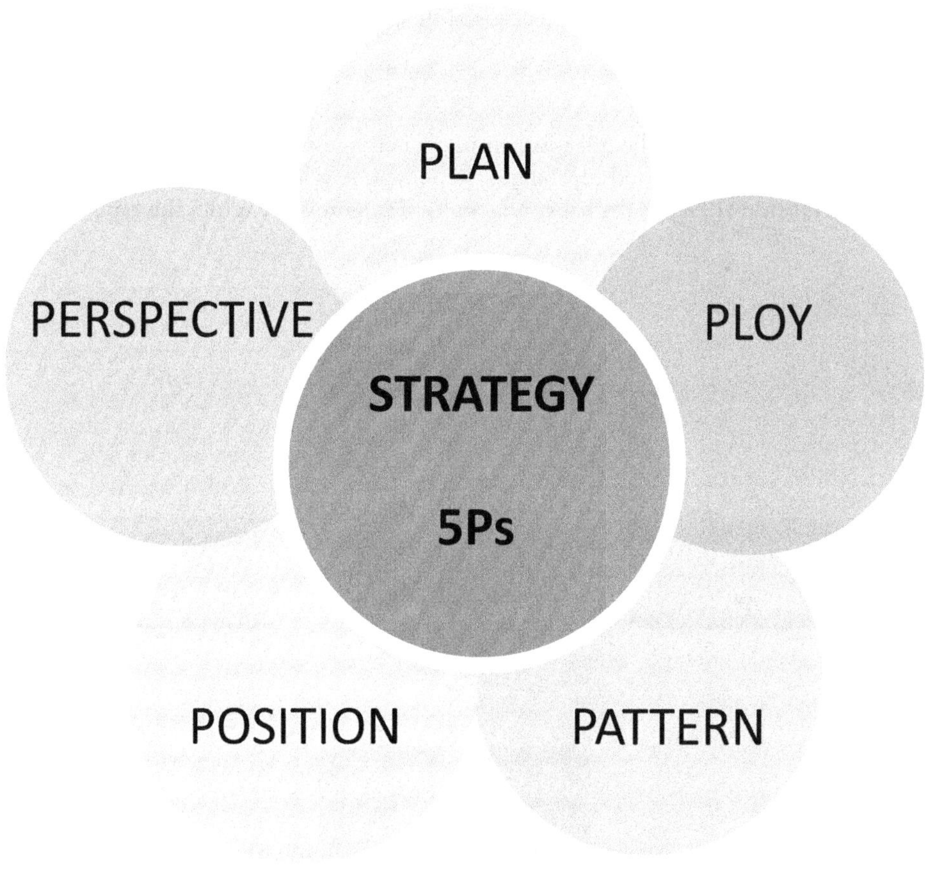

Figure 3.1 The 5Ps.

Source: Adapted from Mintzberg et al. (1998).

- Position – a realistic assessment of the organisation's current situation, especially as viewed by stakeholders within and outside of the organisation.
- Perspective – looking internally at shaping the organisation, such as its culture, for delivering the strategy.

Development of a comprehension of the "5Ps" was considered to be based on answering the following questions (Medenhall, 2019):

- Mission: why does the organisation exist?
- Self-assessments: what are the internal strengths and weaknesses and external threats and opportunities? (SWOT analysis.)
- Vision: where does the organisation want to be in the future?
- Goals and objectives: what are the desired results and measurable outcomes to achieve the mission and vision?
- Strategic plan: how to achieve the strategy in terms of tactics and actions?

Certainly, there is much evidence that decision-makers still do seek these answers, but more than ever, in a rapidly changing business environment, those involved are using the "strategising" processes to make sense of the chaos of their experiences in that environment.

Balanced scorecard

For the adopted strategy to be effective, an integrated assessment of several aspects of the organisation's competencies and capabilities is essential. A valuable tool for this, created by Kaplan and Norton (1992), is the balanced scorecard (Figure 3.2). Whilst this type of model

Figure 3.2 Balanced scorecard.

Source: Adapted from Kaplan and Norton (1992).

is generally employed to establish measures of organisational performance, it can also be helpful in assessing an organisation's condition – in readiness (or not) to pursue desired strategies. In most applications, the model is adjusted to include the elements that the particular organisation deems important to consider in the planning and management of *their* strategy.

Approaches to manage changing strategy

McGahan (2004) suggests there are two pressure points driving strategies, especially when seeking to create reactive change. These are threats to an organisation's core activities and/or threats to their core assets. Changes to strategy, McGahan suggests, then follows one of four trajectories:

- *Radical*. When both core assets and core activities are threatened, necessitating a new strategy entirely. The Kodak case study, in the annex to this chapter (along with the other three case studies), might be regarded as being in this category.
- *Progressive*. Neither core assets nor core activities are immediately threatened, allowing more gradual adaptations.
- *Creative*. Core assets are threatened, but core activities are stable. The organisation's skills and processes can be redeployed in a new direction when their assets are becoming obsolescent. The Remploy and Netflix case studies reflect this.
- *Intermediating*. Core activities are threatened, but the core assets retain ability to create value. The existing assets (manufacturing capability, brands, or knowledge) can be redeployed to revised strategy, most likely new markets. The BAE case study (in chapter annex) could be regarded as an example.

An example of the model is shown in Figure 3.3. The message is clear: corporate change is constant and unavoidable, necessitating constant revision of strategies.

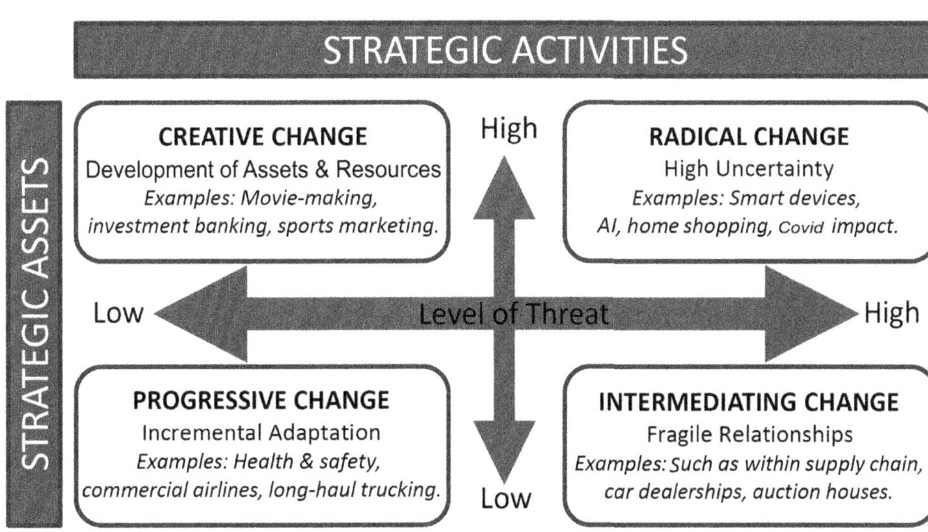

Figure 3.3 Strategic response to threat.

Source: Adapted from McGahan (2004).

Factors affecting strategy development

There are multiple factors that influence and affect strategy, and these are covered in the following sections.

Stakeholders

Classic theory about strategic planning involves a process of the organisation considering what its options are, reducing that to what it would like to do (unavoidably, key stakeholders' opinions are hugely influential at this point), and further reducing that to what it *can* do. Finally, a strategic plan emerges. An example of this is shown in Figure 3.4.

In this decision-making process, stakeholders, both as groups and as individuals, will be influenced by their inherent heuristics, which are largely the products of experience (Redfern, 2006). Human heuristics (not to be confused with the use of the term as applied to expert systems) are the "*rules of thumb*" employed by us all in situations of uncertainty and especially when there is a dearth of data to aid decisions.

What is clear is that the strategy process (Mintzberg et al., 1998) in an established organisation will involve many stakeholders, and usually, whilst there may be a dominant leader, for any determined strategy to be pursued, that strategy must be perceived as appropriate and achievable by the other key stakeholders. In this era, for organisations to develop an achievable strategy, they will commonly have to work with suppliers collaboratively and may also need to involve customers. In the extreme, joint working groups and project teams may be required, or even the creation of joint ventures.

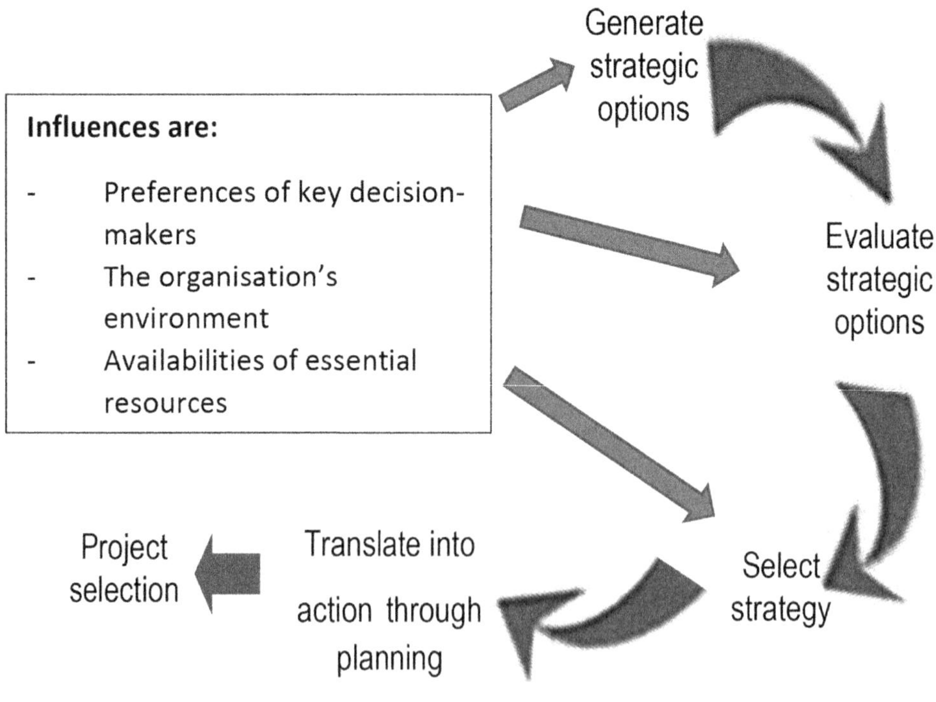

Figure 3.4 The strategy formulation process.

Rate of change in the environment

In some technology-based companies, developments are so rapid, and the opportunities being presented by those developments best understood by the stakeholders actually at the leading edge, that strategy is actually originated at that stratum of the organisation, subsequently to be adopted by that organisation's leaders. In effect, strategy is originated "bottom up". In such situations, it is essential for open and rapid communication conduits to be the norm, so as to enable both those seeing the need for modifications to the strategy (in light of the changing circumstances) and those making the far-reaching strategic decisions. In a fast-moving environment, the management of those programs and projects needs to encourage predictions of future states and concentrate less on current positions.

The evolved, new directions can be the consequences of a wide range of factors, such as new ownership of the organisation, new senior management, disruptive technologies, world events, national and international politics, senior stakeholder pressures, financial constraints, and so many more. That being the case, can organisational strategy ever be stable? Certainly, the business environment in most sectors has become so much more turbulent in the last two decades that the rate of change is accelerating. Even capital-intensive, long-timescale types of industries, such as aircraft manufacture, energy production, metal production, chemical manufacturing, and shipbuilding, have seen rapid environmental changes and disruptive technology advances, challenging their previously long planning cycles. When that is linked with the very large financial investments endemic to those sectors, it is easy to see why planning stable strategies for the necessarily long timescales has become a complex and fraught process. In established and stable, larger organisations with extended supply chains such as these, changes of strategy seem to be most commonly caused by external factors.

Barriers to entry

Organisations involved in highly capitalised, complex operations will obviously have difficulty in changing direction quickly, and there will be less likelihood of new entrants to their market. However, they will be vulnerable to the advent of new market-changing products or technology associated with a disruptive strategy. Organisations look to be the "disrupter" rather than the "disruptee", an example of this is Southwest Airlines, with their low-cost disruptive strategy (Raynor, 2011).

Porter (1979) suggested the now well-accepted model that demonstrates the forces on a market sector and, therefore, the external influences of its members' strategies, with the five competitive forces: competition in the industry, potential of new entrants into the industry, power of suppliers, power of customers, and threat of substitute products shaping strategy (see Figure 3.5).

These external influences affecting competition will and do change. This means some intended strategies will prove to be unachievable, as the original environment the strategy was designed to respond to has changed. Henry Mintzberg observed this in 1985 and offers a model showing the relationships between intended and realised strategy (Mintzberg & Waters, 1985). Developing this, perhaps it should be considered as to when and how it becomes apparent that the intended strategy will be "unrealised". It seems likely this point emerges when the intended strategy meets reality – that's to say when the strategy gets enacted as tactics. Henry Mintzberg described it thus: "[S]trategy emerges over time as intentions collide with, and accommodate, a changing reality" (Mintzberg, 1987, Mintzberg et al., 2008).

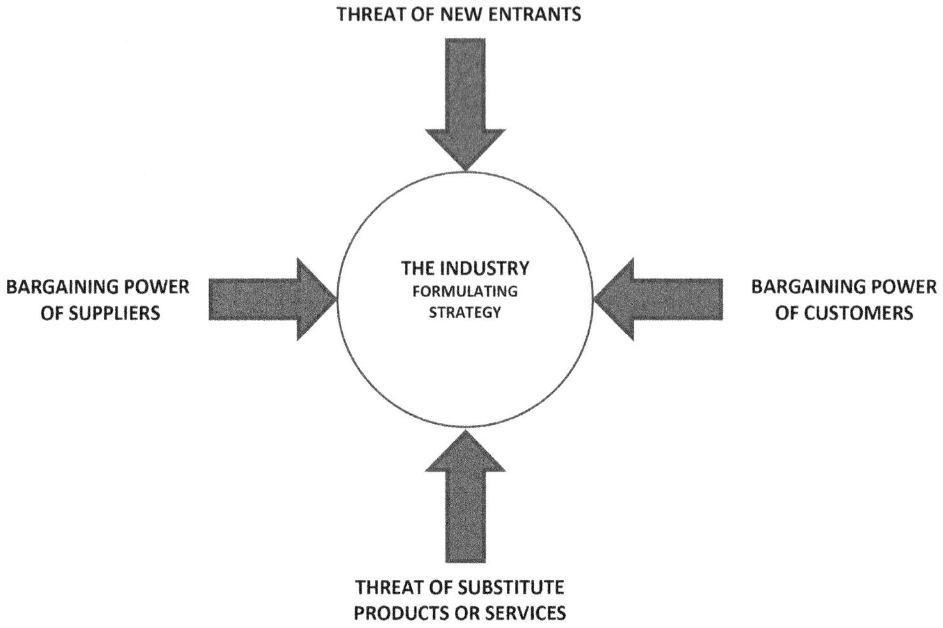

Figure 3.5 Porter's five forces.

Source: Adapted from Porter (1979).

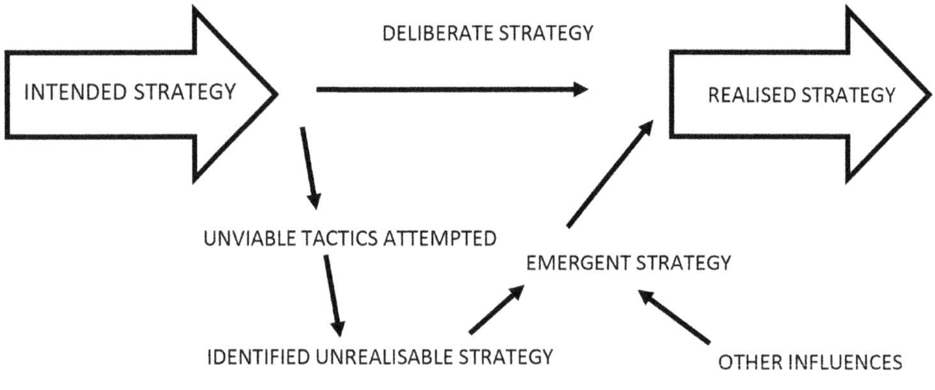

Figure 3.6 Extended view of unrealised and emergent strategy.

Source: Adapted from Mintzberg (1987).

Emergent strategy might result from diverse causes, such as the organisation's own actions, changes in the environment (such as market changes), competitors' actions, new disruptive technology, legislation, or global influences. Emergent strategy informs intended strategy both immediately and in the future. It is arguable that, in this age of rapid and perpetual change, the relatively short-term (< 5 years) strategy is mostly emergent or reactive (see Figure 3.6, an extended view of Figure 2.1).

Porter (1996) differentiates between the long-term, top-down originated strategy that provides stable guidance, which he refers to as "corporate strategy" (planned or deliberate strategy) and "business strategy" that is an adaptable, bottom-up, changeable evolutionary process. It could be argued that almost all the planning becomes the consequence of continuously emergent corporate comprehension rather than being entirely new, except in the less-common cases of new start-ups and complete organisational transformations.

Supply chains

Porter's original business strategy model may work well for smaller, single-market organisations, but in the modern world with complex supply chains, and particularly in the case of multi-company groups, the "isolationist" approach seems likely to lead to competition between those companies for resources, maximisation of *their* profits, and consequentially, an introspective view. Conversely, collaborative strategies may result in co-operative inter-relationships when synergistic activities exploit pooled competencies and capabilities (see the British Aerospace case study). A more developed approach recognises that almost every organisation is positioned in a supply chain, very few being sufficiently vertically integrated to be self-supporting, let alone self-sufficient. Typical of this would be a specialist chemicals manufacturer incorporating a container (to be made by a specialist container manufacturer) that will form part of the product offering because that will then be used as a component of the customers' process machinery. Including the process machinery manufacturer, here we would have four partners linked together in a supply chain, all with a vested interest in the success of the strategy driving the development.

Increasingly, organisations of all sizes are recognising that they are part of a supply chain and dependent on other links in their chain(s) (Chapter 21 discusses in more detail supply chain integration in the context of portfolio management). This ought to lead to a wider perspective and consideration of how their organisational strategy can add value not just to their own organisation but also to customers and suppliers. There is much evidence that in closely linked supply chains, collaborative strategy formulation between partner organisations offers significant benefits (Sandberg, 2007) and is crucial in today's fast-changing business environment (Montoya-Torres & Ortiz-Vargas, 2014). That collaborative strategy is probably most effective when each supplier has a holistic and coordinated perspective on its own situation.

Executing strategy through portfolios of projects and programs

Portfolio management is a management process to reduce conflict on resources and maximise the throughput of projects (and programs), with the aim of achieving strategic intentions and thereby achieving benefits and consolidated value for the organisation (Lock & Wagner, 2019). Portfolio management is defined in this chapter as: "The selection, prioritisation and management of all of an organisation's **projects** and **programs** and may extend to related business-as-usual activities. Portfolios may be established and managed at organisational, program, geographic or functional levels." Based on this definition, an indicative portfolio management structure is shown in Figure 3.7.

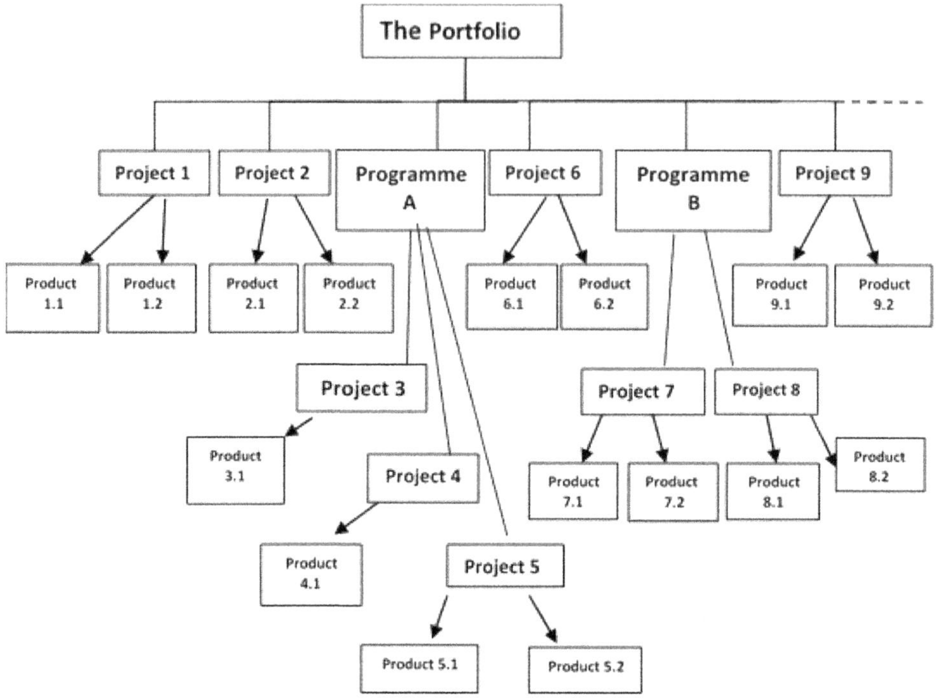

Figure 3.7 Indicative structure of a portfolio.

Source: Adapted from Buttrick (2019).

The challenges of effective strategy execution

The concepts of business strategy planning have been evolving since the early work, discussed earlier by Porter, Drucker, and Mintzberg, amongst others, but there is evidence that much less is understood about effective strategy execution – and there are so many failures of what appear to be good strategies (see the case studies in the chapter annex). Given that the vehicles of strategy execution are portfolios of projects and programs, the problems appear to be either translation of good strategies into correctly formatted portfolios and/or subsequent poor management of the portfolios of projects.

Still ongoing research, started in the UK in 2016, into senior manager's experience of implementation of strategy, reveals some disappointing results (Sull et al., 2015). It was reported that two-thirds to three-quarters of large organisations struggle to implement their strategies. Reported causes were multiple, though the main factors were:

- Despite the larger organisations in the survey having functioning processes to link their strategies to their portfolios, only a small number of respondents were confident that those strategies were achievable – mainly due to lack of collaboration between business units. (See also the case study on the recovery of BAE.)

- Top managers viewed deviations from the established strategic plan as lack of discipline and discouraged portfolio managers from adopting emergent strategies in a reactive and opportunistic mode.
- There was not a cohesive agreement between the senior decision-makers about what they wanted in the first place.
- Organisations were not realistic about what they *could* achieve.

Other reasons for poor strategy execution include lack of realism regarding their position in the market (see the Trump Airlines case study), inappropriate diversification (BAE case study), and deliberate or aversive ignoring of new disruptive technology (Kodak case study).

It is apparent that strategy can (and does) exist at different levels. So far, we have been discussing the highest level of organisational strategy, but at a level down from that, we need strategies for direct enactment of those corporate ambitions. In that way, portfolios of projects (and programs) cascade the enterprise's ambitions down into what is going to actually be *done* to realise those ambitions (Ingason & Jonasson, 2019).

Principles of effective execution

It has been argued that, from a portfolio management perspective, strategy comes down to value management. Hence, once the desired direction has been determined, the organisation's portfolios of projects are to pursue that policy by providing the best results possible, within the constraints of available resources and other factors.

The Association for Project Management's Special Interest Group (SIG) on Portfolio Management (APM, 2019) sees the principles of portfolio management (enactment) as:

- Ensuring strategic alignment of all projects and programs within the portfolio.
- Organisational governance alignment.
- Ensuring senior management engagement and sponsorship.
- Providing active leadership to drive value.
- Facilitating aligned PMOs throughout the portfolio components.
- Ensuring transparency.
- Embracing risk.
- Supporting continuous optimisation of resources.
- Maintaining a delivery mindset.
- Energised change culture.
- Killing early and killing fast.

Most of these could be regarded as self-explanatory, but some require more explanation. The SIG explains "transparency" as trusting people and having the ability to regularly reflect on how the portfolio can be more effective. "Killing early and killing fast" means a preparedness to promptly terminate projects and curtail any activities if these are not likely to deliver benefit, not always a straightforward task in reality. The SIG also argues that, whilst the methodology known as "agile" is embraced by the whole concept of portfolio management, most portfolios should utilise whatever methodologies are appropriate to the particular project(s). Portfolios of projects and programs are most frequently the vehicles used by complex organisations (which probably includes most modern organisations) to bring about change and development of that organisation, even though these collections of ventures are sometimes not recognised as portfolios.

Ultimately, it can be considered that there is a strategy inherent in every portfolio – that is to say, a set of principles will need to be established to ordain governance of it and prioritisation of its elements. Portfolio management is concerned with the *mix* of projects and programs being considered or undertaken by an organisation, prioritised according to agreed criteria, and then executed in a co-ordinated way. This prioritisation is often the subject of much discussion and negotiation, and logically, it should be based on the optimum utilisation of available human and non-human resources to maximise growth and return on investment, whilst ensuring pursuit of strategic initiatives and taking due consideration of risk and issue management. This latter point means balancing risk with the achievability of potential gains, a matter that will be discussed in more detail in chapter 17, but clearly, the collective risk appetites of the organisation's key decision-makers will greatly influence the portfolio strategy. This allows the most important projects and programs to access the required resources and move forward in accordance with their plans.

Advantages of strategy execution through portfolios

It is claimed that the following advantages are gained from using portfolio management to enact strategy (Lock & Wagner, 2019).

- *Economic return.* Prioritisation is an ongoing process. Priorities need to be reviewed in line with project progress, the strategic direction of the organisation, and external influences. Essential to this process is that every project and program has a business case, argued at the same level and with all assumptions stated. Initial prioritisation can then be made on the basis of those that provide the best value for money invested – often referred to as the "desirability" decision. This will continue to be assessed at each checkpoint in the project's life cycle to ensure that only the most appropriate projects are initiated and continue to completion.
- *Risk diversification and distribution.* Once the desirability has been established, the feasibility of the candidate projects and programs needs to be taken into consideration. The emphasis here is on risk diversification and actions to lessen the risk of loss, and coupled with that, each contender needs to be assessed on the amount of resource it requires compared to that available. When this is taken into account with the timescales quoted for delivery of the benefits and the known risks and issues and dependencies, senior management may then make prioritisation decisions. In reviewing risk, the main consideration is level of risk-to-benefits realisation. Only when these are understood should internal project risks be considered. It is important that a portfolio contains projects and programs that have wide-ranging risk profiles. If all projects in the portfolio are high risk and all are economically necessary, the organisation will have no tolerance available should the portfolio need to be adjusted.
- *Capacity (human and non-human).* When a resource pool has to be allocated across a mixture of projects and programs, it is essential that accurate, timely information is held on the assignment and utilisation of those resources. Portfolio management is looking to manage the critical resources that may affect the throughput of the projects and programs and hence the delivery of the expected benefits. These critical resources must be identified, and their use planned, such that there are buffers of time before each allocation, to ensure they are always ready to be used on the due date. Effort must be made to ensure the more strategically important projects and programs have access to these resources, whilst those of a lower priority may have to revise their

schedules and plans, and indeed, some that no longer make a recognisable contribution to the success of the portfolio may be abandoned.

- *Monitoring and control.* Portfolio management is a separate discipline to that of project management, requiring a greater emphasis on interpersonal attributes, communication, and negotiation skills. It is helpful if they are supported by an active portfolio office which collects, analyses, interprets, and presents information covering all projects and programs to allow meaningful decisions to be made. Thus, there is also an important role for project and program managers to play in ensuring their status reports are provided in a timely manner to facilitate this process.
- *Dependencies.* Because the portfolio manager is responsible for ensuring the effective and timely delivery of project products and program benefits, they must ensure that nothing obstructs delivery and that all projects and programs receive inbound constituents, with the considered prioritisation, when required.

Portfolio managers need to adopt a strategic perspective to the management of the individual projects and programs – that is, inputs and outputs are agreed, but the tactical processes are left to the project (and program) managers. At portfolio level, the detail of work being done in each project is not required for decision-making. The projects and programs must agree their deliverables, resources, costs, benefits, and timescales with the portfolio manager but must then be allowed to get on and manage their tasks within agreed tolerances.

The portfolio level focuses on the management of risks, issues, dependencies, change, and overall budgets to remove all obstacles to the successful delivery of the component projects and programs. Remembering from previous discussions that we often find that, for the previously mentioned reasons, portfolios typically include programs as well as projects, with the programs focused on benefit delivery, and especially given that there may be interdependencies between the otherwise "stand-alone" projects in the portfolio, it can be foreseen that communication within the portfolio is the "glue" – and is likely to be complex!

Core elements of successful execution with portfolio management

As with all multi-element endeavours, co-ordination of those elements is obviously essential. However, given the influences of the range of stakeholders affecting the portfolio, or being affected by its conduct or outcomes, it is clear that *how* things are done is at least as important as *what* is done.

Portfolio architecture

Williams and Parr (2004) provide a model for a program management framework. Figure 3.8 shows an adapted model with portfolio architecture and strategic value. In this diagram, the original authors confirm belief in the established hierarchical layering of the elements of strategic initiatives but have added the third dimension that acknowledges the criticality of the co-ordination of *how* it is to be done. They define program, or here shown as portfolio architecture, as "[t]he establishment of leadership, structures, team dynamics, and support mechanisms that enable the delivery of programmes and projects" and describe "change architecture" as "concerned with the human considerations of those in the organisation who will be impacted by programmes and projects, beyond the delivery teams" (*n*ote that Williams and Parr use the word "programme" as an overarching term for major change initiatives and not strictly as we are using it in this text, perhaps

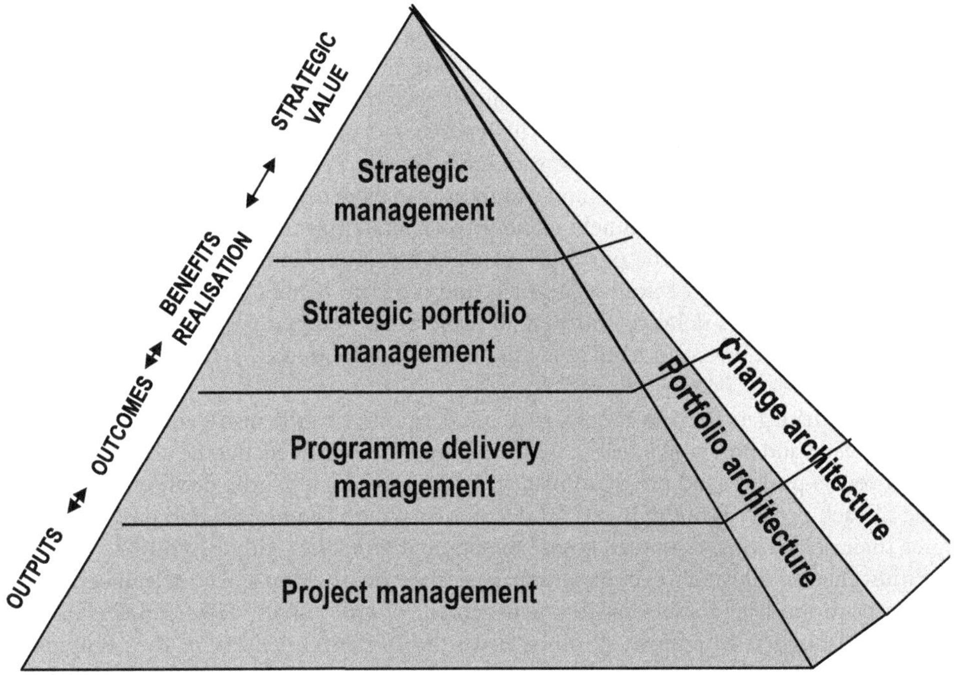

Figure 3.8 The strategic portfolio management framework.

Source: Adapted from Williams and Parr (2004).

here being more aligned with a portfolio architecture, as shown in Figure 3.8). In other words, whereas portfolio (or programme) architecture can be described as *the establishment of support structures and mechanisms that allow effective leadership and provide the teams with the environment, skills, tools, and support they need to operate effectively*, change architecture is interpreted as facilitating the transition from one set of circumstances to a new one – *from the perspective of those whose working lives will be affected by the changes.*

This highlights that, firstly, the organisation must put in place an infrastructure that is conducive to the management of such initiatives and have the necessary resources (of all types) identified and provided. Secondly, that there has to be real emphasis on creating acceptance, if not support, from the community who are going to have the outcomes inflicted upon them – so the "*Hearts and minds*" mantra seems appropriate here.

Strategic alignment

A balanced portfolio could be described as the group of projects that enables an organisation to achieve the objectives of its corporate strategy whilst minimising risks. A common concept in literature on this subject is the categorisation and placement of projects/programs within a value-risk matrix, with the idea that the risky, but high-value, initiatives should be balanced by less-risky ones, although this ignores the reality that many organisations' portfolios are, at times, riskier than is comfortable as a consequence of their adopted strategy.

Organisations in transformation are not likely to have balanced portfolios, and certainly, if Kodak had abandoned their traditional film-based photographic business and embraced the digital technology, they would have had to pass through a very uncertain time, with their portfolio looking very risky for a long period (see case study in chapter annex). Similarly, the pharmaceutical industry has a history of high-risk development portfolios, the risks being bearable only because of profitable ongoing business as a safety net. The idea that high risk equals high gain potential is not always valid; some high-risk ventures, such as technology development, can be high risk and have unpredictable benefit levels.

Portfolio alignment is a process that ensures that all live projects are pursuant to *current* corporate strategy and also ensures that projects that become obsolescent, irrelevant, or excessively risky are terminated so as not to waste scarce resources. In practice, most substantial organisations would probably like to run more relevant projects than they have resources for. This has meant that portfolio management has often been primarily about maximising the throughput of projects and consequent benefits, but that approach can cause neglect of vital co-coordinative or facilitating projects. Whilst maximising value is still a vital part of portfolio management, to achieve an effective portfolio, some priority may need to be afforded to projects with less (or even no) direct benefits potential. Typically, creation of a new IT platform, a building renovation, corporate rebranding, or a revised transport fleet might be in this category. That line of thought leads to the need for a more complex set of criteria for selection of the projects that are to be included in the portfolio at any one time. The challenge is to differentiate between the really essential

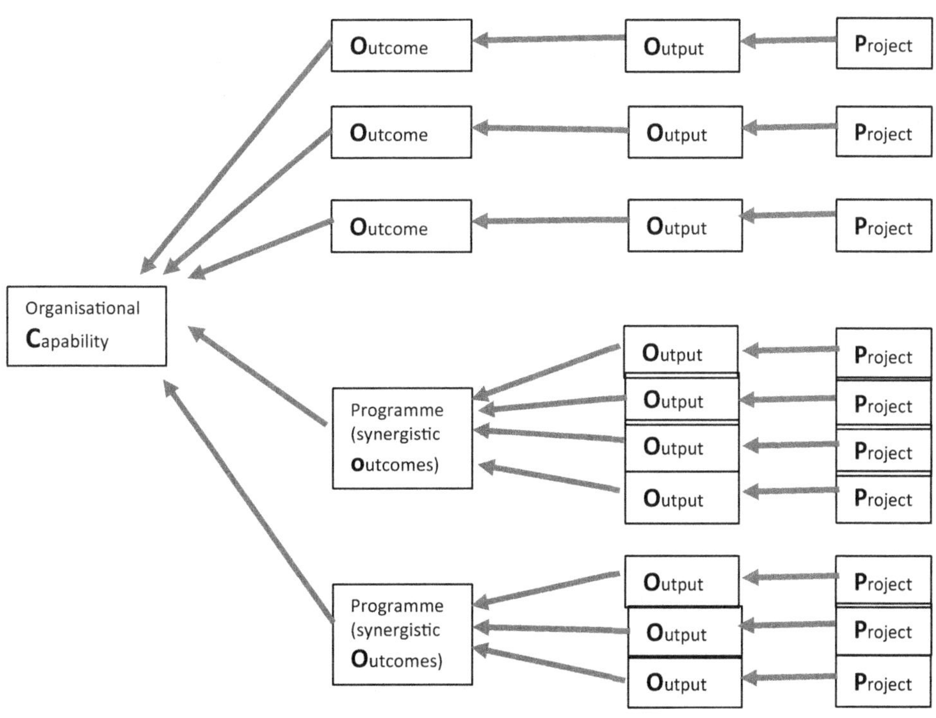

Figure 3.9 COOP mapping process.

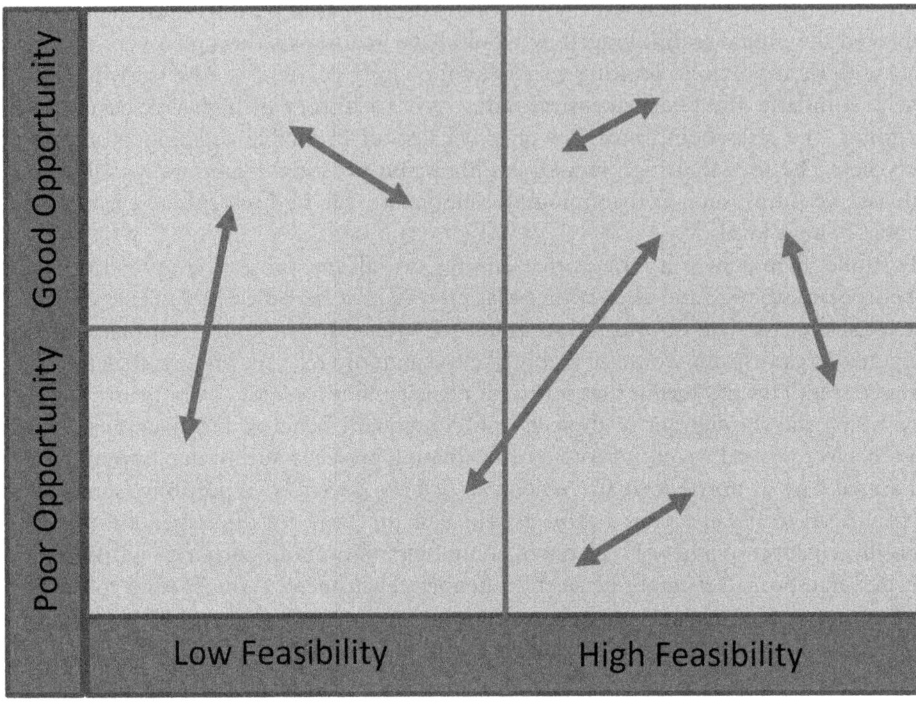

Figure 3.10 Project portfolio mapping.

Source: Adapted from Mitchell et al. (2018).

projects and the "nice-to-haves". Of particular concern are "pet" projects owned and supported relentlessly by very senior managers when it is obvious that those endeavours, whilst not contributing significantly (or even at all) to agreed strategy, will retain scare resources.

Tools such as the COOP (capability, outcome, output, project) diagram (Figure 3.9) are useful initially to establish the array of projects necessary to satisfy planned outcomes. Since, in most such scenarios, all the projects are necessary to achieve the planned strategy, few, if any, will be optional. Obviously, in complex strategic plans, such models will become similarly complex and, therefore, difficult to articulate. It is usually necessary to divide the total corporate strategic ambitions into strands and develop such a model for each strand whilst still being aware of the cross-linkages between them.

Some authors have proposed tools for the prioritisation of optional projects within portfolios, and this can be useful when those projects are not integrated into a network of interconnected projects but could be innovations that may be considered separately. In this case, tools to aid selection can help reduce the influence of cognitive bias (discussed further later) and make selection as logical as possible. The Institute for Management at Cambridge, after analysis of various portfolio matrices, proposed the following visual comparison, for this purpose, in which the length of the bar that represents each project indicates the range of probabilities, shown in Figure 3.10.

Strategic road maps

Strategic road mapping has become a favoured means not only of gathering together information about capabilities and competencies across the organisation but also, thereafter, to aid communication of the strategy behind new initiatives and how these initiatives can exploit and integrate those abilities. To be effective, this necessitates a cross-functional approach.

An established technique for linking together, in logical order, the projects and other initiatives that comprise the portfolio, and aid maintenance of congruency within the portfolio, is the strategic road map. It is a master plan for the execution of the strategic portfolio and fulfils a similar function to the use of a network dependency diagram for a project, as can be seen in Figure 3.11.

Each bar represents a project, program, or other initiative, and as can be seen, some projects cause initiation of others, whereas some have no precedents. Depending on the scenario, the three streams shown might be augmented by other streams or could be divided into subordinate topics. The road map may well include "external" streams, where the organisation's strategy is linked to that of other organisations in a shared supply chain.

Phaal (2019) suggests that the creation of such road maps can be used as group events for the key stakeholders, using the simple discussion mechanism of self-adhesive notes on a wall so as to cause debate and gain agreement on the necessity for, and priorities of, the components. This helps create "buy-in" for this execution plan. Thereafter, the road map can provide visibility of the state of progress (assuming that it is maintained!) and is also a valuable tool to analyse the need for changes to the portfolio when the strategy needs modification. Strategy "road maps" are a good tool to aid tracking of progress towards execution of strategy, and therefore also good for measuring benefits realisation. Road maps can be extrapolated to include the benefits realisation phase. A key role of portfolio management is to ensure that the collection of projects chosen, and being funded, achieve the organisation's goals.

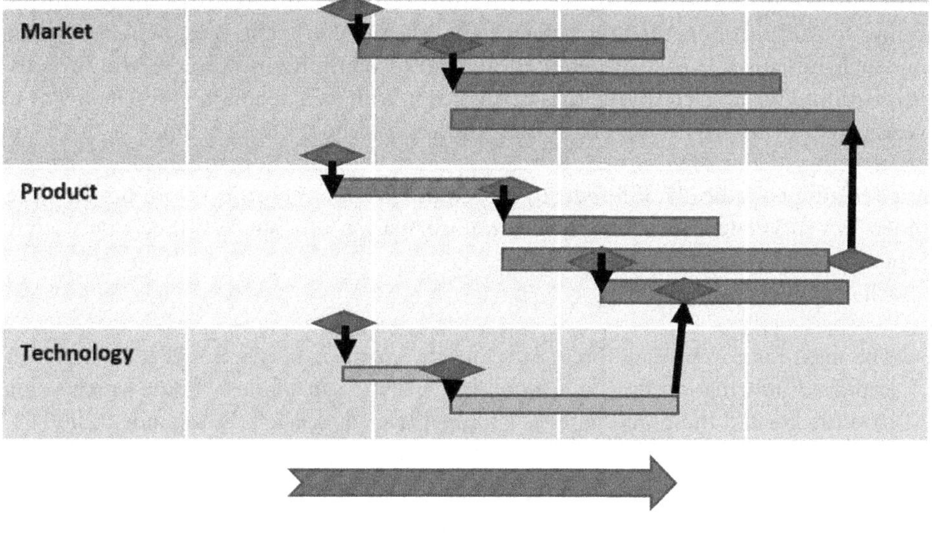

Figure 3.11 Example of a strategic road map.

Benefits realisation management for business benefits and value creation

A portfolio of projects is designed to bring about change that will result in some concept of "gain" for the sponsoring organisation. To that end, evolution of that portfolio needs to start with the end in mind; the portfolio design process must start with a clear set of targeted outcomes and resultant benefits. (Benefits and benefits realisation are covered in more detail in Chapter 7.)

Portfolios are created to fulfil corporate strategy, and therefore to achieve some concept of gain. The visualisation of "gain" – which, in the jargon of project management, is termed "benefits" – is the foundation of a business case, which is an expression of a corporate (organisational) ambition. In well-managed organisations, including those run on a not-for-profit basis, this would be viewed as good management practice. In 1988, two researches, Marilyn Parker and Bob Benson, based in IBM Los Angeles Research Centre, asserted that most benefits could be categorised as one of the following (Cardinali, 1998):

- *Strategic necessity* – necessary to facilitate other initiatives to follow on.
- *Return on investment* – to create new capabilities or improve the profitability of existing capabilities (the latter is often interpreted as cost-reductions).
- *Competitive advantage* – to provide the possibility of the sponsoring organisation to outperform its rivals.
- *Competitive response* – to provide the possibility of the organisation matching its competitors' performance.
- *Asset preservation* – aimed at maintaining the organisation's functionality.

These categories seem to have withstood scrutiny ever since and are often still used as a basis for critical analysis of business cases. However, given the large number of regulatory compliance projects that are run, particularly in the finance sector, but also in some manufacturing industries, "regulatory compliance" could more recently be included in the list, although given that regulatory compliance is usually a requirement for the continuation of the business, it could be argued that it fits within "asset preservation". Given the considerable cost of these legally required projects, many organisations attempt to find real benefits to aid deferment of costs. Since the only benefit resulting from such initiatives is that of being authorised to continue in business, the inventive organisations, when faced with these situations, will seek secondary real benefits to, at least, help defray the costs of running those portfolios. One example of this is the restructuring of the HM Government–supported Remploy organisation, which was forced to adopt a radically different strategy in the face of opposition from hostile stakeholders but succeeded in turning forced transformation into success. (See case study in chapter annex.)

Such examples are:

- The need for compliance forcing the improvement in IT systems that then provide improved information flow and more data analytic capabilities – some organisations have categorised these outcomes as "competitive advantage" (Damianides, 2006).
- The outcome of non-compliance can be fines, which are obvious dis-benefits, but the loss of reputation when non-compliance becomes public knowledge, in some industries, can be even more damaging. Other dis-benefits can include loss of key disenchanted employees and loss of sales contracts. Conversely, effective compliance

projects reassure not only stakeholders but also shareholders, thereby protecting and possibly increasing the perceived worth of the organisation.

Organisations who rely on targeting their strategy on "competitive response" may benefit from the pioneering of those pursuing "competitive advantage" strategies in advance of them but may equally be condemning themselves to always be in "catch-up" mode. Most corporate strategies include more than one category of benefit, and thus several components of their portfolio will be designed to achieve one or more of the targeted benefits.

In particular, strategic execution never finishes if the organisation continues to operate and intends to continue operating. Rather, the strategy continuously evolves whilst the projects deliver their completed products into the business, and the targeted benefits are achieved. It has been suggested that benefit yield can occur in three basic patterns (Schabacker & Vajna, 2008):

- *Sudden and short duration.* Examples would include short-lived "novel" products or new technology deployment prior to competitors emulating those innovations and thereby neutralising the short-lived advantage. Organisations adopting a "leading edge" strategy like this will, necessarily, be continuously running a portfolio that will include a significant number of projects that deliver this pattern of benefits.
- *Slower but persistent.* Examples would be new products or processes that start to create tangible benefits early but are then integrated into the long-term business improvement plan. This is a most desirable pattern of benefits realisation and would be typical of a strategy that is targeting prompt and discernible improvements in the organisation's situation. Typically, efficiency improvement projects, workforce upskilling, and organisation refinancing can yield this type of pattern.
- *Slow build-up.* This pattern of benefits delivery would be typical of a longer-term strategy; typical situations would include business process improvement projects, infrastructure developments, and organisational restructuring.

There are variations on these themes, but this remains a simplistic view – from a "project" standpoint. Taking a more realistic and portfolio management view, benefits are yielded more commonly as a consequence of several projects' outputs being deployed synergistically. Logically, an organisational strategy will require projects delivering in different sequences, delivering benefits to differing patterns. Also, experience suggests that the best scenarios may yield benefits in stages, starting with early benefits that can be hard to quantify – such as better working practices (resulting in improved staff morale), lower error rates (higher efficiencies), then progress to more tangible benefits, such as cost savings and quality improvements, and providing opportunities for longer-term initiatives. An example could be installation of a new IT platform that, firstly, avoids the need for arduous data input processes, then provides faster business processes and reduces errors, and then facilitates new business opportunities being grasped.

Benefits realisation management (BRM) is rightly receiving enhanced attention but is a complex subject, and especially when some projects are enablers to other projects, and also when the timescale of benefits realisation can be years or even decades. Sadly, there are numerous examples of well-considered long-term strategies becoming obsolescent before delivery, and surveys during the last twenty years have suggested that 60–80% of organisations may be failing to achieve their strategy by not completing the benefits realisation process (Kaplan & Norton, 2008). There appears to be a gap between the projects successfully delivering their products and those outputs being deployed to deliver the strategy. The projects' business cases should have been written with clarity regarding the benefits being targeted and so then have aided successful delivery of the correctly specified products. Successful introduction of those outputs into operations to deliver the benefits promised in those business cases should be key to subsequent strategy achievement. For that reason, it is essential that the project managers comprehend the part that their projects play in the achievement of the strategy and so deliver efficacious products. Depending on the positioning of each project within the portfolio, there will be different emphasis on the time/cost/quality criteria, so success cannot be judged simply on achievement of those; the real criterion is how that project actually contributes to overall success.

This problem has too often been seen as a tendency for the project teams to simply hand over their products to operations and expect deployment to occur and benefits to then appear. That is an oversimplistic diagnosis. The fact is that whilst the products' producers might well be most knowledgeable about how best to deploy those products, successful handover can only occur if operations are receptive and prepared to both receive and use the products. Benefits realisation management (BRM) is a multi-stage process that extends from benefits planning, requirements statementing, product development, deployment, and then to gathering the rewards. All stages require willing, active, and committed participants, often from multiple areas of the organisation. One of the key aspects of this model is that the review of outcomes provides the basis for an input into the strategy creation process; in an ongoing business, strategy creation and execution is continuous.

Agility and innovation through governance

Aside from the issue (myth?) of balancing the portfolio, there is the challenge of reacting appropriately to emergent strategy and adjusting the portfolio accordingly. Effective, timely, and responsive governance of the strategy aims to ensure that strategy is realigned to changing situations. Stimulus for adjusting the strategy can be based on real need for changes, and therefore legitimate, or can be misinformed, based on cognitive bias or otherwise illegitimate reasons. Das and Teng (2002) note "a number of heuristics and biases that individuals are subject to in making judgements under uncertainty". Kahnemann (2011) identifies six types of cognitive bias – attribute substitution, when making a complex judgement; availability heuristic looking for immediate examples; anchoring bias, relying more heavily on the first piece of information received; loss aversion, preferring to avoid losses; narrow framing within the context, and hindsight bias – in accepting a theory without prior objective reasoning.

Many portfolio management teams establish portfolio management offices to aid the portfolio manager in overseeing project (and program) progress and delivery and, thereafter, the benefits ensuing (see Chapter 15 in Section III for further discussion). To be effective and provide value, the portfolio office needs to be more than just a data-gathering function. The portfolio office should act as a central co-ordinator of all the elements of the portfolio; this is particularly crucial when, as is usual, those elements span the organisation's functions. Thus, the portfolio office can maintain focus on achieving strategy execution by ensuring continuous strategic alignment of the portfolio's elements, ensuring effective co-ordination at executive level, and efficient integration of the projects' outputs into operations. The last of these aspects is of paramount importance, as highlighted by numerous analysts who report disconnects between project delivery and realisation of the intended benefits (Al-Arabi & Al-Sadeq, 2008; Serra & Kunc, 2014; Kaplan & Norton, 2008).

The end point of any project or program is not its delivery into operations but is when the planned benefits start to be realised by operations. Unless those endeavours have been targeted accurately at the organisation's strategic goals, it is likely that those benefits cannot be realised – and the outcome may even be detrimental to the organisation's ambitions. Project and program success must be translated into investment success. "Strategic governance" is therefore essential to not only delivery of the planned benefits but also of prioritisation of the key projects and programs.

However well the portfolio is formatted initially, it will need to change continuously to adapt to adjusted strategy. Research by Hoffmann et al. (2020) suggests a range of critical success factors to maintain alignment of portfolio management with strategy:

- Agility – the ability of the organisation to be flexible and adaptable.
- The 3Cs – culture, change management, and communications.
- Governance – effective control but reactive.
- Risk management – active risk management processes that enable judgements of risk compared to gain.
- Value – comparing each project's relative contribution to the strategy.
- P3M (portfolio, program, and project) maturity – established effective management methodologies aid effective project deliveries.
- Organisational structure – avoidance of parochial departmental attitudes in favour of a pan-organisational approach.

Strategic realignment

As the portfolio progresses, there will be a need for reaction and realignment to emergent strategy, and this will necessitate new projects and closure of obsolescent existing ones. Of these two, the killing of cherished but redundant projects seems to be a problem for many organisations. Vested interests can lead to the phenomena of "escalation of commitment". However, it is obvious that appropriate project terminations will release resources, thereby enabling vital projects to be better supported, but also avoids those obsolescent projects creating management distractions. Most importantly, judicious cancellation of projects is symptomatic of a portfolio that is being kept focused on the corporate strategy as it continuously evolves. In the words of Porter, "the essence of strategy is deciding what not to do" (Porter, 1996).

Most project managers are probably operating at a level below strategy formulation and are mostly intent on making the deliveries that they have been tasked with, so it is at portfolio management level that the prioritisation decisions need to be taken – but the project managers still need to be understanding which parts of organisational strategy they are contributing to, and therefore what a successful outcome will look like. Trickle-down of high-level requirements statements into meaningful specifications for project deliverables is, consequently, a vital process. Equally vital is the upward communication of information concerning new developments, opportunities, and emerging understandings of the situation "on the ground". However, many organisations experience difficulties even with intra-organisational co-operation and communication, just as indicated by the research by Sull et al. (2015) and others. Consequently, responses to the need for adjustments to strategy are slow, and preparedness to co-operate in those amendments is lacking. If that is compounded by discord within the ranks of the senior stakeholders, obsolete strategy may pervade, and the portfolio's composition may continue unchanged, thus wasting time, effort, and funds.

Conclusion

This chapter begins by discussing strategy formulation and development, setting the scene for discussing how strategy execution is managed within the portfolio. Throughout the chapter, the contrast between planned and emergent strategy is considered, with the accelerated rate of change in the organisational environment and the consequential increasing emphasis on emergent strategies, necessitating managers, at all levels, to develop an ability to be flexible and capable of adjusting the strategies and tactics that they are deploying, in managing their responsibilities within the portfolio. This, then, suggests less reliance on fixed longer-term plans and more utilisation of the sorts of methodologies that encourage flexible portfolio responses to emergent strategy, with the latter part of the chapter emphasising the advantages of executing strategy through portfolio management, as well as its challenges and principles, highlighting the need for strategic alignment and realignment as the organisational strategy evolves.

References

Al-Arabi M. & Al-Sadeq I. (2008) *Establishing a Project Portfolio Management Office*. The Project Management Institute.

APM (2019) *The Agile Portfolio: Fact or Fiction?* Portfolio Management Specific Interest Group.

Barraba V. (2011) *The Decision Loom: A Design for Interactive Decision-making in Organisations*. Triarchy Press.

Buttrick R. (2019) *The Programme and Portfolio Workout*. Routledge.

Cardinali R (1998) Assessing technological productivity gains: Benson and Parker revisited. *Logistics Information Management* 11(2), 89–92.

Damianides M. (2006) Sarbanes-Oxley and IT governance: New guidelines on IT control and compliance. *Information Systems Management* 22, 77–85.

Das T. & Teng B-S. (2002) Cognitive baises and strategic decision processes: An integrative Perspective. *Journal of Management Studies* 36(6), 757–778.

Drucker P. (1993) *Management: Tasks, Responsibilities, Practices*. Heinemann.

Evans R. (Sir), & Price C. (1999) *Vertical Takeoff*. Nicholas Brealey.

Hoffmann D., Ahlemann F. & Reining S. (2020) Reconciling alignment, efficiency, and agility in IT project portfolio management: Recommendations based on a revelatory case study. *International Journal of Project Management* 38(2), 124–136.

Hughes D. (1993) *Moltke on the Art of War; Selected Writings*. Presidio Press.

Ingason H. & Jonasson H. (2019) *Project: Strategy*. Routledge.

Johnson G. & Scholes K. (1993) *Exploring Corporate Strategy*. Prentice Hall.

Kahnemann D. (2011) *Thinking, Fast and Slow*. Penguin.

Kaplan R. & Norton D. (1992) The Balanced Scorecard – measures that drive performance. *Harvard Business Review* 71–79.

Kaplan R. & Norton D. (2008) *The Execution Premium: Linking Strategy to Operations for Competitive Advantage*. Harvard Business School Publishing.

Lock D. & Wagner R. (2019) *The Handbook of Project Portfolio Management*. Routledge.

McGahan A. (October 2004) How industries change. *Harvard Business Review* 82(10), 86–94.

Medenhall M. (2019) Strategic planning failure. www.referenceforbusiness.com

Mintzberg M. (1987) *The Strategy Process: Concepts, Context, Cases.* FT Prentice Hall.

Mintzberg H., Ahlstrand B. & Lampel J. (1998) *Strategy Safari.* FT Prentice Hall.

Mintzberg H., Ahlstrand B. & Lampel J. (2008) *Strategy Safari. The Complete Guide through the Wilds of Strategic Management.* Second Edition. FT Publishing International.

Mintzberg H. & Waters J. (1985) Of strategies, deliberate and emergent. *Strategic Management Journal* 13, 257–272.

Mishra S. & Mohanty B. (2020) Approaches to strategy formulation: A content analysis of definitions of strategy. *Journal of Management and Organization* 1–28.

Mitchell R., Phaal R. & Athanassopouluo N. (March 2018) *Scoring methods for evaluating and selecting early technology and innovation projects.* Centre for Technology Management Working Paper Series no. 2.

Montoya-Torres J. & Ortiz-Vargas D. (2014) Collaboration and information sharing in dyadic supply chains: A literature review over the period 2000–2012. *Estudios Gerenciales* 30(133), 343–354.

Mui C. (2012) *How Kodak Failed.* Leadership Strategy On-line.

Ozdem G. (2011) *An analysis of the Mission and Vision statements on the Strategic Plans of Higher Education Institutions.* Ginesun University.

Pettigrew A., Thomas H. & Whittington R. (2002) *Handbook of Strategy and Management.* Sage.

Phaal R. (2019) *Roadmapping for Strategy and Innovation.* University of Cambridge, Institute for Manufacturing.

Porter M. (1979) How competitive forces shape strategy. *Harvard Business Review*57, 137–145.

Porter M. (1996) What is strategy. *Harvard Business Review.* November, p70.

Raynor M. (2011) Disruptive innovation: The Southwest Airlines case revisited. *Strategy and Leadership* 39(4), 31–34.

Redfern J. (July 2006) Everyone has baggage – But is it yours, 'project'. *Journal of the Association for Project Management.* 16–17.

Sandberg E. (2007) Logistics collaboration in supply chains: Practice vs. theory. *International Journal of Logistics* 18(2), 274–293.

Schabacker M. & Vajna S. (2008) Evaluation of the benefit yield of technology projects. Proceedings paper for 2nd Symposium on International Issues in Engineering Design. DETC2004-57313, 513–520.

Serra C. & Kunc M. (2014) Benefits realisation management and its influence on project success and on the execution of business strategy. *International Journal of Project Management* 33(1), 53–66.

Sull D., Homkes, R. & Sull C. (2015) Why strategy unravels and what to do about it. *Harvard Business Review* 93(3), 58–66.

Viser M. (2016) Donald Trump's airline went from opulence in the air to crash landing. *The Boston Globe.* https://www.bostonglobe.com/news/politics/2016/05/27/donald-trump-airline-went-from-opulence-air-crash-landing/zEf1Er2Hok2dPTVVmZT6NP/story.html.

Williams D. & Parr T. (2004) *Enterprise Programme Management: Delivering value.* Palgrave MacMillan.

Annex

Case studies of different strategic responses to changes in organisational environments

Remploy – turning forced reorganisation into a success story

Remploy was set up by the British government following the Second World War to find employment for ex-servicemen and women with disabilities, and it is still, essentially, the company's mission. As such, it was considered to be a "national institution" by people throughout the UK. By the end of the twentieth century, its employees included those with all manner of physical impairments, included more than just ex-forces employees, and the organisation had grown to ten businesses operating 83 factories. Those businesses ranged from school furniture, packaging materials, and safety equipment through to healthcare and CCTV components.

In the first decade of this century, Remploy was beginning to feel the effects of competitors gaining the cost savings of offshore sourcing and needed to revise its strategy and focus on its most valuable activities. It was also expected to find ways to create more job opportunities for physically impaired people in the future. At that time, the cost of each employee was subsidised by the British government at the rate of £20,000 per person.

The major stakeholders were entirely in disagreement regarding a solution, whereas the National Audit Office was insisting on a drastic reduction in subsidies and stating that the company needed to withdraw from loss-making businesses, yet the trade unions and the general public were totally against any closures or redundancies.

At that time, Remploy had no change management capability, and any project management knowledge was limited to product development within each of its businesses.

A strategy was developed that started with the development of change management and project management competencies, ahead of a major restructuring plan that resulted in the closure or divestment of 29 sites and the redeployment of 2,000 people to other sites or externally. There was to be no compulsory redundancies. The aim was to deliver £90m of benefits over the following five years and to focus on developing routes to placement of people with disabilities into general industry. The whole portfolio of projects needed to be structured carefully, having particular regard for public opinion, and needed to be completed in a very short timescale.

The initial part of the strategy was delivered in less than two years, and Bob Warner, CEO at that time, accredited the achievement to having spent time preparing the organisation, gaining accord with the diverse stakeholders, and acquiring the necessary competencies to undertake such a complete restructuring.

Remploy did develop its people placement capability – operating as a recruitment service, it found 100,000 disabled people jobs in open industry between 2009 and 2014. In 2013, it sold or closed its remaining sites and, in 2015, became part-owned by US service provider Maximus.

This was strategy born of forced change of circumstances and resulted in a completely new direction for the company. However, this strategy could only be executed by this previously rather "staid" organisation learning how to create and manage a portfolio of projects, enabling it to transform itself and thereafter to maintain a modern outlook.

Netflix – an organisation that reinvented itself

Netflix resulted from a late-penalty charge imposed by a video hire company on Wilmot Reed Hastings because he kept the movie too long! That $40 hit caused Reed Hastings and Marc Randolph to consider a different model of DVD hire, in which customers could keep the film as long as they wanted but couldn't rent another until they had returned the existing one. Unlike all the existing movie rental companies at that time, they had no shops – all transactions were done by mail. Users browsed their website and ordered online.

Netflix launched in 1998 and, by 2002, had grown to such an extent that they went public. Not resting on their laurels, they recognised the potential for development of online rentals of films and, by 2007, had completely reformatted the company. By 2012, Netflix was almost global and offering their own movie feature series such as *House of Cards*, being at the forefront of the online entertainment revolution.

Here is a case of an organisation passing through, first, a strategy of "core transformation" (adopting a fundamentally different way of operating) and moving to "strategic transformation" (changing the very essence of the company). The transformation necessitated a diverse and complex portfolio that is also maintained as the organisation progresses forward in a highly competitive media market.

BAE – the strategy behind the saving of British Aerospace Engineering

A story of an organisational rescue involving cultural shift and adopting collaborative working principles.

In 1991, BAE had full order books, was acknowledged for its aerospace expertise (having produced some hugely successful aircraft), and had acquired the synergistic business of Marconi Electronics. Despite having its roots and main expertise in aviation, BAE yet was, in reality, a broad-based conglomerate that included a building company, the Rover car company, a satellite communications company, and a property development company. Yet it was known to have poor customer relations and low workforce morale and motivation. It had operated in a relatively stable environment for many years.

Then in 1992, the global defence industry took a huge downturn, resulting in military aviation companies worldwide cutting their prices – and their workforces. Commercial aircraft builders reduced their prices, which compromised BAE work with Airbus, and it was generally seen that there was overcapacity in the sector. BAE had to stage a £1b asset write-off, and in the words of the CEO, Sir Richard Evans, its future "hung by a thread" (Evans & Price, 1999).

He instigated the organisation-wide initiative "Benchmark BAE", a radical new set of strategies designed to reshape the organisation into a fitter and more agile operator that could cope with a rapidly changing environment. His mentor, the incoming chairman Bob Bauman, had the fierce conviction that only organisations having a talent for perpetual change would be successful in the future.

The aim was to "spring-clean" – focus the organisation's portfolio around their profitable activities. So in early 1993, they adopted a long-term strategy to concentrate on their base of real expertise – their aerospace activities. This must have seemed paradoxical to observers, given the state of the aviation sector, but BAE's strategy was well conceived. The first moves were difficult – in addition to the £1b asset write-off, 60,000 jobs lost from a workforce of 127,000 made the company a pariah to the investors, who had stood by them previously, and a hostile takeover seemed a distinct likelihood. However, the slimming of the workforce left them with the people that they saw as being really needed. As they are technological leaders in the field, rationalisation of design and manufacturing activities proved to not be such an obstacle, and divestment of ill-fitting subsidiaries, such as the building company and Rover cars, yielded useful capital.

There prevailed a culture at divisional level of being merely different companies under common ownership, rather than one of potential to synergistically exploit all the group's capabilities, and competitive, rather than collaborative, attitudes between divisions began to inhibit sharing of competencies and capabilities. Much time was spent by senior managers in winning the hearts and minds of those running the subsidiary companies – the aim was to turn the "independent team" attitudes into a "one company" mindset. At this point, it became obvious that the strategy emphasis needed to change from "technicalities and practicalities" to one of "cultural transformation".

Early executive management work was consequently directed at gaining a common perspective on the objectives, and it took time to achieve the attitudinal shifts. The quest for a new vision statement resulted in:

> At BAE we are dedicated to working together, and with our partners, to become the benchmark for our industry, setting the standard for customer satisfaction, technology, financial performance, and quality in all we do.

A very ambitious statement, given the organisation's predicament at that point!

That statement resulted in the portfolio of programs being focused on five areas:

- Improvements to customer services.
- Behaving as a partner to customers.
- Developing the workforce.
- Innovation and adoption of new technology.
- Improving performance at production-unit level – a quest for better ways of doing everything.

It can be seen that this very major make-or-break initiative was initially driven by a strategy of asset rationalisation, but there followed the realisation that this had to be a cultural transformation – and so the strategy required a very different emphasis. Creation of a coherent vision statement, agreed by all the key stakeholders, was crucial to the focusing of minds on the development of a tactical plan to "make it so".

British Aerospace became British Aerospace Engineering Systems and, over the years of the early twenty-first century, underwent further divestments and acquisitions, gaining strength. Today it is the largest manufacturing company in the UK, at the forefront of military shipbuilding, land-based military vehicles, and security technology involvements, is one of the six main suppliers to the US Department of Defence, and is in a state of constant evolution – which supports Bob Bauman's assertion that successful organisations of the future will have to be capable of perpetual change (Evans & Price, 1999).

Kodak – unable to swallow the bitter pill of disruptive technology

A Kodak engineer, Steve Sasson, is accredited with creating the first digital camera in 1975, but because the organisation was, at that time, *the* global manufacturer of photographic film, which digital photography did not require, he was told to bury the concept.

Kodak management either deliberately ignored this disruptive technology for decades whilst their new competitors exploited it – or were just so immersed in a rapidly obsolete strategy (with all its massive capitalisation) that they were unable to face a change of direction. In 1981, Vince Barraba (2011) conducted a detailed study of this threat to their business and concluded that they had (at most) ten years to catch up. In 1989, a board member, Phil Sampur, proposed a courageous strategy of backing the new technology against their existing film manufacturing capability, but it was considered high risk and dismissed. A replacement CEO was quoted as saying, "Kodak regarded digital photography as the enemy, and a juggernaut that would kill the chemical-based film and paper business that fuelled Kodak's sales and profits for decades" (Mui 2012).

Little remains of this erstwhile-global giant, but a few lessons can be learned from its demise:

- The need to maintain organisational open-mindedness and move with the times.
- An awareness of developing capabilities within the organisation – and exploiting them.
- Preparedness to change the business fundamentally when the need is obvious – and the courage to redesign its portfolio of projects accordingly.

Trump airlines – trying to make a silk purse from a cotton handkerchief at a time when the cotton handkerchief is what is really wanted!

Trump Shuttle Inc. was formed in 1989 by the purchase of a subsidiary of Eastern Airlines. It had established a place in the market as a low-cost air shuttle service operating between New York, Boston, and Washington, DC. This purchase was financed by a syndicate of banks led by Citibank. Donald Trump's strategy was to transform it into a luxury service with features such as maple wood veneer, gold-coloured lavatory fittings, and on-board laptop and phone systems. By the end of the first year, passenger traffic had declined and fuel costs had increased, following the 1990 Gulf War. A recession started, and corporate customers were reducing their travel budgets, just as the airline's running costs increased. The airline defaulted on its debt in September 1990.

On the basis of available information, this failure could be interpreted, at least partially, as the wrong strategy, consequent of the owner's preference for the creation of a luxury brand, when the starting point was a successful position as a budget carrier. That situation was then compounded by a recession, in which the organisation was unable to reposition itself again into a budget airline; its external environment had changed. The company had invested in a portfolio of new sophisticated technology projects when the market was rapidly moving towards low-cost providers (Viser, 2016).

4 Organisational change and portfolio management

Ranjit Sidhu and Pete Harpum

Introduction

This chapter is quite exploratory in nature, reviewing some important ideas and theories about organisational change and inviting some reflection on how these ideas might be used in thinking about the management of strategic portfolios. The intention is that this understanding will facilitate better decision-making at the portfolio level to support more effective delivery of change projects and programs held in the portfolio. This is to propose that strategic portfolio management can play a significant role in influencing the ability of organisations to successfully navigate organisational change. This implies a direct and hands-on role for portfolio management in supporting organisational change.

Change, and the management of change, have been recognised as vital aspects of organisational success for many years. In the context of mainstream management thinking, Kotter (1996) is perhaps most strongly associated with the ideas of how to bring about change in organisations. However, the history, theory, and indeed, practice of the management of change is much older, originating around the end of the nineteenth century – albeit that the theories at that time were about how organisations do, or should, work, not about changing how they work *per se*.

The ideas of organisational change have permeated to the level of projects too. "*Projects deliver change*" has become a virtual mantra, mainly in the normative models, espoused by government, clients, major project delivery organisations, and consultants. On one hand, this statement is true. Obviously true, since projects and programs exist to deliver strategic objectives. In order to do this, they deliver "things" into the environment. This is a fundamental and unavoidable reality. Whenever, and however, something is created, it changes the environment. The magnitude of the impact may be large (megaprojects) or relatively trivial (the roll-out of a piece of software in a start-up business, for example). On the other hand, to insist that project management is all about managing change is to risk trivialising the hugely nuanced, sophisticated, and challenging area of managing organisational change through people (Hornstein, 2015).

Managing portfolios of change programs and projects

A portfolio composed of change programs and projects can be conceived of as "simply" a type of portfolio. In principle, the management of such a portfolio, or sub-portfolio, is no different to the management of portfolios of other types of programs and projects: new product development projects, sales and marketing projects, a portfolio of external

DOI: 10.4324/9780367853129-5

projects (e.g. a contractor's portfolio of construction projects, a consultant's portfolio of consulting assignment projects, etc.). What is important is that the context for such a portfolio needs to be understood to enable good management decision-making – as applies to other types of portfolios.

In order to better understand the context of change, it is useful to look at the various components of organisational change as they are understood in relation specifically to change programs and projects. Note that this chapter reviews some of the basic and mainstream views on organisational change and does this at a very surface level. Readers with an interest in the huge literature on organisational psychology, the dynamics of change, and multiple perspectives on how to conceptualise change may wish to begin their investigations with the following topics:

- *Modern and postmodern thinking* on the topic (there is not a great deal in this topic before the modern period, with organisational psychology really beginning at the turn of the nineteenth century). Burnes (2004) offers a good overview and starting point.
- *Classical*, also called rational-scientific, approaches, with key thinkers being Taylor and the Gilbreths (Cox & Seaton (1992), Fayol (Fells, 2000), and Weber (Mills et al., 2014).
- *Human relations approach*, exemplified through the work of the Tavistock Institute of Human Relations in the UK (Brown, 1967), with writers such as Lewin (1947), Mayo (2004), Emery (1999), Trist (e.g. Pasmore & Khalsa, 1993), Murray (e.g. Murray & O'Mahony, 2007), and others.
- *Contingency theory*, informed with writing by Burns and Stalker (Onday, 2016), Lawrence and Lorsch (1967), Thompson (e.g. Thompson et al., 2017), Woodward (e.g. Kalagnanam & Lindsay, 1999), and Perrow (1961).
- *Culture excellence models* of organisations, underpinned by key writers such as Peters and Waterman (Hitt & Ireland, 1987), McGregor (1966), Moss Kanter (2003), and Handy (2007, 2012).

Planned and emergent strategy and change

Much of the mainstream organisational change management literature is concerned with two main approaches: planned change and emergent change (Bamford & Forrester, 2003). The similarity of this to the central ideas of planned and emergent strategy is not surprising, given the overlap between thinking about strategy and thinking about the impacts of achieving strategic objectives, that is, that organisational change is frequently (perhaps always) needed in order to deliver strategic objectives.

The planned change approach assumes a stable environment (Voet et al., 2014), with clearly defined outcomes, moving systematically from current position to the desired future position in a controlled way (Kotter, 2008). It is no surprise that this has been the central theoretical idea behind the notion that projects and programs are both the ideal vehicles to deliver organisational change and are, in fact, always vehicles for, and of, change. The dominant normative models of project management continue to emphasise effective planning and control as central to project success. Based on the negative-feedback open systems control model, project control is always about returning deviation in project progress and outputs back to the planned (predetermined) progress and outputs (Harpum, 2010).

However, in both the change management and project management literature, these (wistful) ideas are seriously challenged. Critical, chaos and complexity, uncertainty, and human behaviour theories have all brought a generally more realistic set of theories to bear on project management. The classical models of strategy, and hence organisational change, predicated on the scientific-rational ideas of Taylor, the Gilbreths, Fayol, and Weber, have waned, although they still seem to have an undue influence in practice (Burnes, 2004). The planned approach assumes people will all move in the direction planned for by management, enacted through strategy, and then delivered by the portfolio of change projects/programs (Bamford & Forrester, 2003). Burnes (2004) characterises this approach as follows:

- *Organisations are rational entities.* They are collectives of individuals focused on the achievement of relatively specific goals through their organisation into highly formalised, differentiated, and efficient structures.
- *The design of the organisation is a science.* Through experience, observation, and experiment, it has been established that there is one best organisational form for all bodies. This is based on the hierarchical and horizontal division of labour and functions, whereby organisations are conceived of as machines which, once set in motion, inexorably and efficiently will pursue and achieve their preselected goals.
- *People are economic beings.* They are solely motivated by money. This instrumental orientation means they will try to achieve maximum reward for the minimum work and will use whatever bargaining power their skills or knowledge allow to this end. Therefore, jobs must be designed in such a way as to minimise an individual's skill and discretion and to maximise management control.

The problem with planned change is, rather obviously, that people are complex; their emotions and personal interests get in the way, all set within personal, organisational, and societal cultures that are different everywhere (Burnes, 2004). An emergent approach to change considers organisations as complex systems, continually adapting, in response to constantly changing environments, and allows change to emerge from the bottom up (Burnes, 1996). The process is open-ended, evolving iteratively, without a predefined outcome, although the general direction of travel is known (Voet et al., 2014). Greater uncertainty and unpredictability are inherent with emergent change. This approach to change is often referred to as operating at the "edge of chaos" (Stacey, 2001; Hinson & Osborne, 2014). An emergent approach allows change to emerge in response to evolving situations, contexts, and environments.

Mintzberg et al. (2008), following a detailed exposition on the various "schools" of strategic thinking, present the idea of an umbrella strategy, mixing deliberate planned and emergent approaches to strategy. This can be directly applied to organisational change, providing a practical response to the limitations of a purely planned or emergent approach to change. Such a combination of approaches allows responsiveness to uncertainty in the environment, effectiveness of change achieved over time, and changing organisational circumstances, whilst nevertheless helping to set clear direction for the organisation. Again, noting that strategy and achieving the change required to achieve strategic objectives are conflated in this view.

> An umbrella strategy . . . means that the broad outlines are deliberate (such as to move upmarket), while the details are allowed to emerge en route (when, where, and how).

> Thus, emergent strategies are not necessarily bad and deliberate strategies good; effective strategists mix these in ways that reflect the conditions at hand, notably the ability to predict as well as the need to react to unexpected events.
>
> (Mintzberg et al., 2008, p. 11)

Hence, the connection between planned and emergent strategies in and of themselves as distinct strategic approaches and the way change is managed to achieve the strategic objectives envisaged by these approaches are directly related. (It is important to note here that Mintzberg et al. [2008] offer several ways of envisaging strategy and change, with the umbrella strategy being only one of these. The important point is that there are multiple ways to understand strategy, as there are multiple ways to formulate and think about managing the change that strategies inevitably create).

Making sense of change and uncertainty

There is a fundamental reality about life – the future is unknowable. This fact is the motivator and subject of millennia of philosophical thinking, writing, and ideas about how to live life. Change inevitably sharpens the perception of uncertainty – we seek physical and psychological routine in order to reduce the effort expended to protect us from the perception of danger associated with uncertainty of the future (Solms, 2021). In Milliken's (1987) conception, uncertainty is an "individual's perceived inability to predict something accurately". This may stem from ambiguous information or from a lack of it, where ambiguity is understood to be the vague and multi-interpretable meaning of a situation (Abdallah & Langley, 2014).

When change occurs, people interpret information they are receiving in regard to the change based on their mental models (Korzybski, 2000). The clear implication of this is that everyone finds a different meaning, since everyone, definitionally, has a different model of the world. This is just an unavoidable fact of life. Nevertheless, peoples' mental models of how the world "is" will share similarities, since in some ways people have shared experiences. At the very least, within an organisation experiencing or anticipating change, people will share some similar ideas about the organisation – they have ingested the same culturally originated "memes" and integrated them into their mental model (Dennett, 1993). The organisation's culture will have permeated, to some extent or another, the people who are part of the organisation. Since people engage in conversation to make sense of the uncertainty raised by change, there is likely to be some group consensus on the response to the change, all the while those individuals still hold different views in detail to the group-agreed perceptions (Johansson et al., 2014). Leaders are always part of a group, and Weick and Quinn (1999) identify the need for leaders of groups anticipating, or already within, a changing environment to act as sense makers. Weick et al. (2005) suggest sensemaking is about action and interpretation and is a social process. Leaders and managers enact their interpretations with their team members, which in turn leads team members to take action based on their own interpretations.

Creating an environment acceptant of organisational change

To create an environment within an organisation in which there is an acceptance of coming change and willingness to engage with the organisational and personal processes of change, we need to understand, as far as is reasonable and/or possible, the current status of "change readiness". "Change readiness is defined as an individual's beliefs, attitudes, and intentions regarding the extent to which changes are needed and the organisation's capacity to successfully undertake those changes" (Armenakis et al., 1993). To fully understand this in a given organisation, even with only a few people, is really an impossibility. We can only know what is reported by people, not what is actually in their minds (Saploski, 2017), and what is reported is always political. People report about themselves what they believe will lead to the outcome best aligned with their personal desires for the future. To believe there is anything more we can determine than a generalised and actually quite vague idea of the organisational and personal readiness for change is unrealistic, and the vagueness and lack of detail will only increase with organisational size. This is not to say the process of making the assessment has no value. Undertaking a change readiness review can achieve multiple objectives:

- People will feel that their concerns are being asked for and listened to – this alone helps to reduce anxiety related to the unknown future–changed organisation and their role and place in it.
- The process can be used as a communications exercise, sharing with people the anticipated future after the changes, describing the vision for the future, and explaining the benefits and dis-benefits likely to flow.
- Data can be captured that can be fed into both the strategic objective of the change, the strategy for achieving the change, and the detailed plans to enact the change. Emergent ideas can be gathered and worked with.
- The output can be used to support senior- and operational-level decision-making on the change envisaged.
- If the process is carried out several times during the life of the change program, and at the end too, a rolling organisation-wide view can be reported and reviewed as part of the process of managing the change. If appropriate questions are asked and relevant metrics measured, the change readiness review may also be used to assess business benefit achievement.

The factors that contribute to individuals' readiness for change have been proposed to be *discrepancy*, *appropriateness*, *efficacy*, *principal support*, and *valence* (Armenakis & Harris, 2002). These can be reinforced through effective change communication and early participation in change activities.

- *Discrepancy* – individuals believe a change is needed when they recognise the current position is not fit for purpose.
- *Appropriateness* – people must believe the response is appropriate to address the discrepancy.
- *Efficacy* – a belief in one's capability to implement change, as well as the organisation's capability to deliver the change stated as being necessary.
- *Principal support* – confidence that any required support will be available, including social support.
- *Valence* –a psychodynamic term for the propensity an individual has for the role they take up in a group; in this context, valence is seen in the light of an individual's understanding of what is in it for them personally if they support the change (sometimes referred to as WIIFM – what's in it for me).

This list of factors is cognitive. It assumes that people are rational. The response to these factors is relatively straightforward to address. Those responsible for delivering the change can provide information that covers these areas. A well-thought-through communications strategy, built on sensible and logical thinking about the change, is the standard and reasonable response. However, less simple is to address each individual's valence. Nevertheless, the organisational and national culture in which the organisation exists can help predict some general themes about what aspects of the change may lead to higher levels of valence-driven alignment, generally, across the people in the organisation.

For a long time, research into mainstream thinking about managing change has overlooked the affective (emotional) component of change, and both *cognitive* and *affective* aspects of change readiness are important. "Affect factors" influencing an individual's engagement with change are identified as *commitment*, *adaptability*, and emotional responses mediated through *social exchange* activities (Rafferty et al., 2013).

- *Commitment* is a "force (mindset) that binds an individual to a target or course of action" (Herscovitch & Meyer, 2002). They found strong affective commitment to change leads to high levels of compliance and discretionary effort in supporting change.
- *Adaptability* is "the quality of being able to change, without great difficulty, to fit new or changed circumstances" (Savickas, 1997). The emphasis is on an individual's ability to take continuous change in their stride, capable of responding positively to new circumstances and situations.
- *Social exchange*. Commitment to tasks leads to social interactions, which contributes to team cohesion, which is critical for team effectiveness (Kozlowski & Ilgen, 2009). Change readiness needs to be considered at an individual and team level, as social interaction will influence collective interpretation and collective change readiness (Armenakis et al., 1993).

Emotions and social exchange

Organisational psychology research has looked into the emotional and social aspects of how people interact in groups at work. Many of these ideas have found common public acceptance yet are not always seen as either important enough to consider in organisational change or perhaps are believed to be trumped by a rational-scientific model of management. The most important of these emotional, psychological aspects related to managing change are related to dealing with uncertainty and the anxiety it invokes.

The experience of uncertainty is "*particularly aversive and anxiety-provoking*" (Bordia et al., 2004), as human beings seek predictability (Scarlett, 2019) and a state of homeostasis (Lewin, 1947). The implication of this is that when faced with organisational change, people are forced to confront the fact that the future has become more uncertain than they were expecting it to be (there is always some understanding that the future is uncertain). Individuals' normal day-to-day lived experience of managing the feelings about the future are significantly disrupted. The future has become less predictable than it had been presumed to be, and neuropsychological responses occur in all people (Saploski, 2017). Hence, anxiety increases, with the response determined in large part by the person's inherent capacity to manage their feelings of anxiety.

When these personal, largely unconscious responses occur, they are likely to spread from one to many people. Our emotions are contagious and influence individuals, and then as the emotional responses settle and take root, team effectiveness is impacted

(Barsade, 2002; Elfenbein (2014). This is a natural group response. Nevertheless, *conscious* choices about what emotional state to present within a group have been shown to alter the emotional states of others in the group. Endrejat et al. (2020) propose individuals can act as motivational contagions in conversations about change. In simple terms, this means leaders can and should choose to behave and present to groups in ways that are likely to create positive emotional responses to the uncertainties and anxieties associated with organisational change.

Now here is where it can start to become challenging for many managers and leaders of organisations. Robinson and Griffiths's (2005) study of effective responses to uncertainty due to organisational change indicated social support coping (strategies for groups to cope with traumatic experiences) was most often used to deal with stress related to high uncertainty and ambiguity. This is more likely to happen in a caring environment, where others' emotions are recognised and accepted as part of being human (Zak, 2017) and meaningful interactions can take place. Taking the view that caring environments in organisations reflect organisational culture and that culture is established in large part by leaders, the rather-obvious conclusion is that leaders have a responsibility for creating caring environments.

Aside from this being perhaps what leaders ought to aspire to for their organisations in any case, creating such a culture will enable effective change to happen more easily. People will feel cared for; they will have leaders and managers that act as motivators of positive responses towards uncertainty caused by change. Groups within the organisation will more readily engage positively with the work needed to achieve the future. A future that more people can desire, or at least tolerate, rather than hold onto real anxieties and fear. This type of leadership behaviour involves both personal and professional elements and a loosening of boundaries between these elements of the individual leader (Kahn, 1990).

It is worth noting that researchers Ford and Ford (1995) and Stacey (2001) place conversation and interaction at the heart of change. Following the previous discussion, this is not surprising. To give quite a detailed integration of the aforementioned ideas, Stacey (2001) is quoted at some length:

- Both the individual and the collective identities of human beings emerge in the complex interactions between human bodies as they responsively relate to each other. Meaning, that is, knowledge also emerges in that interaction.
- In their responsive relating, people indicate to each other the potential evolution of their intended actions and it is this indication that makes it possible for them to cooperate in sophisticated ways. Responsive relating is a process in which people interweave their actions so that they can go on being and operating together. This circular, responsive process constitutes the joint action that is the social process and it is one in which human bodies act selectively in relation to other human bodies, thereby evoking selective responses from them.
- Bodies are uniquely individual and part of that uniqueness is an individual's self-conscious mind. Mind is the action of an individual's body reflexively directed back to itself so as to call forth in itself bodily responses similar to those evoked by actions directed to other bodies. The responses that a body spontaneously calls forth in itself are simultaneously selected or enacted by that body's history of relating to others. In other words, the human mind is not separate in any way from the body, but neither are processes of mind located in the body. Mind and self are, rather, actions of a whole body, just as, say,

walking is. The action of walking is performed by a body and that action is neither separate from the body, nor is it located in the body. The feature that distinguishes the mind and self from actions such as walking is that the former is directed back to the individual body while the action of walking is directed to the space around the body.

- The social is thus actions that are public and directed by one body to another, while individual mind/self is actions privately directed back to the body.
- Human action, then, simultaneously consists of both the private action directed back at the individual's body, that is, the individual mind/self, and the public action directed between individual bodies, that is, the social.
- A distinguishing feature of human action, both in public and private forms, is that it is communication in the medium of symbols, which makes sophisticated co-operative activity possible.
- All human action is history dependent. Any current action, whether in the medium of symbols or using tools is both enabled and constrained by the actions preceding it. Actions are patterned by both previous history and current context.
- Interaction, or relationship, has intrinsic pattern-forming properties, including the property of emergent novelty when interaction is diverse enough.

Individuals' sense of their psychological safety in organisational settings is always present. This feeling is embedded in the interpersonal actions of everyone on a day-to-day basis. Psychological safety is feeling able to show oneself without fear of negative consequences to self-image, status, or career. A key way in which psychological safety is established and mediated is through so-called psychological contracts between people; in organisations, this particularly means between individuals and their leaders and managers. Arthur and Rousseau (1996) define *psychological contracts* as "good-faith relationships between employees and leaders about what is expected of each other". Psychological contracts that are stable and predictable allow people to feel safe, as trust about how leaders and managers will respond to the individual is established (Kahn, 1990). Edmondson and Zhike (2014, p. 40) suggest that "psychological safety increases collaboration, particularly during uncertainty, complexity and interdependence", proposing that when leaders set expectations of uncertainty, they allow people to be experimental and create a sense of safety and trust. Schein (1997) also emphasises the importance of psychological safety to enable people to learn, without fear and anxiety.

In the case of organisational change, the learning *may* be multi-level: learning will inevitably be about how the organisation will operate in the future, how the individuals will realign their working relationships, how they will do their work if that changes, and to learn about how the organisational culture and the associated psychological contracts will change or have changed. Additionally, people have the opportunity to learn about how they learned, with double-loop learning. The value of this to the organisation (the value to the individual is more obvious) is that people that are "learning to learn" better are likely to become more adaptable in new environments and circumstances. People that learn effectively are valuable assets in an organisation.

However, psychological contracts may become broken during change, especially where there is a job-related impact. This is not always possible to avoid. Significant and difficult-to-predict major changes in organisations may leave leadership with little option than to break the psychological contracts and associated trust that has been built up over time. Procedural and interactional fairness may help counteract the impact of broken psychological contracts (Kickul et al., 2002). This, of course, means that not only must the procedures and interactions set up by the change be fair; they must also be seen to be fair – that is, communication must be clear and accurate and timely about the change and how the organisation will manage the negative impacts on people.

This chapter proposes that those involved in managing organisational change cannot afford to fail to engage with this level of sophisticated thinking about how people interact. To work only with a rational-scientific model of change, where human feelings, and the resultant behaviours, are disregarded or downplayed risks partial or complete failure of organisational change activities.

Organisational response to change and strategic portfolios

Before bringing all the previous ideas together in relation to managing strategic portfolios, there are a few additional important areas of theory to look at that are perhaps more meta-level topics, in some way floating above the "nitty-gritty" of the person-centred discussion so far. The human relations school was mentioned earlier in the chapter as a set of theories that the reader will gain value from looking into. Whilst key ideas of the human relations school include person-centred psychodynamic ideas, such as projection, transference, countertransference, introjection, these are understood and theorised about in the context of individuals and groups within organisational systems, for which there is no room in this chapter to cover. However, there is one construct that is useful to cover here in some detail, in the context of portfolio management. This is the idea that four perspectives can be used to understand organisations (groups) in a simplified manner. This is the "BART" analysis, where what is meant is to look at an organisation's *boundaries, authorities, roles,* and *task*. The strategic portfolio "level" is an ideal place from which to conduct such an analysis and, indeed, to maintain a continuous assessment of the four analytical aspects of BART. These are briefly described as follows (Green & Molenkamp, 2005, pp. 2–8):

- *Boundary* – the container for group work. We encounter boundaries constantly but may not experience them as such. *Time, task,* and *territory* provide the basis for the study of boundaries. . . . Included in this analysis are boundaries of *resources, roles* and *responsibilities*. The most important of these, resources, often determines the capacity of individuals and organisations to complete even the most rudimentary tasks.
- *Authority* – quite simply as the right to do work. . . . When a person takes up their authority, we assume that they take responsibility and that they are accountable for their actions. . . . Formal and [personal] authority are defined separately: *Formal authority* may be derived from a group or body – the Board of Directors . . . – or from an individual such as one's immediate supervisor or manager. The way an individual takes up formal authority we call personal authority. *Personal authority* is how we execute our formal authority. Personal authority is influenced by many different factors, i.e. our psychological make up, our social identity, our cultural background, etc.
- *Role* – People occupy roles. The span of these roles is rather transitory yet robust, ranging from mere moments to a lifetime. Roles can be achieved, acquired, assigned, and/or ascribed to us. According to the goodness of fit, roles can be reflections of, or equated with, our identity.

- *Task* – From a group relations perspective, the next task has never been done before. Yes, we may have a technical "fix" for a variety of circumstances, but the task remains dynamic. While a similar task may have been done previously, the change in the time boundary alone makes it different. (Note, the almost identical definition of task here, and "project" in much of the project management literature, is striking, perhaps even more so in that there is almost no cross-over between the Human Relations (HR) school and project management theory). Each person involved with the task also brings his or her perceptions to the moment. Conflicts arise when perceptions of the task differ from person to person or from group to group. In other words, we tend to import our histories and experiences to a task. Group relations work calls on us to be conscious of what we bring into a situation.

Green and Molenkamp (2005) go on to state that:

> A BART analysis of a workgroup or an organization may assist in preventing loss of valuable resources, off task behaviour, productivity decrease, not to mention stress, frustration and potential interpersonal and intergroup conflicts. The consequences of any of these problem areas are likely to impede or slow down the primary task and may ultimately be destructive for the good of the organization.

(The "primary task" is the task that the organisation sets out to achieve, or a project is set up to deliver, or indeed, by the argument being made in this chapter, the achievement of the set of strategic objectives operationalised through the portfolio and its management.)

Complexity

Complexity theory proposes that paying attention to the degree of stability and control in a system ensures an appropriate balance between chaos and order. With this in mind, Hinson and Osborne (2014) make recommendations for leaders to support people through disruption, including defining what is known, clarifying short-term actions, increasing communication channels, empowering diverse teams, and establishing simple rules to guide decisions and behaviour. Note the similarity to the earlier review of factors related to cognitive and emotional aspects of managing change effectively. They recommend leaders look through the lens of complex adaptive systems to understand the nature of self-organising systems and suggest focusing on the following to create the right conditions for change:

- *Drive for fitness*. This reflects any difference between the current situation and the desired position and indicates the desire or motivation for change. This aligns with the idea of "discrepancy" or "sense of urgency" as described earlier. Suggestions for increasing the drive for fitness include continually monitoring external conditions and emerging trends.
- *Diversity of views*. This is a reminder to ensure diverse perspectives are encouraged and considered with input from multiple levels and wide-ranging groups across the organisation. Different viewpoints help generate fresh insights and innovation. A key factor for this is creating an environment where people feel comfortable in offering different views and ideas (psychological safety and trust).

- *Connectivity*. This refers to the number of different interconnections within an organisation and quality of interactions between them. Strong and far-reaching connectivity enables sharing of ideas, knowledge transfer, and learning.
- *Safety*. This is about psychological safety and how comfortable people feel experimenting, trying out ideas and challenging the status quo. It also impacts the extent to which people will build connections and share ideas with others. A key contributor to this is building trust and making it okay to "fail"; ideas do not always have to work out.
- *Edge of chaos*. This indicates the balance between a sense of stability and being at the edge of chaos. It calls for a core set of standard processes and ways of doing things to give a sense of stability whilst dealing with change and continuous levels of disruption as a normal part of the day-to-day life of the "*organisation in transformation*".
- *Control*. This refers to the degree of autonomy people have. During rapid change, people need to be empowered to act and make decisions quickly, allowing ideas to flourish and be implemented. Control needs to be loosened, but with clear boundaries in place.

Organisational change and strategic portfolio management

People that have professional responsibility for designing and managing change will work with the constructs and ideas presented in this chapter. Almost certainly, change programs and projects are set up to deliver organisational change. Thus, inevitably, programs and projects delivering change will be part of a portfolio, whether it is formalised or not, although hopefully, the programs exist within a structured and managed portfolio. These programs and projects are being defined in such a way as to deliver strategic objectives and selected based on clear and well-understood criteria. In this situation, the portfolio has fulfilled its expected role. Nevertheless, this chapter proposes that a strategic portfolio can undertake an additional role. This role is to play a formal part in ensuring and assuring that organisational change is effective.

Portfolio management itself is essentially a decision-making apparatus. Nevertheless, the criteria against which decisions are made drive behaviour. If a "*portfolio decision criteria*" for a change program to enter the portfolio is, for example, that a formally qualified and experienced expert on organisational change (say, an organisational psychologist) is included in such a program's senior management team, then the portfolio is directly influencing how these programs are designed. It is easy to see, from the theory presented so far in this chapter, that well-thought-through decision criteria can address many aspects of change.

The proposal is not that portfolio managers become experts in change. The proposal is that portfolio management ensures that expertise is brought to bear on deciding appropriate portfolio decision criteria, in the same way that portfolio management cannot, for example, know what are the detailed decision criteria for technical aspects of complex products, but they ensure they are defined and in such a way that these criteria can be applied consistently and rigorously. Portfolio managers work with generalised, industry-specific knowledge about the content of the portfolio and, equally, of the environment, both internal and external, in which the portfolio exists. This chapter proposes this applies just the same to organisational change, for both strategic portfolios and sub-portfolios that contain, for example, only change programs and projects.

The addendum at the end of the chapter offers suggestions for questions that can be addressed when designing the portfolio (*design*) and managing the portfolio (*managing*), working with BART as an organising framework.

Conclusion

This chapter discussed portfolio-enabled change and transformation, looking to bring together the areas of managing change and portfolio management, and, as such, is quite exploratory in nature. The chapter looked at some of the key literature for management of change from the vast array available, considering the uncertainty and complexity of the organisational and strategic portfolio environment with planned and emergent strategy. The chapter continued by establishing the environment for "change readiness", developing the aspects of managing change associated with people's perceptions, emotions, and engagement with change, before finally considering the role of portfolios and portfolio managers when managing change, including a specific example with the BART model for managing change with portfolios of projects and programs.

Further reading

Balogun J. (2003) From blaming the middle to harnessing its potential: Creating change intermediaries. *British Journal of Management* 14(1), 69–83.

Bridges W. (2008) *Managing Transitions: Making the most of change.* Nicholas Brealey Publishing.

DiFonzo N. & Bordia, P. (1998) A tale of two corporations: Managing uncertainty during organisational change. *Human Resource Management* 37(34), 295–303.

Edmans A. (2020) *Grow the Pie: How Great Companies Deliver Both Purpose and Profit.* Cambridge University Press.

Edwards K., Prætorius T. & Nielsen A. (2020) A model of cascading change: Orchestrating planned and emergent change to ensure employee participation. *Journal of Change Management* 20(4), 342–368.

Elving W. (2005) The role of communication in organisational change. *Corporate Communications: An International Journal* 10(2), 129–138.

Edmondson A. (1999) Psychological safety and learning behaviour in work teams. *Administrative Science Quarterly* 44(2), 350–383

Herold D., Fedor D. & Caldwell S. (2007) Beyond change management: A multi-level investigation of contextual and personal influences on employees' commitment to change. *Journal of Applied Psychology* 92(4), 942–951.

Johansson, C. & Heide, M. (2008). Speaking of change: Three communication approaches in studies of organizational change. *Corporate Communications: An International Journal* 13(3), 288–305.

Larkin T. & Larkin S. (1994) *Communicating Change: Winning Employee Support for New Business Goals.* McGraw-Hill.

Lehrer J. (2009) *The Decisive Moment: How the Brain Makes up its Mind.* Canongate.

Lewis L. (2011) *Organisational Change: Creating Change through Strategic Communication.* Wiley-Blackwell.

Pink D. (2009) *Drive: The Surprising Truth about What Motivates Us.* Canongate Books.

Poole M. & Van de Ven A. (2004) *Handbook of Organizational Change and Innovation.* Oxford University Press.

Rousseau D. (1996) Changing the deal while keeping the people. *Academy of Management Executive* 10(1), 50–59.

Ruck K. (2020) *Exploring Internal Communication: Towards Informed Employee Voice.* Fourth Edition. Routledge.

Savickas ML. (1997), Career adaptability: An integrative construct for life-span, life-space theory. *The Career Development Quarterly* 45(1), 247–259

Schein E. (1993) how can organisations learn faster? The challenge of entering the green room. *Sloan Management Review* 34(2), 85–92.

Stouten J., Rousseau D. & Cremer D. (2018) Successful organisational change: Integrating the management practice and scholarly literatures. *Academy of Management Annals* 12(2), 752–788.

Tsoukas H. & Chia R. (2002) On organisational becoming: Rethinking organisational change. *Organisation Science* 13(5), 567–583.

Tsoukas H. & Hatch M. (2001) Complex thinking, complex practice: The case for a narrative approach to organisational complexity. *Human Relations* 54(8), 979–1013.

References

Abdallah C. & Langley A. (2014) The double edge of ambiguity in strategic planning. *Journal of Management Studies* 51(2), 235–263.

Armenakis A. & Harris S. (2002) Crafting a change message to create transformational readiness. *Journal of Organisational Change Management* 15(2), 169.

Armenakis A., Harris S. & Mossholder K. (1993) Creating readiness for organisational change. *Human Relations* 46(6), 681–703.

Arthur M. & Rousseau D. (1996) *The Boundaryless Career: A New Employment Principle for a New Organizational Era*. Oxford University Press.

Bamford D. & Forrester P. (2003) Managing planned and emergent change within an operations management environment. *International Journal of Operations and Production Management* 23(5–6), 546–564.

Barsade S. (2002) The ripple effect: Emotional contagion and its influence on group behaviour. *Administrative Science Quarterly* 47(4), 644–675.

Bordia P., Hunt E., Paulsen N., Tourish D. & DiFonzo N. (2004) Uncertainty during organisational change is it all about control? *European Journal of Work and Organisational Psychology* 13(3), 345–365.

Brown R. (1967) Research and consultancy in industrial enterprises: A review of the contribution of the Tavistock Institute of human relations to the development of industrial sociology. *Sociology* 1(1), 33–60.

Burnes B. (1996) No such thing as . . . a "one best way" to manage organizational change. *Management Decision* 34(10), 11–18.

Burnes B. (2004) *Managing Change: A Strategic Approach to Organisational Dynamics*. Fourth Edition. Financial Times: Prentice Hall.

Cox J & Seaton S. (1992) Systems integrators and implementers: The tools of choice have expanded since the Gilbreths and Taylor. *Computers and Industrial Engineering* 23(1–4), 507–510.

Dennett D. (1993) *Consciousness Explained*. Penguin.

Edmondson A. & Zhike L. (2014) Psychological safety: The history, renaissance, and future of an interpersonal construct. Annual review organisational psychology. *Organisational Behaviour* 1, 23–43.

Elfenbein H. (2014) The many faces of emotional contagion: An affective process theory of affective linkage. *Organisational Psychology Review* 4(4), 326–362.

Emery M. (1999) *Searching: The Theory and Practice of Making Cultural Change*. Fourth Edition. John Benjamins Publishing.

Endrejat P., Meinecke A. & Kuffeld S. (2020) Get the crowd going: Eliciting and maintaining change readiness through solution-focused communication. *Journal of Change Management* 20(1), 35–58.

Fells M. (2000) Fayol stands the test of time. *Journal of Management History* 6(8), 345–360.

Ford J. & Ford L. (1995) The role of conversations in producing intentional change in organisations. *The Academy of Management Review* 20(3), 541–571.

Green Z. & Molenkamp R. (2005) The BART system of group and organizational analysis: Boundary, authority, role and task. www.academia.edu.

Handy C. (2007) *Understanding Organizations*. Penguin.

Handy C. (2012) *The Age of Unreason*. Random House.

Harpum P. (2010) Project control. in Morris P. & Pinto J. *The Wiley Guide to Project Control*. Wiley.

Herscovitch L. & Meyer J. (2002), Commitment to organizational change: Extension of a three-component model. *Journal of Applied Psychology* 87(3), 474–487.

Hinson J. & Osborne D. (2014) Tapping the Power of Emergent Change: The NTL Handbook of Organization Development and Change, Chapter 15, 305–328. Wiley Online Library.

Hitt M. & Ireland R. (1987) Peters and waterman revisited: The unended quest for excellence. *Academy of Management Perspectives* 1(2), 91–98.

Hornstein H. (2015) The integration of project management and organizational change management is now a necessity. *International Journal of Project Management* 33(2), 291–298.

Johansson C., Miller V. & Hamrin S. (2014) Conceptualising communicative leadership. *Corporate Communications: An International Journal* 19(2), 147–165.

Kahn W. (1990) Psychological conditions of personal engagement and disengagement at work. *Academy of Management Journal* 33(4), 692–724.

Kalagnanam S. & Lindsay R. (1999) The use of organic models of control in JIT firms: generalising Woodward's findings to modern manufacturing practices. *Accounting, Organizations and Society* 24(1), 1–30.

Kickul J., Lester S. & Finkl J. (2002) Promise breaking during radical organisational change: Do justice interventions make a difference? *Journal of Organisational Behaviour* 23(4), 469–488.

Korzybski A. (2000) *Science and Sanity*. Fifth Edition. The Institute of General Semantics.

Kotter J. (1996) *Why Transformation Efforts Fail*. Harvard Business Review Press.

Kotter J. (2008) *Leading Change*. Harvard Business Review Press.

Kozlowski S. & Ilgen D. (2009) Enhancing the effectiveness of work groups and teams. *Association of Psychological Science* 7(3), 77–123.

Lawrence P. & Lorsch J. (1967) Differentiation and integration in complex organizations. *Administrative Science Quarterly* 1, 1–47.

Lewin K. (1947) Frontiers in group dynamics: Concept, method and reality in social science; social equilibria and social exchange. *Human Relations* 1(1), 5–41.

Mayo E. (2004) *The Human Problems of an Industrial Civilization*. Routledge.

McGregor D. (1966) *The Human Side of Enterprise*. Cengage Learning.

Milliken F. (1987) Three types of perceived uncertainty about the environment: State, effect, and response uncertainty. *Academy of Management Review* 12(1), 133–143.

Mills A., Weatherbee T. & Durepos G. (2014) Reassembling Weber to reveal the-past-as-history in management and organization studies. *Organization* 21(2), 225–243.

Mintzberg H., Ahlstrand B. & Lampel J. (2008) *Strategy Safari: The Complete Guide through the Wilds of Strategic Management*. Second Edition. FT Publishing International.

Moss Kanter R. (2003) *Challenge of Organizational Change: How Companies Experience It and Leaders Guide It*. Simon and Schuster.

Murray F. & O'Mahony S. (2007) Exploring the foundations of cumulative innovation: Implications for organization science. *Organization Science* 18(6), 1006–1021.

Onday O. (2016) Modern structural organization theory: From mechanistic vs. organic systems of burns & stalker to technology of Burton & Obel. *Global Journal of Human Resource Management* 4(2), 30–46.

Pasmore W. & Khalsa G. (1993) The contributions of Eric Trist to the social engagement of social science. *Academy of Management Review* 18(3), 546–569.

Perrow C. (1961) The analysis of goals in complex organizations. *American Sociological Review* 854–866.

Rafferty A., Jimmieson N. & Armenakis A. (2013) Change readiness: A multilevel review. *Journal of Management* 39(1), 110–135.

Robinson O. & Griffiths A. (2005) Coping with the stress of transformational change in a government department. *The Journal of Applied Behavioural Science* 41(2), 204–221.

Saploski, R. (2017) *Behave: The Biology of Humans at Our Best and Worst*. Penguin.

Scarlett H. (2019) *Neuroscience for Organisational Change: An evidence Based Practical Guide to Managing Change*. Second Edition. Kogan Page.

Schein E. (1997) *Organisational Culture and Leadership*. Second Edition. Jossey-Bass.

Solms M. (2021) *The Hidden Spring: A Journey to the Source of Consciousness*. WW Norton & Co.

Stacey R. (2001) *Complex Responsive Processes in Organizations: Learning and Knowledge Creation*. Routledge.

Thompson J., Zald M. & Scott W. (2017) *Organizations in Action: Social Science Bases of Administrative Theory*. Routledge.

Voet J., Groeneveld S. & Kuipers B. (2014) Talking the talk or walking the walk? The leadership of planned and emergent change in a public organisation. *Journal of Change Management* 14(2), 171–191.

Weick K. & Quinn R. (1999) Organisational change and development. *Annual Review of Psychology* 50(1), 361–386.

Weick K., Sutcliffe K. & Obstfeld D. (2005) Organizing and the process of sense making. *Organization Science* 16(4), 327–451.

Zak P. (2017) *Trust Factor: The Science of Creating High-performance Companies.* Amacom.

Annex

Questions to ask of portfolios using the BART (boundaries, authorities, roles, and tasks)

- Organisational boundaries (design)
  - What part of the organisation does the portfolio cover? Should it be adjusted?
  - Should it include supply chains? If so, how?
  - How many sub-portfolios need to be defined to maximise the overall portfolio management process? How are the decision criteria for sub-portfolios aligned with the strategic portfolio?
- Organisational boundaries (manage) – with the assumption that all organisational change is strategic
  - Do change programs and projects overlap organisational boundaries? Does it matter?
  - If they do, can synergies be maximised, and negative effects mitigated?
  - Is the effect of change in one part of an organisation understood in other parts?
  - Can spillover of the effects of change across the organisation be managed?
- Time boundaries (design)
  - How often are portfolios reviewed? How does this align with strategic review? Are these reviews, in effect, the same thing?
  - How often do projects and programs need to report into the portfolio? Is this optimised for strategy review/progress, portfolio decision-making, AND the programs and projects?
  - What is the deadline for regular reporting from the portfolio to strategic management, and from programs and projects into the portfolio?
- Time boundaries (manage)
  - How are time boundaries for programs and projects managed? For example, how are late-running programs addressed? (This will depend on the anticipated balance between planned and emergent change.)
  - What is the portfolio response to poor time management by programs? For example, what is the response to late reporting?
- Authorities (design) – encapsulated in governance frameworks
  - Who has authority to decide on portfolio decision criteria? Who does not have authority?
  - What authorities (and responsibilities) do portfolio managers have?
  - What authorities (and responsibilities) do change program managers have regarding their programs? How is this aligned with portfolio governance?
- Authorities (management)
  - How is authority assured in portfolio decision-making? For example, when decisions are made that affect resource allocations, how are these decisions enforced

on resource "owners" that may have significant formal authority themselves and disagree with the resource allocation decisions made about staff they control?
    - To what extent does portfolio management enforce/support change program managers' authority?
    - What authorities does the portfolio have to stop change programs/projects or insist on replanning, in the context of emergent change?

- Roles (design)

    - What is the precise role of the strategic portfolio in relation to strategy formation/planning, other portfolios/sub-portfolios, decision-making, managing and communicating emergent strategy and emergent change upwards to strategic management, creating organisational readiness for change, and analysing and assessing the effectiveness of change programs and projects?
    - What are the precise roles of portfolio managers and other staff roles associated with managing and analysing the portfolio?
    - What roles do strategic managers and resource owners (department heads, division heads, etc.) have in relation to the portfolio and portfolio decision-making? (For example, are they part of a portfolio decision-making group or committee?)

- Roles (manage)

    - Can portfolio managers and staff clearly articulate their own roles?
    - Can change program managers and their management teams clearly articulate their roles, both towards the program itself (and the program team members) and towards the portfolio managers?
    - What other roles (formal and informal) do the portfolio managers have within the organisation, and to what extent do such role(s) affect the role carried out for the portfolio?
    - What other roles (formal and informal) do the change program managers have within the organisation, and to what extent do such role(s) affect the role carried out for the change program they lead?

- Task (design)

    - How well defined and agreed is the central task of the portfolio?
    - How well defined and agreed are the tasks that portfolio managers are expected to carry out within their roles?
    - Are these tasks defined in a way that gains acceptance from others in the organisation?
    - A key task for the portfolio is to define tasks to deliver strategic change – programs and projects. Is this task well defined, accepted, and integrated with the strategic management process?

- Task (manage)

    - To what extent is the portfolio responsible for ensuring change programs adhere to their task and benefit realisation as defined?
    - How does the portfolio respond to off-task activity and behaviour? For example, where change programs become ineffective due to inter- and intra-team conflict.
    - To what extent, and how, does the portfolio redesign the change program tasks (or benefits to be delivered) during the execution of the programs, for example, to cater for emergent change?

- To what extent are portfolio managers achieving the primary task? Is there evidence of off-task behaviour by them or within the portfolio management team or the change program leadership? (Defined as dependency, pairing, fight/flight, or oneness – see human relations theory for definitions of these categories, which are called *basic assumptions*).

5 Scenario planning for strategic portfolios

Carol A. Long and Pete Harpum

Introduction

Chapter 2 defined the context for this book, making a clear case for the argument that portfolio management is predominantly an organisational management and strategically orientated activity. Chapter 3 set out what strategy is in some detail and, therefore, what the portfolio has to deliver. This shorter chapter takes one step back, to look at scenario planning and how this strategic activity influences strategy, and hence the portfolio. Whilst it may seem an unlikely sequencing decision, it was intended that, although this chapter is important, it should not interrupt the more significant opening chapters. We suggest to the reader that if you are familiar with scenario planning (although with the relative paucity of research on the topic, you may perhaps not be so familiar), there is the option to skip this chapter. As for the previous chapters, though, this discussion of scenario planning, or what is sometimes referred to as strategic reframing or futures planning, may not necessarily relate to previous understanding within the topic area, particularly in relation to strategic portfolios and portfolio management. This chapter is not intended to provide a comprehensive "how-to" guide for scenario planning but to suggest how this approach may be beneficial for portfolio management.

What is scenario planning?

A *scenario* in terms of strategic planning is *a view of what the future might be related to the particular aspect that the strategists are interested in considering*. Such scenarios might include, for example, ideas about future market conditions, legal and regulatory conditions, national and/or international economic aspects, workforce availability and competencies, environmental and ecological conditions, or different health contexts to the present. A scenario is a view of what the future might be like that is directly relevant to the people that need to make strategic decisions (Ramirez & Wilkinson, 2018).

Since the future is unpredictable, there are many scenarios possible for each organisation to consider (Tetlock & Gardner, 2015). In principle, one might consider there to be an infinite number of scenarios in all cases, some with a higher likelihood of occurrence than others, but all with a greater-than-zero chance of actually happening. What is important is to research carefully the possible scenarios and then arrive at what are believed to be the more likely ones. The "thinking through" processes, for both the scenario development and the strategic responses to the defined scenarios, have been shown to be most effective when people involved "unlearn" (Burt & Nair, 2020). Scenario planning and strategic thinking are most effective when the mind is able to break free from

DOI: 10.4324/9780367853129-6

deeply held assumptions about how the future will play out. Thinking the unthinkable, and holding onto and working with the unthinkable, leads to improved strategic foresight (Wade, 2012).

The critical point about scenarios is that different strategic decisions are needed, depending on the scenarios considered – different futures need different responses. Therefore, scenario planning precedes strategy development. This is too often not understood by strategists, portfolio management, and business and project managers. However, the effort and resources needed for effective scenario development and subsequent analysis and strategic thinking and decision-making are not to be underestimated. Phadnis et al. (2016) describe the work to create scenarios for a large national industry to shape strategic thinking for the forthcoming 30-year period:

> The research began with a symposium in which thought leaders presented the potential future developments in their domains (technology, economics, demographics, etc.) to a few dozen public- and private-sector managers invited to the symposium. The managers were then asked to note their thoughts about the implications of those future developments for the [industry].
>
> A subsequent brainstorming exercise among them distilled the findings into the driving forces shaping the [industry] over the next 30 years. This information was consolidated into 12 snapshot scenarios and presented back to the managers once more for feedback. Based on their feedback, a survey was created, which was administered to public- and private-sector stakeholders whose work pertains to the [industry]. The results of the survey were analysed to identify the key uncertainties and driving forces over the next 30 years – and these findings were used to construct four scenarios.
>
> In addition, narratives were created to describe each scenario. The stories were complemented by various statistics describing the world, presented in charts. The story and the charts were compiled into a 12-page brochure to present a holistic picture of each scenario in words and numbers. Five-minute long videos were also developed presenting a fictional newscast on a day in the distant future (November 2, 2037) in each scenario. The brochure and the video were used together to immerse the scenario users in the respective scenario before asking them to assess long-range investment decisions in particular elements of the [industry].

For single organisations, there may not be the requirement to go to such lengths to create alternative scenarios, but the point is that a lot of work is required to think through possible futures – before strategic objectives and plans are defined, and well before portfolios are defined.

From scenarios to portfolios

Once the first steps of identifying possible and the most probable scenarios have been achieved, the route to defining the strategy and subsequent portfolio(s) can commence from these scenarios. The series of steps linking scenarios and portfolios are shown by the process flow in Figure 5.1, followed by a brief outline of each of the stages.

Possible scenarios. These are a reasonably large number of scenarios that are foreseen as plausible. Putting together such a long list allows for creative thinking to draw on a

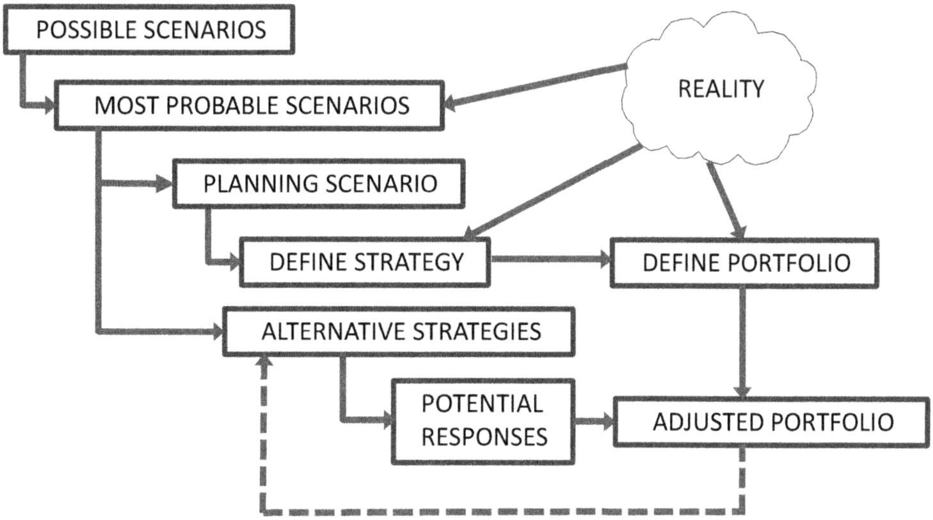

Figure 5.1 The link from scenario development to strategy and portfolio definition.

deepening understanding of what the possible futures are. As the set of scenarios is developed, more research is done, knowledge grows, and the scenarios will evolve to a stable group.

Most probable scenarios. This is when the set of possible scenarios are evaluated, using stakeholders and experts, to assess the more likely scenarios. This process in itself is likely to bring new knowledge forth and allow the probable scenarios to be refined.

Planning scenario. From the probable scenarios, the one considered most likely by external and internal stakeholders and experts, along with organisational leaders and managers, is selected as the planning scenario. This is the scenario for which the organisation will set strategic objectives and a strategy to achieve those objectives.

Define strategy. The strategic objectives and strategy for achieving those objectives are defined, based on the planning scenario.

Alternative strategies. From the other probable scenarios, in at least an outline level of detail, alternative strategies are defined that will match the non-planning, but nevertheless probable, scenarios. An important element of this work is the reflection and thinking through of what might need to be done to adjust strategy – the creation of the potential responses – if reality becomes close to, or even matches, one of the probable scenarios. This helps strategists and portfolio managers approach decision-making with more flexibility, leading to better decisions in both the short and longer terms (Phadnis et al., 2016).

Define the portfolio. The set of work needed to deliver the strategic objectives is defined in the portfolio, drawing on all the previous work and thinking in the scenario and strategy setting processes, as well as input from people that will be responsible for delivering the work in the portfolio, often program and project managers. It is worth noting here that there is a view that the organisational strategic contribution from program and project managers is undervalued and insufficiently brought into the strategy process. These are, after all, the people that face reality every day, leading and managing teams of people delivering into the world. Research by Löwstedt et al. (2018) shows that in some industries, project managers are, in fact, the active organisational strategists, with nominated strategists playing little part in the process.

Adjusted portfolio. As the "real world" impacts on the set of work being done in the portfolio, the results can be monitored, and changes made to the strategy as needed to reflect what is actually happening, compared to what the planning scenario anticipated happening. These changes are part of the stream of emerging strategy discussed in Chapters 2 and 3. Feedback from the adjusted portfolio to the set of alternative strategies allows the organisation to maintain a readiness to accommodate further unanticipated changes in the environment. A different situation occurs when there is a major change in the environment, when the planning scenario has, or is anticipated to, move dramatically away from reality, such as the need to "pivot" in short timescales, as recently seen from the effects of the global pandemic from 2019 to 2022 (Cooper, 2020). With luck, one of the probable scenarios will match the new reality, and one of the associated alternative strategies will be ready, or nearly ready, to be deployed quickly as the organisation responds. A new portfolio can be defined quickly, and the change in the environment catered for without the need for a major review of strategy. This saves time and, with the earlier reflections and thinking built into the process, is likely to lead to high-quality strategic decisions being made and completed more quickly (Wade, 2012).

The planning scenario

The planning scenario is simply the scenario that will be used for future planning for the organisation. The planning scenario chosen by senior decision-makers, supported by the scenario development team, is most likely to be the one *considered* to be the most probable scenario. Clearly, this decision is based on huge uncertainty about the future. Nevertheless, a decision must be made. The planning scenario is then the one against which future strategic decisions are made, with a common mental model (Chermack, 2004). The great advantage of going through the scenario development process is that the organisation has considered in depth other scenarios that may play out in the future. These scenarios are documented, and a continual watch on the emerging future is kept. If it appears that a future different to that anticipated is unfolding, the organisation has two knowledge assets it can draw on quickly: a set of anticipated scenarios that match reasonably closely the emerging reality – then strategy can be reconsidered quickly in the light of the already-contemplated scenario – and the depth of knowledge generated by going through the scenario process itself.

The scenario process creates a big pool of knowledge and ideas about how the future might look – allowing faster and potentially more insightful decisions to be made about the reality that, in fact, unfolds in the environment in which the organisation operates. Strategy can be adjusted quickly, the portfolio can be adjusted to meet the emerging reality, and ultimately, projects and programs can be brought into existence, reorganised, or terminated more quickly. Scenario planning, therefore, drives competitive advantage through an organisation's ability to respond more quickly to a changing future.

Scenarios and vision statements

Having completed the scenario development and analysis, and having decided on the planning scenario, the next step is to describe a vision statement for the organisation's response to the planning scenario, as part of defining the strategy. The vision statement (used at strategic, portfolio, program, and project levels) provides both aspiration for the end state and metaphor to engage on an emotional level. In some cases, this will be a vision statement for processes within an organisation or statements of the culture for the future organisation on completion of a strategic portfolio. This engagement with metaphors and stories provides a reference point for changes and integration effort (Küpers, 2013). When produced as guidance documents for strategic decision-makers and, thereafter, portfolio management, this consistent point of reference unites people around the long-term strategic decision-making and mitigates portfolio scope creep by providing an overall reference point and sensemaking tool. Everyone can understand why the planning scenario was selected, and how the vision and then the strategy to deliver the vision have been developed and agreed, through a multi-level process (Mukherjee et al., 2020).

Scenario development

Scenario development involves significant work on wider environmental, market, technology, and general strategic understanding. The underlying assumptions of the scenario development team will need to be challenged, especially as successful scenario development often relies on expert input to determine which influencing factors are critical to success or most volatile. Some examples include:

- Specific technology development may be beyond the control of the organisation but nevertheless be the foundation of some of the assumptions underlying its business model.
- Emerging national and international political policy may have potential to significantly change the market.
- Changes in social trends may open up new strategic possibilities.
- Climate change and sustainability, which are impacting almost all sectors and all industries.

Scenario development starts with a critical evaluation of the current situation. Drivers such as economic conditions or stakeholder sentiment can be identified using tools usually employed as part of strategy development, such as PESTLE or SWOT. Reviewing the outputs of this type of analysis, the scenario team speculates on, and hopes to tentatively identify, the key drivers of environmental change and sources of uncertainty, opportunity, and risk. Without these drivers, creating the multiple "plausible" scenarios as the precursor to strategy development would not be possible. Fahey and Randall (1998) classify pairs of conditions that help identify change drivers:

- Time based (present v. future).
- Technology or other opportunities development (closed v. open).
- The level of speculation (grounded v. imaginative).
- Holistic consideration (intellectual v. emotional).
- Measurability (qualitative v. quantitative).

Approaches to development and analysis of scenarios

To effectively use techniques for scenario development, it is important to keep an open mind to the possibilities of the future. The nature of scenario development means there is a need to consider non-obvious outcomes for different uncertainties or change drivers within the organisation's context. Scenario development approaches can be identified in three main forms:

- Two-by-two matrices (e.g. Schwartz, 1996)
- Narrative descriptions (e.g. Bontoux & Bengtsson, 2016)
- Decision trees (e.g. Quinlan, 1986)

All three of these approaches are seen in active use in different industries. The sector may have some influence over this; for example, where professionals are drawn from social sciences or education, the narrative form may predominate, as this aligns more readily with habitual practises in those industries. Similarly, those industries that use considerable amounts of mathematical modelling may lean towards decision trees. However, an alternative way of selecting the most appropriate approach to scenario development considers the situation in which the work takes place.

Two-by-two matrix

Where the environment is considered to be relatively stable (bearing in mind that this is often a fallacy), organisations usually seek step-by-step change. In these situations, and assuming two significant drivers of uncertainty can be identified, using the two-by-two matrix is often sufficient.

The two-by-two matrix is common when scenario development sessions are facilitated by external consultants. This approach allows the identified two key drivers for uncertainty to build up four contrasting aspects for development. The disadvantage of this approach is that scenarios significantly outside the current understanding of the organisation's context are less likely to be developed.

This approach to scenario planning was inspired by the Shell oil company model, documented by Schwartz (1996). The two most impactful drivers of uncertainty are placed on the axis, giving four possibilities. Having identified the situation for these two drivers, potential strategies can be simply defined to meet those conditions. Of course, there are risks that the drivers are incorrectly identified, because the organisation's assumptions have not been appropriately tested and, indeed, that the candidate strategies are based on incorrect assumptions about the responses to the situation. One considerable advantage to this method is that it is rapidly understood by most managers. This means that candidate strategies can be identified quickly, and from these four options, a decision can be made. Having identified four key potential strategies, these can be further defined using the narrative format (Bontoux & Bengtsson, 2016).

Narrative descriptions

The narrative approach can handle complexity in the organisation's context and consider multiple drivers of ambiguity or uncertainty. However, it is open to a lack of rigour or missed nuances, as humans make assumptions that are undeclared in their creative thinking and analyses of scenarios. Organisations contemplating the need for significant changes in the environment, and hence, probably also transitional change in the way they operate in that changing environment, are best served by narrative descriptions of scenarios. The descriptive models allow scenarios to be explained in more detail, engaging those reading the scenario with the vision of the future more readily than the non-descriptive forms of scenario planning.

Narrative form scenarios tend to consider broader issues and human factors more readily. The shape of possible futures in these scenarios can be examined in greater depth through narrative description and scientific or mathematical argument. Such scenarios allow multiple changing factors to be discussed over an extended period of time. As part of narrative scenarios, the ability to include structured information and diagrams/tables for orthogonal information increases the ability to summarise information for non-expert readers. It helps to ensure those constructing the scenarios do not miss relevant temporal or other factors; for example, an empty part of a table becomes noticeable, and assumptions can be checked.

Narrative scenarios have been developed to consider the impact of rising temperatures on planet Earth and the transitions needed to manage or mitigate this situation. These are based on complex scientific and public policy matters with broad themes, such as the rise in temperature, the rise in sea level, pollution levels, economic conditions, governmental responses, corporate responses, availability of new technology in various classes (e.g. freshwater supply chain, energy production, sea defences, communications, agriculture), with situations for a range of each factor being considered. In a commercial world, narrative scenarios allow for complexity and complication to be considered, especially where these cannot be firmly quantified. Kurtz and Snowden (2003) published on management decision-making and showed that humans have a high capacity to integrate complex patterns on which they can base decisions. These patterns may be beyond easy comprehension if reduced to mathematical structures (such as decision trees). The narrative form of scenario planning supports such patterns and lends itself to situations that tend towards chaos or with high levels of uncertainty across a variety of factors.

Decision trees

The anticipation of truly transformational change in the environment, with an unknown future state, suits the use of decision trees. The strategic objectives and plans for achievement will likely change as indications of the emerging future become clearer, and further scenario development may be needed to inform the changing strategy. Scenario development in this situation is more likely to need the complexity available from a decision tree approach, as this requires each step to be considered in terms of potential impacts in the environment and in the organisation itself of changes in attitudes, behaviours, as well as the uncertainty and complexity associated with technological advancement.

The stepwise approach of decision trees allows wider possibilities of outcomes to be considered. It may be that, having followed the stepwise process to a series of potential end points, further work is required for the most likely end points. This can then produce a narrative scenario approach to provide sufficient information to decision-makers and leaders developing strategy so that they can understand the changes in mindset and culture that will be required for the organisation to succeed. The narratives are, of course, also valuable to the portfolio design, to achieve the strategic objectives laid out.

The decision tree approach has the advantage of allowing technology, such as machine learning, to be engaged where there is sufficient data. It has the disadvantage of unnecessary complexity if misunderstood by the user. Decision trees can develop into large volumes of possible scenarios, which may make narrowing down the range to most probable scenarios challenging.

In a decision tree, each factor is taken step by step, with each being ascribed a value or attribute, until all have been evaluated and the best options identified. Clearly being able to ascribe values and use maths to calculate value or probability for an option path is advantageous for machine learning. Quinlan (1986) describes how decision trees have been used to represent acquired knowledge, as the options algorithms in machine learning. A similar construct is used to assist the evaluation of values in scenario development, where the options are value- or data-driven. Scenario models of this type can become complex and may need to be divided up to be understood.

The ordering of the steps in these evaluations may be significant. If there are dependencies between factors over assumptions to be made about the relationship between them, then the order needs to be tested to ensure that there isn't the equivalent of mathematical order of operations constraints embedded in the scenario model. This means that decisions made in the past can constrain the options available now. As an example, evaluating market geographies/territories before considering product feature options might give a different result compared to what might be seen if they were evaluated in the reverse order.

The decision tree approach has an advantage of traceability. This is important in more complex situations where there are many options or factors in play. Being able to examine an end result and stepping through the factors to determine how that option becomes viable can be particularly useful, informing the conditions required for a particular product management or policy decision to be made. Similarly, a decision tree can identify when the same outcome serves multiple condition sets. From a strategic management perspective, this can help identify the best paths to success, or where a number of factors can be partly satisfied with the same end result (e.g. a product that might address needs in multiple market niches).

Conclusion

This chapter has discussed the importance of the scenario planning process in defining the environmental context in which strategy should be established. Scenario planning is an important strategic planning tool which ought to precede the setting or resetting of strategic goals and the development of strategy to achieve those goals. The thinking through of potential future environments also builds a pool of knowledge the organisation can draw on as the reality emerges of how the environment will, in fact, be in the future. This allows faster responses to a changing context for the strategy and, of course, therefore, the portfolio of programs and projects that are intended to deliver that strategy.

References

Bontoux L. & Bengtsson D. (2016) Using scenarios to assess policy mixes for resource efficiency and eco-innovation in different fiscal policy frameworks. *Sustainability* 8(4), 309.

Burt G. & Nair A. (2020) Rigidities of imagination in scenario planning: Strategic foresight through 'Unlearning'. *Technological Forecasting and Social Change* 153, 119927.

Chermack T. (2004) Improving decision-making with scenario planning. *Futures* 36(3), 295–309.

Cooper R. (2020) *The Pandemic Pivot: The Need for Product, Service and Business Model Innovation*. Stage-Gate International. www.stage-gate.com.

Fahey L. & Randall R. (1998) *Learning from the Future: Competitive Foresight Scenarios*. Wiley.

Küpers W. (2013) Embodied transformative metaphors and narratives in organisational life-worlds of change. *Journal of Organizational Change Management* 26(3), 494–528.

Kurtz C. & Snowden D. (2003) The new dynamics of strategy: Sense-making in a complex and complicated world. *IBM Systems Journal* 42(3), 462–483.

Löwstedt M., Raisanen C. & Leiringer R. (2018) Doing strategy in project-based organizations: Actors and patterns of action. *International Journal of Project Management* 36, 889–898.

Mukherjee M., Ramirez R. & Cuthbertson R. (2020) Strategic reframing as a multi-level process enabled with scenario research. *Long Range Planning* 53(5), 101933.

Phadnis S., Caplice C. & Sheffi Y. (2016) How scenario planning influences strategic decisions. *MIT Sloan Management Review* 57, 24–27.

Quinlan J. (1986) Induction of decision trees. *Machine Learning* 1, 81–106.

Ramirez R. & Wilkinson A. (2018) *Strategic Reframing: The Oxford Scenario Planning Approach*. Oxford University Press.

Schwartz P. (1996) *The Art of the Long View*. Doubleday.

Tetlock P. & Gardner D. (2015) *Superforecasting: The Art and Science of Prediction*. Crown Publishers.

Wade W. (2012) *Scenario Planning: A Field Guide to the Future*. Wiley.

6 Delivering strategic value through the portfolio

Pete Harpum and Carol A. Long

Introduction

"Value" is one of those words, or concepts, that is often used without much thought as to its meaning, since when the word is used, everyone engaged in the particular conversation usually understands what is meant by it. The same can be said of the word "benefit". According to Wittgenstein (1922), it applies to every word we use: "The meaning of a word hinges on its usefulness in context, not its ideal referent outside of all possible contexts." This is somewhat important to understand in all the chapters in this book (or potentially in all chapters of all books!), but perhaps it is most important in this chapter when defining value and benefits. The delivery of value is something that all organisations are interested in. Value to customers, stakeholders, shareholders, employees, society, and value to the business itself. Becoming blinkered in understanding value as only a measure of money accrued has been, sadly, predominant in some parts of business. The histories of GE (Ocasio & Joseph, 2008) and perhaps Lehman Brothers (Adu-Gyamfi, 2016) are just two egregious examples of what happens when organisations take a very narrow definition of value.

It has been seen in previous chapters that the portfolio is the mechanism by which strategic objectives are converted to sets of actions – projects, programs, or organisational change initiatives. By definition, if strategic objectives cannot be attributed a perceived value for an organisation, they would not exist (or, at least, should not) – why do something for which there is no purpose or no value? A significant aspect of project and program theory and practice rests on the notion that these vehicles for taking action – executing strategy – deliver "*benefits*". In the UK, much of the historic literature issued by the government and the Association for Project Management (APM, 2012) attributes benefit delivery *only* to programs, with projects delivering outputs, or deliverables. However, more recently, others in the project management domain (including, from an academic perspective, Morris, 2013, and the UK government guidance with the more general evaluation in the Green Book, HM Treasury, 2020) contend that the primary objective of programs AND projects is to deliver *benefits*. Yet the delivery of *value* by projects and programs does not seem to figure as much as one might imagine (Morris, 2013).

Keeping in mind Wittgenstein's idea that words mean what we need them to mean, in the context with which we use them, it helps to let go of the idea that "value" and "benefit" have tightly defined and critically important definitions. They do not. This is important because this chapter sets out to integrate the two aspects that follow:

1. A general management/strategic management idea of value.
2. A strategy execution/program and project management view of benefits.

DOI: 10.4324/9780367853129-7

This chapter will present theoretical considerations of value, then of benefits, as they are articulated in the business case. The following chapter on benefits realisation management continues this discussion, establishing how planned benefits are managed within the portfolio, through to being achieved, and with that achievement, the creation of value.

Defining value

The importance of understanding the differences in the meanings and the contextual relevance of the concept of "*value*" is expounded by Pinder (2015), developed from Baudrillard's (Kellner, 2019) ideas, discussing the four sources of value for an object as:

1. *Utility value.* Its function or use: a pencil draws, a refrigerator cools, a management consultant – one hopes – provides good advice.
2. *Exchange value.* An offering's economic or market value: a cow is worth *x* sheep, a pen is worth *y* dollars, an hour of a well-established consultancy partner's time is worth more than an hour of a local consultancy partner's time.
3. *Symbolic value.* The symbolic value of an object – for example, a gift, a wedding ring, a business award.
4. *Sign value.* The value of an object in relation to other similar objects, and what it says about the owner in a social context: a Patek Philippe or Rolex watch signifies different values, status, and taste to a lowlier timepiece. Hiring McKinsey or KPMG consultants, for example, says more about a client enterprise than just the advice provided.

In Pinder's account, the argument highlights that "generally, consumption is driven by the sign value of the object (what it says about the consumer) and this determines the exchange value (what it is worth)." The idea that value is closely related to, and perhaps defined by, what the object (or other "thing" created by an organisation for users) says about the user of that thing is important to understand. The clear implication here is that strategists, portfolio managers and analysts, and program and project managers ought to remain focused on the *contextualised meaning of value in the specific environment in which they are working*. Attention by all organisational actors to the specificity of the value the user is being offered will help maintain a common understanding of how that value will be delivered through the portfolio of work. Although this seems a fairly obvious statement to make, in many organisations, a clear, unambiguous, and widely shared understanding of the value to be created does not exist. "*The trouble with value is that it is a notoriously vague term, not merely subjective in much of its assessment but even having several quite different meanings*" (Morris, 2013). The UK's Financial Reporting Council (FRC, 2018) felt the need to identify sources of non-financial value in publicly held companies' strategy reports, stating:

> The strategic report should also include information relating to sources of value that have not been recognised in the financial statements and how those sources of value are managed, sustained and developed, for example a highly trained or experienced workforce, natural capital, intellectual property or intangible assets, as these are relevant to an understanding of the entity's development, performance, position or future prospects.
>
> Financial Reporting Council (FRC, 2018)

In some parts of engineering (particularly software), the recognition of value as a driving factor in project developments has been evolving since the developers of commercial off-the-shelf (COTS) products recognised that business value could be created from intellectual effort. This was neatly expressed by Gilb (2005) with "value being the benefits the stakeholders consider they will obtain". For example, some software business models are based entirely on the perception of value (e.g. "freemium"), where effort is expended in creating software (or an app) that is then given away with additional functionality or further access after a trial period (e.g. a model commonly used by newspapers). This additional functionality or further access is being monetised as the customer recognises that they have received something they perceive as valuable and wants more of the same.

Value perception

Podolny and Hill-Popper (2004) propose that value can be conceived of in *hedonic* and *transcendent* terms. Hedonic value is essentially a relative assessment of value between two or more "things" (whether tangible or intangible – hedonic value applies just as much in, say, the value of a piece of artwork as in the value of a car). Transcendent value is determined by an individual's engagement with that thing, cognitively and emotionally. It is explicitly not about value in relative terms. Podolny and Hill-Popper (2004) define these two conceptions of value as follows: elaborating and differentiating these two conceptions further as "the hedonic conception of value implies a conceptual decomposition of the object into attributes, the cognitive and emotional connection at the heart of the transcendent conception of value implies a much more holistic approach to valuation".

- Hedonic conception of value "[is] a consumer's perception of the value of an exchange offering [that] is contingent on how the offering directly compares to other exchange offerings on a set of abstracted dimensions".
- Transcendent conception of value "[is] the value that the parties derive from the exchange depend[ing] on the extent to which each becomes invested in the vantage that the other has regarding the object".

Returning to portfolio management, the question is, What does this discussion have to do with value, benefits, and portfolio management? It is useful here to consider some simple comparative examples, as presented next. In all three product categories – smartphones, wine, and cars – enthusiasts in each will argue endlessly about the value attributable to "their" particular favourite.

- All the functionality of most Apple products is available on competitors' products at prices frequently less than 50% of the Apple product.
- A six-litre bottle (mathusalem) of Dom Pérignon Rose Gold 1996 champagne will cost £36,000 today, while Moët & Chandon Brut Imperial Non-Vintage champagne will cost £36.
- A Ferrari 458 costing £170,000 is 1.5 seconds faster around a 2.64 km racetrack than an £85,000 BMW M4, with broadly the same specifications.

The "values" of these significantly higher-priced products are fundamentally not hedonic values. They are transcendent values, based on the buyer's relationship to those things, the attributes of perceived quality, and what those things represent. The strategists in the respective companies making these products will clearly understand the differences in conceptions of value as enacted by people that prefer and buy Apple iPhones, for example, to those that buy Huawei smartphones.

Measuring value

Woodruff (1997) identified that the limits of quality improvement and automation efficiencies (before effective and commercially available artificial intelligence) would reach a point where the marginal improvements would not significantly alter customer perception of product and service values and generate more sales or greater market share. Perceived value, therefore, would be a strategically important consideration in increasing an organisations' dominance of their market. Woodruff also identified that perceived customer value could be measured based on enabling customer goals, the fit between product attributes and satisfaction of tasks (that might be considered as approximating utility [Levy & Markowitz, 1979]), and the consequential satisfaction of the customer. The value to the customer of any product or service may have some foundation in the values they hold, but how they measure value is contextual.

The link here is that organisational strategic objectives are heavily influenced by the concept of value attached to the purpose that the organisation creates and provides to users. This means that in the organisation's internal dialogue about value, those involved must understand how value is being conceived. Strategic objectives are therefore about ensuring the continuation, or the creation, of value delivery to all relevant stakeholders. Value, as understood at the portfolio, must be directly linked to, and understood in, the same manner – otherwise, how will the portfolio effectively and correctly ensure the appropriate sets of actions and activities (the projects and programs created to execute strategy) are defined, assessed, and incorporated? How will the value planned to be created by programs and projects executing strategy be assessed and tested for conformance with the strategic objectives desired?

Part of the challenge for business managers wishing to engage with strategy execution through a portfolio of projects and programs is that the theory and practice in this domain does not reflect the sophistication and nuance recognised at strategic levels, related to the meaning of value. For example, the British Standards Institution (2000) (BS EN 12973) defines *value* as "value for money, i.e. the goods, services or products received are worth the time, cost and effort expended in obtaining them." Other common definitions of value, outside of the more sophisticated literature about market exchange and including benefits, are:

- Value = benefits – costs (Pinder, 2015).
- Value $\propto$ Benefits/Cost (Axelos, 2010).

Comparing these two equations is somewhat disconcerting. One says value is the same as (literally, equal to) benefits subtracted by costs, whilst the other says that value is proportionate to the *ratio* of benefits to costs. However, both permutations connect value and benefits, implying that there is a difference. Pinder (2015) brings strategically orientated and execution-orientated ideas about value, as discussed earlier with the four sources of value, together with his expansion of the simplistic value = benefits – costs equation to:

- Value = benefits (expressed as: utility + exchange + symbolic + sign) – costs (expressed as: utility + exchange + symbolic + sign)

- Here we can start to find a way to engage with the nuance of how value and benefit and cost can be understood and articulated in ways that do not necessarily, or even at all, require monetary allocation to be made to value and cost. This way of looking at value is useful at the portfolio level because strategists or general management (whose primary interest is very much in the value of the strategic objectives to be achieved) can articulate value in a way that execution people (program and project managers or teams) can also engage with. Strategic measures of value are expressed in various forms – as *utility*, *exchange*, *symbolic*, and *sign*. These can then be (re)defined by the portfolio process as benefits that programs and projects need to deliver to the portfolio and hence contribute to achieving strategic objectives. See Chapter 7 for further discussion of portfolio value as the agglomeration of the value of its constituent assets (projects and programs).

Business benefits

The obvious pre-existing crossover between strategists/general management and strategy execution is the program and project business case. Both communities refer to *business benefits* as the vital component of a business case. It is the understanding of the benefits that a program or project will achieve, as articulated in the business case, that determines whether a project or program meets the threshold for entry to the portfolio, as Chapter 12 discusses in further detail.

Despite *business benefits* being a term used both by general managers/portfolio management and the project and program management community, it is surprisingly difficult to find definitions of the term "business benefit" in the mainstream business literature – perhaps because it is considered obvious. Nevertheless, a reasonable and difficult-to-argue-against definition of *business benefit* is, "a tangible outcome of an action or decision that helps meet business objectives" (Schmidt, 2020). Interestingly, it is the project management theorists that have developed the idea of business benefits into a formalised concept, with categorisations for different types of tangible and intangible benefits, along with processes to assess, measure, and track the achievement of those benefits – termed *benefits realisation*. The following chapter discusses this in more detail.

Where we find strategists, general management, portfolio management, and project and program managers coming together, practically and theoretically, is with the business case. This is a document that details the case for investment by the organisation in specific projects and programs. The business case is the critical document for analysis by the portfolio selection process and defines the business benefits intended to be achieved by the project or program.

In summary, the business case is the document where the value of the work to be done is presented and justifies the investment (in cost but also resources, management attention, etc.) in that work. It also forms part of the initial governance and planning documentation when the project or program is still at the initial concept stage. It is maintained and consulted throughout the project life cycle. The information contained in the business case provides data to support reliable decision-making by sponsors around the viability of a project or program. The sponsor should be, as the representative of the organisation accountable for achieving strategic objectives, *formally accountable for the delivery of the project/program value*, and therefore achievement of the benefits delivered through projects and programs. Note that some literature makes the distinction between the portfolio delivering the *business plan* based on the strategic objectives and the projects and programs delivering the *business case* (such as HM Government, 2018).

Value creation in the portfolio

As recently as 2015, the lack of an explicit approach to value creation in organisations was being lamented, with Davidow (2015) noting that "[t]he topic of value creation has become of utmost importance over the last few years; however, most managers have still not implemented it in their organizations". Mahajan (2015) discusses the ideas and explicit articulation and "processualising" of value creation, advocating it "should be at the core of any business system, management philosophy and business practice related to all managerial processes".

Perhaps part of the explanation for the lack of formalised value creation processes, and hence agreement on what is meant by *value* in a given organisation, may be that value is too often not understood clearly enough in terms of market exchange. Podolny and Hill-Popper (2004) say "there has been surprisingly little discussion of the concept of value, which seems so central to any understanding of market exchange". Market exchange is important for understanding value since it is the ultimate interchange or realisation of value to an organisation. This is the point at which the "thing" that the organisation has created (product, service, change in behaviour, new infrastructure, etc.) is passed over to the user of that "thing". This applies equally to non-profit as for-profit organisations, in terms of the value delivered to the consumer.

Figure 6.1 is a model to visualise the flow of value creating activities through an organisation, linking the market (market exchange), with the strategic portfolio, and its constituent projects and programs with benefits. Note that the strategic portfolio does not impact directly on the market – its impact is on the processes and activities that deliver value to the market. The strategic portfolio delivers work that improves the value achievable by the organisation, through improving the way "things" are created for the market or the way those "things are delivered to the market (in project management theory, these activities are often called, perhaps a little pejoratively, 'business-as-usual'[1])". In this conception of the chain of value creation in an organisation, project and program benefits are defined based on a portfolio's need for value, in turn informed by market knowledge. In principle, this model is generally applicable to all organisations making "things" for others to use – *value* being not just synonymous with *money*, as previously discussed.

One area of confusion that arises is where an organisation has a portfolio of "things being made" for the market – for example, construction projects, IT projects, professional services projects, capability building projects, etc. Maintaining clarity about the work of the portfolio helps avoid confusion about the terminology of portfolio management. The strategic portfolio and associated sub-portfolios of projects and programs are not the same as the portfolio of programs and projects being delivered to the market. They are entirely separate groups of work. The processes, decision criteria, and management activities *may* be similar in character but must be defined specifically in the context of the portfolio in hand, such as a strategic, tactical, or sub-portfolio.

Strategic value through benefits realisation

During the concept phase of a project, senior management will have outlined their strategy, intent, expected benefits case, and associated costs and risks. Particularly in large, expensive, or business-critical projects, this early version of the business case is seen as the justification for further investment in project definition and planning (in the early stages of a project, the business case may also document a scheme of delegation for decision-making or

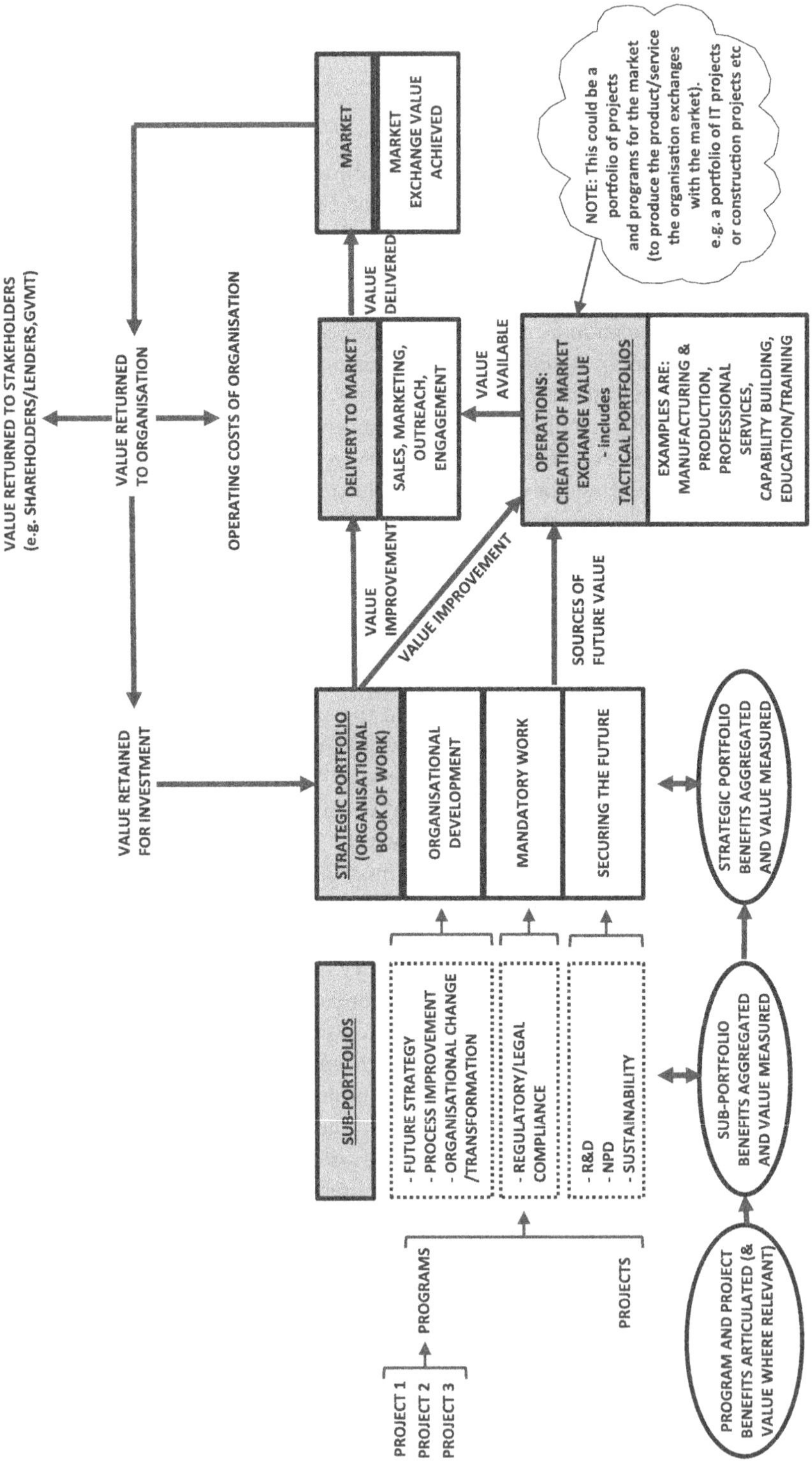

Figure 6.1 The value creation chain and aggregation of benefits and value in organisations.

authorisation authority until this can be transferred to planning or process documentation for the initiative). The concept phase will draw on the strategic situation and business drivers to identify an issue or opportunity to be addressed through the delivery of the initiative. Clearly defining the business issue or opportunity – linking strategic objective to the project objective – is an important part of developing the concept for the project. Feasibility studies and project definition activities will further refine the information on the business drivers or business issue into a problem statement. Guidance on project business cases suggests that at the conclusion of feasibility studies, "senior management and stakeholders will have a good understanding of the robustness of the proposal and the future direction of travel" (HM Treasury, 2018). Having prepared an outline business case and reviewed options through a feasibility study, a full business case reviewing strategic, economic, commercial, financial, and management dimensions of the proposed work can be created to guide the decision-making around continuing work on the project or suspending it as conditions change.

During the project or program, the business case is used in conjunction with the project plan to act as a baseline for monitoring and control of activities. Monitoring of the environment in which the initiative operates will reveal any new significant risks or changes to the profile of benefits that can be expected. In extreme cases, issues arising from the environment may significantly change the expected outcomes or required investment outlined in the business case; this exception should be escalated to the sponsor for a decision on the viability of the continued work. Importantly, this is a portfolio decision, because, by definition, a business case that is no longer believed likely to be achieved (it is no longer possible to deliver the value as planned) is going to fail to deliver that part of the strategy it is supposed to be delivering. A thoroughly developed business case can also identify, based on feasibility studies and the review of options and their associated benefit profiles, contingency actions to support alternative routes to achieving the strategy in this situation. Successful portfolio management practises must include a way to access this collective knowledge when changes of direction are required.

In the early stages, the benefits may not be easily defined and may be stated as headlines with an indication of size. In later project life cycle stages, the business benefits will be more fully defined, estimated, and validated. It is work on the projection of benefits being achieved that potentially changes the viability of the project as it progresses. This leads to the business case being a fundamental document for consideration when the portfolio management and sponsor are reviewing progress and making decisions on whether to continue the project at life cycle stage gates (or other possible review points).

The desired benefits will be defined, and how they are measured must be described sufficiently to provide information towards the appraisal of the investment. Tangible benefits, which can be quantified, can normally be expressed in monetary terms and so are more easily used for investment appraisal when compared to the costs of delivering those benefits. Tangible benefits may include money from new sources of income, increased value of assets, reduced costs, or jobs created. Intangible benefits (e.g. enhanced reputation, compliance, or increased flexibility) are more difficult to quantify in a meaningful way to compare to the costs of delivering them. Process improvements, productivity gains (Chan & Ejohwomu, 2018), and brand equity are examples of benefits that may be tangible in some circumstances, but not others (e.g. productivity gains may happen but are not measurable or useable in some situations). Note also that some benefits may have impacts or unintended consequences that have a negative effect or dis-benefits. Recording and evaluating these in a business case shows a level of maturity and honest appraisal of the initiative. Concealing dis-benefits during investment appraisals for an initiative is an ethical issue. However, dis-benefits may not be an appropriate discussion for some audiences: this underlines the need for the project professional and sponsor to understand the business case sufficiently well to communicate it appropriately for different audiences.

As part of reviewing the investment defined in the business case, potential alternative solutions should be considered, including the option of doing nothing. Different solutions will have a variety of financial benefits or dis-benefits. Part of the options analysis within the business case should consider the sensitivity of these options to risk or business conditions. All options in the business case will need to have costings contrasted with projected benefits. These are likely to be different for different options. Detailed reviews of cash flow, payback periods, internal rate of return (IRR), and net present value (NPV) should usually be included in the cost benefit analysis. (Chapter 12 provides a detailed review of project and aggregated portfolio cash flow and the related calculations for IRR, NPV, and other key financial indicators.)

The timescales, key windows of risk or opportunity, periods of expenditure, and periods of benefit realisation should be noted in the business case. The organisation's strategy will define the duration (or point in time) over which the realisation of benefits and measures of the project's overall value will be assessed. Some of these timings may transfer to planning documents in later phases, but the period over which total net benefit, and hence value created, is assessed will not change.

It is likely any mismatch between the benefits profile and the timescale in which a portfolio's value is assessed will come from the strategic outlook of an organisation (defining the period of assessment) and the life cycle of a product or service. It may be that the initial take-up of that product or service is dependent on wider contextual situations, for example, a product launch during a pandemic or a change in government tax policy reducing raw materials supply, which in turn delays the realisation of benefits. The rate of benefits realisation may vary over different phases of the life cycle for products or services as the innovation gains acceptance (Rogers, 1962). This is why some products or services can be seen as more valuable at the beginning of their life cycle and others become so-called "cash cows" (from the BCG Growth-Share Matrix, Morrison & Wensley, 1991), potentially after the organisation has stopped evaluating the success of the project, program, or portfolio. Any mismatch of this type should be clear in the business case. As conditions change or new strategic options are explored, this information becomes an important knowledge resource in the portfolio.

The business case will almost certainly include financial measures of value, including the benefits being delivered and the costs to achieve those benefits. These financial measures must align with the way in which the value(s) of the strategic objectives of the organisation are being measured. The market exchange value, however it is conceived, will always have some financial assessment. No matter how strategic value is understood and operationalised, hedonic or transcendent, the creation of that value will, in almost all cases, involve a cost in monetary terms. It is hard to conceive of any organisational portfolio in which absolutely no money is exchanged at all. Therefore, assessment of finances is unavoidable and almost always critically important to the achievement of strategic objectives.

Conclusion

This chapter has sought to bring together the notions of value and benefits as conceptualised and used in the domains of strategic management and strategy execution, through strategic portfolios with projects and programs. The fundamental ideas about value – what it means, how it is understood and perceived by various actors in the environment, how it is created and flows through organisations – have been explored. These ideas about value have been connected to benefits, business benefits, and how benefits are described in theory and practice in the domain of strategy execution. The area of inevitable overlap between strategists and execution professionals with the business case has been discussed. The thinking about, and documentation of, the business case is defined as an obvious place where strategic and execution conceptions of value can be jointly discussed and mutual understanding be created about how value needs to be created.

Note

1 The term *business-as-usual* is a non sequitur in organisational terms. For example: Is understanding the market's reaction to the "things" being delivered to it, using that feedback to create future strategic objectives and defining a portfolio of activities to achieve those new strategic objectives, not also "business-as-usual"? If the work on strategy creation was not carried out, there would be no future business! A strategist would surely contend that their work was equally business-as-usual as making the "things" the organisation makes for the market.

References

Adu-Gyamfi M. (2016) The bankruptcy of Lehman Brothers: Causes, effects and lessons learnt. *Journal of Insurance and Financial Management* 1(4).

APM (2012) Body of Knowledge. Sixth Edition. Association for Project Management.

Axelos (2010) Management of Value. OGC The Stationery Office.

British Standards Institution (2000) *BS EN 12973:2000 Value Management*. BSI

Chan P. & Ejohwomu O. (2018) *How does Project Management Relate to Productivity? A Systematic Review of Published Evidence*. Association for Project Management.

Davidow M. (2015) Just follow the yellow brick road: A manager's guide to implementing value creation in your organization. *The Journal of Creating Value* 1(1), 23–32.

FRC (July 2018) The UK corporate Governance Code. *UK Government*. www.FRC.org.uk.

Gilb T. (2005) *Competitive Engineering: A Handbook for Systems Engineering Requirements Engineering, and Software Engineering Using Planguage*. Elsevier Butterworth-Heinemann.

HM Government (2018) *GOVS 002, Project Delivery*. HM Government.

HM Treasury (2018) *Guide to Developing the Project Business Case. Better Business Cases: For Better Outcomes*. UK Government, Welsh Government.

HM Treasury (2020) *The Green Book: Central Government Guidance on Appraisal and Evaluation*. UK Government.

Kellner D. (2019) Jean Baudrillard (1929–2007). *Stanford Encyclopedia of Philosophy*. Winter 2019. https://plato.stanford.edu/archives/win2019/entries/baudrillard/

Levy H. & Markowitz H. (1979) Approximating expected utility by a function of mean and variance. *The American Economic Review* 69(3), 308–317.

Mahajan G. (2015) Interview with professor Luiz Moutinho. *Journal of Creating Value* 1(1), 292–294.

Morris P. (2013) *Reconstructing Project Management*. Wiley.

Morrison A. & Wensley R. (1991) Boxing up or boxed in? A short history of the Boston Consulting Group share/growth matrix. *Journal of Marketing Management* 7(2), 105–129.

Ocasio W. & Joseph J. (2008) Rise and fall – or transformation? The evolution of strategic planning at the General Electric Company, 1940–2006. *Long Range Planning* 41(3), 248–272.

Pinder D. (2015) On 'value' and 'performance'. *Journal of Creating Value* 1(1), 150–158.

Podolny J. & Hill-Popper M. (2004) Hedonic and transcendent conceptions of value. *Industrial and Corporate Change* 13(1), 91–116.

Rogers E. (1962) *Diffusion of Innovations*. Free Press of Glencoe.

Schmidt M. (2020) Business benefits: Measure and value every benefit. *Build the Better Business Case*. www.business-case-analysis.com/business-benefit.html.

Wittgenstein L. (1922) *Tractatus Logico-Philosophicus*. (Trans. Ramsey, F.P. & Ogden, C.K.) Harcourt, Brace, & Co.

Woodruff R. (1997) Customer value: The next source for competitive advantage. *Journal of the Academy of Marketing Science* 25, 139.

7 Benefits realisation management as a driver for delivering strategic value

Carlos Eduardo Martins Serra and Pete Harpum

Introduction

The theoretical concept and practical application of program and project benefits is a staple of the field of project management, with many books and papers written on the topic. The previous chapter highlighted the direct linkages between value, business case, and business benefits and how they operate at the portfolio level. This chapter reviews the literature on, and provides research-based evidence of, the effectiveness of managing the realisation (i.e. the delivery) of business benefits created by projects and programs for the achievement of strategic objectives, from the perspective of the portfolio. This chapter significantly draws upon the ideas based on a paper written by Serra and Kunc published in 2015 (Serra & Kunc, 2015).

Serra and Kunc's research aimed to test the relationship between benefits realisation management (BRM) practices and perceptions of project success and strategic value delivery. In order to elucidate phenomena by testing the relationship between variables, the researchers performed a survey study through questionnaires and data analysis employing analytical survey tools. This chapter does not provide any detail on the research methods or detailed analysis of the results, instead focusing on the relevant literature and the research findings and how they support the need for effective BRM to support the delivery of business value and hence the need for BRM to be maintained within the remit of portfolio management and governance.

Background to the research on benefits realisation management

Although projects and programs in an organisational portfolio can address different objectives (Gray & Larson, 2006; Jenner, 2010; Kendall & Rollins, 2003; Levine, 2005), they are mainly undertaken to support the execution of business strategies (Buttrick, 1997). Therefore, organisations need to ensure the success of their projects and programs in order to succeed in executing their strategy and turn their vision into reality. In order to be successful, project management teams need to clearly define how to evaluate whether each project is successful. However, there is no consensus on the definition of project success (Prabhakar, 2008; Yu et al., 2005), and thus also portfolio success, discussed in Chapter 8. A recent analysis of articles published from 1986 to 2004 in the *International Journal of Project Management* and the *Project Management Journal* found around 30 articles discussing project success, yet with no consensual definition (Ika, 2009). In parallel, surveys performed in the last 20 years have found between 60% and 80% of all organisations are failing in executing their strategies by not delivering the expected outcomes of their portfolio, program, and project processes (Kaplan & Norton, 2008).

DOI: 10.4324/9780367853129-8

Further research up to 2014 focuses on investigating and analysing success with achieving organisational strategic objectives by two different project approaches: project management performance, also called efficiency, which evaluates success mostly based on budget, schedule, and requirements goals, and project success, which evaluates how well projects deliver the benefits required by business strategies in order to meet wider business objectives and to create value (Cooke-Davies, 2002; Serrador, 2013). Despite the clear role projects have in implementing business strategies, organisations were seen to still be evaluating projects only by their efficiency and not by the benefits delivered, with a large group of organisations claiming that project benefits are very hard to measure (Zwikael & Smyrk, 2012), especially benefits realised during product operation, often long after project completion (Yu et al., 2005).

Several scholars (Bradley, 2010; Jenner, 2010; Melton et al., 2008) suggest that BRM should make clear the value created and the strategic relevance of each project, enabling an increased effectiveness of project governance. More than just project governance, "strategic governance" leads organisations to work towards the delivery of planned benefits (Gardiner, 2005). Organisations with mature processes of benefits realisation – and, therefore, arguably stronger governance – have their management boards prioritising and supporting mostly those projects which can deliver the most relevant benefits through the portfolio processes. By increasing the effectiveness of project governance, BRM can arguably reduce project failure rates from a strategic perspective. However, these practices are recognised as not yet widely employed or are alternatively employed as a subset of other project management processes, with scant evidence about its impact on project success (Cooke-Davies, 2002).

Thus, Serra and Kunc's research evaluated the use of BRM as a method of supporting portfolio management and organisational governance to improve the effectiveness of achieving strategic objectives. The research was carried out among the project management communities of three countries, United Kingdom, United States, and Brazil, in order to understand its impact on project success rates and evaluate the impact of projects on the creation of organisational value from a multicultural perspective (Bryde, 2005; Yu et al., 2005; Zwikael & Smyrk, 2012).

Benefits realisation management: project success and strategic value

While there are several different models for the measurement of project success as discussed, several other authors, such as Baccarini (1999) and Pinto and Mantel (1990), agree on the two approaches suggested in the preceding passages for assessment, namely, project management performance and delivery of benefits to the business, clients, and stakeholders. Ika (2009) comparatively splits the benefit-related component of the assessment into, firstly, "project/product success" with satisfaction of end user and benefits to stakeholders and project staff and, secondly, "strategic project management" with business success and achievement of clients' strategic objectives.

In the past, project success was evaluated mostly based on criteria associated with the "triple constraint", cost, schedule, and scope (Ika, 2009; Shenhar & Patanakul, 2012; Zwikael & Smyrk, 2011), which are strongly related to the evaluation of project management performance, usually assessed using key performance indicators (KPIs) designed to measure the adherence to budgets, schedules, and technical specifications (Bryde, 2005).

However, a complete evaluation of success requires a value-related component (Kerzner, 2011), replacing this evaluation method for another focused on the project contribution to the business strategy (Shenhar & Patanakul, 2012), including the creation of shareholder value (Ika, 2009; Levine, 2005).

More recently, consideration of value in relation to benefits becomes more evident. Camilleri (2011) divides benefit between "project success" with outcomes and benefits and "project corporate success" with the achievement of strategic objectives. Zwikael and Smyrk (2011) also separate success into "ownership success" concerning benefits less disbenefits and costs and also "investment success" with financial return to the organisation. Despite these authors having suggested different ways to assess the delivery of benefits and the consequent creation of strategic value to the business, this chapter suggests that *the delivery of benefits to stakeholders has to be related to business strategies and to the achievement of wider business objectives, especially by the financial perspective, considering "project success" as a more comprehensive approach* (Cooke-Davies, 2002).

Defining project success

Although there are several criteria available to evaluate project success, the judgement of success or failure can be taken based on a more situational or subjective basis (Ika, 2009; McLeod et al., 2012). Different perspectives using the same criteria can evaluate the same project as a success and also as a failure. On the other hand, a set of criteria can be suitable to some perspectives but unsuitable for others. For example, project management success, ownership success, and investment success are assessed by different perspectives and criteria (Zwikael & Smyrk, 2011). Nevertheless, project managers are responsible for the alignment of expectations among stakeholders in order to define project success (Kerzner, 2011). Interestingly, these same project managers are usually kept apart from the rationale for project selection and prioritisation, so they may not understand the relevance of their projects in order to deliver the expected benefit to the business (Melton et al., 2008). Thus, a question remains unanswered for them: What value do businesses need?

Strategic objectives and benefits

Serra and Kunc discuss good business strategies as those that deliver stakeholder value, which is the organisation's long-term cash-generation capability or the ability to provide valuable public services, such as in the case of public sector organisations (Johnson & Scholes, 2002). These business strategies set targets of future value, which are met by achieving strategic objectives. Since these objectives are measurable, the difference between the current situation and the target future situation sets the value gap, which is fulfilled by a portfolio of initiatives defined by the organisation in their strategic plan (Kaplan & Norton, 2008). As Figure 7.1 illustrates, strategic initiatives usually fill the value gap by enabling new capabilities – or promoting changes – through the outputs delivered by a set of projects.

Projects are organisational entities which employ resources organised in a new and unique way, for a specific time frame, to enable positive and clearly defined changes in the business (Turner & Müller, 2003). These positive changes aim towards the achievement of organisational objectives, and these strategic improvements in the business are called "benefits". Benefits, which can be seen as improvements, are increments in the business value from not only a shareholders' perspective but also customers', suppliers', or even

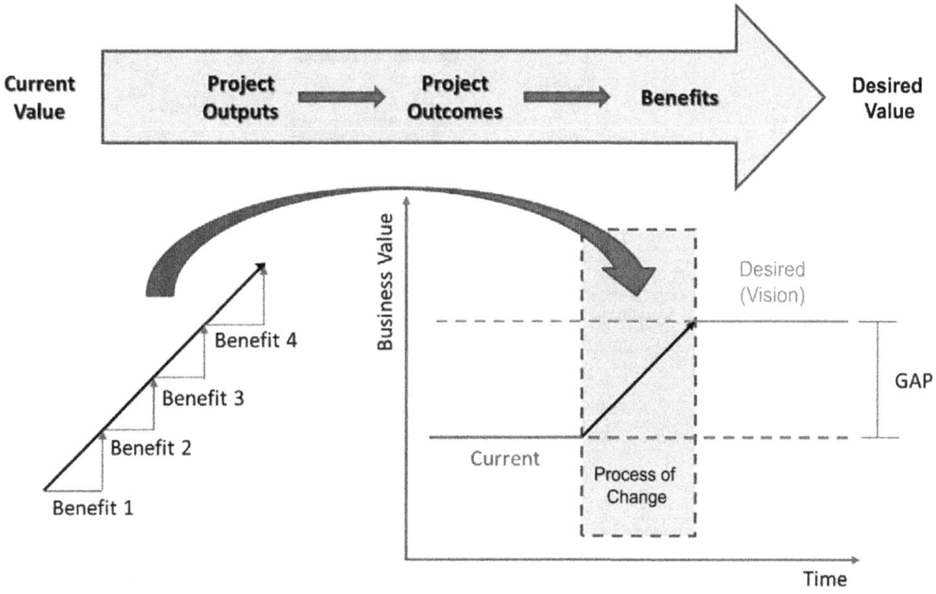

Figure 7.1 Filling the value gap (Serra & Kunc, 2015).

societal perspectives (Zwikael & Smyrk, 2011). Benefits are usually achieved using program and project management techniques. Therefore, the creation of value for business, by the successful execution of business strategy, strongly depends on programs and projects delivering the expected benefits.

Based on the benefit mapping techniques suggested by Thorp (2007), Ward and Daniel (2006), and Bradley (2010) and practitioners' guides (Chittenden & Bon, 2006; Jenner, 2012; OGC, 2007), a conceptual example of benefits realisation, starting from projects and reaching the achievement of business objectives, is presented in Figure 7.2. Conceptually, the process starts on project outputs enabling business changes or directly delivering intermediate benefits. Business changes create outcomes, which prepare operations to realise the expected benefits. Alternatively, business changes can also deliver intermediate benefits, regardless of whether they are enabled by project outputs or not. They can also cause side effects, which are the negative outcomes from change, such as requirements for additional skills or cost increases. These side effects and consequences can also realise further intermediate benefits. Intermediate benefits contribute to the achievement of end benefits (Bradley, 2010), and end benefits directly contribute to the achievement of one or more strategic objectives of the organisation. Usually, end benefits are results of changing processes composed by sets of projects that are managed together as a program (Bradley, 2010), which coordinates work in a synergic way to generate more benefits than individual projects can achieve. (Thiry, 2002).

Therefore, from a strategic perspective, successful projects deliver the expected benefits, thus creating strategic value to the business. Careful management of each project ensures the delivery of outputs, enables outcomes, and then supports the realisation of the right benefits. Noting that benefits are not the only criteria to evaluate project success,

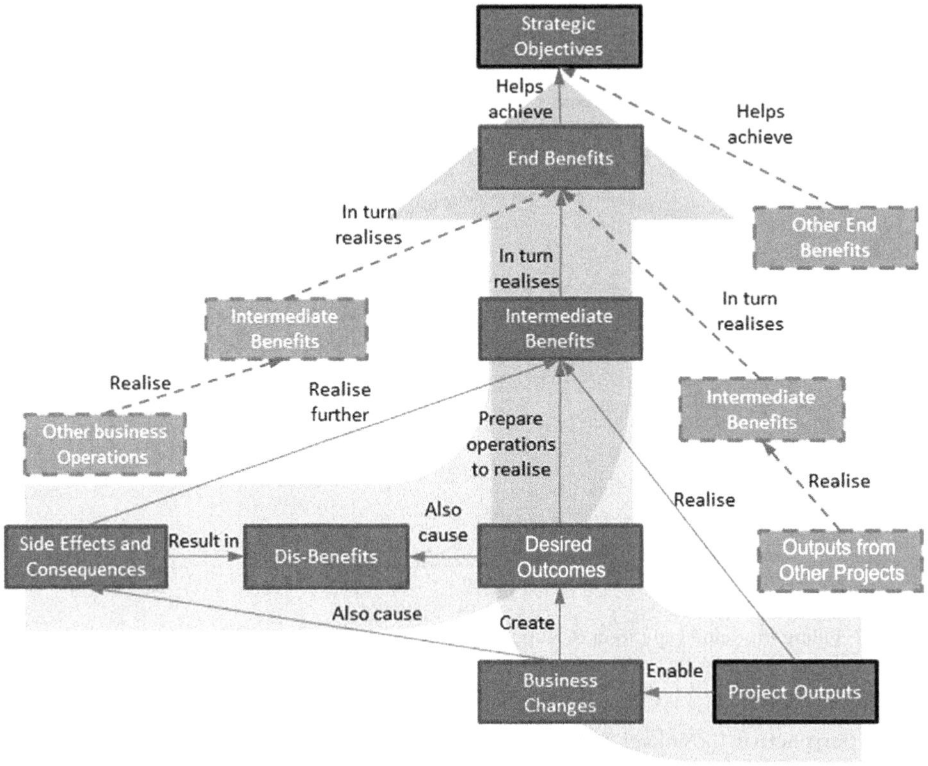

Figure 7.2 Chain of benefits (Serra & Kunc, 2015).

although they are a measurement of how valuable a project is perceived to be. This is the premise of BRM (Serra & Kunc, 2015).

Benefits realisation management and portfolio management

This section of the chapter presents the results of the research with some discussion of both project success criteria and the correlation of these criteria with BRM practices. The connection between these correlations and the portfolio is then explained. The research has identified 12 measures for assessing BRM practices, covering both project success and the creation of value for the business, shown in Figure 7.3 (Zwikael & Smyrk, 2011; Bradley, 2010; Melton et al., 2008; OGC, 2007; Chittenden & Bon, 2006; Buttrick, 1997; Kendall & Rollins, 2003; Levine, 2005; Breese, 2012; Jenner, 2010; Thorp, 2007).

Project management performance: a more relevant success criteria

Seven dimensions were typically identified as the most important for assessing project success: budget, schedule, required outputs, undesired outcomes, expected outcomes, return on investment, and the business case. Only two of these, schedule goals and required outputs, are seen as significant, suggesting a low influence of BRM practices on the overall perception of project success, particularly for the UK and the USA.

BRM1	Expected outcomes clearly defined
BRM2	Value created clearly measurable
BRM3	Strategic objectives clearly defined
BRM4	A business case was approved
BRM5	Outputs and outcomes were reviewed
BRM6	Stakeholders were aware of the results
BRM7	Actual outcomes adhered to the business case
BRM8	Activities aiming to ensure the integration
BRM9	After project closure, kept monitoring project outcomes
BRM10	Performed a process to ensure the integration
BRM11	Benefits management strategy throughout the company
BRM12	Benefits management strategy for the project under analysis

Figure 7.3 Measures for BRM practices (Serra & Kunc, 2015).

The initial analysis of the data collected reinforced the current idea that organisations and professionals evaluate project success immediately after the delivery stage has finished (Atkinson, 1999) and mostly by criteria related to project management performance (budget, schedule, and outputs). Bryde (2005) has previously identified and suggested this practice as a narrow way to measure success by focusing on short-term measures. Besides encouraging project managers to focus on short-term and tactical measures rather than on long-term and strategic improvements on performance (Bryde, 2005), this approach also challenges any attempt to implement BRM practices.

In order to apply BRM in supporting successful implementation of business strategies, organisations need to redesign their success criteria to increase the relevance of dimensions related to the creation of value for the business. Otherwise, any initiatives aiming to increase success rates of the most strategically oriented projects may seem unsuccessful, since organisations are still focusing on the evaluation of success based on project management success rather than evaluating how successful their projects are in creating value for the business.

Benefits realisation management: drivers for the creation of strategic value

Serra and Kunc's (2015) analysis confirmed *BRM practices being much more associated with the creation of value for the business than to project management performance*, as Cooke-Davies (2002) previously identified. The BRM practices that were correlated with value creation, from

Serra and Kunc's work (Table 10), were most notably BRM7, actual outcomes adhered to the business case, together with BRM6, stakeholders aware of the results of reviews; BRM11, benefits management strategy throughout the company; followed by BRM8, activities aiming to ensure the integration; BRM9, after project closure, kept monitoring project outcomes and with less demonstrable correlation with BRM10, performed a process to ensure the integration; BRM12, benefits management strategy for the project under analysis; and BRM1, expected outcomes clearly defined.

Due to a low association found between the creation of value and the overall perception of success, BRM practices were assessed as having a relatively low ability to predict the overall perception of project success, in comparison to the much higher ability they have over a balanced combination of dimensions. Nevertheless, the analysis revealed BRM practices being somehow associated with most dimensions of success (although the results can be different between countries), even to schedule goals and required outputs, which were the only dimensions being significantly associated with the overall perception of project success, both of which are related to success in project management performance.

Another relevant finding is the practice adherence of actual outcomes to the ones planned in the business case, being consistently relevant to predict two dimensions of success across the three countries: the return on the investment and the business case success. These results evidence business cases being effective tools for the comparison of the results between project evaluations, performed at project closure stages, to the results of project appraisals, done at project start for the approval of business cases and updated throughout project execution. They also make the relevance of financial appraisals on business cases clear since these are key elements to support success on the return on investment.

Although the relevance of these BRM practices on influencing the perception of project success seems to be still in its early stages, Serra and Kunc's findings provide evidence of project management, traditionally focused on delivering outputs to a required schedule and budget being able to be expanded to a much broader approach into the strategic management area. In the last decade, project management research has given increasing significance to topics such as strategic alignment and organisational outcomes (Crawford et al., 2006), and the alignment between project management and organisations' strategies has been identified as imperative (Cooke-Davies et al., 2009). In parallel, project management has been increasingly incorporated into the research developed by other management disciplines, especially when related to strategy and project portfolio management (Kwak & Anbari, 2009).

In this scenario, portfolio management has recently emerged as part of a more dynamic and strategic organisational governance (Thorp, 2007), aiming to organise and manage resources in order to ensure the return on a strategically aligned set of investments (Kwak & Anbari, 2009). Thus, BRM becomes relevant to integrating project, program, and portfolio management (Breese, 2012). It also takes the responsibility to the very relevant and previously overlooked phase, or process, of outcome realisation proposed by Zwikael and Smyrk (2012) once these practices aim to embed the outcomes from strategically aligned portfolios into the existing business performance management frameworks.

Conclusion

Although BRM practices are strongly associated with the creation of value for the business, these practices by themselves seem to be insufficient to result in high levels of project management performance, and that has always been and will always be important for project success (Shenhar & Patanakul, 2012). Therefore, BRM needs to be implemented along with other project, program, and portfolio management practices in order to ensure the complete management of project performance in the wider context, as suggested by Bryde (2005).

The findings also suggest that a benefits management strategy integrated into the corporate governance processes helps organisations increase their ability to define and manage their success criteria. More importantly, benefits realisation management helps put in place a key condition for project success identified by Jugdev and Müller (2005). This is the alignment between project management teams, sponsors, and clients (owners) in order to deliver successful and valuable changes to the organisation and its stakeholders, through the development of strategic resources (Kunc & Morecroft, 2010).

References

Atkinson, R. (1999) Project management: Cost, time and quality, two best guesses and a phenomenon, it's time to accept other success criteria. *International Journal of Project Management* 17(6), 337–342.

Baccarini, D. (1999) The logical framework method for defining project success. *Project Management Journal* 30(4), 25–32.

Bradley, G. (2010) *Benefit Realisation Management.* First Edition. MPG Books Group.

Breese, R. (2012) Benefits realisation management: Panacea or False Dawn? *International Journal of Project Management* (30), 341–351.

Bryde, D. (2005) Methods for managing different perspectives of project success. *British Journal of Management* 16, 119–131.

Buttrick, R. (1997) *The Project Workout: a Toolkit for Reaping the Rewards From all Your Business Projects.* First Edition. Financial Times Management.

Camilleri, E. (2011) *Project Success: Critical Factors and Behaviours.* First Edition. Gower Publishing Limited.

Chittenden, J. & Bon, J. (2006) *Program Management based on MSP: A Management Guide.* First Edition. Van Haren Pub.

Cooke-Davies, T. (2002) The "real" success factors on projects. *International Journal of Project Management* 20, 185–190.

Cooke-Davies, T., Crawford, L. & Lechler, T. (2009) Project management systems: Moving project management from an operational to a strategic discipline. *Project Management Journal* 40(1), 110–123.

Crawford, L., Pollack, J. & England, D. (2006) Uncovering the trends in project management: Journal emphases over the last 10 years. *International Journal of Project Management* 24, 175–184.

Gardiner, P. 2005. *Project Management: A Strategic Planning Approach.* First Edition. Palgrave Macmillan.

Gray, C. & Larson, E. (2006) *Project Management: The managerial Process.* International Edition 2006 ed. McGraw-Hill/Irwin.

Ika, L. (2009) Project success as a topic in project management journals. *Project Management Journal* 40(4), 6–19

Jenner, S. (2010) *Transforming Government and Public Services: Realising Benefits through Project Portfolio Management.* First Edition. Ashgate.

Jenner, S. (2012) *Managing Benefits: Optimizing the Return from Investments.* First Edition. TSO.

Johnson, G. & Scholes, K. (2002) *Exploring Corporate Strategy,* Sixth ed. Prentice Hall.

Jugdev, K. & Müller, R. (2005) A retrospective look at our evolving understanding of project success. *Project Management Journal* 36(4), 19–31.

Kaplan, R. & Norton, D. (2008) *The Execution Premium: Linking Strategy to Operations for Competitive Advantage.* First Edition. Harvard Business School Publishing Corporation

Kendall, G. & Rollins, S. (2003) *Advanced Project Portfolio Management and the PMO: Multiplying ROI at Warp Speed.* First Edition. J. Ross.

Kerzner, H., (2011) *Project Management Metrics, KPIs, and Dashboards: A Guide to Measuring and Monitoring Project Performance.* First Edition. John Wiley & Sons, Inc.

Kunc, M. & Morecroft, J. (2010) Managerial decision-making and firm performance under a resource-based paradigm. *Strategic Management Journal* 31, 1164–1182.

Kwak, Y. & Anbari, F. (2009) Analyzing project management research: Perspectives from top management journals. *International Journal of Business Management* 27(5), 435–446.

Levine, H. (2005) *Project Portfolio Management: A Practical Guide to Selecting Projects, Managing Portfolios, and Maximizing Benefits*. First Edition. Jossey-Bass.

McLeod, L., Doolin, B. & MacDonell, S. (2012) A perspective-based understanding of project success. *Project Management Journal* 43(5), 68–86.

Melton, T., Iles-Smith, P. & Yates, J. (2008) *Project Benefits Management: Linking Your Project to the Business*. First Edition. Butterworth-Heinemann.

OGC (2007) *Managing Successful Programs*, Third ed. TSO (The Stationery Office).

Pinto, J. & Mantel, S. (1990) The causes of project failure. *IEEE Transactions on Engineering Management* 37(4), 269–276.

Prabhakar, G. (2008) What is project success: A literature review. *International Journal of Business Management* 3(9), 3–10.

Serra, C. & Kunc, M. (2015) Benefits realisation management and its influence on project success and on the execution of business strategies. *International Journal of Project Management* 33, 53–66.

Serrador, P. (2013) The impact of planning on project success: A literature review. *Journal of Modern Project Management* 1(2), 28–39.

Shenhar, J. & Patanakul, P. (2012) What project strategy really is: The fundamental building block in strategic project management. *Project Management Journal* 43(1), 4–20.

Thiry, M. (2002) Combining value and project management into an effective program management model. *International Journal of Project Management* 20, 221–227.

Thorp, J. (2007) *The Information Paradox*, Revised ed. Fujitsu Consulting Inc.

Turner, J.R. & Müller, R. (2003). On the nature of the project as a temporary organization. *International Journal of Project Management* 21, 1–8.

Ward, J. & Daniel, E. (2006) *Benefits Management – Delivering Value from IS & IT Investments*. First Edition. John Wiley and Sons.

Yu, A., Flett, P. & Bowers, J. (2005) Developing a value-centered proposal for assessing project success. *International Journal of Project Management* 23(6), 428–436.

Zwikael, O. & Smyrk, J. (2011). *Project Management for the Creation of Organisational Value*. First Edition. Springer-Verlag London Limited.

Zwikael, O. & Smyrk, J. (2012) A general framework for gauging the performance of initiatives to enhance organizational value. *British Journal of Management* 23, S6–S22.

8 Rethinking portfolio success

Darren Dalcher

Introduction

The track record of portfolios can sometimes be a little challenging to decipher. Jonas (2010) notes that it remains difficult to determine the overall success or failure of a portfolio, especially as it needs to be realised at different points during the lifespan of a portfolio. Martinsuo and Lehtonen (2007) observe that the performance of a portfolio should not be examined on a single dimension, advocating instead that achievement should be measured at the single project, the portfolio, and the organisational levels. Müller et al. (2008) define portfolio success as a combination of "achieving desired portfolio *results* and achieving project and program *purpose* for the overall portfolio". Marnewick (2015) summarises the main portfolio success criteria in accordance with research completed by Beringer et al. (2013) and Meskendahl (2010) as a combination of:

1. Economic success. Maximisation of the financial value of the portfolio.
2. Strategic fit. Linking the portfolio to the organisational strategy.
3. Portfolio balance. Balancing the projects within the portfolio whilst taking into account the organisation's capacities.
4. Average project success. The average success rate of a project within the portfolio.

Agile portfolio management would encourage a wider focus on value, extending beyond the financial aspects (Ahmad et al., 2017). Indeed, benefits realisation based on utilisation and achievement of intended impacts and outcomes may offer a more valuable utilisation measure. The success of specific projects may also need to be considered in the context of the wider portfolio and the delivery of the intended benefits, expected usefulness, promised impacts, and the overall value that is captured.

Project-orientated organisations rely on their portfolio management and governance systems. "Killing" a specific project may be justified at the enterprise portfolio level (Unger et al., 2012), where there might be better ways of utilising resources, or perhaps other related projects, or initiatives, which may deliver all or some of the benefits. Indeed, some projects may conflict with other initiatives, and hence it would make more sense if they were delayed or cancelled. Yet at the strategic initiative level, specific initiatives should only be terminated if, and only if, they do not jeopardise the wider strategic theme. Clearly, some strategic themes may only be achieved if and when the entire collection of initiatives, which underpins them, is realised.

Furthermore, Kock and Gemünden (2019) recognise the role of longitudinal interdependencies, where new opportunities emerge from existing exploratory projects and

DOI: 10.4324/9780367853129-9

subsequent projects are needed to ensure that such strategic options are duly exploited (see emergent strategy in Chapter 3). Consideration of any specific part of the portfolio can only be determined through understanding the synergy and role that it plays within the wider portfolio and the relationships that exist between different undertakings and the usage points, opportunities that become available, and benefits that are likely to be delivered to the enterprise.

Can success be defined?

Success is a difficult concept. In some research and development (R&D) contexts, the marketability of specific compounds, solutions, or drugs, and how they are perceived by the wider population, may enforce a particular spin on the value or perceived acceptability of proposed solutions. In other set-ups, such as the oil and gas and other energy-exploration endeavours, particular locations, or working with specific regimes and communities, may likewise colour and influence the perceived success of particular initiatives, or even the way the entire company is portrayed. In such settings, the ability to innovate and diversify then feeds into the direct value derived from the portfolio arrangements.

Even within the confines of project-centric portfolios, different definitions abound. Kopmann (2014) advocates that project portfolio success embraces three dimensions: the strategic aspect, the exploitation aspect, and the stakeholder aspect. Corresponding management activities would thus require features of strategic control, stakeholder involvement, and governance for portfolio exploitation. Success would inevitably extend beyond the initial definition phase of the portfolio and may also include an element of preparing for the future as proposed by Meskendahl (2010).

Kopmann et al. (2017) show that portfolios can be used to support both deliberate and emergent strategies. They also demonstrate that "*strategic control activities not only foster the implementation of intended strategies, but also disclose strategic opportunities by unveiling emerging patterns*". Turning their findings around would imply that portfolios may be utilised to develop and explore emergent strategies. Under such conditions, the success criteria would surely also need to reflect the exploration value and the enabled flexibility that comes from the emergent strategy. Indeed, Hoffmann et al. (2020) advocate adding agility as an important design goal for portfolios to allow for rapid adaptations, flexible reprioritisation, and dynamic adjustments in response to changing strategic trajectories and emerging opportunities.

What is portfolio success?

Given the diversity observed in the types of portfolio set-ups, the key criteria applied in establishing the portfolio, and the subtleties of determining success, and failure, at multiple levels and perspectives (Dalcher, 1994, 2014a, 2014b), it should be clear that the key criteria applied in determining success need to be context-specific. Reflecting Engwall's (2003) observation that 'no project is an island", Unger et al. (2014) note that project portfolios as collections of projects are parts and products of their organisations and hence are embedded within their context and culture. Indeed, Martinsuo (2013) reaffirms that "recent studies show evidence that the success of portfolio management is highly dependent on the context".

Undeniably, what appears clear is that we must talk about and measure success in different ways. Success is a complex and multi-layered concept (Dalcher, 2012, 2014a), especially in the context of portfolios. The principles for collecting projects (and programs) into a portfolio must play a key part: the multiple bases, arrangements, and rationales for portfolios demarcate a starting point in the conversation about success in portfolio settings. If there are different reasons for establishing a portfolio, different purposes for grouping key investments together, and different approaches for governing and making decisions, then they must also form the basis for defining what is important and whether the intention and purpose have been achieved.

An interesting omission from the accepted criteria appears to relate to one of the original objectives of applying portfolios – to optimise the deployment of resources across projects. The common theme amongst projects grouped together offers an added synergy and the potential for the sharing of common resources, common technology, or common sponsorship, management, and governance structures. While the case for commonly sharing technology, resources, and arrangements offers the potential for both savings and synergies, there appears to be little effort to quantify or justify such savings. The literature on portfolio success does not directly address the value that comes from such sharing, other than in applicability to organisational strategy. Yet common resourcing, the sharing of expertise, or even the justification of a new technology split across multiple projects can make a compelling case for success.

One potential exception is the area of agile portfolio management, which takes into account portfolio blending, or the bringing together of initiatives that provide economies of scale, alongside the more traditional prioritising and balancing. Agile portfolio management thus suggests that at every portfolio event-driven retrospective or regular stand-up, the performance of the portfolio is evaluated (Horlach et al., 2019). Such evaluation enables adjustments to the prioritisation, blending, and balancing in order to improve the performance of the overall portfolio. While the focus in agile portfolio management may be on the near term, the explicit recognition of blending places it at the core of performance review and assessment (Laanti et al., 2015). Other parts of the portfolio management community are yet to explicitly acknowledge the importance of common grouping to determining the overall value and success of a portfolio (Rautiainen et al., 2011).

The discussion around portfolio success in the extant literature is relatively sparse. Generally accepted criteria appear to offer little pragmatic value or guidance. Moreover, the different needs and requirements of specific arrangements, such as strategic initiatives, imply that specific criteria need to be applied and tailored to each context individually. The mode of execution of the portfolio and the increasing tendency to set up agile portfolios will also require more refined ways of determining success and doing so more rapidly and frequently. The balance between the different components and interests should also be taken into account. The completion of a small part of a portfolio can be significantly less critical than the successful completion of a strategic initiative. Indeed, in a strategic context, specific actions, and their completion, may seem irrelevant against major strategic imperatives.

Achieving the right balance between establishing the variety of projects and initiatives and the selection of appropriate ones is crucial to the success of the portfolio. In a world that increasingly demands doing more with less, the abilities to develop enterprise portfolio capability and to consider projects and initiatives globally are of paramount importance. While portfolio objectives emphasise strategic alignment, or fit, value maximisation, and portfolio balance (Cooper et al., 1997), the exact dimensions of each, and the values that underpin the selections for the portfolio, will also need to feature in the assessment of attainment, especially as organisations endeavour to balance the need to efficiently exploit the known and innovatively explore new opportunities. Identifying the

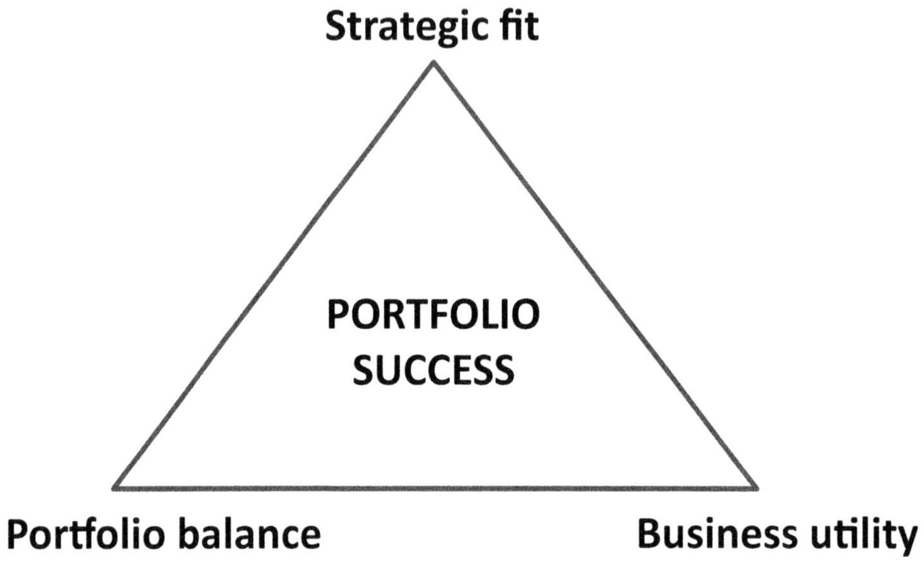

Figure 8.1 The essential portfolio success triangle.

right mix of options and supporting the strategic choice of the options that maximise the enterprise' intentions is critical to success.

While it seems tempting to propose a performance triangle based on fit, utility, and balance of the portfolio as an initial way of mapping success (Figure 8.1), it is also important to recognise that such a scheme would underplay the complexities inherent in portfolio decision-making. Such a triangle would miss the value of common deployment of expertise, skills, tools, and other resources across multiple projects. It would also miss out on contextual issues, such as the balance between exploration and exploitation, the specific types of innovation required, and will not necessarily address the implied critical importance of strategic initiatives.

Overall, therefore, the specific scenario for success needs to be tailored to the specific initiatives and activities that are invoked, and their relative importance to the overall sustained performance of the enterprise should play the key part in planning for and in gauging the achievement of the intended performance, measured in terms of the fit, utility, and balance of the actual portfolio. However, this should be done with the caveat that portfolio success is situated within the direct context of the organisation and the specific benefits sought, including the common sharing of expertise, resources, and tools, and should therefore play a critical part in shaping and influencing any meaningful assessment of portfolio performance.

Perhaps a more sensible approach to defining portfolio success should focus on what we are trying to achieve through the creation and structuring of the portfolio and the competing and overlapping constraints and priorities. According to the Association for Project Management's Portfolio Management Specific Interest Group (APM, 2020), there are multiple values, added benefits, and improved outcomes when portfolio management is implemented and executed properly. Portfolio management can therefore offer the following contributions to business success:

- Ensures early identification of projects and programs that don't add value/benefit, so they are not started/stopped.
- Ensures management of risk at the collective level, increasing success of the "right" projects and programs, and a link to business risk management.
- Ensures visibility of all projects and programs and their interdependence and enables tracking and focus to ensure success.
- Provides better engagement with staff.
- Supports timely decision making and re-orientation of inflight projects and programs so that strategic benefits are optimised.
- Supports effective and optimised allocation of resources to better enable the highest priority 'right' projects and programs to succeed.
- Provides robust governance of change across the whole landscape of change/projects.

(APM, 2020, p. 3)

The list of benefits can be further augmented by additional contributions to the organisation and the business, such as focusing on and optimising the use of scarce resources, emphasising beneficial impact on customers and stakeholders, and encouraging innovation and exploration of new opportunities.

Conclusion

Ultimately, success is contextual and deeply situated. The most pertinent set of contributions that apply to any specific organisation and portfolio set-up should therefore form the basis for evaluating and assessing the success of that specific arrangement. Delivering successful portfolios can thus be informed by and tailored to match the real needs, opportunities, and expectations that relate to a given situation or business environment.

References

Ahmad M., Lwakatare L, Kuvaja P, Oivo M. & Markkula J. (2017) An empirical study of portfolio management and Kanban in agile and lean software companies. *Journal of Software: Evolution and Process* 29(6), e1834.

APM (2020) *Portfolio Management: A Practical Guide*. APM Portfolio Management Specific Interest Group, Association of Project Management.

Beringer C., Jonas D. & Kock A. (2013) Behavior of internal stakeholders in project portfolio management and its impact on success. *International Journal of Project Management* 31(6), 830–846.

Cooper R., Edgett S. & Kleinschmidt E. (1997) Portfolio management in new product development: Lessons from the leaders – II. *Research-Technology Management* 40(6), 43–52.

Dalcher D. (1994) Falling down is part of Growing up; the Study of Failure and the Software Engineering Community. in Diaz-Herrera J. *Software Engineering Education*. Springer, pp. 489–496.

Dalcher D. (2012) Project management for the creation of organisational value. *Project Management Journal* 43(3), 79–79.

Dalcher D. (2014a) Rethinking success in software projects: Looking beyond the failure factors. in Ruhe G. & Wohlin C. *Software Project Management in a Changing World*. Springer, pp. 27–49

Dalcher D. (2014b) What can project success, or failure, tell us about project management theory. in Rietiker S. & Wagner R. *Theory Meets Practice in Projects*. GPM.

Engwall M. (2003) No project is an island: Linking projects to history and context. *Research Policy* 32(5), 789–808.

Hoffmann D., Ahlemann F. & Reining S. (2020) Reconciling alignment, efficiency, and agility in IT project portfolio management: Recommendations based on a revelatory case study. *International Journal of Project Management* 38(2), 124–136.

Horlach B., Schirmer I. & Drews P. (June 8–14 2019) Agile portfolio management: Design goals and principles. in Proceedings of the 27th European Conference on Information Systems (ECIS).

Jonas D. (2010) Empowering project portfolio managers: How management involvement impacts project portfolio management performance. *International Journal of Project Management* 28(8), 818–831.

Kock A. & Gemünden H. (2019) Project lineage management and project portfolio success. *Project Management Journal* 50(5), 587–601.

Kopmann J. (2014) Refining project portfolio success and its antecedents. in *Project Management Institute Research and Education Conference Proceedings*. Project Management Institute.

Kopmann J., Kock A., Killen C. & Gemünden H. (2017) The role of project portfolio management in fostering both deliberate and emergent strategy. *International Journal of Project Management* 35(4), 557–570.

Laanti M. & Kangas M. (August 2015) Is agile portfolio management following the principles of large-scale agile? Case study in Finnish Broadcasting Company Yle. in *2015 Agile Conference*. IEEE, pp. 92–96.

Marnewick C. (2015) Portfolio management success. in Levin G. & Wyzalek J. *Portfolio Management: A Strategic Approach*. CRC Press.

Martinsuo M. (2013) Project portfolio management in practice and in context. *International Journal of Project Management* 31(6), 794–803.

Martinsuo M. & Lehtonen P. (2007) Role of single-project management in achieving portfolio management efficiency. *International Journal of Project Management* 25(1), 56–65.

Meskendahl S. (2010). The influence of business strategy on project portfolio management and its success – a conceptual framework. *International Journal of Project Management* 28(8), 807–817.

Müller R., Martinsuo M. & Blomquist T. (2008) Project portfolio control and portfolio management performance in different contexts. *Project Management Journal* 39(3), 28–42.

Rautiainen K., von Schantz J. & Vähäniitty J. (2011) Supporting scaling agile with portfolio management: case paf. com. in *2011 Janaury 44th Hawaii International Conference on System Sciences*. IEEE, pp. 1–10.

Unger B., Kock A., Gemünden H. & Jonas D. (2012) Enforcing strategic fit of project portfolios by project termination: An empirical study on senior management involvement. *International Journal of Project Management* 30(6), 675–685.

Unger B., Rank J. & Gemuenden H. (2014) Corporate innovation culture and dimensions of project portfolio success: The moderating role of national culture. *Project Management Journal* 45(6), 38–57.

Section II

Developing and managing the strategic portfolio

Introduction

The chapters in this section, written by Harpum, focus on defining capabilities and processes for strategic portfolios (SP). Chapter 9 looks at integration of the portfolio within the organisational structure, systems, and processes, including consideration of the environmental factors. A topic closely associated with program and project management is the delivery of engineered systems, and Chapter 9 includes consideration of portfolios in the context of complex adaptive systems. Chapter 10 looks in detail at the core capabilities required for effective management of strategic portfolios.

Chapter 11 follows the discussion of portfolio management capabilities from Chapter 10, with a discussion of portfolio risk and value for portfolio development, and looks in more detail at alternatives for portfolio process design, including classification and balancing. Chapter 12 concludes this section with an in-depth discussion of selection techniques to determine the contents of a strategic portfolio. Strategic selection decision criteria are defined, reiterating that the choice of the most appropriate methodology is based on the specific organisational context.

Chapter questions

Katy Angliss

Similar to Section I, there are some questions listed to keep in mind when reading through Section II. The material review questions provide an overview of the key messages and approach to consider. The further discussion questions look to help develop thinking about the specific organisational context or for additional student learning.

Chapter 9 Portfolio management integration

Material review questions

9.1 Discuss how considering systems thinking for a strategic portfolio (e.g. as an open system and as a "system of systems") can influence the management of a portfolio.
9.2 Discuss why and how portfolios should be vertically integrated.
9.3 Consider some of the disadvantages of not clearly identifying a portfolio and clarifying suitable processes and responsibilities.
9.4 Assess some of the advantages of an OPM (organisational project management) approach to portfolio management at the business integration layer.

Further discussion questions

9.5 Discuss the importance of capturing emergent strategy within the business integration layer. Following this, consider:

a) How can strategic portfolio controls achieve this by capturing emergent strategy?
b) How does the instability of the portfolio environment affect successful strategic integration?

9.6 Evaluate, for your organisation, some alternatives for the design of integration mechanisms (such as portfolio processes) for ensuring strategic integration and, following this, incorporating portfolio optimisation?

Chapter 10 Environmental factors and portfolio management capabilities

Material review questions

10.1 Suggest alternative models for assessing the environmental interactions of portfolios within their environment.
10.2 Evaluate the environmental factors that can affect portfolio management design (refer to Annexe 1), including the organisational structure (philosophical approach and governance).
10.3 Taking into account the environmental factors, discuss the key elements for portfolio design.

Further discussion questions

10.4 Discuss the organisational capabilities required for high performance of the strategic portfolio?
10.5 Compare and contrast organisational and project management maturity models in the context of portfolio management capability for your organisation, establishing the advantages and disadvantages of each model?

Chapter 11 Portfolio management process design

Material review questions

11.1 Discuss the key process elements of the Padovani and Carvalho portfolio management model.
11.2 Compare and contrast the Padovani and Carvalho model with the PMI model for portfolio process design.
11.3 How can a strategic portfolio be designed to encompass the external environment with projects and programs?

Further discussion questions

11.4 Discuss some of the important factors to consider for classification and balancing in the portfolio design.
11.5 Discuss the potential purposes and alternatives for a classification system (or scheme).
11.6 Consider how the design of the portfolio processes can influence effective decision-making.

11.7 Looking back to the discussion of portfolio success in Chapter 8 and considering portfolio performance in relation to process design in Chapter 11, consider the following:

The need to address portfolio performance specifically and directly in relation to the context is logically identical to the argument put forward for portfolio success: that selection criteria for entry to a portfolio are specifically derived from the strategic objectives the portfolio is intended to deliver. It is therefore perhaps unsurprising that the performance measurement of the portfolio, to make any sense, should follow on from this same criteria-derivation process, that is, portfolio performance should firstly be measured against its ability to achieve strategic objectives.

Chapter 12 Strategic portfolio selection

Material review questions

12.1 Discuss appropriate alternative criteria for the pre-screening stage.
12.2 Compare the different financial metrics available for economic analysis of the elements of the portfolio, including projects and programs.
12.3 How might the five types of real options influence the financial analysis of the portfolio (including projects and programs).
12.4 What is the purpose of the final screening stage, and how may this affect portfolio selection?

Further discussion questions

12.5 Critique the suggested five stages of the portfolio selection process and discuss how they might fit or be improved within your organisation.
12.6 Discuss how CAPEX and OPEX expenditure for the organisation can affect portfolio funding and the process for developing real options.
12.7 Compare and contrast the five example techniques discussed for portfolio selection for your organisation.
12.8 Discuss some of the challenges involved with portfolio selection and optimisation.
12.9 Within the portfolio adjustment phase, evaluate how resource management decisions can affect strategic portfolio performance and benefit realisation within the tactical portfolio(s), including project and program performance.
12.10 Evaluate alternative prioritisation methods and their associated challenges within the portfolio adjustment phase, considering your organisational context.

9 Portfolio management integration

Pete Harpum

Introduction

This chapter sets out to define and explain the ways in which portfolio management can be envisaged to be vertically integrated in organisations – that is to say, how strategy development and planning is connected to the mechanism for operationalising the strategy, that is, delivering the strategic portfolio. The chapter adopts an essentially instrumentalist/rationalist approach to integration, emphasising that management activity can be conceptualised as a set of processes and information flows. In this approach, the assumption made is that it is reasonable to believe organisations work much like machines: people follow policies, processes, and procedures (rules), and that if the rules are matched correctly to the organisation, it will function as intended.

This still tends to be the predominant view of organisational design. Indeed, ensuring that at strategic, portfolio, and project "levels", well-defined sets of processes, etc., are in place (which can be considered to be the outcome of formalisation of management) has been shown to improve overall performance of the organisation. Teller et al. (2012, p. 597) provide evidence of four interconnected outcomes from formalisation at both portfolio and project levels: firstly, there is "a positive relationship between single project management formalisation and project portfolio success"; secondly, a "simultaneous formalisation at both levels has a complimentary positive effect on the quality of the execution of the project portfolio management process"; thirdly, "formalisation becomes even more important for complex portfolios"; and fourthly, "the relationship between formalisation and portfolio success is fully mediated by the PPM [project portfolio management] quality". Setting up strategy, portfolio, and project work within a framework of well-defined "rules" improves performance of the organisation.

It is worth noting that it is not always clear that several levels of portfolios exist in larger organisations. In principle, all the work that needs to be carried out by the organisation to achieve strategic goals is encompassed by the corporate "book of work". This is likely to include sub-portfolios that focus on specific areas of the organisation, for example, internal IT programs and projects, new product development work, organisational change, and in organisations whose reason for existence is delivering projects to clients, the portfolio of deliverable work to those clients. Figure 9.1 shows the existence of various portfolios within an organisation, with the outer box itself representing the entire corporate "book of work" or strategic portfolio (also refer to Figure 1.1).

A word of warning: Outside of abstract models, in real life, there is a need to take account of the fact that people are not rational. Or at least they do not adhere to the behaviours expected of them by those designing the "rational" models of managerial

DOI: 10.4324/9780367853129-11

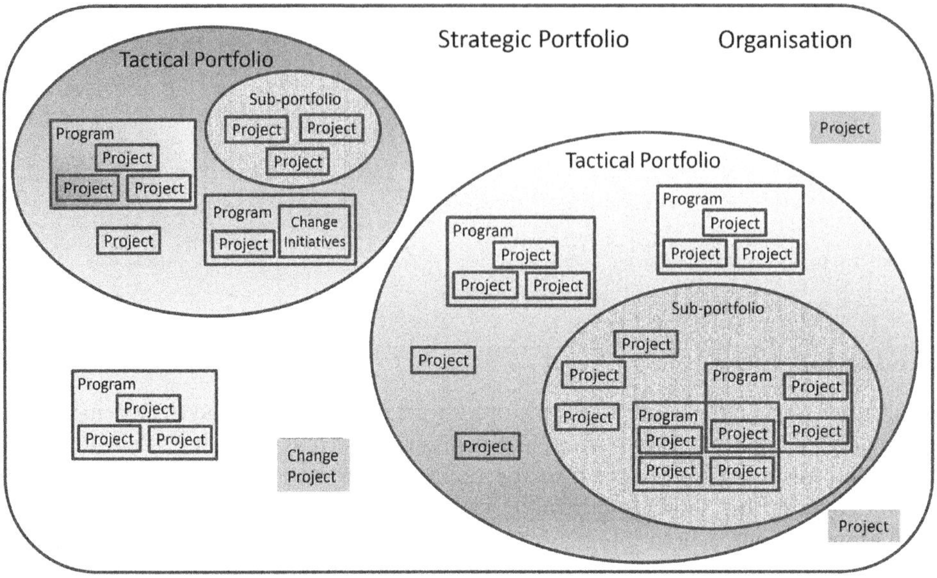

Figure 9.1 The relationship between portfolios, programs, and projects.

Source: Adapted from Lock and Wagner (2016).

processes. In the practical use of these integrated models for strategy execution, an enormous range of factors are at play that appear to frustrate a "perfectly designed" set of processes. Power, politics, ethics, interpersonal behaviour, multiple stakeholder interactions, the nature of complexity, fundamental uncertainty, risks and opportunities, competitor behaviour, the economic environment, amongst many others, all contribute to the "moment-to-moment" behaviour of individuals managing and being managed by these processes. It is vitally important not to fall into the trap of believing that the machine we design to deliver strategy is actually a machine. It is not. The integrated set of processes is, at best, a "good enough" way to try to get work done, and flexibility in use, openness to the emergence of new information, and a willingness to continually adapt the "machine" to the exigencies of organisational reality. (For a critical view of the issues associated with designing human systems, using a socio-technical systems perspective, see Cherns, 1993.)

A system's perspective on controlling work

The application of general system theory to organisations started in the 1950s with work on socio-technical systems at the Tavistock Institute (Emery, 1993). This work, in turn, had a significant influence on the development of ideas about managing project work, leading to the fundamental mechanistic perspective on project control processes (Harpum, 2004). (Harpum provides a detailed account of the application of systems theory to project control in Morris and Pinto [2004], and key elements of that discussion are drawn on in this chapter.) In simple terms, the basic open systems model is shown in Figure 9.2.

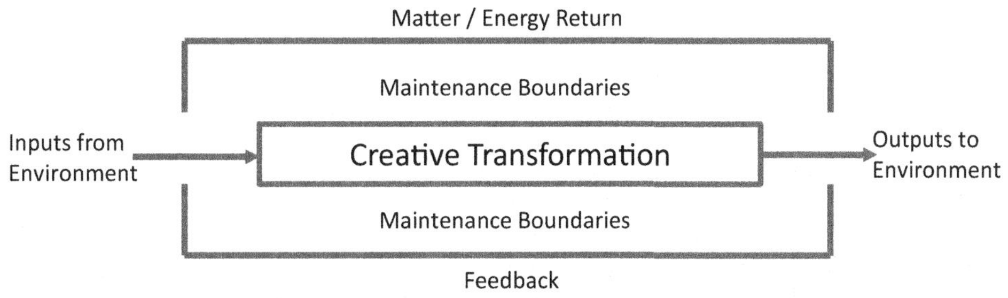

Figure 9.2 The basic systems model.

Source: Adapted from Harpum (2004).

The elements of the system are described as follows:

The system: a set of components that are interrelated, acting in a unified way, to achieve a goal.	**The creative transformation:** the process(es) that act on the energy, resources, and materials from the environment to turn inputs into outputs.
Inputs: energy, resources, and materials from the environment.	**Outputs:** products, knowledge, or services that help the system achieve its goals.
Maintenance boundaries: the mechanism which defines the transformation process(es) and therefore creates the system's unique identity.	**Matter/energy return:** matter and energy are returned to the environment in order to ensure the system remains in equilibrium.
Feedback: the negative feedback required to ensure the system stays on course to deliver its goals.	**The environment:** These are all the influences which act on the system and that the control system attempts to mitigate.

An important feature of an open system is that the boundaries are, to a large extent, set arbitrarily, depending on the observer's perspective (or, more pertinently, perhaps for us, the organisational designer). Wherever system boundaries are placed, they are always permeable to energy and information from the outside. This quality is fundamental in allowing the relationships between the system and its environment to be considered in the context of change, from an initial condition to a final one: to allow a movement towards strategic objectives, informed by strategy. "A critical part of this theory that is useful when considering management control is that the open system always moves towards the achievement of superordinate goals" (Harpum, 2004, p. 8).

If the generic system diagram is redrawn to represent the portfolio of work, delivering strategic objectives into the environment, the relationship of management control to the strategic plans and the portfolio of work to be completed is made clear, as in Figure 9.3.

The value of the open systems model of the portfolio shows how the "mechanistic" control meta-process attempts to ensure that the portfolio continues towards achievement of its strategic objectives. The social issues (behaviours, relationships, roles, etc.) are

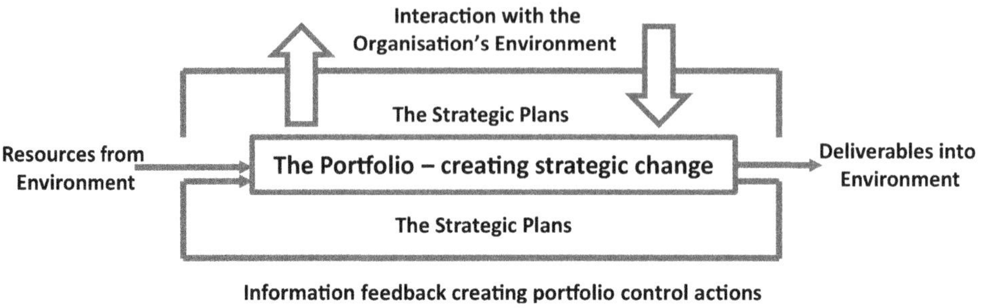

Figure 9.3 The portfolio as a system.

evident throughout the project system: within strategy and portfolio decision processes, acting across the permeable boundaries with the organisational stakeholders and wider environment, and indeed, around the "outside" of the portfolio system, but nevertheless affecting the strategic goals – and hence the strategic direction the organisation needs to move in to reach those goals: all as manifest by the composition and ongoing management of the portfolio. Martinsuo and Geraldi (2020) adopted an open systems model for the analysis of the way in which portfolios can be assessed as an organisation in themselves and how such an organisation is responsive to environmental factors.

The feedback loop measures where the organisation is deviating from its strategic plans to achieve the strategic objectives and provides inputs to the system to correct the deviation. Control is therefore central to the organisational system; it tries to ensure that the strategy – enacted in and through the portfolio – stays on course to meet its objectives. The deviation away from achieving the objectives can be caused by suboptimal strategic processes (poor strategy definition, for instance) or by positive or negative influences from the environment penetrating the permeable boundaries and affecting the processes or goal (poor productivity in the projects/programs, failures of technologies to perform as expected, market changes, political influence, poorly considered changes in strategic objectives, etc.).

Another fundamental characteristic of systems is that systems exist within systems – often in many levels of hierarchy. Think of air transport: aircraft engines exist within the bigger system of the aircraft and are controlled by that superordinate system; the aircraft has multiple systems within it (flight controls, power, fuel, air, the pilots, etc.); the aircraft operates within the air traffic control system, which itself is made up of multiple systems; the air traffic control system operates within national regulatory policies (e.g. Federal Aviation Authority in America, European Aviation Safety Agency in Europe, etc.), which then are coordinated through an overall seamless set of policies supervised by the International Civil Aviation Organization. In this example, the systems incorporate technical systems (engines, aircraft, etc.) and managerial systems (the regulatory authorities). Social systems could equally have been included – how the aviation industry operates within local, national, and international societal systems.

Managerial systems within systems

This *systems-within-systems* approach is applicable when looking at the managerial processes of vertically integrating strategy, through the portfolio, into programs and projects, and then further to work packages (referring back to Figure 2.3). To simplify the open systems diagram, we can signify the central box (*creative transformation*) as a "black box". This means we are not concerned with the "how" of the transformation that takes place within the black box and so can avoid an overly messy and complicated diagram. Now we can stack the open systems representation of the strategy-portfolio-program-project in a vertical hierarchy with Figure 9.4.

What is needed is a way of ensuring that the strategic objectives formulated in the strategy setting process flow accurately into the portfolio and that the strategies of the programs and projects created in the portfolio faithfully align to the achievement of the strategic objectives. In turn, the program and project strategies must be correctly turned into scopes of work that achieve project strategic objectives (and hence program objectives). The scopes of work for projects comprise the work packages, and so it should be possible to identify a clear line linking work package to project to program strategies to the strategic objectives of the organisation.

It is then clear that at each of these levels of management, there is a planning process, and it is this planning (and monitoring of progress) process that provides the basis for vertical integration. This process assures, as an example, alignment between objectives of work at different levels (between the portfolio and programs, between programs and projects, and within projects to align work packages).

At the next level of detail in the development of this system within a system, various critical processes in the project and portfolio control systems can be modelled. Figure 9.5 brings out several aspects of the integration processes. It shows how strategy, risk, and value are integrated vertically. The corporate strategy control and reporting processes define policy and procedure at the high level, regarding how, firstly, value will be managed, ensuring it is constantly under review and sought after at each level; secondly, risk will be identified, managed, escalated, and reported/tracked; and thirdly, strategy is transmitted into each level and used to determine correct scopes of work.

The diagram also identifies that at the portfolio level, there are two primary organisational roles. Firstly, the portfolio leadership is accountable for portfolio strategy (i.e. that the corporate strategy is correctly manifest in the portfolio strategy), including that the correct programs and projects are in the portfolio, and that the analysis of the portfolio reflects the strategic objectives set for the portfolio to achieve. Portfolio directors then manage the implementation of the portfolio strategy in the programs and projects, through various mechanisms, including resource allocation, monitoring program/project performance against portfolio expectations, and taking responsibility for value, risk management, and assurance at the portfolio/program/project interfaces.

Horizontal integration occurs across the "system-within-system" model, such that at each level the same (or adequately aligned) processes operate. Value and risk management can only be effective if these processes are carried out the same in each portfolio, each program within a portfolio, and each project within a program (and in a way that allows these processes to also suit large projects that are not programs). At the very least, consistently defined, presented, and transmitted information up and down the system requires that the same approach across the organisation to information tracking and reporting is happening in all the portfolio's programs and projects.

What this and other models show is an abstract overview of how the various components of the integration work together. The specifics of all these processes must be defined in a way that is consistent with the organisational culture, overarching strategic objectives, and environmental factors (users, regulators, owners, financiers, etc.). What is important in terms of integration is that there is a clear communication of principles on

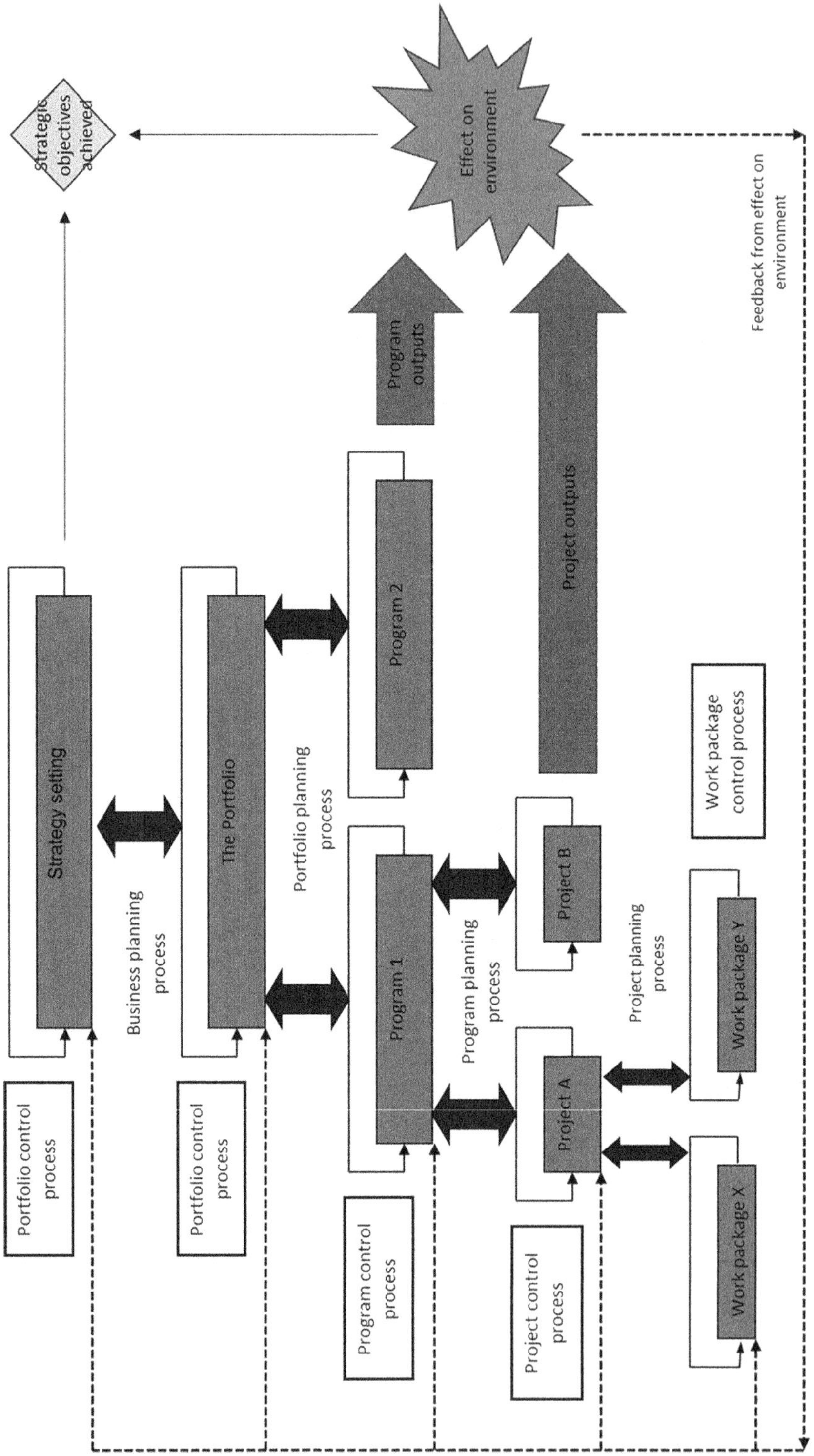

Figure 9.4 The hierarchical nature of work control systems for the implementation of strategy.

Source: Adapted from Harpum (2004).

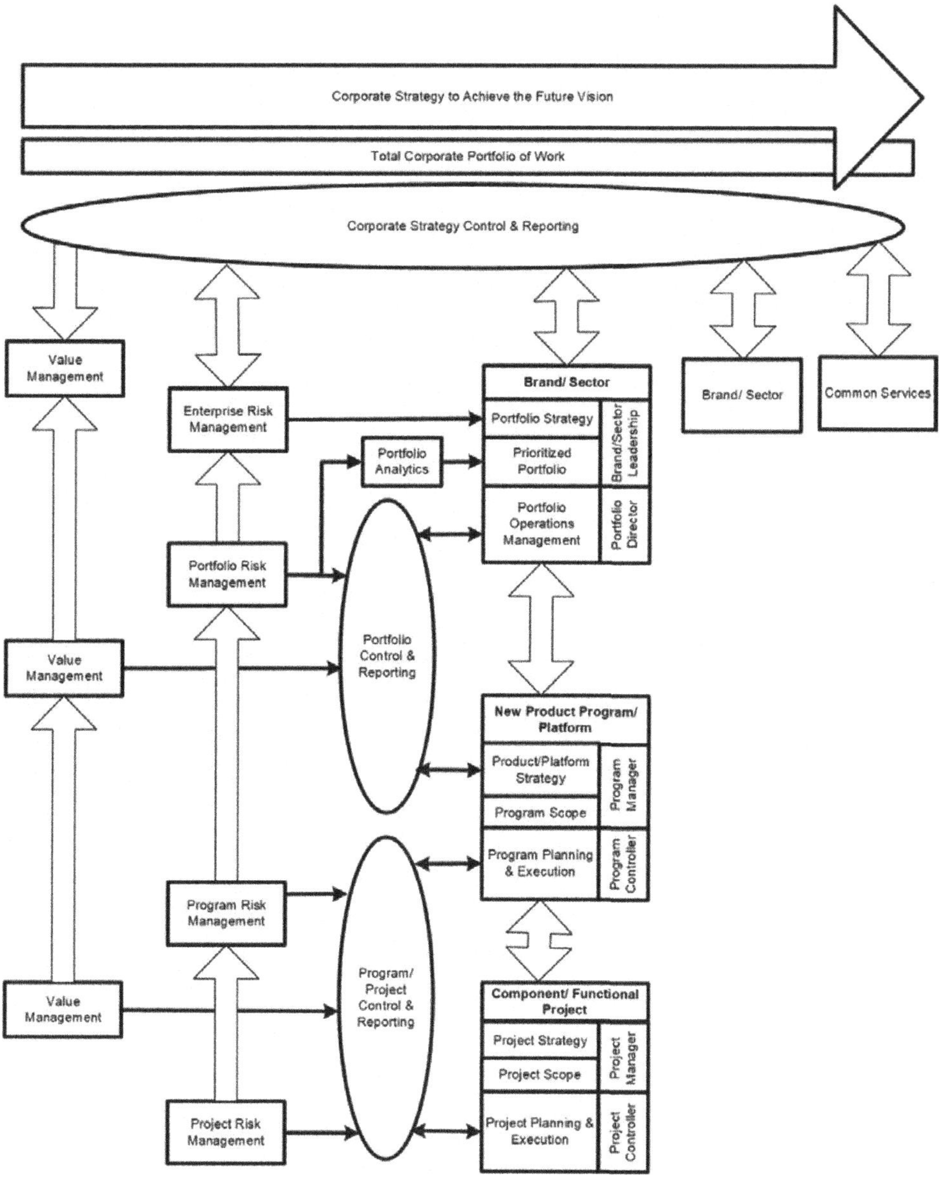

Figure 9.5 System-of-systems integration of portfolio management.

Source: Adapted from Harpum (2010).

decision-making, common processes (if even at a fundamental level, with different detail in process to match differing needs across the organisation), and that the topmost level of the portfolio (which is often not, in fact, put in place formally as the corporate book of work) maintains accountability for alignment through the sets of portfolios.

If there is no formal top-level portfolio, there is a real danger that the organisation will fail to coordinate the work in the various portfolios, and that programs and

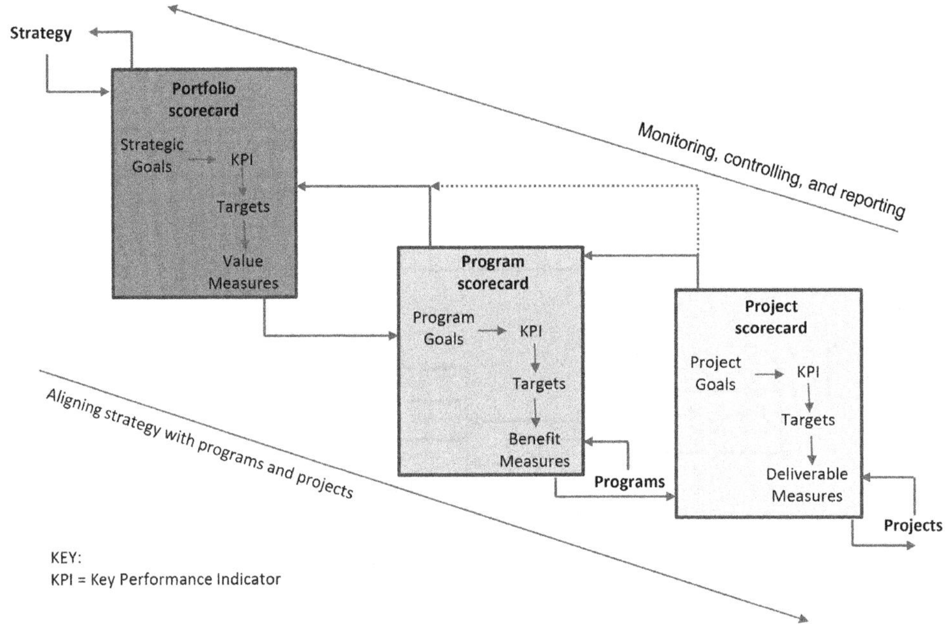

Figure 9.6 Linking strategy, information flow, and control processes for portfolios.

Source: Adapted from Lock and Wagner (2016).

projects across the business will fail to stay aligned to organisational strategy and will then begin to conflict with each other in terms of program/project objectives: and then the allocation of assets across the organisation becomes conflicted and subject to local power and not subject to the overall role of the portfolio function(s) to deliver strategic objectives.

A practical example of the way that it can be assured that strategic objectives are accurately cascaded down through the organisation is shown in Figure 9.6 (also referred to in Figure 2.5). Here it is clear that strategic goals, key performance indicators, targets, and measures of progress are aligned vertically and across the hierarchy.

Organisational project portfolio management

A crucial element of successful portfolio management is integrating the strategic portfolio within the organisation and business processes. Organisational project management (OPM), or enterprise project management, is a way of looking at and understanding how project management, as a method to manage the delivery of strategic objectives, is integrated into the organisation in which it exists. OPM was developed initially to understand how portfolios of programs and projects (definitionally temporary organisations) are integrated into the permanent organisation in which they reside, with an emphasis on processes and policies.

More recent work by Müller and colleagues (Müller et al., 2019) has expanded OPM into a normative model that includes many more aspects of portfolio, program, and project management (see the example in Figure 9.7). Their work has provided a better

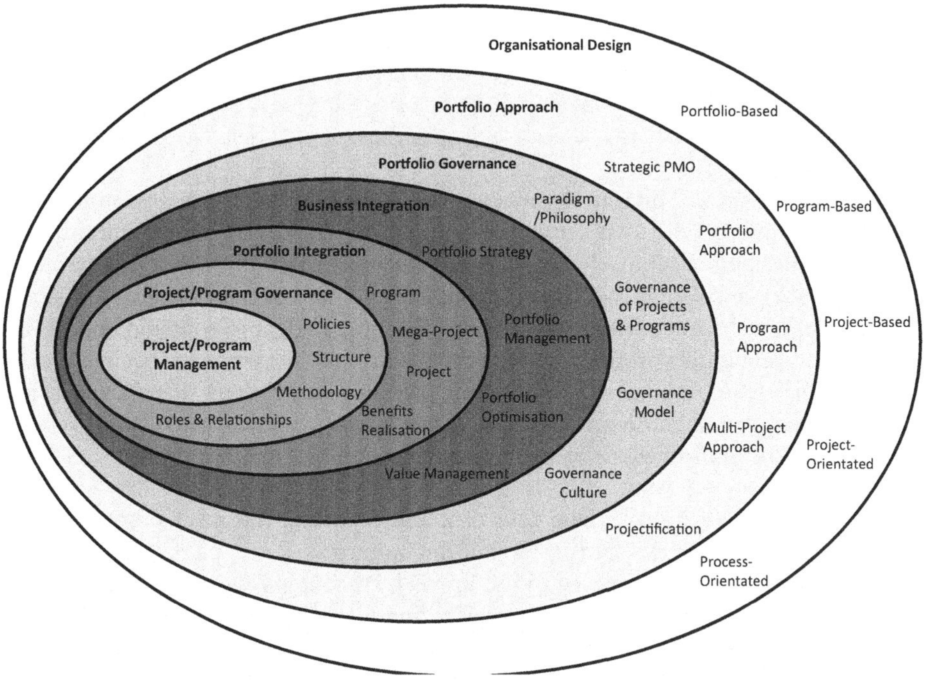

Figure 9.7 The onion model of portfolio management.

Source: Adapted from Müller et al. (2019).

understanding of the integration between various levels of the organisation. In this model each layer sets parameters in the next innermost layer by defining certain attributes that shape the elements in the next layer. They describe this as follows with regard to the business integration layer (comprising portfolio strategy, portfolio management, portfolio optimisation, and benefits realisation):

> [The OPM governance] layer explained governance of groups of projects to facilitate their effective management leading to the business integration layer. For example, a process-based governance paradigm and rule-based governance models are often associated with more numbers-driven portfolio strategies and optimization techniques. Contrarily, more outcome-related governance paradigms, principles-based governance models, and liberal and neo-liberal governmentality are often paired with more results-oriented portfolio strategies and more strategy-related optimization techniques and benefits sought after.
>
> (Müller et al., 2019, pp. 502–506)

This model of how project management works in organisations is based on contingency theory. Hence, the specifics of how, in this case, the way the elements within the business integration layer are designed, are contingent on the elements in the layer "above" it. In this model the four elements in the business integration layer are defined by Müller et al. (2019) as follows:

- *Portfolio strategy.* Defines what the project portfolio is expected to achieve and guides day-to-day management of the portfolio. It links project selection with the strategic objectives of the organisation.
- *Project portfolio management.* Informed by the portfolio strategy element and "*deals with the coordination and control of multiple projects pursing the same strategic goals and competing for the same resources, whereby managers prioritize among projects to achieve strategic benefits*" (Martinsuo, 2012).
- *Portfolio optimisation.* This is an element with widely varying approaches and meanings – that is, optimising what? Müller et al. cite Cooper et al. (2001) in defining three different optimisation approaches: value maximisation (typically financial), balancing (selection against several weighted parameters that are non-financial, such as risk, technology, etc.), and strategic alignment (allocating budget to strategic buckets and only allocating money from those buckets to work that fits within a specific bucket).
- *Value management.* Appropriate projects and programs are selected, shaped, and scoped to optimise their alignment with business needs, ensuring delivery of the associated benefits and cumulatively delivering strategic value.

In the OPM portfolio model, these four elements comprise the mechanism by which vertical integration is achieved at this level of the business.

Horizontal integration is achieved in this model by the interaction of the four elements above with each other. The portfolio strategy defines how the portfolio will be managed: how projects are selected, how resource allocation decisions are made, the rules governing project prioritisation, and the sets of rules for use at decision gates throughout the projects' life cycles. Portfolio strategy and portfolio management, in turn, influence and are iteratively related to the way in which the portfolio is optimised: optimisation to assure achievement of the strategic objectives also clearly requires that portfolio management rules are referenced in deciding which of the three optimisation approaches are used. Benefits realisation requires that project and program delivery is tracked to ensure that the desired benefits are constantly evaluated through the life cycle to assure that they will, in fact, be delivered, or adjustments made to the projects and programs to match achievable benefits to a changing environment, and hence, this feeds back into the portfolio strategy. Ensuring these four elements are tightly linked leads to effective performance of the organisation at the business integration layer.

The reality of integration

The various models described previously depend on the assumption that people will "follow the rules", that the processes themselves can adequately meet the challenges of integrating the strategy execution hierarchy, and that, broadly speaking, the organisation and its people will behave rationally. In reality, this simply doesn't happen.

> Strategy does not flow straight from conception to execution in an idealised trajectory so much as become enacted though numerous, recursive and reflexive enactments and translations. To be able to be creatively engaged in enactment, an organisation's design and personnel must allow for organisational agility, because objectives change as implementation proceeds in dynamic contexts and environments.
>
> (Clegg et al., 2018, p. 767)

Those creating strategy do not have perfect knowledge of the present and past, and obviously not the future either. Strategies are always based on the interpretation of the (insufficient) information available. The enactment of strategy into a portfolio of programs and projects is always a judgement call. The number of variations of sets of programs and projects that, it is hoped, will deliver the strategic objectives is certainly more than one! The finally selected set, and the management of that set thereafter, is influenced by peoples' perceptions, judgements, and less-than-complete information.

This non-rational reality occurs at every level of the hierarchy, as for instance when program managers strive to define and deliver strategy, aligned and linked to the strategic requirements set for them by the portfolio: "Projects rarely unfold according to plan: instead, they are translated in situ through practices enacted by leaders through negotiations, conflicts and improvisations" (Clegg et al., 2018). The use of tools in portfolio, program, and project management is another area in which non-rationality is encountered. Tools are used to do work – meaning, they are what is used in carrying out processes. Particularly at interfaces (or boundaries in systems language) between each level, tools are used for transferring information and for ensuring process compliance. However, tools are not "machines", and so, continue Clegg et al., "enable politics to be played by others means, by hampering shared meaning, particularly across hierarchical levels, by structuring and shaping information and legitimising powerful interest, obscuring when and how project portfolio decisions actually occur" (Clegg et al., 2018, p. 768).

In a very real sense then, formal processes that aim to vertically and horizontally integrate the execution of strategy, through a portfolio of programs and projects, are "necessary but insufficient". The reality of non-rational behaviour must be accounted for in managing the overall dynamics of the system, however imagined in the abstract and configured through the artefacts of management process. Of course, an alternative view is that assuming a rational-based view of organisations and the people in them is wholly irrational!

Emergent strategy

Although so far, the discussion has considered strategy as a top-down process, the systems model hints at the existence of emergent strategy – that is, strategy that emerges as the strategy is executed. As each level of the strategy execution hierarchy delivers outputs into the environment, the model includes the feedback loop (Figure 2.2) to take information on the deviation for the planned impact and feeds it back into the creative transformation processes (the project, the program, and the overall strategy-setting process). If this information is interrogated rather than simply used as an input to try to make the project create the original desired impact (which may well be something that is not possible, given the strategic objective of the project), it is possible to see alternative strategic objectives and ways of achieving modified objectives are possible. This is one basis in which emergent strategy may be initiated.

Emergent strategy also arises from the very process of carrying out the work at each level. Research identifies that the source of emergent strategy also includes portfolio, program and project planning, and the implementation of those plans, including resource allocation, autonomous strategic behaviour (by managers), and interactive strategic control systems (Kopmann et al., 2017). Planning to capture emergent strategy rather than leaving it to chance that strategic insight will be fed up the vertical hierarchy to change corporate strategy is a relatively new idea, despite Mintzberg (see Chapter 2) having identified the concept in the 1980s. Nevertheless, the evidence of the ability to build processes that are designed to capture emergent strategy is clear. Kopmann et al. (2017) found that strategic controls in portfolio management "can play a positive role in enhancing emerging strategy recognition, and in turn in enhancing project portfolio success."

Strategic portfolio controls are essentially the topic that is being discussed in this chapter and which are demonstrated in the several figures so far presented. How the controls and processes are designed and integrated into the overall hierarchical system depends on the specifics (the contingencies) of the particular environment of the organisation. Additionally, the real non-rational aspects of the way the system's hierarchy delivers strategy must be fully built into the system design – typically meaning that flexibility is needed in terms of compliance.

The importance of moving beyond a belief that strategy can be simply formulated and cascaded down for flawless implementation is underlined by case studies of the real world. In contrast to Teller et al. (2012), who identified that increased formalisation leads to increased portfolio success, Young et al. (2012) find that the instability of the environment in which projects are delivering strategic objectives, and the difficulty of predicting the future environment, means "[s]trategy formulators are therefore often not fully informed and the environment is too unstable to implement plans without frequent reformulation". Young et al. (2012) see that:

> Project manager's perspectives on strategy are largely focussed around the concept of aligning the project with a pre-existing documented strategic plan . . . project and portfolio managers have a passive role in formulating strategy and there is little or no recognition of the entrepreneurial role they must play in adapting strategy to emergent events.

These researchers found that best practice project management and investment frameworks in the state of Victoria (Australia) were not preventing serious failures to implement state strategies. They believed that systemic deficiencies in the best practice program and portfolio governance processes (which were enacted in their state "system of systems" to execute strategy) are likely to be the cause. The biggest area of integration failure, however, did not seem to be that between the portfolio and the programs, but "a failure to clarify how individual projects contribute towards strategic goals" (Young et al., 2012, p. 889).

One implication that can be drawn from this is that program and project integration processes need to better reflect the instability of the environment, through more effective feedback loops, with program and project managers confident to work more flexibly whilst fostering emergent strategic thinking. The overall system must be integrated with an acceptance that strategy is rarely able to be executed exactly as it was planned. Therefore, the management system integration must be designed in such a way that unstable and messy reality is the starting point rather than a nicely ordered world in which it is possible to formulate and execute strategy predominantly driven top down.

Defining integration processes

Described so far is that what is critical for integration is not the specifics of how each aspect of portfolio management is set up for a particular organisation but how effectively the processes are linked vertically. This is a matter both of process/structural design and effective behaviours. The best-designed processes and structures cannot bring the intended value to integration if people cannot or will not use the processes as designed. The degree

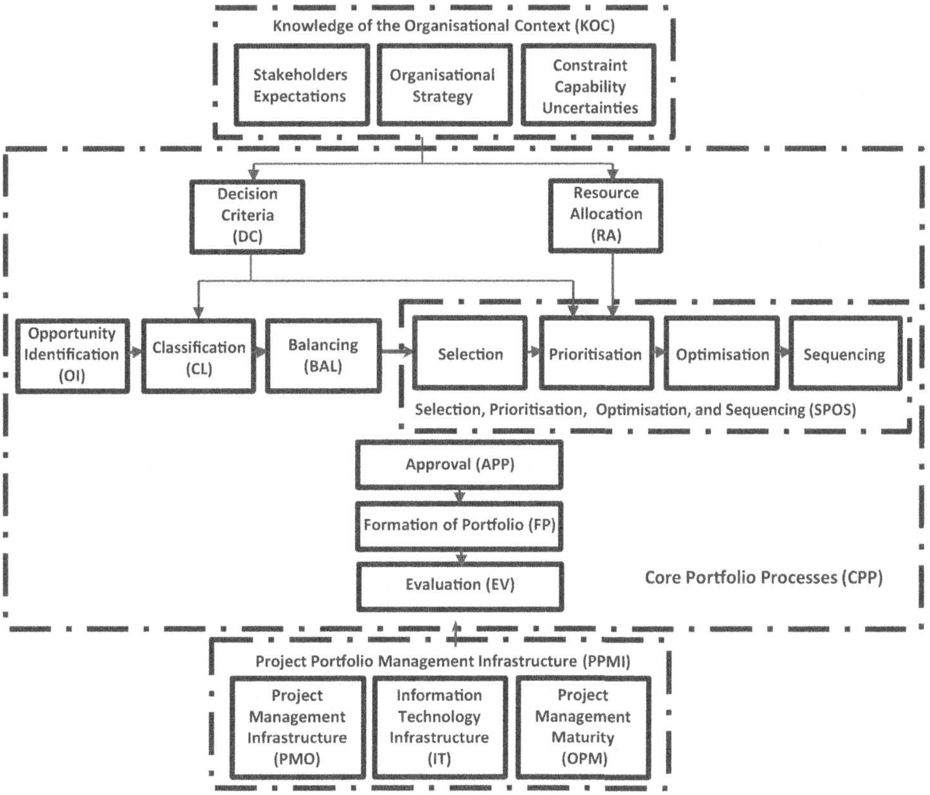

Figure 9.8 Core processes in portfolio management.

Source: Adapted from Padovani and Carvalho (2016).

of choice available to people in organisations to follow process varies, depending on many factors, but particularly, for example, culture around use (and misuse) of power (Lukes, 2021). Some sectors with a need for very highly qualified specialists struggle the most with process compliance – because failure to adhere to process brings little to no consequence for an individual. These people are needed too much by the organisation to fire them, and so process is suboptimally enacted, but with the pay-off of maintaining motivated staff that feel empowered in their disregard for management processes.

But what are the full set of core processes? As recently as 2016, it was still possible to state that "there is still a lack of consensus on which are the core processes of project portfolio management" (Padovani & Carvalho, 2016). They identified from research the processes that could be considered to comprise portfolio management (see Figure 9.8). This diagram presents much more detail of what happens inside the "black box" or creative transformation than the open systems model works with. The abstract models presented earlier by Harpum and Müller et al. are filled in, at the portfolio level at least, and the vertical connections are identified from strategy to the portfolio, and the portfolio to the project organisation. A fuller discussion of this model is included in Chapter 11. Risk does seem to be a rather-obvious missing process.

Integration of fundamental processes

Having discussed the importance of vertical integration, this section provides a high-level view of the fundamental work that the portfolio needs to undertake in order to show how the processes are integrated vertically.

Defining the work needed to deliver strategic objectives

The portfolio process creates a set of projects (and, if necessary, programs) that will deliver the strategic objectives of the organisation, following a strategic approach defined by strategists working in the organisation. The portfolio may also include all the operational activities, although the need for this is logically doubtful. (Operations are steady state, doing the intended work of the organisation. Strategic objectives are about getting to a new place beyond the current steady state – the argument is, therefore, that the portfolio contains work that brings about change. If operations need to change, then that work of change is included in the portfolio, not the operations work itself.) The process of correctly defining the specific work needed in the portfolio is covered in other parts of this book.

The integration aspect to ensure the programs, projects, and indeed, work packages are correctly developed to ensure the strategic objectives are assured is about confirming, at each level, that strategic objectives are correctly set. This is in fact an aspect of program and project management that is frequently overlooked or insufficiently emphasised. The mechanism to assure this process happens is to firstly ensure clear and accurate strategic information is given to the program and project managers. That these people understand the strategic goals is vital – one-way communication of the information is insufficient. The portfolio management function must work closely with the program/project managers to be certain that strategic objectives are clearly understood, and understood in the context of the organisational strategy. See Figure 9.9 for an example of how strategy can be cascaded. Morris and Jamieson (2003) also provide multiple models in which strategy is turned into programs and projects.

With this strategic portfolio-level understanding, the program/project managers are then able to formulate, with their stakeholders and specialist teams, strategic objectives that will deliver all, or a correctly identified part of, the specified organisational strategic goal for which the program/project exists to achieve. This is likely to be an iterative process and should, in most situations, involve the creation of multiple alternative strategies (see next subsection). A program/project strategy-creation process is required, and this must be developed in collaboration with the portfolio function.

The process finally must also include a review, where the programs/projects present the proposed strategies (and alternatives) to the portfolio function (and other senior leaders if they are not already included in the portfolio management team) for review and approval. This interaction allows the thinking behind the program/project strategy and objectives to be exposed, and tested for accuracy of the translation of organisational strategic objectives into work that contributes directly (and only) to those objectives. The presentation of alternative program/project strategies allows for a rich insight to be generated on how the portfolio mix of programs and projects may be optimised to take account of uncertainty and internal asset allocation to the work.

As the program/project proceeds along its life cycle, the strategy is brought before the portfolio function at regular intervals, typically ensured by the organisation's stage gate control process for programs and projects. In this way, the correct formulation of program/project strategy is tested and validated over time. It also allows for changes in organisational

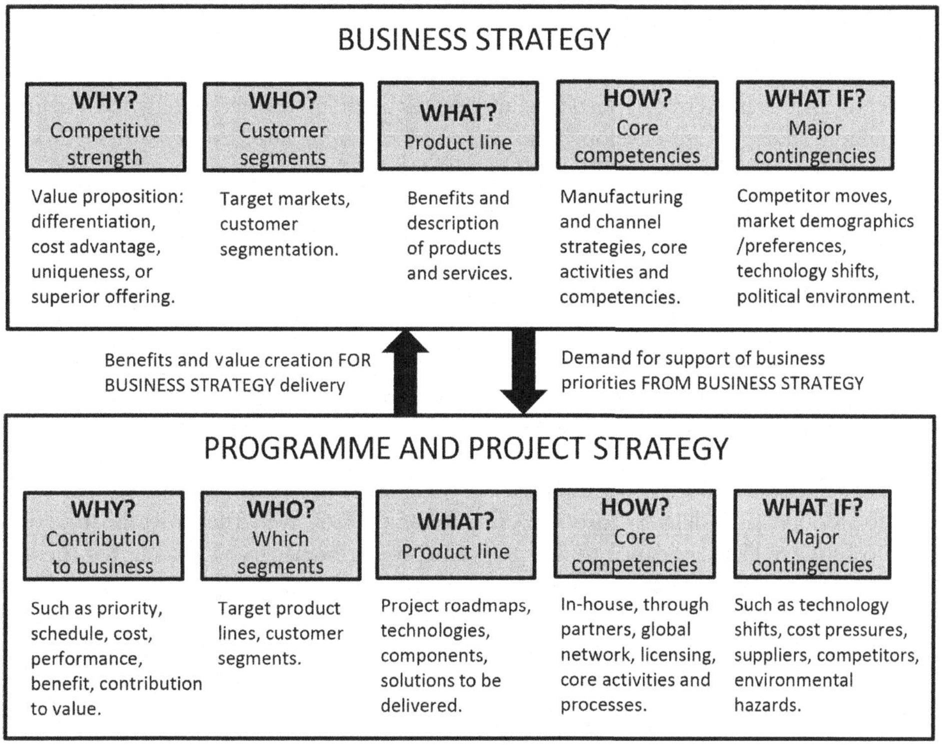

Figure 9.9 Strategic cascade model based on five questions.

Source: Adapted from Loch and Kavadias (2012).

strategy to be reflected in program/project strategy and may mean the portfolio function decides to change, remove, or indeed, add scope to the programs/projects. As mentioned in the introductory section of the chapter, the important difference in the process expounded here and in other literature is that the strategic alignment process is, by definition, a top-down process. The portfolio function is *accountable* for correct translation of strategic intent down through the hierarchy of programs and projects – this is not a program/project management accountability. Nevertheless, it is the program/project managers that are *responsible* for building correctly "strategised" programs and projects. They also have a responsibility to feed information upwards that helps identify emergent strategy.

Portfolio optimisation

Setting up a portfolio of work to achieve a set of strategic objectives is inevitably a process of compromise. Trade-offs are essential between usage of internal assets, interactions between the programs and projects (including dependencies between them), uncertainty in the external and internal environments, and attempts to manage risks associated with the specific programs and projects. The process of optimisation of the portfolio is discussed elsewhere in the book, and this section is about how to ensure portfolio optimisation is possible and can be achieved effectively. In order to understand what trade-offs are possible within the set of work defined in the portfolio, it is desirable to have available from all the programs and projects multiple strategic options for delivering their objectives. This is the integration mechanism that supports portfolio optimisation, noted in the preceding section.

The processes defined by the portfolio function for program/project strategy must require that multiple strategies are developed and may also offer guidance on how these various strategies should be structured. This will be different for each organisation, although the type of work carried out by the firm is likely to have a strong influence on what type of alternatives the programs/projects should investigate when defining alternative strategies. For example, in fast-moving new product development businesses, alternative strategies for getting products to market quickly are likely to be important (e.g. fast to a single market, slower to several markets simultaneously, slower but to all markets at the same time). In industries where safety is critical, alternative strategies to ensure a safe product are likely to be relevant (e.g. different ways to protect patients from adverse effects of medical devices, alternative approaches to ensure safety of aircraft operations).

The relevant issues that alternative program/project strategies need to take account of may seem rather obvious, depending on the organisation's main "products" (whatever assets it produces and delivers into the environment). However, the portfolio function needs to produce clear guidance to the program/project managers to ensure that there is uniformity of thinking on the types of alternatives that are required by portfolio management, to allow effective optimisation of the portfolio to be achieved. If there is little or no coherence in the way alternative strategies are defined, it becomes impossible to make comparisons across the set of programs/projects in the portfolio, and hence optimisation is seriously hampered.

It is worth noting that program managers must have accountability for ensuring that projects in their program also create multiple strategic options, and that these are considered when defining the final program. This aspect of optimising a program's strategy by optimising its constituent's projects strategies (by insisting the projects all create multiple strategic options for program-level consideration) is barely mentioned in the program management literature. The portfolio management function must ensure this process happens.

Optimisation of internal asset allocation (resource allocation)

The effective and efficient allocation of internal assets to the work to deliver strategy is critical; hence, the vital role that the portfolio management function plays in ensuring that asset allocation is optimised across the organisation. The organisational structures, power distribution, management processes all impact on asset allocation. Power over asset allocation can reside in many places, and understanding how the overall "system" works is critical in developing asset allocation processes. Functional matrix; weak, balanced, and strong matrix; and pure project organisations all share asset allocation power and authority differently, with widely varying stakeholders having inputs and influence on the process. As with previous sections in this chapter, we are not concerned here with the specifics for any particular organisation but with the general needs for integration to support effective allocation.

The most important information required by the organisation in decision-making about asset allocation is:

1. The absolute importance of a program or project to achieving strategic goals – for example, is a particular program/project mission critical? Will failure to achieve the strategic objective mean the organisation does not survive?

2. The relative importance of programs and projects in relation to each other – for example, of several new product development projects, which are more important? Which are less so?

Transparency of the decision-making process about asset allocation is vital so that people throughout the business (certainly in managerial positions) understand why assets have been allocated to certain programs/projects, and the decision criteria that those decisions were based on. The decision criteria for program/project inclusion in the portfolio, and relative priority of them, are discussed elsewhere in this book (Chapter 12) – the point here is that the criteria must be accepted by the organisation, which is a communication and often negotiation process and activity when agreeing the criteria, and the application of the criteria is made transparent and communicated.

Tracking of the allocation, and ongoing use of assets, against the programs and projects is highly beneficial in allowing the efficiency of the portfolio to be monitored, and control decisions made/remade where necessary. This reporting must flow upwards through the entire organisation, from work packages (where, in fact, the vast majority of the assets are actually allocated – the work packages create the outputs, after all!) to the projects, programs, and into the portfolio. Once again, this means the portfolio function should be accountable for the effectiveness of the asset allocation decision and tracking processes, with program and project managers responsible for accurate reporting of asset usage, and for maintaining maximum efficiency of asset allocation – where assets are no longer needed, the program/project managers should release the assets immediately.

The way in which the portfolio function interacts with operations' allocation of assets depends entirely on the specifics of the organisation. Where the majority of the assets employed in a business are in operations work (e.g. a bank), probably in a functional or weak matrix structure, the portfolio is likely to have relatively limited influence over final asset allocations. In organisations where the raison d'être is to deliver a portfolio of programs/projects (e.g. new product development–driven organisations or construction firms), the portfolio will have a strong and direct contribution to allocation decisions, since the firm's financial success is dependent on effective and efficient allocation of assets to the portfolio. Once again, what is important is that this is understood clearly when developing and managing the portfolio function, to ensure the integration processes are fit for purpose.

Managing risk

Risk impacts on the portfolio from two directions: from the impact of risks in the environment affecting the viability of strategic goals and the strategy devised to achieve them, and from the risks associated with the ability to execute the strategy, via the portfolio of programs and projects (see Chapter 17). Integration of the way risk is managed must then deal with risks flowing both down the structures, from strategy to programs/projects via the portfolio, and upwards, from projects and programs to the portfolio (and indeed the impact of risks of execution on the viability of the strategic goals that are intended to be achieved).

Integration and management of downward-flowing risk is achieved firstly by the creation of various scenarios in which programs and projects can successfully plan. A *scenario* is a description of a possible future environment, and the creation of scenarios for an organisation to consider is strategic work. Defining scenarios ensures that strategic goals and the strategy for achieving them are rooted in a clear sense of what the possible futures could be for the organisation (refer back to Chapter 5, dedicated to scenario planning as a strategic activity). Understanding how risks may impact the organisation in this way allows the portfolio function to provide to programs and projects the relevant scenario for which they should define their strategies. Different strategies will be needed to deliver strategic goals in different scenarios. Hence, the downward setting of expected risks is managed.

As risks becomes certain – real life happens in the environment – the impacts on the organisation's strategic goals and strategy can be assessed, and adjustments made in the goals/strategy. These changes will impact the portfolio: programs and projects will need to be adjusted (or cancelled, and/or new programs/projects added to the portfolio) to account for the change. For relatively slow changes, the normal program/project life cycle (stage gate) process can be utilised to maintain alignment. The implication, of course, is that program/project strategy is always assessed/reassessed in the stage gate process. Where change is needed to maintain alignment, revised program/project strategies need to be revalidated within the portfolio function.

Where change is often faster within the environment and the portfolio must be able to respond quickly, a process must be put in place to track changes in the environment and quick assessments made of the viability of current program/project strategies, with speedy responses from programs/projects to changes in strategy. This also implies other portfolio processes must be agile and responsive – reprioritisation of programs/projects and reallocation of internal assets must be highly responsive to change.

Risks that flow upwards from the impact of reality-hitting program/project plans as they are executed are managed through the process of risk management at the program/project level. Once again, the specifics of how risk is managed are not particularly important for integration, but what is important is that the risks associated with program/project execution are transparent to the portfolio.

The escalation and reporting aspects of risk management from programs/projects need to ensure the most important risks are reported upwards so that an integrated view is possible across the entire portfolio. The complete set of execution risks can then be assessed, and control actions checked, where these are put in place by program/project managers. It is also likely that overarching portfolio-level control actions need to be put in place, typically to manage, for example, very significant risk that requires portfolio-level or other senior management input, or category risks that are better managed in a coordinated manner for all programs/projects at the portfolio level. This process relies on a robust risk management process at program and project levels, rigorously applied, with accurate reporting upwards, and effective escalation for control action where needed.

Conclusion

This chapter has focused on the importance of integrating the work of strategy execution – that is, the set of processes starting with defining strategy, operationalising it in the portfolio as a set of programs and projects, and ensuring that these strategic objectives are accurately translated into program and project strategies. The chapter provided an overview of the rationale behind taking a system-of-systems approach to strategy execution. Abstract models are described that lead to the development of more detailed and practice-based sets of integrated processes. Finally, a high-level view of how the fundamental portfolio processes are integrated is discussed. The following chapters in this section will further develop these higher-level views.

References

Cherns A. (1993) Principles of socio-technical design. in Trist E. & Murray H. *The Social Engagement of Social Science*. Vol 2. The University of Pennsylvania Press.

Clegg S., Killen C., Biesenthal C. & Sankaran S. (2018) Practices, projects and portfolios: Current research trends and new directions. *International Journal of Project Management* 36(5), 762–772.

Cooper R., Edgett S. & Kleinschmidt E. (2001) *Portfolio Management for New Products*. Second Edition. Basic books.

Emery F. (1993) Characteristics of Socio-Technical Systems. in Trist E. & Murray H. *The Social Engagement of Social Science, Vol. II: The Socio-Technical perspective*. University of Pennsylvania Press.

Harpum P. (2004) Project control. in Morris PWG. & Pinto, J. *The Wiley Guide to the Management of Projects*. Wiley.

Harpum P. (2010) *Portfolio, Program, and Project Management in the Pharmaceutical and Biotechnology Industries*. Wiley.

Kopmann J., Kock A., Killen C. & Gemünden H. (2017) The role of project portfolio management in fostering both deliberate and emergent strategy. *International Journal of Project Management* 35(4), 557–570.

Loch C. & Kavadias S. (2012) Implementing strategy through projects. in Morris P., Pinto J. & Soederlund J. *The Oxford Handbook of Project Management*. Oxford University Press.

Lock D. & Wagner R. (2016) *Gower Handbook of Program Management*. Routledge.

Lukes S. (2021) *Power: A Radical View*. Third Edition. Macmillan International.

Martinsuo M. (2012) Project portfolio management in practice and in context. *International Journal of Project Management* 31(2), 794–803.

Martinsuo M. & Geraldi J. (2020) Management of project portfolios: Relationships of project portfolios with their contexts. *International Journal of Project Management* 38(7), 441–453.

Morris P. & Jamieson A. (2003) *Translating Corporate Strategy into Project Strategy: Realizing Corporate Strategy through Project Management*. Project Management Institute.

Morris P. & Pinto J. (2004) *The Wiley Guide to the Management of Projects*. Wiley.

Müller R., Drouin N. & Sankaran S. (2019) Modelling organizational project management. *Project Management Journal* 50(4), 499–513.

Padovani M. & Carvalho M. (2016) Integrated PPM process: Scale development and validation. *International Journal of Project Management* 34(4), 627–642.

Teller J., Unger B., Kock A. & Gemünden H. (2012) Formalization of project portfolio management: The moderating role of project portfolio complexity. *International Journal of Project Management* 30(5), 596–607.

Young R., Young M., Jordan E. & O'Connor P. (2012) Is strategy being implemented through projects? Contrary evidence from a leader in new public management. *International Journal of Project Management* 30(8), 887–900.

10 Environmental factors and portfolio management capabilities

Pete Harpum

Introduction

This chapter sets out, firstly, to identify the relevant environmental aspects that impact on and, in turn, are influenced by portfolio management and, secondly to look at the capabilities required for effective portfolio management.

It is a reasonably established truism that "organisations do not exist in a vacuum. They are part of a large number of complex interrelated systems such as the social system, the economic system, etc." (Aubry et al., 2007). Contingency theory has long determined that to be effective, portfolio structures and processes (the portfolio organisation) must be designed according to the environment in which they exist (Cherns, 1993). Much work, based on contingency theory, has been done researching the design of all aspects of portfolio management. Amongst many others, Müller and colleagues note that "project-based organisations need idiosyncratic organisational designs, which are resilient to constant change" (Müller et al., 2019, p. 500). This means that each portfolio management organisation must be designed to suit the unique characteristics of its environment.

Portfolios as systems-within-systems

Open systems theory, described in some detail in Chapter 9, again provides a helpful starting point in thinking about how the creative transformation process of portfolio management can be understood. Drawing on several strands of theory, Harpum (1998) combines an open systems model based on Jackson's anthropological perspective (Jackson, 1993), Walker's model of macroeconomic factors (Walker, 1996), and Porter's microeconomic analysis of competitive forces (Porter, 1998) to assess organisational fitness for purpose (Figure 10.1).

Logically, if we accept the premise that open systems have porous boundaries (what is outside and what is inside affect each other in a reciprocal manner), influence must flow both ways through the boundaries. External factors are impacted by changes in the transformation process, as well as from the outputs from the creative process (here, the portfolio processes). Inevitably, then, "the need for structural change . . . arises from the substandard performance that comes from the mismatch of structure and contingency (their contextual elements)" (Müller et al., 2019, p. 501). Indeed, it is clear that an effective portfolio management process is, by definition, intended to impact on several of these elements: competitors, intermediaries (e.g. the chain delivering products to market), clients (and users), shareholders, suppliers, and perhaps economic behaviour of the market. Other elements may be less easily impacted but nevertheless will be so.

DOI: 10.4324/9780367853129-12

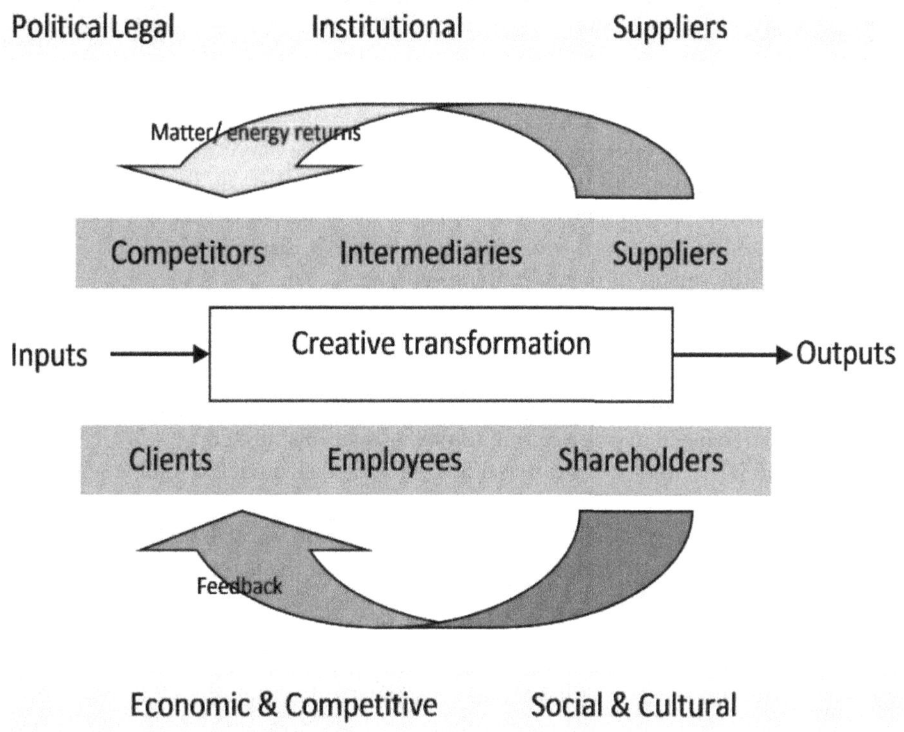

Figure 10.1 The macro and micro environmental factors in the organisational system.

Source: Adapted from Harpum (1998).

In brief, and by way of context setting for the remainder of this chapter, the macro factors are outlined as follows, the model often referred to as the PESTLE or PEST in marketing analysis:

- *Political.* Political forces are essentially those which are influenced by government policy either directly or indirectly. For example, governments of all countries use national construction industries as a significant control on such issues as unemployment and government expenditure. The provision of infrastructure to facilitate services such as healthcare is another, perhaps more indirect political activity in the environment. In essence, the political forces will be shaped primarily by a government's political ideology. The effects of global or quasi-global institutions may also be a major factor.
- *Legal.* The legal environment is closely related to the political environment since government enacts statutory legislation. Political ideology in many parts of the world is also a strong influence on common law. Legal factors in the environment will affect both the relationships of the overall organisation with the environment and the way in which the portfolio management structure and processes are designed.

- *Institutional.* These are forces that are due to institutions in the environment and may affect issues such as behaviour of members of these groups and rules of conduct. These are likely to include professional institutions, industrial associations, and the context of the organisation, for example, the corporate regulators of for-profit organisations, the regulators of charities for not-for-profit organisations and NGOs, etc.
- *Economic and competitive.* These factors are also dependent to a great extent on the political forces in the environment. They will influence client demand, the type and extent of competition, and the potential profit margins that can be earned. The economic and competitive environment will also affect the micro factors greatly. Pressures generated by macroeconomic forces will have a major impact on the strategic and operational aspects of portfolio management.
- *Social and cultural.* The effect of these forces within the system's environment is a key consideration. These factors influence the way the portfolio organisation is designed – who is involved in design decisions, the power allocated to the portfolio process and those managing portfolios, and also whether a decision-making process is capable of being operationalised in practice due to power relationships, etc.
- *Technological.* The rapid technological advances that characterise much of the business environment in all markets create huge forces for change within the system. The increasingly fast rate of market creation and destruction is attributable directly to the introduction of new and improved technologies. Most organisations are highly susceptible to these pressures to produce ever more added-value outputs, however that value is measured.

The micro factors are more straightforward to understand, although the analysis of them when designing portfolio management requires no less effort and insight: the competitive environment clearly must be understood; how the supply chain in the sector and, specifically, for the organisation is structured and operating is important to understand; where intermediaries and agents exist, how their role affects the way the portfolio needs to work; the specific factors needed to be taken into account regarding employees (education, culture, expectations, etc.); and how the technology of the sector affects decision-making and project selection criteria.

The open systems model combined with contingency theory then provides a way of getting a high-level oversight of the environmental elements that are in a reciprocal relationship with portfolio management structures and processes. More recently than Harpum, Martinsuo and Geraldi (2020) rely on an open systems model of the portfolio as an organisation in itself within the parent organisation to reflect on ways of theorising about the environmental interactions of portfolios with their environments (Figure 10.2). The diagram indicates more than one external context (environment) impacting on a given portfolio and clearly shows the permeable boundaries between successive systems-within-systems, making explicit the bidirectional influence of environmental factors.

A thorough analysis of portfolio management design and its impact on, and reaction to, the environment would take far more space than this book allows for. Nevertheless, several studies provide evidence of what needs to be considered in detail with regard to the environment of a portfolio management organisation. The annex to this chapter has a tabulation by Martinsuo and Geraldi (2020) of future academic research ideas for portfolio management. (Note here that Martinsuo and Geraldi look to extend the methodological research theories beyond contingency theory, which they see as limiting, proposing other

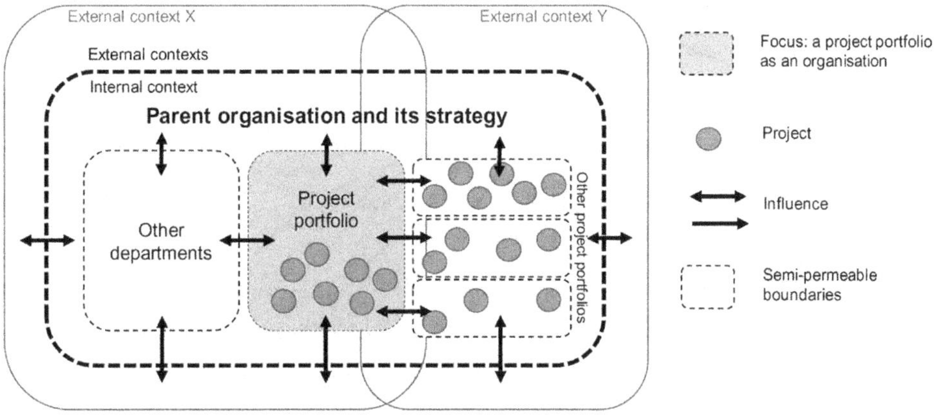

Figure 10.2 Project portfolios within the context of their organisation (Martinsuo & Geraldi, 2020).

theoretical viewpoints as being useful and relevant for future researchers to use in this field: institutional theory, stakeholder management theory, resource dependency theory, and sensemaking theory.)

In fact, this provides an effective high-level perspective of multiple different lenses through which the design of portfolio management can be considered in relation to the environmental factors of the organisation. The ideas in the annex can be used as a template against which to analyse the environment and strategic drivers of portfolio management when looking for a holistic assessment of these factors to ensure the design is fit for purpose to achieve the strategic objectives of the organisation.

Returning to the organisational project management (OPM) onion model introduced in Chapter 9 (Figure 9.7), but this time investigating the outer layers (the outer systems-within-systems) to understand the environment, the following three aspects that determine the environment are identified: organisational design, the portfolio approach, and the portfolio governance approach (Figure 10.3).

Organisational design is shaped by the market the organisation delivers into, the purpose of the organisation itself (what it makes and does, and for whom), and the cultural factors that exist in this marketplace, both outside the organisation and within it (people tend to work in sectors that fit their personal characteristics – called "self-selection for employment"). Müller et al. (2019) identify three predominant types of organisations that are determined by the market environment (hence defining their purpose): process-orientated, project-orientated, and project-based. These types reflect the extent to which the organisation sees projects as the default way of delivering strategy.

- *Process-orientated.* "[A]re typically structured by functional lines and work is done in permanent organizational entities in pursuance of production processes. This is beneficial in relatively stable markets, for mass production, and building of economies of scale. Projects in these organisations are few and mainly undertaken to optimize production in terms of costs or other economic measures."
- *Project-oriented.* "[A]re typical for more dynamic markets. Management decides to run the business by projects, even though a process orientation would also be possible.

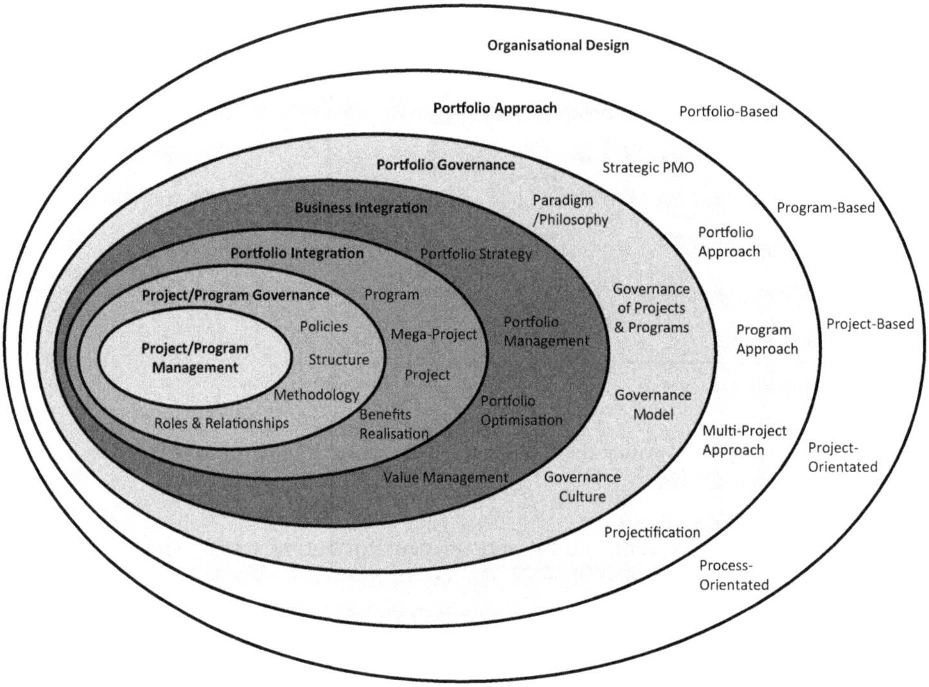

Figure 10.3 The onion model of portfolio management.

Source: Adapted from Müller et al. (2019).

These organizations consider management by project as their strategy. They use temporary organizations as a strategic choice for value delivery to clients. These organisations empower their employees and use flat structures and strong customer orientation to achieve competitive advantage."

- *Project-based.* "[A]re required by the nature of their deliverables to work in projects. Their unit of production is projects, which brings about the need for project-specific control systems and associated higher transaction costs . . . the more project-oriented/based the organizational form, the more innovative and flexible organizations are in their response to customer requirements. However, this reduces their ability for efficient task execution, building economies of scale, and promotion of organization-wide learning."

(Müller et al., 2019, p. 504)

The way the organisation understands itself in its market and cultural environment shapes the next level in the organisation, the portfolio approach, which is described in terms of the strategies employed in designing the portfolio itself. Again, Müller et al. (2019) have four approaches:

- *Multi-project strategy.* "[O]rganizations accept any project they can get, neither the resources are necessarily shared nor are the objectives aligned across projects. Project personnel is hired when a project gets awarded and made redundant when the project ends."

- *Program strategy*. "[O]rganizations prefer projects that contribute to higher level objectives, such as program objectives. This often implies that project goals interlink, but resources cannot be shared across projects."
- *Portfolio strategy*. "[O]rganisations prefer projects that predominantly use their existing employees. Hence, the resources are shared, but project objectives might vary."
- *Hybrid strategy*. "[O]rganisations balance the program and portfolio strategies in an attempt to maximize both utilization of existing resources and accomplishment of higher-level objectives."

(Müller et al., 2019, p. 504)

The link between market environment shaping the philosophical approach to how an organisation thinks about projects in relation to how it delivers strategy is then clearly linked directly to how that organisation chooses programs and projects, which defines the portfolio process (since the portfolio translates organisational strategic objectives into programs and projects to deliver those objectives).

The final layer that is strongly influenced by the environment (the other layers are, too, but less so going further "into" the onion) is portfolio governance. Whilst the role of governance is significant in shaping various aspects of how portfolio, programs, and projects are structured, set up, and operationalised, perhaps the most critical impact it has, that influences all the other aspects, is the paradigm adopted by governance – shaped and motivated by the portfolio strategy. Müller et al.'s four paradigms are:

- *Conformist*. "[E]xemplifies organizations with a shareholder orientation (as opposed to a stakeholder orientation) with strict behaviour control of the project manager (i.e. process compliance), in an attempt to lower overall project costs."
- *Flexible economist*. "[E]xemplifies shareholder-oriented organizations with a control focus toward expected outcomes. Here the aim is also to keep project costs low, but through careful selection of project management methodologies."
- *Versatile artist*. "[E]xemplifies organizations with a stakeholder focus and output control. These organizations balance the multitude of requirements stemming from the many different stakeholders of the organization's projects. Hence their focus is more on value creation than lowering costs."
- *Agile pragmatist*. "[E]xemplifies stakeholder orientation and controlling by process compliance, in order to maximize the usability and business value of a project's product, through a time-phased approach to product release of functionality over a period of time."

(Müller et al., 2019, p. 505)

These varying paradigms directly set the parameters and expectations of the management structures and processes of portfolio management in the specific circumstances of each organisation – the "idiosyncratic" designs referred to earlier. Portfolio management designs that attempt to ensure the organisation executes its strategy through a set of programs and projects that meet the strategic need and that are managed at the portfolio level in a way that matches the environmental contingencies most effectively. Ultimately, these environmental factors, informed by the philosophical orientation of the organisation through to the governance paradigms, must be responded to accurately to ensure the strategic objectives are achieved.

Portfolios as complex adaptive systems

Complexity science has become a central concern of research into project management for over 20 years, with Baccarini's (1996) seminal paper spearheading a huge research effort, and many papers and books published on the subject. The research has encompassed portfolio management as well and helps identify important aspects of the environment that need to be considered when designing portfolio management.

In combination with systems theory, complexity theory defines the idea of complex adaptive systems – systems that adapt to the effects of complexity in their environment, as well as the effects of complexity within the system being analysed, in this case.

> Complexity theory can be defined broadly as the study of how order, structure, pattern, and novelty arise from extremely complicated, apparently chaotic systems and conversely, how complex behaviour and structure merges from simple underlying roles. As such, it includes other areas of study that are collectively known as chaos theory, and non-linear dynamical theory.
>
> (Cicmil et al., 2009, p. 22)

In order to make sense of this set of ideas, to allow practical action to be taken, the components of a complex adaptive system can be identified and then used as the basis for reflection on, and design of, the portfolio organisation. Aritua et al. (2009) outline the main characteristics of these components and what they mean for the realisation of effective portfolio management, as follows, and with Figure 10.4:

- *Inter-relationships.* "The concept of inter-relationships or inter-relatedness . . . implies that in a system, individual components affect each other and influence actions. A system is complex if it consists of many varied interrelated parts. In relation to multi-project environments, projects that are bundled as a portfolio and are co-ordinated as programs of projects are often interdependent and a degree of interrelatedness

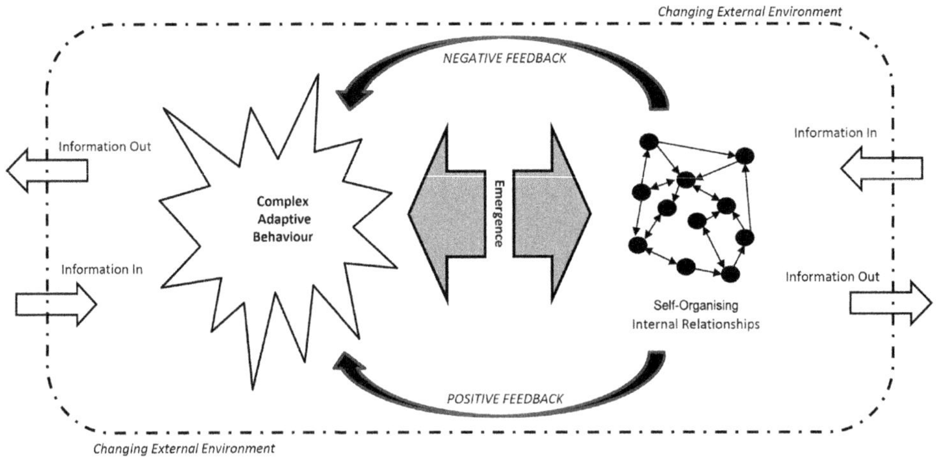

Figure 10.4 Complex adaptive system.

Source: Adapted from Aritua et al. (2009).

between projects exists. One of the obvious challenges for the simultaneous management of projects as a bundle is the co-ordination of resources, schedules and costs. More importantly however, is the maximising of value from the combination while optimally managing the risks of the combination."

- *Adaptability*. "[A]ccording to this concept, in an open system, information flows in and out. New information enters into the feedback loops and influences the behaviour of the individuals, and thus the overall behaviour of the system adapts to the external environment. Systems that are continuously open to new information from the environment and circulate the information within the system will continuously change in response. In terms of the multi-project approach the benefits of program/portfolio management are obvious as a deliberate effort is made to manage risk and obtain value in response to changing business environments and the evolving needs of projects within a multi-project environment."
- *Self-organisation*. "Complexity theory argues that some systems tend toward order or self-organisation – not disorder – as individuals decide to act in similar ways in proximity to and in concert with each other; for their own reasons. This concept dispels the idea that programs and portfolio management should simply be viewed as scaled up versions of single project management. By using appropriate approaches, individual projects can be better coordinated. This aspect of the relationship between complexity theory and multi-project management would imply that program managers and portfolio managers should not be 'bogged down' with detail and should allow and enable competent project managers to act more creatively and on their own. This understanding also influences multi-project managers on the one hand to seek a balance between trusting project managers and allowing them to concentrate on details, whilst seeking the necessary level of control and accountability".

(Aritua et al., 2009, p. 76–77)

- *Emergence*. "[T]he concept behind the principle of emergence may be summarised as 'the whole is greater than the sum of the parts'. From a systems point of view the group behaviour is distinct from the individual behaviour. Application of this principle reinforces the implications of self-organisation discussed above and supports the view in the standard for portfolio management (PMI, 2017) that better risk and value management is achieved by multi-project management than would be possible if the single projects were delivered as autonomous projects."
- *Feedback*. "[I]nformation circulates, is modified by others, then comes back to influence the behaviour of the originator either positively (amplified) or negatively (dampened). This principle should influence organisational structures, information management frameworks and communication channels in a multi-project environment. It also emphasises the need for the multi-project management to react to the changing business environment to keep the strategic objectives at the fore, while providing relative stability for the delivery of individual projects."
- *Non-linearity*. "[C]omplex systems often display non-linearity whereby small changes in the initial conditions or external environment can have large and unpredictable consequences in the outcomes of the system. Non-linearity in multi-project environments means that different tools and techniques are needed for management of multi-projects as contrasted with current tools that assume linearity."

(Aritua et al., 2009, p. 77)

In short, the design of the portfolio should respond to the need to:

1. Manage risks arising from interrelatedness of programs and projects whilst optimising value (finding and proactively managing opportunities).
2. Allow program and project managers to work flexibly within managerial constraints and control parameters so they can maximise their and their team's creativity in delivering their work.
3. Build risk and value management disciplines and processes that are integrated from projects, to programs, to portfolios (and thus to the strategy organisation also).
4. Create communication channels and information management processes and systems that are resilient to distortions created by positive and negative feedback loops.
5. Ensure corporate strategic objectives remain highly visible to all actors in the strategy execution structures.
6. Recognise that unpredicted outcomes will occur from small (and often unnoticed) changes inside or outside the portfolio organisation, and create management tools that help the decision process rather than hinder them (as processes that anticipate linear/predictable responses in the system often do).

This chapter now moves on to look at how the capabilities of portfolio management can be understood as a response to the environment. The needed capabilities make explicit the way in which the portfolio needs to be designed to operate. The environmental factors already discussed impact in a two-way interaction on the portfolio management capabilities and do so in a dynamic manner, as the environment changes over time (due to, say, changes in competition, economics of production, technology, regulation, etc.).

Portfolio management capabilities

The capability to manage a portfolio, irrespective of what that portfolio comprises, must be dynamic: to be effective, it needs to respond to changes in the environment. This has been conceptualised already by looking at portfolio management as an open system, delivering into and being affected by its environment. There is a second source of change that motivates the dynamic adaptation of the PPM capabilities in addition to changes in the environment. This is an ongoing attempt to improve the capabilities themselves. As the portfolio capabilities are applied to the management of the portfolio, people learn what works well and what doesn't. This leads to ongoing optimisation of the structures, competencies, and processes. A quite-complex situation evolves then as the organisation adapts dynamically to both changing external factors and new learning from within the system. As such, the adjustments to the portfolio capabilities may well become an aspect of organisational change that itself must be managed (and must be managed within the overall organisational portfolio – the corporate book of work or strategic portfolio).

"Dynamic capabilities" has a specific meaning in the research literature, coming from a strategic perspective on how organisations respond to environmental change. Typical dynamic capabilities include alliance management capabilities, new product development capabilities, entrepreneurial capabilities, reconfiguring activities capabilities, and marketing capabilities (Sicotte et al., 2014). What is really interesting is how many of these dynamic capabilities directly affect and play vital roles in portfolio management (for example, decisions on which new product projects to include and which to exclude from the portfolio). Of those listed, only marketing could be considered truly outside the

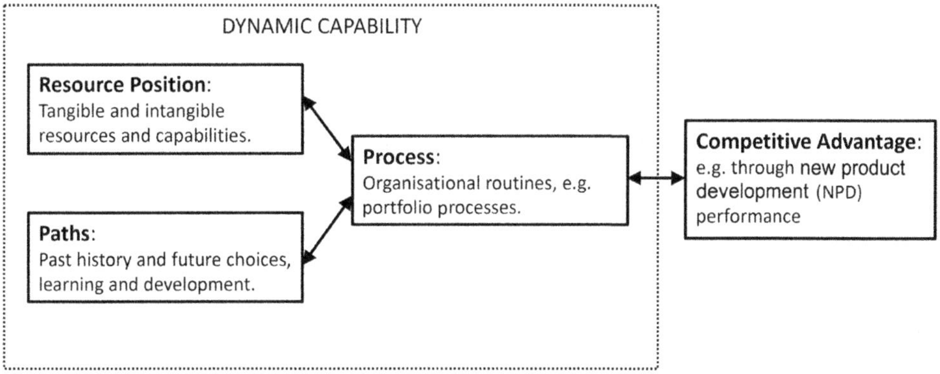

Figure 10.5 The development of dynamic capability for portfolio management.

Source: Adapted from Killen and Hunt (2013).

portfolio as such, yet the marketing decisions, driven by strategic objectives, must have a direct impact on the project selection criteria.

Where portfolio management is functionally operating as the primary mechanism to translate strategy into work to be done and then managing that set of work over time in a manner that responds effectively to the changing environment, it must become a critical dynamic capability itself. Sicotte et al. (2014) suggest the portfolio management capability responds to "sensing opportunities and threats; making timely decisions; making market-oriented decision; changing the firm's resource base." There is also clear evidence of two high-level (i.e. that can be used to guide portfolio management organisational design) capabilities that ensure high performance of the portfolio: *absorptive capabilities*, which encourage high-quality information flows into and out of the portfolio processes, and *adaptive capabilities*, which foster the ability of portfolio management to adapt quickly and effectively to changing environmental factors (within and external to the portfolio organisation) (Beidenbach & Müller, 2012).

Organisational maturity models can help bring an overview and some order to the development of capabilities. In the project management context, several capability development models exist (e.g. OPM3 from the US-based PMI [2013], P3M3 from the UK OGC [Axelos, 2021], and Pennypacker [2005] for project portfolio management amongst other public and commercial maturity models for project management), and a similar model of organisational development has been applied to portfolio management by Killen and Hunt (2013) (see Figure 10.5). They find in the literature and their own research that the development of portfolio management capability depends on the resources available in the environment: people, technology, competitive factors; the historical context of portfolio (and project) management in the organisation; and the existing and likely future organisational routines, such as strategy formulation, governance structures and processes, and portfolio processes themselves.

The argument for a model that guides the dynamic development of portfolio management capabilities is that a consistent pattern in how capability develops can be established from research, and that competitive advantage can be gained by optimising the development of the capabilities. The benefits of "maturity assessment lie in setting direction, prioritizing actions, and beginning cultural change rather than primarily identifying the current level at which an organization is performing" (Killen & Hunt, 2013). There are many capability models for portfolio management available, but beware, the idea that there is a best practice-based model that has any general applicability is contested. Whilst the models give useful guidance on how to develop capability, it is vital that the specifics of the environmental factors are taken into account.

There is often no reason that any particular portfolio organisation has to proceed in the stepwise fashion described by these models to develop capability, and there is often no reason that particular capabilities themselves are even relevant. Remember, these models are for general guidance in practice. It is recommended to always go back to the original construct – Figure 10.5 – to be reminded of the first principles of matching dynamic capability to the specific environment. The earlier note about absorptive and adaptive dynamic capabilities is also relevant here – highly effective capabilities to absorb information and to adapt to changing environmental circumstances must be predicated on thorough analysis and responses to the specifics of the organisation, not through enforcing an organisation with a general capability development model, until it perhaps "fits" what is uncritically assumed to be the "best practice".

Portfolio management capability can be envisaged as a complete, albeit high-level, account or framework of what needs to be in place to manage a portfolio successfully (see figure 10.6). For example, Cooper et al. (2001), looking at portfolio management of new product development, integrated the portfolio and project management processes. The design of the portfolio management organisation includes structures (hierarchies, roles and responsibilities, reporting, etc.), people (competencies, attitudes, technical knowledge, orientation to certain cultural values, etc.), and processes. Each of these aspects is covered in detail in later chapters of this book.

Figure 10.6 links the portfolio capabilities to the project life cycle, showing how projects may be controlled within the portfolio through a stage gate process. Ensuring consistent application of portfolio processes to all projects in the portfolio is fundamental to effective control. (It is worth noting here that arguably the stage gate process is, in fact, a portfolio process, not a project process – to be effective across the portfolio, it is essential that the parameters and criteria that drive the stage gate process are defined and managed [and adjusted dynamically if required] by those managing the portfolio.) If a core function of the portfolio is to allocate resources in a manner that optimises the value of the portfolio (however that is defined), then every project and program must be understood against the same set of parameters. This, in reality, is not always so easy. For example, power and politics intervene, and processes may be bent to suit political motives, with interdependencies evident. Indeed, the processes themselves could be designed to ensure manipulation to meet political objectives by senior management. Such input to process and/or application of process is nevertheless an environmental factor to be considered in designing the portfolio organisation. The capabilities are intended to be dynamic, after all, responding effectively to environmental factors, including those aspects of, *mutatis mutandis*, power and politics.

Figure 10.6 also implicitly brings out another critical aspect of portfolio management – the two requirements to manage at the strategic and operational levels. Strategic management means translating strategy into projects and programs, according to consistent processes and decision-making (say, on decision criteria), maintaining alignment, balancing, etc. Operationally, portfolio management has to make short-term resource allocation decisions, track project and program progress, manage stage gates, etc. Patanakul (2015) lists attributes of portfolio management effectiveness as follows:

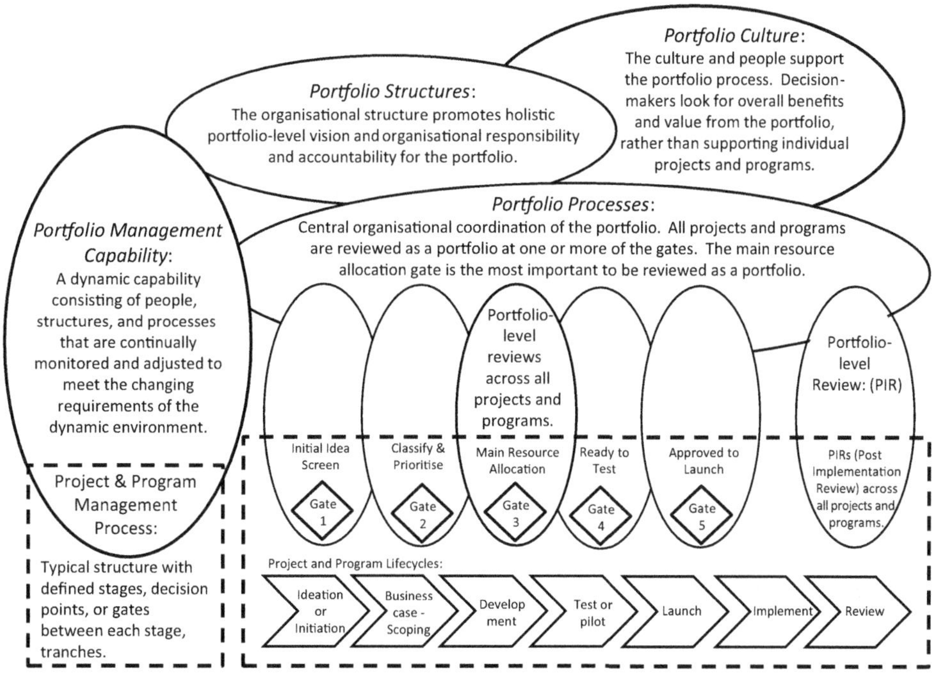

Figure 10.6 Portfolio management capabilities aligned to the project life cycle.

Source: Adapted from Cooper et al. (2001).

Strategic attributes

- "Strategic alignment – the alignment of the portfolio with the organisation's strategic direction.
- Adaptability to internal and external changes – the ability to address risks and uncertainties within the environment.
- Expected value – the consideration of expected value of projects in order to form a portfolio with an acceptably high expected value."

Operational attributes

- "Project and program visibility – the degree of exposure of a project or program to its stakeholders.
- Transparency in portfolio decision-making – the stakeholders' clear understanding of the reasons behind portfolio decisions.
- Predictability of project and program delivery – the ability to predict project and program performance."

(Patanakul, 2015, p. 1095)

These two sets of attributes of effective portfolio management must be enacted via processes but may also be split structurally, with different roles responsible for strategic management and operational management of the portfolio(s). For example, in the pharmaceuticals industry, separation of strategic and operational roles has significant history in portfolio management.

Conclusion

This chapter provides a relatively high-level view of the multiple aspects of the environments in which portfolio management exists in organisations. Three theoretical perspectives are used to draw out the many factors, including sustainability, that need to be considered in the design of portfolio management: systems theory and systems-within-systems, contingency theory, and complexity and complex adaptive systems. The chapter gives no recommendations on what factors are most important or advice on how these factors should be accounted for in the way portfolio management is designed and operationalised. The need for unique, idiosyncratic portfolio management design, with adaptability and flexibility to make continuous change to the design, in maximising the effectiveness of the portfolio management capabilities and the strategic portfolio, is central to the ability of the organisation to maintain competitive advantage and/or maximise its contribution to the environment.

References

Aritua B., Smith N. & Bower D. (2009) Construction client multi-projects – A complex adaptive systems perspective. *International Journal of Project Management* 27(1), 72–79.

Aubry M., Hobbs B. & Thuillier D. (2007) A new framework for understanding organisational project management through the PMO. *International Journal of Project Management* 25(4), 328–336.

Axelos (2021) Portfolio, Programme and Project Management Maturity Model (P3M3). www.axelos.com/for-organizations/p3m3 (correct at time of print).

Baccarini D. (1996) The concept of project complexity – A review. *International Journal of Project Management* 14(4), 201–204.

Beidenbach T. & Müller R. (2012) Absorptive, innovative and adaptive capabilities and their impact on project and project portfolio performance. *International Journal of Project Management* 30(5), 621–634.

Cherns A. (1993) Principles of socio-technical design. in Trist E. & Murray H. *The Social Engagement of Social Science*. Vol 2. The University of Pennsylvania Press.

Cicmil S., Cooke-Davies T., Crawford L. & Richardson K. (2009) *Exploring the Complexity of Projects: Implications of Complexity Theory for Project Management Practice*. Project Management Institute.

Cooper R., Edgett S. & Kleinschmidt E. (2001) *Portfolio Management for New Products*. Basic Books.

Harpum P. (1998) Chinese Design Institutes: Analysis of their Options for Internationalisation, Using a Systems Approach. Unpublished MSc. Dissertation, University of Manchester.

Jackson T. (1993) *Organisational Behaviour in International Management*. Butterworth-Heinmann.

Killen C. & Hunt R. (2013) Robust project portfolio management: Capability evolution and maturity. *International Journal of Managing Projects in Business* 6(1), 131–151.

Martinsuo M. & Geraldi J. (2020) Management of project portfolios: Relationships of project portfolios with their contexts. *International Journal of Project Management* 38(7), 441–453.

Müller R., Drouin N. & Sankaran S. (2019) Modelling organizational project management. *Project Management Journal* 50(4), 499–513.

Patanakul P. (2015) Key attributes of effectiveness in managing project portfolio. *International Journal of Project Management* 33(5), 1084–1097.

Pennypacker J. (2005) *Project Portfolio Management Maturity Model*. Centre for Business Practices.

PMI (2013) *Organizational Project Management Maturity Model (OPM3)*. Third Edition. Project Management Institute.

PMI (2017) *The Standard for Portfolio Management*. Fourth Edition. Project Management Institute.

Porter M. (1998) *The Competitive Advantage of Nations*. Second Edition. Macmillan Press.

Sicotte H., Drouin N. & Delerue H. (2014) Innovation portfolio management as a subset of dynamic capabilities: Measurement and impact on innovative performance. *Project Management Journal* 45(6), 58–72.

Walker A. (1996) *Project Management in Construction*. Blackwell Science.

Annex

Aspects of the environment to consider when designing portfolio management (Martinsuo & Geraldi, 2020)

Themes Theoretical perspectives	Project portfolios, strategy, and success	Project portfolios in complex stakeholder contexts	Managing the project portfolio
Institutional field	Processes of how organisational templates become acceptable or rejected within industries Dynamics of evolving organisational templates (including agile)	Isomorphic pressures on portfolios Deviant behaviours in managing project portfolios	Portfolio responses to isomorphic pressures Processes for legitimising and maintaining portfolio decision-making
Stakeholder management	Portfolio strategies, related stakeholder analyses, and value priorities Portfolio-level considerations of value and value management (acknowledging different stakeholders' views)	Stakeholder landscapes for different types of portfolios (e.g., product development, investment, and delivery) mPortfolio stakeholders and project competition (for funding), e.g., in public infrastructure development	Managing the two-directional links between the portfolio and stakeholders (potentially specific to certain project types) Managing the links between levels of analysis (project, portfolio, parent organisation, business network)
Resource dependence	Resource-specific consideration of portfolio value Real organisational effectiveness as the success measure—differentiated success measures based on specific strategies (e.g., growth, survival, cost-efficiency, differentiation)	External actors with power: Who has power over the portfolio? What are the interdependencies or power relations? Resource dependence caused by the different activity types in the same organisation (e.g., projects vs. services vs. sales)	Interplay between the portfolios of a certain parent organisation, including conflicts and strategic decisions between portfolios Portfolio governance (the level between the project and the parent organisation)
Enactment and sensemaking	Visualisation, to connect project portfolios with competing strategies Strategic learning and capabilities for managing project portfolios	Crises, and turbulence and its effects at the level of the project portfolio Social mechanisms for making sense of the context Narratives and stories in the construction and negotiation of meaning across stakeholders	Sensemaking and behavioural decision-making in project portfolios Practice-based view on managing project portfolios

Figure 10A.1 Aspects of the environment to consider when designing portfolio management (Martinsuo & Geraldi, 2020).

11 Portfolio management process design

Pete Harpum

Introduction

The preceding chapters have laid out a path from strategy formulation, its contextualised relationship to portfolio management, the overall integration of strategy through the portfolio into strategy execution through programs and projects, and the environmental factors and dynamic capabilities needed to respond to a given environment for portfolio management. This chapter continues the development of the argument in the previous chapters and focuses on the definition of the processes of strategic portfolio management, through critiquing some of the existing literature on project portfolios and offering a wider range of ideas than is found in the normative literature.

Defining the portfolio processes

In Chapter 9 (portfolio integration), a construct of portfolio management was presented from Padovani and Carvalho (2016) in Figure 9.8, showing how the various vertical and horizontal integrating processes can be combined into the basis for designing the portfolio management processes. With that model as a starting point, this chapter looks in more depth at the various ideas that inform the design of the processes themselves. Introducing the basis for the model, Padovani and Carvalho (2016, p. 628) note that "[d]espite some efforts towards achieving an integrated framework for portfolio management, there is still a lack of consensus on which are the core processes of project portfolio management." This chapter also contrasts this view with the PMI model of the processes of portfolio management before moving on to review several other ideas and models that inform portfolio management process design.

Portfolio management process design – based on Padovani and Carvalho model

The research-based Padovani and Carvalho (2016) is reproduced again here in Figure 11.1, and a detailed explanation of each set of processes follows, drawing heavily from their description of the model (all work quoted in this subsection is from this work, and citations are not repeated "*ad nauseum*").

Knowledge about the organisational context (KOC)

All the environmental and contextual factors covered in earlier chapters are included in this set of processes. "KOC drives the portfolio decision-making. It is essential for the alignment of portfolio management, enabling the strategic plan to be deployed,

DOI: 10.4324/9780367853129-13

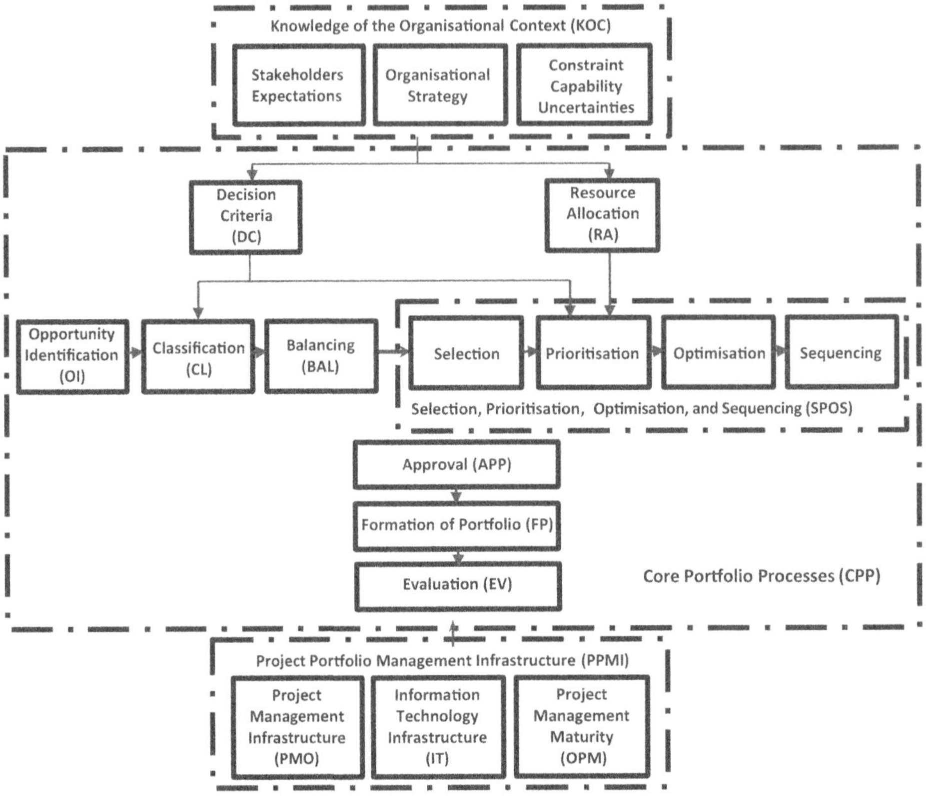

Figure 11.1 Processes for portfolio management.

Source: Adapted from Padovani and Carvalho (2016).

communicated, known and monitored at all the levels of the organization." The key to an effective process at this level is clarity of information, accurate analysis, and obviously, the existence of a strategic planning process.

Core group of portfolio management processes

The connection with the KOC is via the decision criteria (DC) and resource allocation (RA) processes. The design of both of these processes is defined by the KOC processes (the outer layers of the OPM onion described previously in Chapter 10, Figure 10.3). The DC and RA are effectively the brain of the portfolio decision-making processes that are connected to them. Decision criteria and resource allocation are discussed in detail in subsequent chapters in Section III.

Decision criteria is:

> To select and prioritize the most feasible projects, obtaining a portfolio with the highest value and which meets the needs of the organisation, requires clarity about the organization's goals and objectives and decision criteria (DC) that are aligned and defined with the main stakeholders.

"Resource allocation (RA) is an important activity of portfolio management, and should be included in the prioritization step, given that human resources are usually limited and constitute constraints."

The DC and RA processes interact with the heart of the portfolio process, that is, the processes that decide what projects and programs will comprise the portfolio. These are the processes through which the strategic objectives and strategy plan to deliver those objectives are translated into the correct set of projects to execute the strategy.

Opportunity identification (OI) captures all the relevant information needed about the set of projects that will become/maintain the portfolio: "scope, objective, value, earnings, market and other information about the candidate proposals in a single place, to provide a global vision of the entire portfolio of projects, which is needed for decision-making." In order to make balancing the portfolio easier, it is often useful to classify (CL) projects and programs, and in some cases, it is essential. For example, R&D projects never have high NPVs (net present values) because their return is so far in the future compared to other near-term financial returns from projects delivering more quickly. Hence, it can be a serious mistake to misunderstand the types of projects in the portfolio by not recognising categorical differences between them – and then make poor selection decisions as a result. These preceding activities are about balancing (BAL) the portfolio.

It is important to have a balanced portfolio to ensure the portfolio achieves short-, medium-, and long-term strategic objectives in response to changing environmental factors. Balancing the portfolio is fundamental to ensure that the strategic objectives remain aligned, irrespective of the projects/programs that the decision criteria and resources allocation processes suggest are the preferred ones. Balancing is a feedback loop process to make sure that the portfolio delivers what is needed, correcting the inherent biases that the DC and RA processes create.

Project selection, prioritisation, optimisation, and sequencing (SPOS) requires an overview and analysis of the entire portfolio. Balancing ensures the correct categories of potential projects/programs are analysed coming into SPOS, and also, over time, as the portfolio delivers strategic objectives and real impacts on the performance of the projects/programs, ongoing analysis of the portfolio is required. Hence, it is critical to ensure the portfolio continues to be aligned to strategy, both planned, intended strategy and emergent strategy. It also has to reflect the parts of planned strategy that become unrealised – projects/programs that are found to be infeasible once started for whatever reason and need to be removed from the portfolio.

Selection and prioritisation require both decision criteria and resource inputs (not just people, but also organisational capabilities, technology, facilities, infrastructure, etc.) to choose the correct projects. This is essentially a purely analytical process, which is then normally mediated by the input of senior leaders who bring knowledge and experience of the sector, the business, and the people in it and make final selection and prioritisation decisions that implicitly or explicitly involve so-called "gut feeling".[1]

Optimisation of the portfolio is typically a process that adjusts both the portfolio and the projects/programs selected. Optimisation at the portfolio level "seeks to understand how to make the best use of available human resources, considering their qualifications and information about the expected and actual time spent developing a task in order to reduce downtime, project waiting queues, and consequent delays." Portfolio-level-driven optimisation of projects/programs may mean adjustment of the project/program strategies and plans to reflect the needs of other projects and programs in the portfolio. This might mean "re-strategising" a project to take account of the fact that particular resources are needed on other projects and not available for the project under consideration.

At the point at which the set of projects/programs in the portfolio has been established, the focus shifts to the operational aspects of portfolio management. Approval (AP), formation of portfolio (FP), and evaluation (EV) processes are where the portfolio and project/program processes overlap, as shown in Figure 11.1. The stage gate process is, in effect, the manifestation of these three processes. When the stage gate process is well set up, the three processes are in fact incorporated into each stage gate review as the projects/programs progress through their life cycles.

Stage gates are designed to check progress of the project (once started), ensure correct and relevant processes have been completed, check selection relevance/ongoing relevance once past the start gate, evaluate plans for the next phase, and then make an accept/reject decision for progression of the project/program into the next stage. Gates typically allow for several decision states: continue to next stage, continue but rework aspects that are not accepted, stop and rework and come back for approval to proceed, stop completely. The criteria against which these decisions are made are identical to, or directly derived from, those that are used in the DC process.

Portfolio management infrastructure

These processes are designed to support the core portfolio processes. They are also part of the overlap between portfolio and projects/programs. In organisations where a project management office (PMO) exists, this group is often responsible for collecting and collating project data (plans, progress, risks, expected value, etc.). This data is then fed into the portfolio processes to support ongoing prioritisation and optimisation of the portfolio. The PMO may also be home to the stage gate process, therefore acting directly as the interface between the portfolio and the projects/programs. The PMO may also be the functional "home" for specialists that support projects/programs, such as risk management, value management, planners, etc. (see Chapter 15 for further discussion of the portfolio office). By definition, then, these resources are also (or should be) interfacing between the portfolio and specific projects/programs. Another really useful and important role for the PMO is to capture decisions made throughout the portfolio process: "A decision tracing support package increases the ability to trace the decisions made, reduce risk, promote earlier management buy-in and establish a reliable and valid methodology for capturing and storing information about actual decision-making events" (Bennett, 1999).

A portfolio of any significant size will also be heavily dependent on information technology. The IT infrastructure will span across large parts of, if not all, the vertical and horizontally integrated processes, from strategy development, portfolio analytics and decision-making, portfolio value analysis, project progress, value per project, financial and economic analysis, risk, and much else. There are many fully integrated portfolio and project management software platforms that incorporate a wide range of process automation and analytics. They also interface effectively with enterprise resource planning (ERP) systems and other key business process automation software. This provides a very strong set of data – the challenge, then, is data accuracy, which is where a well-designed and efficient PMO should bring high value (see Chapters 14 and 16 for further discussion of effective data management).

Portfolio management maturity

There is research evidence that higher maturity in project management is also a factor for higher performance of portfolios, meaning, that strategic objectives are achieved as needed, including the incorporation of emergent strategy. In a real way, this is rather self-evident – if the projects/programs are not effectively delivering the outcomes that achieve strategic objectives, the portfolio cannot be high-performing, no matter how well it is designed and managed. Nevertheless, some aspects of project management maturity that relate to interacting with the portfolio are often incorporated in the maturity model. Hence, higher maturity includes being good at the interaction and interface with portfolio management. (Portfolio management maturity is demonstrated further in the case study in Chapter 29.)

Portfolio management process design – based on the PMI model

The PMI approach to portfolio management is built along the same lines as their project and program management documents, with process groups (called "performance domains") organised around a portfolio life cycle (Figure 11.2). In contrast to the Padovani and

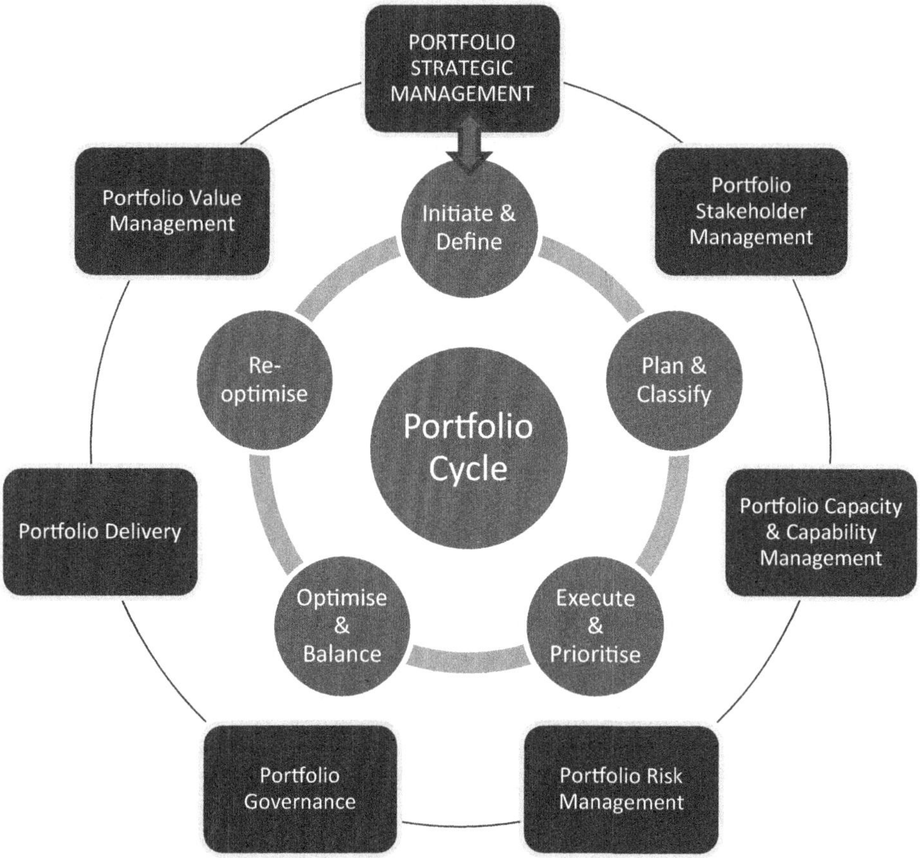

Figure 11.2 PMI model of portfolio management.

Source: Adapted from PMI (2017).

Carvalho model, it is unclear what the supporting research evidence is for the standard for portfolio management (PMI, 2017), nor is the methodology made clear about how the processes of portfolio management were decided on. Nevertheless, there is significant concordance between the PMI model and much of the academic literature, including Padovani and Carvalho, and so it provides a useful point of comparison.

Organising a model of portfolio management around a concept that PMI promotes as defining projects and programs[2] (PMI 2013a, b), that is, the life cycle, is arguably perpetuating the idea of portfolio management as an extension of project management theory: "like programs and projects, portfolios go through a life cycle that includes initiation, planning, execution, and optimisation" (PMI, 2017). Conversely, portfolios have life cycles only in so much as any business process has a life cycle – something or other begins and ends. Portfolios are, in essence, a set of processes that continuously define and redefine the set of work needed to deliver strategic objectives. Once the set of projects and programs within a portfolio is defined, it is highly unlikely that the entire set will be discarded, and a new set defined to refill the portfolio. Rather, there is an ongoing iterative cycle of review of the portfolio against strategic objectives, analysis of the portfolio to continuously assess fitness for purpose, expected value, and decisions on incoming and outgoing projects/programs.

A disadvantage of this instrumentalist approach to portfolio management is that it can restrict thinking, pulling the designers and managers of portfolios into an overly mechanistic and deterministic approach to what is a highly organic and complex set of capabilities, processes, behaviours, and interactions. Indeed, it is such an approach to project and program management itself by PMI and other institutional bodies that, some argue, slowed the development of both theory and practice for decades (Cicmil & Hodgson, 2006). Locating the construct of portfolio management around a highly generic "plan-do-act-check" life cycle is reminiscent of the relevant and long-standing criticisms of the PMI guides to the bodies of knowledge for projects (Morris, 2013). The model also may deceive the organisational designer into downplaying the critical importance of context and environment. PMI mentions these factors only in passing and not as fundamental aspects of design and management of portfolios (although the document does mention that what is presented should not be seen as a methodology and the environment must be taken into account in design). Despite these potential shortcomings, these groups of processes encompass many of the processes described in the previous model, and the document is a useful reference for a detailed review of how each process may be designed.

Both the Padovani and Carvalho and the PMI models are normative – they describe how things ought to be done, with or without empirical evidence for why said things should be done as the model describes. Postmodern critical theory has been applied to many areas of management theory to test and challenge normative ideas, including those of rationality and universal truths (meaning, theories of general application of practice and process – such as portfolio management). These studies include a drive to understand how organisations actually carry out work in practice, rather than in theory. Blichfeldt and Eskerod studied the enactment of portfolio management and found that "many project-oriented companies do not perform well when it comes to PPM" (Blichfeldt & Eskerod, 2008). They identified the following three problems, noting these observations as particularly interesting because the companies included in the research project were supposed to be especially experienced in PPM and engaged in PPM according to the extant body of literature on PPM.

1. Projects are not completed according to plan (or they even peter out during their project life cycle).
2. Management and employees feel they lack a broad overview of ongoing projects (especially when the number of ongoing projects increases as more and more projects are not completed according to plan).
3. People experience stress as resources are continuously reallocated across projects in order to make ends meet.

This reinforces the exhortation that the specifics of how portfolio management processes are designed *must be determined by the specifics of the environment and context.* Blind adherence to normative models of how portfolio management should be designed is likely to lead to underperformance of the portfolio, leading to failure to achieve strategic objectives.

This is not an argument to not formalise the processes; it is an argument to *formalise the processes to meet the specific needs of each specific organisation* – refer back to Chapter 9, where findings from Teller et al. (2012) giving empirical evidence that formalisation improves performance is presented.

Portfolios of external projects

The previous discussion of portfolio management processes all assumes that the organisation is delivering a portfolio of projects/programs that are internal. The portfolio is derived directly from the strategic objectives, and all processes and metrics are designed to ensure the projects/programs deliver those strategic objectives or are removed from the portfolio. It is also designed to identify emergent strategy, feed it into the strategy process, and define projects/programs that will deliver on agreed emergent strategic objectives.

A sector that is critical for the well-being of people across the world is construction, with a global construction output in 2020 of US$10.7 trillion, forecast to rise by 42% or US$4.5 trillion between 2020 and 2030, to reach US$15.2 trillion (Marsh & GuyCarpenter, 2021). That is approximately 13% of total global GDP and is a very large sector of the world economy. Construction projects are almost exclusively designed and built by third parties to the owner – the construction contracting industry. These construction companies have a portfolio of projects that are not internal – they are external. Therefore, these types of organisations have two portfolios, an internal portfolio, striving to achieve strategic objectives (become more efficient, M&A, enhanced IT systems, organisational change and transformation programs, etc.) and a portfolio of construction projects they are building for others – that is, the raison d'être of the organisation.

This double-portfolio model applies to all sectors where work is done on behalf of another organisation, whether it be creating an artefact (deliverable, product, output, such as a road, house, office, dam, etc.) or delivering a service (design consulting, management consulting, third-party management services, advisory services, etc.). In this scenario, the process for deciding upon what work to undertake – normally, but not always, in a competitive bidding situation – has to be directly linked to strategy as well as the portfolio process. Bidding is a significant and important set of processes and knowledge, and its effectiveness is critical to organisations that deliver third-party projects/programs. Simister (2003), Bernink & Turner (1995), and Steel (2004), amongst many others, provide overviews of the bidding process for external projects delivered to others. Figure 11.3 shows a general view of the bidding process.

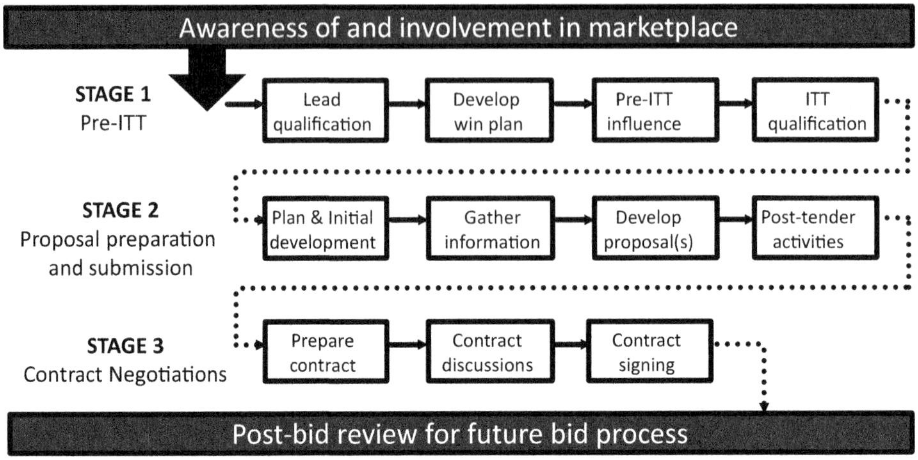

Figure 11.3 Overview of bidding process.

Source: Adapted from Simister (2003).

From the diagram it is clear that organisational strategic aims and strategy are important inputs to much of the process: being aware of the marketplace is surely a strategic activity, as is knowing what leads to be interested in and how the organisation goes about influencing potential owners in the pre-proposal phases. In fact, the ITT (invitation to tender) qualification is the portfolio selection process for the external portfolio – what projects will the organisation choose to have in its portfolio (assuming it wins the bid). The processes for deciding what work to do (what to bid for) and how to assess the opportunity (bid pricing, commercial terms, etc.) become, in effect, the portfolio decision processes for the external portfolio processes. (Additionally, once work is incorporated into the external portfolio, it generally must be completed – the choice to remove the projects/programs does not exist usually, since a contract is in place for delivery of the work to the owner/buyer.) Figure 11.4 shows how the marketing infrastructure provides input into the early external portfolio stages, and then the bidding process itself is the *de facto* portfolio selection process.

For any contracting organisation, bidding is a sophisticated set of processes, involving financial, resource, commercial, market, and other strategic inputs. Winning work that the organisation cannot deliver with the appropriate value to itself is obviously counterproductive.[3] In some industries like construction, winning a project that cannot be delivered effectively may be a fast route to going bust (see case study in Chapter 27).

Classification and balancing

There are many classifications and typological models for projects and programs. These have various uses, including being able to identify needed competencies in sets or groups to ensure projects are deliverable, allocating appropriately competent and qualified people to the projects/programs, helping shape organisations' self-perceptions of the types of projects they deliver, defining for the market the types of projects/programs the organisation can deliver externally (i.e. as contractors), and many others.

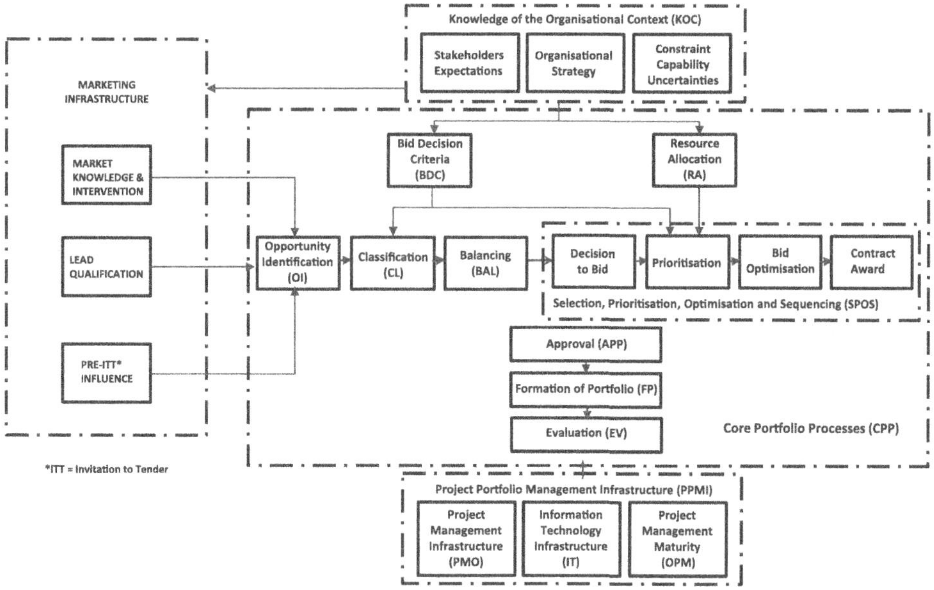

Figure 11.4 The external portfolio processes.

Source: Adapted from Padovani and Carvalho (2016).

With regard to portfolio management, the need for classification is rather different. The central reason to classify is to make portfolio balancing decisions more effective. This must be achieved against a reality that project/program selection is always political:

> Any portfolio management system will have to deal with the desire of every business unit to fund as many of its projects as possible. . . . In companies with a decentralised business unit structure, the politics are especially rough: inter-business competition is very keen; BU's [business units] have little understanding of project resource constraints.
>
> (Nandurdikar, 2015, p. 14)

Starting from first principles of portfolio management for assets, what is needed is the most efficient portfolio achievable that will deliver the strategic objectives: "A portfolio is inefficient if it is possible to obtain higher expected (or average) return with no greater variability of return, or obtain greater certainty of return with no less average or expected return" (Markowitz, 1991, p. 129). In other words, the locus of decision-making in portfolios of investment assets is an understanding of the expected return from each asset and the risk associated with that return. Since projects/programs are fundamentally representative of assets (they are intended to create value through the production of a tangible output,[4] howsoever defined), this approach to balance is substantiated. Intuitively, it seems reasonable to be deeply interested in the value trade-off against the risk being taken with a set of projects/programs in a portfolio. (The importance of understanding value and risk throughout the integrated processes of strategy development down to the projects delivering the strategy is covered in Chapter 6. The value and risk processes must be vertically integrated and recognised as critical to the ability to effectively manage the portfolio.)

Translating asset (investment) portfolio theory into that of portfolios of projects and programs means that each project/program must be assessed according to its value/risk profile. Value is expressed in the way the organisation needs to define it to match its strategic objectives and its raison d'être. So for example, the value/risk analysis of a not-for-profit organisation could be "impact in a given community compared to risk of failure". For a new product development organisation, it might be "expected (e)NPV compared to normalised (i.e. industry-reported) probability of technical failure" of the particular product. This measure may or may not be part of the typology of the projects/programs in the portfolio but will almost certainly be a key decision-making criteria. Classification might be, say, high value/high risk, low value/high risk, high value/low risk, low value/low risk.

Other alternatives of simple binary measures include[5]:

- Ease versus attractiveness.
- Strength versus attractiveness.
- Cost versus timing.
- Strategic fit versus financial benefit.
- Cost versus financial benefit.

(Moustafaev, 2017, p. 34)

The portfolio also needs to be balanced to take account of the need to include (often widely) varying types of projects/programs. This merely reflects that strategic objectives require a wide range of projects/programs to deliver them; some with high cash needs, some with low profitability, some with no profitability (e.g. mandatory projects required by regulators/legislation), some lasting six months or one year, others possibly lasting ten years or more before they create any value to the organisation, and of course, some with higher risks than others.

Returning briefly to Markowitz (1991) and efficiency of the portfolio, his work demonstrated that there is typically more than one set of assets (more than one version of a portfolio) that can achieve the strategic objective of an investor in assets. This is directly translatable to a portfolio of project/program "assets". There are normally multiple ways of achieving strategic objectives. Firstly, that means the organisation must acknowledge this fact – getting obsessed on a view that there is only one way to deliver strategic objectives and no other is likely to lead to inflexibility in decision-making and difficulties adjusting the portfolio contents over time as risks and uncertainties of the real world play out in relation to the projects and programs being executed. There is clear evidence that successful new product development firms look at alternative sets of projects/programs:

> [T]he goal of strategic portfolio management is not to pick which projects are best but to pick the best set of projects to achieve the organisation's goals.
>
> (Smith & Sonnenblick, 2015)

The balance of a portfolio, then, is critical to understand not only in and of itself for the given portfolio but also to allow comparison of alternative portfolio compositions. Working "backwards" from the need to understand the portfolio balance means that the classification created for the organisation's projects/programs needs to be defined so as to allow that balance to be understood in terms that are contextualised to the environment of the organisation and its specific strategic objectives.

Markowitz and the rational-economic view of man (which predicates his and others' neoclassical economic theories) have been strongly challenged, not least by Taleb (2010). Taleb points out that highly unlikely but extremely high-impact events (black swans) create the most significant change[6] and that man is simply not rational. The combination of these two facts determines that black swan events combined with people's inability to intuitively grasp the effect of black swans lead to poor responses to the unlikely event happening – often driven by irrational belief in the certainty of plans for the future. Clearly, a portfolio is the embodiment of plans for the future. The point, then, is that whilst it is sensible to use value/risk assessment when assessing portfolio balance, it is also sensible to take into account the possibility of black swan events impacting projects and programs in the portfolio.

Classification helps decision-makers to see what groups of projects/programs exist in a given portfolio, with expected values and risks associated, and so ensure that the relevant strategic objectives are prioritised in line with strategic requirements, whilst not losing sight that some low- or no-value (i.e. no financial value) projects are essential to the business strategy.

To return to the early 1950s again[7] (see Chapter 2), Dean (1951) already understood and was advising on the need for classification of projects to support decision-making on the allocation of capital and proposed several illustrative classifications for different sectors.

Automobile manufacturer:

1. *Replacement investments.*
2. *Expense-saving investments, generally in the form of equipment-obsolescence investments.*
3. *Expansion and new business investments, lumped together, even though they are recognised as different.*
4. *New model investments, which are, for the most part, tools and dies whose economic life is as short-lived as that model.*

Petroleum company:

1. *Essential investments, that is, those required by law, by contractual obligations, or to meet competitive standards of product quality. Oil drilling investments are put in this category because they are considered essential for the company's future.*
2. *Replacement investments, that is, replacement of assets that wear out with other substantially similar ones (e.g. delivery trucks). These investments are also viewed as essential, since operations would break down without replacements, although they do not meet profitability tests.*
3. *Profitability investments, which are of two main types, expense saving and product upgrading (i.e. converting waste or low-value petroleum products into products of higher value).*
4. *Desirable investments, that is, low-payout investments and those for which no payout can be conveniently calculated.*

Building materials manufacture:

1. *Necessary replacement investments.*
2. *Cost-reducing investments.*
3. *Product-obsolescence investments.*
4. *New product investments.*
5. *Expansion investments.*
6. *Working conditions improvement investments.*

Henderson (1970) defined the now-eponymous growth share matrix ("the Boston box") to demonstrate that organisations needed to understand the financial aspects of products they had in their portfolio to achieve balance, in terms of profitability, cash flow, and market position sustaining these cash and profitability indicators.

> To be successful, a company should have a portfolio of products with different growth rates and different market shares. The portfolio composition is a function of the balance between cash flows. High-growth products require cash inputs to grow. Low-growth products should generate excess cash. Both kinds are needed simultaneously.

Henderson (1970) defined four rules to determine the cash flow of a product.

- *Margins and cash generated are a function of market share. High margins and high market share go together. This is a matter of common observation, explained by the experience curve effect.*
- *Growth requires cash input to finance added assets. The added cash required to hold market share is a function of growth rates.*
- *High market share must be earned or bought. Buying market share requires an additional increment of investment.*
- *No product market can grow indefinitely. The pay-off from growth must come when the growth slows, or it never will. The pay-off is cash that cannot be reinvested in that product.*

The classification for the portfolio is about helping decision-makers balance the portfolio – getting the right mix of projects/programs (and testing that mix against the strategic objectives) – and prioritisation of the projects/programs in the portfolio to ensure the more strategically important work gets allocated resources preferentially. This ability to balance the portfolio through understanding categorisation is important especially where there are widely different financial returns from projects. One danger is of only funding high-NPV, fast-return-on-investment work and not funding low-NPV, later-return-on-investment projects. This is classically a challenge in new product development organisations with long lead times to market. NPV is a very poor indicator of financial performance over long time periods due to the discount rate compounded over many years, reducing the NPV hugely compared to returns gained in a year or two. This is discussed in more detail in Chapter 12 on portfolio selection.

At a rather-abstract level, several authors have attempted to create generic classification models based on project and program typologies, in contrast to strategy-driven classification. These may be of use when thinking through the classification model needed for a particular organisation, if for no other reason than they offer a starting point that may fit the contextual needs. Pellegrinelli et al. (2011) offer various literature-based categorisation models for programs and projects:

- *Strategic change, business cycle related, and single objective (from Ferns, 1991).*
- *Derivative, breakthrough, and R&D – for product development programs/projects (from Wheelwright & Clark (1992).*
- *Portfolio, goal orientated, and heartbeat (Pellegrinelli, 1997).*
- *Co-located projects, distributed projects within a program, traditional projects (from Evaristo & van Fenema, 1999).*
- *Sequential projects in a program, concurrent projects in a portfolio, and network projects, which are entirely independent of each other (from Maylor et al., 2006).*

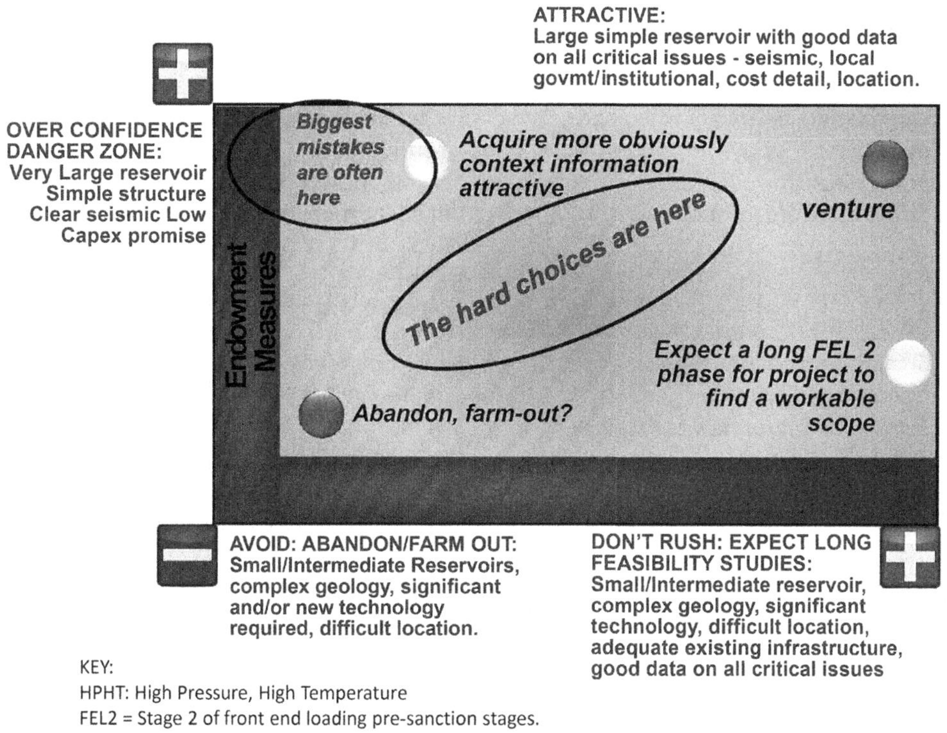
ATTRACTIVE:
Large simple reservoir with good data on all critical issues - seismic, local govmt/institutional, cost detail, location.
OVER CONFIDENCE DANGER ZONE:
Very Large reservoir Simple structure Clear seismic Low Capex promise
Biggest mistakes are often here
Acquire more obviously context information attractive
venture
The hard choices are here
Endowment Measures
Expect a long FEL 2 phase for project to find a workable scope
Abandon, farm-out?
AVOID: ABANDON/FARM OUT:
Small/Intermediate Reservoirs, complex geology, significant and/or new technology required, difficult location.
DON'T RUSH: EXPECT LONG FEASIBILITY STUDIES:
Small/Intermediate reservoir, complex geology, significant technology, difficult location, adequate existing infrastructure, good data on all critical issues
KEY:
HPHT: High Pressure, High Temperature
FEL2 = Stage 2 of front end loading pre-sanction stages.

Figure 11.5a Example of categorisation for upstream oil and gas.

Source: Adapted from Nandurdikar (2015). KEY: HPHT, high pressure, high temperature; FEL2, stage 2 of front-end loading pre-sanction stages.

The decision-making processes must align strategic objectives with the content of the portfolio, by definition. This means the classification being used to support the decision-making must also be defined by the strategic objectives. Therefore, the classes used by every organisation must be defined to suit the organisation specifically – whilst also reflecting the sectoral thinking, such that it is possible to understand how one organisation's portfolio compares to other organisations' portfolios. This is "knowledge of the organisational context" (KOC) in Figure 11.1 and is (should be) built into the decision criteria process. Figures 11.5a and b demonstrate another set of criteria, used in the upstream oil and gas sector, to support decision-making on what oil/gas field assets to take into development/production, helping to create understanding of which decisions are simpler and which are more difficult.

The derivation of the categories from the project information diagram in Figure 11.5a (by Nandurdikar, 2015) starts to make visible the link to decision criteria (Figure 11.5b), which are highly likely to be at least some of the criteria shown on the diagram's axes.

Crawford et al. (2006) unsurprisingly find that project classification (or categorisation) systems have multiple purposes; nevertheless, it was also identified that the classification system may be created to fulfil three purposes:

OVERCONFIDENCE DANGER ZONE "Acquire more context information"	OBVIOUSLY ATTRACTIVE "Obviously attractive venture"
Large simple reservoirs with good seismic data Small capex Straightforward location	Large simple reservoir with good data on all critical issues: Seismic, local content, institutional, cost detail, location.
AVOID "Abandon, farm-out?"	DON'T RUSH "Expect a long FEL 2 phase..."
Small/intermediate reservoir Complex geology Significant and/or new technology required Difficult location	Small/intermediate reservoir Complex geology Significant technology needed Difficult location Adequate existing infrastructure Good data on all critical issues

Figure 11.5b Example categorisation table for upstream oil and gas.

Source: Adapted from Nandurdikar (2015).

1. *Strategic alignment.* Organisations need to categorise projects to:
   - Assign priority for projects within their investment portfolio.
   - Track the efficacy of their investment in projects.
   - Create strategic visibility.
2. *Capability specialisation.* Organisations need to categorise projects to:
   - Develop project delivery capability within the organisation.
   - Assign appropriate resources and tools to the management of projects.
3. *Promote the project approach.* The minor need is to:
   - Decide that the work being done is projects, and differentiate projects from operations.
   - Differentiate projects, programs, and portfolios of projects.
   - Provide a common language for project management within the organisation.

Figure 11.6 shows an example of a specific classification schema for an organisation, originally developed by Crawford et al. (2006). This model allows the decision-makers to see what projects exist in the portfolio and at what stage of their life cycles they are. New entries to the portfolio can be assessed against the existing portfolio, stage gate decisions for specific projects can be informed by the overall portfolio composition and prioritisation, and the balance of projects/programs is clear.

The three italicised points from Crawford et al. (assign priority for projects within their investment portfolio, track the efficacy of their investment in projects, and assign appropriate resources and tools to the management of projects) are the keys to defining each aspect of categorisation, specific to the organisation. Figure 11.6 shows the decision criteria as an input to the classification process, and these criteria shape the classification descriptions.

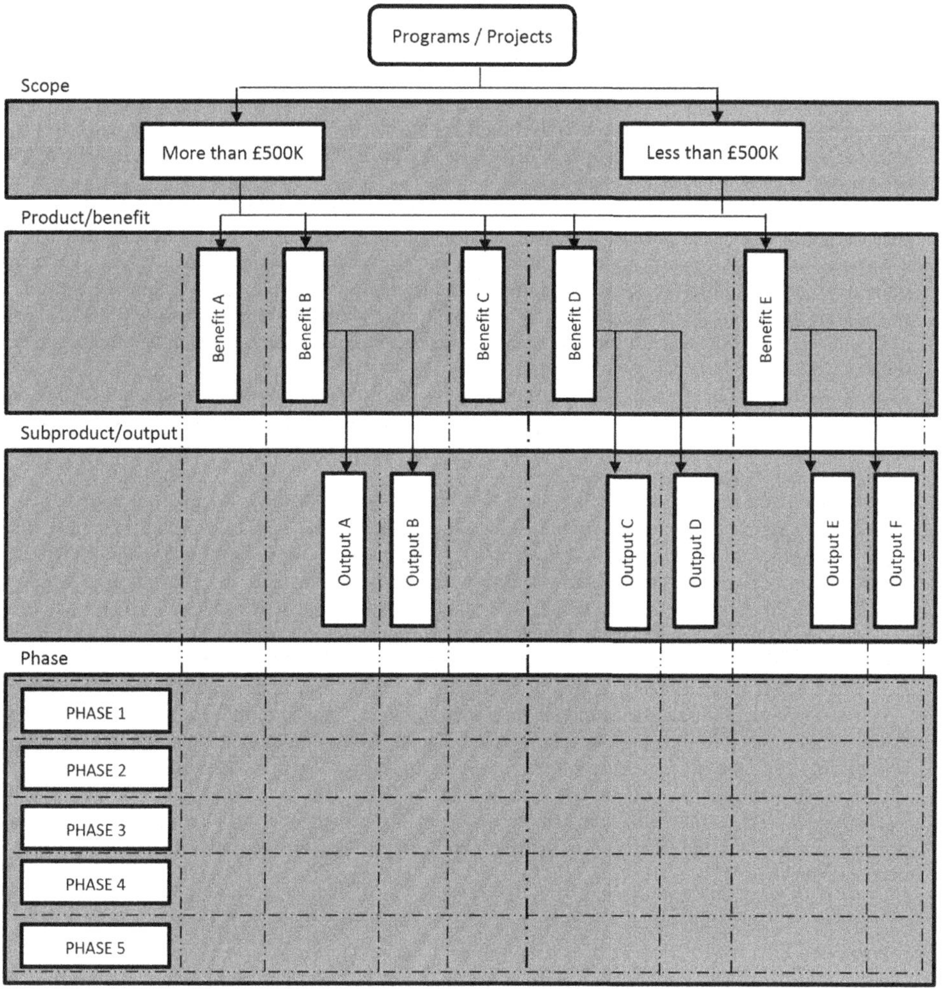

Figure 11.6 Example composite categorisation system.

Source: Adapted from Crawford et al. (2006).

Conclusion

This chapter has delved into the process design required to manage a strategic portfolio in more depth, looking at the way the processes are dependent on context and environment. The process models presented are based on evidence from research on real applications of portfolio management and compared to alternative theoretical models. The differences in portfolio processes between internal and external portfolios are discussed, as is the importance of understanding that there are normally several alternative sets of projects/programs within portfolios that can all achieve the strategic objectives, and the challenge is to find the most efficient set. Classification and balancing are covered in some detail, including a relatively high-level discussion of risk and value, in readiness for subsequent chapters in the book to go into more detail on these subjects.

Notes

1 This "gut feeling" input is another feedback loop. The DC and RA process designs must incorporate as much of this type of expertise as possible in order to be effective. The "gut feel" can be built into the analytical processes, and the output decisions of the analysis checked again by the same people that provided portfolio process design input. This is how a high-quality process is designed – portfolio analysts can at times be frustrated that their beautiful analyses are disregarded by senior leaders applying gut feelings to decisions, yet arguably *this is part of the process*. (This is further discussed in subsequent chapters).

2 "Project management is accomplished through the appropriate application and integration of 47 logically grouped project management processes, which are categorised into five process groups . . . initiating, planning, executing, monitoring and controlling, and closing" (PMI, 2013a). The program management life cycle sits at the centre of the program management performance domain diagram, introducing program management in "the standard for program management" (PMI, 2013b), in an entirely analogous way to the centrality of the portfolio life cycle in the portfolio management standard (PMI, 2017).

3 *Value* is not defined here exclusively as money – an organisation may seek to win a bid for reasons such as maintaining a pipeline of future projects with the same buyer, to maintain cash flow at low or zero margin, etc. Again, these are thoroughly strategic issues and directly operate in the external portfolio decision-making processes.

4 By *tangible* what is meant is something that is real and exists: new knowledge in an organisation and its people is tangible; financial products are tangible; an improved market opposition is tangible. The point is stressed since much of the literature on the benefits created by projects and programs emphasises a difference between tangible and intangible benefits, with normally an exhortation to focus on tangible benefits, being something that can be touched – that is, an artefact. This is an argument for looking instead at value as the key output measure of projects/programs and not benefits.

5 Interestingly, all these pairs include, implicitly or explicitly, value of the output.

6 Part of the effect of irrationality is people's difficulty in recognising that black swan events actually occur more frequently than is considered "rationally" possible. This is reinforced by neoclassical economic theory that is founded on the assumptions that all risk can be modelled on Gaussian distribution of risk (a.k.a. the normal distribution curve). "Simply, if you remove their Gaussian assumptions and treat prices as scalable, you are left with hot air" (Taleb, 2010).

7 With the aim to continue reinforcing the historical reality that theory and practice about managing portfolios of projects and programs are neither a new area of knowledge nor an extension of project management theory.

References

Bennett J. (1999) Portfolio management in the pharmaceutical industry. in Harpum P. *Portfolio, Program, and Project Management in the Pharmaceutical and Biotechnology Industries*. Wiley.

Bernink B. & Turner R. (1995) *Winning Contracts: The Commercial Project Manager*. McGraw-Hill.

Blichfeldt B. & Eskerod P. (2008) Project portfolio management – There's more to it than what management enacts. *International Journal of Project Management* 26(4), 357–365.

Cicmil S. & Hodgson D. (2006) Making projects critical: An introduction. in Cicmil S. & Hodgson D. *Making Projects Critical*. Palgrave Macmillan.

Crawford L., Hobbs B. & Turner R. (2006) Aligning capability with strategy: Categorizing projects to do the right projects and to do them right. *Project Management Journal* 37(2), 28–50.

Dean J. (1951) *Capital Budgeting*. Columbia University Press.

Evaristo R. & Van Fenema P. (1999) A typology of project management: Emergence and evolution of new forms. *International Journal of Project Management* 17(5), 275–281.

Ferns D. (1991) Developments in programme management. *International Journal of Project Management* 9(3), 148–156.

Henderson (1970) *The Product Portfolio*. Boston Consulting Group. www.bcg.com/publications/1970/strategy-the-product-portfolio.aspx.

Markowitz H. (1991) *Portfolio Selection*. Blackwell.

Marsh & GuyCarpenter (2021) *Future of Construction: A Global Forecast for Construction to 2030.* Oxford Economics.

Maylor H., Brady T., Cooke-Davies T. & Hodgson D. (2006) From projectification to programmification. *International Journal of Project Management* 24(8), 663–674.

Morris P. (2013) *Reconstructing Project Management.* Wiley-Blackwell.

Moustafaev J. (2017) *Project Portfolio Management in Theory and Practice: Thirty Case Studies from around the World.* CRC Press.

Nandurdikar N. (February 2015) *Retooling portfolio management methods.* BIS Oil & Gas Exploration & Production Conference Paper.

Padovani M. & Carvalho M. (2016) Integrated PPM process: Scale development and validation. *International Journal of Project Management* 34(4), 627–642.

Pellegrinelli S. (1997) Programme management: Organising project-based change. *International Journal of Project Management* 15(3), 141–149.

Pellegrinelli S., Partington D. & Geraldi J. (2011) Program management: An emerging opportunity for research and scholarship. in Morris, PW, Pinto, J. & Soederlund. *The Oxford Handbook of Project Management.* Oxford University Press.

PMI (2013a) *A Guide to the Project Management Body of Knowledge.* Fifth Edition. Project Management Institute.

PMI (2013b) *The Standard for Program Management.* Third Edition. Project Management Institute.

PMI (2017) *The Standard for Portfolio Management.* Fourth Edition. Project Management Institute.

Simister S. (2003) Bidding. in Turner R. *Contracting for Project Management.* Gower.

Smith D. & Sonnenblick R. (2015) From budget-based to strategy based portfolio management: A six year case study. Innovation portfolio management. *Research Technology Management* 56(5), 45–51.

Steel G. (2004) Tender management. in Morris P. & Pinto J. *The Wiley Guide to the Management of Projects.* Wiley.

Taleb N. (2010) *The Black Swan: The Impact of the Highly Improbable.* Penguin.

Teller J., Unger B., Kock A. & Gemünden H. (2012) Formalization of project portfolio management: The moderating role of project portfolio complexity. *International Journal of Project Management* 30(5), 596–607.

Wheelwright S. & Clark K. (1992) *Revolutionizing Product Development. Quantum Leaps in Speed, Efficiency and Quality.* Free Press.

12 Strategic portfolio selection

Pete Harpum[1]

Introduction

Following on from the preceding discussion of process design and classification (and balancing) of the content of portfolios, this chapter will look at the next stage in the portfolio management process – selecting projects for the portfolio. Whilst there are swathes of literature on selection models and methodologies, there is relatively little on how the scope of the portfolio is defined – the decisions on which projects are needed in the portfolio to deliver the strategic objectives. Almost all the selection models assume explicitly or implicitly that the projects arrive at portfolio selection from a bottom-up process, with some kind of influence from strategy. In reality, and as predicted by the dual process of planned and emergent strategy (see Chapter 3), work that needs to be incorporated in the portfolio, that is, programs and projects, arrives both top-down (planned) and bottom-up (emergent).

Much of this overemphasis on bottom-up delivery of projects/programs for assessment for selection could be attributed to the dominant theme of much project portfolio management writing – that is, that from a project management theoretical perspective, the natural tendency is to write from a project/program position. Yet understanding how strategy gets turned into work in organisations shows this is only a partial view.

The source of projects for external projects was covered in Chapter 11, with Figure 11.3 showing how projects arrive at opportunity identification from the marketing infrastructure of the contracting organisation. In organisations that only deliver internal portfolios, where do projects and programs arrive from when they come from "above"? This depends on the organisation's environment. Many projects/programs come from marketing in many organisations – for example, new product development, professional services, and financial products firms all understandably deliver many strategic goals through getting the right products to market. Additionally, strategic goals often include requirements to improve operating efficiency of the organisation through IT systems, process improvement, revised structures, sustainability, etc. Other strategic drivers of work in an organisation include fundamental transformations (recently including that of digital transformation), mergers and acquisitions, financial structuring (e.g. share buy backs, issuing shares, bond issues, etc). The point is that turning these requirements into projects is a top-down process, not a bottom-up process, where projects/programs somehow materialise from the organisation and merely need to be put through the selection process to decide what is accepted into the portfolio and what is not.

It is this work to define projects and programs that meet the needs of the organisation's strategy that is one primary concern of the strategic level of portfolio management. Working with the strategy definition part of the organisation, different sets of projects

DOI: 10.4324/9780367853129-14

need to be defined and then run through selection to test the most effective set to achieve the strategic objectives, with the highest value return and the lowest risk. Of course, the sets of projects and programs also need to go through categorisation and balancing as well so that a full and rounded view of each set of projects is gained, leading to an optimised portfolio. Optimised to achieve organisational strategic objectives. This is why the decision criteria must be defined according to strategic needs.

The use of specific program and project characteristics for portfolio selection is situation-dependent. Each organisation tends to choose methodologies that suit its own culture and operating environment (Archer & Ghasemzadeh, 2004). This inevitably means there are many possible project portfolio selection models and methodologies.[2]

At this juncture, it is worth noting that risk is a fundamental characteristic of the portfolio selection process, as was discussed with regard to benefit/risk assessment in the previous chapter. This chapter will discuss risk in general terms and indicate where its assessment is incorporated into selection. However, this is such an important element of portfolio management that a separate chapter is devoted to its coverage in Chapter 17.

High-level model of selection

Returning to Chapter 11, the overall portfolio management process model was presented (Figure 11.1), showing that the selection process required input from both decision criteria and resource allocation processes. Archer and Ghasemzadeh (1999) have also developed a detailed model for project selection (Figure 12.1) that suitably matches the broader Padovani and Carvalho portfolio management process model that effectively structured the previous chapter. The naming and ordering of the processes are slightly different but in fact remarkably consistent.[3] The original model by Archer and Ghasemzadeh has been adjusted to indicate that project proposals are derived from the strategy development process and the flow of emergent strategy.

Apart from showing a high level of concordance between general models of portfolio management, the Archer and Ghasemzadeh model includes additional process information. It shows that the choice of methodology for the screening process requires a decision to be made. The screening methodology (for project selection) needs to be defined so that it integrates with the guidelines and resource allocation processes. The selection methodology brings together both these processes and ensures there is a consistent transfer of criteria and resource aspects through the selection stages. For completeness, Archer and Ghasemzadeh's list of selection techniques is included in Table 12.1., providing a structure for the rest of the chapter. The chapter annex also includes a comprehensive list of additional techniques used for portfolio selection.

The pre- and post-processes listed in Table 12.1 will not be covered in this chapter. The pre-processes correspond to the discussions in Chapter 11 on the strategy processes, and the post-processes are matters for project and program management, not portfolio management, whilst recognising that these processes must be properly integrated with the portfolio processes.

Portfolio selection processes – the five stages

The five portfolio selection processes are discussed in this section in more detail: pre-screening, individual project analysis, screening, portfolio selection, and portfolio adjustment. Most of these processes have an extensive literature, and looking up the works

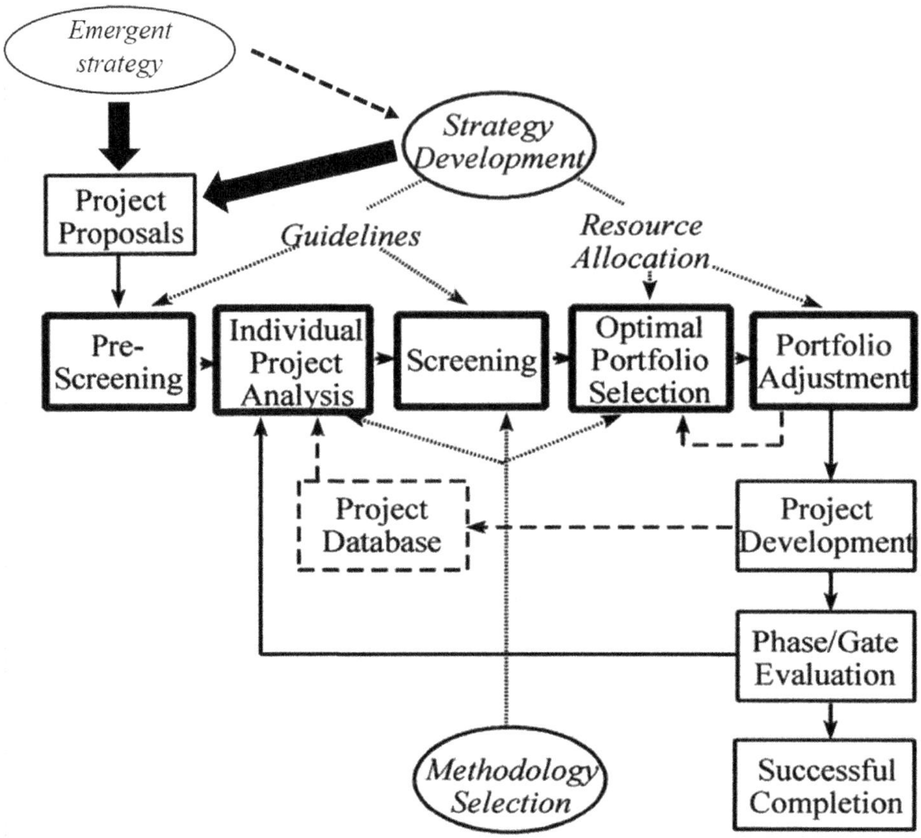

Figure 12.1 Framework for project selection.

Source: Adapted from Archer and Ghasemzadeh (1999).

cited will pay dividends when designing the portfolio selection processes for a particular organisation.

Pre-screening

Once the set of projects/programs identified to deliver the strategic objectives is defined, which will inevitably be an ongoing process, and as new projects/programs are identified from emergent strategy, they must be tested against strategic sorting criteria first – the pre-screening stage. The point of this process is to ensure that projects meet a set of core criteria for inclusion, or that can be adjusted based on feedback from testing them against the criteria. These criteria are about ensuring projects/programs will deliver against strategic objectives, and as such, they must be derived from strategic objectives. It would be unusual to not include significant elements of market research in this process, no matter the market for the organisation, including not-for-profit, for-purpose, and other third sector organisations; those receiving the outputs of the organisation may not strictly be

Table 12.1 Activities and methodologies in the portfolio selection framework

Process stage	*Selection stage*	*Activity*	*Potential methodologies*
Pre-process	Methodology selection, strategy development	Choice of modelling techniques, development of strategic focus, budgeting, resource constraints	Business strategy correlation and allocation, cluster analysis, etc.
Portfolio selection process	**Pre-screening**	**Rejection of projects that do not meet portfolio criteria**	**Manually applied criteria; strategic focus, champion, feasibility study availability**
	Individual project analysis	**Calculation of common parameters for each project**	**Decision trees, risk estimates, NPV, ROI, resource requirements, etc.**
	Screening	**Rejecting non-viable projects**	**Ad hoc techniques**
	Portfolio selection	**Integrated consideration of project attributes, resource constraints, interactions**	**AHP, constrained option, scoring models, sensitivity analysis**
	Portfolio adjustment	**User-directed adjustments**	**Matrix displays, sensitivity analysis**
Post-process	Final portfolio	Project development	Project and program management techniques, data collection

Source: Adapted from Archer and Ghasemzadeh (2004).

paying "customers", but delivering outputs that are not of value to those likely to need them is surely a complete waste of resource.

It is inevitable that these criteria are highly dependent on the organisation's context and environment, purpose, stakeholders, market, etc. Compare a heavy engineering contractor delivering EPC[4] contracts to external clients and a pharmaceutical company looking to feed new drug compounds into its new product development pipeline. The EPC contractor will put invitations to tender through their bidding process, entering at the lead qualification process and then continuing into opportunity identification (see Figure 11.3, Chapter 11). Strategic decision criteria will be applied in these stages, and these might include, for lead qualification: geographic location, ability to cross-sell equipment made by the contractor or its affiliates, ability to offer non-compliant bids with superior technology, and/or significant prior influence on bid development by owner. The opportunity identification process might then refine the testing of the bid to get to a preliminary bid/no-bid decision, such as past experience with the owner, potential for future projects with the owner, likely competition, commercial clauses in contract terms, ability to negotiate technological solutions, familiarity with any pre-feasibility design, and/or FEED (front-end engineering design, often done by third-party designers directly for the owner), cash flow implications for the business, risk envelope, and/or likely range of profitability, etc.

A pharmaceutical company, for example, either does early research (often called discovery[5]), to identify compounds that might lead to successful drug products, or brings in these compounds from third parties (there are multiple ways they may do this). At the point at which it appears the compound has enough attributes that it has not already been discarded, it will begin its journey into the portfolio for development. Decision criteria at this point are likely to include several technical measures of the compound's suitability for development specific to the type of compound/disease, risk envelope as far as known (based on specific organisation criteria), probability of success based on internal and external metrics, ease of designing and executing the "killer experiment" – an experiment that can determine as quickly as possible if the compound can progress (the quicker the "kill," the less money is wasted working on a compound that will eventually not progress later), relative fit to other compounds in development, in-organisation experience of the type of compound/disease area, knowledge of market for the disease, etc.

Clearly, *every organisation has different views on these criteria*, no matter the sector(s) they operate in and, indeed, what the criteria needs to be for their specific circumstances and strategic objectives.

Defining these criteria is an art in itself. As was alluded to in Chapter 11, defining the criteria means understanding what the senior decision-makers believe to be the key criteria, and this is normally captured through a research project gathering data, interviewing, facilitating workshops, and offering alternative sets of criteria for discussion and refinement. Once there is agreement across the senior stakeholder group for ensuring strategic objectives are achieved, the criteria can be trialled and then becomes the standard single reference source of entry criteria to the portfolio. Note that the same organisation may have to have different decision criteria for their internal and, where applicable, external projects. Both sets of criteria need to go through the same process to determine what they are and achieve senior management agreement and commitment to abide by the criteria. Senior decision-makers bringing their "gut feelings" into the final decision process is completely legitimate:

> [S]trategic decision makers display behaviour that is simultaneously rational and intuitive. They make plans and strategies, but they act quickly on incomplete information; they develop many alternatives, but they do not analyse them thoroughly or just focus on a few. Furthermore, it is believed that heuristics and inductive logics that decision makers use often lead to effective decisions.
>
> (Gutiérrez & Magnusson, 2014, p. 32)

The criteria are guidelines for ensuring alignment to strategic objectives and for creating a consistent process for all projects/programs to be assessed against, *not* a final binding and unchallengeable set of rules, the outcome of which is sacrosanct.

Individual project analysis – project evaluation at portfolio entry

Only projects/programs that have been assessed as meeting strategic criteria should be evaluated in detail. Such an evaluation is done using information and data that is included in what is usually called a business case (the document in which the case is made to demonstrate that the project/program is viable and meets organisation-specific business criteria). This almost always includes an assessment of the financial metrics of the project, again specifically matched to the organisational strategic criteria, as well as other key indicators of financial (and also often commercial) performance.

Project evaluation normally includes the following sets of criteria/evaluation testing:

1. *Economic analysis.* These techniques typically require financial estimates of investment and income flows over the time frame of the project, often based on experience with similar projects. The following section will provide detailed information on the set of criteria and their use in analysis.
2. *Simulation.* Simulation can be used to look at all the events on a project and assess the likely outcome of the project and benefit to the organisation. The most commonly used method is *Monte Carlo* simulation, which produces a probability profile of the likely finish time and profile of final cost (the tool is often used for detailed risk analysis, but profiles can be used for project selection). Other simulation techniques include sensitivity analysis, decision theory, Bayesian statistical theory, and decision theory combined with influence diagram approaches (Archer & Ghasemzadeh, 1999). All these techniques are sophisticated and require a detailed explanation beyond the scope of this book to do them any justice.
3. *Cost/value.* A more generic development from cost/benefit; *benefit* has unfortunately become synonymous with the definition of the outcomes of programs in the UK within the project management practitioner community.[6] Measuring the ratio of cost to value can of course be done in many ways, and value may or may not be a financial metric – for example, it could be numbers of people helped out of poverty for a not-for-profit organisation – as a fairly straight forward measure. Chapter 6 is devoted to understanding value in the context of portfolio management.
4. *Risk.* It is important in the use of numeric (quantitative) models to keep a focus on the objective and not get lost in the numbers. Project risk can dramatically affect the likely outcome of a project, and taking a clear-eyed view of the qualitative assumptions underlying quantitative assessment of risk can help prevent serious errors in decisions about project acceptability in the portfolio. See Chapter 17 on risk management for portfolios.
5. *Risk/value.* As for cost/value, this is a more generic measure than risk/benefit for the same reason. It is frequently used as a financial ratio of value at risk (in money terms) versus potential value to be achieved by the project. This is one of the directly translatable metrics from investment portfolio analysis, where the two criteria for portfolio assessment are expected return on investment and risk of that return (called variability in investment terms[7]).

Economic analysis

The portfolio level is concerned with comparisons between projects as well as absolute values of the various financial metrics that can be calculated for projects/programs. Comparing financial metrics allows us to understand:

- Which projects should be funded, and which should not, based on their relative ranking and the total availability of money/funding.
- In what way the projects/programs should be prioritised to maximise the financial efficiency of the portfolio.

- Which projects should receive additional funding if priorities change or the portfolio content changes (e.g. through addition or loss of projects/programs).

Having available absolute financial information allows us to understand:

- The overall make-up of the portfolio in terms of financial returns (the sum of the portfolio's financial returns from projects/programs), which can then be assessed against strategic objectives for the organisation – for example, will organisational financial metrics be achieved, with what cash flow, and with what impact on funding?
- The specifics of each project/program's financial situation to feed into the portfolio decision process.

Financial information is also critical for the management and control of each project/program by their managers and teams.

Since portfolio and program financial information is based on the economics of the constituent projects, we will begin with a look at those.

Project economic analysis needs to be carried out to enable the project investment appraisal to be completed.[8] There are various key metrics used to analyse project economics. It is important to recognise that no one metric alone (generally speaking) is sufficient to understand the complete picture. It is usually the case that the following information is calculated:

- Return on investment (ROI).
- Payback period.
- Cash flow for the project, to the end of the project outputs' operating lives.
- Discounted cash flow (DCF), for the same periods as the previous.
- Maximum capital lock-up.
- Net present value (NPV).
- Internal rate of return (IRR).

The *return on investment* (ROI) is simply the ratio of required investment in a project to the financial benefit generated by the project's outputs, over the lifetime of the project's outputs. ROI is measured on actual (nominal) cash value.

The project cash flows are no more than the negative and positive cash flows needed by, and created by, the project. As is customary for projects, expenditure to create the project and its outputs are treated as negative cash flows, and the monetary benefit created by the project outputs are positive cash flows. Negative and positive cash flows are measured at specific points in time and plotted cumulatively. The time interval to plot cash flows is clearly dependent on the duration of the project, as well as the financial and management accounting cycle time of the organisation funding (and receiving benefit from) the project. A six-month high-intensity information technology platform implementation may work on monthly cash flows (at least during implementation), whereas the construction and operation of a nuclear power station is likely to work on annual cash flows.

A simplified project cash flow curve is shown in Figure 12.2. The key information is included and shows how the payback period is calculated (discounting and net present value are discussed in the next subsection).

When cash flow is plotted, it is obvious when the net negative and positive cash flows are equal. This time period from the beginning of the project is the *payback period*. The

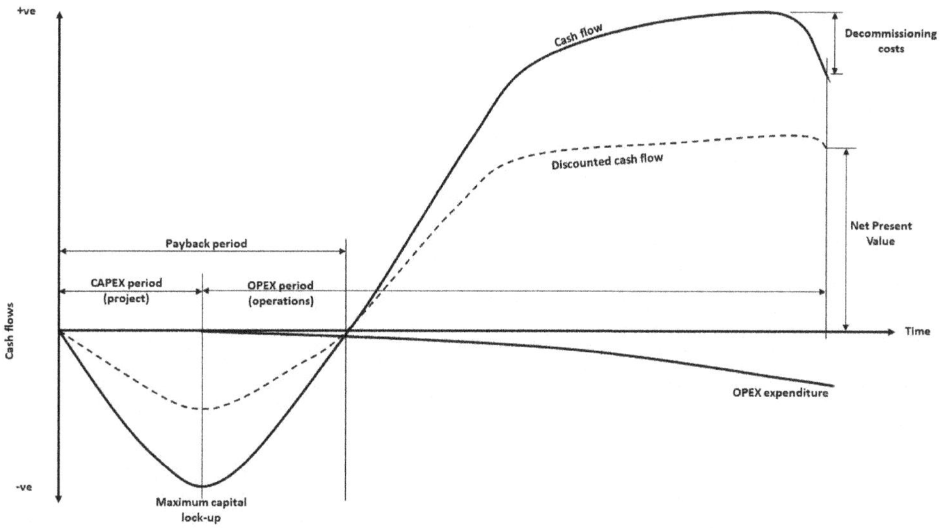

Figure 12.2 Single-project cash flows.

project deliverables at this point have created enough benefit to "pay back" the money invested. The maximum negative cash flow is known as the *maximum capital lock-up*. At the organisation level, this is the maximum amount of cash that will be "locked up" in the project (and therefore not available to the business for other purposes, such as funding working capital or, if the funding is from external sources, indicates the maximum monies borrowed from the lender).

The curve and associated cash flow calculations show at any point after payback is achieved the net positive cumulative inflow of cash to the organisation. The exact shape of the positive cash flows will be dependent on a wide range of factors, including how the benefit is being created. A technology product output from a new product development project will have a cash flow that is likely to have a fast ramp-up of cash inflow, followed by a flattening of cash flow rather quickly (perhaps as competitors race their own products to market). A major organisational change project product, such as an organisation-wide training output, will likely have a slower ramp-up of positive cash flow, but one that steadily continues to increase over a longer period.

Discounted cash flow, present value, and weighted average cost of capital

Cash flow calculations analyse cash at today's value – no account has been taken of the time value of money. Over time, a sum of cash reduces in value as inflation reduces its buying power.[9] A euro today is worth more than a euro in one year's time. At an inflation rate of 2%, one unit of currency is reduced by 2% in a year. To account for this reduction in value over time, cash flows are *discounted*. The value of future cash today is called *present value*. The rate at which cash is discounted is based on anticipated interest rates. The present value, PV, of a single transaction (cash into, or out, of the project) at the end of year n is given by the equation in Figure 12.3.

$$PV = P_n/(1+i)^n = P_n/q^n$$

Figure 12.3 Present value equation – single transaction.

Where: PV = present value; P_n = nominal value of a single payment in year n; i = discount rate, annual interest rate; n = number of years; and q = (1 + i): discount factor.

$$PV_n = \sum_{t=1}^{t=n} P_t/(1+i)^t = \sum_{t=1}^{t=n} P_t/q^t$$

Figure 12.4 Present value equation – unequal cash flow.

Where: PV_n = present value; P_t = single payment due at time t; i = interest rate/discount rate; n = number of years; and q = (1 + i): discount factor.

In real life, project negative and positive cash flows are a series of unequal payments. The present value of a series of *n* unequal cash flows is found by multiplying the time values of each individual cash value by the corresponding present value factor $1/q^t = 1/(1 + i)^t$ and subsequently adding up the present values of the individual payments (Figure 12.4).

When discounting is applied to large projects with significant capital expenditure (CAPEX), a discount rate is used that reflects the particular circumstances of the high CAPEX demand for the investment required in the project. The selection of the discount rate is critical to assessing the costs and benefits of high-CAPEX projects, as small variations in the discount rate can have large effects on the NPV calculations (and hence viability of the expenditure compared to the expected benefits). Also important is that cash flows later in the life of the project's outputs reduce quickly when modelled using discounted cash flows.

Discount factors for large projects are based on the cost of money used to finance the project. Large project finance is often made up from a mixture of sources, typically the organisation's own capital and bank loans. The cost of this project finance is based on the weighted average cost of capital (WACC) for the organisation. Weighted average cost of capital is a calculation of a firm's cost of capital in which each category of capital is proportionately weighted. The WACC determines the minimum acceptable discount rate of an investment, also known as the *hurdle discount rate*.

All sources of capital, including common stock, preferred stock, bonds, and any other long-term debt, are included in a WACC calculation. A firm's WACC increases as the beta[10] and rate of return on equity increase, because an increase in WACC denotes a decrease in valuation and an increase in risk.

To calculate WACC, multiply the cost of each capital component by its proportional weight and take the sum of the results. The method for calculating WACC can be expressed in the following formula (Figure 12.5).

Net present value and internal rate of return

In order to make a complete assessment of the investment case for a project, the *net present value* (NPV) needs to be calculated. This is the difference between the total benefit delivered by the project's outputs (present value of cash generated by project) and the total cost

$$WACC = E/V * Re + D/V * Rd * (1 - Tc)$$

Figure 12.5 Formula for weighted average cost of capital (WACC).

Where: Re = cost of equity; Rd = cost of debt; E = market value of the firm's equity; D = market value of the firm's debt; V = E + D = total market value of the firm's financing (equity and debt); E/V = percentage of financing that is equity; D/V = percentage of financing that is debt; and Tc = corporate tax rate.

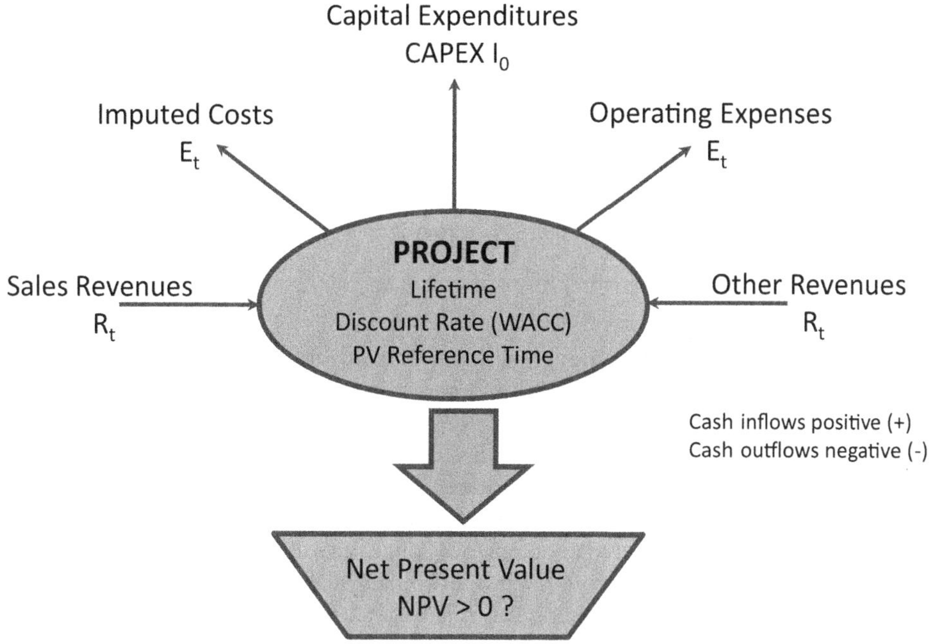

Figure 12.6 Project cash flows in and out.

Source: Adapted from Konstantin and Konstantin (2018).

of delivering the project (present value of project cost), with cash flows for both benefit and cost discounted. In order to be completely accurate, the compounded value of benefits delivered by the project's outputs must also be included in the final NPV calculation. Figure 12.6 shows all the cash flows that are considered when assessing NPV.

Following is the calculation, with a formal definition of NPV (Konstantin & Konstantin, 2018) (Figure 12.7).

> The NPV of an investment is calculated by discounting the time values of all payments during the lifetime of an investment project and adding their cumulative present value of the invested capital. This is mathematically expressed with the following equation:

All projects with an NPV greater than zero can be considered for funding – simply put, if $NPV < 0$, then the organisation will deliver financial benefits by investing in (delivering)

$$NPV = -I_0 + \sum_{t=1}^{t=n} (R_t - E_t) / q^t$$

Figure 12.7 NPV equation.

Where: I_0 = capital expenditures present value (CAPEX); R_t = time value of sales revenues of the year t; E_t = time value of expenses at the year t (OPEX); q = discount factor q = (1 + i); i = discount rate %/a; n = lifetime of the investment project in years and number of years; and t_0 = reference year for discounting (start of commercial operation).

$$NPV = -I_0 + \sum_{t=1}^{t=n} (R_t - E_t) / q^t = -I_0 + \sum_{t=1}^{t=n} (R_t - E_t) / (1 + IRROI)^t$$

Figure 12.8 Internal rate of return on investment.

Where: I_0 = capital expenditures, present value; R_t = sales revenues of the year t; E_t = expenses of the year t (OPEX); q = discount factor q = 1 + IRROI.

the project. In real life, organisations will have a list of projects in their portfolios they wish to run (and this may also apply to programs) but insufficient financial resources to fund all projects and programs. Hence, the NPV, along with other financial and resource assessments (people, time, space, equipment, etc.), is used to prioritise projects.

It is worth repeating: large-CAPEX projects often have long design and implementation periods (two to five years or more for mega-projects), with benefits (positive cash flow) only starting to be delivered at completion, after the initial high negative cash flows. Early negative cash flows are discounted proportionately less than later positive cash flows in large projects – inherently skewing the calculation and leading to possibly marginal NPVs, which may seem unattractive for investment. Hence, great care must be taken with the use of NPV figures in analysing the project economics.

The *internal rate of return* (IRR) of a project is defined as the *annualised effective compounded return rate* or rate of return that sets the cumulative *net present value* of all cash flows from the investment equal to zero.[11] IRR is designed to account for the time preference of money and investments, but in terms of a return on investment rather than a cash sum (as in NPV). A given return on investment received at a given time is worth more than the same return received at a later time, so the latter would yield a lower IRR than the former, if all other factors are equal. The calculation for IRR (in this example, IRR is represented by IRROI[12] = internal rate of return on investment) (Figure 12.8).

IRR is calculated by inference – a rate is estimated, inserted to check for the NPV result, and then adjusted by trial and error until NPV = 0. Microsoft Excel and other software can make direct calculations, where a single input gives the result for IRR.

IRR helps to understand the effective rate of return of the project and is usually measured against a *hurdle rate* set by the organisation. The hurdle rate is set in relation to the organisation's WACC. The difference between the WACC and the hurdle rate accounts for the risk the organisation is prepared to take with projects. As with NPV figures for projects, IRR can be used to prioritise projects based on their financial metrics. Projects with higher IRRs are preferred to projects with lower IRRs.

Note that IRR and NPV give different views of projects' economics. NPV is a measure of total value created at present values, whereas IRR gives a return-on-investment measure. Due to this, these two measures may not give the same order of prioritisation of projects.

Risk

The financial metrics calculated for projects do not, as they stand, incorporate a view of risk (albeit that revenue risk may already be built into the revenue projections). A risk-and-opportunity analysis is needed for each project to understand the profile of uncertainty around various aspects of each project (risks and opportunities associated with technical, funding, market demand, environmental regulations, availability of contractors, stakeholder behaviour, political environment, etc.). The risk-and-opportunity profile can then be used to make an informed assessment of the risks and opportunities in relation to the financial metrics. The calculated figures may then be adjusted (weighted) to take account of the risks/opportunities. Thereafter, the projects are likely to fall into a different place in the prioritisation list/portfolio (see Chapter 17).

Real options

One more financial metric, or rather a way of modelling the projects for further financial analysis, is the incorporation of real options pricing. This has been identified for many decades[13] as a useful way of assessing projects as a series of capital investment decisions that occur over the lifetime (life cycle) of the project.

> [T]he real option framework facilitates decision makers with the options to invest, grow or abandon a project contingent upon the arrival of new information. Similarly . . . a simple capital budgeting model for finding the portfolio of options that has maximum value and fulfils the capital expenditure constraints.
>
> (proposed by Helga et al., 2001 in Padhy & Sahu, 2011)

Five types of real options are generally considered for this method (Trigeorgis & Reuer, 2016):

1. *Growth (or expansion).* Where there are options to grow the project value at certain decision points in the project/program, through various mechanisms (change technology, bring partners in, etc.). An expansion option is valuable because it gives the decision-maker the right, but not the obligation, to increase production (increase scope) if project conditions turn out to be favourable (Farrell, 2002).
2. *Defer or stage.* Delay the project for strategic reasons or for market entry optimisation.
3. *Alter scale.* Significantly change the scope of the project/program to change the scale of the output.
4. *Switch.* Significant changes to supply chain, major alteration to production methods (e.g. change from "stick build" [construct all facilities on site] to modularisation [building large modules in a fabrication yard, then shipping to site and connecting the modules together]).
5. *Abandon/exit.* Abandon a project/program at the point that abandonment value is higher than value of project taken to completion[14]: "The abandonment option is

valuable because liquidation value establishes a minimum project value. A project that can be sold if it becomes unprofitable is worth more than that same project without the possibility of abandonment" (Farrell, 2002).

Whilst the mathematical modelling of real options becomes complicated quickly, the basics are straightforward. Each of the options listed in the preceding passages – and there may be multiple options within each group – has a potential value that diverges from the project value in its planned form. Understanding in advance what value each option could add/subtract to the project when sufficient information is available to make the decision allows the project to be seen as a series of investment decisions. In effect, the organisation is buying the next phase of work in order to gain information that leads to higher-quality decisions on the set of options that have then become available as "real" options. The complete set of decisions is modelled with a decision tree, and multiple futures can then be understood as background to decisions that need to be made at each portfolio decision point (i.e. project entry to the portfolio and subsequent project stage gates).

A summary of the process to develop real options for a project/program is as follows, drawing again on Trigeorgis and Reuer (2016).

1. *Problem structuring*. This involves a qualitative, strategic depiction of the problem structure indicating the various managerial decisions or options, their timing and linkages, the main underlying uncertainties, and the key value drivers. An option map can be developed that is analogous to a decision tree representation but focuses on option characteristics and interlinkages among options.
2. *Valuation and modelling*. At its core, this analysis involves collection of the primary input data to enable a standard discounted cash flow (DCF) estimation and determination of a base-case net present value (NPV) as a base (benchmark). After estimating additional option-driven input estimates, the analysis proceeds with use of an option valuation model, such as binomial trees or simulation, to estimate the expanded-NPV (E-NPV) of an investment. This captures the value of active management represented by the set of embedded options.
3. *Implementation planning*. After arriving at a recommendation for a strategic investment, (project) management can develop a contingent decision plan specifying conditions for the exercise of major options in different circumstances and develop an operating policy and decision milestones across investment stages.

It is likely that the project/program management community will need analytical support for this work, but it is hoped they would already be interacting significantly with finance/portfolio analysts during the development of the business case, anyway. The stages in the development and decision-making for real options for projects/programs is shown in Figure 12.9.

The diagram shows the interaction between the portfolio and project/program communities in order to develop the real options per project. This book takes the view that project managers have a critical role to play in contributing to organisational strategy[15] (which varies depending on the nature of the organisation), and therefore to the portfolio decision-making process. This is normally exercised through the stage gate process but may happen in other organisation-specific ways too. This contribution changes over the development of the real options, with both a period of supporting portfolio management and later periods of leading on the decision process (at the project level).

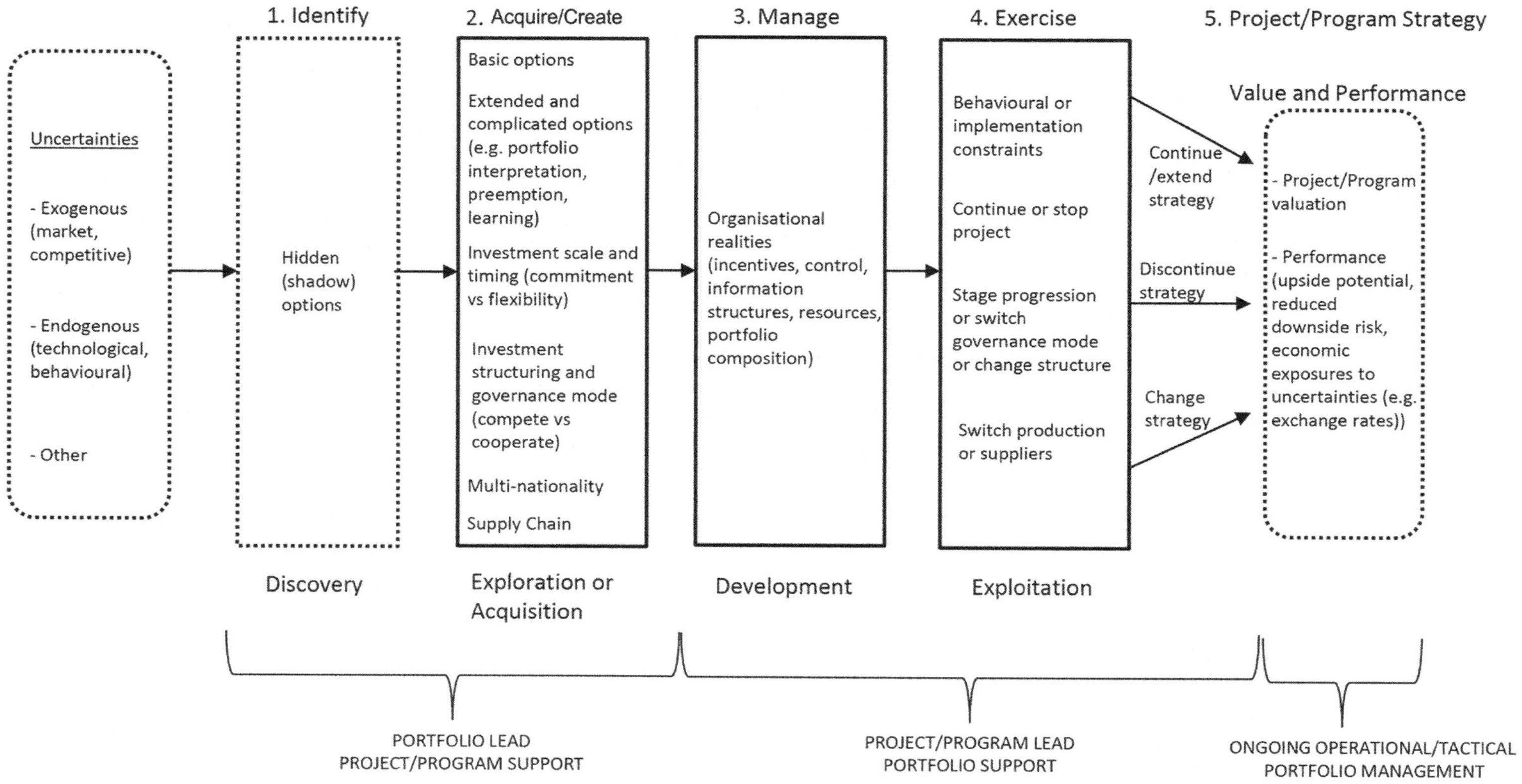

Figure 12.9 Stages of real options development for projects/programs in a portfolio.

Source: Adapted from Trigeorgis and Reuer (2016).

CAPEX, OPEX, and financial management

Capex, or capital expenditure is, definitionally, *a business expense incurred to create future benefit* (i.e. acquisition of assets that will have a useful life beyond the tax year). Capital expenditures can include everything from repairing a roof to a building to purchasing equipment, building new facilities, and can include large software installations. (This type of financial outlay is also made by companies to maintain or increase the scope of their operations.) All significant projects will be financed through capital expenditure.

Expenditures required for the day-to-day functioning of the business, like wages, utilities, maintenance, and repairs, fall under the category of OPEX, or operational expenditure. OPEX is the *money the business spends to turn inventory into throughput.* Operating expenses also include depreciation of plants, machinery, and other assets which are needed to run the company to produce its outputs.

The main differences between CAPEX and OPEX are shown in Table 12.2.

Table 12.2 CAPEX and OPEX compared

	CAPEX	*OPEX*
Definition	Capital expenditures are expenditures creating future benefits. A capital expenditure is incurred when a business spends money either to buy fixed assets or to add to the value of an existing asset with a useful life that extends beyond the tax year.	OPEX (operational expenditure) refers to expenses incurred in the course of ordinary business, such as sales, general and administrative expenses, maintenance, etc. (and excluding cost of goods sold – or COGS, taxes, depreciation and interest).
Also known as	Capital expenditure, capital expense.	Operating expense, operating expenditure, revenue expenditure.
Accounting treatment	Cannot be fully deducted in the period when they were incurred. Tangible assets are depreciated, and intangible assets are amortised over time.	Operating expenses are fully deducted in the accounting period during which they were incurred.
In throughput accounting	Money spent on inventory falls under capex.	The money spent turning inventory into throughput is OPEX.
Examples	Buying machinery and other equipment, acquiring intellectual property assets like patents.	Wages, maintenance and repair of machinery, utilities, rent, SG&A expenses.
In real estate	Costs incurred for buying the income-producing property.	Costs associated with the operation and maintenance of an income-producing property.
Procurement involvement	Purchasing rarely takes the lead but will likely assist in the procurement of assets/ contracts. The negotiation process also takes much longer.	Everyday items bought on a regular basis and minimum stock levels kept. It also does not incur any maintenance cost or repair.

Project and program CAPEX considerations

In terms of accounting, an expense is considered to be a capital expenditure when the asset is a newly purchased capital asset or an investment that improves the useful life of an existing capital asset. If an expense is a capital expenditure, it needs to be capitalised. This requires the company to spread the cost of the expenditure (the fixed cost) over the useful life of the asset. If, however, the expense is one that maintains the asset at its current condition, the cost is deducted fully in the year the expense is incurred.

CAPEX can be found in the cash flow from investing activities in a company's cash flow statement. Different companies notify and manage CAPEX in different ways, and it may be listed as capital spending; purchases of property, plant, and equipment (PPE); acquisition expense; etc. The amount of capital expenditures a company is likely to have depends on the industry. *Capital-intensive* industries have the highest levels of capital expenditures: oil exploration and production, telecommunication, manufacturing, utility industries, etc.

Revenue expenses are shorter-term expenses required to meet the ongoing operational costs of running a business, and therefore they are essentially identical to operating expenses. Unlike capital expenditures, revenue expenses can be fully tax-deducted in the same year in which the expenses occur.

Understanding the total CAPEX needs for an organisation's annual and multi-year financial planning cycle is vital for the efficient management of any organisation (for-profit, not-for-profit, and public). The organisation must be able to determine whether it is able to fund CAPEX from operating profit or whether it needs to access external funding. Furthermore, the timings of the cash demand for CAPEX are also critical, to enable the cash position of the firm at any point in time to be matched to the cash needed to fund OPEX. This applies equally to funding from external sources – it is important to know when funds will need to be made available, what the drawdown profile of that cash will be, and how repayments against these funds will be timed in relation to the CAPEX and OPEX situation of the organisation.

At the organisation level, the total cash demand for all CAPEX outlays at any point in time needs to be known. This essentially means understanding the *aggregated cash flow at the portfolio level* for all the constituent projects and programs. Hence, the project cash flow curve is not only of use to the project/program manager for control of the project/program finances but also for the corporate finance managers to control the organisational finances. This understanding is often missing from people working at the project level, and therefore relatively little attention is given to this aspect of project control. Project cash flow is information that should be included in the business case for all CAPEX-funded projects/programs.

OPEX expenditure can be allocated against specific projects in some cases – for example, asset-specific operating costs, maintenance costs, etc. These OPEX costs may be of interest to project economics and ought to be of concern to organisational finance management. Bringing the necessary attention to OPEX needed to operate the outputs of the project is relevant to the project team – project design decisions may be influenced by the post-project-completion OPEX. It is also quite possible that OPEX may begin before the project is completed if project outputs begin to be used in advance of project completion (this is particularly the case in large multi-phase mega-projects[16]).

For a program, the cash flow is the aggregated cash flow for all projects in the program. Lining up the project cash flows, both negative (CAPEX expenditure) and positive (revenue or benefits), against the program timeline, and in the period in which benefits are accrued, is important and takes care. Factors impacting on this are:

- The initiation of negative cash flows for each project in the program will be at different points in the program life cycle.
- Some benefit will begin to accrue from project outputs before the program has finished.
- It may be the case that some benefits will have different realisation profiles than others; for example, some benefits may continue to be delivered for many years after the program has completed, whilst other benefits may stop after a relatively short time.
- Some projects may deliver no financial benefit as they are enabling projects that allow other projects later in the program to be initiated.

The concern of the program manager is to create a financial monitoring and control process that allows the economics of each project to be clearly understood both at the projects' level and as those project level economics relate to the overall program. This could be particularly important for enabling projects with no benefit directly associated with them. (Finance managers may be very keen to understand the business cases for projects with no directly attributable financial returns!)

The same process is used to create a CAPEX profile for the portfolio. An example of a typical CAPEX profile is shown at Figure 12.10 for a program to build a water treatment facility. Training of operators begins after the project has started, and process optimisation begins after the facility is complete and in operation.

Most significant CAPEX projects have a duration longer than one year, and hence longer than most organisation's financial management cycle of one year. Almost all projects of any significance at all will last longer than the typical large organisational quarterly financial management cycle. A detailed understanding of the cash flows at project, program, and portfolio level is crucial to accurately predict, and thereafter report, cash flow into the organisational financial management cycle. This information allows the financial management of the organisation to be optimised for many factors, including tax, cash flow, profit and loss, depreciation, amortisation, dividend payments, etc. Understanding the financial constraints at a portfolio and organisational level will help project and program managers in their decision-making in planning and implementing projects/programs. Portfolio managers should look to avoid double-counting of project costs and benefits, where the same project is associated with more than one program (see, for example, the tactical portfolio in Figure 9.1, Chapter 9).

Screening

Once the detailed analyses are completed, the project/program is again assessed for strategic fit. Rework of a project's business case as part of optimisation, based on the analysis carried out, may lead to a better analytical outcome in terms of the narrow financial and other measures used but may mean it strays from the strategic criteria. Therefore, the projects/programs are again screened for strategic fit, using many of the same strategic decision criteria used previously, and possibly additional metrics (e.g. gross and net financial contribution). At this stage of the process, the decision being made is, notwithstanding other projects in the portfolio, would the organisation accept the project as it stands in isolation?

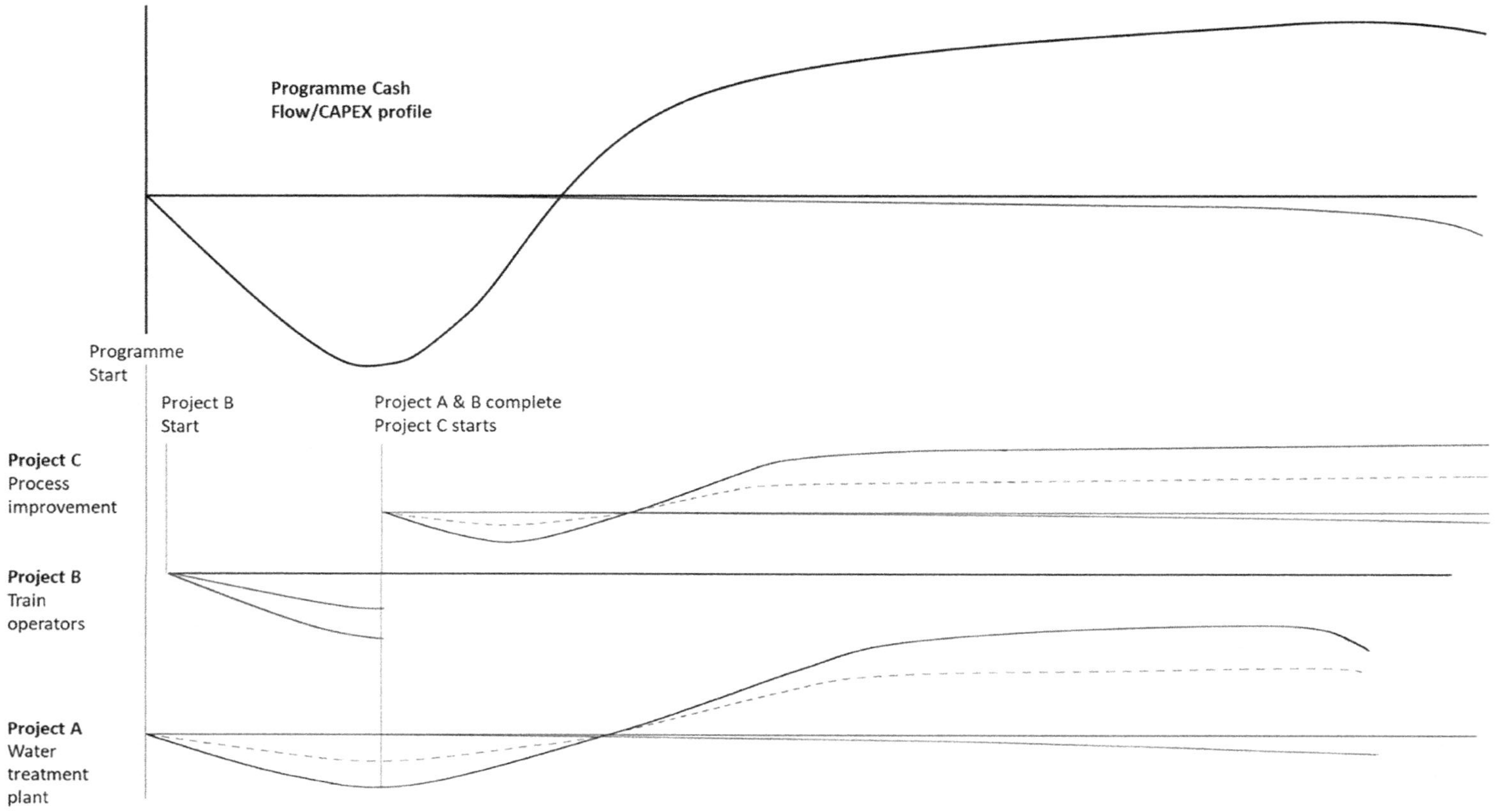

Figure 12.10 Profiled CAPEX for a program.

Once past this final screening, the projects/programs are then assessed against the other projects/programs as a set forming (or reforming) the portfolio (Harpum et al., 1999).

As Table 12.1 indicates, the processes used for screening are ad hoc. This means every organisation will have quite-simple screening tests for projects that will allow inclusion or preclusion in the portfolio, based on the outputs of the project analysis. For new product development portfolios, it seems rather obvious that no new project should enter the portfolio unless it is anticipated to make money – and that means a return at some predetermined level above the cost of the project – often assessed as a certain percentage return above the internal rate of return. For a portfolio of projects delivered to external clients, it is more obvious that cash flow considerations must be accounted for to ensure that potential periods of negative cash flow per project can be accommodated (a critical concern for example in construction projects). Profit-based organisations will also have financial and other performance expectations from projects that the preceding analysis will provide evidence to make a decision against.

Portfolio selection

Once again, there are multiple techniques used in this process, most requiring significant mathematical operations. The following list is by no means comprehensive,[17] but a selection of the methodologies that have, in one way or another, made it into practical application (in some cases, only rarely) and will be discussed are:

1. *Portfolio matrices, also known as portfolio mapping*. Portfolio matrices use bubble diagrams to display values on three or four data dimensions (e.g. risk, NPV, margin, time to deliver, time to pay back, etc.), allowing for simpler decision-making using graphical presentation of project data. This is by far the most common method for selecting the portfolio composition.
2. *Mathematical optimisation models*. Optimisation models select from the list of candidate projects a set that provides maximum benefit (e.g. maximum net present value).
3. *Portfolio decision support systems*. Decision support systems in portfolio selection are typically based on a mixed quantitative and qualitative optimisation approach that involves decision-makers in the process (compared to mathematical optimisation, which does not).
4. *Comparative approaches*. Included in this classification are Q-sort, analytic hierarchy process (AHP), and data envelopment analysis (DEA).
5. *Cognitive modelling*. Cognitive modelling seeks to understand the decision-making process used by project management experts to select projects. This is modelled using artificial intelligence techniques and the method then applied for the selection of projects.

Portfolio matrices

Portfolio matrices are extended from the growth matrix idea (Cooper et al., 2001; Abdallah & Sicotte, 2018; Whittington et al., 2020), with a two-dimensional diagram displaying up to three variables mapped in space: one on the x-axis, one on the y-axis, and another by the size of a bubble. This can be further modified and extended by such techniques as colouring the bubbles to indicate, for example, project categorisation, overall risk level (say, red, yellow, green for different risk levels – each colour defined as part of the process), and many other representations of data. Hence, four criteria could be presented in such

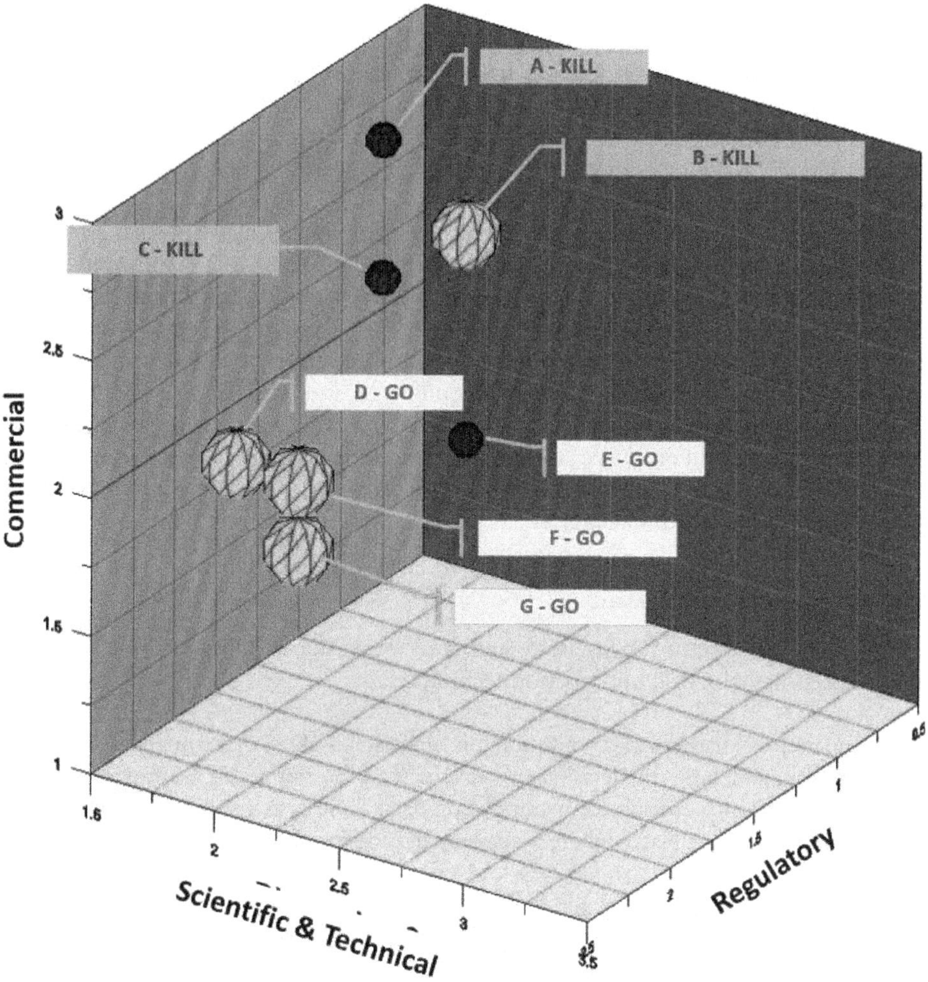

Figure 12.11 Example of five data dimensional representation in a portfolio matrix (bubble diagram).

a diagram. Adding a z-axis allows another dimension to be modelled. That means such a bubble diagram is capable of presenting project data of five criteria, mapped against other projects in the portfolio. Adding cut-off zones to the bubble diagram and other decision notation provides an intuitive approach to project selection for the portfolio. Figure 12.11 provides an example from a biopharmaceutical company. Cut-off for inclusion in the portfolio can be seen with the red lines on the commercial and scientific axes, and the bubbles represent risk (size) and classification (colour). Further information on the practical use of matrices in portfolio selection can be found in the case study in Chapter 24.

Mathematical optimisation models

There are various techniques used in mathematical modelling for portfolios, and this was a major area of interest in the 1970s. Techniques such as linear and mathematical programming, statistical decision theory, and probability theory were applied to solve the optimum portfolio. However, the number of factors that can be accounted for are limited, and often the technique is only able to solve for small numbers of factors (e.g. profitability, costs) (Cooper et al., 2001). Most of these models have not been widely adopted in industry. The mathematics involved requires significant knowledge of the techniques, making them difficult to understand, and therefore difficult to trust by non-specialists. Portfolio selection and optimisation needs to take account of many factors, not just a few straightforward metrics. In effect, complicated mathematical models were originally offered that only solved for simple problems.

Nevertheless, it is important to not dismiss all complicated mathematical approaches to solving for selection and optimisation. Real options pricing uses sophisticated binomial methods (Padhy & Sahu, 2011), combinatorial optimisation algorithms, and integer programming methods (Montajabiha et al., 2017). These techniques are developed with the limitations of earlier work taken into account. The point is not that mathematical modelling is not used or useful; it is that early models that optimised on small numbers of variables are not useful. Nevertheless, the challenge of getting senior decision-makers to engage with the use and outputs of selection and prioritisation models they are not able to fully understand remains problematic, even considering current computational advances. This is discussed further in Chapter 16.

Portfolio decision support systems

Decision support systems (DSSs) are designed to overcome the limited applicability and use of earlier mathematical optimisation techniques.

> Compared to mathematical optimisation approaches, DSSs are much more flexible because they include the decision maker as part of the system. DSSs provide information, models, and/or tools for manipulating data; these systems solve part of the problem and help isolate places where management judgement and experience are required.
>
> (Cooper et al., 2001)

DSSs use a mixture of qualitative and quantitative techniques, involve decision-makers, and are able to optimise for a wide range of factors, such as from Caballero and Schmidt (2014):

- The resources the company needs to develop the project, including investment, people, and equipment.
- Technical requirements, such as productivity, quality, degree of risk, and environmental regulations.
- Relationship between projects, including complementary, disjoint, and mandatory projects.

Although DSSs still require significant mathematical underpinnings, the selection of types of data needed and the particular methods used in the model should be easily understandable by senior decision-makers. If not, this becomes a real problem of legitimacy. The model needs to be simple and transparent in operation, use multiple criteria that have been captured from and agreed by senior management (as for the strategic decision criteria selection noted earlier in the chapter), and be able to produce reliable results even when there is incomplete data (Dutra et al., 2014).

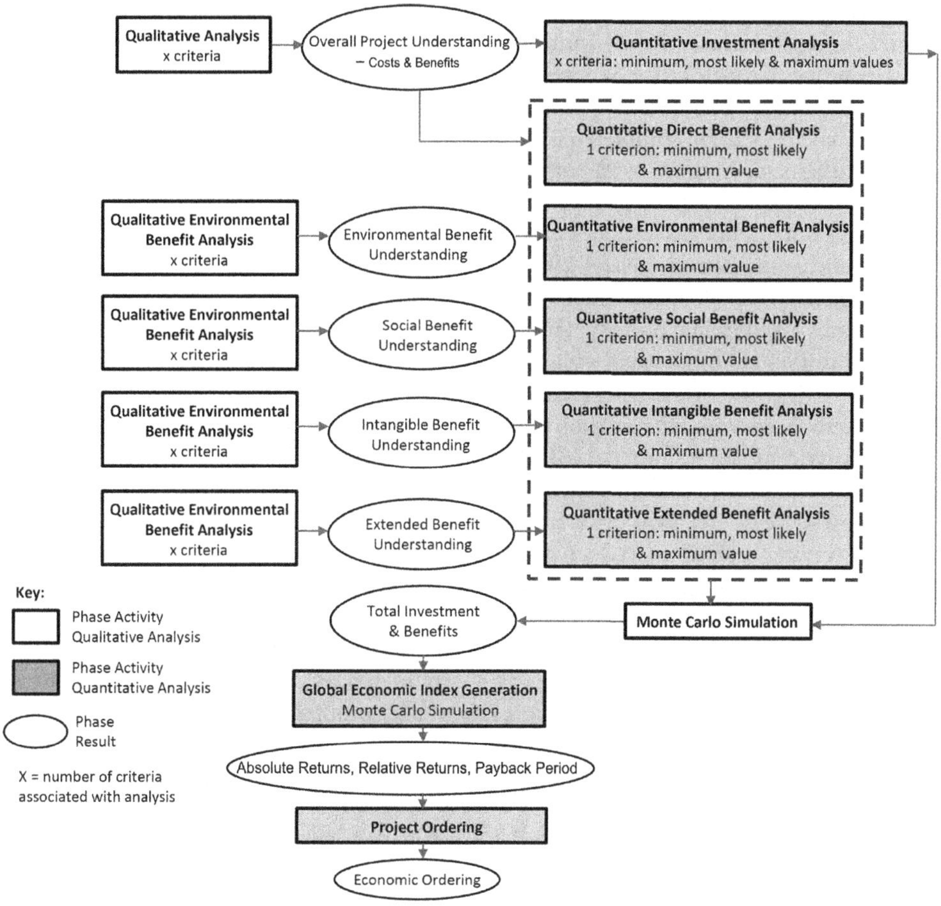

Figure 12.12 An example decision support system process model.

Source: Adapted from Dutra et al. (2014).

An example of a DSS is shown in Figure 12.12. This shows the series of process steps rather than a detailed set of mathematical models employed in each stage. The operations research literature provides rich insight into the detailed applications of the models. Indeed, the project management academic literature also has many papers describing the details of how portfolio DSSs are designed and used.

Comparative approaches

Included in this classification are Q-sort, analytic hierarchy process (AHP), and data envelopment analysis (DEA).

Q-sort has a history in social science research going back to 1935. It is a methodology that combines quantitative and qualitative methods in such a manner that the strengths of both are combined. Although the methodology behind Q-sort is highly mathematical (factor analysis), it provides a way "to reveal the subjectivity involved in any situation – for example, in aesthetic judgement, poetic interpretation, perceptions of organisational role, political attitudes, appraisals of healthcare, experiences of bereavement, perspectives on life and the cosmos, etcetera ad infinitum" (Brown, 1996, p. 561) and, of course, project selection for portfolios – where politics, perceptions, interpretations of value, and alignment to strategy judgements are all fully present (despite the claims of many senior decision-makers of their complete rationality and "observance of what the data shows").

The mathematical aspect of Q-sort is designed to reduce a complicated set of data to a small number of correlated groups of data. "The interest is not the degree to which a series of measurements are related, but instead the degree to which Q-sorts of the people participating in the activity relate" (Rieber, 2020). This means that the group of senior decision-makers use Q-sort methodology to rank projects/programs based on relevant data and questions asked by the process. The questions need to be created carefully by an analyst familiar with the technique, and with care taken not to bias the results through biasing the questions – this is one of the chief criticisms of the method (see Rieber, 2020, and Sneegas, 2020). There are several software tools available for Q-sort analysis, as well as online options.

The analytic hierarchy process (AHP) is a common technique used to prioritise and sort[18] a series of data/artefacts through comparing pairs. This is a method that can be used in selecting strategic decision criteria as well as for the actual portfolio selection process itself. By forcing selection between pairs, the relative importance of each is eventually established after running through all pairs. Once again, reasonably sophisticated mathematical procedures underlie the methodology.

The method assesses the relevance of criteria in the real world and determines interactions between the criteria and relatively large number(s) of alternatives. AHP is reported to be recommended for tender selection in several European Union member countries to ensure conformance with tendering policies for public works (Atanasova-Pachemska et al., 2014, p. II-375). This indicates its reliability and effectiveness for multi-criteria analysis in portfolio decisions.

Data envelopment analysis (DEA) is the most mathematically demanding of the techniques for comparative analysis for portfolio selection. It is used frequently in investment portfolio selection, where it is shown to overcome some of the deficiencies of Markowitz's mathematical modelling.

> This non-parametric method is based on linear programming. It is used to measure the relative efficiency of several decision-making units (DMU) which can be stocks, mutual funds, bonds or other assets where several inputs and outputs are taken into account. . . . Its objective is to compare the inputs and the outputs of DMUs by establishing an efficient frontier and by comparing the efficiency of individual DMUs relative to that frontier.
>
> (Dia, 2009, p. 72)

Ghapanchi et al. (2012) applied fuzzy DEA to portfolio selection for IT/IS projects and found that it can effectively incorporate uncertainty and in-portfolio project dependencies into the decision-making process. Despite this, the mathematics are still fairly daunting.

Cognitive modelling

Cognitive modelling is frequently used in research in the field of decision sciences (into which portfolio selection decision-making falls fair and square). Once again, the mathematics is complicated and not easily accessible to non-expert mathematicians. Nevertheless, it seems reasonable to assume that as this technique is amenable to artificial intelligence (AI) applications, it could well become a common methodology in portfolio selection. Fuzzy cognitive mapping (FCM) has been used to assess risk interdependencies in portfolios, using expert inputs. FCM develops cognitive modelling through the use of language inputs, derived from answers to questions asked of experts of the risks in specific portfolios – that is, real examples have been used to test FCM in portfolio decision-making scenarios, using decision-makers' inputs (Gónzalez et al., 2016). The application with AI simplifies the process for the users and decision-makers, although the nature of the black box process is likely to be a barrier to wider adoption.

Portfolio adjustment

Resource allocation to projects/programs determines how effectively the work can be carried out in terms of schedules, budgets, and the level of risk that can be sustained. If one or a small number of projects receive all the most effective staff, most of the funding available, and preferential access to equipment, space, senior management focus, etc, then what happens to the other projects that are approved in the portfolio but probably cannot hope to deliver to the business case initially put forward in the selection process? This occurs because the business case at the time of the individual project analysis stage could not take account of the final agreed prioritisation – because that decision comes after portfolio selection, logically and in practice.

As usual, the challenge is highly context-dependent. New product development portfolios are internal and, in many sectors, will be affected by attrition, as projects drop out of the portfolio through "failure" (technology doesn't work, likely value does not appear to be materialising, market changes, etc.). External portfolios of projects/programs being delivered to clients are unlikely to "fail" in the same manner. Engineering, construction, IT projects, once under contract, must be taken to completion. Both types of portfolios benefit from prioritisation – which are the most important projects to the organisation. However, the criteria will be vastly different, depending on context and informed by, or identical with, the criteria used for selection for that specific organisation.

Directly related to the impact of resource allocation decisions is the overall value achieved by the portfolio. The value calculated is based on the value each fully achieved project delivers. The less highly ranked projects may not receive sufficient resources to achieve their value, and hence, the overall value of the portfolio may be compromised. If the high-ranked projects achieve their value but the lower ones do not, then the higher-ranked, and better-resourced, projects must, logically, deliver *more* value than they were originally intended to, to ensure the overall portfolio value is achieved.

The previous sections in this chapter have discussed in some detail the various approaches to selecting projects for the portfolio, which in most cases involves ranking projects through different combinations of criteria. Post-selection, the projects may be categorised or not. If they are categorised, as part of balancing and optimising the portfolio, ranking within the category is also possible. Figure 12.13 shows an example of criteria where financial performance is not directly measured (although the scoring criteria of benefit and risk – high, medium, low – may have metrics associated with them). This, of course, is a set of criteria that may be used for selection as well but, by default, provides a ranking, since the overall scores for each project/program can be compared. Whilst this is a rather-simplistic example, no matter the criteria used, there is likely to be a ranking created.

Priority	Change name	Budget	Benefit	Risk	Priority score
1	Proposed change 2	£5.1 m	H	H	10
2	Proposed change 6	£1.6 m	H	M	10
3	Proposed change 5	£4.1 m	H	M	10
4	Proposed change 1	£1.1 m	M	M	7.5
5	Proposed change 8	£550 k	M	M	6
6	Proposed change 7	£100 k	M	L	5
7	Proposed change 3	£2.1 m	H	H	2
8	Proposed change 4	£3.1 m	L	H	2

Figure 12.13 Ranked list of change programs.

Source: Adapted from Axelos (2015).

Priority	Change name	Budget	Benefit	Risk	Priority score	Group
1	Proposed change 2	£5.1 m	H	H	10	Priority 1
2	Proposed change 6	£1.6 m	H	M	10	Priority 1
3	Proposed change 5	£4.1 m	H	M	10	Priority 1
4	Proposed change 1	£1.1 m	M	M	7.5	Priority 2
5	Proposed change 8	£550 k	M	M	6	Priority 2
6	Proposed change 7	£100 k	M	L	5	Priority 2
7	Proposed change 3	£2.1 m	H	H	2	Priority 3
8	Proposed change 4	£3.1 m	L	H	2	Priority 3

Priority 1 = Fully resource to ensure success at all costs
Priority 2 = Resource as far as possible to meet objectives unless priority 1 overrides
Priority 3 = Reduced resourcing, dynamically varying with resources not allocated to higher priority projects

Figure 12.14 Prioritisation groupings within a ranked list of change programs.

Source: Adapted from Axelos (2015).

In reality, even with a relatively small number of projects in a portfolio (say, upwards of five), the allocation of resources is unlikely to be finely gradated to rank. What is more likely is that groups of projects in the portfolio will be created (if not already created through categorisation), shown in Figure 12.14. Resources will then be allocated to those groups, depending on the group/category, without differentiation between projects in the groups.

Of course, within categories of projects that themselves contain large numbers of projects, there may be further grouping and allocation of resources by group within the category. For example, within a construction company's "book of work", it may have 15 projects in its external portfolio (delivered to clients) and 7 in its internal portfolio (organisational development projects/programs, bidding, marketing, etc.). A split in resource allocation between the two portfolios needs to be decided upon. That will probably be a dynamic and changing split over time, as the demands of the two portfolios change. If the external portfolio is running short of resources, it seems likely that the internal portfolio may have resources transferred to the external portfolio until the demand drops in the projects in the external portfolio. When the demand is relatively well managed in the external portfolio or there is perhaps excess capacity due to reduced external projects, the organisation may wish to maximise the return on its internal portfolio while waiting to secure new work for external clients. These decisions about resource allocation are tactical in nature and would be managed by the operational part of the portfolio management team (see further discussion of portfolio leadership, governance, and responsibilities in Section III).

For a pharmaceutical company, the "book of work" or strategic portfolio may have sub-portfolios, including separate research and development portfolios, marketed product portfolio(s) (for, say, brand development), an internal development portfolio, and perhaps others. Allocating budget across the portfolios in both types of company is a strategic decision of the highest order – get this wrong and the organisation's performance could suffer significantly. The construction company that, for example, under-resources important projects for clients gets in contractual difficulties and loses money; the pharmaceutical firm that over-resources research, leading to a lot of potential development projects, in so doing, under-resources the marketed products portfolio, leading to loss of market share and therefore loss of revenue.

After the decisions about allocating resources to portfolios within an organisation, there are the decisions about resource allocation within the portfolios, based on prioritisation using the agreed selection criteria. In practice, there is also likely to be an interaction between portfolio/sub-portfolio allocation of resources (inter-portfolio allocation) and the allocation of resources within the portfolios (intra-portfolio allocation), reducing resources allocated to a sub-portfolio, then needs to be reflected in the allocation of resources to projects in the portfolio – that is, are all projects reduced equally, or are some maintained at their resourcing level whilst others lose much or all their resourcing?

There are several examples in the research literature of prioritisation processes used in industry, including for aviation safety projects at NASA (Sharma et al., 2009) and service life extension of offshore oil platforms (De Melo et al., 2019). These two examples both extend the set of criteria used for selection into the portfolio to take account of the relative importance of projects to each other, measured by additional criteria. As noted previously, Chapter 24 provides detail of the development of selection and prioritisation criteria for a pharmaceutical company. See also Bennett (2010) for a detailed discussion of portfolio management processes, including prioritisation, in the pharmaceuticals industry.

Conclusion

This lengthy chapter has provided a significant amount of information on the selection techniques and methodologies used throughout the portfolio selection process. Strategic decision criteria and their formulation are the starting point for decisions on project/program inclusion in the portfolio, followed by detailed project analysis of business cases, then decision-making on the final set of projects that should comprise the portfolio to optimise it for its job – to deliver the organisation's strategic objectives.

Notes

1 With acknowledgement for text review and insights from Lee Griffin at the University of Warwick on the financial analysis section of the chapter.
2 The literature quite often states that despite much research on selection methods and criteria, there is no consensus on which are the most effective. This seems rather obvious, since the design of these must, by definition, be context- and environment-dependent. Many standardised techniques (e.g. financial calculations) will be incorporated into the *overall selection model,* but each model is unique to meet the needs of the organisation (Paquin et al., 2016).
3 Project proposals maps to opportunity identification. Pre-screening is similar to classification (although in this model there is more emphasis on financial metrics for classification). Optimal

project selection and portfolio adjustment map to selection and optimisation. Portfolio adjustment maps to formation of portfolio. Guidelines and resource allocation are identical to decision criteria and resource allocation. Individual project analysis connected to phase/gate evaluation is the same process as evaluating (EV), which is about evaluating the projects and programs themselves for viability, both as they stand alone and as they fit into the portfolio.

4 EPC contracts (engineer procure construct) are typically large or megaprojects – over $1bn in value – where a contractor is responsible for engineering design, procuring the materials for the contract, and constructing the facility.

5 If discovery is done in the organisation, there is almost certainly a portfolio of discovery compounds that is being worked on, although they are often not projectised at that point – entering the next phase of development is about becoming a drug development project.

6 That *benefit* has become definitional of what programs deliver, due in the main part to the UK's Office of Government Commerce (now called Axelos) guidance publication "Managing Successful Programmes" (Axelos, 2015), and their arguably dogmatic assertion on publicly funded programs following such guidance has led to debate about whether a project can deliver benefits.

7 Note that only accepting a portfolio that overall contains the lowest risk and the highest return does not imply the most efficient portfolio. Markowitz showed this with the expected return/variance (risk), called the E-V rule: "The portfolio with maximum expected return is not necessarily the one with minimum variance. There is a rate at which the investor can gain expected return by taking on variance, or reduce variance by giving up expected return" (Markowitz, 1952).

8 Economic analysis and investment appraisal are often used synonymously. They are subtly different: economic analysis is the work to determine financial metrics for a project; investment appraisal uses the financial metrics for investment appraisal of the opportunity provided by the project.

9 Other aspects of the reduction in value of money in the future also may be included, such as the opportunity cost of not investing money now, say, in government guilts.

10 In finance, the beta (β, or beta coefficient) of an investment indicates whether the investment is more or less volatile than the market as a whole. Beta is a measure of the risk arising from exposure to general market movements as opposed to idiosyncratic factors. The market portfolio of all investable assets has a beta of exactly 1. A beta below 1 can indicate either an investment with lower volatility than the market or a volatile investment whose price movements are not highly correlated with the market. An example of the first is a treasury bill: the price does not go up or down much, so it has a low beta. An example of the second is gold. The price of gold does go up and down a lot, but not in the same direction or at the same time as the market.

11 Equally, IRR is the discount rate at which the net present value of future cash flows is equal to the initial investment, and it is also equal to the discount rate at which the total present value of costs (negative cash flows) equals the total present value of the benefits (positive cash flows).

12 In strict terms, there are two measures of IRR in use. IRROI = internal rate of return on investment, and IRROE = internal rate of return on equity. IRROE only calculates the return on the equity portion of the investment, where equity is invested.

13 By way of an example for how long sophisticated and rigorous portfolio decision-making for sets of projects has been understood as critical to organisational performance, see Dean (1956). Project abandonment options are discussed in 1967 in mainstream financial journals; see Robichek & Van Horne (1967). Note: this is before the existence of the Association for Project Management, 1972, or the Project Management Institute, 1969.

14 "In general, the greater the variance of returns on a project, the greater the expected value of the abandonment option. Other factors that influence option value include: current project value, project residual value or exercise price, time to maturity of the abandonment option and the risk-free interest rate" (Farrell, 2002)

15 From Löwstedt et al. (2018) with their research "*Who is then to be considered a 'strategist' in ConstCorp?*" (Anonymised name for case study organisation). There were indeed some actors who engaged in strategy in the traditional sense: some had developed and formulated strategy plans (often a CEO), some had commissioned strategy workshops as a means to facilitate strategy-making and operationalising the strategy plans on projects, and some had approved of hiring a group of designated strategists that were fully engaged in strategy-related work. While they can be seen as the formal strategists, they were unable to contribute to the creation of significant organizational outcomes. Being empowered to do so was less about which formal role they had and more about being part of a certain informally structured community of practice. "Those managers who had project experience

and foregrounded its related practices and logics were collectively empowered to act as strategists. That is, they were provided with the legitimacy to define what the 'real problems' and 'real solutions' in ConstCorp were . . . would qualify them as 'strategists' and thereby, also giving them the power to reject (or ignore) the practices and tools proposed by various (il)legitimate strategists."

16 For example, a three-unit power station with a CAPEX of £2Bn will likely have unit 1 in operation, generating and selling power, well before units 2 and 3 are built and operating – hence, OPEX for unit 1 starts midway through the project schedule. Some of the OPEX may be included in the project budget, albeit that part of the budget is treated as OPEX, not project CAPEX.

17 Some technical models are reviewed in this chapter, but by way of examples, others such as multi-objective particle swarm optimisation for project selection, artificial neural networks, and problem and analytic network processes are not. See Costantino et al. (2015).

18 Standard AHP is not considered that effective for sorting, but AHPSort has been developed specifically to overcome the shortcomings of the standard approach (Ishizaka et al., 2012).

References

Abdallah S. & Sicotte H. (2018) A real options analysis of project portfolios: Practitioners' assessment. *Journal of Modern Project Management* 6(2), 37–53.

Archer N. & Ghasemzadeh F. (1999) An integrated framework for project portfolio selection. *International Journal of Project Management* 17(4), 207–216.

Archer N. & Ghasemzadeh F. (2004) Project portfolio selection and management. in Morris P. & Pinto J. *The Wiley Guide to the Management of Projects*. Wiley.

Atanasova-Pachemska T., Lapevski M. & Timovski R. (November 21–22, 2014) Analytical hierarchical process (AHP) Method application in the process of selection and evaluation. Conference Proceedings Unitech 2014. GABROVO.

Axelos (2015) *Managing Successful Programmes*. Fourth Edition. The Stationary Office (TSO).

Bennett J. (2010) Portfolio management in the pharmaceutical industry. in Harpum P. *Portfolio, Program, and Project Management in the Pharmaceutical and Biotechnology Industries*. Wiley.

Brown S. (1996) Q methodology and qualitative research. *Qualitative Health Research* 6(4), 561–567.

Caballero H. & Schmidt E. (2014) Decision support system for portfolio components selection and prioritizing. Paper presented at PMI® Global Congress 2014 – North America. Project Management Institute.

Costantino F., Gravio G. & Nonino F. (2015) Project selection in project portfolio management: An artificial neural network model based on critical success factors. *International Journal of Project Management* 33(8), 1744–1754.

Cooper R., Edgett S. & Kleinschmidt E. (2001) Portfolio Management for New Products. Second Edition. Basic books.

De Melo R., Gomes L. & Filardi F. (2019) Project portfolio prioritization strategy to extend the service life of offshore platforms – A Prométhée V approach. *Independent Journal of Management & Production* 10(5), 1421–1445.

Dean J. (1956) Capital Budgeting: Top-Management Policy on Plant, Equipment, and Product Development. Columbia University Press.

Dia M. (2009) A portfolio selection methodology based on data envelopment analysis. *INFOR* 47(1), 71–79.

Dutra C., Ribeiro J. & Monteiro de Carvalho M. (2014) An economic – probabilistic model for project selection and prioritization. *International Journal of Project Management* 32(6), 1042–1055.

Farrell M. (2002) Financial engineering in project management. *Project Management Journal* 33(1), 27–36.

Ghapanchi A., Tavana M, Khakbaz M. & Low G. (2012) A methodology for selecting portfolios of projects with interactions and under uncertainty. *International Journal of Project Management* 30(7), 791–803.

Gónzalez M., Barrionuevo De La Rosa C., & Cedeño Moran F. (2016) Fuzzy cognitive maps and computing with words for modelling project portfolio risks interdependencies. *International Journal of Innovation and Applied Studies* 15(4), 737–742.

Gutiérrez E. & Magnusson M. (2014) Dealing with legitimacy: A key challenge for project portfolio management decision makers. *International Journal of Project Management* 32(1), 30–39.

Harpum P., Merna A. & Pearson B. (1999) Traceability of strategic decisions throughout the project life-cycle. Proceedings Projects and Competencies. University of Economics and Business Administration.

Helga M., Nicos C. & Gerry S. (2001) Capital budgeting under uncertainty–an integrated approach using contingent claims analysis and integer programming. *Operations Research* 49(2), 196–206.

Ishizaka A., Pearman C. & Nemery P. (2012) AHPSort: An AHP-based method for sorting problems. *International Journal of Production Research* 50(17), 1–18.

Konstantin P. & Konstantin M. (2018) *Power and Energy Systems Engineering Economics*. Springer.

Löwstedt M., Raisanen C. & Leiringer R. (2018) Doing strategy in project-based organizations: Actors and patterns of action. *International Journal of Project Management* 36(6), 889–898.

Markowitz H. (1952) Portfolio selection. *Journal of Finance* 7(1), 7–91.

Montajabiha M., Khamseh A. & Afshar-Nadjafi B. (2017) A robust algorithm for project portfolio selection problem using real options valuation. *International Journal of Managing Projects in Business* 10(2), 386–403.

Padhy R. & Sahu S. (2011) A real option based six sigma project evaluation and selection model. *International Journal of Project Management* 29(8), 1091–1102.

Paquin J., Gauthier C. & Morin P. (2016) The downside risk of project portfolios: The impact of capital investment projects and the value of project efficiency and project risk management programmes. *International Journal of Project Management* 34(8), 1460–1470.

Rieber L. (2020) Q methodology in learning, design, and technology: An introduction. in *Education Technical Research Development*. https://link.springer.com/content/pdf/10.1007/s11423-020-09777-2.pdf.

Robichek A. & Van Horne J. (1967) Abandonment value and capital budgeting. *The Journal of Finance* 22(4), 577–589.

Sharma V., Coit D., Oztekin A. & Luxhøj J. (2009) A decision analytic approach for technology portfolio prioritisation: Aviation safety applications. *Journal of Risk Research* 12(6), 843–864.

Sneegas G. (2020) Making the case for critical Q methodology. *The Professional Geographer* 72(1), 78–87.

Trigeorgis L. & Reuer J. (2016) Real options theory in strategic management. *Strategic Management Journal* 38(1), 42–63.

Whittington R., Regner P, Angwin D, Johnson G. & Scholes K. (2020) *Exploring Strategy*. Twelfth Edition. Pearson.

Annex

List of methods for project evaluation and selection for portfolio management

Following is a list of methods used in portfolio selection and optimisation. A list of these methods together with relevant references in the literature for further reading can be found in Dutra et al. (2014).

Table 12.3 Portfolio evaluation and selection methods

Approach	*Method*
Qualitative	Balanced Scorecard (BSC)
	Quality Function Deployment (QFD)
	Bubble Chart
	Fuzzy Logic
	Delphi Method
	Promethee Multi-criteria Method
	Technological Road Map
	Score Technique
	Multi-Attribute Utility Theory (MAUT)
Hybrid	Decision Tree
	Analytic Hierarchy Process (AHP)
	Analytic Network Process (ANP)
	Neural Networks
Quantitative	Data Envelopment Analysis (DEA)
	Financial Analysis
	Dynamic Programming
	Integer Programming
	Linear Programming
	Non-linear Programming
	Programming by Objectives
	Monte Carlo Simulation

Source: Adapted from Dutra et al. (2014).

Section III

Portfolio management capabilities

Introduction

This section focuses both on the practical aspects of managing portfolios covering portfolio management capabilities, interspersed with some further academic research, such as for leadership with four chapters, 16 and 18–20, relating to portfolio leadership in this section.

The section begins with Carol A. Long covering an important area within portfolio management, that of managing resources, with Chapter 13 including discussions on the challenges of managing shared assets and resources, decision-making for prioritisation, and managing data. Chapter 14 follows the theme of integration within the organisation, David Dunning introducing the business integrated governance (BIG) model as an example of managing portfolio governance. This is followed by a related topic in Chapter 15, managing the portfolio office, by Adam Skinner, discussing how to operationalise the functions of portfolio management with the example of a service catalogue. Chapter 16 relates to both the two previous chapters in visualising data and also to portfolio leadership when using data for effective decision-making. This chapter by Catherine Killen examines a set of research case studies in supporting the use of visuals for portfolio management and some guidance when adopting visualisation. It is worth noting here for Chapter 16 that the term PPM (project portfolio management), which the research is based upon, relates to a portfolio of projects.

It is also worth noting within this section the different terms used for the two different areas of portfolio, typically referred to in other sections of this book as portfolio development and portfolio delivery. For example, the governance chapter (Chapter 14) refers to portfolio direction and progress, whilst the portfolio office chapter (Chapter 15) refers to portfolio optimisation and delivery. Following one of the themes of this book, the terminology used is less important than establishing what works in the specific organisational context, recognising that the strategic portfolio will need to be developed and, when established, will need processes in place for effective delivery of the strategic objectives, as discussed in the previous section within Chapters 11 and 12.

Chapter 17 discusses a key capability of portfolio risk management with the example of the efficient risk frontier by David Hillson. Chapter 18 is the principal chapter on portfolio leadership, where Stuart Forsyth and Carl Gavin examine two models based on an engineering sector case study. For Chapter 18, it is useful to note the context within which the projects and programs are organised within the large-scale engineering environment. Other industries and organisations, for example, may consider a £1Bn project larger in scale and therefore more complex than a £10M change program, demonstrating that it is presumed, but may not always be the case for every organisation, that programs are larger and more complex than projects, requiring a higher level of leadership. Within this chapter, the CP3 (complex projects, programs, and portfolios) model is discussed in relation to leadership. This is not related to other acronyms for projects, programs, and portfolios, such as P3M.

Chapter 19 supports the previous chapter from an academic perspective, with Martinsuo and Vuorinen considering key portfolio leadership roles, comparing two case studies for effectiveness. Note that the term "actors" is used in several sections in this chapter and, in an academic context, refers to roles that personnel, or groups/teams of personnel, may hold within an organisation. This can be compared within a project management context with the alternative term of "stakeholders". Chapter 20 is the final chapter relating to portfolio leadership and returns to a more practical perspective, with MacNicol and Dooley considering the styles of leadership in adopting portfolio management, based on the example DISC model.

The final two chapters in this section continue to develop the wider organisational perspective for portfolio management. Nikolov and Harpum, in Chapter 21, discuss supply chain integration with construction industry examples whilst recognising that the principles of supply chain integration are applicable more generally to most supply chains. The final chapter in this section, Chapter 22, covers agile portfolio management with Messenger and Angliss. The chapter is fairly experimental in nature, considering whether strategic portfolio management ensues the same principles as agile portfolio management, based on the agile organisation and organisational agility.

Finally, it is worth noting when reading through these chapters that if this book has met one of its own strategic objectives of reaching senior managers and c-suite executives, the hope is that people in these roles can already recognise strategic portfolio management as the critical linkage between strategy development and strategy execution, and thus the important role of strategic portfolio management at all levels within the organisation.

Chapter questions

Katy Angliss

Once again, similar to the previous sections, there are some questions to consider when reading through Section III, covering for each chapter initially the material review questions, followed by the further discussion questions. (As previously noted, where references are included in the questions that follow, these relate to the references in the relevant chapter).

Chapter 13: Asset and resource management

Material review questions

13.1 Discuss some of the areas to consider for effective asset management within the portfolio.
13.2 Discuss some of the areas to consider for effective resource management within the portfolio.
13.3 What are the optimisation challenges for both asset and resource management within the portfolio?

Further discussion questions

13.4 Discuss the key challenges for a portfolio manager when managing assets within the portfolio.
13.5 Discuss the key challenges for a portfolio manager when managing resources within the portfolio.
13.6 Debate whether data is an asset or a resource and how data can be managed in the portfolio.

Chapter 14: Business integrated portfolio governance

Material review questions

14.1 What are some of the requirements for, and the benefits of, effective portfolio governance?
14.2 What are the different types of portfolio archetypes discussed, and what is the distinction between each?

14.3 Identify some of the main roles and responsibilities of a PDG (portfolio direction group) and PPG (portfolio progress group).
14.4 What are the important aspects of MI (management information) to consider for the BIG model to be effective?

Further discussion questions

14.5 How can the role of the main board influence the success of the portfolio?
14.6 How can the method of data collection and collation affect the establishment and operation of the data model as part of the governance framework?
14.7 What are the advantages of a business integrated governance model for effective portfolio management?
14.8 What are some of the considerations involved with establishing a robust, but not overburdened, reporting cycle with effective management information and data to maintain a focus on strategic portfolio delivery?
14.9 How could the *business integrated governance (BIG) framework* be adapted for your organisation? Or suggest an alternative integrated governance model that may be more appropriate for your organisation – consider within this the accountability nodes.
14.10 After reading the following statement, critique the BAU portfolio archetype. Is it appropriate for your organisation?

The operational portfolio is sometimes called the BAU (business-as-usual) portfolio. The concept of business-as-usual is challenged in earlier sections, where the distinction between business-as-usual and the content of portfolios of projects and programs is considered to be false (delivering a portfolio of projects and programs is business-as-usual; otherwise, how would organisations survive if they didn't carry out such work?).

Chapter 15: Portfolio office

Material review questions

15.1 Compare and contrast the advantages and disadvantages of a portfolio office.
15.2 What are the aspects to consider for service operationalisation?
15.3 Consider how optimisation and delivery sub-functions can affect the portfolio structure and portfolio leadership. How important is effective decision-making in the portfolio?

Further discussion questions

15.4 Discuss how the *optimisation* services sub-functions influence high-quality *optimisation* decisions.
15.5 Discuss how the *delivery* services sub-functions influence high-quality *delivery* decisions.
15.6 Where and how should resourcing and capacity management decisions be made in the organisation?

Chapter 16: Visualising data for portfolio decision-making

Material review questions

16.1 How can the adoption and understanding of portfolio visuals (and data) help with effective decision-making?
16.2 How does human cognition and "cognitive load" affect portfolio decision-making?
16.3 What are some of the key factors to consider when designing effective visuals to support portfolio decision-making?
16.4 What are the three types of interdependencies between projects when considering cognitive fit, and what are some of the different methods for displaying these interdependencies?

Further discussion questions

16.5 Discuss some of the disadvantages of using mathematical modelling for data visualisation.
16.6 Discuss whether visualisations can reduce bias and the reliance on heuristics for portfolio decision-making.
16.7 How might visualisations be designed or improved for portfolio management decision-making within your organisation?

Chapter 17: Portfolio risk management

Material review questions

17.1 Why is it important to manage portfolio risk effectively?
17.2 How is managing portfolio risk different from managing program(me) or project risk?
17.3 What can be the different origins of portfolio risks?
17.4 How can portfolio risk be managed using the risk efficient frontier?

Further discussion questions

17.5 Discuss the recommended differences for the portfolio risk management process when compared to a typical project risk management process.
17.6 Consider some of the difficulties with managing portfolio risk and/or implementing a portfolio risk management process within your organisation.
17.7 Refer back again to the discussion of value and benefits in Chapters 6 and 7 and consider the following in terms of portfolio risk management in this chapter.

> *"Benefits" is a term frequently used in project management and risk management in various domains. The relationship between the meaning of the word "benefit" and of "value" is not always clear, and therefore some attention is needed when*

understanding exactly what is meant by the meaning of both these words in the context of portfolio risk management.

17.8 After having read through this chapter, look to discuss the following argument, with reference to the alternative sources as suggested and, from a practical perspective, considering the following three questions:

a) Do you agree with this perspective?
b) How might applying risk efficiency influence the management of portfolios?
c) Can you suggest other ways of managing portfolio risk management?

In line with the perhaps perceived view of the "discovery" of portfolio management by the professional bodies for project management, there is beginning to be some recognition of the concept of risk efficiency in portfolio risk management.

However, detailed guidance on implementation and application is still arguably mostly missing. For example, the risk management section of the PMI Standard for Portfolio Management *(Project Management Institute, 2017b) includes clear statements about balancing risk and value but does not explicitly mention the term "risk efficiency". Perhaps even more importantly, the suggested portfolio risk management framework reverts to the traditional approach of risk management planning, risk identification, risk analysis, and risk response, without explaining how a risk-efficient portfolio can be achieved or maintained.*

The same situation is found in APM Portfolio Management: A practical guide *(Association for Project Management, 2019b), which also does not mention risk efficiency. Detailed guidance is not given on how to assess the overall risk profile of a portfolio or determine whether it is within limits, and the section on constructing a portfolio seems to mention risk only in passing.*

Chapter 18: Portfolio leadership

Material review questions

18.1 What types of skills are important for a portfolio leader to possess?
18.2 How complex is portfolio leadership when compared to project and program leadership?
18.3 What is the typical role of the portfolio sponsor?
18.4 When is it more appropriate to use fact-based management and pattern-based management?

Further discussion questions

18.5 How does complexity affect portfolio leadership, and how can the portfolio leader adapt to different complex systems?
18.6 What is an equivalent role to the portfolio leader in your organisation?

18.7 Critique the four areas of Ancona et al.'s (2007) model: sensemaking, relating, visioning, and inventing?

18.8 How could the portfolio leaders in your organisation (or for your own portfolio leadership) improve performance considering Ancona's model (or the CP3 model), the portfolio leadership model (Cynefin framework), and portfolio complexity?

Chapter 19: Managers' roles in strategic portfolio management

Material review questions

19.1 Considering the two case study organisations, ConstructionCo and SoftwareCo, how can manager's involvement in SPM differ between organisations and be context-specific?

19.2 How does the manager's involvement affect the success of SPM?

Further discussion questions

19.3 How is it suggested that managers can relate to SPM (strategic portfolio management) as opposed to PPM (project portfolio management), and how could senior managers engage with SPM in your organisation?

Chapter 20: Enabling adoption of portfolio management

Material review questions

20.1 How can the DISC model be applied to initiating a portfolio?

20.2 What are some of the potential challenges and biases for the adoption of portfolio management, with reference to personal styles?

Further discussion questions

20.3 What are the typical phases for adopting portfolio management discussed in this chapter, and how do they compare with earlier discussions (e.g. within Section II)?

20.4 Referring back to Section II of this book, covering alternative perspectives on the naming, structuring, and managerial philosophies for portfolio structures, critique the two types of structure, "standard" and "structured", discussed in this chapter and the advantages and disadvantages of each.

Chapter 21: Supply chain integration in portfolio management

Material review questions

21.1 How does supply chain integration (SCI) differ from supply chain management (SCM)?
21.2 Discuss the advantages and challenges of supply chain integration.
21.3 How can the four types of portfolio archetypes, suggested for managing supply chain integration, establish value for the organisation?
21.4 What are some of the aspects to consider for the four dimensions of supply chain management (SCI) – strength, scope, duration, and depth – in realising value through the portfolio?

Further discussion questions

21.5 How does the portfolio life cycle discussed in this chapter when considering SCI (screening, selection, and prioritisation) compare to the portfolio life cycle discussed in earlier chapters?
21.6 How could SCI be, or is, managed within your organisation for projects, programs, and the portfolio(s)?

Chapter 22: Agile portfolio management

Material review questions

22.1 Discuss the basic premise of the Agile Manifesto and how the agile philosophy can relate to agile portfolio management.
22.2 Consider alternative strategic development tools and techniques, other than "VMOST", that may be appropriate for an agile strategy.
22.3 What are the key agile behaviours, based on continuously creating value for the organisation, to consider for effective agile portfolio management?

Further discussion questions

22.4 Critique the agile portfolio management flow proposed by the Agile Business Consortium, and consider any alternative approaches that may be appropriate in this context.
22.5 Suggest how resource management and portfolio governance can be integrated with agile portfolio management.

13 Asset and resource management

Carol A. Long

Introduction

Asset and resource management are fundamental to portfolio management. Without assets as enablers and resources to execute the work, then any portfolio would be impossible to deliver. In many organisations, as Wagner (2018) notes, "[a]sset portfolio planning is impossible without the planning information from projects, programs and project portfolios". This bottom-up approach has benefits in short-term planning. However, portfolio management and strategy development often have longer time horizons that cannot wait for the details from the projects these processes will initiate. This top-down, bottom-up dichotomy is difficult to resolve if asset and resource managers are not given sufficient foresight of demand. For some assets or resources, the lead time from order to delivery can be substantial – for example, a new building, a redeveloped manufacturing plant, or time in the diary of an expert skilled in a rarefied area of technology.

Yet in PRINCE2 (Axelos, 2017) and other project management methods, assets and resources are rarely mentioned as something to be managed beyond the tasks and activities in which they are involved. For the most part, attention is given to the resources of money or humans and assets under a configuration management plan (see ISO 10007:2017 for a definition of configuration management). There is a focus on defined roles and responsibilities and measurement in terms of time, cost, and quality. For a project, this may be entirely appropriate, as ownership of assets is likely to be short-term or beyond the management level of the project manager.

Program management is often defined in terms of the activities (which may be in projects) that are undertaken to deliver a change for the organisation (Axelos, 2020). The construct of process, organisation, technology, and information (POTI), which is used to describe what might change, may include assets or resources. Again, the processes in program management methodologies do not provide any particular focus for asset or resource management.

In contrast, portfolio management methodologies often focus on resources as the business capacity to deliver the overall strategic aim. Pennypacker (2008) noted much of this resource management focus is the management of human resources. This is incomplete thinking about the problem of how to develop, deploy, and dispose of assets and resources towards strategic aims.

There are some benefits in the separation of assets and resources in the thinking of portfolio managers. This recognises that some factors are expected to be resources that will be depleted (used and expended) during a portfolio, whereas assets will be under stewardship (used and cared for), and this thinking may be an advantage in planning. There will be

DOI: 10.4324/9780367853129-16

responsibilities and activities required to ensure that assets are maintained and enhanced, responsibilities that are beyond those tasks required for managing resources. For portfolio management, the task with resources is to ensure that they are stored (accommodation), used, and released (either for work or outside the portfolio) when appropriate and available in the right place in a timely way. This chapter is not intended as a full briefing on human resource management, asset, or capacity management but covers some aspects that are particularly interesting in the context of portfolio management.

Capacity management

It is worth noting here that the terms *asset*, *resources*, and *capacity* can be seen as overlapping and/or used interchangeably. For the purposes of this chapter, *resources* predominantly refer to human resources, with *assets* referring to non-human assets. Both resources and assets can be tangible or intangible. For example, tangible assets could be machinery, and intangible assets could include software, contracts, or copyright. Intangible resources could be intellectual property or supply chain capability. *Capacity* is often used in the context of primarily human resources but can also be used to cover both human and non-human resources or assets. As such, *capacity* and *capacity management*, in this context, will refer to the availability and utilisation of both resources and assets as an overarching capability.

Capacity management is defined as covering both the planning and control of capacity, that is, capacity must first be planned, and then, once capacity is made available, it must be managed to meet the actual needs – as opposed to the needs assumed during the planning process (Harpum, 2010). A generic capacity management process is shown in Figure 13.1. The reality is that capacity management of human resource is difficult, many-faceted, and still quite immature compared to other capacity management processes, for example, production machinery utilisation and IT network infrastructure capacity management.

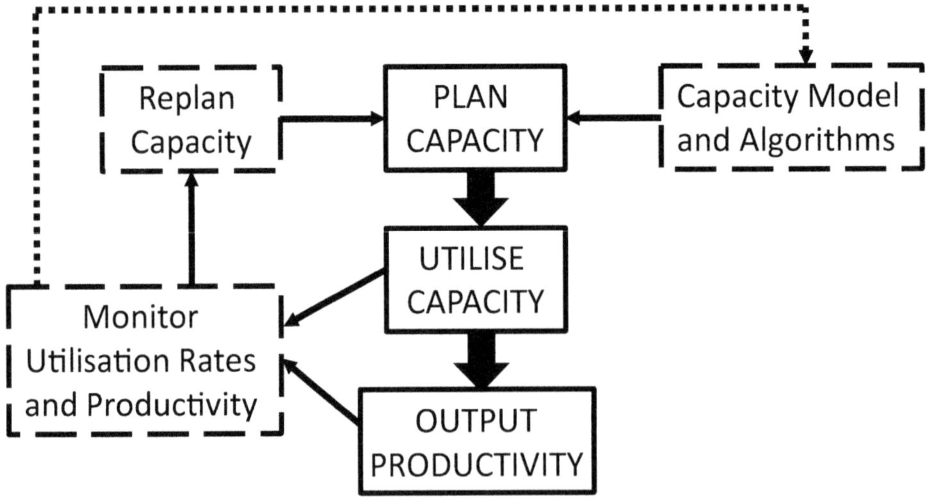

Figure 13.1 Generic capacity management process.

Source: Adapted from Harpum (2010).

Asset management in portfolios

Wagner (2018) poses a number of questions about asset management for the planning of the strategic portfolios, such as: Which assets are to be built next year? Do we have enough resources to perform the asset development projects on time, to quality, and to budget? What are the priorities for the multiple projects to be completed in a sub-portfolio or a portfolio? How do we balance the available financial and human resources between the requirements and assets of respective project portfolios?

These demonstrate an interesting perspective from project management:

- It is short- to mid-term in timescales.
- It focuses on prioritising projects or sub-portfolios (it is about work).
- It only considers financial and human resources (and not other resource types).
- Assets are output (not enablers).

Thus, asset management is a broader topic than the project management community may acknowledge, and it sits well beside the wider view of strategy.

Changes in the business context, where corporations had a single purpose of "profit maximisation" to the focus on "stakeholder capitalism" (Gleeson-White, 2020), have changed how managers see value (refer to Chapter 6 for further discussion on value). This drives a change in strategy, which in turn is likely to change the way in which companies determine measures of effective use of their assets and resources. This move towards recognising sustainability is not just about raw materials or organisational longevity, as it encourages the minimisation of waste overall. Thus, effective stewardship of assets and sustainable use of resources is somewhat different to the culture suggested by the project management perspective, that is, only an interest in the shorter-term delivery. Portfolio management will continue to be the place in which care of assets and management resource is manipulated to fit the delivery of both strategic aims and tactical outcomes.

Gavrikova et al. (2020) reviewed the current literature on asset management in the strategic context and highlighted the apparent optimal approach to asset management as holistic and strategically aligned. This provides the portfolio manager with some difficulties:

- It is unlikely the portfolio manager will have long-term exclusive ownership or stewardship over all the strategic assets used within their portfolio.
- The underlying temporary nature of projects, programs, and strategic intents (that once they are achieved, they expire) suggests that project portfolios are also temporary organisations.
- Each portfolio manager's concern may be their own portfolio, but at an organisational level, there may be more than one portfolio that requires use of a strategic asset, giving rise to internal conflict between strategic aims.
- While some assets have relatively short life cycles, more enduring strategic assets are likely to outlive the portfolio, for which they are critical enablers or strategic developments.

This suggests that the assets that are most important to a tactical or project portfolio may not be effectively within the management scope of the portfolio manager. An organisation that has multiple portfolios may have portfolio managers competing for the use of strategic assets. Prioritisation or scheduling issues may need to be resolved at the more senior management level, that is, at the strategic portfolio level, above project portfolio managers, to ensure that effective use of the asset aligns with the overall strategy of the organisation. Resolving these questions may have serious impacts on the achievability of some portfolios, and how these decisions are made will be industry-dependent, as the nature of an asset, or the constraints around its use, may relate to that industry. One example of this is the research asset of a wind tunnel and competing portfolios within that organisation to (a) develop a new product and (b) upgrade or relocate older research facilities. Alternatively, in other industries that are less asset-intensive and rely more on intellectual property, it may be possible for two portfolios to use the same intellectual assets (e.g. proprietary research or patents) without any discernible impact on each other.

Strategic use of an asset may have a contextual bias. What is seen as the strategic direction at corporate strategy level may be different from the asset management strategy over portfolios or at odds with the technical asset management strategy within any specific discipline. This is implied in Gavrikova's (Gavrikova et al., 2020) separation of strategic asset management, based on levels of management, following their choice of the Thompson-Peteraf-Gamble-Strickland observations of strategy divisions (Thompson et al., 2020). Considering the projectised organisation, portfolios tend to sit at a level that may equate with a business group (i.e. may be aligned with a product suite or supply chain) or functional group (e.g. a technical renewal) or may have a scope that covers the whole organisation in parts (e.g. a "root and branch" diversity and inclusion improvements portfolio). Sub-portfolios may be split out to compartmentalise risk or accountability (e.g. within a program or for a business location).

In strategic terms, the decision-making around the assets assigned to a portfolio may thus be assumed to be constrained by the expectations of the organisation's stakeholders and also compliance placed upon the organisation, as this often frames corporate-level strategy. However, from the author's personal observations in practise, the achievement of a strategic portfolio can sometimes be attained only by departing from these expectations and operating in another field of compliance. This is particularly so where a portfolio is designed for transformative business change, and so to pivot the organisation from one area of operation to another. This deviates from Gavrikova's unstated assumption that certain aspects may not apply in the management of assets between operations, management of individual (or classes of) assets, and organisational management. In practice, a portfolio manager may be accountable for a part or whole of an asset life cycle and its specification or its performance, knowing that the asset has a life outside of their portfolio. Thus, the accountability of a portfolio manager may cut across all levels of management regarding the assets allocated to their portfolio.

The duration of the life cycle of an asset is dependent on that asset. Intellectual property or nuclear reactor life cycles are measured in decades. In contrast, a building, vehicle, or factory machinery, and perhaps software, may be envisioned, created, used, and disposed of within a smaller number of years. Alternatively, knowledge creating strategic advantage can be an asset that lasts mere days before it becomes of limited value. Thus, conceptual processes or abstract standards might not be able to deal with some types of assets. There are, however, some consistent themes around the care of assets that a portfolio manager should pay attention to so that the asset maintains its value in the organisation. These include:

- Basic information about the asset, such as its identifiers, asset class, condition (or life cycle stage), location, and value on receipt of the asset.
- Maintenance obligations and schedule, maintenance, or disposal protocols.

- Obligations around tracking (e.g. location or performance), compliance, potential liability, security or protection, and associated continuity plans.
- Operation information and operational constraints.
- Expected class, status, and residual value after the portfolio has handed the asset back to the organisation.
- Risk management plan(s) for the asset, its life cycle, and its use.

This is a simplified list to start the thinking process around risk and how an asset should be stewarded. The asset will arrive with management expectation that it will be used within the portfolio and has been allocated to that portfolio for strategic benefit. During the execution of the portfolio, that asset will be needed in a particular state for each activity, and that state needs to be managed both before and after the activity. There may be some operating risks that need to be managed in specific ways for each type of asset (e.g. the location of a building may not need to be protected, but access to that building may need to be restricted, whereas the existence of a company secret design may need to be protected from any form of disclosure, as well as access to the design documentation being restricted, and access to specialist equipment may need to be restricted to approved operators only).

At the outset of a portfolio, paying attention to the end state required of an asset may change the options available to the work of the portfolio. For a building, there may be a need to return it to the state received as part of the dilapidations clause of a lease, or the purpose of the portfolio may be to replace it and other buildings, or to leave it in a state where colleagues working in another portfolio may take up residence. Similarly, equipment may need to be retired, repurposed, or improved as part of a portfolio of work. Financial assets can be used to generate financial resources, although there may be constraints around what is allowable within the financial controls of the organisation (e.g. investment may be allowable, whereas loans against the capital may not be possible without further approval, and liquidation may not be an option).

Reflecting on the previous paragraphs, a portfolio manager will note that there are a range of stakeholders that may be associated with each asset. As the asset ages through its life cycle, the condition and resilience of the asset and these stakeholders and their expectations, may significantly change. The management plan for an asset may need to be phased for these factors.

Each asset will need some active management and monitoring. This activity will require resource and possibly a separate budget from the main work of the portfolio. Assuming the asset has strategic value, it will need to be easily located and evaluated, against the organisation's process demands. The management plan will also need to include any specific risks around failure, deterioration, faults, or replacement that are the responsibility of the portfolio outside of the expected maintenance obligations. The portfolio risk management plan may be an appropriate place to search for, or record, such asset life cycle–related potential work. There may be an existing organisational framework for managing risks associated with assets.

The accountability for an asset and the responsibility for its use may need to be carefully considered, as it is employed within the portfolio – are there any specific handover requirements, tracking and monitoring, or reporting lines that need to be informed as part of the management of the asset? If the asset is of strategic value, there might be reporting lines outside of the portfolio that also need to be considered.

Some assets, including manufacturing and wearable design and devices, will require technical management to be included in the asset management plan. The increasing growth of IoT (internet of things) sensors and the associated statistical process control or artificial intelligence need to be considered carefully to ensure effective and ethical use of the data collected and any conclusions drawn. This may require the engagement of some deep specialist capability within the portfolio management team.

Asset allocation and assignment to activities within the portfolio will be a key driver for effective and timely delivery of the activity within the portfolio. Care must be taken to ensure that the appropriate assets are available in the right condition as required by those activities in a timely matter. The inclusion of a risk factor to allow for schedule delays and dependencies between those activities must be balanced against effective overall use of the asset. The balance between efficiency and effective use of assets and the difficulty of assuming the possibility of optimisation is discussed later in this chapter.

Asset availability can shape the selection of activities within a portfolio. If assets required for a particular strategy are not available within a suitable timeframe, then that strategy will fail, as the enabling activities will not be able to deliver. Allocation of assets can therefore shape the activities and projects within a portfolio, as tactical alternatives modify the activities based on the assets that are available. Simple prioritisation or scheduling techniques may not consider this predicament, so a more holistic view of strategic need might be required. With physical assets, this becomes a "management art" of working with what is available, rather than a mathematical allocation or scheduling problem (Harpum, 2010).

Gavrikova et al. (2020) note that several of the papers they reviewed also conflated decision-making around assets, particularly regarding make-or-buy decisions. This is unsurprising, given that some portfolios (or programs) are specifically established around creating assets (lasting business capabilities or products to generate future resources), typically through the conversion of intellectual property and raw materials with tools and human effort. Some of these tools will be assets in themselves. Note also that conflating both the methods by which the outputs or outcomes are produced and those outputs or products themselves signals a commonality in how assets are viewed by the project management community.

For some organisations, all products are treated as assets, and the configuration management around those assets recognises the value, status, and current and future ownership (perhaps a customer or another part of the organisation). There are difficulties, however, with this approach, especially if the practical management is extended into financial management, when considering capitalisation and disposal or sale of such assets – obviously, the details of this specialist area is beyond the brief for this book – but portfolio management practitioners may need to consider this as a practical question: What is an asset and what is a resource in this organisation, and does it matter to our corporate value? The following section assumes resources are discussed in the more generally accepted categories.

Resource management in portfolios

As discussed earlier, resources can be both tangible and intangible. Intangible resources include intellectual property and ideas, reputation and esteem, or potential. These factors can at best be estimated in an imprecise way and are particularly difficult to measure effectively. Tangible resources are those that can be seen or touched and counted, such as supply chain capability, data, financials (e.g. cash), and equipment that isn't classed as an asset.

Human effort is usually included as the main tangible resource category, because time or energy can be quantified. However, humans should be recognised for unique variability and talents. To pretend that all humans have equal value for a particular task, while admirable in the human context, is inaccurate when considering professional capital, motivation, knowledge, and skills. The work of an individual can vary with task and context. The work of different individuals in those same contexts will also be variable. This makes humans one of the most complex resource categories to manage effectively.

Resources require scheduling, accommodation (or storage), deployment, and maintenance and are to be released when no longer required. While much of the resource is being used through projects and the main detail of the scheduling may be held within that project, the overall resource supply will need to be consolidated at the portfolio level. This provides the portfolio manager with choices around the autonomy of their management teams' ability to source materials, equipment, and other resources. For some portfolios, it is appropriate that those managers are empowered to make decisions around what they will source, whereas in other situations, consolidated supply chains provide significant advantages in terms of contract management, product definition, simplicity of supply, relationship with suppliers, and (hopefully) costs. Figure 13.2 shows a typical process for resource management decision-making.

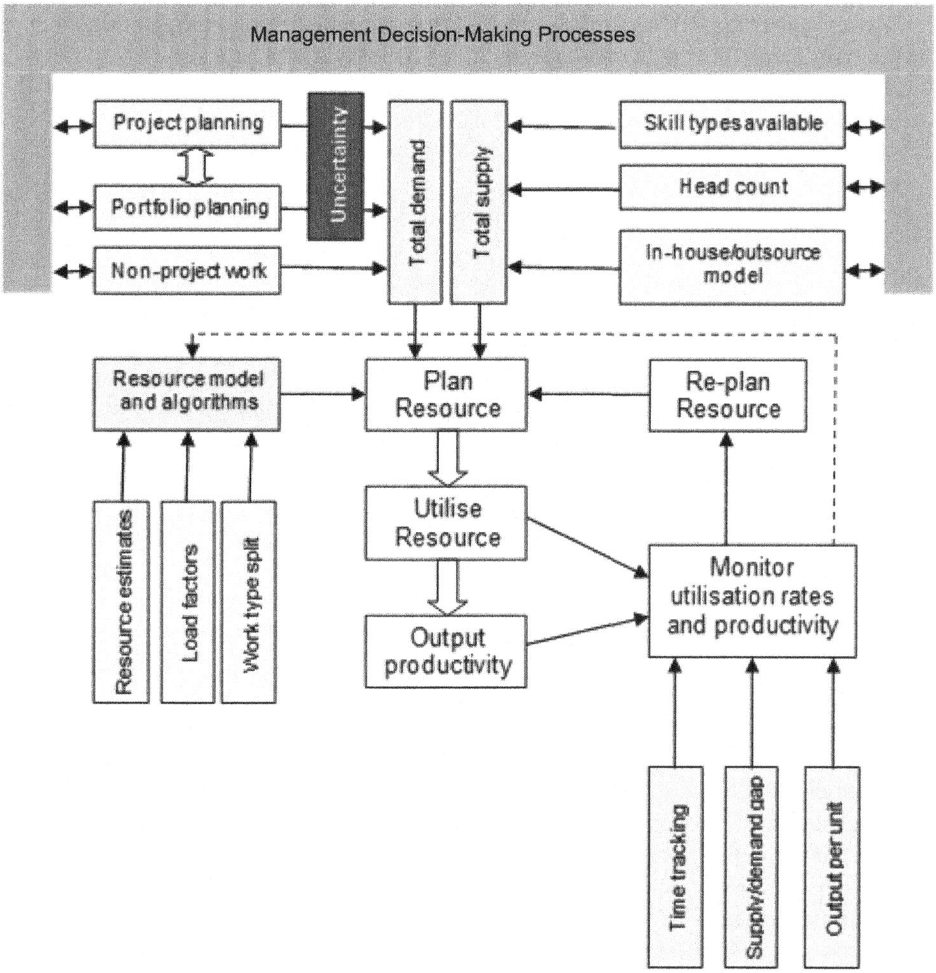

Figure 13.2 Resource management decision-making process.

Source: Adapted from Harpum (2010).

The process shown in Figure 13.2 is not intended to be definitive. The process required for a particular organisation will depend on the contextual factors influencing the capacity management process. These factors may include:

- *Objectives of the process* – supply/demand integration, optimise utilisation rates, transparency of resource planning and use, resource efficiency, productivity.
- *Remit of capacity to be managed* – people, equipment, materials, computing power, space, money, supply chain, and others dependent on context.
- *Degree of granularity* required for work disaggregation and role hierarchy.
- *Existing/legacy processes for CP* (capacity planning), CM (capacity management), and RM (resource management).
- *Maturity of related processes* – project management (most critically work estimating and project planning, risk and uncertainty management, and change control), portfolio management, people and project performance management, project and corporate budget management.
- *Urgency of need* for RM in the business, and therefore degree of phasing of the change program required to deliver an effective, positive ROI, RM process.
- *Acceptance at all levels*, but particularly at middle and senior management, of the importance of behavioural change to enable the RM process to be:
    - Rolled out effectively, and then,
    - To work properly as an established business process.

Ineffective resource management can lead to wastage or increased costs. Resource management that applies the wrong resource to a situation is likely to result in inappropriate outputs. This increases the likelihood of any rework or missing an opportunity that was strategically important to the portfolio. This is especially true where the resource (or similarly for an asset such as a material or part) appears to be like-for-like but is significantly dissimilar and not fit for purpose. The specification and definition over resource needs can, therefore, be as important to portfolio activities and projects as the clear definition of a product or outcome.

Inefficient resource management can lead to unplanned periods of overload (work unexpectedly waiting), processes starved of raw materials, or times where resources are on hold awaiting work. The knock-on effect of this can be unnecessary delays, and probably additional costs in recouping lost scheduled time. Where the supply or allocation of resource is not efficient, extra work or other waste (e.g. waiting times) can add to the overall cost of an activity (Hendriks et al., 1999).

Efficiency of resource and asset usage is often associated with throughput. That is, the amount of work that can be completed in a specific time. It has long been established that multitasking is likely to be less effective in the completion of tasks than with a focus on minimising work in progress. The start time of multitasking efforts may be brought forward, but the completion of nearly every task will be delayed (Goldratt, 2002).

Some resources require particular care and attention. Like assets, they may need to be tracked and allocated with specific processes. Generally, this is industry-specific, such as biological samples in the health sector or chemicals for industrial processes. However, there are two generic classes of resources that depend on their classification, as they can be seen as assets in certain context, these being data and humans, because by their nature they can either be held and developed or used and expended.

Human resources or assets

As with any asset or resource, the care of a human resource (or "asset", as some organisations prefer) can be quite complex. Consideration needs to be beyond the completion of the task in hand. Longer-term care and development of the humans in the portfolio are a consideration. Well-being, professional development, and succession planning are aspects of human resource management within the portfolio context.

- *Well-being* includes physical and mental health, encompassing aspects such as health and safety arrangements, workplace stresses, and culture.
- *Professional development* is the maintenance and extension of knowledge and skills through education, training, and experience. The aim of professional development in the portfolio context is to allow the existing humans to be more productive within the portfolio (and their wider careers). Communication skills, attitudes, and professional behaviours may also be developed, as these can have a significant impact on key aspects of portfolio management (see Chapter 4 discussing effective organisational change and culture).
- Succession planning considers the longer-term human resource needs of the portfolio in skills and management capability. The plan considers the future path for each key resource and robustness of the resource pool for the mid- and long-term demands of the portfolio. Part of this will be professional development and retention of the existing humans, and part will be attraction and recruitment of others. This may include release of groups of resources that are over capacity or do not have the skills needed as the portfolio progresses.

There is also a need for individual resource management of assignment to activities and projects within the portfolio, management of that work, monitoring of performance (both behaviours and work on tasks), and prioritisation of competing demands on these resources. Each human's skills and experience are subtly different. This can lead to different approaches to work, insights, specialisms, and apparent talents. As mentioned earlier, any one individual may be more productive over a specific task than another. Others may have a broader skill set and be more productive over a range of tasks. The work in hand may require a specialist approach for certain tasks and a generalist approach for other tasks.

This individuality may prove to be both a difficulty in allocation and a benefit in problem-solving. Most portfolios include projects that require creative thinking or unique approaches. The right combination of human resource applied to a problem can produce innovative solutions, yet there is debate around how to form appropriate teams for creative problem-solving or difficult tasks. Unlike machine parts, humans cannot be snap-fit into larger assemblies. Human teams need to evolve through a cycle of development before they become truly productive (Tuckman, 1965; Lencioni, 2012). Thus, productivity of a team or an individual within a context is unlikely to be at full strength from the first hour of their allocation to a task. Scheduling human resource needs to include time for this human process to take place. This scheduling would normally take place within the projects or other activity – the portfolio manager must ensure that such time is included in plans and that the team members are available for these processes.

The scheduling of human resources across a portfolio allows the portfolio to support expertise across all work that the projects or other activities in themselves may not be able to justify. A common example is a technical specialist employed at portfolio level, where the consolidated demand justifies a salary, which would not be affordable as a series of short-term contracts at project level. The presence of such an expert may skew project planning, to assume that all work within that expertise should fall upon the expert. Managing this resource bottleneck falls within the portfolio to avoid unnecessary dependencies or constraints.

The productivity of individuals can be variable based on the specific situation or other outside factors. Efficient utilisation of a person's capacity means that everything required for their next task is ready for use and they are in a sound state to apply it. In theory, the efficient utilisation rate of a person could be 100% of contract time. In practice, this is highly unlikely, as time is required to:

- Coordinate work with teams (cannot be credited as productive for the activities but is aiding the smooth running of the portfolio and organisation).
- Refresh and maintain skills and techniques at optimal levels (professional development).
- Provide slack periods of intellectual rest and create the environment for creativity (as documented by De Marco, 2002).

Each organisational context will have variations on these needs to identify what is possible for utilisation of human resources. Later in this chapter, we look at the fallacies of resource optimisations, particularly for human resource, where the unpredictable nature of the environment may also have additional impacts with regards to productivity being reduced, such as workplace stresses.

Minimising WIP (work in progress) is considered a more effective approach with humans (and machines). There may be a cost or time delay associated with task switching, as discussed with multitasking. Restarting a machine that has been idle for maintenance is analogous to the time taken by most humans to refocus at a level of high productivity. Wylie and Allport (2000) noted these "switch costs" and the interference of proactive thinking (doing one task and distractedly thinking ahead to another) in human performance.

Even where switch costs are negligible, distraction changes productivity (Mark et al., 2008) and quality of work (Altmann et al., 2014). What may appear faster work may be more stressful and of lower quality. In some contexts, fast throughput of work is more important than quality, and the amount of stress on workers can be limited. In those situations, distractions are continual, and optimisation is an illusion. The general business of the situation hides the potential for greater productivity. In other situations, the productivity is distinctly low and extensive rework to rectify the poor quality caused by distraction will be demotivating, further reducing effective output.

The other aspect of optimisation which is particular to human resources is the disengagement between "craftsmanship" and the work in hand (this also applies to intellectual work). "Ownership" of work and engagement has been seen as a better path to overall productive quality for organisations. Where workers take responsibility for the whole solution, engagement tends to increase with pride in work and conscientiousness (Halkos & Bousinakis, 2010). This increase in productivity may outweigh any productivity benefits from traditional work planning, such as with traditional approaches focused on piecework and the division of responsibilities using specialist skills, an example being Ford's original car manufacturing system (Wilson, 1995). This divided all work into specific tasks that allowed focused training on limited tasks, and thus speed of work, as "experts" performed each step. The focus on engagement suggests a more holistic approach to work that is more akin to a craftsmanship or generalist approach that demands an understanding of the wider context of the task in hand (Sorenson, 2013). In this approach wider training may be required.

The balance between specialist skills and generalist capability is interesting in balancing the human resource demand and supply for a portfolio. The unique advantage of having an expert or specialist in a skill is that their level of practise is likely to ensure that tasks happen at high quality and pace in that specialist area. However, there may be a wait time for the availability of that specialist – capacity being a constraint. A generalist may have greater availability but may not be as skilled or expert in a particular task. Resource levelling (i.e. balancing workload without increasing resources) needs to be used with great care in these situations. The distinction needs to be drawn between those tasks which are appropriate for the specialist and those that offer opportunities for others to aspire to that level of skill, with professional development.

Alternatively, where there is overcapacity of specialists, they may be asked to perform a generalist function, bringing their average performance down. This averaging down might easily happen within a project context, where resource smoothing has been used to smooth out peaks and troughs of resource demand while not intending to affect the overall duration of the project or wider activity. In the short term, this may have no overall impact, but continued practice separates the specialist from their specialist area and may erode their effective skill level and throughput to tasks when they return to their specialist duties.

Engagement is having an interest in, and commitment to, the work. To a certain point, adding a level of workplace stress or incentives can support this engagement but can easily lead to reduced productivity (Halkos & Bousinakis, 2010). Persistent or high levels of workplace stress can result in exhausting the human resource (burnout) or mental health issues. Maslach and Leiter (2016) provide a summary of these issues. Increased satisfaction leads to increased productivity, provided that the work does not impinge on the workers' lives outside of the work context. Quality work is more related to conscientiousness and personal satisfaction than workload. Energetic and active individuals, who are likely to be influenced by involvement in interesting work in a self-reinforcing cycle, are likely to affect productivity positively.

Some questions a manager may ask about optimising human resources are these:

- Will the productivity gain from using A's specialist skills on this task outweigh the overall productivity (and professional development) gain from allowing B to complete the whole task at a less-expert level?
- Are we using our specialists in the most effective way?
- How do we "average up" the productive value of our team rather than averaging down?
- Are we giving each person the tools, knowledge, skills, resources, processes, environment, and support they need to be productive in this situation?

Optimisation illusions

Optimal use of assets or resources may not be 100% efficient, as is sometimes assumed. Assets or resources seen as efficient at low level may cause waste or other issues at higher levels of abstraction in the portfolio or organisation.

Many assets require time to configure for use, need maintenance work, or to become acquainted with by operators. Thus, in some circumstances, it might be more effective to allow an asset to lie idle and await a more resource-constrained activity to complete than to attempt to squeeze in another use of that asset elsewhere in the portfolio, or indeed from a different portfolio. The difference between effective asset use and efficient asset use may be markedly different. The measure of efficiency tends to be seen at a lower level (e.g. constant use of a machine) compared to effectiveness, which certainly will be measured at or above portfolio management level (e.g. supporting effective delivery of strategic objectives within optimal cost or time constraints).

There are other circumstances in which optimal utilisation is an illusion or fallacy. This is the fallacy of busywork and can be seen in organisations that are incentivised for productivity over effective use of resources. This is a particular problem where the product produced by assets is perishable or difficult to store. Overproduction through high utilisation may waste more raw materials and may have environmental damage factors significantly greater than for allowing idleness. This provides us with a hint that full productivity and resource optimisation may be an inappropriate goal in some circumstances. Examples to consider include overproduction as the equivalent of a vehicle sat in a traffic jam emitting unfriendly chemicals into our atmosphere, or the overproduction of butter and beef to stockpile, under previous regulations of European agriculture.

Inventory management issues are particularly noticeable when there is a mismatch between productivity in one area of an organisation and another. Raw materials may be in short supply, delaying a portfolio's work, and finished products may need additional storage space in advance of customer orders. The associated additional costs (or potential quality issues) with rush-ordering raw materials and additional storage can be particularly painful to the financial health of a portfolio. There are two areas of familiar research that look to address such difficulties:

- ToC (theory of constraints) considers scheduling of work, recognising that critical paths may need adjustment with inbuilt "buffers" to allow effective orchestration of assets and resources (Goldratt, 2002).
- JIT (just-in-time) supply chain management, where a customer order prompts scheduling of supply chain delivery such that there are minimum resources on hand while maintaining sufficient stock to ensure the main measure of productivity (utilisation of the main processes in the organisation) remains high.

More recently, the increasingly VUCA (volatile, uncertain, complex, ambiguous) (Bennis & Nanus, 1985) conditions in some parts of our economy and society highlight how difficult it is to make decisions about what is the most efficient use of any asset of resource. By the time the work has been completed based on any decision about the employment of asset or resource for a specific purpose, the conditions will have changed. This makes it impossible to provide a meaningful comparison between ways of working in some conditions. This lack of comparison stems from the inability to recreate what might have been if a different decision had been made, as time had passed (see Chapter 3 discussing emergent strategy), or as with humans, the actions taken responding to the decision has subsequently changed the asset or resource.

Each portfolio manager must contemplate that there is effort and time associated with optimisation studies (for an evidence-based approach) and decision-making. They will need to balance speed of decision (agile and opportunistic approaches) against a more evidence-based approach that will take some time to establish a framework, take measurements, and draw conclusions. The evidence-based approach can provide a framework of guidance in which to make future flexible decisions around the management of assets or resources, indicating predictive maintenance schedules, resource allocation, process estimation/tolerances, or effective capacity limits within which decisions can be based. However, there must be recognition that any evidence-based model enshrines the assumption of a stable environment, in which the same activity will have the same result. In a VUCA setting, speed of action and the ability to correct erroneous decisions may seem more appropriate to the less-stable and predictable conditions.

Data as a resource or asset

Many business processes revolve around the collection and processing of data as a resource. In consolidating this data, an organisation may build something of lasting value: in terms of reuse for commercial gain or to build intelligence around its own operational risk. This has been observed in the current century with the rise of internet-based companies and social media platforms. It is a continuing trend from the 1970s and the computerisation of the financial services sector (Anderton et al., 1995). In the 1980s, the transactional systems were being reconfigured to provide a customer-centric view of the companies' business. This capability transformed transactional and operational data for strategic purposes, as this was seen as adding value to certain companies within the sector. For example, a bank that could see all its customer's information when that customer contacted the bank for a decision was seen as intrinsically more valuable than the bank that held the same data account by account and, therefore, could not provide an on-the-spot risk evaluation upon which to base its decisions.

The portfolio manager should see data as a resource to be used in a transactional way, and data as an asset providing intelligence. With the increasing use of artificial intelligence (AI), the line between data as an asset or resource may blur even further. The management of data as a particularly valuable asset or resource will continue to increase in importance. Data quality (in terms of accuracy, timeliness, currency, and completeness) will be just as important as the security and protection of this data.

The portfolio manager must also become aware that not all data is of equal commercial or compliance value. Data that can be used for security purposes, or data about specific individuals, needs special attention and control. The cost of non-compliance in this area will be too important for the organisation to make assumptions that projects and other activities are aware of the implications of the data they use. Hence, portfolio managers may need access to data and data protection specialists as part of their team.

The data available to a portfolio is likely to need a catalogue, which as a minimum will provide a single source of information around the technical and business assets aspects of the data, its location and sources, who is responsible for the data, data design rules and associated systems, specific security constraints, and its legal uses and data protection protocols.

Conclusion

This chapter has established that asset and resource management are key areas of portfolio management, as part of a comprehensive capacity management strategy for the organisation. The responsibility and challenges for the portfolio manager when managing shared assets is discussed, including the consideration of decision-making for asset management. The discussion of resources focuses on human resource management and the challenges and the possibilities for managing these as either a resource or an asset. The responsibilities and challenges for the portfolio manager when managing human resources is discussed, and the constraints of aiming to achieve resource (and asset) optimisation. The chapter concludes by considering the management of data as a resource from the portfolio manager's perspective.

References

Altmann E., Trafton J. & Hambrick D. (2014) Momentary interruptions can derail the train of thought. *Journal of Experimental Psychology: General* 143(1), 215–226.

Anderton B., Davis J, Hussain G. & Staley A. (1995) The impact of information technology on the financial services sector. in Anderton B. (eds) *Current Issues in Financial Services*. Palgrave.

Axelos (2017) *Managing Successful Projects with PRINCE2*. Sixth Edition. Stationery Office.

Axelos (2020) *Managing Successful Programmes*. Fifth Edition. Stationery Office.

Bennis W. & Nanus B. (1985) *Leaders: The Strategies for Taking Charge*. New York: Harper and Row.

De Marco T. (2002) *Slack: Getting Past Burnout, Busywork, and the Myth of Total Efficiency*. Broadway Books.

Gavrikova E., Volkova I. & Burda Y. (2020) Strategic aspects of asset management: An overview of current research. *Sustainability* 12(15), 5955.

Gleeson-White J. (2020) *Six Capitals: Capitalism: Climate Change and the Accounting Revolution that Can Save the Planet*. Revised Edition. Allen and Unwin.

Goldratt E. (2002) *Critical Chain*. The North River Press.

Halkos G. & Bousinakis D. (2010) The effect of stress and satisfaction on productivity. *International Journal of Productivity and Performance Management* 59(5), 415–431.

Harpum P. (2010) *Portfolio, Program and Project Management in the Pharmaceutical and Biotechnology Industries*. Wiley.

Hendriks M., Voeten B. & Kroep L. (1999) Human resource allocation in a multi-project R&D environment: Resource capacity allocation and project portfolio planning in practice. *International Journal of Project Management* 17(3), 181–188.

ISO 10007:2017 (2017) Quality management – Guidelines for configuration management. www.iso.org/obp/ui/#iso:std:iso:10007:en.

Lencioni P. (2012) *The Five Dysfunctions of a Team: Team Assessment*. Second Edition. Pfeiffer.

Mark G., Gudith D. & Klocke U. (April 2008) The cost of interrupted work: More speed and stress. CHI'08: Proceedings of the SIGCHI Conference on Human Factors in Computing Systems, pp. 107–110.

Maslach C. & Leiter M. (2016) Understanding the burnout experience: Recent research and its implications for psychiatry. *World Psychiatry: Official Journal of the World Psychiatric Association (WPA)* 15(2), 103–111.

Pennypacker J. (2008) Portfolio resource management: the most significant challenge to project management effectiveness. Paper presented at PMI® Global Congress 2008 – North America. Project Management Institute.

Sorenson S. (2013) How employee engagement drives growth. *Gallup Business Journal* 1, 1–4.

Thompson A., Peteraf M, Gamble J. & Strickland A. (2020) *Crafting and Executing Strategy: Concepts*. Twenty-Second Edition. McGraw-Hill.

Tuckman B. (1965) Developmental sequence in small groups. *Psychological Bulletin* 63(6), 384–399.

Wagner R. (2018) The interrelations between asset and project management. www.ipma.world/interrelations-asset-project-management/.

Wilson J. (1995) Henry Ford's just-in-time system. *International Journal of Operations & Production Management* 15(12), 59–75.

Wylie G. & Allport A. (2000) Task switching and the measurement of "switch costs". *Psychology Research* 63(3–4), 212–33.

14 Business integrated portfolio governance

David Dunning and Katy Angliss

Introduction

This chapter provides a practical perspective on how portfolios can be governed and does so through a particular lens of organisational governance, rooted in a "real-world" response to the challenges found in business in assuring portfolio performance. This chapter focuses on the management of the portfolio, that is, once the portfolio is initiated. In discussing portfolio governance, the model presented discusses the management of portfolios from two aspects, *portfolio direction* and *portfolio progress* (Axelos, 2011).

The model (*business integrated governance framework*) that is applied to portfolio governance presented in this chapter has been developed through an organisation called the *Core P3M Data Club (2021)*. Information about the club is in this chapter annex 1, enabling the opportunity to contextualise the model presented and aid with understanding the extent to which the model is generalisable and applicable in specific organisational circumstances.

Critical to the development of the model has been a desire to be innovative in how portfolio governance can be defined, not to stifle innovation in the projects and programs in a given portfolio, but to enhance the innovation capability and to start from the position that there is a need for a truly integrated approach to governance and assurance from a business perspective – not a project management theory-driven approach to portfolio management. The Core P3M Data Club was formed to address one very specific concern: in many organisations, the data available to manage portfolios of projects and programs is not collated, integrated, or reliable. This has two consequences:

1. There is huge effort, cost, and extended time frame required to collate data that is actually available.
2. A significant disconnect happens between articulated strategic intent and what is communicated through the portfolio in terms of instructions to projects and programs (as well as distortions in the feedback to strategic management through progress tracking and other communications).

This can affect many stakeholder groups, with several examples given here:

- Shareholders, main/executive board can lose confidence that strategic instructions are effectively tasking the business and that progress is being made against the right priorities.
- Portfolio groups can become disconnected by leadership changing priorities and become frustrated with task-orientated progress tracking from projects and programs.

DOI: 10.4324/9780367853129-17

- Projects and programs can become frustrated using organisationally mandated but ineffective methods or tools and thus potentially struggle to acquire and retain resources and carry a painful administration overhead.
- Product leadership can get frustrated that the business is not agile enough to take advantage of emerging market opportunities and/or respond to threats quickly enough and struggle to collate reliable overall performance data to warrant ongoing investment.
- Management teams can struggle to balance BAU (business-as-usual) work with shifting resource, time, and energy needs from projects, leading to a struggle to realise benefits from change programs.
- Finance can find it difficult to support parochial performance modelling tools, provide specialist resource for unpredicted finance expertise requirements, and provide adequate input for effective investment appraisal or outcome measurement.
- Assurance and support functions struggle to attain effectiveness and efficiency with multiple tools and operations used across the range of projects and programs in the portfolio (and may try to force "one size fits all" approach).

These issues can prove very costly for organisations in several ways, including serious sub-optimisation of portfolio value delivered, poor agility in decision-making, major problems allocating resources effectively, and many other issues. However, recent advances in methods, governance, support, and technology have provided more options to address these issues more easily than could have been achieved even in recent years. Examples of developments that enable better governance include:

- Cloud-based information management and analysis solutions and data services, meaning accessible sophistication across a business.
- Advances in management information (MI) capability – that is, the content enabled by the solutions noted previously.
- Rapid changes in thinking about business models, operating models, and various strategic drivers of transformation (not the least being digitalisation).
- Advances in thinking about portfolio management in the project management community.
- Increasingly sophisticated models and methods for project and program management support.
- Agile methods and tools for project design and delivery spreading from the world of software to other domains.
- Advances in integrated portfolio and project management information and analysis tool capability and continuing reduction in cost of these tools.
- More recent opportunities with AI – artificial intelligence (for example, business intelligence tools that provide information based on verbal questions) and machine learning (for example, applications filling in parts of forms based on rules provided).

Despite these changes in how we think about organisations and how we use technology to support new designs and operating models, there has not been much progress made recently with a unified and integrated approach to managing strategy execution, business-as-usual, finances, and resources, that is, portfolio management in the wider business environment. This perhaps remains a future challenge. However, as part of the move towards this utopia, the need to share data over boundaries and collaborate across competing priorities continues to be addressed, and solutions developed – to facilitate high-quality governance and hence more effective decision-making.

Portfolio archetypes

Before moving onto the governance model itself, it is useful to look at some distinct portfolio archetypes that were identified while developing the integrated governance model. This is important as different types of portfolios require a tailored application of the governance model. It is noted here that strategy advancement or transformation portfolios can be seen as a strategic portfolio, as discussed in earlier chapters, whereas the other types of portfolios can be classified as tactical portfolios.

Strategy advancement/transformation portfolios

This a traditional corporate-level portfolio domain, or a strategic portfolio. There are, however, several other titles used for this type of portfolio, such as a change portfolio (although, arguably, change portfolios can be seen as an alternative for one of the tactical portfolios that follow, dependent on the organisation's perspective on change management; see operational portfolios that follow). Such strategic portfolios are characterised as:

- Significant business case.
- Corporate risk.
- High priority.
- Top-down budgets and high-level sponsorship.
- Delivery primarily through clear projects and programs.
- Benefit realisation, value drivers, and strategy attainment goals.

Operational portfolios

The terms of reference for the person leading the operational (sometimes called business-as-usual, BAU) portfolio may be different from someone who is running a portfolio of projects and programs. Just because some work is not classified as project or program does not mean it cannot be identified within a portfolio. For example, if there are several service delivery workstreams within a department, those workstreams could arguably constitute a portfolio, as the workstreams often offer cost versus value choices that can be prioritised. An alternative perspective is that the operational (or "BAU") portfolio includes change workstreams (which can then be balanced with operational workstreams; thus, all workstreams – finite or continuous delivery – can be balanced). The operational portfolios will have:

- Definition of accountability, which for operational purposes is usually a director or line manager who has a management team.
- Remit and definition of related responsibility.
- Finance and resources.
- Priority within the business.
- Business cases implied in business or operating plans and accountability.
- Targets – a portfolio of projects and programs may have objectives, and an operational portfolio may have operational targets (service level, customer satisfaction, volume, revenue, KPI, etc.).

Innovation portfolios

While this may be considered part of the operational activities, a business may, nonetheless, want to have visibility of finance and resources that are being spent on any non-prioritised items. This may be contentious, and if a management team has a remit to locally achieve its targets, it should have a remit to improve using its operational budget and may have included local innovations into the operating plan. These may be delivered by professional development activities or small bottom-up projects – perhaps accountable to line managers. They may be delivered in the background or in an agile approach or larger investments which need a specific business case, primarily through projects and programs. Another reason for seeking visibility of these initiatives is to prevent duplication or to stop initiatives that, while they could be locally productive, may be left as obsolete by a new corporate initiative. In any case, they may consume the same resources and budgets as strategy advancement or operational workloads and therefore be included in re-prioritisations if necessary. The innovation portfolio can enable riskier or less obviously value-generating workstreams to be contained within a boundary of funding and resources to separate these kinds of entity from the more certain operational or change delivery.

Customer portfolios

This may also be considered part of operations (but a special case) because of the need to capture costs accurately and the capability to generate revenue directly. They also have the capability to affect corporate metrics, such as customer satisfaction. Defined as portfolios or not, the customer portfolios typically have a business manager accountable for sales and revenue and, depending on whether they have a delivery team, quality and customer satisfaction. Business managers will have a business plan and targets and manage delivery via service management or tactical use of projects or programs, usually including contract management.

Product portfolios

The distinction between an asset and a product is that the creation of products for the market is the reason the organisation exists, as opposed to assets which are business enablers. There are many types of products. Product portfolio managers may be accountable for product performance, which may be supported by a dedicated team, or a flexible team drawn from across the business. The product will have a business plan and targets to justify its consumption of finance and resources and may be delivered via projects or continuous releases. The product portfolio has the challenge of coordinating many business units in the business, unless the organisation is set up as a product-based structure, where integrated teams combine the skills needed to manage products without using other business units.

Asset management portfolios

This final type of portfolio, although worth a mention, is less well practiced or defined. The term "asset" is defined in many ways but, for the purpose here, is defined as an item that enables business. It is normally the case that asset management is fundamental to the business plans and is the responsibility of management teams. Similar to the product portfolio, specific managers may be accountable for product performance and supported by a dedicated team, or a flexible team drawn from within the business matrix. The asset will have a business plan and targets to justify its use of finances and resources and may be delivered via finite or continuous delivery. For example, a key asset can be something with a business case of its own, such as a business technology solution or a major organisational facility. These asset management activities are often included in the product portfolio if the products are dependent on shared assets.

Which portfolios an organisation wants to manage together is a choice. Some may want to focus only on "change", others on "customer" and "asset/product". Hopefully, by now, most will want to oversee all activities within a strategic portfolio. With organisations doing more work in "project like" but not project ways, the term *project portfolio management* is becoming a less of an all-encompassing term, and more are looking to "modern work management" and "agile" approaches as the definitions of projects and programs blur or become unnecessary. What remains is the need to manage priorities, dependencies, resources, risks, benefits, and finances irrespective of an entity being a "project", "product", or an "initiative". If organisations define these portfolios in common ways, then the items can be visualised together.

Thus, if businesses design all the appropriate types of portfolios for their organisation in common ways, then the multiple aspects, issues, processes, etc. can be understood as a whole, allowing a more effective and efficient governance model to be defined, leading to:

- Value being maximised – as spending is focused on the best options and duplication is reduced.
- Problems solved without causing chaos in the portfolio – the implications of decisions that change prior business decisions that lead to an impact on the portfolio can be managed.
- Business agility facilitated – the ability to understand the impact of business decisions on the portfolio before the decision is made (portfolio modelling) allows faster, more effective decisions to be made.

Identifying and defining the requirements for effective portfolio governance

There are some obvious benefits to joining up governance through an integrated model that meets the intended requirements in an efficient way. These include:

- Better connection of strategy to delivery and back again for portfolios and main or executive boards.
- More effective integration of finance and cost management within projects, programs, and portfolios.
- Priority-based resource allocation across operations or business-as-usual, corporate changes, customer work, and local projects.
- Enablement of local tools and processes for parochial P3M needs while supporting the wider business governance needs.
- Efficient and effective business (e.g. project) support and assurance.
- Efficient and effective data-based decision-making across the portfolio.

In order to define a model for portfolio governance that will be available for widespread application, it is important to define the requirements the model needs to meet. A list of requirements, including issues to overcome, are shown in Table 14.1, broken down

Table 14.1 Requirements for a portfolio governance framework

Stakeholder group	*Requirements/issues to overcome*	*How the business integrated governance framework delivers the requirements*
Main board	Maintained connection of board-level concerns (*opportunities, threats, imperatives, and goals* – OTIG).	Language set to describe concerns (OTIG).
	Resolution of OTIG into a vision cognisant of current state into clear enabling factors and sequence – this defining the strategy.	Connection of OTIG to enabling factors to derive strategy.
	Visibility of accountability for objectives resultant from strategy; targets and challenges (*objectives, targets, and challenges* – OTC) that emerge from OTIG.	Connection of enabling factors to operations, change, challenge (OTC) within strategy.
	Confidence in translation of OTC into business plans – for operations, portfolio mandates for change, and terms of reference for challenges.	Assignment of OTC into business plans – portfolio direction group to convey change instruction to the organisation.
	Confidence in delivery instruction through the organisation against business plans.	Portfolio progress group to focus on accomplishment.
	Confidence in progress and accomplishment information to enable (re)direction to be implemented.	Other groups (finance, management teams, programs, project, and assurance) coordinated to deliver, with appropriate performance management, finance management, and resource management, to assure effective prioritisation.
	Lack of visibility of board-level relevant delivery information.	Visibility of board-level portfolio information confident that underlying delivery is in control.
Portfolio board(s)	Unclear remit, lack of engagement on the drivers behind remit, lack of empowerment and support with clear priority and resources.	Clear presentation of remit in relation to OTIG, enabling factors, strategy, accountability for OTC encapsulated into business plans, providing empowerment and resources.
	Lack of reliable mechanism to communicate agreed/measurable objectives and targets, focus in delivery teams on progress to task rather than accomplishment.	Control over issue of delivery instruction through the organisation against business plans with clear protocol for prioritisation and management against that, and an escalation path to main board where needed.
	Disconnect with board concerns, leading to unexpected direction changes or invisible/unexpected priority shifts.	Ongoing maintenance of portfolio alignment with Main Board vis Portfolio Direction Group.
	Unreliable feedback loops from delivery, with lack of focus on benefit and alignment to OTC.	Reliable operational feedback loops to enable changes in both remit "top down" and opportunity/threat "bottom up" to be dealt with in the best interest of the business.
	Portfolio caught between a master that doesn't include it in thinking and a slave that can't speak business language.	Portfolio definition and progress groups assure the translations occur.

Program boards	Unclear remit, lack of engagement on the drivers behind remit, lack of empowerment and support with clear priority and resources.	Clear presentation of remit in relation to accountability for OTC encapsulated into a program business case providing empowerment and resources.
	Lack of reliable mechanism to communicate agreed/ measurable objectives and targets to projects.	Control over issue of delivery instruction through the organisation with project business cases, with clear protocol for prioritisation of resources/funding against that, and an escalation path to portfolio progress group where needed.
	Disconnect with portfolio concerns leading to unexpected direction changes or invisible/unexpected priority shifts.	Reliable operational feedback loops to enable changes in both remit "top down" and opportunity/threat "bottom up" to be dealt with in the best interest of the business.
	Inability to coordinate workstreams that all talk different language and use different data/tools.	Justifiable, common business support services can be clearly defined to support the program and its peer programs.
	Unreliable feedback loops from delivery, with lack of focus on benefit and alignment to OTC as delivery teams focus on progress to task rather than accomplishment.	Greater focus all round on keeping the business objectives in mind and connected.
	Business support services seen as an overhead.	Greater clarity on what is needed to support decision-making around which business support services can be aligned.
Product boards	Unclear remit, lack of engagement on the drivers behind remit, lack of empowerment and support, with clear priority and resources.	Clear presentation of remit in relation to accountability for OTC encapsulated into a product business plan providing empowerment and resources.
	Lack of reliable mechanism to communicate agreed/ measurable objectives and targets to design delivery teams.	Control over issue of delivery instruction through the organisation with design delivery business cases, with clear protocol for prioritisation of resources/funding against that, and an escalation path to a product portfolio group where needed.
	Disconnect with portfolio concerns leading to unexpected direction changes or invisible/unexpected priority shifts.	Reliable operational feedback loops to enable changes in both remit "top down" and opportunity/threat "bottom up" to be dealt with in the best interest of the business.
	Inability to coordinate workstreams that all talk different language and use different data/tools.	Justifiable, common business support services can be clearly defined to support the product and its peer/constituent programs and projects.
	Unreliable feedback loops from product development and product delivery, with lack of focus on benefit and alignment to OTC as delivery teams focus on progress to task rather than accomplishment.	Greater focus all around on keeping the business objectives in mind and connected.
	Business support services seen as an overhead.	Greater clarity on what is needed to support decision-making around which business support services can be aligned.

(*Continued*)

Table 14.1 (Continued)

Stakeholder group	*Requirements/issues to overcome*	*How the business integrated governance framework delivers the requirements*
Project boards	Unclear remit, lack of engagement on the drivers behind remit, lack of empowerment and support with clear priority and resources.	Clear presentation of remit in relation to accountability for OTC encapsulated into a project business case providing empowerment and resources.
	Lack of reliable mechanism to communicate agreed/measurable objectives and targets to team members, suppliers, supporting business teams.	Clear understanding of the "why".
	Disconnect with program concerns leading to unexpected direction changes or invisible/unexpected priority shifts.	Control over issue of delivery instruction through the organisation using local tools to issue clear tasking, with a reliable protocol for prioritisation of resources/funding against that, and an escalation path to program board/portfolio progress group where needed.
	Inability to coordinate workstreams that all talk different language and use different data/tools.	Reliable operational feedback loops to enable changes in both remit "top down" and opportunity/threat "bottom up" to be dealt with in the best interest of the business.
	Unreliable feedback loops from delivery with lack of data on progress and remaining work, ineffective resource allocation, poor dependency management, and limited access to support for problems.	Justifiable, common business support services can be clearly defined to support projects.
	Business support services seen as an overhead.	Greater clarity on what is needed to support decision-making around which business support services can be aligned.
Commercial and finance	Limited engagement from the business on the potential finance needs from portfolios.	Finance and cost performance core to main board, portfolio program, project and management teams operating agendas, and MI needs.
	Difficult to satisfy ad hoc demands for financial expertise support pre-project.	Greater visibility of finance needs and finance resource needs leading to effective planning of finances and finance support.
	Unreliable estimating of costs, risk, and benefits diminishes the viability of investment appraisal and downstream financial controls	Greater focus on accountability means better estimating or greater honesty on uncertainty, meaning financial analysis more reliable.
	Late-in-the-day requests to set up accounting processes and data capture for portfolio items.	Enterprise reference data is key to the whole portfolio – including finance, meaning simpler cost/schedule reporting.
	Poor data quality on cost performance data from ineffective timesheet, procurement, and invoicing data capture.	Focus on issues possible once data is clean.
	Lack of resources to provide financial expertise into projects to enable best practice.	Resources that exist can be deployed more effectively in accordance with priorities.
	Lack of accountability for poor cost/benefit performance on portfolio items, meaning financial guidance not taken.	Greater accountability leading to more effective financial performance and finance performance.

Business units	Limited engagement from the business on the potential resourcing needs from portfolios (change/customer/product).	Single reliable demand and resource allocation model.
	Difficult to satisfy ad hoc demands for resource support pre-project.	Ad hoc needs better anticipated and managed.
	Unreliable estimating effort/start for potential work means resource modelling for effective acquisition, deployment, and disposal more difficult.	Accountability for estimating or honesty about uncertainty senable more effective resource modelling.
	Late "slippages" and urgent "unforeseen demands" cause management time and ineffective resource usage.	Project and programs in control mean less surprises and slippages.
	Inconsistent communication of priorities and demand means effective allocation more difficult.	Consistent priority communication and "why" reasoning, visibility of allocations against priority, mean less arm twisting for suboptimal resource usage.
	Accountability for benefits, and benefit planning not always factored in to business unit resourcing.	Benefit planning and realisation scheduled into business unit plans.
	Lack of accountability for benefit performance on portfolio items, meaning investment return potential diminished.	Greater likelihood of business unit target hitting via constant focus to task.
Assurance	Not built into board processes.	Fundamental to board confidence in information. Provides confidence to enable board members to focus on key matters, not reading all the details.
	Seen as overhead.	Clear component to risk avoidance strategy.
	Data not easily available.	Data easily available through the core data models.
	Analysis time-consuming to compile.	Time saved in not having to compile data.
PMO/business support	More work than just projects to organise.	Fundamental confidence in information.
	Seen as overhead.	Joined up support across all areas a clear enabling factor to the operation.
	Multiple support functions – not joined-up?	Data easily available through the core data models.
	Parochial towards methods and tools?	Time saved in not having to compile data.
	Analysis – time-consuming to compile information.	Provides confidence to enable board members to focus on key matters, not reading all the details.
	Difficult to define service levels to enable effective delivery operation in areas where business support has not authority.	Framework provides cadence and data needs, meaning capability requirement is clear and support service can be sized correctly.
	Separation of outputs and change-focused support does not simplify business messages to executives.	Boards provide executive focus which support services can be clearly defined to support – which includes PMO.

by the stakeholder group requirement(s) and a high-level description of how the model meets those requirements. The following sections then expand on the business integrated governance model in more detail.

Business integrated governance framework

Having defined the various types of portfolios and discussed the requirements for a model, the chapter now turns to examine one example of a governance model for integrating portfolios within a business governance structure, with the *business integrated governance (BIG) framework*, shown in Figure 14.1.

The key business domains included within the framework, referred to in the model as *accountability nodes* are the *business domain*, with the main board, operations group, and change group; *portfolio domain*, with portfolio direction group(s), portfolio progress group(s), and assurance group; *program and project domain*, with program board(s) and project board(s); and *central function domain*, with commercial/finance and management team(s).

The generic structure includes a main board that delegates strategy execution to a subcommittee and operational matters to an operations subcommittee. It is assumed that each main board subcommittee tasks portfolio direction groups and management teams (which includes finance) respectively with objectives for change, targets for operation, and challenges to be addressed cross-functionally – at which level directions are prioritised for action. A relatively high-level view of the accountability nodes is presented here. A fuller description of each node, including for each its background and typical issues, expected operation, example agendas, and a link to examples of relevant management information (MI) and definitions, can be found in the Praxis framework (Praxis, 2020).

The model presented assumes that portfolio and business operations are carried out within an organisation that has clear roles and responsibilities, operating model, decision-making processes and provides business support to enable people and processes

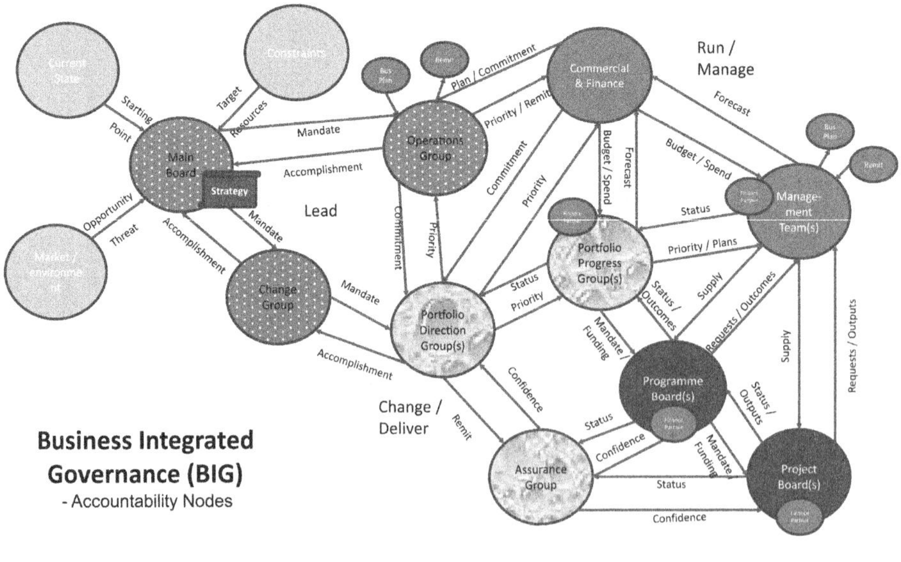

Figure 14.1 Business integrated governance framework.

with the appropriate technology and data management. The model does not go into capability, competence, or methods related to portfolio, program, and project management and does not encompass support models or the need to harmonise operations. It does, however, make assumptions about business support provided and has a node for assurance within the project and program domain, which provides a discussion of compliance management and a range of assurance services that an assurance function would be assumed to provide for the example scenario (noting that each specific organisation can have different needs). An example of external portfolio assurance is provided in this chapter annex 2.

The model is not prescriptive about what a commercial and finance team delivers within its organisational terms of reference, but it does state assumptions and suggest a model for how the portfolio(s) could work effectively with parts of the finance operation, especially the areas of financing, such as specific expertise, cost performance, and assurance. Likewise, the model is not prescriptive about what management teams deliver within their organisational terms of reference. It does, however, state assumptions and suggest a model for how the portfolio(s) could work effectively with parts of the finance operation that deals with delivering BAU and customer projects, alongside transformation work, benefit realisation, and resourcing to projects. It is assumed that management teams have performance targets to achieve and also have local change needs to be managed, which may not be visible at main board level but can still be consuming resources and delivering local benefits.

Additionally, there will be participation for management teams in corporate transformation initiatives, which can also consume resources and perhaps primarily deliver corporate, but not local, benefits, which may create a conflict between focusing on achieving performance targets and collaborating with corporate transformation imperatives. Hence, it is assumed that an allocation model is maintained to assure effective visible prioritisation.

Portfolio roles and responsibilities

A portfolio requires an accountable leader who may be an individual or a committee exercising authority through its chairperson. Accountability covers setting goals and allocating resources. To do this, the portfolio is likely to follow values and principles that it interprets and delegates as policy. Goals and values are primarily achieved through decision-making that combines a view of the future with the present and the past, together with opinion, preference, values, meaning, and pressures.

Governance at the strategic portfolio level consists of balancing response to pressures in order to return the maximum benefit to stakeholders. Portfolio functions are thus determining who stakeholders are, and their influence and interests; establishing agreed-upon objectives; agreed-upon paths to objectives; and the status of actions on those paths, with projections of where continued action will be likely to deliver the portfolio.

In the past, separate processes, governance, and systems for customer delivery, engineering management, and transformation planning, etc., may have allowed for optimised performance of those aspects. However, these may now be seen as "islands of automation" which prevent the "big picture" being achieved. Hence, more organisations understand that an operational workstream is just an accountability node the same as a project, except that it has a different plan shape, leadership, and accountability. To manage both work

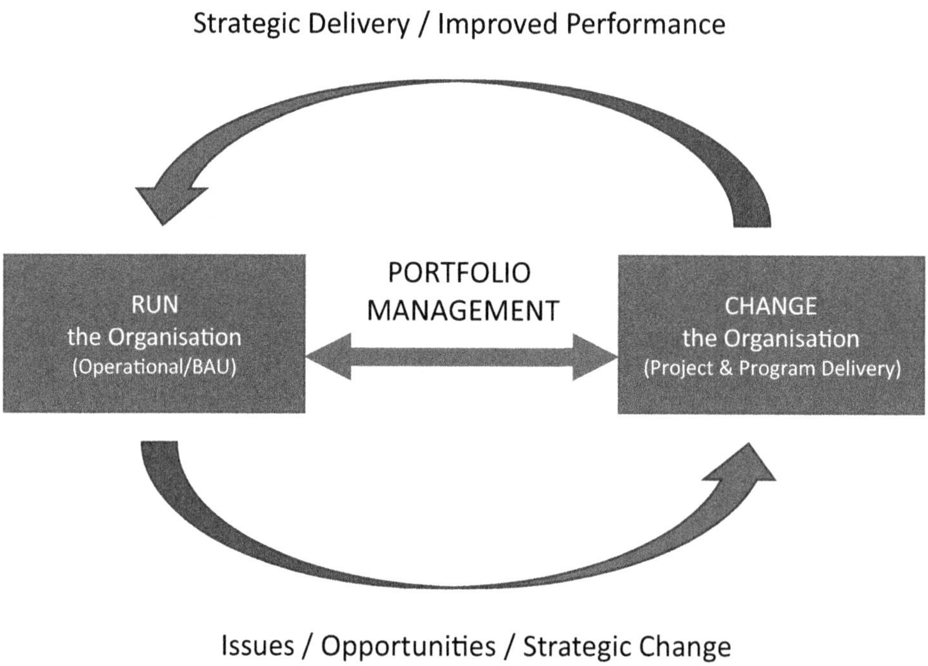

Figure 14.2 Managing operational and change activities in the business.

Source: Adapted from Axelos (2011).

types effectively, for operations and projects, that is, the "run" and "change" aspects of the business in Figure 14.2, both must be brought together to enable overall prioritisation, dependency mapping, resource, and financial management so that, for example, the "change lead" can see work commitments and dependencies for people in their project and the "line manager" can see when external commitments are required in their teams.

Business domain

The main board and sub-groups in the integrated governance model turn *opportunities, threats, imperatives,* and *goals* (OTIGs) into *objectives, targets,* and *challenges* (OTCs), shown in Figure 14.3. The main board maintains confidence that strategic instructions are effectively tasking the business, and that progress is being made against the right priorities.

Portfolio domain

Working with the portfolio definition group(s) (PDG) are portfolio progress groups (PPG) that, as the name implies, focus on delivery oversight and benefit realisation. Portfolio definition and progress groups are tasked with translating objectives into projects, programs, and other associated activities as appropriate. The make-up of these groups depends on the nature and scale of the portfolio business. Portfolio groups remain connected with leadership priority changes and, while supported with task-orientated progress from projects and programs, are responsible for outcomes, benefits, and value.

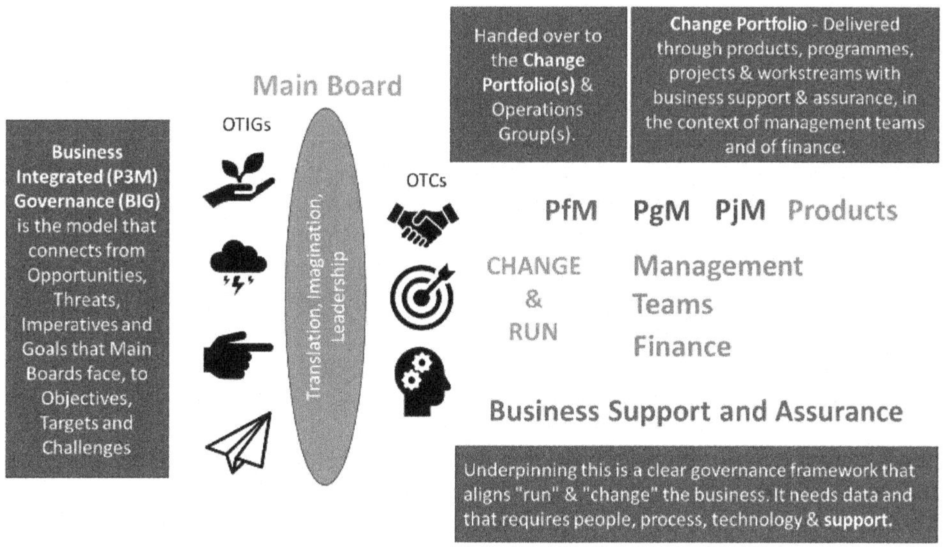

Figure 14.3 Example of main board portfolio governance structure.

Portfolio definition group

The portfolio definition group (PDG) focuses on strategic matters in relation to the main board, of which members of the PDG may be a part. The assumptions underlying the portfolio direction group are (Axelos, 2011):

- PDG consists of the main board members and management team heads, who are collectively accountable for ensuring that the portfolio delivers the changes, outcomes, benefits, and organisational value desired within the organisation's strategic objectives.
- Makes proactive decisions and provides oversight, direction, and leadership that energises the delivery teams and the organisation to achieve the objectives of the strategy.
- Meetings may be attended by additional members where required, including others within portfolio management, senior business change, or program management roles.
- Accountable to the main board (or its change sub-group) for realisation of strategic outcomes from the portfolio.

The PDG has the following assumed responsibilities:

- Constantly monitor the environment and market for impacts on the strategic direction of the portfolio.
- Ensure that the portfolio remains on course (or direction is changed) to deliver the desired strategic benefits and outcomes.
- Overall ownership, oversight, and direction of the portfolio. Set the strategic vision for the portfolio.
- Set criteria for portfolio inclusion.

- Ultimate decision body on content of the portfolio – inclusion, removal, priority of initiatives in the portfolio, and the strategic balance.
- Ensure that operational/business-as-usual and the change portfolio are aligned effectively to deliver the strategic objectives.
- Ensure that any conflicts between the portfolio delivery and operations/business-as-usual that cannot be resolved by the PPG are addressed.
- Delegate translation of strategic objectives into specific prioritised, balanced, and planned portfolio items and oversight of delivery to the PPG.
- Review the status of the portfolio regularly via management dashboards, focusing on prediction and forecast of achievement of strategic outcomes, benefits, and value within the medium- to long-term environment and market.
- Review recommendations and issues from portfolio progress group (PPG) and make decisions accordingly.
- Manage expectations of strategic stakeholders.

The key information that the PDG needs to provide effective oversight for is contained in an agenda dashboard covering three distinct areas:

Progress and status. This section looks backwards and picks up overall portfolio progress, performance and accomplishment, escalations and exceptions, review of cost, and resource performance.

Enablers. This section covers a restatement or review of the overall strategic goals and imperatives, stated as objectives and challenges (i.e. have there been any changes in underlying drivers?), and their status. The section highlights new ideas, input from the market in terms of satisfaction, threats, opportunities, and trends, and also the trend in risk appetite, customer feedback, and health, environment, and safety metrics.

Prediction. Prediction of outcomes and trend towards the achievement of those outcomes – the PDG meeting would focus heavily on outcomes (but would take input from the PPG on forecast outputs). This section of the dashboard and meeting includes review of forecast strategic outcomes and strategic value, overall costs, resource issues, review of risks, and confirming priorities, balance of finance, and resource commitments.

Decisions based on the previous information would then be taken, such as to commence, slow down, speed up, change, or stop existing portfolio items and to review resources and funding position. A key aspect of the PDG review is benefits, outcome realisation, and ascertaining strategic value. While it may be within the role of a program board to manage benefit realisation at a program level, the PDG takes accountability for overall business change and benefit realisation achievement in their portfolio and sub-portfolio. However, some portfolios are business-wide, which means that management team leaders who are not PPG leaders will deliver (at least part of) some change projects and their related benefits (although arguably all strategic-related activity should be included in the PDG as part of the strategic portfolio). Benefits are also therefore included within the management team review example, especially bearing in mind a management team may become accountable for ongoing benefits once a program or project and its related sub-portfolio are disbanded.

Portfolio progress group

The portfolio progress group (PPG) maintains a relationship between projects and programs, PDG, and management teams (from where resources may be provided, and benefits realised within). The assumptions underlying the portfolio progress group are (Axelos, 2011):

- Accountable to the PDG.
- Oversee, understand, and categorise portfolio items through prioritisation, balance, and planning to the point of handover to their program and/or project boards.
- Monitor portfolio progress and resolve issues for the portfolio strategy and delivery plan (outputs, benefits, and strategic outcomes).
- Delivery cycle process (change authority) and operation checking – ensure initiatives comply with delivery standards.
- Approve communications on portfolio progress and successes.

The PPG has the following assumed responsibilities:

- Orchestrate the identification and definition of programs, start-up, and initiation of projects to the point of handover to their program/project boards.
- Ensure that PDG strategic priorities are reflected in the portfolio delivery plan.
- Monitor portfolio output: delivery progress, status, and resolving delivery issues, including:

    1. Program and project progress, exceptions, and escalations.
    2. Achievement of deliverables.
    3. Dependencies and interdependencies alignment and interlocks agreed and on-track.
    4. Spending, and action, on overspend or underspend (reallocation) and timescales.
    5. Review portfolio issues, escalate as appropriate to PDG.
    6. Overview of risks and dependencies.
    7. Resources and allocation oversight.
    8. Reforecast of benefits and alignment to strategic objectives.
    9. Approving minor changes to portfolio and constituent programs and projects.
    10 Recommending major changes to portfolio to PDG, including:

        i. New projects or programs.
        ii. Termination of projects or programs.

    - Ensure that delivery plans are agreed with operational areas to cause minimum disruption.
    - Approve communications on portfolio status and progress.

The key information that the PPG needs to interrogate, for effective actions and decision-making, is contained in the PPG agenda dashboard, typically comprising:

Progress and status. This section looks backwards and focuses on historical trend and last period delivery performance and issues. Overall accomplishment, escalations and exceptions, review of cost and resource performance, review of additional and "front door" proposals for potential inclusion in the portfolio, and review of assurance escalations.

Enablers. This section covers review of objectives (have there been any changes in underlying drivers?), key people performance review (e.g. sponsors, program, and project manager effectiveness), efficiency and effectiveness trend reviews, lessons learned realisation, culture and ethics implications review, satisfaction reviews (staff, customers), and review of current portfolio balance.

Prediction. This section looks forwards and reviews risk and confidence – in delivery, outputs, outcomes, cost, and resource estimates to confirm priorities, balance of finances, resources commitment – and enables portfolio items to commence, take escalations, finalise decisions, confirm actions, and any associated communications.

These two roles (PDG and PPG), however, may be carried out by one combined portfolio group in some organisations, dependent on the situation. Also, not only may PDG and PPG overlap, but they may well also overlap with main board functions too. Clearly, roles and responsibilities need to be defined and agreed so that accountability can be properly allocated.

Central function domain

The management team's accountability node ensures effective resource allocation management and benefit realisation with the PPG while delivering business targets of their own. Operations management is outside the remit of the model, except once again for how the assurance node interacts with the business. Where a business unit is not the "lead" business unit for a sub-portfolio, a management team leader might still support a PPG led in a sibling or peer management team and can be responsible for some resourcing and benefit delivery.

Tactical or sub-portfolios can also be led by a management team (business unit) leader who takes on a PDG role for initiatives contained within their domain – the management team leader is effectively the sub-portfolio sponsor. Management teams lead the operation but also make ultimate decisions about resourcing and benefit realisation within their domains. The management team can also take on the PPG role for their sub-portfolio, but this may be delegated to a subcommittee or direct report of the management team. Management teams may of course use different language and recoil at the P3M-based terminology. For example, the sales director may, in effect, run the portfolio direction group for their customer portfolio, but instead of "programs", there may be "business streams" with a "business manager", and instead of "projects", there may be "accounts" with a "relationship manager", etc. Notwithstanding, ensuring clear accountabilities and roles, no matter the title, is crucial for successful portfolio management.

Finally, the commercial and finance accountability node provides expertise, funding sources, and cost performance services. Finance can more easily support common performance models, resource more predictable finance expertise needs, and support effective investment appraisal and outcome measurement. Finance management is again outside the remit of the model, except for how the assurance node interacts with the business. The assurance accountability node provides compliance and independent checks and balances.

Management information and reporting

By defining the respective accountability nodes and deriving their governance operation, as part of any governance framework, a common data model can be compiled against which to configure all the systems, aggregating these systems into a common data model. The overall environment for such a data model is shown in Figure 14.4, relating to the accountability nodes in the integrated governance model. The following sections in this chapter set out how data can be integrated for collation of management information (MI) and how the data is defined in relation to the accountability nodes.

Having established that data is needed for the MI to support the governance operation, there are several ways this data can be collected, ranging from traditional P3M data collated manually, followed by more recent developments with project portfolio management (PPM) software solutions, and the latest thinking and developments with modern BI (business integrated) tools. The traditional manual collation, from local data sources, is time-consuming, expensive, inflexible, and frequently unreliable (even the perception of unreliability is destructive of trust in the data). The subsequent PPM software solutions deliver an improved level of efficiency compared to manual collation, but they are not always effective due to lack of committed sponsorship, unclear or uncommitted governance, and usually a poor connection to business governance operations. In most cases, they also have no connection back to the strategic level, where opportunities, threats, imperatives, and goals for strategic decision-making are managed.

Collation of MI from source data for business integration

There are several different system architectures for the most recent BI (business information) solutions. One method uses integration toolsets, where the sources of MI data are connected, allowing a picture of the source data to be maintained, as shown in Figure 14.5A. An alternative method is a snapshot taken from a data lake (or data warehouse), shown in Figure 14.5B. Toolset B is often an attractive option, but there is a sustainment implication in that the integration connections need to be maintained when tools and configurations change. In this configuration of the system, data is harvested and collated as a snapshot at a given time, providing to users of the MI an integrated picture at that moment. This means that connectors are needed, and the data is not real time, but the source systems would still have live data.

These two options demonstrate the need for integrated data, and adopting either of these two architectures, with integration toolsets and connectors, is the starting point for the management, production, and collation of MI data. There is merit in also using local toolsets like PPM software or agile delivery tools. It should be reasonable for different parts of the organisation to operate their own customised PPM toolset, for example, in areas that deliver customer projects and may require contract management capability, projects delivering integrated solutions will need effective dependency management, and agile product delivery requires a focus on backlog and sprinting.

Future integration options

Often, data is summarised or aggregated through the collation process in order to provide viable and useful MI, but data underpinning portfolios often needs to be transformed or connected to other data too, with examples shown next. This suggests future evolution

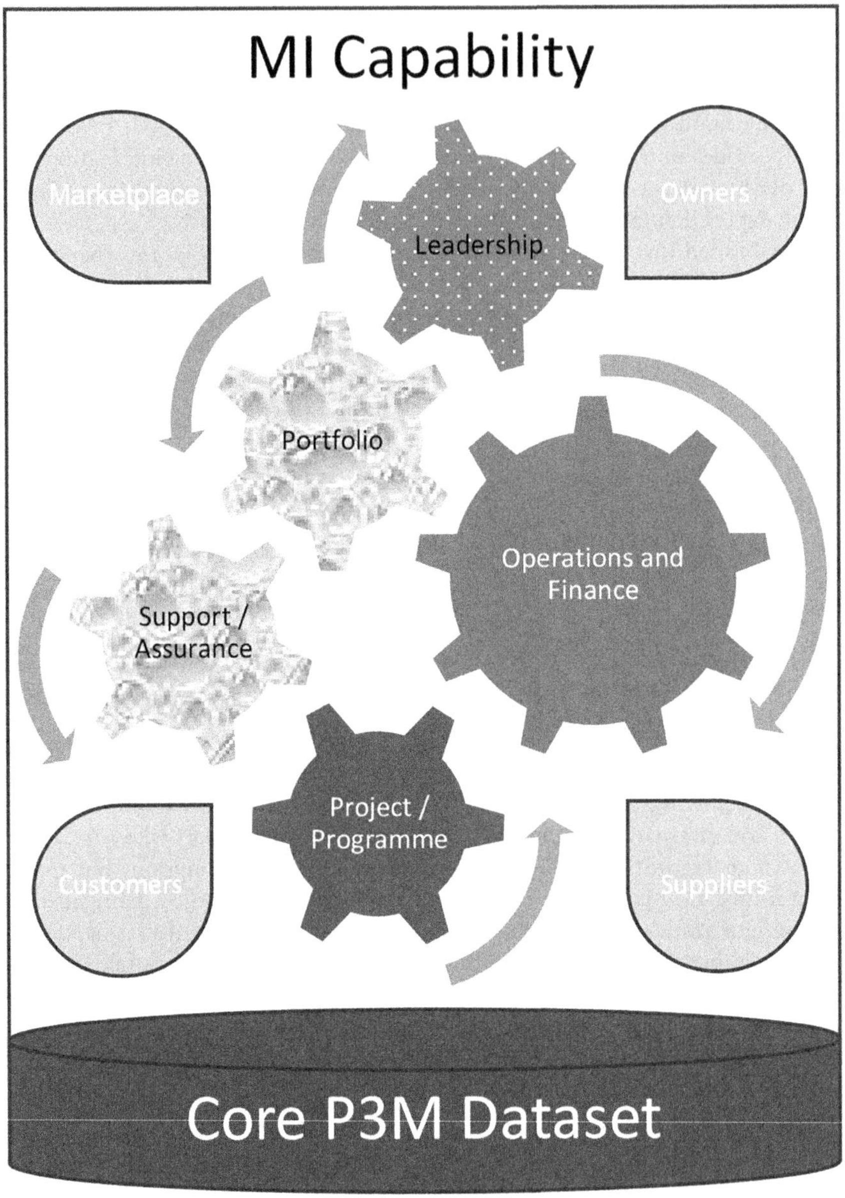

Figure 14.4 Overall environment for a common data model.

for MI is with greater integration and collation of data, such as within a manufacturing environment, incorporating "whole value chain collaboration".

- Translation of main board opportunities, threats, imperatives, and goals to objectives, targets, and challenges.
- Translation of portfolio objectives into high-level planning items.

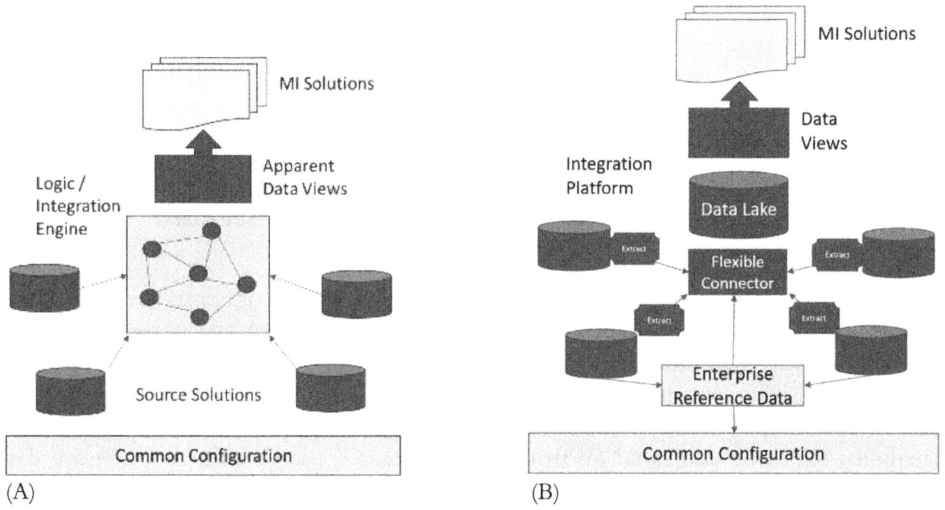

Figure 14.5 A and B Collation of MI from source data comparing integration Toolset A and a snapshot in time Toolset B.

- Aggregation of project and program data to enable compliance checking, dependency management, assurance, and cross-business analysis.
- Relation of resource models maintained locally within projects and programs (e.g. demand) to resource models maintained within management teams (e.g. competing demands, benefit delivery demands, and operations).
- Planning, ownership delegation, and delivery of benefits, and related performance data.
- Integration of finance, actuals, and cost projections between finance and the portfolio management teams.
- Ongoing integration of changing main board OTIGs to OTCs and progress or attainment reported back against these, with resulting portfolio direction changes affecting programs and projects.

Defining the data needed for management information

The approach to data definition is determined by what MI is to be derived from it. Typically, this is approached by asking users what reports they want and collating implications, engaging the process owners and asking what their process implies, asking users what data they currently keep, and finally, taking the standard set of reports from a vendor (assuming this dataset will be sufficient).

In order to define the data needed for the *business integrated governance framework*, interrogating the framework itself and the accountability nodes should provide the answers required for MI. For each node type in the governance framework, the question is: What is the generic activity they should be carrying out? For example, although the specific work of a project board may vary, the structure and operation are generalisable, and hence the core MI can be derived. Having defined the core MI needs for each accountability node, it is possible to clarify the data model supporting the MI. In the particular case of the work for the *business integrated governance framework*, for example, the starting point was a core data model implied from the Praxis framework documents and reports (Praxis, 2020), which was merged with a core planning data model, typically used in planning tools, like *Microsoft Project*. The data needs implied from the core MI needs were then "superimposed", being careful to distinguish between core data (e.g. task ID) and metadata likely to be organisation-specific (e.g. location).

Establishing the data model to support the business integrated governance framework

It is likely that the first delivery of core data capability an organisation makes will be for a part of the organisation, not the whole, and therefore only a part of the full dataset. Not only will the data model need to change with learning during first implementation and use, but it will also need to be extended. Clearly, the business need will have to drive what gets addressed, but the IT design for the underpinning data capability has to be addressed up front. It may make sense to look at the entire data vision around governance to avoid short termism in design. Questions like these will undoubtedly appear:

- *What is our MI and data strategy?* Sometimes, if an organisation has not delivered a data solution before, it may not have an MI and data strategy. This can be a problem, as the requirement may appear to be very difficult to capture and understand. Without a strategy, parochial solutions may emerge, which may seem simple at the time, but this can also cause later integration issues.
- *Where are the sources for this data?* If there is a need to take feeds into a data model, where will this data come from? Are there connectors to it?
- *What are the enterprise reference data items, and where are they?* For example, with code schemes and metadata, where is it mastered, and how is this shared across systems?
- *What is the current quality of data, and what assurance and support are in place to enable the necessary data quality?* For example, is there a quality assurance process established within the business?
- *What is the strategy to assemble data?* For example, manual copy and paste, data warehouse, or systems integration.

Once it is clear what data is needed (to start with, at least, and to support governance and operation, not just operation) and the capability is enabled, the business can start to run its governance meetings using the core dataset. Governance can feel safe in the knowledge that it is possible to extend its data sources, serve its regular and ad hoc MI needs, and most importantly, enable more informed decision-making throughout the portfolio.

Repeatable decisions and review cycles exist in the portfolio that the business needs to coordinate MI around, such that management can rely on integrated views of progress, cost, and forecasting at a common moment in time. Operating with decision and review cycles can still allow the use of local tools, data, and reporting for real-time analysis, which are different to the governance requirement. Business support, information quality management, assurance, and decision support can then be orchestrated to be available in peaks and troughs within the cycles. The principles of participation, procedures, data gathering, analysis, and decision-making repeat within the portfolio

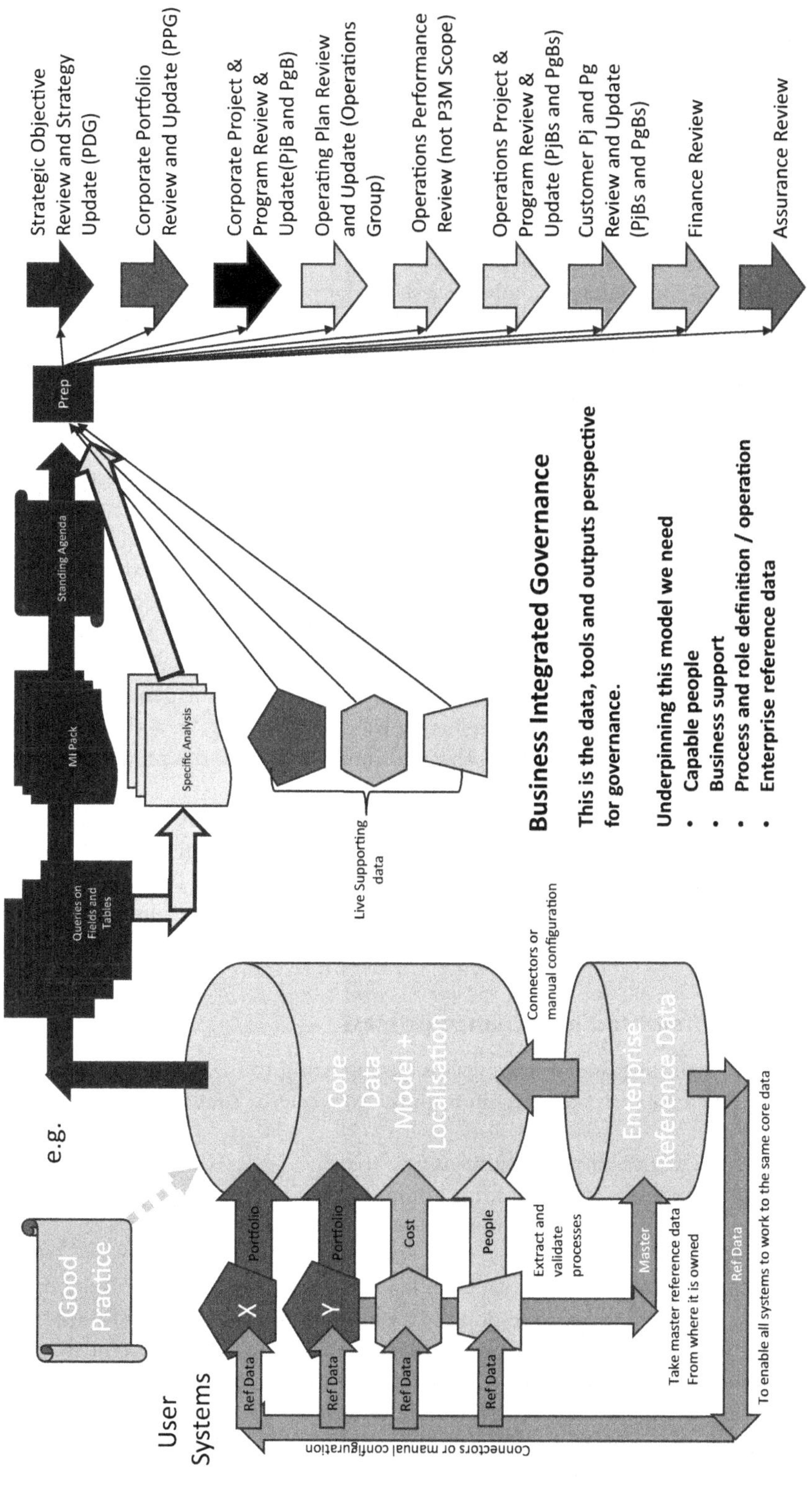

Figure 14.6 Flow of data for effective MI linking strategic concerns to delivery.

for operational and calendar-driven activities, with major events or change driven at the scale of program (change from idea, through selection, to stabilising impacts on operations) and project (development of solution to need). The Core P3M Data Club has sought to place the right data into the right analysis processes to support timely (and hopefully excellent and improving) decision-making. The complete flow of data for MI for the *business integrated governance framework* has been identified, and the result is the ability, through effective MI, to link strategic issues and concerns through to delivery, shown in Figure 14.6.

A key implication of this fully integrated data architecture is that the organisation can identify and supply core enterprise reference data. For portfolios, this can include simple information, like project code, resource ID, as well as local, specific data, like location, business unit, etc. If we can collect and maintain the collation of this reference data, then our component toolsets and data stores can be configured to use these code schemes to enable integration of data from other systems. Referring to a resource with a different code in the PPM system, HR system, and finance system can lead to a struggle to connect their data. Therefore, connecting the tools used with common data classifications enables data to be used effectively and enables "golden threads" to be defined and tracked though the organisation rather than losing these connections across organisational boundaries.

For example, it becomes possible to track a threat that the main board is interested in to an objective given to a portfolio, which enables its priority to be recognised. This then enables easy decomposition into various planning items for a program so that the project can pick up clear, related deliverables and the management team can allocate resource to it. Finance can also then track cost against it. Ultimately, the management team is able to be certain that the threat has been reduced, by understanding how the actions taken have played out across the organisation, through interrogation of the relevant MI, shown in Figure 14.7.

Importantly, this means the business can adjust if the threat diminishes in importance, as the items claiming priority from work to address the threat can easily be seen. The investment in methods and tools that an organisation has made in local areas can therefore be exploited rather than discarded as failed parochial solutions, eliminating conflict between incompatible peer domains.

Operating an integrated governance process

With cloud-based tooling and simple, accessible reporting tools, many parts of the business expect and receive real-time data in response to requests, such as:

- How many enquiries have we had today?
- What support requests are open from our customers?
- Where are our deliveries on the road?

To answer these questions, it makes sense to have live data. For example, there may be a need to reroute deliveries today to respond to an important customer. Portfolios, projects, and programs, however, are typically less live, although it may be important to schedule and control some tasks to the hour or minute, for example, in plant shutdowns, where down time is very expensive. Therefore, people on some projects might like a "to-do list" to track their specific task details. Typically, the reporting and tracking time frames for the framework are:

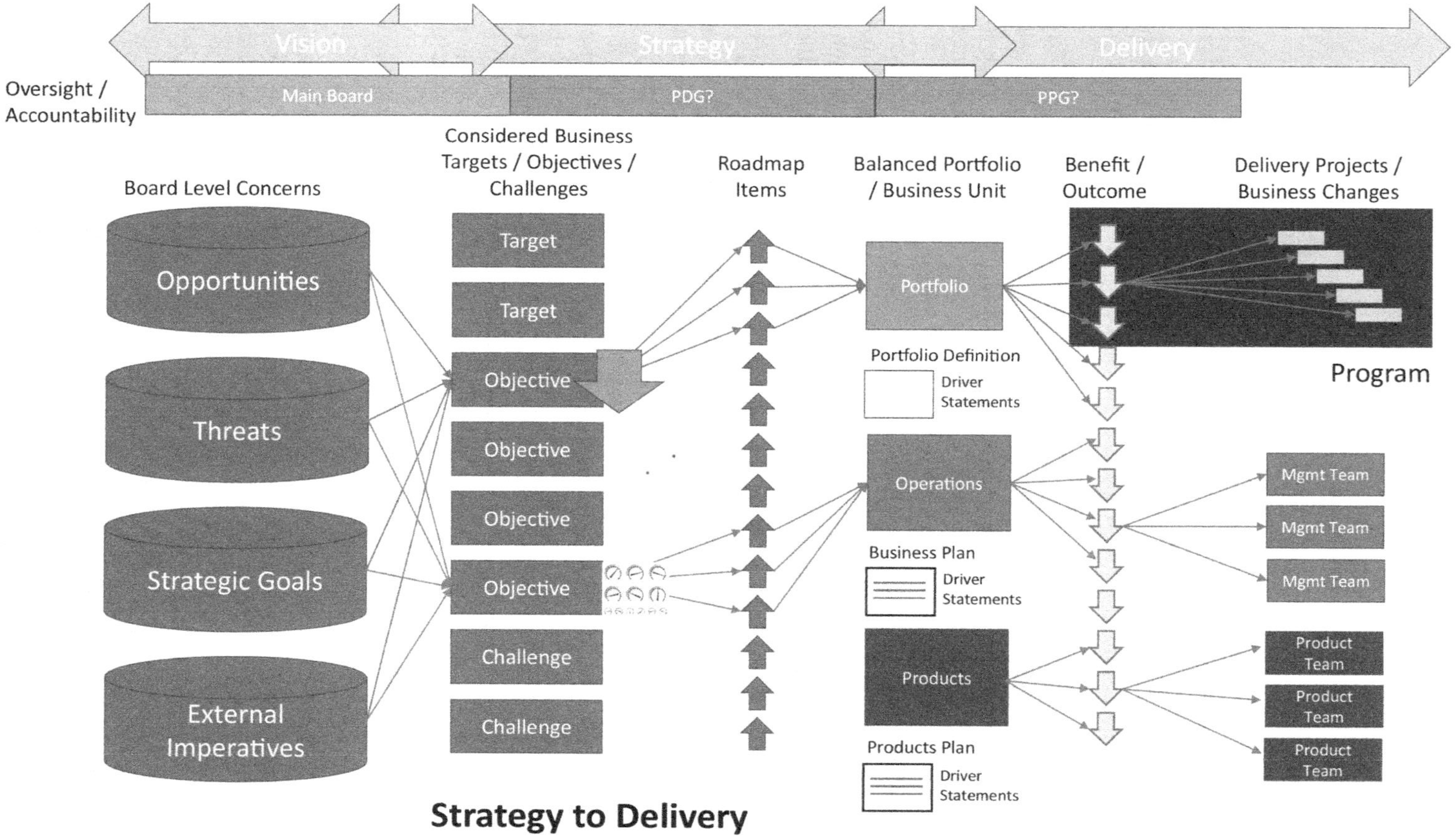

Figure 14.7 Effective MI linking strategic concerns to delivery and tracking actions across the organisation.

- Delivery teams track daily.
- Project teams track weekly.
- Portfolio progress groups, program teams, and project boards monthly.
- Management teams status monthly.
- Finance teams operate monthly cycles.
- Main board, portfolio direction group, and program boards quarterly.

An annual pattern may look something like Figure 14.8:

The logic is as follows: assuming the main board runs a quarterly review of performance to targets and objectives, then the quarterly portfolio progress group (PPG) meetings need to happen before the main board review, and therefore, program performance boards need to have completed before the PPG meetings and project boards need to have completed before program performance boards.

Based on this, quarterly management team meetings on performance need to happen before main board meetings, quarterly management team meetings for benefits delivery need to happen before program performance boards, and finance operations (such as any end-of-month or end-of-quarter processes) for revenue and cost performance need to have completed before management team meetings and/or main board meetings.

Following this, and assuming the main board releases new objectives and targets for portfolios and management teams, respectively, from main board meetings, then portfolio direction group meetings need to happen just after them, and management teams resourcing meetings and finance allocation management meetings could happen after them as well.

Without governance cadence or commonality of process, standards for data, status capture, and "snapshotting" of portfolio status, each accountability node would have to seek from the business the information it needed when it needed it, potentially causing management inefficiency (this is expensive to support), and ineffectiveness can result (as the pictures would be unreliable and possibly out of date).

Cadence-based operations should enable participating business units to be part of the *integrated framework* approach, but organisational capacity and capability vary, so business support functions are often needed. These, themselves, may need to be supported or led to make them effective, which is often achieved with a hub-and-spoke model for business support. Clearly, aspects of the operation are dependent on services outside of the portfolio management domain, so cross-business support may go wider than the governance framework in some organisational structures.

Conclusion

The case for an integrated approach to portfolio governance has been discussed in this chapter, using the *business integrated governance framework* as a model, noting that the model is generic and can be adapted to suit the specific organisational context. It has also been discussed that effective management of data for management information and reporting is important for a successful integrated governance framework, and hence effective portfolio management.

The high-level plans that link the current state to the future vision equates to the strategy, with objectives, targets, and challenges providing the tactics, and with portfolio mandates, business plans, and innovation challenges giving assigned business units terms

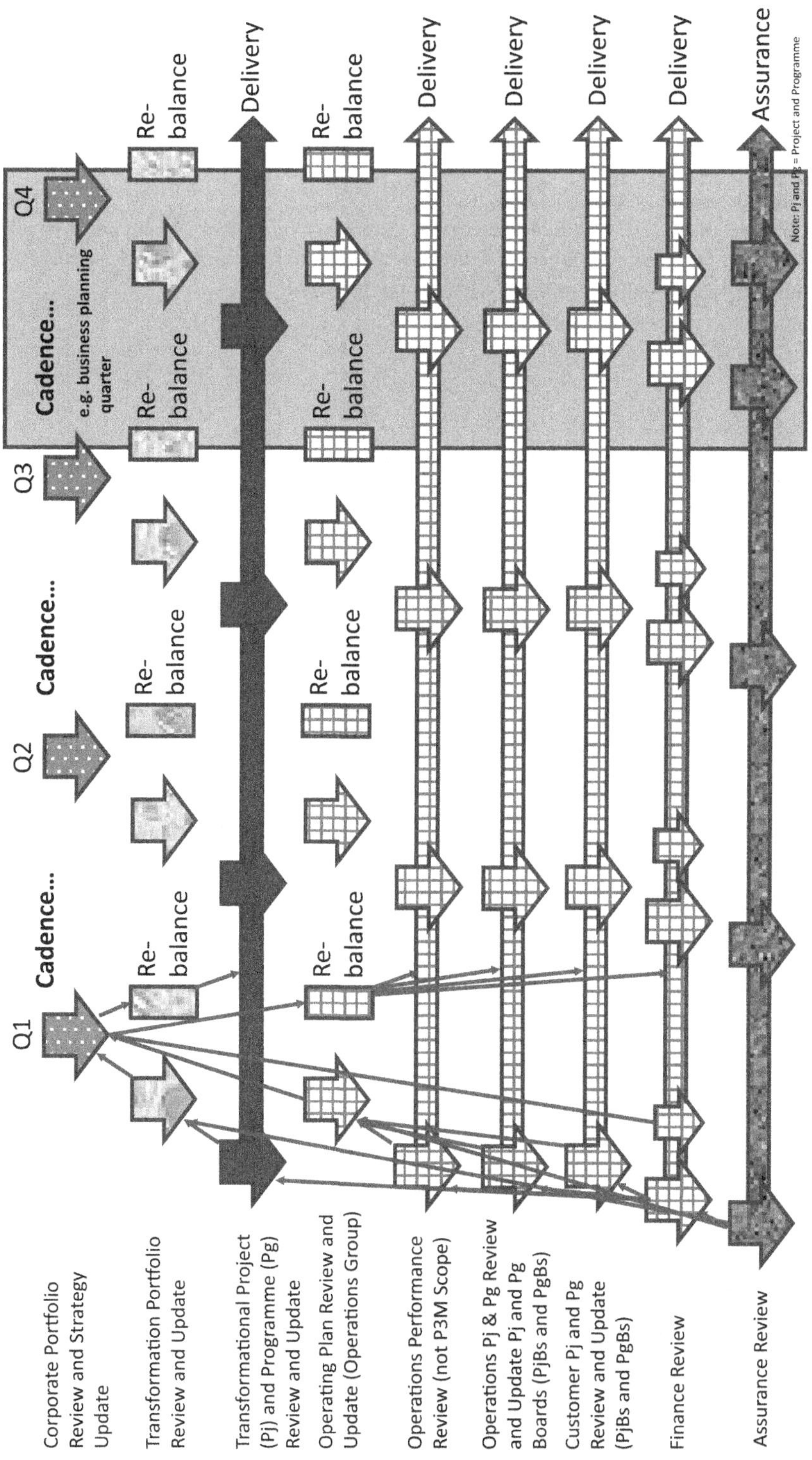

Figure 14.8 A typical annual reporting cycle.

of reference, in which to make a response within known and accepted accountability. Hence, this results in strategy execution.

If the organisation can develop its own accountability nodes, tease out the MI needs each of these nodes have, and collate the data, then there is a basis for a data model.

References

Axelos (2011) *Management of Portfolios (MoP)*. TSO.

Core P3M Data Club (2021) The business integrated governance framework. www.corep3m.club

Praxis (2020) *Praxis Framework: An Integrated Guide to the Management of Projects, Programmes and Portfolios*. Association for Project Management. www.praxisframework.org.

Annex 1

The Core P3M Data Club

This addendum provides a brief background on the Core P3M Data Club.

The club was formed to create a data standard for portfolio, program, project (and product) management (P3M) to enable delivery of business integrated governance more effectively across business-as-usual *and* change. It was started in November 2018 and has delivered a core governance and data model for P3M, with extensions for main board, finance, management teams, and product management.

The founders of the club are all portfolio, program, project, and/or product management professionals, each of whom have been frustrated by their organisations' lack of will and ability to integrate governance around portfolio (and program, project, and product) delivery. While many talk about poor tools, an under-resourced PMO, lack of training, inadequate methods, etc. for ineffective delivery and accomplishment, the club believes it is primarily down to ineffective governance and an overarching ecosystem within organisations to enable governance. It believes this strongly and passionately, so its founder (David Dunning) started a process to provide a framework to solve this endemic concern.

The process began by brainstorming a realistic organisation and governance model. The MI assumptions and the associated data model are based on the standards from a respected P3M framework (Praxis, 2020). These collective outputs are referred to as the *business integrated governance model*, shortened as BIG.

It means the journey from main board objectives, targets, and challenges can be delivered through portfolios, programs, and projects, regardless of a functional perspective. Key club goals are to deliver more strategic outcomes, greater business agility, lower management overhead, and better efficiency.

The team is proud to be volunteer-based, and the content is delivered into the public domain. To date, over 80 members (client organisations, tool vendors, data specialists, consultants) have been personally recognised for contribution to leadership, content development, or review of the materials for the club. The club created material containing thinking to enable others to address the issues they face in operating governance around their portfolios, including:

- A core P3M data model and supporting material.
- Example reports which can be delivered from the data model.

- Accountability node business definitions and example agendas for main board, finance, portfolios, programs, projects, management teams, and assurance.
- An overall framework for accountability nodes.
- An example organisation structure to enable discussions and to visualise stakeholder groups.
- A network of consultants, service providers, and software vendors who have contributed, reviewed, and advised.
- The material about the model and how to use it posted in the Praxis framework for open access (Praxis, 2020).

The club took an innovative approach to addressing these concerns, and this approach is recommended to other organisations to adapt to their own circumstances:

- Rather than brainstorm all the data elements that might possibly be needed, the decision was taken to create an example imaginary scenario.
- The club brainstormed a simple organisation model that would illustrate a scenario that had a mix of workloads across corporate transformation, customer work, business-as-usual (including services, products, and assets), and local innovation.
- A governance framework was "imagineered" that would connect the main board to portfolios (projects and programs to management teams and finance) – consisting of defined "accountability nodes".
    - "Main board" recognised opportunities/threats/imperatives/goals (OTIGs) would be translated into objectives for change, targets for business-as-usual, and challenges to be addressed (OTCs) that could be given to a main board sub-group for change and another for operation.
    - It assumed the sub-group for change would form portfolios to deliver objectives and engage on challenges.
    - The sub-group for operation would work with management teams running business units to deliver the operational requirements to meet targets.
    - "Portfolio(s)" would address objectives and be directed by portfolio direction group(s) and tracked by portfolio progress group(s) – and provide the interface between main board and delivery teams.
    - "Programs" and "projects" would provide the mechanism to deliver the road map towards objectives via benefit delivery, outcomes, and outputs.
    - "Management teams" within the organisation would focus on their BAU targets (and local innovations related to those), support portfolios with objective delivery resources, deliver benefit realisation and customer portfolios.
    - "Commercial and finance" would support all accountability nodes when making a business case or plan, supporting business planning, providing

  investment appraisal, financial assurance, and providing reliable performance data to enable control.
  - "Assurance" would provide independent review of business cases, operations, and performance.

- Each of these nodes was described in terms of its assumed governance operation with high-level assumptions in relation to portfolio, program, and project management operation. It was not the club's objective to define main board, finance, or management team operational details but instead to offer suggestions for operational aspects that would make P3M governance more effective.
- For each of these accountability nodes and the operation of them, the club then started to collect examples and suggestions for best practice management information.
- It was decided to take the backbone of data implied from the Praxis framework, a core planning data definition used in common planning tools (plan to task to assignment and resource and dependencies) and to superimpose what the group agreed were "core fields" to create a core P3M dataset.

Whilst applicable as examples, the outputs of the club do not offer a blueprint to copy and deliver as "install.exe", but it offers a framework for a thought process to deliver an organisation's version of it.

Annex 2

A construction portfolio assurance case study example

Hedley Walls

Introduction

This case study looks at portfolio assurance within the construction industry, developed by an external assurance team, examining portfolio performance and its associated effect on organisational performance, together with considering the impact of organisational change and strategic alignment.

Assessing a portfolio out of control

As a new CEO arrived at this large, well-established international company in the construction sector, senior management were concerned, as justification for cost over-runs had become interwoven with an inherent systemic lack of cost control, within a "silo-ism" culture. The construction business at that time was divided into four key divisions, each with their own managing director and operational management teams. These quite-separate divisions focused on different construction markets, which included residential housing, highways, and large-scale municipal civil engineering developments. At a macro-level, the company was battling with a reduction in market demand and pressured margins, bouncing between break-even and losses across its divisions.

To move the company forward and to make changes to answer the headwinds, there had been, through a number of singular stand-alone initiatives, very sensible investments initiated – particularly in IT infrastructure. However, these change investments had yet to be tracked and managed, which, coupled with a portfolio management office that was in its infancy, were not on the radar or agenda of the most senior management levels in the business.

Six months earlier, an assurance team from a tier 1 consultancy was engaged by the newly appointed head of portfolio management to carry out what appeared initially to be a fairly standard piece of checking and portfolio assurance work. The end result turned out to be anything but standard. It followed previous project assurance work carried out for the same manager in previous organisations. The manager was driven by a desire to pursue opportunities for rationalisation and prioritisation of projects, which to date the company had failed to achieve. Not untypically, the engagement objectives were vague and high level but sought to provide:

- Confirmation that the £80m portfolio of ongoing change programs was indeed the correct portfolio requiring management.
- Validation that all change programs under delivery were strategic in nature and that the business impact of initiatives was understood.
- And assurance that management were fully in control of timescales, cost, and quality.

These were broad objectives of the assignment, which the consulting assurance team decided to approach by answering some simple key questions:

- What live projects and programs are being delivered today?
- What are their individual budgets?
- Are they strategically aligned?
- Do they have a named project sponsor?
- Does a business case exist for each?
- Who signed off each project or program?
- Is a plan in place for each?

The approach taken to the portfolio assurance was a typical three-stage approach of (1) plan, (2) analyse, and (3) report. Planning involved initial evaluation and scope development. Analysis followed with capturing data, validating information, and reviewing and assessing findings, with the reporting phase bringing this together in a final delivery document for the client. Following agreement on scope with the sponsor, the approach taken by the team was to identify the key senior points of contact and then canvas each with a survey request to answer the previous questions, supplemented by a handful of more detailed questions. These included points on capacity and resourcing; likely capability to deliver; outcomes, scale, and complexity; and a subjective view on the likely impact of changes being delivered to the business. The survey was then followed up with a small number of interviews of the program sponsors of the largest programs and each of the four business divisional leads.

Portfolio assurance

The assurance team collated a large set of qualitative and quantitative information over a four-week period. This was used to build a picture of the overall portfolio, its costs, and its components. Additionally, in order to try to use the qualitative evidence effectively, a maturity score was applied to certain question outcomes in order to be able to compare across all live projects and programs – for example, the degree to which a project or portfolio was truly strategically aligned. (For further discussion of portfolio maturity, see Chapter 28).

The results from the exercise were startling. Instead of an £80m portfolio of "live" change activity, it was found in reality that this was nearer £200m of ongoing change investment, spanning 86 different projects and programs across the organisation; 18% of the portfolio could not demonstrate a sign-off for their investment or initiation, indicating poor operational controls of spend on capital-intensive activities outside of normal business. Towards 20% of the identified projects and programs were not led by a senior manager or appropriate sponsor, and 32% could not demonstrate genuine strategic alignment. Nearly half the portfolio declared the need for further support in order to deliver, and 30% stated they were unlikely to meet their current delivery plan. It was as if strategy and cost did not matter.

Conclusions focused on the need to improve strategic alignment of change initiatives, actions in relation to cross-project and program dependencies, advice on designing the portfolio management function, and a broader suite of specific recommendations for improvements to project and program performance. The final report shocked the portfolio manager and the new CEO. The strength of the financial and quantitative analysis meant that the conclusions were hard to dismiss. The results of the work were duly used to start to reshape the portfolio, and as this highlighted a significant need for change to financial control, a number of senior leaders in the change organisation began a plan of remedial action. Key strategic programs were closed down with immediate effect; there was internal reorganisation, financial controls were implemented, and the outflow of cash was effectively stemmed.

This portfolio assurance exercise demonstrated why portfolio management needs to be strong, that close attention to management controls (particularly in relation to appropriate project and program initiation and subsequent cost) is key, and that when delivering assurance work, resilience is a much-needed strength. In this case, the assurance team employed a powerful qualitative analysis that provided sound evidence and enabled action in the organisation as a result.

Conclusion

In summary, a strong portfolio management approach and associated controls, through portfolio assurance of projects and programs, can work to avoid difficulties, as experienced by the business highlighted in this case study, and look to ensure that strategic intent has a stronger likelihood of being successfully realised.

15 The strategic portfolio management office (SPMO)

Adam Skinner

Introduction

This chapter discusses how to operationalise the functions of portfolio management within a specific organisation. The main focus of the chapter is with the development of a service catalogue for an organisational group, to ensure all the needs of portfolio management are achieved, from a practical perspective. Such a group, sitting between strategic management and general management (or, perhaps, depending on the overall organisational structure, between the board and the general management levels), is needed in any significantly sized organisation to run the portfolio management activities.

The chapter begins with a brief review of structural options for the development of a portfolio office. Several alternative names (and acronyms) for the function of the portfolio management office or strategic PMO exist, including PoMO, PfMO, PPMO, and P_TMO. However, in this chapter a term that aligns with the key themes of the book and is applicable to most organisations is discussed, the *strategic portfolio management office* (SPMO), or more simply the portfolio office (in some organisations referred to as the corporate portfolio office).

The chapter then introduces the idea of a service catalogue for what the SPMO might do for an organisation. This is the "guts" of how the SPMO will transform strategic intent into discrete activities to achieve the intended outcomes and how the activities will be managed at the portfolio level thereafter. This is followed by a detailed discussion of the various services provided, concluding with a short note on how these services are typically further developed into a detailed operating model for the SPMO.

Context and structure for a portfolio office

Before an organisation can begin to build a validated service catalogue for an SPMO, there are a number of important steps to go through, and these steps reflect both an understanding of the design of the SPMO and the organisational change that may be needed to implement the services catalogue through the SPMO. These initial steps are:

1. *Understand the customer need.* Identify the key customers of the SPMO, discuss with them what is good and bad about the current management of the portfolio (does it even happen?), and ask them what they need to be in place to make efficient and effective decisions for the portfolio. From a change management perspective, it cannot be emphasised enough how critical this first step is and how important it is to go into this discussion without any preconditions around what the SPMO should and

DOI: 10.4324/9780367853129-18

could do. The SPMO lives or dies based on senior stakeholder engagement and their needs, and subjective experience of the SPMO is paramount.

2. *Understand the "as-is" situation.* Map out the current capability to manage the portfolio in terms of:

   - The capability and training of the individuals performing the portfolio management.
   - The process and tooling to deliver the portfolio and the decisions needed.
   - The leadership and culture around and within the management of the portfolio, decision-making, the hierarchical structures, etc.

3. *Define the "to be" future set of services the SPMO is required to deliver to the organisation.* Based on the customer/stakeholders asked, what is the end point of the services in terms of the information it provides, and the enablers of that information?
4. *Build the implementation road map.* Working with all key stakeholders for the SPMO services, plan the stepwise journey that gets the service from the "as-is" to the "to be". Each step should lead to an increase in information and decision-making capability.

A useful method when building the road map is to plan "show-and-tell" activities for each maturity increase into the established governance structure, as this becomes a useful validation point for the service. This also ensures a steady stream of "new things" into the governance approach to maintain senior stakeholder interest. As with all road maps, the short-term wins, and improvements are critical for achieving the "to be" end point. The goal is to drive continuous improvement in maturity of services and portfolio decision-making whilst maintaining flexibility based on the changing needs of the organisation and services.

There are a number of different organisational structural options for the SPMO. Portfolio management has often been rather narrowly focused on optimisation. However, a full-spectrum SPMO can deliver a much larger scope of services than solely optimisation of the portfolio, including having a much deeper reach into the ways in which projects and programs within the portfolio are managed. This leads to several structural options:

Centralised. A centralised SPMO is the simplest concept – a single centralised team, most often under a single lead, that delivers all the services from one place. The background and functional orientation of this lead role can be based on the specific services and areas the SPMO predominantly delivers into. The role may be filled by the CEO, CFO, CIO, or more recently, chief strategy officer (CSO) or even chief transformation officer (CTO). Usually, this model struggles when trying to deliver a large number of services – particularly when those services require reach into the projects (such as resource and capacity management) – but has strengths in terms of co-ordination of information and engagement with stakeholders. This model usually favours a service framework that leans towards one or other of the sub-functions (i.e. purely focused on portfolio optimisation to support the chief strategy officer with decision-making).

Hub and spoke. This model has become increasingly popular in recent years, particularly where the services of the SPMO require good insight and access to the activity within the projects. The typical hub-and-spoke model has a hub which acts as a central point for policy, information collation, reporting, and best practice linked to hubs of activity (usually within the projects) that implement policy and information management. This model has huge strength, particularly where the SPMO sits over the project capability and implements a resource and capacity management service. In this structure, the SPMO can both define best practice and ensure it is implemented via its hubs, whilst also directly accessing project information via those hubs. Such a set-up here would see the SPMO as the hub, and a separate centre of excellence as a spoke sitting within the project community.

A logical extension of this model is to have the "hub" as the SPMO and the "spokes" as project management offices within the major projects implementing delivery best practice and capturing information on behalf of the portfolio office. This is an increasingly popular combination.

Virtual SPMO. With modern data management and analysis techniques, it is entirely possible for the services of the SPMO to be provided without any part of the organisation being a traditional "SPMO". As with so much in modern business, it is the output that matters, and as long as the output that drives strong decision-making occurs, it does not matter whether a centralised function called an SPMO enables it or otherwise. Having said that, this is a high-risk approach – particularly in an organisation that has not attempted portfolio management before. The focus provided by setting up a dedicated entity to carry out portfolio management can be invaluable in driving the services forward. When moving towards a virtual SPMO, a clear service catalogue is essential from the start of the operation. It is also essential that there is a clear understanding of the *modus operandi* of the SPMO.

Hierarchical fit for an SPMO. Figure 15.1 articulates one view of how "offices" can support, and organisations work at, different levels in the organisation – from the project support office aligned at the project and workstream level, through to the program management office aligned at the program/outcome level, up to the strategic/portfolio level. Even at the strategic level, there are a range of levels where the portfolio management office can sit – whether genuinely linked into the board/organisational strategy or aligned to a particular business unit's investment portfolio. There is no right answer here. The SPMO (sometimes called the strategic PMO) should ideally be as close to both the key customer/stakeholders and the sources of information as possible. These will depend on the services offered.

The service catalogue

Before delving into the detailed services the SPMO can develop and deliver, it is worth taking a functional look at such an organisation, based on portfolio leadership, with the model shown in Figure 15.2 as an example. Ultimately, the SPMO needs to provide leadership to the portfolio through a range of criteria, including enabling decision-making and acting as a sounding board for senior leadership – but how does it do this? The leading portfolio management methodologies – for example, management of portfolios (Axelos, 2011), portfolio management guide (APM, 2019), AIPMO certification (AIPMO, 2021), or portfolio, program, and project offices (Axelos, 2013) – break the provision of portfolio management leadership down into two sub-functions (see Chapter 11 for a detailed discussion of portfolio optimisation and balance):

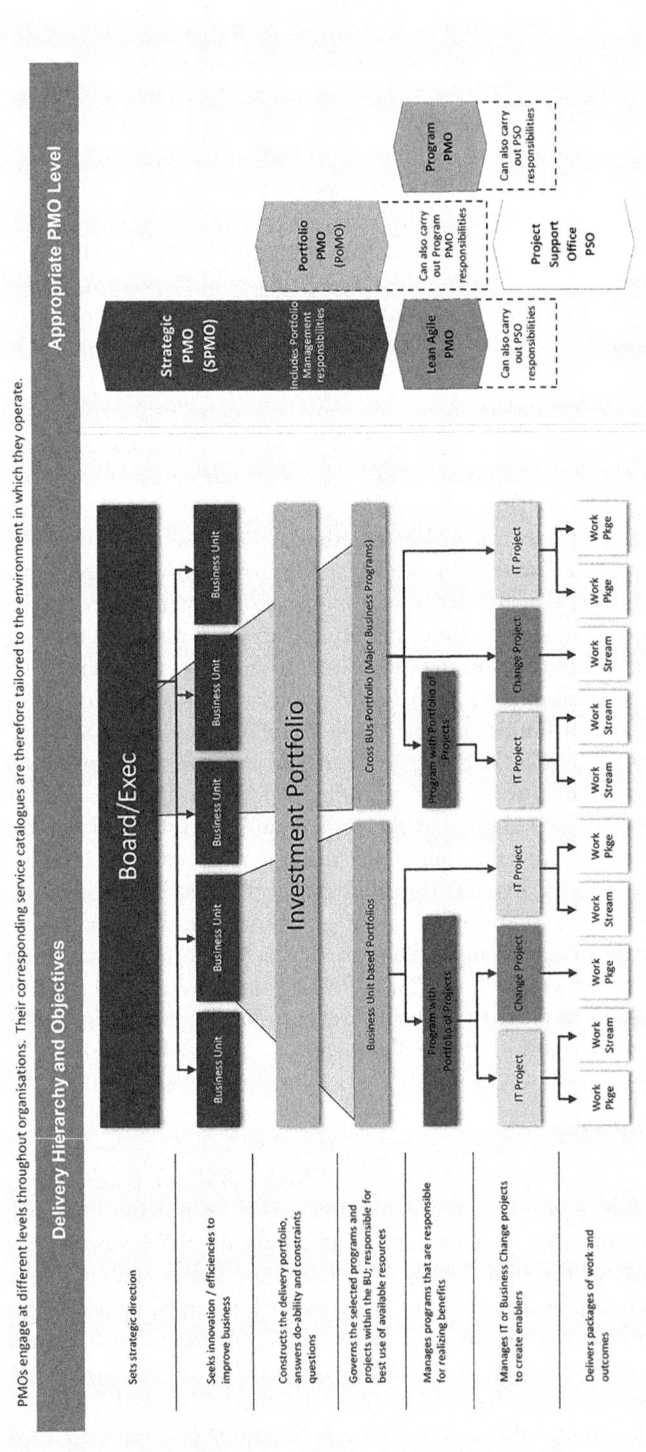

Figure 15.1 Hierarchy of PMOs.

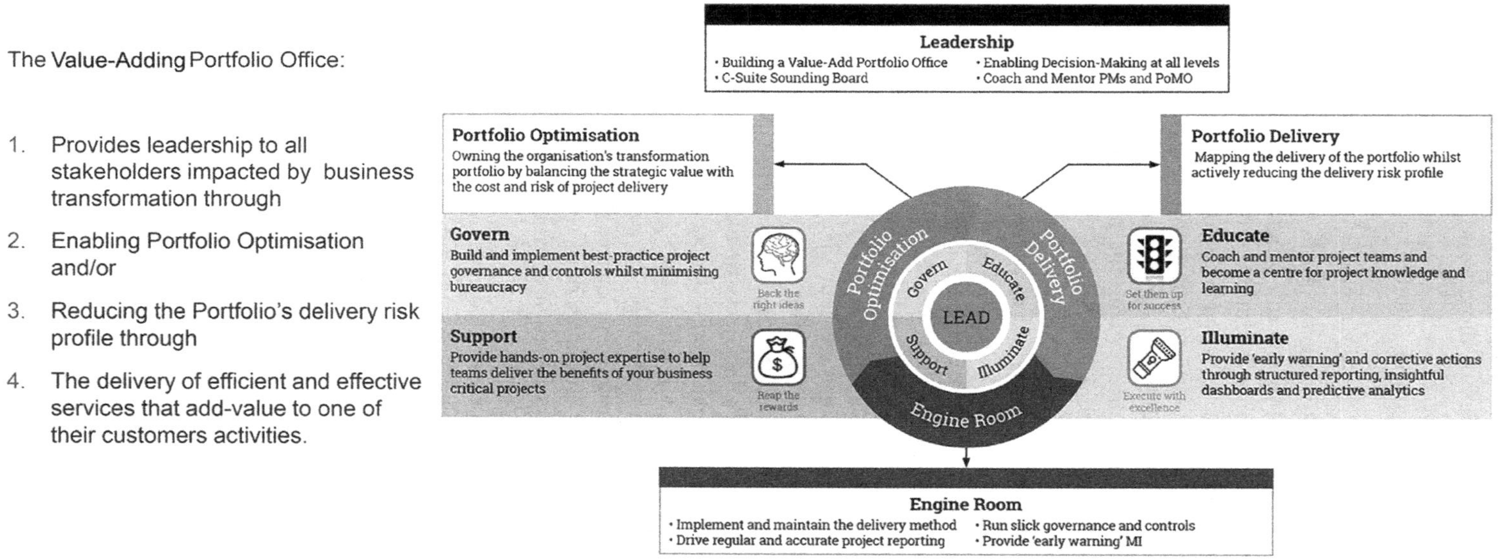
The Value-Adding Portfolio Office:
1. Provides leadership to all stakeholders impacted by business transformation through
2. Enabling Portfolio Optimisation and/or
3. Reducing the Portfolio's delivery risk profile through
4. The delivery of efficient and effective services that add-value to one of their customers activities.
Leadership
• Building a Value-Add Portfolio Office
• C-Suite Sounding Board
• Enabling Decision-Making at all levels
• Coach and Mentor PMs and PoMO
Portfolio Optimisation
Owning the organisation's transformation portfolio by balancing the strategic value with the cost and risk of project delivery
Portfolio Delivery
Mapping the delivery of the portfolio whilst actively reducing the delivery risk profile
Govern
Build and implement best-practice project governance and controls whilst minimising bureaucracy
Back the right ideas
Support
Provide hands-on project expertise to help teams deliver the benefits of your business critical projects
Reap the rewards
Portfolio Optimisation
Portfolio Delivery
Govern
Educate
LEAD
Support
Illuminate
Engine Room
Educate
Coach and mentor project teams and become a centre for project knowledge and learning
Set them up for success
Illuminate
Provide 'early warning' and corrective actions through structured reporting, insightful dashboards and predictive analytics
Execute with excellence
Engine Room
• Implement and maintain the delivery method
• Drive regular and accurate project reporting
• Run slick governance and controls
• Provide 'early warning' MI

Figure 15.2 A functional SPMO model.

1. *Optimisation* – which defines which projects should be in the portfolio based on the cost, risk, and value parameters of those projects and the strategic appetite of the organisation.
2. *Delivery* – which supports the organisation in taking actions that reduce the delivery risk of the portfolio.

Portfolio optimisation is the sub-function of portfolio management that looks to answer the question, What are the right projects and programs to attempt to deliver, based on the strategic direction of the organisation, and the cost and risk parameters of the individual projects? It is a common error when balancing the portfolio to prioritise purely based on the cost and value parameters, as cost is notoriously difficult to estimate to any degree of certainty, whereas risk estimation can give a more accurate picture of the overall achievability of a particular portfolio. So here the term "portfolio optimisation" means building a portfolio based on the three variables of value, cost, and risk. The goal of this sub-function is a balanced portfolio that broadly meets with the approval of the key stakeholders, as achievable within their cost and risk envelope, whilst delivering the strategic and tactical needs of the organisation.

Portfolio delivery is the sub-function of the SPMO that acts to reduce the overall delivery risk of the portfolio. It does this through a series of services that monitor and manage key areas of portfolio health that are, in many cases, exclusively accessible when viewed from the portfolio level, as opposed to from the project or program level. For instance, the service of demand management identifies, tracks, and removes impediments created by project dependencies on organisational resources. An example would be if more than one project needs simultaneous access to a particular IT system testing environment resource, the individual projects are likely to struggle to identify that there will be a clash ahead of time. Indeed, even if the clash is identified, the projects will lack the prioritisation information to say which one gets precedence. From the portfolio level, the portfolio manager can more easily see which projects need which particular resources and, more critically, work to prioritise those projects and identify needed mitigation approaches. An analogy often used for the SPMO is that of "air-traffic control for the portfolio" – it has a high-level view of all the projects, which is necessary to avoid project demand clashes.

Figure 15.2 has a number of other important components – beyond the two sub-functions mentioned previously. The third sub-function is called the engine room, and this contains the actual activities that deliver the services that make up the optimisation and assurance sub-functions.

Whereas the optimisation sub-function consists of a series of services that build on each other to support portfolio optimisation decisions, the delivery sub-function tends to consist of services that support various different stand-alone elements of the portfolio. There can be huge variation in the delivery services performed by an SPMO. Few of these services deliver their full value in isolation, and even more critically, the services that sit under the portfolio delivery sub-function vastly enrich the activities that sit under the portfolio optimisation sub-function. As with all organisational activity, the real value-add comes from how one integrates the learning and information from the individual services. Figure 15.3 shows the complete set of services that an SPMO may offer.

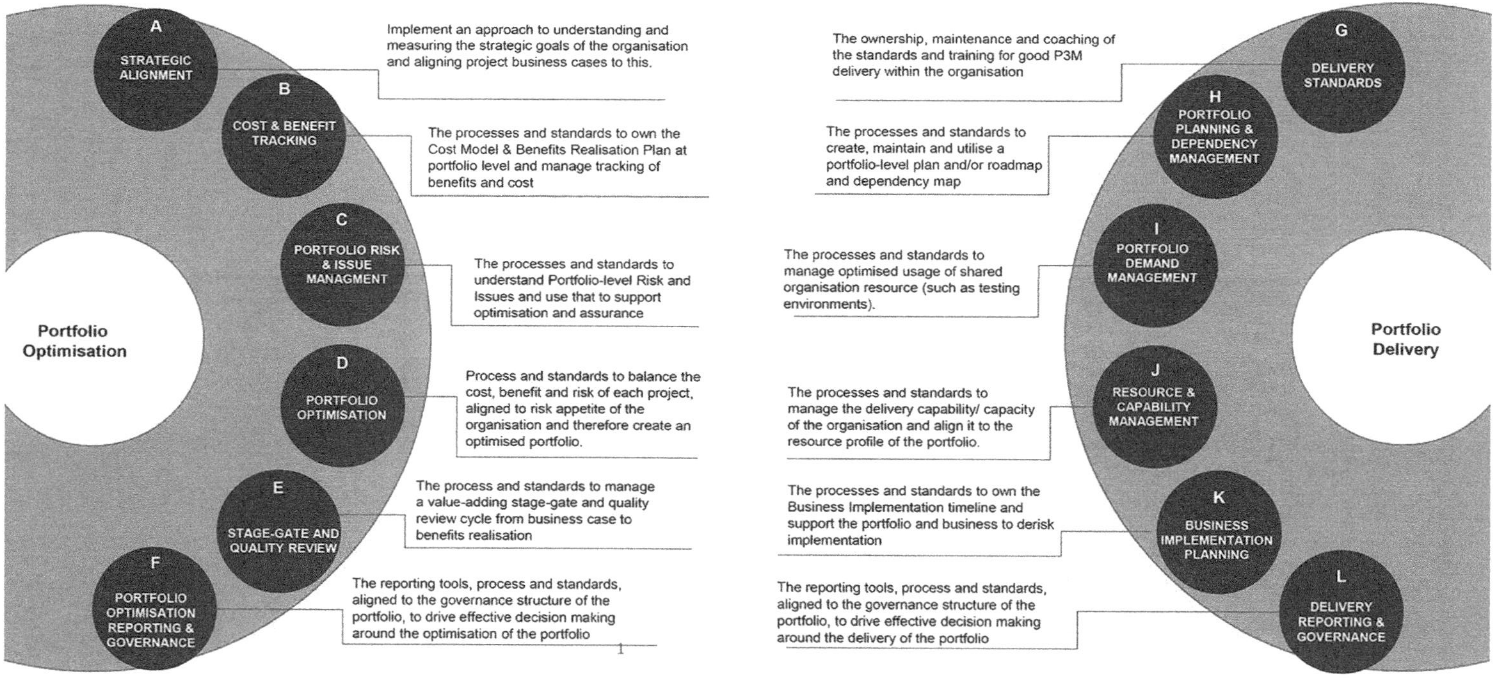
Portfolio Optimisation
A
STRATEGIC ALIGNMENT
Implement an approach to understanding and measuring the strategic goals of the organisation and aligning project business cases to this.
B
COST & BENEFIT TRACKING
The processes and standards to own the Cost Model & Benefits Realisation Plan at portfolio level and manage tracking of benefits and cost
C
PORTFOLIO RISK & ISSUE MANAGMENT
The processes and standards to understand Portfolio-level Risk and Issues and use that to support optimisation and assurance
D
PORTFOLIO OPTIMISATION
Process and standards to balance the cost, benefit and risk of each project, aligned to risk appetite of the organisation and therefore create an optimised portfolio.
E
STAGE-GATE AND QUALITY REVIEW
The process and standards to manage a value-adding stage-gate and quality review cycle from business case to benefits realisation
F
PORTFOLIO OPTIMISATION REPORTING & GOVERNANCE
The reporting tools, process and standards, aligned to the governance structure of the portfolio, to drive effective decision making around the optimisation of the portfolio
Portfolio Delivery
G
DELIVERY STANDARDS
The ownership, maintenance and coaching of the standards and training for good P3M delivery within the organisation
H
PORTFOLIO PLANNING & DEPENDENCY MANAGEMENT
The processes and standards to create, maintain and utilise a portfolio-level plan and/or roadmap and dependency map
I
PORTFOLIO DEMAND MANAGEMENT
The processes and standards to manage optimised usage of shared organisation resource (such as testing environments).
J
RESOURCE & CAPABILITY MANAGEMENT
The processes and standards to manage the delivery capability/ capacity of the organisation and align it to the resource profile of the portfolio.
K
BUSINESS IMPLEMENTATION PLANNING
The processes and standards to own the Business Implementation timeline and support the portfolio and business to derisk implementation
L
DELIVERY REPORTING & GOVERNANCE
The reporting tools, process and standards, aligned to the governance structure of the portfolio, to drive effective decision making around the delivery of the portfolio

Figure 15.3 A set of integrated portfolio management services (P2 Consulting, 2021).

The optimisation sub-function and its services

Looking now in more detail at what the set of services may be in each sub-function, Table 15.1 links the various questions that need to be answered in making high-quality optimisation decisions with the optimisation service in this sub-function. These services are then described following the table.

Strategic alignment. This involves identification of what value means to the organisation, what value increase is expected over a strategic timeline, and how this will be quantified as benefits and measured. It means taking the organisation's strategy and turning it into key performance indicators (KPIs) that the delivery of project benefits, and therefore their intrinsic value, can be measured against over agreed time frames. Ideally, the KPIs should be quantifiable to aid optimisation but may be qualitative (such as small, medium, large) or relative (such as project 1 is "more valuable" than project 2).

Portfolio cost and benefit measurement. This is measuring the likely cost and benefit of potential and actual projects. Cost measurement should involve all the potential expenses in delivering projects and operating the resultant deliverables (in other words, both capital and operating expenses – CAPEX and OPEX). A major factor of any cost discussion in any business or program is resourcing – the actual people who make up the teams and their various logistic and system needs. This, therefore, creates a strong link between this service and the resource and capability management service (which should be providing the resource) and is a critical one to manage carefully to keep costs under control (i.e. to avoid a large influx of expensive temporary workers due to poor resource management). The flip side of cost measurement, benefit measurement, means tracking the benefits defined in the project business cases, and assessing whether they will deliver on the organisational KPIs identified under strategic alignment. A good SPMO needs to track these metrics both prior to a project's kick-off (to assess whether it should enter the optimised portfolio), during execution (to keep an accurate record of what the portfolio is likely to cost and deliver), and post-closure (to track what the portfolio has achieved).

Table 15.1 Portfolio optimisation services

Service to support optimisation sub-function	*Key questions the service answers*
Strategic Alignment	What does value mean to the organisation, and how do I measure it?
Portfolio Cost and Benefit Measurement	What is the likely cost and benefit of the portfolio and its potential projects?
Risk and Issue Management	What is the likely risk profile of the portfolio and its potential projects?
Portfolio Optimisation	What is the combination of projects, based on the cost, benefit, and risk information, that creates the optimal portfolio?
Portfolio Quality Assurance	What is the current status of the portfolio against our optimisation metrics of cost, risk, and value?
Governance and Reporting	What are the right decisions to make to optimise the portfolio based on the available data?

Portfolio risk and issue management. Looks at quantifying the level of risk within the portfolio and monitoring activity to reduce that level. Understanding the level of risk held in the portfolio, and the level of risk inherent in potential projects, is a critical factor in optimising the portfolio. Therefore, the logical extension of this is the activity required, not simply to monitor the level of risk, but to facilitate the mitigation and management of those risks and issues identified at portfolio level (see Chapter 17 for a more detailed discussion). Clearly, there is a significant crossover between this activity and the sub-function of portfolio delivery – where many of the risks that impact optimisation will be identified and managed. A critical point here is that portfolio risks are not project and program risks and issues. Risks that impact projects and programs are managed at the project and program level – those risks become portfolio risks when a pattern is identified across a range of project and programs that can only be mitigated at the organisational level.

Portfolio optimisation. Involves using the raw value, risk, and cost information around all the portfolio to create a balanced and optimised portfolio that has a realistic chance of delivering the organisation's strategic objectives to an agreed level of confidence and within specific cost parameters. This could be done as simply as the key stakeholders talking through the projects during an all-day workshop and agreeing "what feels right" or, alternatively, engaging a complex, high-end portfolio management system creating the optimal portfolio based on raw data and cutting-edge algorithms. The critical point here is that portfolio optimisation is treated as a service.

Portfolio quality assurance (stage-gating). Performs regular reviews of the portfolio's projects and programs to assess portfolio health. Usually, this involves an assessment/reassessment of project and program key documents, such as the plan and business case, primarily with the goal of identifying areas of risk, and assessing the accuracy of a range of metrics, including expected cost, risk, and benefit. This (re)assessment of metrics should then play back into portfolio optimisation decisions. This service will often make an overall assessment of health and risk levels, as well as making recommendations for risk reduction. However, the primary goal of this activity, from a portfolio optimisation point of view, is to reassess the key variables of cost, risk, and benefit to ensure the "as-is" view of the portfolio is maintained for optimisation activity.

Portfolio optimisation governance and reporting. Capturing, interpreting, and presenting information on the portfolio and organising and operating the governance in order to support and enable decision-making around the optimised structure of the portfolio. (See Chapter 14, "Portfolio governance," and Chapter 16, "Visualising data for portfolio decision-making", for further discussions of these two topic areas.)

The delivery sub-function and its services

When considering the portfolio delivery sub-function, it is important to ensure the SPMO is finding ways to use its overarching position to support the delivery teams (i.e. the projects and programs) in reducing their delivery risk. This means using the fact that they have sight of all project activity to help those projects deliver. This is traditionally done through leveraging the SPMO's overview to spot risks and bottlenecks the projects themselves cannot spot; when done correctly, a good SPMO adds as much value to the projects as it does to the portfolio decision-making, which is the mark of a high-value SPMO. A good guide as to whether a service is appropriate within the SPMO is to ask,

"Is this genuinely a portfolio problem, or is it better resolved/managed within the project?" The portfolio delivery sub-functions are:

Delivery standards. These are the project and program delivery methodologies for the organisation and the templates, tools, and subject matter experts that underpin that delivery methodology. Traditionally, this links heavily to the reporting and quality assurance services and involves saying what must be done in the process (i.e. reporting on key milestones monthly) and what best practice is (i.e. where possible, ensure a project has a clear communication plan). However, more mature services may include subject matter experts, community of practices, and a full suite of training and coaching to ensure those delivery standards are adhered to.

Portfolio planning and dependency management. This involves defining what good planning and dependency management looks like within the organisation and what standards are to be adhered to. Many SPMOs will also define and own the portfolio-level milestones and dependency points (often called "*level 0 milestones*" in project planning parlance). Traditionally, this will be a higher level of milestone than a project would operate on but would allow construction of a portfolio delivery plan (or a strategy delivery plan). It is common practice for the SPMO to be accountable for developing and maintaining these higher-level milestones and be the point of authorisation for changes to these milestones and any dependency points. Critically, dependency management is one of the key SPMO functions that can only be done effectively at the portfolio level, given its overarching view of all major projects and programs.

Demand management. It is associated with arranging access to shared organisational resource required to deliver the projects and programs (execute strategy). A classic example of this would be IT software testing environments, where the SPMOs' overarching view of all project demand makes it the ideal place to manage access to this organisational resource and also to make priority calls for the project community where a clash is inevitable. Other resources that may come under a demand management service might be business experts, specialist design groups, software testing and release environments, legal/HR/operational experts, space, laboratory equipment, pilot plants, access to product/business-specific technical expertise – in fact, any part of the organisation that is in limited supply.

Resource and capacity management. It is managing the supply and demand for resources needed to deliver the portfolio. This can be as simple as having a resource profile of the portfolio to as complex as overseeing the entire capacity within the organisation available to the portfolio. It may even include human resource aspects, such as training, promotion, and allocation. Given the significance of this service, it is discussed in more detail in Chapter 13.

Business implementation management. This encompasses managing the readiness of the business to receive organisational change and transformation products. At its most basic, this involves managing the schedule of organisational change interventions and deliverables so as not to swamp a particular business area with too much concurrent change. At more advanced levels, it can involve taking regular change stress checks of different parts of the business to assess readiness to receive change and overseeing the coaching/training design in the portfolio to ensure it is of sufficient quality for the business. This is another area where, with a little effort, the SPMO can provide a unique view, and significant value, to the business with respect to organisational performance improvement.

Delivery reporting and governance. This facilitates effective decision-making through the operation of portfolio governance and the provision of information and analysis for decision-making. The purpose of the decision-making is almost always to focus on reducing the delivery risk of the portfolio – raising questions such as "What is the right resource profile to deliver the portfolio?" and "Which business implementation timeline gives the portfolio the best chance of success?" This is a broad area, however, and what is reported on, and what decisions need to be made, will be fundamentally driven by the services being delivered for the customers of the SPMO. Traditionally, organisations only have one governance framework linked to the portfolio that covers both optimisation and delivery question. However, it is becoming increasingly popular to have one governance focused on optimisation and one focused on delivery, reflecting the differences in the information and decision-making requirements for each sub-function.

Aspects of service operationalisation

So far, this chapter has explored some of the key services that an SPMO may choose to offer, given all SPMOs will deliver different services to different maturity levels, based on the culture of their organisation and the requirements of the organisation. However, a *description* of a service is not an operationalised service. To effectively operationalise a service, we need to have four aspects identified and described in a level of detail appropriate to the service and the organisational cultural context:

1) *Service description* – a clear description of the service, who it serves, what it produces, and what the output is to be used for.
2) *People* – what the roles that operationalise the service are, what their seniority and location in the structure, the responsibilities, and information interfaces they must interact with are.
3) *Process* – what process the service follows, what the inputs to the service, the flow of activity, the process branches, and the outputs of the service are.
4) *Tools* – what the tools and templates used during that service are, where they can be found, and how the users can be trained and coached in their use.

Anyone familiar with an organisational architecture will be familiar with these components of a service. It is helpful to codify these items within an SPMO handbook, which can be accessed by both the SPMO and its key stakeholders, giving a clear understanding of what the SPMO does, who does it within the SPMO, and how it is done. This also forms the basis for service/function reviews and continuous improvement and/or transformation of the SPMO.

The next two sections of this chapter expand on and give some further insights on two fundamental aspects of portfolio management: high-quality decision-making enabled and supported by the SPMO services, and effective and organisationally efficient resource allocation and capacity planning.

Decision-making enablement in the SPMO

At this stage of the chapter, it can be assumed the SPMO is set up with clear services, is supported by relevant stakeholders in the organisation, is operated and managed by well-trained and motivated people, has effective and efficient processes and tools, and has available a clear and easily accessible description of the way the SPMO operates. Of course, success is a well-functioning portfolio, but what exactly is the SPMO doing that enables portfolio success? Capturing data on portfolio dependencies or project benefit delivery does not, in itself, directly lead to portfolio success. There is one critical step between the data and the positive outcome – *good decisions*. More than any other measure we can use to define success in any kind of support office, the enablement of high-quality decision-making is pre-eminent.

Let's begin with a definition of a good decision: a good decision is one taken in a timely and objective manner, using relevant and up-to-date data, made by appropriate and accountable decision-makers, following effective challenge from relevant stakeholders. The ability to make effective decisions is grouped under three headings: *good governance*, *good information*, and *good psychology*.

Good governance means having available a good decision-making forum. Some critical aspects of a good decision-making forum are:

- It is composed of the right people, who either have relevant information or responsibility (i.e. they have, as the saying goes, "skin in the game" – Taleb, 2019).
- All roles in the forum have clear responsibilities in the decision-making process.
- Clarity over the forum's authority and responsibilities (i.e. it is actually able, organisationally, to make the decisions it needs to).
- The regularity of the forum, influenced by its role in the overall organisation, where it could range from a short-cycle, very hands-on activity in the week-to-week life of the organisation to an annual forum for making high-level strategic portfolio decisions, or it may even be ad hoc, assembled when it is deemed necessary.
- There is sufficient lead time and advanced warning of decision-making, both for those in the forum and those impacted by the decisions made.
- Ensuring the organisational culture is understood well enough to enable high-quality decisions to be made and acted on (of course, this is fundamental to the definition of the SPMO and its services in the first place). Absolutely critically, the forum must have clarity over the question/decision it is established to answer.

Good information. Entire books have been written on what it means to provide good information, so here it is just worth noting that good information is never about providing more information. Good information for decision-making must be:

- *Trusted*. Even if the information is right, if it is not trusted, it is useless. Being clear about how much trust/weight can be placed on the data is critical.
- *Informative*. It must tell the decision-maker something they do not already know or provide insight that helps understand other information.
- *Appropriate*. It must provide just enough information on the relevant decision to help, without drowning the user in data.
- *Engaging*. The information must tell a story about reality that the viewer can engage with, and therefore understand it, in their own context.
- *Contextual*. The information must clearly state what problem/question the decision is intended to resolve, how the information supports the decision process, and what gaps in information may remain.

Making information obviously useful is not always easy in the SPMO – the charge of simply passing on information provided by the projects is often levelled at the SPMO and must be guarded against. The best way to do this is to be extremely clear about the role of the SPMO in supporting decision-making. It is also vital to focus on how to add value to the raw data provided by the projects and programs – integrating data in a way the projects cannot, that is, either across projects (as discussed in the services section to provide an overview) or across information streams (e.g. combining cost, risk, and milestone data to create a portfolio-level cost quantitative risk assessment to support better apportionment of the portfolio contingency pot).

Good psychology. Again, much has been written on the psychological aspects of organisational change, such as Scarlett, 2019; Kahnemann, 2011; Taleb, 2010, 2013. Both Kahnemann and Taleb explore, and arguably have popularised, the science linking psychology to organisational change, with an increasing awareness of the many heurisms that bound a leader's decision-making and the impact these have in the area of program and portfolio management. Heurisms, such as optimism bias and lock-in (Murray & Häubl, 2007), can fundamentally impact good decision-making, despite the strength of the governance framework or the quality of the information. Indeed, the Dunning-Kruger heurism (Coutinho et al., 2021) implies the more informed you are about something, the harder you find it to make a decision, as you realise how much more there is to know. Flybjvberg (2013) argues that these types of biases cannot be overcome, and so an outside source of information should be sought – as opposed to a decision made by the group, or "inside" source, sometimes called groupthink – and suggests the use of a technique known as "reference class forecasting".

Putting heurisms to one side, another area of psychology that is growing in focus as a way of driving strong organisations and strong decision-making is psychological safety. Nembhard and Edmondson (2012) identify the importance of teams and decision-makers trusting and respecting each other, feeling they can disagree, and even make errors without retribution, and that ultimately success and failure are collective endeavours with cognitive diversity seen to benefit decision-making (Syed, 2021). Further research in this space looks at the organisational impacts of psychological safety, such as Mckinsey (2021), rather than more specifically investigating the impact of psychological safety in governance forums. However, anecdotal evidence from a community of portfolio directors (APM, 2021) supports psychologically safe governance forums as being likely to be effective for quick, efficient, and optimised decision-making. This psychological safety will depend on the governance structure, for instance, whether the portfolio manager is heavily involved with the decision-making or is primarily responsible for presenting the information and the potential options to the decision-makers, that is, for decision support. Many aspects of psychological safety can only be developed over time, that is, the growing trust between decision-makers (Edmondson, 2018), but it is an interesting exercise to explore, with a decision-making forum, how to accelerate the development of a psychologically safe environment.

Resourcing and capacity management

Resource and capacity management has the potential to be the largest and most resource-intensive service within the SPMO. In simplistic terms, it is the activity required to ensure the capability exists to deliver the optimised portfolio – essentially to ensure the supply of all resources (not just humans) equals or exceeds the demand to deliver the portfolio at any given time. To understand the resource demand, the SPMO must be able to understand:

1. The projects' schedules, at the project level and integrated at the portfolio level.
2. The resource requirement for projects at the individual capability level (both role and experience).
3. The level of certainty around the resource estimates.

Effective resource management means having in place a service that can review and adjust the portfolio resource demand timeline dynamically as factors change and milestones shift. In order to understand the capability of the resources available to support the portfolio, the SPMO must have:

- A resource capability framework against which to assess specific capability (e.g. for human resources, a competence model for all roles, and where on that model the human resources in the organisation sit).
- A dynamic resourcing tool that allows the SPMO to see what activity each resource is allocated to and for how long.

By combining the demand and the supply view, the SPMO will have established the capability gap it has to fill. It then needs to address this gap via four options:

1. Adjust the demand by slipping milestones, reducing scope, or closing projects to free up and redirect existing resource.
2. Adjust the supply through permanent changes to capability availability (recruitment, buy machinery, lock-in service providers, etc.).
3. Adjust the supply by using third-party providers (either as subcontractors, leasing or hiring process capability, using consultants, and all manner of other third-party suppliers).
4. Increase or adjust capability through training and coaching of people, adding process improvement projects to the portfolio, etc.

All these activities must be carried out dynamically and responsively to the changes and slippages that are normal in most portfolios. None of the aforementioned options are easy, and all involve more effort and skill from the SPMO, such as supporting recruitment, training, commercial and contracting for third-party services, process improvement teams in technical functions, and supporting specialist functions in the organisation as they work to develop a high level of capability.

Given the level of effort, expertise, political will, and process development needed to provide an SPMO service that effectively supports and delivers resource management, most SPMOs do not include this service in their catalogue, despite the service arguably being a critical role for effective portfolio management. Obviously, the balance of supply and demand is considerably harder when the SPMO does not have direct control over the capability within the organisation, and a powerful and overarching SPMO is a rarity in most organisations. A skilled project team is regularly cited as one of the most important factors driving traditional project success, yet a key failure point for projects is often identified as poor knowledge at the portfolio level of resource and capability demand (Williams & Vo 2015). Often being challenging to achieve, when effective resource and capacity management fails, the typical result is both cost inflation and project failure, as expensive external resources are sought to bridge the gap in the resourcing profile, caused by poor resource planning and management, negating both the budget and potentially the business case for the affected project(s).

Conclusion

An SPMO can range from a small organisational group dedicated to portfolio analysis and decision support, through to an overarching structure, with a wide range of business services, intended to not only ensure the portfolio has correctly translated strategic intent to action but also to take accountability for delivering the strategy. These extremes are a long way apart. Nevertheless, no matter the size and role of the SPMO, adopting a service catalogue approach brings significant advantages to the execution of strategy.

Two important points about the effectiveness of an SPMO are:

Firstly, SPMOs provide a service that is only as valuable as the subjective experiences of its senior stakeholders – it lives and dies by their patronage. Engaging with stakeholders early and often is vital: ensure understanding of their needs and drivers and deliver to them.

Secondly, the value of the SPMO is in how it enables those stakeholders to make more efficient and effective decisions for the portfolio to support effective strategy execution. Anything that improves this is value-adding; anything else – no matter how clever – is not. Plan the services, resources, and SPMO improvements accordingly.

References

AIPMO (2021) IPMO practitioner and expert courses. www.aipmo.org

APM (2019) *Portfolio Management: A Practical Guide*. Association for Project Management.

APM (2021) APM Portfolio Management specific interest group (SIG) 6th annual conference: Portfolio management in a digital age. www.apm.org.uk

Axelos (2011) *Management of Portfolios*. TSO The Stationery Office.

Axelos (2013) *Portfolio, Programme and Project Offices*. OGC.

Coutinho M., Thomas J, Alsuwaidi A. & Couchman J. (2021) Dunning-Kruger effect: Intuitive errors predict overconfidence on the cognitive reflection test. *Frontiers in Psychology* 12, 603225.

Edmondson A. (2018) *The Fearless Organization: Creating Psychological Safety in the Workplace for Learning, Innovation and Growth*. Wiley.

Flybjvberg B. (2013) From Nobel prize to project management: Getting risks right. *Project Management Journal* 37(3), 5–15.

Kahnemann D. (2011) *Thinking, Fast and Slow*. Penguin.

Mckinsey (February 2021) Psychological safety and the critical role of leadership development. www.mckinsey.com

Murray K. & Häubl G. (2007) Explaining cognitive lock-in: The role of skill-based habits of use in consumer choice. *Journal of Consumer Research* 34(1), 77–88.

Nembhard I. & Edmondson A. (2012) Psychological safety: A foundation for speaking up, collaboration and experimentation in organizations. *The Oxford Handbook of Positive Organizational Scholarship*. Oxford Handbooks.

P2 Consulting (2021) *Portfolio Office Model* ™. www.p2consulting.com

Scarlett H. (2019) *Neuroscience for Organisational Change: An Evidenced based Practical Guide to Managing Change*. Second Edition. Kogan Page.

Syed M. (2021) *Rebel Ideas: The Power of Thinking Differently*. John Murray publications.

Taleb N. (2010) *The Black Swan: The Impact of the Highly Improbable*. Second Edition. Penguin.

Taleb N. (2013) *Antifragile: Things that Gain from Disorder*. Penguin.

Taleb N. (2019) *Skin in the Game: Hidden Asymmetries in Daily Life*. Penguin.

Williams T. & Vo H. (2015) *Conditions for project success*. APM Research Report. Association for Project Management.

16 Visualising data for portfolio decision-making

Catherine Killen

Introduction

Visualisations of portfolio data are making an increasing impact on the management of portfolios of projects. Project portfolio management (PPM) approaches provide decision-makers with a high-level strategic view of the projects in a portfolio to promote decisions that provide the best overall benefit. In industries where strategy is primarily delivered through projects, PPM is an essential capability; PPM decisions bridge strategy with its delivery through projects (and programs). Such decisions require analysis of information about a wide range of factors, including strategic objectives, project performance, risks, resource requirements, and relationships between projects.

Visualisations of data are regularly used in PPM to assist decision-makers to understand the data and "see" the project landscape. The increased use of such visuals can be partially attributed to the increasing ease in creating graphical displays. Creating visuals was once a time-consuming manual process; now visuals can be almost instantly generated by software programs. Dashboards of multiple visuals have become a common feature of PPM and other management systems. However, the ease of creation does not ensure the visuals will be useful. Visuals can confuse, mislead, and waste time when not created well, tailored to context and understood by the users. Research is important to understand whether and how visuals can enhance decision-making – and to provide guidance for the effective use of visualisations in PPM.

Established PPM capabilities provide organisations with competitive advantages that enable them to compete and adapt to changes in the environment (Killen & Hunt, 2010). The decision environment and the processes that support decision-making are central to PPM. A primary goal of a PPM process should be to support the decision-makers and enhance their ability to make good decisions; such decisions affect the implementation of strategy, the development of competitive advantages, and survival and success of the organisation.

Portfolio-level decisions are often made by a group of experienced managers and executives in portfolio review meetings – this group is often called the portfolio review board (PRB) (Killen et al., 2008a; Mosavi, 2014), although alternatives are available, such as portfolio direction and/or progress group discussed in Chapter 14. Decision boards that are made up of experienced and accountable representatives of different perspectives (finance, marketing, technical, operations, etc.) are most often recommended by research findings (Killen et al., 2008a). The goal is to gain input from multiple perspectives to best understand the project landscape and generate robust discussions that lead to well-informed and balanced decisions. Visuals have a growing influence in this process; visual

DOI: 10.4324/9780367853129-19

representations of data are often provided to decision-makers in advance and referred to during the PRB meetings (Cooper et al., 2001). Evidence is mounting on the ways that visuals can enhance the ability of decision-makers to understand and discuss the relevant portfolio data. For example, a case-based study of six organisations emphasised the importance of the dialogue during PRB meetings and how visuals can generate valuable discussions (Killen & Hunt, 2010).

This chapter outlines research on the use of visuals in PPM. It firstly introduces some of the theories and concepts that underpin the research and then explains three programs of research that explore the role of visualisations of data for PPM decision-making. Practical implications from these research studies are brought together in the concluding section to guide managers in improving the ways visuals are used to support PPM.

The role of cognitive limits in portfolio decision-making

Portfolio management decisions are challenging – decision-makers must absorb a wide range of information about the projects (and programs) in the portfolio to support their decisions. When allocating resources to projects or changing the priority or scope of projects, decision-makers need to understand how each project fits with other projects in the portfolio on multiple dimensions. For example:

- How does this project fit with our strategy?
- Does this project complement or conflict with other projects?
- How strong and reliable is the need for this project (markets, customers, changing demographics)?
- What resources are required (funding, skills, equipment)?
- What benefits are expected (financial return on investment, strategic or reputational advantages)?
- Are other projects or external factors important for this project (Does this project depend on another project? Do regulations affect the project? Will the project or its supply chain be affected by international events?).
- What are the risks involved (financial, safety, legal, reputational)?

These and other questions factor into the complex portfolio decision-making task of choosing and supporting the best overall set of projects (and programs) to meet short- and long-term objectives. This volume of information about the projects and the portfolio presents a cognitive challenge for decision-makers: How can they absorb and make sense of all the data to make good decisions? The research presented in this chapter explores the role of visuals in enhancing the ways decision-makers understand, analyse, and discuss information.

Concepts of cognition, cognitive fit, and bounded rationality help explain why making good decisions in such environments is challenging and how visuals can be of assistance. Cognition refers to the mental processes required for learning, solving problems, making decisions, absorbing information, and forming memories (Newell, 1990). These mental processes represent a "cognitive load" on the working memory of decisions-makers. There are limits to the amount of information that can be handled by individual decision-makers. These limits are often compared to limits in computer processing power; when the load is too high, information cannot be processed effectively. Similarly, in portfolio decision-making, once the cognitive load required to absorb and analyse portfolio information increases too much, cognitive capability becomes overloaded, and the quality of decisions is affected.

Although the analogy with computer processing can be useful, human cognition is much more complex than computer processing. In particular, humans possess nuanced perception capabilities and superior abilities to recognise patterns. When designed well, visual representations of data can complement human cognitive capabilities and improve decision-makers' ability to understand the data (Tergan & Keller, 2005; Ware, 2012). Recent research on the use of visuals for PPM has drawn on two main theories related to cognition: cognitive fit theory and the theory of bounded rationality.

- *Cognitive fit theory* proposes that visuals are most effective when the elements used in the design of the visuals correspond to the problem at hand – in other words, when there is a high level of "cognitive fit" (Vessey, 1991). The second research theme discussed next provides further information on cognitive fit theory and its application in research on PPM visuals.
- *The theory of bounded rationality* aims to provide a holistic way of understanding cognitive limits and decision-making (Simon, 1955). According to the theory, human decision-making is flawed due to the "bounded rationality" resulting from three main impediments to making "perfect" decisions. These are (1) limits in the reliability of the information (incomplete, inaccurate, or outdated data), (2) limits in the amount of information that can be absorbed by the human decision-maker (cognitive limits), and (3) limits in the time available to make a decision (Simon, 1955). According to the theory, decisions will be improved if the impact of one or more of these limits can be minimised.

Many of the efforts to improve portfolio decision-making aim to address these limits. Ensuring the reliability of the data is an essential part of PPM, as nothing can compensate for inaccurate data – and an effective portfolio process requires that decision-makers trust the information at hand. In response, PPM frameworks have a strong focus on processes designed to collect and maintain relevant, current, and reliable data about projects and to compile that data to support decision-making. Much of the PPM guidance and literature documents methods for collecting, maintaining, and collating data – including the use of visuals to display the data. In addition, PPM research repeatedly confirms that considerations on what types of data to collect and how often to collect and update information will depend on the context, the nature of the decisions in that environment, and the time and effort involved. Tailoring and customising PPM often focuses on the mechanisms related to collecting and compiling data to reduce the effect on decisions from limits in the data. This tailoring includes the design and use of visuals to display data that is relevant for the decision context.

While many PPM processes aim to ensure accurate, up-to-date, and reliable information to support better decision-making, there is less attention given to the other aspects of the theory of bounded rationality (limits in cognitive capabilities and limits in available time). Two distinct streams of PPM research aim to reduce the impact from cognitive limits and to speed up the decision process, in very different ways. One of these streams involves the development of mathematical optimisation models to make or support project portfolio decisions, and the other stream explores the use of visuals in PPM decision processes (the focus of this chapter).

Mathematical models assign numerical values to measure and provide weighting factors for the many considerations in PPM decisions and employ a range of algorithms to generate "optimal" portfolios of projects. Despite the volumes of research in this area and the increasingly sophisticated algorithms applied (see, for example, Abbassi et al., 2014; Mohagheghi et al., 2020; and Wu et al., 2019), such models are rarely used in practice. One drawback of such mathematical modelling is that the quantification of subjective information (such as the degree of strategic alignment) or information projecting the future (such as the expected NPV) can obscure the nuances of the situation. Executives and managers are often uncomfortable with using such models to support decision-making; they expect to bring their experience and perspectives to discussions about strategic portfolio options at PRB decision meetings. Decision-makers in one study expressed concerns that computer-based tools that reduce opportunities for face-to-face dialogue may jeopardise the process (Killen & Hunt, 2010).

In contrast, executives and managers embrace the use of visuals to enhance decision-making. Research demonstrates the power of visuals in a range of strategic management and business activities (Bresciani, 2019; Bresciani & Eppler, 2015; Kernbach et al., 2015; Warglien & Jacobides, 2010). An increasingly influential stream of research on the use of visual representations of portfolio data reveals how visuals can address the limits in cognitive capability and the time available and improve portfolio decisions. Three themes of PPM research on visuals are summarised here: (1) research findings on the design of PPM visuals, (2) cognitive fit and visualising project interdependencies as a network, and (3) the role of the decision-maker, bias, and heuristics in PPM decisions.

Theme 1 – designing visuals: research findings on the design of portfolio visuals

Visualisations have long been used in PPM decision-making; however, the prevalence and types of visuals employed are increasing. The most prominent type of PPM visual is the portfolio map (also called a bubble chart; see Figure 16.1.) Such two-by-two, matrix-based visuals show the spread of project options (current and/or proposed projects) on two dimensions, with other information provided through graphical means and text labels, to provide a holistic view to support PPM decision-making (Mikkola, 2001). Other PPM visualisations include scorecards, dashboards, radar charts, pie charts, bar/stack graphs, bubble diagrams, etc. (Cooper et al., 2001; Kodukula, 2014; Wideman, 2004). Research confirms advantages from the use of portfolio maps (Cooper et al., 1999, and Killen et al., 2008b) and that the use of multiple types of visuals (rather than just one) can enhance the benefits (Killen et al., 2020). Not all visuals are beneficial, however – advantages are obtained when the visuals are well designed (Geraldi & Arlt, 2015) and decision-makers are familiar with the visuals (Killen et al., 2020).

Guidance on the design of visuals has been developed based on an extensive research study (Arlt, 2010; Geraldi & Arlt, 2015). Researchers tested a range of PPM visuals through experiments and interviews with 204 participants. The findings enhanced the understanding of which elements and options produced the most effective visuals to support decision-making. Based on their in-depth research and the resulting insights on how the design of PPM visuals influence the decision process, Geraldi and Arlt (2015) offer five principles for the design of effective visuals to support strategic PPM decision-making:

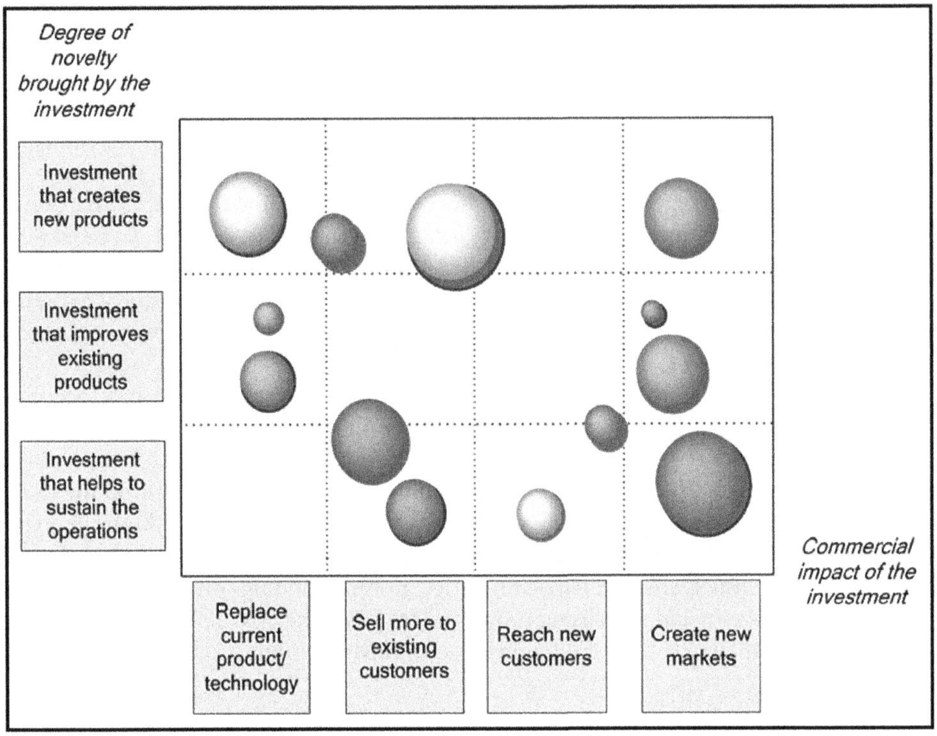

Figure 16.1 Example portfolio map (Arlt, 2010).

- *Interactive.* Organisations obtain greater benefits from visuals when the user is able to interact with the visuals by creating and customising the format or data. However, too much interactivity reduces benefits – for example, when users do not have a standard framework to guide their use of the visuals. The limits of interactivity are also explored in other studies; too much interactivity can be a negative if it overwhelms or distracts the decision-maker or obscures relevant information (Van der Land et al., 2013).
- *Purposeful.* Visuals should display a subset of the data in order to provide focus on information that is relevant to the PPM problem at hand. Whether a visual is purposeful will depend on the context – PPM visuals need to be tailored to suit the decision environment.
- *Truthful.* The underlying data should be accurate and trusted by users. User perceptions are important – the benefits from visuals will be decreased if users suspect deceit designed to manipulate perceptions. It is important to clearly portray the data using expected conventions, such as standard formats for labelling axes and selecting the end points and range.
- *Efficient.* Visuals should be designed to take advantage of the natural human capacity to recognise patterns and interpret meaning. This principle aligns with the concept of cognitive fit, although the concept was not mentioned by Geraldi and Arlt (2015). Cognitive fit is discussed further in the next section.

- *Aesthetic.* Research confirms that visuals that are pleasing to look at produce better outcomes. This principle aligns with prominent guidance on visuals (Tufte & Robins, 1997).

Theme 2 – cognitive fit: visualising interdependencies between projects using network mapping

The theory of cognitive fit proposes that a visualisation will be more effective if the nature of the representation "fits" with the nature of the problem. A high level of cognitive fit reduces the amount of cognitive energy required to interpret the visualisation by reducing the steps that must be done cognitively. For example, a line chart tracking sales volume over time has good cognitive fit for evaluating an increase or decrease in sales (the slope of the line directly shows the degree of increase or decrease), whereas a table of sales figures requires a number of cognitive steps to select and compare individual items of data in order to determine whether there is an increase or decrease in the sales.

The concept of cognitive fit is demonstrated through research on visualising interdependencies between projects. To make the best decisions, it is essential to understand how projects and project decisions affect other projects in the portfolio. However, standard PPM approaches often represent each project or project idea as an independent entity, with little recognition of the ways that projects affect each other in the portfolio (Bathallath et al., 2016; Killen & Kjaer, 2012). The ability to incorporate information on dependencies between projects is a recognised weakness in common PPM approaches (Elonen & Artto, 2003). This section summarises research findings on the role of cognitive fit in supporting PPM decision-making, by using network mapping to represent project interdependencies (Killen, 2017; Killen & Kjaer, 2012).

Dependencies between projects can take many forms. Common types of dependencies are *outcome dependencies*, where a project depends on the outcomes from another project; *resource dependencies*, where a project depends on resources that are used by another project; or *learning dependencies*, where a project depends on the availability of knowledge that is developed through another project (Bathallath et al., 2016; Killen, 2017). When such interdependencies exist between projects, decisions made about one project will affect the success of other projects. The impact can cause delays or affect the quality or scope of project outcomes and can even be critical, preventing successful completion of the project. Managing dependencies between projects requires, firstly, understanding where dependencies occur (between which projects, what type, and in what direction) and where dependencies and their effects cascade through a chain of dependent projects.

Visual project maps: a network mapping approach to visualise interdependencies

Traditionally, dependencies between projects have been recorded in spreadsheets or databases and in some environments displayed visually using a grid-based visual display, called a dependency map (Danilovic & Browning, 2007, and Dickinson et al., 2001). Dependency maps list all projects on both the x- and y-axis of the grid and provide marks or dates to indicate dependencies on the relevant cells of the grid (see the top half of Figure 16.2). Although dependency maps can be useful, users must take several cognitive steps to analyse the information. For each dependency marked in the grid, users must check the row and column headers to determine which projects have interdependencies. In addition, the

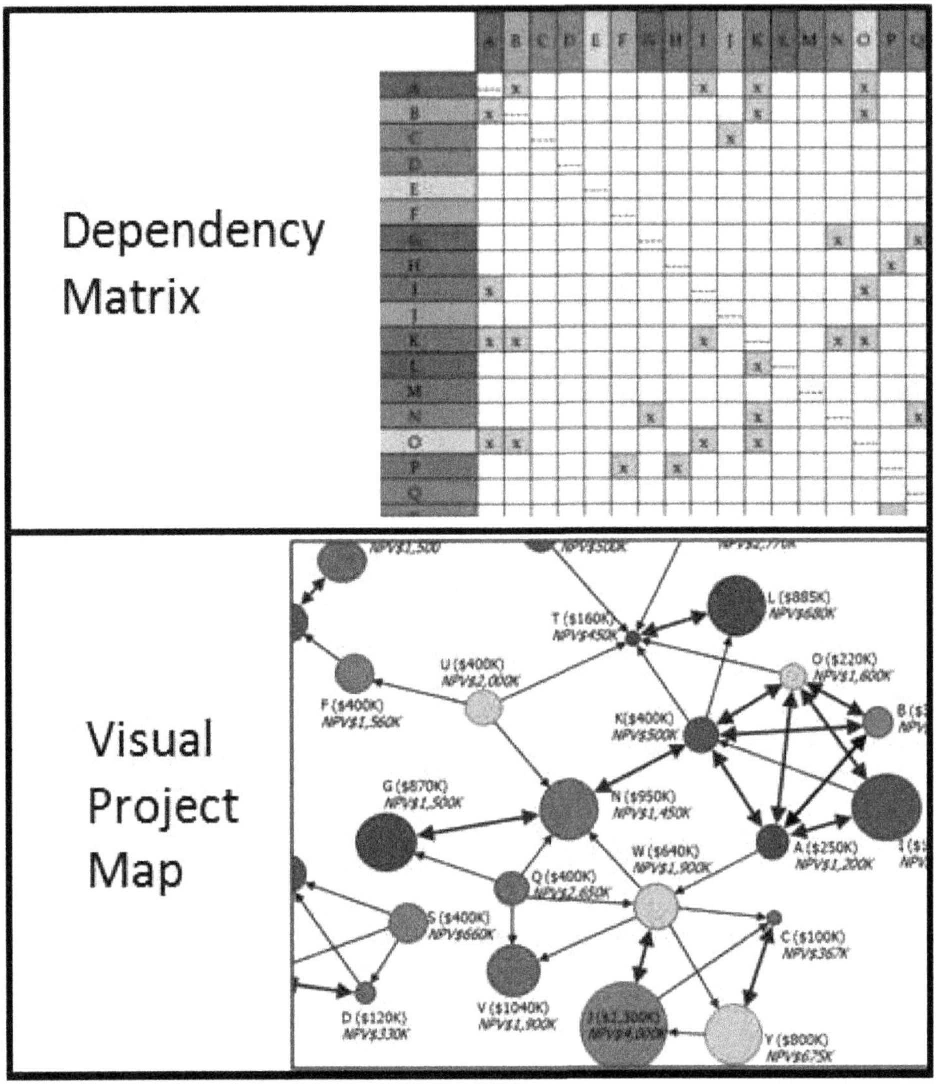

Figure 16.2 Example dependency matrix and visual project map (VPM).

information is provided based on a pair of projects; additional steps are required to check for chains of flow-on dependencies.

Another way of viewing the interdependencies between projects is as a network. Similar to approaches used for social network analysis, a network mapping approach has been developed to improve understanding and managing of project portfolio dependencies. Drawing upon the cognitive fit perspective, the network mapping approach was designed to have a strong "fit" between the nature of the task and the visual representation. Using this approach, projects are the "nodes" in the network (represented by circles), and the interdependencies between projects form the "connections" between the projects (represented by arrows). Projects can be connected to multiple other projects in a "network" of connections, where the arrows indicate the direction of dependencies and chains of dependencies can be followed by tracing connections (dependencies) across nodes (projects). The visual project map (VPM) approach was developed with a goal to better support more accurate and faster decision-making by reducing the cognitive effort required to understand interdependencies. The bottom half of Figure 16.2 shows a portion of a VPM that displays the same data as the dependency matrix in the top half of the figure.

Extensive experimental research with 480 participants (Killen, 2017) complemented findings from implementing VPM in organisations (Killen & Kjaer, 2012) and provides strong support for using VPM to manage interdependencies. The experiments compared decisions made based on displays of the same data, represented using different formats. The results revealed that the choice of visual format affected the decisions. Decisions were more accurate and made more quickly when interdependency data was displayed in the VPM format instead of through a dependency matrix or a spreadsheet (Killen, 2017). Evidence that the format of the visuals can affect decisions also raises concerns about potential bias or undue influence from the format of the visuals. There is a danger that visuals will be formatted in a way to intentionally skew decisions in a particular direction or that poorly designed visuals will inadvertently affect decisions. The power of visuals is clear; the challenge is to design visuals that enhance decision-making without creating additional bias.

Participants in organisations that trialled the VPM approach felt that the project mapping displays were an excellent device for communicating the relationships between projects to support strategic decisions and to explain the decisions to others (Killen & Kjaer, 2012). Decision-makers noted that the VPM displays enabled them to gain a holistic perspective and understand flow-on effects from portfolio decisions. One senior decision-maker commented that the maps provided the ability to "see the connections and where the work needs to be done . . . it does add value to me and I can see [relationships] that I had not seen before" (Killen & Kjaer, 2012).

These positive findings on the use of visual project maps can be explained by the high level of cognitive fit between the problem and the nature of the visual representation. The findings from research on using network mapping to evaluate portfolio interdependencies offers these implications for practitioners:

- Network-based visualisations of project interdependencies should be considered to support faster and better decision-making.
- Cognitive fit between the task and the visuals should be a goal in the careful and purposeful design of visuals.
- Visuals are powerful. The findings serve to remind practitioners that the choice and design of visuals can influence or bias decisions.

Theme 3 – bias and heuristics: the role of individual decision-maker's experience and preferences

Research and practitioner publications regularly discuss the many different types and styles of PPM visuals and their application (Cooper et al., 2001; Geraldi & Arlt, 2015). Less attention is paid to the other side – to the qualities of the decision-makers who view and use the visuals. While most research has focused on the actual visuals to determine what is most effective, recent research explores the impact from the individual decision-makers' characteristics and how they use visuals (Killen et al., 2020). The study involved 138 organisations, each with between two and five participants who completed a detailed survey. The multi-informant study collected different types of survey data from respondents in different roles to reduce bias and increase reliability and confidence in the findings. For example, a decision-maker from each organisation reports on their experiences, their decision-making preferences, and the outcomes of the PPM process, while people closer to the PPM activities report on the details of the process.

The findings reveal that the decision-makers' experiences and preferences affect the success of the decisions. Experience with visuals is associated with increased decision-making success, supporting propositions that familiarity with visuals reduces the cognitive load (Killen et al., 2020). When a decision-maker is familiar with a visualisation, the degree of mental energy required to understand the format of the visualisation is reduced and more time can be spent on analysing and discussing the data, thus increasing the benefits afforded by the visualisation (Paas et al., 2003).

The study also evaluated the decision-maker's tendency to use heuristics – the "rules of thumb" or "simple rules" often developed from experience that speed decision-making. While such heuristics can provide benefits by capturing experience and embedding expert knowledge (Bingham & Eisenhardt, 2011; Kahneman & Klein, 2009), these simple rules often embed biases and detract from the quality of the decisions. Analysis of the survey results confirmed the negative influence on decision-making when decision-makers have higher levels of reliance on heuristics. However, the use of visualisations of data reduced this negative effect. By presenting the data from a new perspective, in an engaging and easy-to-interpret form, visuals may help "break thorough" the bias associated with heuristic use. Visualisations can thus dampen the negative effects from decision-makers' reliance on heuristics.

These findings are reinforced by another study involving two related experiments testing the use of decision support tools and the effect on heuristics for decision-making (Schiffels et al., 2018). Although the tools in this study were sorting tools rather than visual tools, the findings on heuristic use and cognitive load align. Schiffels et al.'s (2018) study found stronger evidence of heuristic use (and associated negative impacts on decisions) when cognitive limits are challenged. Decision support tools can help reduce the negative impact of cognitive limits and the reliance on heuristics. The study also confirms that familiarity with methods and tools is important for gaining the desired benefits. Findings from both studies suggest that a training program should accompany the introduction of new tools or visuals in decision processes (Killen, 2017; Schiffels et al., 2018).

Implications for practice

All indications suggest that visualisations will continue to play an increasing role and make a growing impact on society – and that visuals will continue to be a part of management environments and processes, such as PPM and portfolio management. Research combining academic and practice-based interests has increased our understanding of the impact of visuals in PPM. Findings from the research provides practical guidance for improving the way that visuals are used to support strategic PPM decisions.

This chapter has summarised three themes of research that demonstrate the power of visuals and the benefits for strategic PPM or portfolio decision-making. Theories of cognitive fit and bounded rationality help explain how visuals enhance the ability of

PPM decision-makers to absorb and understand information and to make good decisions. The research findings provide strong support for implementing visuals to enhance PPM results; the use of visuals is associated with better project portfolio performance and has been demonstrated to save time, support better decision-making, and promote valuable dialogue during strategic portfolio review board meetings. Actionable guidance is offered to practitioners for improving the design and use of visuals to best support portfolio decision-making.

In conclusion, derived from the collective findings reported in this chapter, the following five recommendations are offered to practitioners.

Consider where and how to use visualisations to improve portfolio outcomes

Remember that visuals can help or hinder portfolio decision-making. They can act as a cognitive aid, enhancing the ability of decision-makers to understand the problem under consideration, or they can reduce decision quality by introducing bias or by confusing or overwhelming decision-makers if the visuals are not designed well and implemented appropriately. Design visuals purposively and only use visuals that are designed to serve a need and help decision-makers understand the information required to make effective decisions.

Most portfolio processes will benefit from multiple (but not too many) visuals

Research findings repeatedly demonstrate that visual displays of information can enhance PPM decisions. The use of multiple different types of visuals provides a range of perspectives to promote balanced considerations and can assist with reducing bias. Managers should be aware of the potential for bias from the use of heuristics in decision-making and the potential for visualisations to reduce such bias. However, managers need to pay careful attention to the design of each visual and avoid introducing bias through poorly designed visuals or increasing decision-makers' cognitive load by implementing too many different types of visualisations.

Design the visuals carefully

Design visualisations to ensure they are fit for the task and tailored for context – considering visual aspects (layout, colours, and shapes) as well as information aspects (what subset of information is most relevant) and whether the nature of the visual fits with the decision problem (cognitive fit) (Geraldi & Arlt, 2015; Killen, 2017). Each visualisation should have a purpose and a place in the portfolio process. When designing visuals, consider these questions: (1) What is the visualisation meant to convey? (2) What types of decisions will it support? (3) What is the context of the decision? And (4) what are the experiences, preferences, and tendencies of the decision-makers?

Testing, implementation, and familiarisation

Test potential visualisations with decision-makers to iterate and improve the format and check whether and how the visual supports decision-making. When introducing new visualisations, include guidance and training and allow time for decision-makers to develop familiarity with the visuals. Limit the number of visuals used, and do not change the format of visuals too often. Only introduce new visuals that provide significant advantages, considering the "costs" of the training and the time required for users to become familiar with the visuals.

Use visuals to enhance and support decision-makers' dialogue about portfolio decisions

Finally, remember the important role visuals can play in decision meetings. Design the visuals and the process so that visuals can be referred to in the meetings to support a robust discussion about the portfolio decisions; such dialogue will bring out the wealth of knowledge and wisdom embodied in the decision-makers to enhance strategic decision-making.

Conclusion

This chapter brings together research on the use of visuals for project portfolio management (PPM) and offers actionable insights for practice. The insights and recommendations are substantiated by the research findings. However, it is important to recognise that no research study is perfect – every research study has strengths as well as limitations. Findings from qualitative case-based studies provide depth but may not be representative of other environments (Killen & Hunt, 2010; Killen & Kjaer, 2012). Experiment-based studies allow specific questions to be explored in a controlled situation but can be subject to bias due to the experiment design and the selection of the participants and may not reflect real-life situations (Arlt, 2010; Geraldi & Arlt, 2015; Killen, 2017; Schiffels et al., 2018). Large-scale quantitative studies by Cooper et al. (1999) and Killen et al. (2008b) are able to identify a positive correlation between visualisation use and portfolio success; however, these studies focus on the impact of only one type of visualisation (portfolio maps) and are subject to single-informant bias as they involve a single respondent from each organisation. A recent large-scale quantitative study by Killen et al. (2020) provides improved confidence in the findings by extending the study to multiple types of visualisations and multiple informants; however, as with most survey-based studies, it only captures one point in time and cannot determine the reasons behind the correlations.

By bringing together diverse studies, this chapter has provided a balanced view of the use of visuals for strategic portfolio decision-making. The combination of multiple studies that use a variety of methods with differing (and non-overlapping) strengths and weaknesses provides enhanced levels of understanding and confidence that could not be achieved through any one study alone (Tashakkori & Teddlie, 1998). Taken together, these studies support the use of visuals for portfolio management and provide guidance to enhance the benefits when adopting visualisation.

References

Abbassi M., Ashrafi M. & Sharifi Tashnizi E. (2014) Selecting balanced portfolios of R&D projects with interdependencies: A Cross-Entropy based methodology. *Technovation* 34(1), 54–63.

Arlt M. (2010) *Advancing the Maturity of Project Portfolio Management through Methodology and Metrics Refinements*. Doctor of Project Management (DPM), RMIT University Royal Melbourne Institute of Technology.

Bathallath S., Smedberg Å. & Kjellin H. (2016) Managing project interdependencies in IT/IS project portfolios: A review of managerial issues. *International Journal of Information Systems and Project Management* 4(1), 67–82.

Bingham C. & Eisenhardt K. (2011) Rational heuristics: The 'simple rules' that strategists learn from process experience. *Strategic Management Journal* 32(13), 1437–1464.

Bresciani S. (2019) Visual design thinking: A collaborative dimensions framework to profile visualisations. *Design Studies* 63, 92–124.

Bresciani S. & Eppler M. (2015) The pitfalls of visual representations: A review and classification of common errors made while designing and interpreting visualizations. *Sage Open* 5(4), 2158244015611451.

Cooper R., Edgett S. & Kleinschmidt E. (1999) New product portfolio management: Practices and performance. *Journal of Product Innovation Management* 16(4), 333–351.

Cooper R., Edgett S., & Kleinschmidt E. (2001) *Portfolio Management for New Products.* Second Edition. Perseus.

Danilovic M. & Browning T. (2007) Managing complex product development projects with design structure matrices and domain mapping matrices. *International Journal of Project Management* 25, 300–314.

Dickinson M., Thornton A. & Graves S. (2001) Technology portfolio management: Optimizing interdependent projects over multiple time periods. [yes]. *IEEE Transactions on Engineering Management,* 48(4), 518–527.

Elonen S. & Artto K. (2003) Problems in managing internal development projects in multi-project environments. *International Journal of Project Management* 21(6), 395–402.

Geraldi J. & Arlt M. (2015) *Visuals Matter! Designing and Using Effective Visual Representations to Support Project and Portfolio Decisions.* Project Management Institute.

Kahneman D. & Klein G. (2009) Conditions for intuitive expertise: A failure to disagree. *American Psychologist* 64(6), 515–526.

Kernbach S., Eppler M. & Bresciani S. (2015) The use of visualization in the communication of business strategies: An experimental evaluation. *International Journal of Business Communication* 52(2), 164–187.

Killen C. (2017) Managing portfolio interdependencies: The effects of visual data representations on project portfolio decision making. *International Journal of Managing Projects in Business* 10(4), 856–879.

Killen C., Geraldi J. & Kock A. (2020) The role of decision makers' use of visualizations in project portfolio decision making. *International Journal of Project Management* 38(5), 267–277.

Killen C. & Hunt R. (2010) Dynamic capability through project portfolio management in service and manufacturing industries. *International Journal of Managing Projects in Business* 3(1), 157–169.

Killen C., Hunt R. & Kleinschmidt E. (2008a) Learning investments and organisational capabilities: Case studies on the development of project portfolio management capabilities. *International Journal of Managing Projects in Business* 1(3), 334–351.

Killen C., Hunt R. & Kleinschmidt E. (2008b) Project portfolio management for product innovation. *International Journal of Quality and Reliability Management* 25(1), 24–38.

Killen C. & Kjaer C. (2012) Understanding project interdependencies: The role of visual representation, culture and process. *International Journal of Project Management* 30(5), 554–566.

Kodukula P. (2014) *Organizational Project Portfolio Management: A Practitioner's Guide.* J. Ross Publishing.

Mikkola J. (2001). Portfolio management of R&D projects: Implications for innovation management. *Technovation* 21(7), 423–435.

Mohagheghi V., Meysam Mousavi S. & Mojtahedi M. (2020) Project portfolio selection problems: Two decades review from 1999 to 2019. *Journal of Intelligent & Fuzzy Systems* 38(2), 1675–1689.

Mosavi A. (2014) Exploring the roles of portfolio steering committees in project portfolio governance. *International Journal of Project Management* 32(3), 388–399.

Newell A. (1990) *Unified Theories of Cognition.* Harvard University Press.

Paas F., Renkl A. & Sweller J. (2003) Cognitive load theory and instructional design: Recent developments. *Educational Psychologist* 38(1), 1–4.

Schiffels S., Fliedner T. & Kolisch R. (2018) Human behavior in project portfolio selection: insights from an experimental study. *Decision Sciences* 49(6), 1061–1087.

Simon H. (1955) A behavioral model of rational choice. *Quarterly Journal of Economics* 69(1), 99–118.

Tashakkori A. & Teddlie C. (1998) *Mixed Methodology: Combining Qualitative and Quantitative Approaches.* Sage.

Tergan S.-O. & Keller T. (Eds.). (2005) *Knowledge and Information Visualisation.* Springer-Verlag.

Tufte E. & Robins D. (1997) *Visual Explanations: Images as Quantities, Evidence and Narrative.* Graphic Press.

Van der Land S., Schouten A., Feldberg F., van den Hooff B. & Huysman M. (2013) Lost in space? Cognitive fit and cognitive load in 3D virtual environments. *Computers in Human Behavior* 29(3), 1054–1064.

Vessey I. (1991) Cognitive fit: A theory-based analysis of the graphs versus tables literature. *Decision Sciences* 22(2), 219–241.

Ware C. (2012) *Information Visualization: Perception for Design.* Elsevier.

Warglien M. & Jacobides M. (2010) The power of representations: From visualization, maps and categories to dynamic tools. Paper presented at the Academy of Management Meeting, August 6th, 2010, Montreal.

Wideman R. (2004) *A Management Framework for Project, Program and Portfolio Management.* Trafford Publishing.

Wu Y., Xu C, Ke Y, Tao Y. & Li X. (2019) Portfolio optimization of renewable energy projects under type-2 fuzzy environment with sustainability perspective. *Computers & Industrial Engineering* 133, 69–82.

17 Portfolio risk management

David Hillson

Introduction

As we have seen in previous chapters, portfolios are the means of translating strategy into action, via programs, projects, and other activities, and as in Chapter 2, Shakespeare's *The Merchant of Venice* demonstrates that portfolio management is not a new concept. It is also clear that the need for a diversified portfolio is inherently related to the risk associated with the ability of the contents of the portfolio to deliver what is expected, Shakespeare once again advising, "My ventures are not in one bottom trusted." In 1939, Hicks (Hicks, 1939) was explicitly theorising portfolio value calculations using risk, and Markowitz (1959) noted that *risk* and *variance-of-return* of an asset are essentially synonymous. The expected outcome of each asset not being 100% predictable (the future is unknown!). Taleb (2007) has more recently explored the concept of the "black swan" for risk events in considering the "highly improbable" in relation to portfolios, as well as much more widely in a general sense.

Thus, managing a portfolio means, implicitly, managing the risk inherent in the portfolio, no matter whether the contents are, for example, financial assets, new product development projects, change programs, or construction projects delivered externally to clients. In managing portfolio risk effectively, it is important to define the portfolio clearly (APM, 2019a, PMI, 2017b, Axelos, 2011, AIPM, 2019), as the scope of the area under consideration defines the scope of risks to be identified, assessed, and managed. This discussion on portfolio risk emphasises the critical position occupied by portfolios, sitting between strategy and its implementation, with portfolios as the means of translating strategy into action, via programs, projects, and other activities.

What is risk?

In order to be clear about terms, we need to know what we mean by "risk". In simple terms, *risk* can be described as "uncertainty that matters", since all risks are uncertain, but not all uncertainties are risks. This proto-definition can be expanded to explain how and why risk might matter, by linking the definition to objectives, as shown in Table 17.1. This allows us to produce a generic definition of *risk*: "*any uncertainty that, if it occurs, will affect achievement of objectives.*"

The definitions in Table 17.1 reveal another important element of the nature of risk: not all risk is bad. Almost every standard and guideline includes the idea that risk is a broad concept that encompasses both threat (downside risk, uncertainty with negative effect) and opportunity (upside risk, uncertainty with positive effect). This has been

DOI: 10.4324/9780367853129-20

Table 17.1 Definitions of risk as "uncertainty that matters"

Source of definition	*"Uncertainty . . ."*	*". . . That matters"*
Standard for Risk Management in Portfolios, Programs and Projects. (Project Management Institute, 2019)	"An *uncertain* event or condition . . ."	". . . that, if it occurs, has a positive or negative *impact on one or more objectives.*"
APM Body of Knowledge, seventh edition. (Association for Project Management, 2019a)	"The *potential* of a situation or event . . ."	". . . to *impact on achievement of specific objectives.*"
ISO31000:2018 *Risk Management Guidelines.* (International Organization for Standardization, 2018)	"Effect of *uncertainty* . . ." "Note: An effect is a deviation from the expected. It can be positive, negative or both, and can address, create or result in opportunities and threats."	". . . on *objectives.*"
A Guide to the Project Management Body of Knowledge [PMBOK® Guide], Sixth Edition. (Project Management Institute, 2017a)	"An *uncertain* event or condition . . ."	". . . that, if it occurs, has a positive or negative *effect on one or more project objectives.*"
The Standard for Portfolio Management, fourth edition. (Project Management Institute, 2017b)	An *uncertain* event, set of events, or conditions . . ."	". . . that, if they occur, have one or more *effects*, either positive or negative, *on at least one strategic business objective of the portfolio.*"
PM² Project Management Methodology Guide – Open Edition. (European Commission Centre of Excellence in Project Management, CoEPM², 2016)	"An *uncertain* event or set of events (positive or negative) . . ."	". . . that, should it occur, will have an *effect on the achievement of project objectives.*"
Risk Analysis and Management for Projects: A strategic framework for managing project risk and its financial implications, third edition. (Institution of Civil Engineers and Institute & Faculty of Actuaries, 2014)	"A *possible* occurrence . . ."	". . . which could *affect* (positively or negatively) *the achievement of the objectives* for the investment."
Management of Risk [M_o_R®]: Guidance for Practitioners, Third Edition. (Axelos, 2010)	"An *uncertain* event or set of events . . ."	". . . that, should it occur, will have an *effect on the achievement of objectives.*"

promoted in the P3M (portfolio, program, and project) world for many years (Wideman, 1992; Chapman & Ward, 1997, 2011; Ward & Chapman, 2003; Olsson, 2006, 2007, 2008; Hillson, 2002a, 2003a, 2009, 2019), but practice lags somewhat behind theory. Nevertheless, the ability to manage proactively both aspects of the double-sided nature of risk is an essential contributor to success, since the purpose of risk management is to minimise threats, maximise opportunities, and optimise achievement of objectives.

What is portfolio risk?

The generic definition of *risk* as "*any uncertainty that, if it occurs, will affect achievement of objectives*" allows us to define any level of risk in terms of the level of objectives that would be affected. Thus, strategic risk affects achievement of strategic objectives, project risk affects project objectives, personal risk affects personal objectives, and so on.

Similarly, we can define *portfolio risk* as "*any uncertainty that, if it occurs, will affect achievement of portfolio objectives*".

Despite the attractive simplicity of this definition of *portfolio risk*, managing portfolio risk is complicated by the fact that it arises from three different directions: above, below, and sideways. This is illustrated in Figure 17.1, which shows risks at portfolio level coming up from lower levels (via *risk escalation* or *risk aggregation*), down from the levels above (via *risk delegation*), or sideways from the same level as the portfolio itself.

1. **Risks from below**. There are two main ways in which the portfolio can be affected by risks from portfolio components at lower levels.
   - *Risk escalation*. Some lower-level risks are so large that they can affect the achievement of higher-level objectives. The term "large" needs to be defined clearly and carefully, of course, since not all lower-level risks are relevant at the higher level. Escalation criteria are therefore required that will define the thresholds at which a lower-level risk should be passed up to the next level. This is discussed in the following passages. These criteria need to include risks which impact higher-level objectives, as well as risks requiring responses or action at the higher level.

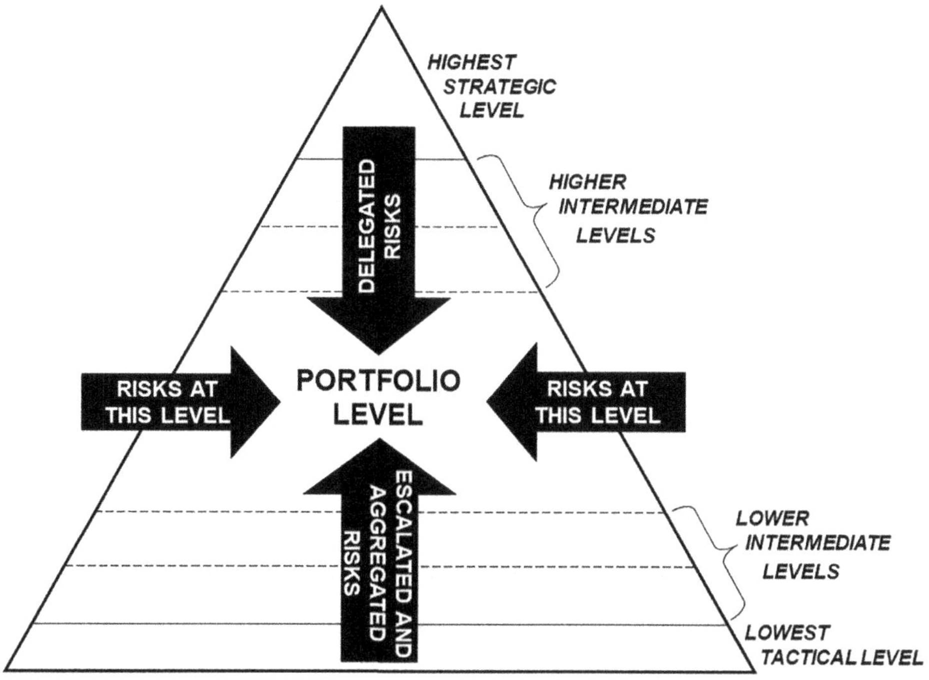

Figure 17.1 Sources of risk at portfolio level.

- *Risk aggregation*. It is also necessary to be able to aggregate lower-level risks, where a number of similar and related risks might combine to create a higher-level risk, either by simple summation (ten insignificant lower-level risks may equal one significant higher-level risk) or as a result of synergy (the whole may be greater than the sum of the parts). Suitable risk categorisation schemes are required to facilitate such aggregation by identifying commonalities and possible synergies, and a generic risk breakdown structure (RBS) may be used for this purpose (Hillson 2002b, 2003b). When a group of aggregated risks becomes sufficiently significant, it is escalated in the same way as an individual large risk.

2. **Risks from above**. Organisational strategy is delivered by decomposing strategic objectives into lower-level objectives, creating an essential link between intermediate levels and those above them. There are strategic risks associated with the overall direction of the organisation, and many of these can and should be addressed wholly by the senior leadership of the organisation. However, some strategic risks will have implications for those lower levels which are used to deliver the strategy and create the business benefits, including portfolios. Strategic risks which can affect lower-level objectives or which require action at a lower level will need to be *delegated*. This requires well-defined delegation criteria and thresholds, as well as clear channels of communication, to ensure that management of strategic risks delegated to lower levels is reported back to senior management. The goal is to achieve delegation without abdication.
3. **Risks at the same level**. In addition to risks escalated and aggregated from below or delegated from above, each level in the organisation is affected by specific uncertainties arising at that level. These include both threats and opportunities across the full range of risk types, including technical, management, commercial, and external risks. Examples include conflicting objectives between portfolio components, resource constraints across portfolio components (particularly arising from incompatible resource requirements), changes in the external context of the portfolio (such as the regulatory or market environment), potential issues arising from dependencies between portfolio components, or at the interfaces between components. These need to be managed by application of the traditional generic risk process, as discussed next.

Portfolio risk management needs to address risks that arise from all sources in order to optimise the chances of achieving the strategic objectives for which the portfolio was established.

How is portfolio risk managed?

The preceding section describes *risks that could affect successful execution of the portfolio* once it is launched. However, portfolio risk management has an additional risk challenge, which arises before the portfolio is initiated for the first time and which re-emerges when an existing portfolio is reviewed at key points during its life cycle. This is the challenge of *building and maintaining a risk-efficient portfolio* within the other constraints of portfolio construction. A mature approach to portfolio risk management needs to address both challenges (Hillson, 2011).

Building and maintaining a risk-efficient portfolio

When shaping a portfolio to achieve optimal prioritisation of work, there is a need to balance a number of factors, including "*the risk profile of each project or program in the portfolio*". Other factors include relative priority of strategic objectives, timing of benefits realisation, external constraints (regulatory, legal, technological), and resource availability.

The following steps are involved in building or reshaping a portfolio to ensure that an appropriate balance is achieved of risk against the desired portfolio value (in financial terms, to optimise the variance-of-return in such a way that the strategic objectives are most likely to be achieved effectively):

- **Understand risk thresholds for the portfolio.** It is important that the overall risk exposure of the portfolio remains within the risk thresholds set by senior management, which in turn will reflect corporate risk appetite (Hillson & Murray-Webster, 2012). This vital first step is often poorly understood or executed in many organisations. Without knowing how much risk is too much risk for the portfolio, it will be impossible to know which components to include.
- **Assess potential portfolio components using a common risk/benefits framework.** The list of candidate components to be included in the portfolio should be well defined and understood, including the level of risk exposure associated with each one, and the extent of promised benefits. Both of these parameters need to be quantified using a common framework so that they are directly comparable. This requires a good understanding of how to determine overall risk exposure for programs, projects, and other portfolio components (Hillson, 2014).
- **Select components to balance risk exposure with benefits.** When each candidate component has been assessed for both risk exposure and potential benefits, the portfolio can be constructed (if this is prior to launch of a new portfolio) or reshaped (at key review points during the life cycle of an existing portfolio), using the principles of *risk efficiency*. This was first described by Markowitz in his description of modern portfolio theory for financial investment portfolios (Markowitz, 1952, 1959), and it has more recently been proposed for use with projects (Chapman & Ward, 2004, 2011).

  Risk efficiency involves developing various alternative portfolios, each containing a different mix of candidate components. For each portfolio, the total overall risk exposure is determined, as well as the total expected return/benefit. Alternative portfolios are then plotted on a graph that shows risk exposure against potential benefits. The *risk-efficient frontier* is also shown on this graph, separating portfolio options that have acceptable levels of either risk or benefit from other options. The region to the left of the frontier is *infeasible*, where the level of return cannot be achieved at the associated low levels of risk exposure. The region to the right of the frontier contains feasible portfolio options, and those portfolios that lie closest to the frontier have optimal combinations of risk and benefit. Positions further to the right of the frontier are *inefficient*, where levels of promised benefits are too low to justify the associated level of risk.

  An example risk efficiency graph is shown in Figure 17.2, plotting five alternative versions of the same portfolio, each with different components. In this example, portfolio options A, C, and D could all achieve higher returns for the given level

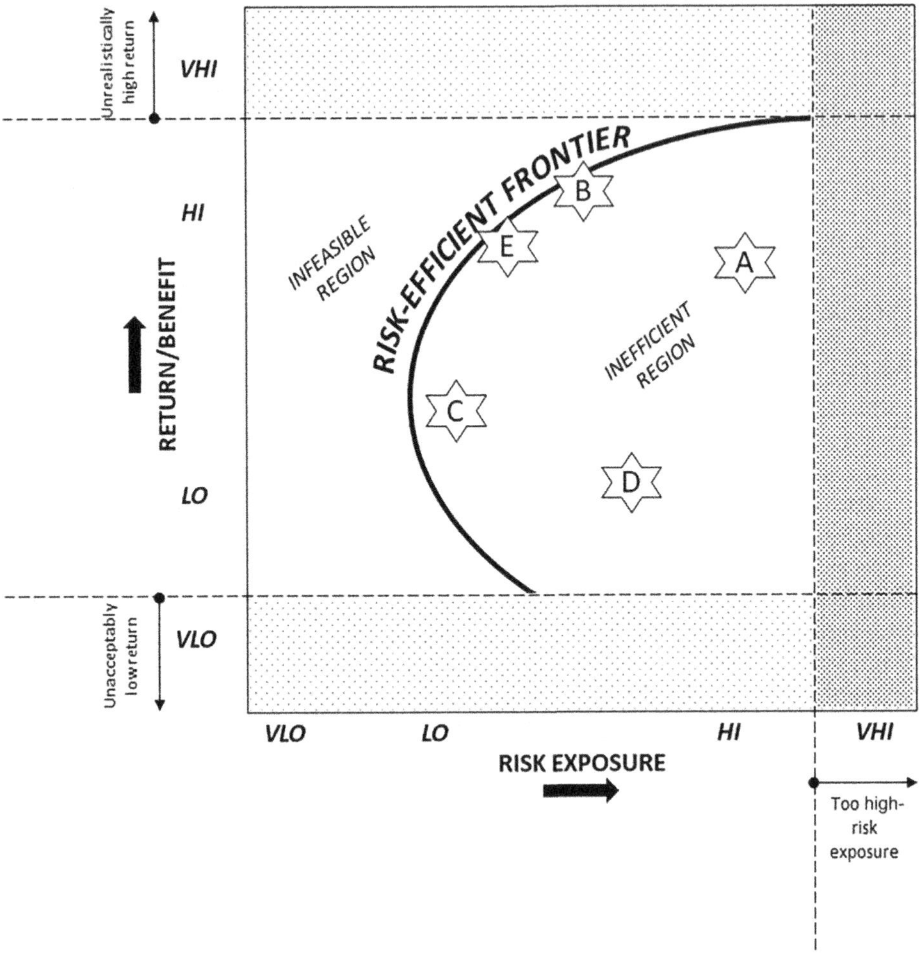

Figure 17.2 Example risk efficiency graph (Hillson, 2014).

of risk (i.e. they are inefficient), whereas portfolio options B and E lie on the risk-efficient frontier, with the maximum feasible return for the given level of risk.

Each portfolio option on the risk-efficient frontier should be considered as viable, but the actual portfolio selected for execution will have a position on the frontier where the level of risk lies at or below the defined risk threshold for the portfolio. In Figure 17.2, if the risk threshold lies between portfolio options B and E, then E should be selected.

Where review of an existing portfolio shows that it has fallen outside the risk-efficient frontier, due to either an unacceptably high level of risk exposure or an infeasibly low level of achievable benefits, or both, then the mix of components in the portfolio should be reviewed and changed as necessary to restore risk efficiency. The same is true for an existing portfolio that has become inefficient, moving away from the risk-efficient frontier.

Managing risk during portfolio execution

In addition to ensuring that the portfolio is risk-efficient when it is initially constructed and at key review points in the portfolio life cycle, there is a requirement to explicitly manage risks that emerge during the execution of the portfolio. This requires a structured portfolio risk management process analogous to the project risk management approach, which must iteratively identify risks, assess their significance and importance, develop appropriate responses, implement those responses, and monitor subsequent changes. This needs to address risks that arise by escalation or aggregation from portfolio components, risks that are delegated from the strategic level, and risks that originate at the level of the portfolio itself (see Figure 17.1).

Many current approaches to portfolio risk management are limited to this type of explicit risk process, and most simply recommend adopting or adapting the methods of project risk management. While the structure of the risk process for managing risks during portfolio execution is similar to that for projects, there are some important differences, as outlined in the following.

- **Initiation/risk management planning.** This step launches the risk process for the portfolio and defines the scope of the risk process, within which risks will be identified. Risk thresholds are set for the overall portfolio and for each portfolio objective, against which risks will be assessed. Criteria are agreed for risk escalation, risk aggregation, and risk delegation, as discussed previously. Process parameters are defined, including roles and responsibilities, and review and reporting requirements. This planning step is initially performed at portfolio launch, but it should be revisited at key points during the portfolio life cycle, to ensure that the portfolio risk process responds to the changing risk profile associated with the evolving and emergent nature of portfolios. Initiation decisions should be documented in a portfolio risk management plan.
- **Risk identification.** Before the portfolio is launched, the level of overall portfolio risk exposure will have been identified and assessed, as part of the risk efficiency exercise discussed previously. Individual portfolio-level risks should also be identified as part of the explicit portfolio risk management process, both on a regular basis and ad hoc as they arise, taking account of the three routes by which such risks arise (see Figure 17.1). Risks may be escalated or aggregated from lower component levels or delegated from higher strategic levels, and the portfolio requires clear criteria to determine whether these should be accepted for management at portfolio level. In addition to these, the usual risk identification techniques can be used to find portfolio-level risks, including brainstorming, checklists, assumptions analysis, Delphi groups, etc. Risk identification at portfolio level should seek both threats and opportunities and should consider the full range of potential risk sources defined in the portfolio risk breakdown structure. Risks will be recorded in a portfolio risk register.
- **Risk assessment/analysis (qualitative/quantitative).** Identified risks should be assessed and prioritised based on their likelihood of occurrence (probability and/or frequency) and their impact on one or more portfolio objectives. Risks escalated/aggregated from component level and risks delegated from strategic level will need to be reassessed against portfolio-level risk thresholds to allow them to be prioritised on a common basis. Quantitative risk analysis techniques can be used to provide an overall assessment of portfolio risk exposure, combining the effects of all types of

risk at portfolio level and taking account of risk dependencies. The results from this analysis can be used to estimate the overall level of portfolio risk exposure discussed previously.

- **Risk response development.** Response to the overall level of portfolio risk exposure is handled by adjusting the portfolio composition to maintain risk efficiency. Explicit responses are also required for individual portfolio risks, and these match the options available at project level, including avoid/transfer/reduce/accept for threats and exploit/share/enhance/accept for opportunities. Additional response options available at portfolio level include escalation of a risk to strategic level (where the impact affects strategic objectives and/or senior management action is required) and delegation of a risk to component level (where the primary impact and/or risk ownership is at a lower level), with suitable escalation/delegation criteria required.
- **Risk review/risk monitoring and control.** Risk is a dynamic challenge within portfolios, and the portfolio risk process must be iterative in order to maintain an appropriate degree of attention to managing risks. Regular risk reviews must be held at portfolio level, usually as part of the routine portfolio management process, but the scope of these risk reviews must be rigorously controlled to avoid discussing component-level risks or strategic risks outside the scope of the portfolio.
- **Risk lessons learned.** When a portfolio is terminated, it is important for the organisation to capture knowledge to benefit future portfolios. A formal lessons-learned workshop should be conducted, and risk must be considered as part of this exercise. It would also be useful to hold interim lessons-learned workshops at key points during the portfolio life cycle, to identify lessons that might be implemented in later phases of this portfolio, as well as benefiting other portfolios if appropriate.

Compared to the challenge of building and maintaining a risk-efficient portfolio, the management of risk throughout the life cycle of an existing portfolio is relatively straightforward, because it largely follows the traditional risk management process. It is, however, dependent on the ability to establish clear risk thresholds at which risks will be escalated from component levels or delegated from strategic levels, as well as defining clear risk assessment criteria for portfolio-level risks.

Where are we now, and what's missing?

This chapter has presented a structured approach to the management of risk in portfolios, including ensuring that risk efficiency is achieved during the initial construction of the portfolio and that it is maintained throughout the portfolio life cycle, as well as implementing a more traditional portfolio risk management process to address portfolio risks arising from a variety of sources. Although the principles described here are clear, a number of challenges exist in ensuring that they are implemented effectively. These challenges are briefly outlined next.

Defining risk thresholds

Effective management of portfolio risk requires a clear understanding of how much risk is acceptable within the portfolio. It is not possible to answer this question without understanding how to define corporate risk appetite and then express that risk appetite as quantified risk thresholds. Corporate risk thresholds must then be translated down to portfolio level. In addition, clear and agreed thresholds must be defined for escalation and delegation of risks between levels.

Implementing risk efficiency

Building a risk-efficient portfolio using the techniques described previously requires an ability to turn the theory of risk efficiency into practice. Although the principles of risk efficiency have been known for over 60 years (Markowitz, 1952, 1959) and their application to financial portfolios is well established, it is not always immediately clear how such an approach should be applied at portfolio level. In particular, there may be challenges in deriving the measures required to build and operate a risk efficiency model, including both the ability to quantify the overall risk exposure of portfolio components on a consistent basis and the ability to quantify promised benefits. Even when these two parameters are defined, many organisations are unsure how and where to define a risk-efficient frontier that reflects the risk appetite of key stakeholders for a particular portfolio. Nevertheless, industrial sectors with very high capital investment requirements use sophisticated analytical models to understand the efficient frontiers of their portfolios (e.g. petroleum industry, see Tyler & McVean, 2001; pharmaceuticals, Rogers et al., 2003). More recently, the domain of event planning has also used risk efficient frontier portfolio models (Andersson et al., 2017). The key for effective implementation is understanding properly the context for the portfolio, the selection criteria for entry to the portfolio, and how the value of projects and programs is calculated (see Chapters 12 and 6).

Avoiding a project mindset

Many of the existing portfolio management guidelines have been developed by organisations and practitioners who come from a project management background. As a result, their departure point in terms of both thinking and process is the project mindset. This inevitably affects their recommended approach to managing portfolio risk.

A good example are the current PMI guidelines for portfolio risk management (Project Management Institute, 2019), which opens by saying that:

> *One of the main goals of portfolio management is to build a risk-efficient portfolio, where the organization chooses to take an appropriate amount of risk with the portfolio in order to achieve the required value in the overall organizational strategy. This is achieved by adding or removing portfolio components, based on their contributions to the overall risk exposure and strategic value.*
>
> (Project Management Institute, 2019)

Despite this promising start, the section continues by describing a portfolio risk management life cycle that mirrors the project risk process precisely (compare Project Management Institute, 2019, Section 5.1, with Project Management Institute, 2017a, Section 11), and the remainder of the section does not mention *risk efficiency* again. The same situation is found in *APM Portfolio Management: A practical guide (APM, 2019b)*, which also does not mention *risk efficiency*.

There are many pitfalls associated with taking a project-based view of portfolios, most of which arise from limitations in the underlying thinking, as Teller et al. (2014) agreed when discussing risk management in project portfolios. This is likely to remain a challenge for as long as portfolio management is seen as an extension of project management theory and practice, or at least until the concepts and practice of portfolio risk management become better established.

Building consensus on portfolio risk management

Unfortunately, a cursory reading of available guidelines and textbooks confirms a worrying lack of consensus among key players and opinion-formers in the field concerning the purpose and nature of portfolio risk management or the process and techniques required to achieve it. This is reinforced by a review of the limited academic literature addressing management of risk in portfolios of projects. The approach outlined in this chapter is gaining traction and acceptance, but it remains one view among several. Professional bodies and practitioners alike need to give attention to this important area and develop an agreed position on where portfolio risk comes from, why it matters, and how it can be managed proactively and effectively.

Conclusion

There is no doubt that portfolios are risky undertakings and that successful delivery of strategic benefits through portfolios depends on effective portfolio risk management. Although there are similarities and parallels between the process for explicit management of individual portfolio risks and the well-established project risk management process, portfolio risks can arise from above and below the portfolio as well as within it, and the process must tackle all these sources. In addition, portfolio risk management must manage overall portfolio risk exposure through application of a risk-efficient approach to the construction and ongoing execution of the portfolio.

References

Andersson T., Getz D., Gration D. & Raciti M. (2017) Event portfolios: Asset value, risk and returns. *International Journal of Event and Festival Management* 8(3), 226–243.

Association for Project Management (2019a) *APM Body of Knowledge*. Seventh Edition. Association for Project Management.

Association for Project Management (2019b) *Portfolio Management: A Practical Guide*. Association for Project Management.

Australian Institute of Project Management (2019) *AIPM Glossary of Terms*. https://my.aipm.com.au/info-hub/glossary.

Axelos (2010) *Management of Risk, MoR®: Guidance for Practitioners*. Third Edition. The Stationery Office.

Axelos (2011) *Management of Portfolios, MoP®*. The Stationery Office.

Chapman C. & Ward S. (1997) *Project Risk Management: Processes, Techniques and Insights*. Wiley.

Chapman C. & Ward S. (2004) Why risk efficiency is a key aspect of best practice projects. *International Journal of Project Management* 22(8), 619–632.

Chapman C. & Ward S. (2011) *How to Manage Project Opportunity and Risk*. Wiley.

European Commission Centre of Excellence in Project Management (CoEPM) (2016) *PM² Project Management Methodology Guide – Open Edition*. European Commission.

Hicks J. (1939) *Value and Capital: An Inquiry into Some Fundamental Principles of Economic Theory*. Clarendon Press.

Hillson D. (2002a) Extending the risk process to manage opportunities. *International Journal of Project Management* 20(3), 235–240.

Hillson D. (June 2002b) The Risk Breakdown Structure (RBS) as an aid to effective risk management. Proceedings of Fifth European Project Management Conference (PMI Europe 2002), Cannes.

Hillson D. (2003a) *Effective Opportunity Management for Projects: Exploiting Positive Risk*. Routledge/ Taylor & Francis.

Hillson D. (2003b) Using a risk breakdown structure in project management. *Journal of Facilities Management* 2(1), 85–97.

Hillson D. (2009) *Managing Risk in Projects*. Routledge/Gower.

Hillson D. (2011) *Managing Risk in Project Portfolios*. www.risk-doctor.com/docs/64%20Managing%20 risk%20in%20project%20portfolios.pdf.

Hillson D. (2014 May) Managing overall project risk. Presented at the PMI Global Congress EMEA, UAE.

Hillson D. (2019) *Capturing Upside Risk: Finding and Managing Opportunities in Projects*. Routledge/ Taylor & Francis.

Hillson D. & Murray-Webster R. (2012) *A Short Guide to Risk Appetite*. Gower.

Institution of Civil Engineers, Institute and Faculty of Actuaries. (2014) *Risk Analysis & Management for Projects (RAMP)*. Third Edition. ICE Publishing.

International Organization for Standardization. (2018) *ISO 31000:2018: Risk Management Guidelines*. International Organization for Standardization.

Markowitz H. (1952) Portfolio selection. *Journal of Finance* 7(1), 77–91.

Markowitz H. (1959) *Portfolio Selection: Efficient Diversification of Investments*. J Wiley.

Olsson R. (2006) *Managing Project Uncertainty by Using an Enhanced Risk Management Process*. Mälardalen University.

Olsson R. (2007) In search of opportunity management: Is the risk management process enough? *International Journal of Project Management* 25(8), 745–752.

Olsson R. (2008) Risk management in a multi-project environment. *International Journal of Quality & Reliability Management* 25(1), 60–71.

Project Management Institute (2017a) *A Guide to the Project Management Body of Knowledge (PMBOK® Guide)*. Sixth Edition. Project Management Institute.

Project Management Institute (2017b) *The Standard for Portfolio Management*. Fourth Edition. Project Management Institute.

Project Management Institute (2019) *The Standard for Risk Management in Portfolios, Programs and Projects*. Project Management Institute.

Rogers M., Gupta A. &. Maranas C. (2003) Risk Management in Real Options Based Pharmaceutical Portfolio Planning, Proceedings Foundations of Computer-Aided Process Operations (FOCAPO2003).

Taleb N. (2007) *The Black Swan*. Penguin Publishing.

Teller J., Kock A. & Gemunden H. (2014) Risk management in project portfolios is more than managing project risks: A contingency perspective on risk management. *Project Management Journal* 45(4), 67–80.

Tyler P. & McVean J. (March 25–28, 2001) Significance of Project Risking Methods on Portfolio Optimization Models. Society of Petroleum Engineers, Latin American and Caribbean Petroleum Engineering Conference, Society of Petroleum Engineers

Ward S. & Chapman C. (2003) Transforming project risk management into project uncertainty management. *International Journal of Project Management* 21, 97–105.

Wideman R. (1992) *Project and Program Risk Management: A Guide to Managing Project Risks and Opportunities*. Project Management Institute.

18 Delivery leadership of complex portfolios

Stuart Forsyth and Carl Gavin

Introduction

This chapter focuses on the leadership of portfolios and achieves this through discussing, from direct experience, a case study for delivery leadership of a complex portfolio. Following the introduction of the case study for BAE systems, a model for portfolio delivery leadership based on distributed leadership (CP3 model) is discussed, together with a model relating to a complex system for portfolio leadership (based on the Cynefin model), bringing together a discussion of the complexities of portfolio leadership and the resulting capabilities required for leading the delivery of these complex portfolios.

The Association for Project Management (APM) defines "portfolio management" as "*the selection, prioritisation and control of an organisation's projects and programs in line with its strategic objectives and its capacity to deliver*" (APM, 2019). The Project Management Institute (PMI, 2017) has a similar definition, in that "portfolio management" is:

> [T]he coordinated management of one or more portfolios [of projects and/or programs] to achieve organisational strategies and objectives. It includes interrelated organisational processes by which an organisation evaluates, selects, prioritises, and allocates its limited internal resources to best accomplish organisational strategies consistent with its vision, mission and values.
>
> (PMI, 2017)

In both previous cases, these leading professional institutions recognise that portfolio management is concerned with delivering company strategy and implementing processes for evaluation, selection, and prioritisation of projects and/or programs. However, these definitions and processes tend to make us think of portfolio managers as being abstract from the projects and/or programs they are responsible for and that the decision-making is similar to decision-making in financial investments, such as for stocks and shares. What is unclear is the role of the portfolio manager in "*delivery leadership*" – the APM definition mentioned prior uses the word "*control*", and the PMI definition uses "*coordinated management*", yet these do not suggest that the portfolio manager should lead the delivery of projects and programs in their portfolio.

Delivery leadership is a necessary element of portfolio management, in addition to evaluation, selection, and prioritisation processes. The decision-making could be perfect in terms of evaluating, selection, and prioritisation, but if leadership of delivery is lacking, the end result could be failure, or at least less-successful outcomes than otherwise

DOI: 10.4324/9780367853129-21

expected. This is particularly the case where the projects within the portfolio are complex, such as product or service development projects.

Hereinafter, the term *project* will be adopted, but in the knowledge that this term could refer to projects, programs, or a combination of both within the portfolio.

Leadership of projects has been researched extensively over the past decade with the overwhelming conclusion that competent leadership is essential for successful projects – evidence from various studies indicates a significant link between project leadership and project success (Turner & Müller, 2005; Yang et al., 2011; Nixon et al., 2012; Morris, 1994). Leading an uncertain, temporary, unique venture requires someone to own the project vision, inspire and motivate the team, and foster collaboration and commitment with the stakeholders – creating the environment where projects succeed.

As projects become more complex, leadership becomes a differentiator – in recent research, Merrow and Nandurdikar (2018) state that leadership is the defining factor in whether or not complex projects are successful. They argue that large complex projects are, in many respects, fundamentally different to simpler projects. The complexities associated with scope, organisation, and stakeholder alignment all dictate the challenge of leading such projects. As Merrow and Nandurdikar (2018) state:

> [O]ur point is a simple one: the complex project leader's job is really quite difficult, and the skill set required to navigate this position well is quite remarkable . . . as projects become more complex the leadership role not only expands, it becomes progressively more important to project success. The complex project has many more paths to failure than a simple (or standard) project . . . complexity makes the project leader's job bigger, more varied, and more difficult.

This is true for groups of projects as it is for single projects. Leadership of challenging complex portfolios is a differentiator in ensuring successful delivery, and yet leadership of portfolios of projects and programs is seldom discussed. As our premise is that *delivery leadership* is a required additional competence of portfolio managers, particularly for portfolios containing complex projects, hereinafter this role will be referred to as the *portfolio leader*. The subsequent models in this chapter are based around the following BAE case study.

Case study – BAE Systems portfolio management

BAE Systems PLC is an international company providing some of the world's most advanced, technology-led defence, aerospace, and security solutions and, at the time of writing, operating in over 40 countries with a skilled workforce of 86,000 people. Working with customers and local partners, it develops, engineers, manufactures, and supports products and systems to deliver military capability, protect national security and people, and keep critical information and infrastructure secure. BAE Systems is involved in several major defence projects, including the Lockheed Martin F-35 Lightning II, the Eurofighter Typhoon, the Astute-class submarine, and the Queen Elizabeth–class aircraft carriers.

BAE Systems is a federated organisation with multiple businesses, with each business being a portfolio of projects. These projects are mostly to deliver against customer-provided contracts, with documented terms and conditions and a technical specification, although in some cases the projects are internal investment projects, for example, to deliver a new IT system or to research and develop a new technology or product.

Regardless of the type of projects, in almost all cases, the portfolios are highly complex, delivered by teams operating across functional, business, geographical, national, and cultural boundaries, sometimes within challenging contractual relationships and for "intelligent" customers. The complexity of the portfolios derives from projects containing many interconnecting parts that can change in ways which are unpredictable, compounded by rapidly evolving technologies, shifting geopolitical priorities, customer relationships (both directly with users and with procurement bodies), supply chain collaborations, the diversity of stakeholders engaged, and resulting complexity with the organisation of the portfolio itself.

An interesting point is that the portfolios of projects delivering against customer contractual requirements have subtly different evaluation and selection processes applied to those advocated for standard portfolio management. Evaluation and selection are completed through the bidding process via pursue/do not pursue decisions (i.e. evaluation) and bid/do not bid decisions (i.e. selection). (Note: For comparison of a model for portfolio definition, refer back to Chapter 11). Once secured, however, all requirements for quality and delivery will be defined by the customer: there are no degrees of freedom if all contracts are to be satisfied. Only resource prioritisation forms the basis for decisions to be taken, with the objective of satisfying all contracts. The ability to stop a contracted project without being penalised in contractual and reputational terms is limited.

Groups of contracted projects are considered as portfolios – within the company, portfolio leaders have the title of managing directors because the portfolios are managed as businesses and the portfolio leaders have profit and loss accountability. Where internal investment projects are also included in the portfolio, it is very difficult to keep focus on achievement, because contracted projects will always get resource priority.

In 2018, BAE Systems conducted a survey of the leaders of a range of portfolios across the company to determine the expected competences for portfolio leaders. The results of the survey indicated that portfolio leaders should demonstrate the following capabilities:

- Active oversight, being visible, and taking an active interest in people.
- Afresh perspective from a wider long-term viewpoint based on diverse experiences.
- The appropriate organisational tone, for example, encouraging collaborative behaviours, fact-based decisions, openness and honesty, no surprises, and "*truth to power*" conversations.
- Coaching and development of project leaders.
- Empowerment of people to solve problems.
- A consistent approach using positive constructive language, setting clear expectations, and using articulate communication.
- Tolerance of mistakes and encouraging learning from mistakes.
- Sensitivity to early warning signals of risks and issues.
- Management of stakeholders not accessible to project and program leaders.

The results of this research, and other research conducted on project and program leaders within the company (Forsyth & Gavin, 2017; Browning & Ramasesh, 2015; Morris, 2013), helped Alliance Manchester Business School to propose a leadership model for project, program, and portfolio leaders within BAE Systems, titled the CP3 (complex projects, programs, and portfolios) leadership model. This was based on the model of distributed leadership developed by Deborah Ancona and her team at MIT Sloan (Ancona et al., 2007). The Cynefin framework (Snowden & Boone, 2007) was also utilised in the analysis of portfolio complexity. Both of these models, and their applicability to delivery leadership of complex portfolios, will be discussed further.

A model for portfolio delivery leadership

A number of well-known leadership thinkers at MIT Sloan Management School, led by Professor Deborah Ancona, developed a proposition that championed the "*incomplete leader*". This proposition challenges the traditional, and often ingrained, view of the leader as hero, that those who lead us know all and can do all, with great intellectual capacity, future visioning powers, operational know-how, and interpersonal skills to lead, influence, and motivate their staff. However, no single person is a perfect leader, possessing all these skills in great measure.

> It's time to end the myth of the complete leader: the flawless person at the top who's got it all figured out. . . . In today's world, the executive's job is no longer to command and control but to cultivate and coordinate the actions of others at all levels of the organization. Only when leaders come to see themselves as incomplete – as having both strengths and weaknesses – will they be able to make up for their missing skills by relying on others.
>
> (Ancona et al., 2007).

In the past, leadership success came from knowing the answer and sharing it through the management and direction of others. Experience, knowledge, and critical analysis were prized above all other skills. As most company's projects become more complex – with increases in risk and uncertainties – in response to more demanding customers and operating in a more competitive and volatile market, we cannot pretend that our leaders are "*complete*" and have all the answers. In the future, leadership success will come not from not knowing the answers but from knowing how to get to the answers and working with others – through networking and asking effective questions – to do so.

To counter the myth of the complete leader, Ancona and her team proposed a model of distributed leadership which summarised leadership thinking and research into four leadership capabilities:

- *Sensemaking* – understanding the context in which a company operates.
- *Relating* – building relationships within and across organisations.
- *Visioning* – creating a compelling picture of the future.
- *Inventing* – developing new ways to achieve the vision.

It is unlikely someone will be equally skilled in all four capabilities, but a leader who acknowledges that they are "*incomplete*" will realise that they have their own strengths and weaknesses and need to work with others to build on their strengths and compensate for their limitations.

> Sensemaking, relating, visioning, and inventing are interdependent. Without sensemaking, there's no common view of reality from which to start. Without relating, people work in isolation or, worse, strive toward different aims. Without visioning, there's no shared direction. And without inventing, a vision remains illusory. No one leader, however, will excel at all four capabilities in equal measure.
>
> (Ancona et al., 2007)

BAE Systems adopted Ancona's model of distributed leadership (more widely known colloquially as the *Sloan leadership model*, although Ancona refers to it as the *4-CAP model*)

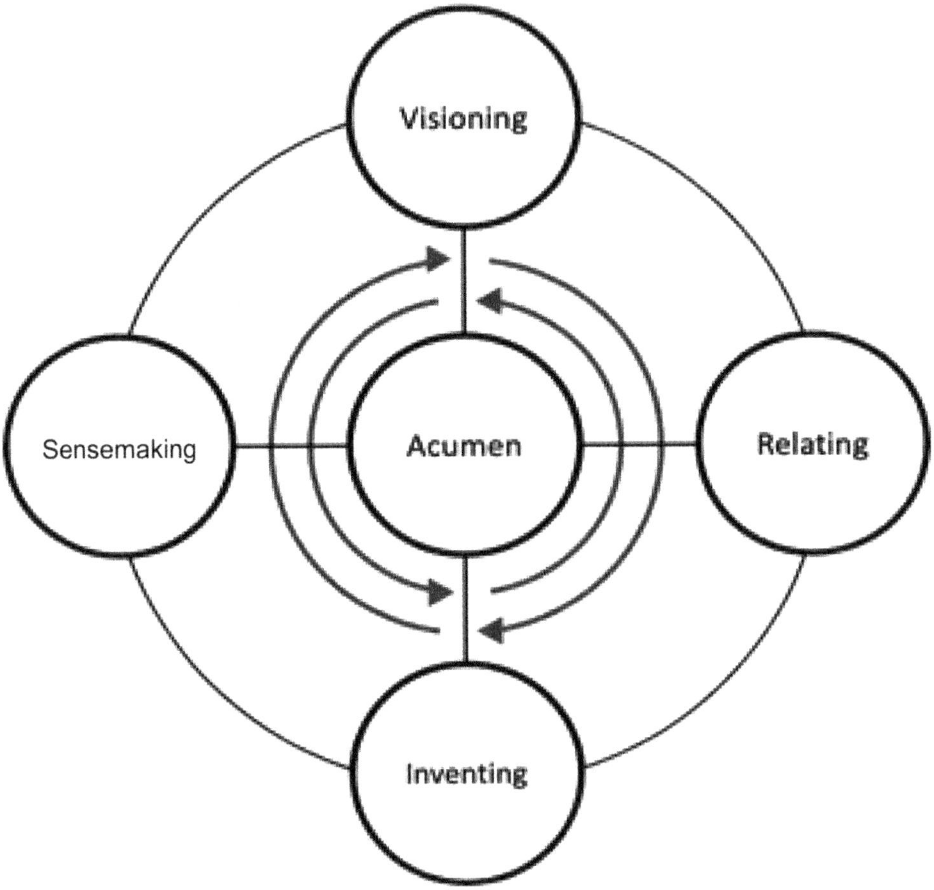

Figure 18.1 Portfolio leadership capabilities model.

Source: Adapted from Ancona et al. (2007).

for portfolio leadership training because it emphasises what leaders actually do and how they do it – it is about leadership capability and behaviour and suited to the leadership of complex portfolios. The leadership model was further enhanced for portfolio leadership by adding a fifth capability, *acumen*, at the centre of the distributed leadership model, shown in Figure 18.1. *Acumen* emphasises the experience of the leaders and their ability to make good judgements and decisions – it underpins, contextualises, and enables the other four capabilities of the leadership model.

Sensemaking: understanding the context in which a company and the portfolio operate

Portfolio leaders need to make sense of the world around them and understand the contexts they are operating in and what is changing, that is, develop a map of the project terrain. The portfolio leader should quickly capture the complexities of the portfolio environment – getting data from multiple sources and stakeholders, involving others, and being open – and ensure everyone is working from this same map. The map may be imperfect and not conform to dominant views so must highlight what the portfolio leader believes to be critical.

Relating: building relationships within and across organisations

Portfolio leaders need to build effective and trusting relationships with all stakeholders – and in a world where portfolio leaders don't know the answer, they have to work with others to explore options and determine the answers. Ancona et al. (2007) state three key methods to do this are inquiring (asking questions and listening to understand), advocating (giving their view of the world, with explanation of the reasoning), and connecting (cultivating a network of confidants who can help the portfolio leader accomplish a wide range of goals). Relating is a factor of how much you listen and not how much you advocate for your own analysis and perspectives; the key is to ask yourself one question every time you interact: *"Am I listening to understand, or am I listening to reply?"*

Visioning: creating a compelling picture of the future

Visioning creates the compelling images of the future; sensemaking creates a map of what is. Visioning produces a map of what could be: the portfolio leader's intent. The vision gives people a sense of meaning in their work and inspires and motivates them to help bring about the portfolio leader's vision – if the vision is compelling and realistic, the team will discover ways to make it real. The portfolio leader should be prepared to explain the vision and what can be achieved through it. As the vision is a key tool in orchestrating change through others, portfolio leaders must be highly skilled at articulating and communicating it.

Inventing: developing new ways to achieve the vision

Inventing transforms the vision of the future from an idea into reality. Rather than using the term "*execution*", "*inventing*" implies creativity and innovation in determining what is needed, including new ways of organising and interacting. Implementing a new vision is very rarely reliant on "*doing the same things we've been doing*" – the portfolio leader should encourage creative ways of getting it done and be asking, "*What other options are possible?*" The portfolio leader should "*test and learn*": encourage the use of hypotheses informed through deep customer and market insight to experiment to find the best way forward – actively testing new approaches and ideas before significant decisions are made. The portfolio leader should also champion the importance of diversity of voices and ideas in looking for options that may resolve key issues, ensuring a full understanding of risk and options.

Acumen: drawing on experience, judgement, and gut feeling

Acumen comes from experience and the exposure to the widest possible combination of internal and external influences – *acumen* is the synthesis of this experience and exposure over time into the thinking about business, its challenges, and its opportunities. Acumen provides portfolio leaders with a "*sense*" of a situation. It is a "*gut feeling*" based on experience and enables the leader, for example, to know when to challenge and when not to, when to trust and when not to, when to dive deeply into a problem and when to sit back. The ability to sit back and reflect on the situation is critical for leaders operating in complexity. The portfolio leader should reflect on and identify the key challenges by taking in the "*whole*" and identifying where the issues might be – one way of thinking about this is to think of the portfolio as a crowded dance floor; the patterns and disturbances only become evident if you can watch it from a balcony. Acumen is developed by applying the other four capabilities in real-life, project-based situations.

Portfolio leadership capabilities

As stated, the portfolio leadership capabilities model (or CP3) is a model of distributed leadership – portfolio leaders should not be expected to be highly skilled in all capabilities but should rely on their team and their project and program leaders to complement and compensate for their strengths and weaknesses.

Portfolios contain multiple projects and programs, with the common aspect being that they are all in some way linked to delivering the company strategy and they are also likely to be linked by the need to access a common resource pool. Leading such groups of projects and programs is different to leading a single project or a program.

With a project, the project leader is focused on delivering an output, using well-established project management processes along a well-established project life cycle. The competence of project leaders tends to be associated with the technical subject matter being developed, coupled with some level of leadership expertise.

For a program – which is, in essence, a collection of interdependent projects, linked in such a way that the outputs from the projects integrate together to create the overall program output or outcome – the program leader manages the project leaders towards achieving this integrated result: they are therefore a "*leader of leaders*" (or a leader of project leaders). The competence of the program leader is mostly about integrating and will generally require higher levels of leadership expertise than with project leadership (noting context dependency discussed in the section introduction).

Managing groups of projects and programs requires a wide understanding of the collective project scope and a very clear understanding of how each one influences and delivers the strategy of the organisation. The portfolio leader is also *a "leader of leaders"*, but in some ways, this is more challenging because the subject matter of the projects could be highly diverse. The competence of the portfolio leader is to have a clear understanding of the company strategy and to lead the collection of individual projects and programs to deliver this. The competence of the portfolio leader is therefore required to be higher than that of the project or program leader.

At this point, it is also worth considering the role of a *sponsor*. APM (2019) defines a *sponsor "as an important senior management role. The sponsor is accountable for ensuring that the work is governed effectively and delivers the objectives that meet the identified needs*". PMI (2017) defines a *sponsor* as "*the person or group that provides the financial resources, in cash or kind, for the project and provides an escalation path for issues beyond the control of the project manager*". Unlike the definitions of project, program, or even portfolio manager, these definitions are somewhat different, highlighting that the role of the sponsor is currently not clear across the professional organisations. Our working definition suggests that a sponsor is someone who is accountable for the results of a project, program, or portfolio but who does not manage or lead the day-to-day aspects.

The sponsor is the person who should provide a clear vision and direction; will support program or portfolio managers to take decisions, offering the benefit of experience through application of a wider, longer-term view; set the overall operating environment; and manage stakeholders not accessible to the project, program, or portfolio leaders, with the most senior sponsor focusing on ensuring the contribution to organisational value for strategic delivery. These responsibilities suggest that a good sponsor will play an active role. They also suggest that sponsorship could be on the same competence continuum as project, program, and portfolio management, as suggested in Table 18.1. Within BAE Systems, the sponsors will be the group managing director of multiple portfolios, that is, multiple product- or service-related business entities.

Understanding that the leadership of portfolios is different to the leadership of projects or programs implies that the competence of portfolio leaders is different to the competence of project or program leaders and that of sponsors. This may be subtle, but in our view, the competence will increase going from project to program to portfolio to sponsor, as shown in Table 18.1.

Portfolio leadership and complexity

Snowden and Boone (2007), in their studies, found that good leaders tailor their approach to fit the complexity of their circumstances, identifying the context they are working in at any given time and changing their behaviour and their decisions to match that context. Good leadership is not a one-size-fits-all proposition – best practice is, by definition, past practice, and leaders need to react to the context they find themselves in.

Snowden and Boone (2007) state that a complex system has the following characteristics:

- It involves large numbers of interacting elements.
- The interactions are nonlinear, and minor changes can produce disproportionately major consequences.
- The system is dynamic.
- The elements of the system evolve with one another and with the environment, and evolution is irreversible.
- Though a complex system may appear to be ordered and predictable, the external conditions and system constantly change.
- An inability to forecast or predict what will happen in a complex system with certainty.

Snowden and Boone (2007) developed the Cynefin framework (Cynefin, pronounced ku-nev-in, is a Welsh word that means "*habitat*" or "*environment*") to help leaders determine the context they are operating in and to make appropriate choices based on that context. They identified four contexts defined by the nature of the relationships between cause and effect, each requiring different actions. Figure 18.2 shows a complex system model for portfolio leadership based on the Cynefin framework.

Standard and *complicated* contexts assume an ordered environment, where cause-and-effect relationships are discernible and right answers can be determined based on fact. *Complex* and *chaotic* contexts are disordered, with no immediately apparent relationship between cause and effect, and the way forward has to be determined based on emerging

Table 18.1 Capability evolution from project to program to portfolio leader to sponsor

	Project leader	*Program leader*	*Portfolio leader*	*Sponsor*
Sensemaking	• Understands the context in which theroject will operate. • Makes sense of complexity, risk, and uncertainty within project and surrounding the project in the internal and external context. • Creates a "map of what is".	• Understands the context in which the program will operate. • Makes sense of complexity, risk, and uncertainty within program and surrounding the program in the internal and external context. • Understand and synthesise complexity, risk, and uncertainty from dependent projects. • Creates a "map of what is" for the program.	• Understands the context in which the portfolio will operate. • Makes sense of complexity, risk, and uncertainty within portfolio and surrounding the portfolio in the internal and external context, particularly as linked to strategy. • Understand and synthesise complexity, risk, and uncertainty from independent projects. • Create a "map of what is" for the portfolio.	• Understands the context in which the wider organisation will operate. • Making sense of complexity, risk, and uncertainty from the overall organisational environment. • Creates a "map of what is" for the wider organisation.
Relating	• Builds and maintains trusted relationships with internal and external stakeholders. • Creates a network of confidants. • Encourages appropriate behaviours, for example, collaboration, honesty, truth to power.	• Manages stakeholders not available to the project managers. • A leader of leaders. • Challenges, coaches, mentors project leaders. • Creates a network of confidants. • Encourages appropriate behaviours, for example, collaboration, honesty, truth to power.	• Manages stakeholders not available to the project or program managers. • A leader of leaders. • Challenges, coaches, mentors project and program leaders. • Creates a network of confidants. • Encourages appropriate behaviours, for example, collaboration, honesty, truth to power.	• Provides a long-term view from a wider perspective. • Provides active oversight and interest in people. • Manages stakeholders not available to the project, program, or portfolio managers. • A sponsor of leaders, with no direct line of sight to people doing the work. • Challenges, coaches, mentors project, program, and portfolio leaders. • Creates a network of confidants. • Encourages appropriate behaviours, for example, collaboration, honesty, truth to power.

Visioning	• Creates a compelling forward view to the end of the project. • Creates a sense of purpose, beyond the task delivery.	• Creates a compelling forward view to the end of the program. • Creates a sense of purpose, beyond the task delivery. • Sets the "tone" of the program.	• Creates a compelling forward view of the portfolio from a longer-term perspective. • Creates a sense of purpose, beyond the task delivery. • Sets the "tone" of the portfolio. • Aligns projects and programs with organisation's strategy and objectives.	• Creates a compelling long-range view of the wider organisation. • Sets the "tone" of the organisation. • Ensures that projects, programs, and portfolios are aligned with the organisation's strategy and objectives.
Inventing	• Be creative in tailoring processes and tools for the needs of the project.	• Be creative in tailoring processes and tools for the needs of the program.	• Be creative in tailoring processes and tools for the needs of the portfolio – it could be that different projects require different ways of operating to respond to different levels of complexity.	• Be creative in organisational design.
Acumen	• Limited acumen based on limited experience, with limited ability to make decisions based on judgement.	• Increased acumen based on significant experience, with significant ability to make decisions based on judgement.	• Increased acumen based on significant experience, with significant ability to make decisions based on judgement, but with a wider viewpoint.	• Wide experience and capable of making decisions from a long-term point of view.

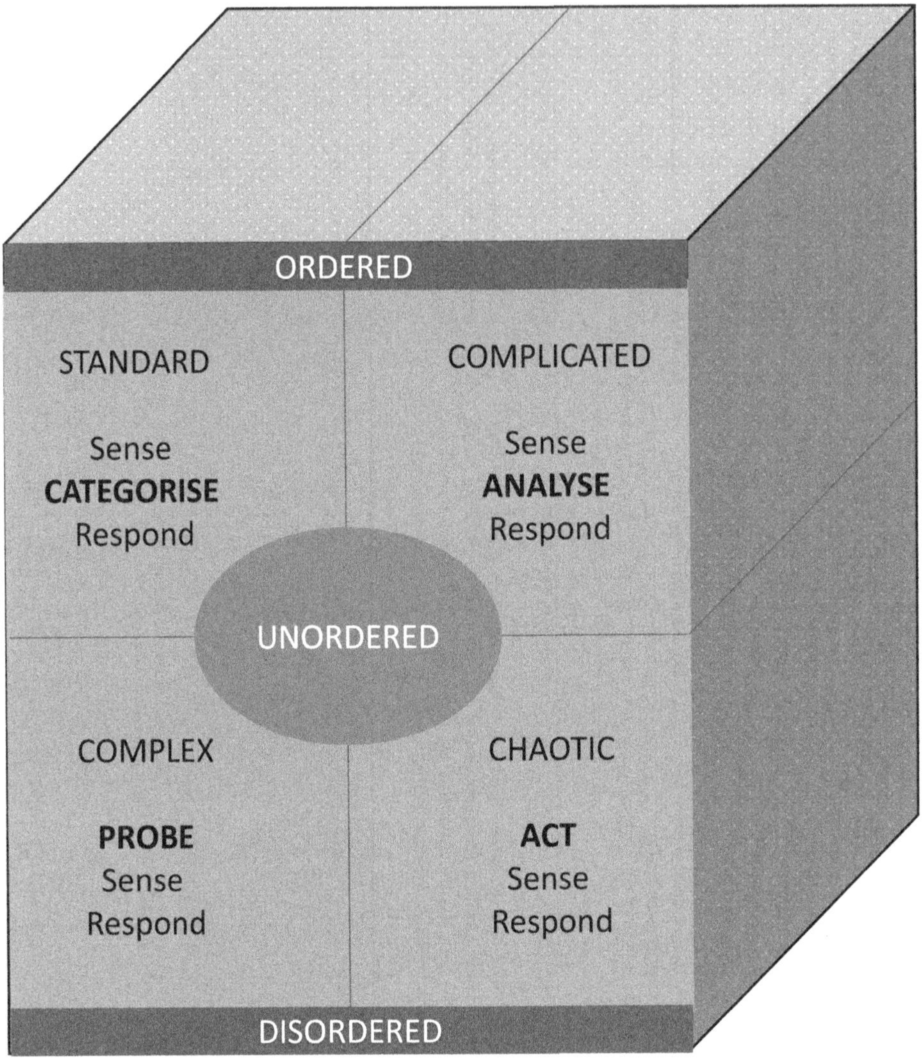

Figure 18.2 A complex system model for portfolio leadership.

Source: Adapted from Snowden and Boone (2007).

patterns. Similar to Snowdon and Boone, the ordered world is the area of fact-based management, whereas the disordered world represents pattern-based management.

Standard contexts: the domain of best practice

Standard contexts are characterised by stability and clear cause-and-effect relationships that are easily discernible – the right answer is self-evident and undisputed. This is the realm of "*known knowns*". Standard contexts, if properly assessed, require straightforward management and monitoring. Here, leaders *sense, categorise, and respond* – they assess the facts of the situation, categorise them, and then base their responses on established practice.

Complicated contexts: the domain of experts

Complicated contexts may contain multiple right answers, and although there is a clear relationship between cause and effect, it may not be perceived by everyone. This is the realm of "*known unknowns*". Leaders in a complicated context must *sense, analyse, and respond* – this approach is not easy and often requires a level of expertise.

Complex contexts: the domain of emergence

In complex contexts, major change introduces unpredictability and flux, and outcomes are unpredictable. Right answers are not easily discernible. This is the realm of "*unknown unknowns*". There is only an understanding of why things happen in hindsight. Instead of attempting to impose a course of action, leaders must allow the way forward to reveal itself. Leaders need to *probe first, then sense and then respond.* A complex domain requires a more experimental mode of management – leaders who try to impose order in a complex context will fail, but those who allow patterns to emerge and determine which ones to take action on will be successful.

Chaotic contexts: the domain of rapid response

In a chaotic context, relationships between cause and effect are impossible to determine because they shift constantly and no manageable patterns exist. This is the realm of "*unknowables*". Searching for right answers is pointless; the leader must instead *act, sense, and respond* – act to establish order, sense where stability is present and absent, and respond to move the situation from chaos to a complex context. The aim is to quickly prevent a crisis.

Adapting to the relevant context

Snowden and Boone argue that effective leaders learn to shift their decision-making styles and responses to match the relevant contexts and environments. "*A deep understanding of context, the ability to embrace complexity, paradox and ambiguity and a willingness to flexibly change leadership style will be required for leaders who want to make things happen in a time of increasing uncertainty*" (Snowden & Boone, 2007).

Portfolio leaders need to understand the complexity of the projects within their portfolio. There may be a mixture of projects: some may be standard, others complicated, and some complex, and hopefully none in chaos. With this understanding of complexity, the portfolio leader should establish different ways of operating for each project: this is an additional complexity that does not exist at a project or program level. The recommendation is to conduct such a portfolio analysis using the portfolio leadership complexity model (or Cynefin framework) to highlight which projects are in which category and therefore require different ways of operating.

The challenges of reducing complexity in complex portfolios

Complexity drives risk and uncertainty; in a complex project, where there are many interdependent elements – each carrying risk and uncertainty – that interact in unpredictable ways, it is difficult to create a plan with any expectation of predictable outcomes. In a portfolio of complex projects, the overall risk and uncertainty is likely to be even more complex than any single individual project.

BAE Systems categorises the drivers of complexity into three aspects: structural complexity, sociopolitical complexity, and emergence:

- *Structural complexity* arises where there are many interdependent elements, for example, components, lines of code, equipment, sub-systems, deliverables, geographic locations, time zones, businesses involved, suppliers, interdependencies, people, disciplines, tools, processes, stakeholders, requirements, etc.
- *Sociopolitical complexity* relates to the quantity and quality of relationships with internal and external stakeholders, with potential conflicts due to interests, agendas, politics, and power.
- *Emergent complexity* arises from changes over time due to uncertainty, technical novelty, poor definition and planning, inexperienced team and team changes, etc.

It is the responsibility of the portfolio leader to understand complexity within their portfolio and take actions to reduce it, on the basis that this will reduce delivery risk and uncertainty. This may require creative and innovative approaches.

To reduce portfolio complexity, it is necessary to reduce individual project complexity. The overall complexity of a portfolio, which is the sum of individual projects, is likely to be higher than the sum of the complexity of the individual projects and could pose significant leadership challenges (Geraldi et al., 2011). Not least where the portfolio consists of projects with different levels of complexity and therefore requires different responses to reducing the complexity.

Reducing structural complexity can be achieved by good basic project management. Ideally, the projects in the portfolio should be defined early in the project life cycle as part of a front-end loading (FEL) strategy (Merrow, 2011; Morris, 2009). For example, systematically decomposing the project using a work breakdown structure (WBS), organisational breakdown structure (OBS), and cost breakdown structure (CBS) to form appropriate project control systems, forming appropriately detailed plans for project execution and having an effective governance system that will independently scrutinise and challenge these plans. Most of this type of work should be done by the project leaders and not the portfolio leader. However, the portfolio leader should have adequate understanding of the importance of planning and control and ensure that it is done – establishing an effective project control system for all projects within the portfolio along with appropriate governance is fundamental to successful delivery.

Reducing sociopolitical complexity can be achieved by effective stakeholder management and good communications, with good interpersonal skills (negotiation, persuasion, relationship development, conflict resolution). This is often an area that is not allocated enough time by portfolio leaders. Some people are naturally good at this, but others will require training and development. Portfolio leaders should allow adequate time to network inside and outside the organisation, to ensure support for the project and program leaders. As the number of suppliers, partners, and customers increase, then more time should be allowed, and the relating competences of the portfolio leader may need to be stronger.

Reducing emergent complexity can be more difficult, particularly for complex projects, programs, and portfolios. Approaches to reducing emergent complexity include having an experienced team who will make less mistakes than an inexperienced team; using a robust change management process, ideally strongly linked to the customer to avoid requirements creep; deploying effective independent technical reviews along the project life cycle and a solid risk management process. In addition, an "alert culture" where "early warning signs" of potential emergent difficulties are actively identified and responded to is recommended (Haji-Kazemi et al., 2013). Such an alert culture is one where the people within the project teams are educated to understand that complexity results in emergent problems, risks, and uncertainties and are encouraged to behave in such a way that these are illuminated and brought to the surface rather than remaining hidden – it is a culture where it is normal practice to "*probe, sense, respond*" in line with the recommendations for complex environments in the portfolio leadership model.

Having an alert culture within the portfolio should be the right culture regardless of whether the projects are standard, complicated, complex, or chaotic. However, it could be that certain aspects are emphasised or de-emphasised, depending on the category of the project.

Delivery leadership of complex portfolios

Portfolio leaders and their team will exercise all the leadership capabilities (Figure 18.1), to some degree, in order to establish and manage a portfolio, with the appropriate operating model and an appropriate culture. The portfolio leadership complexity model(Figure 18.2) suggests that a "probe, sense, respond" approach is best for leading complex projects and that this is enabled by setting up and maintaining an alert culture within the portfolio.

This section will integrate the two models (portfolio leadership capabilities and portfolio leadership complexity model) and make practical recommendations for delivery leadership of a portfolio containing complex projects. The following text uses some of the key points from the "portfolio leader" column in Table 18.1, and Table 18.2 cross-refers the portfolio complexity model "probe, sense, respond" approach to the leadership capabilities needed to achieve it and then the activities required for set-up and delivery phases of the portfolio.

Table 18.2 "Probe, sense, respond" in set-up and ongoing delivery

Complexity model	*Leadership capability*	*Set-up phase – create the alert culture*	*Delivery*
Probe	Sensemaking Relating Acumen	Emphasise: • Value of experimentation. • Openness to asking and answering questions. • People feeling safe to speak "truth to power".	• Ask questions.
Sense		• Regular discussions of problems and risks.	• Seek early warning signs and patterns of behaviour. • Allow time for reflection.
Respond	Visioning Inventing Acumen	Value: • Learning from mistakes. • Diversity of thought. • Openness and honesty – no surprises.	• Increased levels of interaction, communication, and discussion. • Encourage dissent and diversity.

Visioning

The portfolio leader must start off with a vision, that is, a high-level impression of what they want the future to look like, ideally captured in a short vision statement. A portfolio leader will have a longer-term, wider view than the project leaders within the portfolio, so they should use this knowledge to create a compelling view of the future that provides a sense of purpose beyond the scope of any particular project but is still consistent with the strategy and objectives of the company. It should engage the heart as well as the head and be easily understood by a wide group of stakeholders. It should be time-independent, contain no technical jargon, and be flexible enough to accommodate changes in the portfolio. It should set the operating culture for the portfolio and be consistent with the business strategy. A vision for an alert culture will require the team to understand the behaviours expected from them. It will also require the portfolio leader to consistently operate in a particular way and for the sponsor and the organisation in which the portfolio resides to provide unstinting support.

Sensemaking

The portfolio leader must understand the context in which the portfolio will operate. Both the internal context and the external context are important so that they can make sense and help the project leaders with their own sensemaking and indeed to support their own higher-level decision-making.

Portfolios contain multiple projects, and the portfolio leader must make sense of the complexity, risk, and uncertainty of the individual projects and synthesise this into a portfolio leader's view. There are many techniques for making sense of complexity, for example, mind maps, cognitive mapping, but for this chapter, we focus on the most simple and intuitive method of asking open questions, that is, probing, with the intent of understanding and building up a "map" of the current situation or problem.

As part of an alert culture, the portfolio leader should constantly probe by asking questions and constantly reflecting on the answers in order to seek patterns that identify risks, uncertainties, and early warning signs. For such an alert culture to work, it must be safe for people to be honest and open about project challenges and progress. By asking open questions to as many people as possible, continually as part of an alert culture, the portfolio leader will build up an understanding of the problems, risks, and uncertainties around the projects and synthesise these into portfolio problems, risks, and uncertainties and provide a much more complete understanding of the complexities.

A study into the identification of early warning signals in complex projects (Williams et al., 2012) reported that project leaders are, in general, not very good at picking up early warning signs; often, they are conveniently overlooked or simply not envisaged. Early warning signs can be "*hard*" – measurable and based on numbers and progress – and soft – people issues; indeed, many early project problems are "*soft*" indicators, for example, attitudes and values which are harder to measure. "*Hard*" issues are identified typically through formal assessments, and reviews and "*soft*" issues are identified through gut feeling–based assessment.

Williams et al. (2012) asserted that early warning signs are possible to identify but are often not acted upon due to time pressures, a tendency to optimism ("*it will all be fine in the end*"), little motivation to scan for warning signs, and political pressure to stick to a given solution. Formal project assessments and reviews have an implicit focus on "*hard*" issues (e.g. risks, progress, finances) but can be "*blind*" to softer issues, which are just as important. The portfolio leader should seek patterns in technical results, process results, and people's behaviours – linking these together into patterns may provide an indicator that something needs to change.

The portfolio leader has the best possible overview and so is in the ideal position to detect early warning signs. For the portfolio leader, the focus should be on noticing early deviations, detecting weak signals, using intuition, management by walking about, and taking appropriate actions. Detecting a warning sign only contributes to project success if the portfolio leader makes an intervention as a result; otherwise, there is no point. Making a project intervention on the basis of an early warning sign takes experience, knowledge, and judgement – it also requires courage. To be of any use, an intervention must happen early enough to avoid the potential consequences, and this means while the warning sign is still imprecise, waiting for a definitive signal probably may mean the interventions are already too late.

Relating

Building and maintaining trusted relationships is a vital capability for portfolio leaders. Probing requires the use of a questioning style by the portfolio leader and the team members. This style encourages full participation and teamwork and helps to surface problems, risks, and uncertainties that may otherwise remain hidden. It requires trust throughout the portfolio organisation, which can only be achieved through a focus on building strong relationships.

The portfolio leader must support the project and program leaders by managing stakeholders that are not available to them. It is expected that the portfolio leader will build a network of trusted confidants inside and outside the organisation.

The portfolio leader is, in fact, a "*leader of leaders*" and should mentor and coach but should also challenge their behaviours and performance. They should consistently encourage appropriate behaviours of openness, honesty, and collaboration within the team. The portfolio leader should try to ensure that their teams contain people with maximum diversity of thought, as this results in new ideas. By the nature of the role of the portfolio leader, they come at problems from a longer-term viewpoint, giving advice and guiding project leaders to solve their own problems.

Portfolio leaders can foster a culture of honesty and improve portfolio delivery by communicating a commitment to fostering more candid dialogue, lowering the hurdle for speaking up, and ensuring that there are no negative repercussions for doing so – to make it easy and make it safe to overcome a "*crisis of silence*" (Grenny et al., 2007) and to "*speak truth to power*". Speaking up and challenging others, including senior leadership, should be encouraged and supported by the underlying culture, a "*culture of honesty*", of the organisation. Speaking candidly about concerns related to the project should not be "*career-limiting*"; otherwise, the organisation is setting itself up to fail.

Inventing

The inventing capability is very important at the early stages of designing and developing the portfolio organisation, systems, processes, and culture. We recommend a flat organisation structure, that is, all project leaders reporting directly to the portfolio leader. This will aid alertness and agility within the portfolio. Systems and processes should be tailored to support the culture. For example, an appropriate project control system should be implemented to minimise structural complexity.

A learning and development plan should also be implemented to educate team members in understanding and managing complexity and, in particular, stakeholder management to minimise sociopolitical complexity. The ability to ask questions is a further capability that can be taught in order to reduce emergent complexity.

Acumen

Acumen comes with experience of applying the other portfolio leadership capabilities with time – the more experience of managing a portfolio, the more likely one is to increase acumen. If this experience is lacking in the portfolio leader, the sponsor may be able to bring their experience and acumen to help the portfolio leader. As acumen improves, judgement and decision-making will improve.

The key to responding in an alert culture is speed. To respond with speed, you need confidence in your decision-making. Confidence comes with experience, and experience results in acumen. It is important to reflect on the consequences of action, including experimental action. We know that patterns can emerge in complex systems, but it is important to know when you have enough information to act. However, with quick decisions, some may not be the right ones, and therefore the overall portfolio organisation should be set up to accept mistakes. It is very important that the culture accepts a level of failure, in that failure should be a means of learning for the future – if decisions made are wrong, iterate and try again.

Thus, the culture should be experimental and encourage trying new ways of doing things – tailoring processes, using new tools, allowing inexperienced people to take responsibility. However, this should be done in a safe and controlled environment.

Issues, risks, and uncertainties should be discussed as much as possible. Only by doing this will early warning signs surface. The role of project leaders is to identify these, and the role of the portfolio leader is to identify those that impact multiple projects in the portfolio and take a bigger integrated view.

Conclusion

Delivery leadership is a seldom-discussed competence of portfolio managers but, in our view, is critical for the successful delivery of portfolios, particularly where they contain groups of complex projects, for example, product or service development projects arranged into portfolios. It is recommended that portfolio leaders are encouraged to develop capabilities – both in themselves and their team – in line with the portfolio leadership capabilities model and to understand project complexity and the responses needed to lead and manage the resulting portfolio complexity.

References

Ancona D., Malone T, Orlikowski W. & Senge P. (2007) In praise of the incomplete leader. *Harvard Business Review* 85(2), 92–100.

Association for Project Management. (2019) *APM Body of Knowledge.* Seventh Edition. Princes Risborough, APM.

Browning T. & Ramasesh R. (2015) Reducing unwelcome surprises in project management. *MIT Sloan Management Review* 2015, 53–62.

Forsyth S. & Gavin C. (2017) Developing 'third wave' project leaders. *Project Journal* 2017, 54–55.

Geraldi J., Maylor H. & Williams T. (2011) Now, let's make it really complex (complicated): A systematic review of the complexities of projects. *International Journal of Operations and Production Management* 31(9), 966–990.

Grenny J., Maxfield D. & Shimberg A. (2007) How project leaders can overcome the crisis of silence. *MIT Sloan Management Review* 48(4), 46–52.

Haji-Kazemi S., Andersen B. & Krane H. (2013) A review on possible approaches for detecting early warning signs in projects. *Project Management Journal* 44, 55–69.

Merrow E. (2011) *Industrial Megaprojects*. Wiley.

Merrow E. & Nandurdikar N. (2018) *Leading Complex Projects: A Data – Driven Approach to Mastering the Human Side of Project Management*. Wiley.

Morris P. (1994) *The Management of Projects*. Thomas Telford.

Morris P. (2009) Implementing strategy through project management: The importance of managing the project front-end. in Williams T., Samset K. & Sunnevaag K. *Making Essential Choices with Scant Information*. London: Palgrave Macmillan.

Morris P. (2013) *Reconstructing Project Management*. Wiley-Blackwell.

Nixon P., Harrington M. & Parker D. (2012) Leadership performance is significant to project success or failure: A critical analysis. *International Journal of Productivity and Performance Management* 61(2), 204–216.

PMI. (2017) *A Guide to the Project Management Body of Knowledge (PMBOK Guide)*. Sixth Edition. Newtown Square: Project Management Institute.

Snowden D. & Boone M. (2007) A leader's framework to decision making. *Harvard Business Review* 85(11), 68–76.

Turner J. & Müller R. (2005) The project manager's leadership style as a success factor on projects: A literature review. *Project Management Journal* 36(2), 49–61.

Williams T., Klakegg O., Walker D., Andersen B. & Magnussen O. (2012) Identifying and acting on early warning signs in complex projects. *Project Management Journal* 43, 37–53.

Yang L., Huang C. & Wu K. (2011) The association among project manager's leadership style, teamwork and project success. *International Journal of Project Management* 29(3), 258–267.

19 Managers' roles in strategic portfolio management

Miia Martinsuo and Lauri Vuorinen

Introduction

This chapter explores the involvement of managers in implementing organisational strategic portfolio management (SPM), especially in highly innovative contexts. There is, firstly, an introduction of the current knowledge of managers' practices and roles in SPM. The main part of the chapter then reports on recent research that investigates two illustrative examples of portfolios in highly innovative contexts and managers' involvement in portfolio management in these differing contexts (Yin, 2009). Both organisations are medium-sized firms, representing completely different industries (construction and software), different degrees of innovativeness of the portfolio (radical vs. incremental), and different ways of organising the management of the portfolio (less vs. more formal). Through a discussion of the cross-case findings, it is clear that context-specific management approaches to SPM are adopted, primarily related to the radicalness of the innovations and formalisation of routines reflected in the managers' portfolio management practice.

This chapter focuses on portfolio management in innovation, that is, selecting, steering, and reconfiguring project portfolios that deal with innovation projects. It specifically concerns managers' involvement, that is, their ways to implement portfolio management based on their individual judgement and situation-specific information. Despite routines and structures for project assessment, prioritisation and selection, resource allocation, and decision-making, possibly intended for (and orientated at) the formalisation of PPM practices and processes in organisations, these practices are seen to change due to the strategic insight and knowledgeability of the managers, their awareness of the past, imagination of the future, and responses to present circumstances.

In order to understand different approaches to portfolio management in highly innovative organisations, *managers' involvement in implementing* portfolio management is explored. While the typical attention is either on the portfolio managers or project managers, it is acknowledged that managers on various levels of the organisation may be differently involved in portfolio management, depending on the industry and context. Our focus is specifically on highly innovative contexts, where it is possible that the dynamic and evolving nature of the environment requires high degrees of management involvement. Also, the focus is on innovation project portfolios, to clarify that the firms in the empirical study also have other types of projects ongoing (i.e. a delivery project portfolio) in their project-based business.

The successful management of innovation project portfolios is of interest as a way of implementing the innovation strategy of the firm. Various good practices have been identified for successfully carrying out project portfolio management (PPM) (Cooper et al.,

DOI: 10.4324/9780367853129-22

1999; Dye & Pennypacker, 1999), and in general, firms are starting to design their PPM processes and routines using such good practices. The focus of this, however, tends to be on operative PPM, that is, assessing, prioritising, selecting, and coordinating projects, whereas strategic portfolio management (SPM), focusing on overseeing and governing the entire portfolio, from selection and steering to reconfiguration, tends to receive less attention.

Due to uncertainties and changes taking place in the portfolio content or context, it is typical that some flexibility is needed in managing portfolios (e.g. Korhonen et al., 2014; Martinsuo et al., 2014; Petit, 2012). Managers should use their strategic insight and capabilities to ensure successful portfolio management. Some studies indicate that managers and employees can improvise without warning, based on situation-specific information (Jerbrant & Karrbom Gustavsson, 2013), and can then enact sometimes other than planned practices (Blichfeldt & Eskerod, 2008; Christiansen & Varnes, 2008). Conceptual studies encourage further empirical research concerning the routines and actual practices in managing project portfolios (Clegg et al., 2018; Martinsuo, 2013; Martinsuo & Geraldi, 2020).

Routines and dynamics in portfolio management

A significant amount of previous research has endeavoured to identify and test practices that can explain project portfolio success. Most of these practices are operational routines that are repeated, including multiple interdependent actions requiring multiple actors' involvement. For example, standards and bodies of knowledge list specific structures, including governance bodies and actor roles, techniques for assessing and planning projects, selecting and prioritising projects, and controlling and optimising the portfolio (PMI, 2008, 2016). Also, the early studies on PPM success have identified various techniques and processes for the purposes of driving PPM success, including the assessment and prioritisation of projects in line with strategy (Cooper et al., 1999; Dye & Pennypacker, 1999).

Many studies, however, have pointed out that it is not specific techniques as such that explain success but rather the way in which managers use these techniques. For example, Jonas et al. (2013) draw attention to management quality as the nature of the processes in which the techniques are applied. Similarly, Unger et al. (2012a, 2012 b) use the concept of PPM quality as an antecedent to success, with influence from various project management office–related routines. Martinsuo and Lehtonen (2007) cover goal setting, availability of information, and systematic decision-making as antecedents of portfolio management efficiency – not the specific techniques used for them. Kopmann et al. (2017) report the relevance of anticipation of the future in the form of emergent strategies as part of PPM.

Studies have increasingly paid attention to uncertainties and how managers deal with uncertainties and changes, possibly due to the dynamic, evolving contexts typical to innovation portfolios. For example, Petit (2012) and Petit and Hobbs (2010) portray PPM as a dynamic capability that deals with how managers take the uncertain environment into account (also Killen & Hunt, 2010). This attention to uncertainties is reflected also on how managers interpret the environment (Martinsuo et al., 2014), control the project portfolios (Korhonen et al., 2014), and combine evidence, power, and opinions in the decision processes (Kester et al., 2011, 2014). These previous studies draw attention to what managers actually do (instead of describing the official portfolio management approach) when implementing PPM.

In our view, routine-centric PPM is operational, whereas strategic portfolio management (SPM) deals specifically with governing the portfolio as a whole, in relation to its context (Martinsuo, 2013; Martinsuo & Geraldi, 2020): selecting its composition, steering and monitoring its content and relation with strategy, and reconfiguring it as a possible response to, or anticipation of, uncertainty in the environment. Strategic portfolio management is particularly sensitive to how managers act and relate to the dynamic business environment.

Managers' involvement in strategic portfolio management

Various actors have a role in PPM and SPM, ranging from senior managers and portfolio owners to coordinators, controllers, project managers, and employees. The focus here is on managers at the different levels of the organisation. Some specific studies have already covered managers' roles and practices in PPM, although not necessarily explicitly focusing on innovation projects or SPM.

Table 19.1 summarises the key findings. Having a dominantly qualitative orientation, previous research significantly draws attention to what roles and dispositions managers have in PPM (Korhonen et al., 2014; McNally et al., 2009), what managers actually do, instead of what they ought to do (Blichfeldt & Eskerod, 2008; Christiansen & Varnes, 2008), and the variety of decision-making processes they can use in PPM (Kester et al., 2009; 2011). Also, the project personnel's viewpoint has been covered in more recent research, indicating their active role in multi-project situations (Karrbom Gustavsson, 2016; Vuorinen & Martinsuo, 2018; Näsänen & Vanharanta, 2016).

The analysis of previous research in Table 19.1 reveals that managers differ from each other in many ways, affecting how they face uncertainties and demands from the environment and how they implement strategic portfolio management in their organisation. Differences exist particularly in the following domains:

- Managers' personal traits, previous experience, and behavioural and leadership styles.
- Managers' sensemaking processes, both within the organisation and in relation to the business environment.
- Managers' strategies to cope with uncertainty and demands of each situation (also the willingness to control uncertainty).
- Managers' collaboration with each other and employees, in justifying and making decisions.
- Managers' use of evidence and information in making judgements.

With this background, our exploration with portfolio management in innovative organisations started with the interest to understand how the organisations differ from each other in the managers' involvement in implementing portfolio management and what contextual and portfolio issues might explain such differences (Teller & Kock, 2013; Teller et al., 2012).

Two highly innovative organisations with strategic portfolios

This research has focused on highly innovative, growth-orientated organisations that represent a dynamic context and acknowledged innovativeness in their industry. Medium-sized organisations were selected in order to focus on the firms' innovation

Table 19.1 Examples of previous research drawing attention to managers' involvement in PPM

Reference	*Data and method*	*Key findings on PPM routines and managers' roles*
Blichfeldt & Eskerod, 2008	Qualitative interview-based study with 30 companies in different industries and project types.	Managers may be selective in including projects in the official (enacted) portfolio, but also target resources to projects outside of it.
Christiansen & Varnes, 2008	Qualitative, multi-method, single-case study in one organisation.	Official PPM rules are only partly followed; decision-making in meetings is affected by the formal system and rules, observations of others, the organisational context, and organisational learning. Signals from top management influence the decision-makers' interpretations of the organisational context and frame the decision-making.
Karrbom Gustavsson, 2016	Interview study in three project-based organisations.	Employees involved in multiple parallel projects experienced overload and used multiple (unofficial) strategies to cope with the situation, including the use of boundary objects, informal communication, and other mechanisms that supported sensemaking.
Kester et al., 2009	Qualitative interview study in 11 multinational firms.	Identified three genres of portfolio management decision-making at the level of the firm: formalist-reactive, intuitive, and integrative. Firms using the intuitive genre rely on flexibility, qualitative assessment criteria, and decision-makers' experience and expertise.
Kester et al., 2011	Qualitative multiple-case study, four companies in different industries.	Identified three portfolio decision-making processes: evidence-based, power-based, and opinion-based, each with their practices and consequences. Particularly power-based and opinion-based processes rely on individuals' and groups' judgement (instead of objective criteria).
Korhonen et al., 2014	Qualitative multiple-case study, six companies in machine manufacturing.	Managers involved in PPM have different roles and experience the sources of uncertainties differently. They also engage in different control activities to manage the uncertainties.
McNally et al., 2009	Qualitative embedded single case study with multiple methods in three business units of one company.	Explored managers' dispositional traits (change resistance, ambiguity tolerance, analytic cognitive style, and leadership style) and their connection with portfolio management performance, offered propositions for further testing.
Vuorinen & Martinsuo, 2018	Qualitative two-case study in multi-project programs, two different industries.	Investigated the approaches to integration within multi-project programs and towards the parent organisation. Discovered the centrality of program actors' agency in preparing for and implementing the integration practices, including program managers, project managers, employees, and parent organisation.

Table 19.2 Background information of the case companies

	ConstructionCo	*SoftwareCo*
Industry and business type	Construction and related services and software Project-based	Software solutions Project-based
Net sales 2017	> 200 MEUR	> 50 MEUR
No. of employees	> 250	> 400
Radicalness of innovations in projects	Higher (new business openings and business models)	Moderate (traditional product development)
Number of simultaneous projects	Lower	Higher
Resources for innovation projects	Fewer resources dedicated specifically to innovation projects	More dedicated resources and experience for innovation projects
Formality of innovation project portfolio management	Less formal; processes are vaguely defined or being defined	More formal; structured and formally defined processes in use

activities holistically, through the strategic innovation project portfolio (i.e. one innovation portfolio per firm). Two firms representing different industries were chosen to enable cross-case comparison; they are here called ConstructionCo and SoftwareCo. Both are project-based organisations that carry out project business and implement their innovation activities as projects and, thereby, would have an active innovation project portfolio. Some background information of the firms and their innovation portfolios is presented in Table 19.2. Both companies have grown fairly fast and continue to grow and hire new talents, and they have recently developed innovative solutions and innovation strategies for the future.

ConstructionCo offers solutions, services, and software for the construction industry, both in commercial construction and private sector (housing and renovations). Their approach is very innovative as they perceive construction "as a service" instead of "assembly", and they strive for leadership in service and software business in the construction industry. The company has received external funding for their innovation activities and consider innovation as a strategic process. The business is divided into three main areas: construction, services, and smart solutions. ConstructionCo wants to be perceived as visionary in the very conservative construction industry, and they have established an innovation-orientated strategy, reflected also in the definition of related management roles.

SoftwareCo sells, develops, and implements software for other firms and organisations in a business-to-business market. They have a very innovative core product that they use for tailoring and versioning for different uses. The company has various technology partners with whom they develop compatible software solutions. They also offer technical support, consultancy services, and training related to their solutions. The company's core product was a major innovation when it was first released, and the product is still considered innovative compared to their competitors. SoftwareCo released a new, innovative artificial intelligence–based feature to their core product recently. The company has received several awards and recognitions for being innovative and visionary in their field. It is also among the fastest-growing European companies in its industry.

Both companies' innovativeness (with respect to the industry) is evident in the companies' external communication (e.g. web pages and marketing). They promote an open atmosphere and culture, for example, by encouraging development ideas from all personnel and using a flat organisational structure. The main differences between the companies relates to the nature of the innovation project portfolio (more radical business model innovation vs. more incremental product development) and the formalisation of the innovation process (under development vs. more established and formalised).

Data was collected through interviews with business developers or leaders, chief innovation and technology officers, development managers and experts, and R&D directors. In analysing the interview data, dominant, recurring practices specific to the two case firms were sought, particularly concerning the involvement of managers in the strategic goal setting and selection of the portfolio and steering and monitoring its status over time. The two cases show quite different firm-specific patterns in these issues, so each case narrative is reported separately before concluding with a cross-case comparison on the potential explanations for the similarities and differences.

ConstructionCo: managers' hands-on involvement in portfolio management

ConstructionCo's innovation projects include both more radical innovations (e.g. new business models) and incremental development of the core business (i.e. the construction projects). The research focus was on the more radical innovations of new business openings.

An overarching characteristic of managing the innovation project portfolio at ConstructionCo is the strong involvement of the company's top management. The important decisions are made, and the innovation portfolio is monitored and steered, by the top management of the firm. The high involvement of top management was justified by the need to enable an overall understanding of the innovation project portfolio. As interviewees described:

> "In our company, the top management is strongly involved in the daily business. They communicate very directly what should be done and where the focus should be."
>
> "All the innovation projects are managed as one project portfolio – the goal is that at least the top management would be aware of what is happening in our company [regarding innovation projects]. That is why all the innovation projects are in one portfolio."

The hands-on involvement of top management is reflected in a fairly flexible and informal approach to innovation project portfolio selection. It has contrasting implications on the degree of autonomy for the innovation projects in the portfolio as well.

ConstructionCo: strategy, goal setting, and innovation project portfolio selection

ConstructionCo does not have a separate innovation strategy. Instead, many aspects related to innovations are included in the company's business strategy. The business strategy is defined by the management group and the company board. The innovation project portfolio is built around three development programs whose goals are derived from the business strategy. The company has stated visions for the future of the industry that also guide the innovation work.

To communicate the strategy and the vision statements and to involve the personnel in the strategy work, several strategy events take place annually. Such events are organised separately for the different levels of the organisation, that is, the top management, management of the business units, and the company personnel.

Some of the innovation projects are clearly developed based on the business strategy. This implies setting goals and approving innovation projects that fulfil strategic objectives. The goals for such innovation projects are derived from the business strategy and from the goals of the development programs. As an interviewee described:

> "*We have defined our long-term vision in the company strategy. The company strategy defines what kind of innovations are pursued – so those kind of innovation initiatives are then specified into projects, resources are allocated to them, and so on . . .*"

However, this top-down approach does not apply to all innovation projects. ConstructionCo also very typically enables the initiation of innovation projects in a more bottom-up manner, based on the employees' creative ideas and proactiveness. In such events, the alignment of project goals and the business strategy is ensured on a more case-by-case basis. The following two quotations exemplify this issue:

> "We have had cases where someone has come up with an idea, developed that idea further to a concept and then got it approved as an innovation project."
>
> "I feel that the overall direction [for the innovations] comes from the strategy work, but the innovation projects themselves arise more bottom up. At least to my understanding, there isn't really a formal process for project-level goal setting."

The alignment of innovation project goals and strategy is verified as part of project planning and approval. Although the company is developing a more structured model for forming the portfolio, the current approach is seen as rather ad hoc and based on informal discussions and interpersonal relationships. Project initiation typically requires approval from a senior manager, but this approval may be based on interpersonal relationships and informal or unofficial influence. An interviewee exemplified this form of managerial involvement:

> "There aren't really formal or official decision-making processes. Instead, project approval is more to do with you knowing the right people and discussing with them. It is a bit of an unofficial channel for influence."

ConstructionCo: steering and reconfiguring the innovation project portfolio

The main actor for steering and decision-making at ConstructionCo is the management group. The management group includes representatives of the business units, the development programs, and top management. The management group monitors the status of the innovation project portfolio and the progress of the larger innovation projects and makes strategic portfolio decisions if reconfiguring is needed.

The life cycle of single innovation projects is divided into three phases: discovery phase, go-to-market phase, and scale-up phase. A dedicated project steering committee is formed at least for all the larger innovation projects. Routines typical to agile development are followed in the innovation projects, and project work is organised in two-week sprints.

Between those sprints, project progress is assessed either by the management group or the project steering committee. This kind of a reasonably structured process is followed in the larger or strategically more important projects; the practices are more varied and flexible in the smaller and more incremental innovation projects.

The top managers – especially the heads of the business units – have a significant role at the level of the single innovation projects, besides portfolio-level monitoring and steering. As ConstructionCo does not have dedicated resources for innovation work, business unit managers need to transfer resources for the innovation work from other duties, making resource allocation of high importance in portfolio steering.

The strong top management involvement has contrasting implications on innovation project portfolio management. On one hand, it implies a simple and low hierarchy for innovation portfolio management and gives managers good visibility to the innovation projects. On the other hand, it may restrict the autonomy of the project managers. Due to the informal and flexible approach, different top managers may sometimes drive projects in different directions. Two interviewees described the issues of contrasting steering and the reduced project autonomy:

> "At the portfolio level, there is a coherent understanding because it is managed by the top management, but at the level of the single innovation project, there can be contrasting steering from different directions. The head of the business unit and the innovation manager may have different goals for the project for example, so there are always two sides to the coin, you know [regarding the strong involvement of the top management]."
>
> "I feel that the top managers are maybe steering the projects at a too detailed level, while their steering should be a bit more strategic – what I have discussed with product owners or project managers, they would prefer a bit more autonomy and more guidance or support, instead of very detailed micromanagement."

SoftwareCo: managers' guidance for portfolio management through product road maps and innovation processes

The majority of SoftwareCo's innovation projects are related to software product development. The company has a software-based core offering, and the focus of innovation project portfolio management is mostly on managing the development of that offering, its versions, and customer-specific adaptations. As the offering is very specialised and innovative, patenting and intellectual property rights (IPRs) also have a significant role in SoftwareCo's innovation projects.

Managers have a significant role in managing the innovation project portfolio at SoftwareCo. In contrast to the strong involvement of top management at ConstructionCo, the role of middle managers, especially product managers, is more evident at SoftwareCo. The delegation of authority for selecting and steering the projects in the portfolio occurs through jointly agreed product road maps and a structured, formalised innovation process.

SoftwareCo: strategy, goal setting, and innovation (project) portfolio formation

Similar to ConstructionCo, SoftwareCo does not have an explicit innovation strategy, but the company's business strategy work led by the top management has direct implications on the innovation project portfolio. Besides guidance through business strategy, innovations are governed through product road maps for which the product development and product management functions have a focal role. Product road maps specify the technologies and applications featured in product versions, as well as the timing, order, and priorities of their development. The head of R&D and product managers collaborate to define and plan these road maps, and they also involve personnel in road mapping. An interviewee described these two levels of strategic planning:

> "Of course, if we are talking about the strategic priorities of the whole company, they are not decided by a single product manager [but the top management of the company, instead]."
>
> "The product manager, or the product management function, is responsible for a product and the product road map – so the product manager has to participate in and facilitate all of those discussions [with different stakeholders] to create the understanding for the future."

SoftwareCo has a more structured approach for generating innovation project ideas and selecting the portfolio than ConstructionCo. The company has a specific information system (idea system) for collecting and storing the project ideas. They also organise regular events for idea generation (e.g. an innovation hunt). These systems and events are supported by the top management – *"the top management enables or approves these kinds of events"* – and are typically facilitated by the R&D unit (e.g. the product managers). Software developers are also encouraged to use some of their work time for developing their favourite ideas towards potential new innovation projects.

An important characteristic of the portfolio formation and selection in SoftwareCo is the variety of different sources and the high number of innovation project ideas. Consequently, there is a need to analyse, prioritise, and develop further project ideas when managing the product road maps. The project ideas are handled systematically and regularly by the product managers:

> "It is the responsibility of the product managers to manage the idea system, in order to include development ideas in the product road map. We have the difficulty that there are the development tasks in the product road map, there are also customer requests and we might have direct steering from the top management . . . all of this should be balanced in the product road map."

SoftwareCo: steering and reconfiguring the innovation project portfolio

Among top managers, the steering of the innovation project portfolio involves the chief technology officer (CTO), who handles the issues related to patents and IPRs, and the head of R&D, who focuses on the key products and technologies. While the senior managers are in charge of the key processes for prioritising and steering the innovation projects in the portfolio, the practical prioritisation and project setting is delegated to product managers. This, as well as the bottom-up approach to new idea generation, implies that reconfiguring the portfolio occurs as part of product management. Two interviewees described the distribution of responsibilities:

> "The head of R&D does, of course, facilitate the innovation project work in some way but, on the other hand, it is the product management and the product managers who are responsible for those project prioritisation decisions."

> "I'd say that the product manager plans the features of upcoming releases, the head of R&D is responsible for the overall processes and the top management of the company defines the overall strategy."

Single innovation projects and day-to-day innovation work follow an agile development process (with some modifications), that is, the product managers and project managers lead work scheduling and task allocation, innovation work is planned for two-week sprints, and progress is evaluated, with planning for the next sprint taking place between the sprints.

Some additional guidance and steering take place from the perspective of patents and IPRs. Such innovation projects that involve patenting follow a specific process with the following phases: collection of project ideas, evaluation of project idea, and filing of the patent applications. Specific evaluation routines are in place for these kinds of processes, with CTO as the leader and potential external firms as partners. An interviewee described this process as follows:

> "If people come up with good innovative ideas, we encourage people to submit patent ideas [in an internal IT system]. The patent ideas follow the IPR process, where a panel evaluates the ideas and decides whether a patent application should be filed or not. If a positive decision is made, an external partner is used for filing the official patent application and for managing the communication with the relevant authorities."

Cross-case findings

The findings show two quite-different approaches to managers' roles and activities in selecting and steering innovation portfolios. While both companies are innovative and successful in their own industries, they differ in the radicalness of the innovations, the scope of the innovation portfolio together with its dedicated resources (Engwall & Jerbrant, 2003), and the formality of PPM routines and processes. Even if various PPM frameworks advocate the use of formalised routines (Cooper et al., 1999; Dye & Pennypacker, 1999; PMI, 2008, 2016), it is assumed and shown that innovative contexts can also allow a flexible approach to implementing such routines. Both case firms had similar kinds of PPM routines – including those regarding idea development, decision-making, prioritisation and resource allocation, and the agile development process – but they differed in how managers handled the strategic alignment and selection of the portfolio and its steering and reconfiguration as part of strategic portfolio management. Table 19.3 summarises the key differences in the key aspects of strategic portfolio management across the two companies.

One of the key differences dealt with the division of work across management levels. ConstructionCo, with a smaller, more radical business-transforming innovation portfolio and a less-formal approach in its PPM, relied on stronger, hands-on involvement from top management in portfolio management. SoftwareCo, with a larger but incremental product innovation portfolio, had established formal processes for PPM and, thereby, had built managerial guidance into the product road map and innovation process, delegating much of portfolio selection and steering to lower levels within the organisation. These two innovation portfolios may be selective examples of innovative firms in their industry, but their specific approaches illustrate the potential variety of managers' involvement in implementing strategic portfolio management and leading strategic portfolios.

Table 19.3 Comparison of managers' involvement in SPM between the two companies

	ConstructionCo	*SoftwareCo*
Strategy, goal setting, and innovation project portfolio selection	Top management has a focal role in project approval and project goal setting.	Top management sets the overall direction, but managers of R&D lead road mapping and thereby guide portfolio selection.
	The approaches to project approval are more informal.	There are more formal processes in place for project idea generation.
	Resource allocation is a critical task due to the limited dedicated resources and personnel's other work priorities.	Project prioritisation is a continuous task of product management.
Steering and reconfiguring the innovation project portfolio	Top management is strongly involved in managing the innovation project portfolio. They are involved even in single (larger) innovation projects.	Product road maps and the agile project management framework guide the innovation projects.
	The strong involvement of managers ensures visibility to the innovation project portfolio, but it might jeopardise project autonomy.	Product management is in charge of steering the innovation portfolio, together with the project managers.
	Reconfiguration based on monitoring.	Bottom-up reconfiguration.

Conclusion

The findings have some implications for portfolio management practitioners. Firstly, the research attempts to draw attention to portfolio management specifically in the form of strategising, setting goals for, steering, and reconfiguring the project portfolio, as a contrast to more operative-level PPM that centres on assessing, prioritising, selecting, and coordinating projects in the portfolio. Strategic portfolio management implies that top management necessarily should be involved, as the project portfolio is expected to fulfil and renew the business strategy of the firm. Secondly, the findings emphasise the necessity to align the managers' involvement in portfolio management with the requirements of the organisational context and culture. Specifically, this study proposes the nature of the innovation portfolios (radicalness, resource dedication, and formalisation of routines) as a factor which should be evaluated when the managers' responsibilities and tasks are planned in portfolio management.

Thirdly, when involved in strategic portfolio management, companies should prepare for a change in the responsibilities and tasks particularly between top management, middle management, and project-level actors when changes take place in the portfolio context. If the degree of radicalness, resource availability, and formalisation in the innovation portfolio change, so should the managers' involvement. As SPM is expected to guide and give direction to more operative-level PPM, their interplay should be explored further, by not studying just managers but also other actors' involvement and exploring the purposive use of routines and improvisation in different portfolio circumstances.

Acknowledgements

We would like to thank the case study companies for offering access to their innovation portfolios and businesses, and Ida Levón for collecting the data. We gratefully acknowledge the financial support of Tampere University of Technology Support Foundation and Yrjö and Senja Koivunen Foundation. The inspiration for this study stems from our collaboration with Professor Catherine Killen at the University of Technology Sydney. We express our warmest appreciation for her insight and support before and during this study.

References

Blichfeldt B. & Eskerod P. (2008) Project portfolio management – there's more to it than what management enacts. *International Journal of Project Management* 26, 357–365.

Christiansen J. & Varnes C. (2008) From models to practice: Decision making at portfolio meetings. *International Journal of Quality and Reliability Management* 25(1), 87–101.

Clegg S., Killen C., Biesenthal C. & Shankaran S. (2018) Practices, projects and portfolios: Current research trends and new directions. *International Journal of Project Management* 36, 762–772.

Cooper R., Edgett S. & Kleinschmidt E. (1999) New product portfolio management: Practices and performance. *Journal of Product Innovation Management* 16(4), 333–351.

Dye L. & Pennypacker J. (1999) *Project Portfolio Management. Selecting and Priortising Projects for Competitive Advantage.* Center for Business Practices.

Engwall M. & Jerbrant A. (2003) The resource allocation syndrome: The prime challenge of multi-project management? *International Journal of Project Management* 21(6), 403–409.

Jerbrant A. & Karrbom Gustavsson T. (2013) Managing project portfolios: Balancing flexibility and structure by improvising. *International Journal of Managing Projects in Business.* 6, 152–172.

Jonas D., Kock A. & Gemünden H. (2013) Predicting project portfolio success by measuring management quality – A longitudinal study. *IEEE Transactions on Engineering Management* 60(2), 215–226.

Karrbom Gustavsson T. (2016) Organizing to avoid project overload: The use and risks of narrowing strategies in multi-project practice. *International Journal of Project Management* 34, 94–101.

Kester L., Griffin A., Hultink E. & Lauche K. (2011) Exploring portfolio decision-making processes. *Journal of Product Innovation Management* 28(5), 641–661.

Kester L., Hultink E. & Griffin A. (2014) An empirical investigation of the antecedents and outcomes of NPD portfolio success. *Journal of Product Innovation Management* 31(6), 1199–1213.

Kester L., Hultink E. & Lauche K. (2009) Portfolio decision-making genres: A case study. *Journal of Engineering and Technology Management* 26(4), 327–341.

Killen C. & Hunt R. (2010) Dynamic capability through project portfolio management in service and manufacturing industries. *International Journal of Managing Projects in Business* 3(1), 157–169.

Kopmann J., Kock A., Killen C. & Gemünden H. (2017) The role of project portfolio management in fostering both deliberate and emergent strategy. *International Journal of Project Management* 35, 557–570.

Korhonen T., Laine T. & Martinsuo M. (2014) Management control of project portfolio uncertainty: A managerial role perspective. *Project Management Journal* 45(1), 21–37.

Martinsuo M. (2013) Project portfolio management in practice and in context. *International Journal of Project Management* 31(6), 794–803.

Martinsuo M. & Geraldi J. (2020) The management of project portfolios: Relationships of project portfolios with their contexts. *International Journal of Project Management* 38(7), 441–453.

Martinsuo M., Korhonen T. & Laine T. (2014) Identifying, framing and managing uncertainties in project portfolios. *International Journal of Project Management* 32(5), 732–746.

Martinsuo M. & Lehtonen P. (2007) Role of single-project management in achieving portfolio management efficiency. *International Journal of Project Management* 25(1), 56–65.

McNally R., Durmusoglu S., Calantone R. & Harmancioglu N. (2009) Exploring new product portfolio management decisions: The role of managers' dispositional traits. *Industrial Marketing Management* 38, 127–143.

Näsänen J. & Vanharanta O. (2016) Program group's discursive construction of context: A means to legitimize buck-passing. *International Journal of Project Management* 34, 1672–1686.

Petit Y. (2012) Project portfolios in dynamic environments: Organizing for uncertainty. *International Journal of Project Management* 30(5), 539–553.

Petit Y. & Hobbs B. (2010) Project portfolios in dynamic environments: Sources of uncertainty and sensing mechanisms. *Project Management Journal* 41(4), 46–58.

PMI Project Management Institute (2008) *The Standard for Portfolio Management.* Second Edition. Project Management Institute.

PMI Project Management Institute (2016) *Governance of Portfolios, Programs and Projects. A Practice Guide.* Project Management Institute.

Teller J. & Kock A. (2013) An empirical investigation on how portfolio risk management influences project portfolio success. *International Journal of Project Management* 31(6), 817–829.

Teller J., Unger B., Kock A. & Gemünden H. (2012) Formalization of project portfolio management: The moderating role of project portfolio complexity. *International Journal of Project Management* 30(5), 596–607.

Unger B., Gemünden H. & Aubry M. (2012a) The three roles of a project portfolio management office: their impact on portfolio management execution and success. *International Journal of Project Management* 30(5), 608–620.

Unger B., Kock A., Gemünden H. & Jonas D. (2012b) Enforcing strategic fit of project portfolios by project termination: An empirical study on senior management involvement. *International Journal of Project Management* 30(6), 675–685.

Vuorinen L. & Martinsuo M. (2018) Program integration in multi-project change programs: Agency in integration practice. *International Journal of Project Management* 36(4), 583–599.

Yin R. (2009) *Case Study Research: Design and Methods.* Sage Publications.

20 Enabling adoption of portfolio management

A practitioner's perspective

Donnie MacNicol and Adrian Dooley

Introduction

The previous chapter identifies from academic research that the manager's role and level of active engagement in the portfolio can differ between organisations and begins to suggest that this can affect the success of the portfolio. This current chapter builds on this research, looking from a practitioner's perspective at the effects of personal style when managing or involved with a portfolio, considering in particular the role of the portfolio leader.

Any organisation that has more than one project or program has, by default, a portfolio (Lock & Wagner, 2019). It may seem an obvious statement that in realising the benefits of a formal project portfolio management approach, an organisation must firstly initiate a portfolio, by collecting and inducting their projects and programs into the portfolio structure, and then by governing or managing the portfolio, so that the portfolio continues to run smoothly, delivering benefits and value to the organisation that would not be achieved by simply managing projects and programs independently. Getting the buy-in to collecting and inducting is challenging for a range of reasons, including the active or passive resistance of senior managers, perhaps perceiving it as some form of threat, such as the need to relinquish power and control. Implementing portfolio management is a business change program in its own right. Change is something that involves a lot of people and has many opportunities to go wrong if we don't appreciate and accept the people involved, their individual motivations, and their personal needs.

People are also at the heart of effective portfolio management – how they perceive the value, adopt, and practice it. In this chapter the focus is on how people and, in particular, their personal styles and preferred ways of doing things have a direct and often significant impact on the success of portfolio management – from initiation through a change program and ongoing governance of portfolios. The chapter will also suggest some tools to help in understanding and working with those involved with portfolios more effectively.

The chapter will cover:

1. Key concepts around portfolio management (as promulgated by the Praxis framework) – to set the context of the philosophy behind the framework.
2. Distinguishing between people using personal styles.
3. How personal styles impact initiation of portfolio management.
4. How personal styles impact the practice of portfolio management.
5. Ways a portfolio manager can take advantage of these insights.

DOI: 10.4324/9780367853129-23

The substrate for this chapter is the widely available Praxis framework, on which both chapter authors have worked extensively. Praxis is a free framework for the management of projects, programs, and portfolios. It includes a body of knowledge, methodology, competency framework, and capability maturity model. The framework is supported by a knowledge base of resources and an encyclopaedia for P3M. The Praxis website is online and free at www.praxisframework.org. Praxis was used as the foundation to develop the thinking that is presented in this chapter, not only because of its quality and unified nature, but also because its use is covered by the terms of the Creative Commons Licence, meaning, that it has been incorporated into the website for the benefit of others and the profession as a whole.

Establishing the context: key concepts around portfolio management

It is useful initially to distinguish between two types of portfolios, as both have unique people challenges (Praxis, 2020; Lock & Wagner, 2019). Noting that an organisation may have multiple portfolios distinguished by environment, geography, or operating division creating a diverse range of people challenges unique to each portfolio. The need for a professional, centralised function that is aware of and actively managing these challenges is critical.

- A "*standard portfolio*" comprises a set of independent projects and/or programs. The main objective of co-ordinating a standard portfolio is to ensure that the component projects and programs are managed in a consistently effective way. From a people perspective, this can be a challenge, as there is likely to be a very diverse group of people involved. An example would be a construction company that is performing a number of independent projects, all for different clients. This type of portfolio is seen as synonymous with a tactical portfolio.
- A "*structured portfolio*" comprises a set of projects and/or programs that are united by a set of common strategic objectives. Structured portfolios will have many more interrelationships between the component projects and programs, and governance must therefore be more rigorous – something that people may or may not welcome. An example would be an organisation that repeatedly implements the objectives of its strategic planning cycle through a rolling portfolio life cycle. To be effective, this type of portfolio requires a high level of collaboration and coordination, and therefore, the portfolio manager has a need to focus on engaging key stakeholders from the outset to ensure it is a success. This type of portfolio is seen as synonymous with a strategic portfolio.

It is also helpful to consider ways of presenting the portfolio life cycle. One example, in addition to those discussed in Section II, is shown in Figure 20.1 (Praxis, 2020). This life cycle shows a closure, but in reality, most portfolios only evolve and change with time, meaning, that over an extended time period, a large diverse group of people will most likely be directly or indirectly involved and impacted by portfolio management.

While the life cycle represents the fundamental structure of a portfolio, a set of processes are also useful in managing the portfolio throughout its life cycle. Once again, the process model in Figure 20.2 is taken from the Praxis framework. This chapter will therefore broadly focus on the two elements of this process model and the impact that personal styles have on each, although firstly, the discussion returns to focus on the people aspects, in discussing a simple model for distinguishing between broad personal styles.

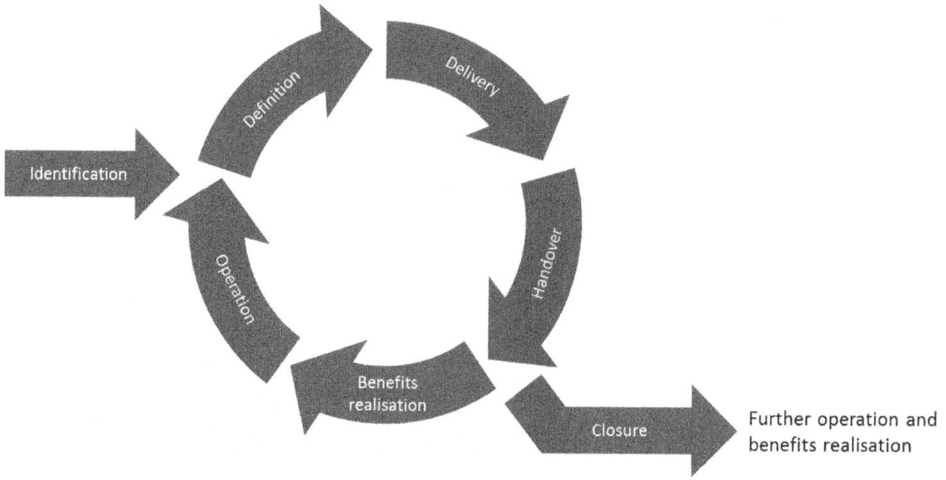

Figure 20.1 Portfolio life cycle (Praxis, 2020).

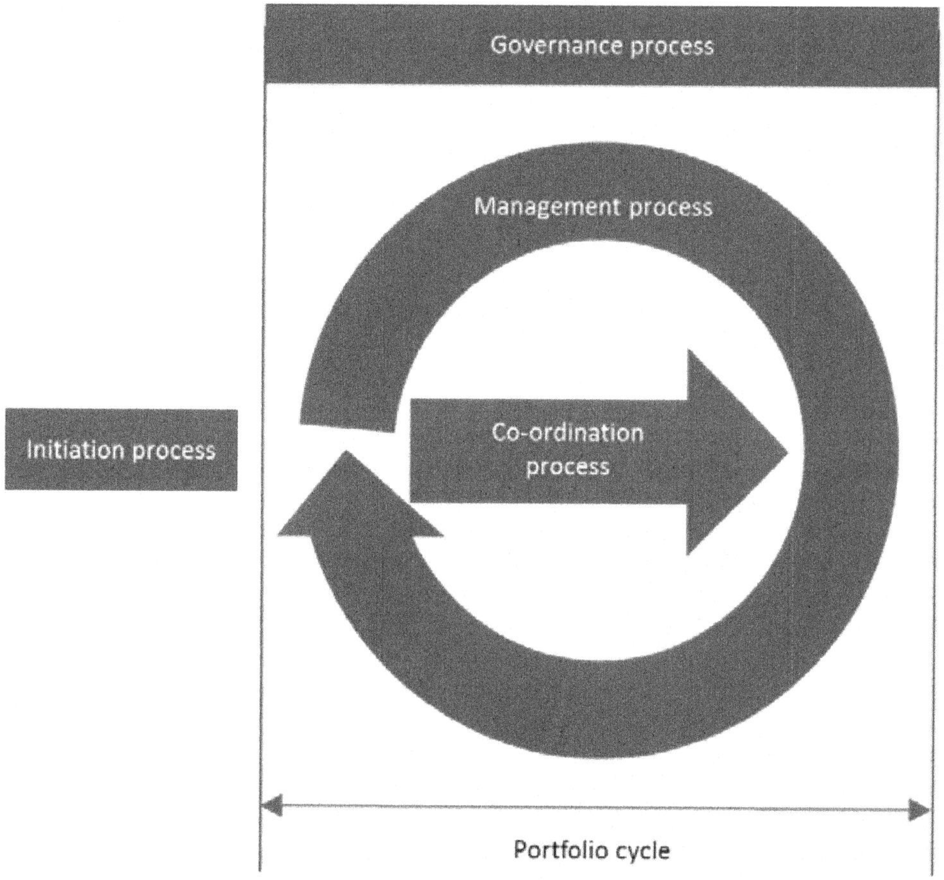

Figure 20.2 Portfolio management processes (Praxis, 2020).

1. The initiation of the portfolio – and hence the initiation of formal portfolio management.
2. The management process – which most people relate to as "being" portfolio management, although intuitively it requires far more than simply managing.

How to distinguish between people using personal styles

To establish the impact that people have on portfolio management, it is useful to firstly identify some way of distinguishing between different personal styles. Distinguishing between people can be done in many different ways using one of hundreds of personal characteristics that go into making us an individual. Simple tools are often used to help us objectify these differences (Lock & Wagner, 2019).

Some people, in applying these tools, identify with the idea that they are being pigeonholed into a particular type of behaviour. However, such tools only indicate a preference and, ultimately, as such are only an indicator. The reality is that as individuals, we typically have a range of responses to a situation and that we work across a spectrum, often depending on the context. Being aware of your typical approach and being able to flex it as the situation and context requires is one of the key attributes of successful professionals and leaders.

The model chosen for discussion here is DISC, a public domain model of human behaviour developed by Marston (1928) and based on the work of Jung (1921), who created a groundbreaking model for human behaviour. Jung recognised that people can be divided into four main styles. Marston's work built upon Jung's and named the four main behavioural styles as D, I, S, and C:

- Dominance (D)
- Inducement (I)
- Submission (S)
- Compliance ©

Marston's work focused on psychological phenomena that could be both observed and measured, concentrating on the way the individual perceives their environment and the way they react to that perception. In the original work, the environment is classed as either favourable or antagonistic, and the individual's typical response as either passive or active, and when presented as axes, these reveal the four primary types of behaviour for D, I, S, and C. Marston himself never created an assessment instrument based on the DISC model. Clarke, an industrial psychologist, was the first person to create such an instrument (personality profile test) using Marston's theory (Merenda & Clarke, 1965). Since 1928, the model has evolved considerably, and a plethora of proprietary assessment tools have been developed. DISC is now, arguably, the most common psychometric profiling tool in use today. Some tools explicitly reference DISC, but even those that do not still have its underlying structure at their core.

The character traits are now more generally referred to as dominant, influential, steady, and conscientious – clearly retaining the DISC acronym, although many other terms have been applied. The two axes are also described in several different ways in modern versions of DISC. Figure 20.3 brings typical terminology together and shows how the four behaviours relate to the axes. Current approaches to the DISC model invariably colour-code the four quadrants – typically red, yellow, blue, and green. The attribution of colours to the four behaviours is not consistent, so when moving between products, it is always wise to focus on the letters D, I, S, C (when used) rather than the colours.

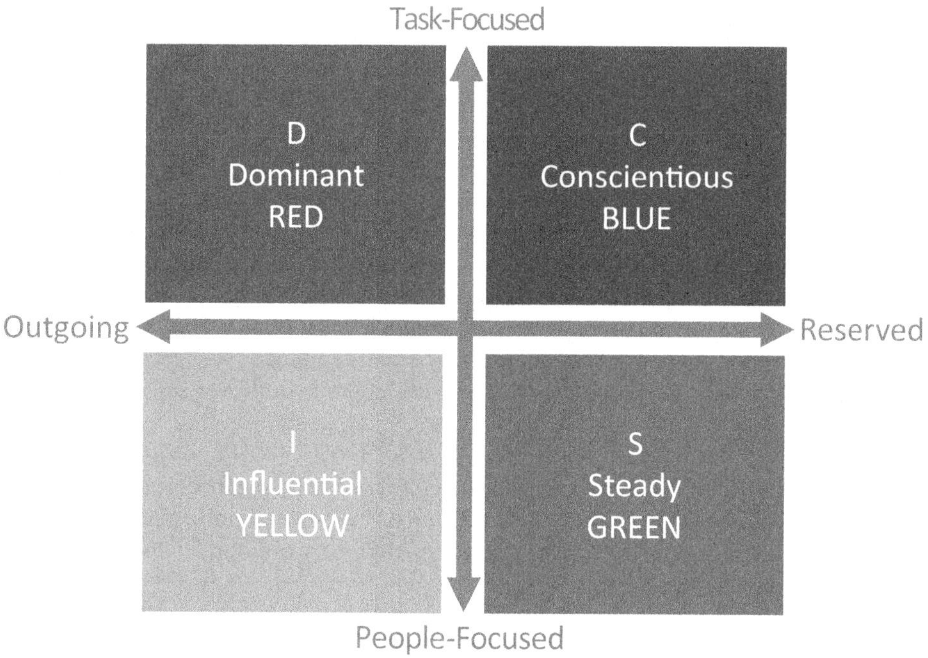

Figure 20.3 The four primary DISC types.

Source: Adapted from Jung (1921).

A description of each "typical" style is provided in the following passages using meetings as an example for the context. The context being provided only as a generic description to highlight the distinction. As meetings are, rightly or wrongly, a key element of initiating or delivering a portfolio, the description provides reference to this. It is important to note that people do not fit entirely into one quadrant or another. At different times and in different circumstances, it is possible to exhibit all four behaviours, but it is most likely that one will be strongly preferred and more common than the others.

- **Dominant**
  - *D*s are likely to be vocal and direct in meetings. They will assert the points they wish to discuss and are independent-minded. If they are the leader by seniority or title in the meeting, they will seek to cover points as quickly as possible and prefer decisions to be made without extended analysis or discussion.
  - *D*s are generally comfortable with conflict and can even thrive and may push harder than other more passive profiles to assert their will and take control of a meeting or situation. They may appear pushy and critical if conflict arises.
- **Influential**
  - *I*s are lively contributors to meetings, providing new ideas, and will look to keep an informal approach. If they are the leader by seniority or title in the meeting, they will be enthusiastic leaders and be open to a broad range of topics being discussed and different opinions and options explored.

- They are happy for the structure of the meetings to evolve and change as they see the value in other people's input. *I*s are generally comfortable with conflict and aware of the social dynamics of a situation and will look for alliances to be formed. They will seek to defuse conflict with humour and may appear opinionated and impulsive in such situations.

- **Steady**
  - *S*s are reserved and supportive and may not actively contribute but will be sympathetic to others' perspectives, as well as excellent active listeners. If they are the leader by seniority or title, they will seek meetings to be consistent and people to have delivered what they had committed to.
  - *S*s are generally uncomfortable with conflict, seeking out calm, steady environments, and will help resolve conflict by being diplomatic and generally supportive. They may appear indecisive and withdrawn if conflict arises.
- **Conscientious**
  - *C*s are reserved and reflective and therefore may not actively contribute to meetings until they believe they can add value or have a strong objection to a particular point. They prefer to work independently so would prefer individual rather than joint actions.
  - If they are the leader by seniority or title in the meeting, they will have prepared for the meeting and expect others to have done the same, demand a structure that is followed and discussions focused on objective discussions. *C*s are generally uncomfortable with conflict and will use logic to resolve the situation. They may appear withdrawn and slow to act if conflict arises.

Projects and programs in the portfolio (P3M) environment involve all kinds of people coming together to achieve stated objectives. It involves many processes, techniques, and plans that suggest how these processes and techniques should be applied. The issue for many P3M teams is that people with different behavioural preferences will perceive and implement the processes and techniques in several different ways. Naturally, we all tend to think that people will look at a plan or a situation and see it in the same way that we do. That is not the case. Members of a project or program team need to understand how colleagues and stakeholders will perceive even the fundamentals of project, program, and portfolio management in alternative ways. In doing so, individuals will become more productive, gain from the diversity within the team, and reduce conflict, in turn leading to better outcomes.

Understanding the preferred colour style of different people within a portfolio is important both in terms of what is delivered and in the way it is achieved. As an example: if the portfolio leader is a high red and a business executive who acts as a project sponsor to a number of projects is a high blue, the project leader should understand that their sponsor may see them as pushy and insensitive if all they focus on in their discussions is the delivery of outcomes, without any regard for the impact on people.

How personal styles impact the initiation of portfolio management

One aspect that is common to all best practice is that it assumes the content is all viewed by everyone in the same way. People perceive, design, adopt, deploy on the portfolio, practice, involve others, adapt, sustain its use, and learn from and share knowledge differently. Surprisingly, these differences are typically not taken into account in defining good practice and how it should be practised, with this being a potential area for improvement through future research. This part of the chapter will look at the initiation of portfolio management from a people perspective, considering, firstly, what is initiation in providing some context as to what adoption involves, followed by the different perceptions of the goals of portfolio management, discussing how personal bias might affect the adoption of portfolio management.

What is initiation?

Initiation is one of the most challenging aspects of the process due to the many people-related issues that must be addressed. Before considering these challenges, it is worth considering what is required for successful initiation and adoption by the organisation of portfolio management. There are four key steps to the initiation process within this critical stage (Praxis, 2020):

1. Establish a mandate.
2. Design the portfolio structure, including processes and team structure, by developing a proposal. (An authorisation request is required to move to the next stage.)
3. Prepare the portfolio, including establishing portfolio-wide standards.
4. Mobilise the team and adopt portfolio management.

Just like projects and programs, a portfolio will start with some form of mandate, which will give an individual the task of initiating a portfolio. Initiation is usually a one-off process. It represents the point at which the host organisation makes the decision to manage its projects and programs as a portfolio. Often, this is not a simple, one-off decision impacting the whole organisation, but rather, individual leaders deciding to implement portfolios within part of an organisation. This inevitably leads to complex stakeholder engagement and adoption issues. Broadly speaking, the decision to create a portfolio, or consider the projects and programs as part of a portfolio, has three purposes (Praxis, 2020):

1. To maximise the efficient use of available resources and avoid conflicts in resource requirements wherever possible.
2. To promote a consistent approach to project and program management that focuses on developing individual competency and organisational maturity.
3. To manage a set of projects and programs that collectively achieve a set of strategic objectives.

The person responsible for the design of the portfolio may be a board member or, suitably, senior manager who typically becomes the portfolio's sponsor. The "sponsor designate" will need to assemble a small team to investigate the way a portfolio should be constituted and governed to best suit the needs of the host organisation. The result will be a proposal that is submitted for authorisation to the issuer of the mandate. Portfolios are rarely created from scratch. It is more likely that an organisation having several projects and programs decides to collect these into a portfolio to improve management and/or focus on strategic objectives. If the proposal is accepted, then preparatory work is commenced. Depending upon the type of portfolio and its context, this could include multiple activities. Examples include:

- Identifying and documenting managerial processes and documentation.
- Setting up a competency framework.
- Reviewing existing projects and programs to capture good practice and baseline capability maturity.

It is highly unlikely that the preparation stage will start with a totally blank sheet of paper. The organisation will be managing projects and possibly programs, and these will already have processes, procedures, and documentation standards in place. All existing methods should be assessed, and the current best practice should form the basis of the new portfolio-wide standards. People may be very connected to the existing ways of working, have divergent opinions as to what is and is not best practice, and there will likely be many personal biases. Therefore, it is important to seek input, engage with all stakeholders, objectively assess as effectively as possible, and openly communicate why decisions have been made and the impact these may have.

The implementation of a portfolio will often require significant change management activities, and it is important that these are adequately resourced. If the systems and processes of portfolio management are to be embedded for long-term benefit, the existing organisation and the people in it will have to undergo change, not just in terms of physical infrastructure, but also in terms of attitudes and behaviour. The mobilisation stage may include aspects such as:

- Setting up clear governance structure and clearly identifying activities and roles and responsibilities.
- Initiating training programs and briefings that address the real needs.
- Amending recruitment and appointment processes to ensure that the people moving into the profession have the necessary skills.

Once initiated, how the portfolio will be managed in practice is then considered, with a management plan developed as part of the initiation phase.

The different perception of the goals of portfolio management

It is worth considering how people with different communication styles (using DISC) perceive the goals of portfolio management. The goals of portfolio management initiation according to Praxis (2020) are to:

- Decide what type of portfolio is required.
- Design the portfolio infrastructure.
- Obtain senior-level approval and commitment.
- Implement the portfolio.

When implementing these goals, the different colours tend to focus on different areas, have different priorities, and wish to see varying levels of justification, etc., keeping in mind that people are rarely solely "dominant" or "influential" as the attributes are only typical of each type. Note that the list of attributes in Table 20.1 are not intended to be exhaustive; they are indications of different attitudes that need to be taken into account when working with others, or to provide a fresh perspective. The attributes are written as definitive statements to reduce the use of "in most situations or cases", "primarily", or "has a preference for", etc. It should therefore also be noted that the most frequent preference is identified and, as such, is not an absolute characteristic.

Table 20.1 Typical personal attributes associated with the main DISC profiles

(C)onscientious	*(D)ominant*
BLUE	*RED*
Conscientious behaviour would typically propose or want to see:	**Dominant behaviour would typically propose or want to see:**
A rational explanation of what portfolio management is aiming to achieve.	Action taken quickly to complete the initiation process.
A consistent and systematic approach to initiating, governing, managing, and co-ordinating a portfolio.	A pragmatic view of the achievability of the perceived value.
A long-term commitment to maintaining and monitoring the portfolio.	They have maximum freedom to take action as they believe necessary to complete the initiation process.
Tangible and detailed financial benefits which are measurable and can be shown to be realised from the investment.	Resources being identified and committed to portfolio management in the short term.
Someone exhibiting conscientious behaviour would typically be perceived as:	**Someone exhibiting dominant behaviour would typically be perceived as:**
Increasing bureaucracy and delay when insisting on evidence and facts to justify the adoption of portfolio management.	Focusing on short term wins and the demonstration of value as quickly as possible;
Discounting intangible/non-financial benefits and relying solely on tangible/financial benefits for the justification.	Focused primarily on quantifiable/financial benefits of portfolio management and potentially dismissing those benefits that cannot be described in this way.
(S)teady **GREEN**	**(I)nfluential** **YELLOW**
Steady behaviour would typically propose or want to see:	**Influential behaviour would typically propose or want to see:**
Key individuals are given the opportunity to input and influence the decision.	Clear communication on the importance of portfolio management and its role in improving team motivation and thereby performance.
Equal consideration to intangible and non-financial benefits when considering the potential value.	Short-term responsibilities for portfolio management identified and clarified with people.
A clear understanding of the positive and negative impacts on people of introducing portfolio management.	Encourage early interaction within the team and with stakeholders as part of the adoption process.
Caution regarding how quickly portfolio management can be adopted, especially where it involves a change in people's attitudes and behaviours.	A broad view of the benefits of portfolio management adoption – intangible and non-financial.
Someone exhibiting steady behaviour would typically be perceived as:	**Someone exhibiting influential behaviour would typically be perceived as:**
Being empathic to the impact of the proposed changes on people.	Overestimating the value in some intangible and non-financial benefits of portfolio management to the organisation.
A leader who wishes to ensure that there is adequate investment in managing the change associated with implementing portfolio management.	Being overly optimistic regarding the ease with which portfolio management can be adopted.
Focusing on the attitudes and behaviours of those impacted versus the tangible benefits of adopting portfolio management.	
Focusing on dis-benefits of portfolio management as well as benefits.	

Personal bias of leaders in adopting portfolio management

Portfolio management should be established from an objective and rationale perspective, yet as has been seen so far in this chapter, the perceptions of individuals involved with the initiation of portfolio management can vary. There may be variances in how the portfolio is perceived, causing a lack of good practice for adoption or lack of engagement. The underlying causes could be a lack of understanding of portfolio management and how it might work in practice, or perhaps it's not seen as a priority. Alternatively, there might be a reluctance for additional potential workload without clear sight of the value of portfolio management, or portfolio management is seen as a threat to existing leadership, such as a lack of control or reduced power. Table 20.2. shows where some of these biases may arise, by recognising some of the perceived challenges of adopting portfolio management.

How personal styles impact the practice of portfolio management

Effective collaboration and teamworking are a key to success in portfolio, program, and project management (P3M). However, teams are made up of individuals, each of whom have their own communication and working style. Having awareness of personal styles provides insights that improve cohesion and performance. The P3M frameworks currently available take a "one size fits all" approach. They provide good practice in knowledge and process but make minimal allowance for the various ways that different people perceive, understand, and implement that practice. The aim is to enhance our ability to implement and benefit from portfolio management by understanding how to adapt it, not only to the context of the organisation's portfolio, but also for the people involved, including all types of associated stakeholders.

The management process

Following initiation of portfolio management, how these attributes are manifested in the functions and processes of portfolio management on an ongoing basis can be considered within the management process. The process is shown in Figure 20.4 and is similar in nature to many other approaches (refer to Section II). The management process assesses the suitability of projects and programs for inclusion in the portfolio and maintains a beneficial and manageable mix of projects and programs. Needless to say, the inclusion or not and what is classed as beneficial can often end up as a subjective assessment; thus, the impact of people can be a major influencing factor.

Select projects and programs. The main criterion for inclusion of a project or program in a standard portfolio may be simply that it exists, whereas a structured portfolio would likely have a quite sophisticated system (see Chapter 12) for selecting projects and programs to achieve strategic organisational objectives that could be achieved by various means.

Categorise. Categorisation is useful on particularly large portfolios and are typically defined to make it easier for senior decision-makers to understand the nature of the portfolio, for example, mandatory or discretionary, short- or long-term investments, high or low risk, significant or marginal change, and so on. This categorisation will inevitably be influenced by the people who conceive and implement the categories as their personal priorities may be biased.

Table 20.2 Sources of bias for adopting portfolio management

Sources of bias	*Impact on portfolio practice*
Lack of Understanding and Distinction	There may be an assumption that everyone knows what portfolio management is: Are there different meanings evident? Is portfolio management seen as distinctive enough to add value, or is it too similar to other management constructs?
Integral System	Portfolio management should not be a "bolt on" to the organisational system but rather an integral part. If not integral, then it may be easy to work around. It should fit seamlessly with strategy setting (benefits and value), finance (budgets and costs), and HR (resources and performance).
Perception of Value	Different people within and outside the organisation can perceive its value and its use in multiple ways, impacting effective adoption.
Demonstrating Value	Is the value of portfolio management clear and not seen as additional unnecessary work? Leaders can understand and build on the research that demonstrates its value to organisations and society.
Loss of Power	Having resources can equal power, and losing control of those resources and associated decision-making can be challenging. Are resources being managed at the appropriate level?
Fit with Culture	Does the portfolio culture fit with the organisational culture? Designing the strategic portfolio to fit with the organisations' culture can increase people's willingness and ability for adoption and sustainability.
Maximising Energy	A strategic portfolio can be "brought to life" by removing barriers (friction) and bureaucracy and energising the organisation.
Differences in Practice	Do those involved understand and apply portfolio management in different ways, impacting on the consistency of approach?
Poorly Communicated – What, Why, How, and the Associated Processes and Approach	Is portfolio management shrouded in mystery and not fully objective? Is there a lack of transparency? Is communication effective?
Poor Adoption of Appropriate Technologies	Is there a capability to realise a positive impact of technology?
Timely Data and Information	Is the need for reliable and real-time data to aid decision-making realised?
Complexity of "Nesting"	Not always "one ring to rule them all"; therefore, is "nesting" evident such as with local controls (e.g. lack of clarity and overlapping processes)? Does the portfolio fit with the organisational structure and culture?
Show Leadership	Leadership is needed to overcome the aforementioned challenges and to demonstrate value to the organisation and customers.

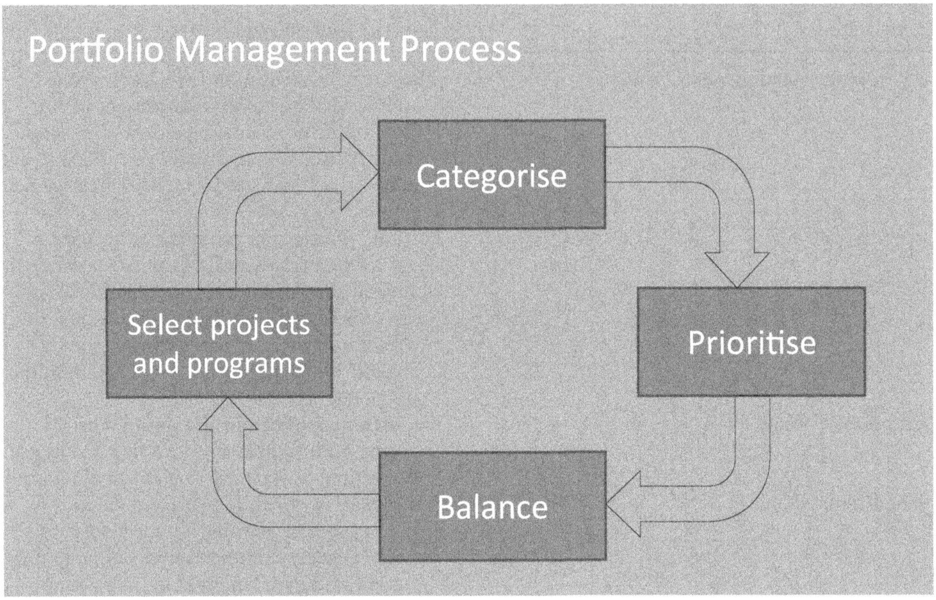

Figure 20.4 Simplified portfolio management process.

Source: Adapted from Praxis (2020).

Prioritise. When multiple initiatives compete for finite resources, conflicts will occur and choices will need to be made. The first priority of any organisation is to continue to exist, but beyond this the priorities of the leaders, often linked to their own personal priorities, will have a major impact; for example, is it to innovate, secure position, benefit the employees, etc.?

Balance. Whereas categorisation and prioritisation can be relatively objective, finding the right balance can be even more subjective, as ultimately personal preferences and priorities of individual decision-makers can have a disproportionate impact, driven by the context and values of the host organisation. In a young and dynamic business, it may be acceptable and feasible to have a high proportion of the portfolio generating significant change. In an entrepreneurial organisation, for example, it may be desirable to have higher overall levels of risk (with associated potential for high return).

The impact of different styles on portfolio practice

When implementing or carrying out the steps in the portfolio management process, the different colours and styles would typically focus on different areas, demonstrated by the examples in Table 20.3 that follows.

How can a portfolio manager take advantage of these insights?

As a portfolio manager, there are a number of aspects to consider based on the insights shared earlier, such as how the portfolio might fit within the organisation and, principally, the advantages of initiating and practicing portfolio management for the organisation,

Table 20.3 Desired portfolio management outcomes for the different DISC profiles

(C)onscientious	*(D)ominant*
BLUE	*RED*
Conscientious behaviour would typically propose or want to see:	**Dominant behaviour would typically propose or want to see:**
The consistent use across the portfolio of methodical, fact-based tools and techniques that provide quantitative data to facilitate objective decision-making.	The use of portfolio management tools and techniques that are quick to implement and provide short-term value.
Principles and details of the way valuation tools should be used.	A focused set of data around which logical decisions can be made.
A methodical and evidence-based approach to measuring the before and end states, which objectively demonstrates the value of the portfolio.	That lessons learned are taken into account and acted upon.
A high proportion of information that is robust, verifiable, and against which measurement can take place.	Quantitative rather than qualitative output from the portfolio processes that allows speedy decision-making.
Performance quantitatively judged during the management process.	Flexible approaches which are there to act as guidance for those responsible for implementing the processes.
A comprehensive and robust portfolio plan linking outputs to the necessary changes that will realise the benefits and all steps for a successful transition.	Sufficient and verifiable information against which measurement can take place and progress can be easily monitored across the portfolio.
	Accountabilities for managing the portfolio processes made clear and formally recorded.
	Timely monitoring and control to ensure that people are being held to account against their responsibilities.
(S)teady	**(I)nfluential**
GREEN	**YELLOW**
Steady behaviour would typically propose or want to see:	**Influential behaviour would typically propose or want to see:**
The involvement of people, ideally through one-to-one discussions in the selection, categorisation, prioritisation, and balancing phases.	The involvement of team members and stakeholders through discussion and workshops to ensure a broad mix of views is considered.
Benefits and dis-benefits that are people-centric (often intangible and non-financial).	Communication with people from other portfolios, typically in a workshop setting, to obtain lessons learned.
Communication with people from other portfolios to obtain lessons learned, focusing on the impact on people of the practice of portfolio management.	Less focus on dis-benefits where they don't consider them significant.
The use of qualitative techniques as well as quantitative.	Information for the portfolio processes created with minimal level of formality.
Comprehensive portfolio processes that clearly identify responsibilities, including their own.	Resources being deployed to ensure sufficient performance information is available across the portfolio.
An approach that has been agreed by all parties with clear responsibilities that are fairly allocated across the portfolio management team.	The adoption and use of qualitative techniques for valuing benefits.

(*Continued*)

Table 20.3 (Continued)

(C)onscientious	*(D)ominant*
BLUE	*RED*
Resources being deployed to communicate with all those impacted by the decisions made through the management process.	Flexible processes that are there for guidance, allowing people to tailor and adapt.
A focus on minimising the negative impact on people and ongoing operations if prioritisation/balancing results in major changes within the business.	Effort put to marketing and communicating the portfolio to a broad audience to ensure their support.
	A personal role in this, potentially acting as a spokesman for the process and helping people understand the impact of the changes implemented by the portfolio.
	A flexible and simple means of monitoring actions.

accounting for individual personal styles. By reading this far, it can be assumed that there is already some assessment of the value of portfolio management; there may be further interest in considering its application in either an individual's current role or looking to add a fresh perspective and capability to improve future performance in an area of the business or the organisation as a whole. As a leader, it is useful firstly to identify an individual's own style and how adapting this style, given the context, may be advantageous to the effectiveness of initially the individual's role and then the portfolio and the wider organisation. The figures included throughout this chapter are framed around implementing and adopting portfolio management, through initiation and management, although the principles can be applied to all aspects of the portfolio and other management processes (see the Praxis framework for further discussion).

Reflecting on your own style and strengths

In assessing your own personal style, identify what you would typically propose or want to see, such as the example of a conscientious style shown in Figure 20.5. Consider if this is appropriate given the context, and then consider others involved with the portfolio, identifying how their colour styles would tackle the same activity. Question whether this style and approach add value to portfolio development, and then modify as appropriate. Having a flexibility of style and approach is often critical to being a leader in complex environments. The approach discussed here was developed to help professionals who are willing to do the preparatory work necessary to reflect and understand their own style and then consider and test different strategies.

Working with others – individuals or teams

In assessing the styles of others, a suggested approach is to identify a colleague's colour style, consider the implications in terms of the relationship and in achieving the task, then consider how other colour styles may tackle the task or deal with the situation. Subsequently, evaluate how this will impact your style, and modify as appropriate. Using such

(C)onscientious BLUE	(D)ominant RED
Conscientious behaviour would typically propose or want to see: • a rational explanation of what portfolio management is aiming to achieve; • a consistent and systematic approach to initiating, governing, managing and co-ordinating a portfolio; • a long term commitment to maintaining and monitoring the portfolio; • tangible and detailed financial benefits which are measurable and can be shown to be realised from the investment.	**Dominant behaviour would typically propose or want to see:** • action taken quickly to complete the initiation process; • a pragmatic view of the achievability of the perceived value; • that they have maximum freedom to take action as they believe necessary to complete the initiation process; • resources being identified and committed to portfolio management in the short term.
(S)teady GREEN	**(I)nfluential YELLOW**
Steady behaviour would typically propose or want to see: • key individuals are given the opportunity to input and influence the decision; • equal consideration to intangible and non-financial benefits when considering the potential value; • a clear understanding of the positive and negative impacts on people of introducing portfolio management; • caution regarding how quickly portfolio management can be adopted especially where it involves a change in people's attitudes and behaviours.	**Influential behaviour would typically propose or want to see:** • clear communication on the importance of portfolio management and its role in improving team motivation and thereby performance; • short term responsibilities for portfolio management identified and clarified with people; • encourage early interaction within the team and with stakeholders as part of the adoption process; • a broad view of the benefits of portfolio management adoption - intangible and non-financial.

Figure 20.5 Reflecting on expectations from others based on DISC profiles (Praxis, 2020).

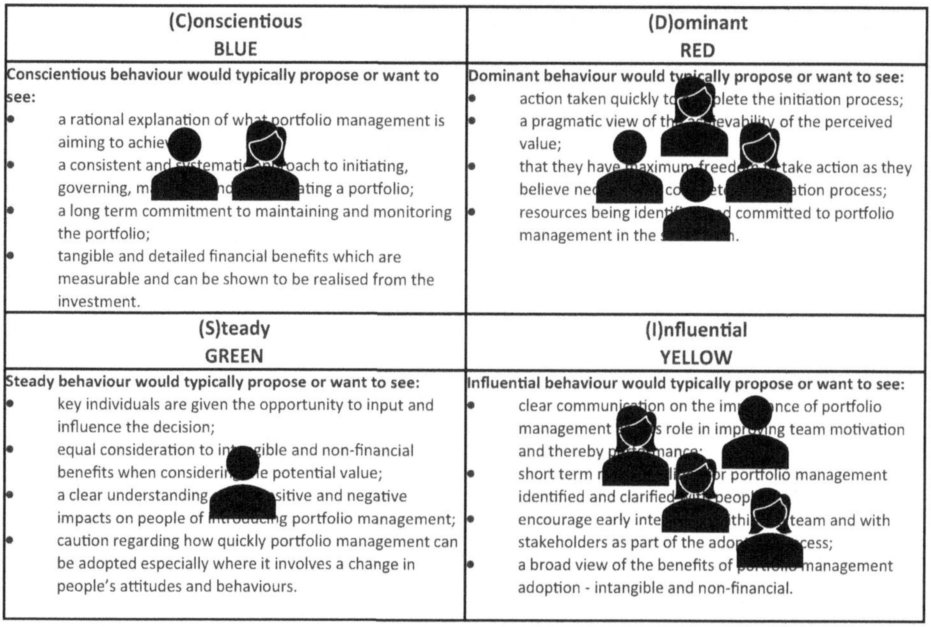
(C)onscientious
BLUE
Conscientious behaviour would typically propose or want to see:
a long term commitment to maintaining and monitoring the portfolio;
tangible and detailed financial benefits which are measurable and can be shown to be realised from the investment.
(D)ominant
RED
(S)teady
GREEN
Steady behaviour would typically propose or want to see:
key individuals are given the opportunity to input and influence the decision;
caution regarding how quickly portfolio management can be adopted especially where it involves a change in people's attitudes and behaviours.
(I)nfluential
YELLOW
Influential behaviour would typically propose or want to see:
adoption - intangible and non-financial.

Figure 20.6 Using DISC profiles to understand team behaviour when adopting portfolio management (Praxis, 2020).

insights can help build greater understanding of colleagues and thereby improve relationships and performance. Being aware of the differences and the value that each style brings allows challenges to be tackled from multiple perspectives. A similar approach can be taken for entire teams. Understanding the style of each member of the team allows leaders to explain the resulting dynamics and decision-making. For example, if Figure 20.6 represented a portfolio management team, then certain behaviours may be predicted or explained from the analysis – such as a more outward-facing approach – through a higher number of D and I styles (4D and 4I as opposed to 1S and 2C).

Conclusion

People are at the heart of effective portfolio management – how they perceive the value, adopt, and practice it. It is hoped that the arguments provided earlier have demonstrated this. Personal styles and preferred ways of completing activities have a direct and often significant impact on success. Through identifying personal differences, in this case using DISC as the example, and by providing the tools and insights presented in this chapter, it is intended that this can offer the opportunity to positively impact the practice of portfolio management within your organisation.

References

Jung, C. (1921) *Psychological Types* (Trans. Baynes, H.G.) Martino Fine Books (Latest Publication 2016).

Lock D. & Wagner R. (2019) *The Handbook of Project Portfolio Management.* Routledge.

Marston, W. (1928) *Emotions of Normal People.* First Edition. Routledge.

Merenda, P. & Clarke, W. (1965) Self-description and personality measurement. *Journal of Clinical Psychology* 21(1), 52–56.

Praxis (2020) *Praxis Framework: An Integrated Guide to the Management of Projects, Programmes and Portfolios.* Association for Project Management. www.praxisframework.org.

21 The role of supply chain integration in portfolio management

Aleksandar Nikolov and Pete Harpum

Introduction

Supply chain management (SCM) is a way of understanding how to manage the entire set of organisations that supply a final customer – it is the sequence of these firms, supplying into each other, with a final deliverable or product reaching the customer, that forms the supply chain (SC). In theory, the supply chain begins with firms producing all the raw materials that work their way through the various operations carried out in the supply chain to create the output of the chain. In practice, it is rare for the entire supply chain to fall under one management approach, all the way back to raw materials. However, in some fully vertically integrated industries, such as international oil, this has been commonplace (the major oil companies extract the oil, process it through a long series of different plants and facilities, and deliver the final product to the customer – petrol sold through company-owned filling stations being the most obvious example). Venkataraman (2004) defines SCM as:

> *[A] set of approaches utilised to efficiently and fully integrate the network of all organisations and their related activities in producing/completing and delivering a product, a service, or a project so that systemwide costs are minimised while maintaining or exceeding customer-service-level requirements.*

Typical SCM activities and approaches, applied through several layers of the supply chain, include formal partnering arrangements, information and risk sharing, sharing of specialist expertise in production and manufacturing with less technically advanced members of the supply chain, implementing total quality management (TQM) philosophies, and the now-ubiquitous just-in-time logistical delivery approach to eliminate inventory standing in stock.

Figure 21.1 shows how internal and external portfolios have supply chains feeding them, with various levels of suppliers, called tiers, feeding towards the customer sequentially. Some suppliers may supply a firm's internal and external supply chain, as well as feed the customer directly – software houses are typical of this situation, as shown as "H" in Figure 21.1.

Supply chain integration (SCI) in the context of managing portfolios of projects is a different concept to the integration of a single supply chain as described previously. By supply chain integration in the context of portfolio management, what is meant is the *integration of multiple single supply chains feeding each of the projects in the portfolio.* In some industries, particularly those delivering external projects as their business

DOI: 10.4324/9780367853129-24

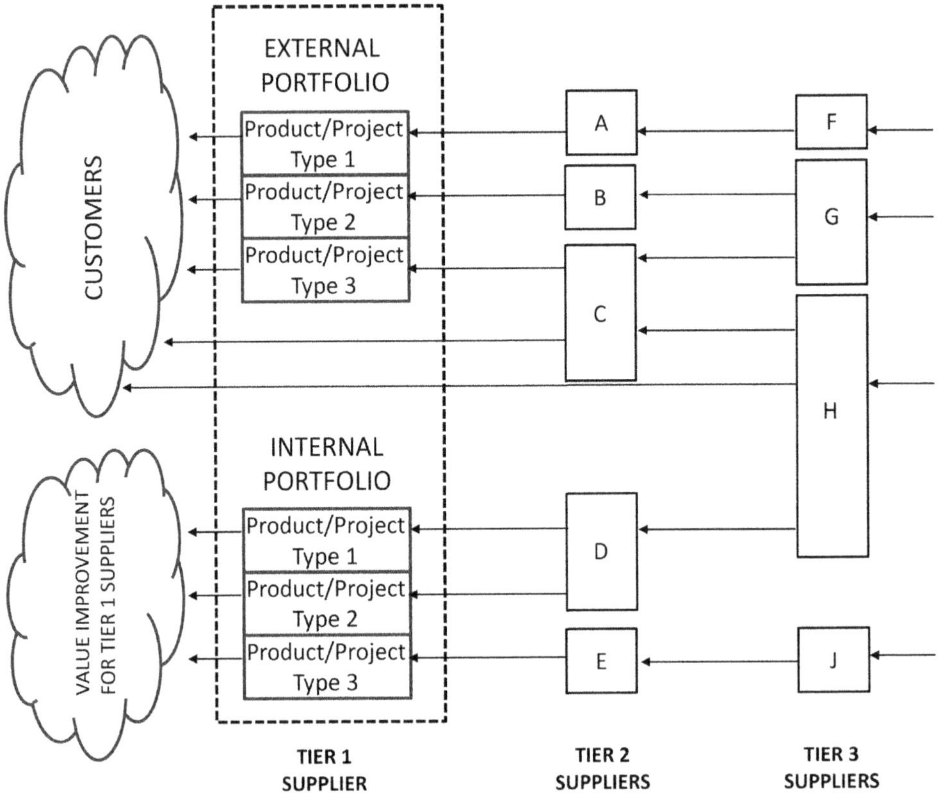

Figure 21.1 External and internal portfolios in relation to SCM.

(e.g. construction, IT project delivery, and engineering firms), the supply chains for each project in the portfolio are set up separately, often with little or no reference or integration, with other supply chains feeding different projects in the same portfolio. This is wasteful. For example, price optimisation from suppliers is more difficult, suppliers may become overburdened trying to supply multiple projects in an uncoordinated manner, and frequently inefficient where different policies, procedures, and regulations and standards are applied by different projects in the same portfolio to the same supplier working in different supply chains.

This chapter discusses several aspects of SCI in the context of portfolios, highlighting the benefits SCI can realise. Actors referred to in this chapter can be defined as any stakeholder involved with the supply chain or project-based organisation.

Applying supply chain integration to improve portfolio performance

Regarding its application in practice, SCI is particularly challenging because it relies on collective understanding and practice of a particular philosophical orientation. It requires a change in mindset of supply chain actors towards practical understanding of its strategic implications, how it realises value, and what aspects to focus on integrating collectively. Traditional SCM (supply chain management) focuses on its supporting functional role in delivering individual projects, driven by their individual requirements. This approach is reactive in nature to the stream of projects coming out of the portfolio pipeline. Taking into account the need to realise effectiveness and efficiency from a project portfolio, SCM requires a different approach, one that is proactive in pursuing the strategic objectives of project-based organisations (PBOs).

In this context, the role of SCI is not to create a number of supply chains for each project, thus increasing complexity, but instead to integrate these supply chains towards unlocking value. Utilising portfolio archetypes (discussed in the following section) serves as a basis for integrating supply chains into supporting both the entire portfolio and subsets of the portfolio. Instead of individual project requirements, SCI uses demand profiling to integrate requirements, improving effectiveness and efficiency of delivery. The strategic planning process of the PBO develops patterns in the project portfolio, and supply chain integration enables the embedded efficiency and effectiveness in realising value from such patterns. Using an SCI approach allows pursuing the strategic objectives of the PBO proactively, as supply chain (SC) partners are already positioned in production channels, to realise value once demand comes through. The role of SCI as an overarching goal of SCM improves alignment between PBO's strategic objectives and supply chain fulfilment.

In addition, as supply chain partners integrate, they develop objectives between themselves, resulting in outcomes such as, but not limited to, increased production volume, secure and stable demand for future project work, and development of new project competencies. In such ways, partners are actively involved in collectively developing improved value realisation for the PBO, as well as generate profit based on their individual specialisation and value drivers. This approach enables the role of SCI as an antidote to fragmentation, as partners develop an active interest in both individual commercial and joint performance aspects. Developing joint practical understanding of the interdependence actors share in project performance is critical for the success of SCI. The inability to meet performance criteria on projects in a demand profile can lead to missed strategic objectives for the PBO. This, in turn, results in a strategic planning process unable to aggregate value based on "economies of repetition" and "economies of recombination".

Underperformance inhibits value generation from strategic planning, detaches SC actors from the overriding strategic planning process, and creates demand for small-in-size, dispersed work packages suitable for execution by a limited number of individual SC actors. In such instances, actors are unable to aggregate demand, develop production flows, and bid on multiple criteria associated with individual work packages that may not necessarily be aligned with their value drivers. The outcome is disintegration of actors from the strategic planning process and loss of commercial position. It is thus in the best interest of SC actors to perform well collectively.

SCI can be thought of as largely a self-organisation process between SC actors, given the presence of the right conditions (i.e. portfolio characteristics); however, the PBO's role in integration should not be overlooked. This is especially critical in the SCI dimensions of duration and depth (discussed next). From the duration perspective, securing a stable stream of a series of projects is a critical link between PBO's strategic planning process and supply chain integration. It is the baseline to which individual project performance can be benchmarked with actual SCI performance over a series of projects. Such practices can serve as valuable indicators for the PBO in evaluating the extent SCI is improving efficiency and realising value from the strategic planning process. Through the depth dimension, the PBO can actively get involved in and influence integrative activities. For instance, depending on the management characteristics of projects, the PBO can establish a set of suitable criteria for the integrated SC.

First, through value identification in the portfolio, the PBO can set a number of value improvement criteria in line with demand for projects. These can be introduced formally through bidding on a series of projects and/or enforced by the right personnel representation in integrative activities. Criteria can include interactive planning (i.e. concept select planning), contract and procurement strategy, design class, value engineering, availability assurance/reliability, selection of standards and specifications, and constructability. Setting the right criteria can indicate to the integrated SC what factors differentiate a project in the demand profile and how top quartile (TQ) performance is to be achieved, that is, achieving top quartile performance in a category of projects in the PBO's portfolio (in other words, a set of benchmarks between projects, usually associated with cost, schedule, and production, with quality and safety as a given).

Once criteria are identified and clear to SC actors, the integrated SC can realise value by achieving TQ performance, utilising each actor's nature (i.e. their key competitive drivers). Lastly, the role of SCI as a means of implementing sophisticated strategy is also considered. It requires partners to think how to create long-term win-win relationships and improve their joint performance (Wood & Ellis, 2005). Such strategic intent can be characterised by improved productivity on one hand and revenue growth on the other (Kaplan & Norton, 2000).

From the productivity perspective, an integrated SC strengthens the links between actors. Thus facilitating benefits, such as managing costs collaboratively, better definition of client values, and development of continuous improvement. Such an approach can result in improved cost structuring and asset use. Practical examples can include improved efficiency in collaborative procurement and processes; improved cash flow operating cycles, which may be particularly important for SMEs with limited access to finance; and improved flow of information, resulting in effective cost allocation practices. From a revenue growth perspective, through the scope dimension (discussed later), for example, SCI positions actors to capture collective opportunities presented and better adapt to and respond to changing customer project demand.

As the number, nature, and interdependencies between actors align, this allows value-creation activities to take place and increases end value to the PBO, as enacted through the portfolio. Relevant benefits may include competing through superior value, establishing supplier relationships and mobilisation, and development of people. In this context, because of its highly integrated state, the SC can quickly adapt to revenue from new sources and focus on which projects to compete.

Characteristics of projects within portfolios from an SCI perspective

In this context, portfolio management as a decision-making framework assumes a life cycle involving the initial *screening*, *selection*, and *prioritisation* of project proposals – see Chapters 11 and 12 for a more detailed account of this process. Developing an operations-informed initial screening of projects involves identifying what their intrinsic characteristics are.

Operations-informed characteristics

Firstly, following Davies and Brady (2016), projects can be classified into routine and innovative. Routine projects "exploit the existing base, utilise proven technologies and mature products, and address current customer demands" (Davies & Brady, 2016). Innovative projects, on the other hand, "support base-moving strategies that explore innovative alternatives, experiment with new ideas, schemes and approaches, and create entirely new technologies and markets". Secondly, following Syntetos et al. (2005), projects can exhibit different demand patterns in a portfolio. These patterns are dependent on the projects' lumpiness (size of demand when it occurs) and intermittence (frequency of demand). Such characteristics can indicate appropriate batching processes for required resources, in line with the sequence of, and consolidation between, portfolio components.

Thirdly, following Godsell et al. (2018), projects in a portfolio can also differ in the extent of their repeatability, predictability, and budget. These three criteria can be used for segmenting the portfolio, forming distinct demand profiles that can facilitate planning processes. The segmentation process is conducted based on cut-off points that allocate projects in their respective portfolio component clusters. Repeatability is "*a measure of whether the projects of a specific type generally follow the same design, use the same (or similar) materials, resources and equipment, and are implemented according to a similar plan*". Project *repeatability* can be expressed in percentages. The project estimator can set a cut-off point that characterises the project as non-repeatable, partially repeatable, or repeatable. For instance, again considering Godsell et al. (2018), the estimator can decide that a project is partially repeatable if its repeatability is higher than 50%, and repeatable if its repeatability is higher than 70%. *Predictability* is a "*measure of whether the projects are planned well in advance with a high degree of certainty, vs being scheduled on an ad hoc basis*". The estimator can set a cut-off point that characterises the project as predictable or not predictable. For instance, the estimator can decide that a project is predictable if it has been planned one year before its start date. *Budget* is a measure of "*the budget allocated to the project, and cut-off points should be based on the individual history and context of the particular organisation*" (Godsell et al., 2018).

Management characteristics

Conducting an initial screening of a portfolio based on operations-informed analysis can reveal project characteristics that facilitate the identification of alternative ways of managing the portfolio components. Portfolio management, as a decision-making framework, can then formulate informed decisions based on which and what type of projects can benefit from efficiency. In practice, this may involve grouping projects with similar demand profile characteristics into programs, sub-portfolios, or executing them as distinct groups of operations. Depending on the industry the specific PBO operates in, the portfolio analysis can reveal different management approaches are suitable. In a case study of water engineering projects, for instance, Godsell et al. (2018) identified large commonality between projects, pointing to efficiencies to be gained by managing them as programs of repetitive projects.

Establishing four portfolio management archetypes from an SCI perspective

Screening represents the evaluation or investigation of portfolio components as part of a methodical survey in order to assess their suitability for a particular role or purpose in the portfolio. As part of the screening process, using projects' operational and management characteristics can facilitate establishing four distinct portfolio management archetypes. These archetypes, in the context of SCI, can enable better-informed decision-making processes within the PBO's portfolio management framework.

Single project management

Firstly, single project management (SPM) as a distinct portfolio archetype is characterised by a small number of projects, but of large size. Such projects are usually strategic in nature and can be routine or innovative. In general, projects within this archetype do not appear in the portfolio frequently (low intermittence) and, when they appear, because of their large size, create high spikes in demand for resources (high lumpiness). In line with their strategic nature, such projects are usually not emergent, can be planned well in advance, and thus are predictable. SPM projects often tackle a unique issue, which is why they are usually not repeatable, although in some cases they can be routine in nature and adopt repeatable elements from other portfolio components. Due to their large allocated budget and scale of change introduced, projects within this archetype are often classified as major projects. In terms of their nature in line with the objectives of the PBO, projects within this archetype play a significant role in introducing change. Thus, they can be thought of as an "agency for change" and create opportunities for developing PBO's capabilities and knowledge.

Functionally, because SPMs are often managed as stand-alone project organisations, they can provide an impetus to overcome the inertia of the PBO, build momentum in introducing change, prototype successful change processes, and offer organisational flexibility required to respond to uncertainties in the change process and change objectives. Projects within this archetype are value drivers, not only because of their expected benefits, but because their size can offer innovation windows, where PBOs can mobilise integrated actors, together with processes and activities, to leverage value (Davies et al., 2015), in accordance with changing customer needs and market dynamics (Pillay & Mafini, 2017). Due to their high value, these projects need to be closely managed by the PBO.

Multiple project management

Secondly, multiple project management (MPM) as a distinct portfolio archetype is characterised by a series of small-in-size, one-off projects. Projects within this archetype have a tactical role and are usually unrelated to one another. The basis of clustering projects within this grouping is determined by their tendency to be routine in nature and exhibit low variability in their demand profile, typically emerging through the portfolio pipeline. They do not appear in the portfolio frequently (low intermittence) and are individually small in size (low lumpiness). From a scope perspective (discussed later), portfolio components within this grouping usually deal with "debottlenecking" and reservoir capacity issues of existing assets or their maintenance. As such, it is important to differentiate between production and non-production impact projects.

This differentiation can serve as a basis for determining which components in this category can in fact benefit from being managed as projects and which as groups of operations. Within this grouping, projects can exhibit different levels of predictability. In general, projects dealing with production-related interfaces can show high levels of predictability, while low-priority maintenance works are less predictable, as resources are committed on an ad hoc basis and often reprioritised. Projects within this archetype are not repeatable, because of their unique scope, and can be dependent on integration of specific information and knowledge of other pre-existing capital assets.

Functionally, this grouping of projects can benefit from viewing them as a temporary organisation, focusing on their transience. This is in line with their tactical nature in the PBO's portfolio, calling for good timing of execution, within the timescale the project opportunity exists. The combined characteristics of low commercial value, non-repeatability, and timing pressure create relatively low probability of technical success in such projects. This archetype requires to first clearly identify if such projects can be avoided and, if not, then to carefully define the ones that are in fact necessary for meeting the PBO's objectives. Once such projects are selected, the PBO needs to adopt a "no change" mindset. The effective management of this archetype requires cost discipline, because of their low expected commercial value, and risk tolerance discipline, as a large number of such projects can accumulate high risk to the portfolio value.

Traditional program management

Thirdly, traditional program management (TPM) as a distinct portfolio archetype is characterised by sets of projects that are linked to the delivery of a specific strategic goal. By definition, program management involves the centralised, coordinated management of resources and activities in this group of interdependent projects towards defined strategic objectives and benefits (PMI, 2017). The basis of clustering projects within this grouping is determined both by the need for pooling sets of interdependent individual projects towards a strategic goal and by the need for efficiency in resource utilisation.

Within this archetype, individual projects in a program can vary in the type of solution delivered (routine or innovative). In addition, individual projects tend to be discrete (low intermittence) but could vary in size (low/high lumpiness). From a scope perspective, for instance, in water engineering projects, these project archetypes are usually addressing resource challenges (e.g. climate and demographic changes) through applying technological solutions in line with an engrained need for engineered flexibility in the operations phase. Here, examples of projects can include wastewater treatment plants, water filtration plants, and carbon efficiency projects, amongst others. Within this archetype, projects are usually not emergent and highly predictable. However, such projects are complex, as they can develop new technologies or require tailoring of existing technologies to various conditions, circumstances, or operating contingencies. As such, they are non-repeatable or only partially repeatable.

Functionally, projects within this category can benefit from viewing them as an agency for resource utilisation. A narrow selection of projects included in this distinct archetype enables the PBO to differentiate between sets of strategic goals in order to shape project resources into effective programs. In addition, this allows the PBO to investigate what are the optimum levels of resource allocation and management reserve in line with defined goals, rather than individual projects. Moreover, this approach can also facilitate through-life costing initiatives (TOTEX) as the PBO can adopt a long-term view, taking into account the operation phase stemming from the project objectives. In this archetype, projects are of high commercial value and offer opportunities for maximisation of portfolio return.

This can be achieved through growth opportunities from leveraging selection of best and "doable" concepts and technologies and branching out into other projects. Additionally, this archetype can maximise value for the PBO through identifying and assessing ways for improved cost structuring and asset use, by grouping projects into goal-driven programs. The effective management of this archetype can benefit from a value-driven convergent thinking approach, where projects are evaluated from a goal-driven, sub-portfolio perspective.

Program management of repetitive projects

Fourthly, program management of repetitive projects (PMRP) as a distinct portfolio archetype is characterised by projects that have a strategic objective (e.g. to provide the upgrade of a particular type of asset) but differ from TPM in that, within a program, the projects are necessarily routine and repeatable. Projects within this archetype require high-value outcomes to compensate for their low individual value and, as such, rely on developing economies of scale. In addition, such projects can benefit from "economies of repetition" (Davies & Brady, 2000), where the organisation can deliver a series of similar projects at lower cost and more effectively, taking advantage of the learning opportunities that this offers. As such, the basis for clustering projects within this archetype is in the interest of improved operational efficiency, through grouping them into programs of repetitive projects as well as infusing stability in the portfolio value realisation. Within this archetype, individual projects exhibit high intermittence but could vary in size (low/high lumpiness). From a scope perspective, projects within this archetype are addressing well-known engineering challenges that use repeatable design and have limited constructability considerations.

Examples of types of projects can include flood protection, tunnelling, and excavation works. Within this archetype, projects are of both predictable and repeatable demand pattern, thus offering opportunities for removal of costly buffers of uncertainty in the portfolio. In addition, projects in this grouping are not technically complex and functionally can be viewed as a production function. Establishing programs of repeatable projects can strategically utilise this productivity perspective for establishing informational, material, and financial flows through improving cost structuring and asset use within the archetype. The effective management of this archetype requires a focus on stable productivity by developing efficiency gains through scalability by the number, or size, of projects within the program.

The four portfolio archetypes in relation to their operational and management characteristics with their strategic implications are summarised in Figure 21.2.

Realising value from supply chain integration

Realising value from the strategic planning process of the project portfolio requires a supply chain that is aligned to deliver effectiveness and efficiency. Using a traditional approach to SCM as a fulfilment function proves inadequate for PBOs' needs, as poorly planned demand for projects creates complexity in processes, leading to poor SC performance and missed strategic objectives. Engineering projects, in particular, consistently overrun in terms of cost and time (Olawale & Sun, 2010). Contributing factors include lack of demand visibility, late involvement of contractors and suppliers, design changes, risk transfer upstream, adversarial relationships, lack of trust, and reliance on large, fragmented supply base of small- and medium-sized enterprises (SMEs) (Ireland, 2004; Bankvall et al., 2010; Hartmann & Caerteling, 2010; Polat et al., 2014). Such factors lead to disjointed effort and creation of new SCs for each project, which in turn

Archetype	*Operational Characteristics*			*Management Characteristics*			*Strategic Implications*
	Following Davies and Brady (2016) projects can be classified into ***routine and innovative***.	Following Syntetos *et al.* (2005) projects can exhibit different demand patterns in a portfolio. These patterns dependent on the projects' ***lumpiness (size of demand when it occurs) and intermittence (frequency of demand)***.	Following Godsell *et al.*(2018) projects in a portfolio can differ in the extent of their ***repeatability, predictability and budget.***	Following Patanakul and Milosevic (2009) and Godsell et al. (2018) four types of project ***management groupings*** can be used for clustering projects on the basis of their operational characteristics.	Following Turner and Müller (2003) a ***project's nature*** can be associated with use of different project management techniques. Projects' nature relates to the different portfolio management role in line with the business objectives of the PBO.	Following Cooper (2000) Projects can exhibit different ***management classification according to the project value and probability of technical success***.	***Portfolio Management implications***
Single Project Management (SPM)	Can be routine or innovative	Projects do not appear in the portfolio frequently (low intermittence) and when they appear, because of their large size, create high spikes in demand for resources (high lumpiness).	In line with their strategic nature, such projects are usually not emergent and are predictable. SPM projects often tackle a unique issue, which is why they are usually not repeatable. Projects in this archetype have large, allocated budget and introduce change of large scale.	Managed as single projects. These projects are of high value and require close management. Managing them as single projects enables the PBO to be effective and flexible in delivering change objectives.	Can be thought of as an "agency for change". Functionally, because SPM are managed as standalone project organisations, they can provide "an impetus to overcome the inertia" of the PBO, build momentum in introducing change, prototype successful change processes and offer the flexibility required to respond to uncertainties in the change process and change objectives.	Projects within this archetype are regarded as "pearls" or in cases where considerable technical complexity exists as "oysters". However, regardless of their technical complexity, because of their high value, these projects require to be managed closely by the PBO.	Usually not a large number of projects but of large size offering innovation windows. These projects are critical in developing competencies and build up the knowledge, capabilities, and resources of the PBO. SPM projects are of high value and require close management.
Multiple Project Management (MPM)	Tend to be routine	Individual projects do not appear in the portfolio frequently (low intermittence) and are individually small in size (low lumpiness).	Within this grouping, projects can exhibit different levels of predictability. Generally, projects dealing with production-related interventions can show higher predictability, while low-priority maintenance works are less predictable, as resources are committed on an ad hoc basis and often reprioritised. Projects within this archetype are not repeatable, because of their unique scope, dependent on integration of specific information and knowledge of other pre-existing capital assets. Estimated budgeting of projects in this archetype can be inaccurate (incur sunk costs), as projects can demonstrate considerable cost variance.	Multiple Project Management (MPM) as distinct portfolio archetype is characterised by small, series of one-off projects. Projects within this archetype have a tactical role and are usually unrelated to one another. The basis for clustering projects in this archetype is for collecting all project proposals and then make better informed decisions on selection of individual projects.	Functionally, this grouping of projects can benefit from viewing them as a "temporary organisation", focusing on their transience. This is in line with their tactical nature in the PBO's portfolio, calling for good timing of execution, within the timescale the project opportunity exists.	The combined characteristics of low commercial value, non-repeatability and timing pressure, create relatively low probability of technical success in such projects. Thus, projects within this archetype are regarded as "white elephants".	This archetype requires to first clearly identify, if such projects can be avoided and if not, then carefully define the ones that are in fact necessary for meeting the PBO's objectives. Once projects are selected, the PBO needs to adopt no change mind-set. The effective management of this archetype requires cost discipline, because of their low expected commercial value and risk tolerance discipline as large number of such projects can accumulate high risk to portfolio value.
Traditional Programme Management (TPM)	Within this archetype, individual projects in a programme can vary in the type of solution delivered (routine or innovative).	Individual projects tend to be discrete (low intermittence) but could vary in size (low/high lumpiness).	Within this archetype, projects are usually not emergent and highly predictable. Such projects are complex, as they can develop new technologies or require tailoring of existing technologies to various conditions, circumstances, or operating contingencies. As such, they are non-repeatable or only partially repeatable. Allocated budget is dependent on the type of solution offered and functionality.	Traditional Programme Management (TPM) as distinct portfolio archetype is characterised by sets of projects linked to the delivery of a strategic goal. The basis of clustering projects within this grouping is determined both by the need for pooling sets of interdependent individual projects towards a strategic goal and by the need for efficiency in resource utilisation.	Functionally, projects within this category can benefit from viewing them as an "agency for resource utilisation". Allocating projects into this distinct archetype, enables the PBO to differentiate between sets of strategic goals in order to shape project resources into effective programmes.	In this archetype, projects are of high commercial value and offer opportunities for maximisation of portfolio return. This can be achieved through growth opportunities from leveraging selection of best and "doable" concepts and technologies and branching out into other related projects. Can benefit from identifying and assessing ways for improved cost structuring and asset use by grouping projects into goal-driven programmes. Projects within this archetype can be regarded as "oysters".	Allocating projects into this distinct archetype, enables the PBO to differentiate between sets of strategic goals in order to shape project resources into effective programmes. The effective management of this archetype can benefit from value-driven convergent thinking approach where evaluation of projects is from goal-driven sub-portfolio perspective.
Programme Management of Repetitive Projects (PMRP)	Consist of projects that have a strategic objective (e.g. to provide the upgrade of a particular type of asset) but differ from TPM in that, within a programme, the projects are necessarily routine and repeatable.	Individual projects exhibit high intermittence but could vary in size (low/high lumpiness).	Within this archetype, projects are of both predictable and repeatable demand pattern, thus offering opportunities for removal of costly buffers of uncertainty in the portfolio.	The basis for clustering projects within this grouping is in the interest of improved operational efficiency through grouping them into programmes of repeatable projects and for infusing stability in the portfolio value realisation.	Projects in this grouping are not technically complex and functionally can be viewed as a "production function". Establishing programmes of repeatable projects can apply strategic approach to productivity perspective by improving cost structuring and asset use within the archetype.	In this archetype, the type of projects can be regarded as "bread and butter". Individual projects have high probability of technical success but relatively low commercial value individually.	The effective management of this archetype requires focus on stable productivity through developing efficiency gains by scalability in number and size of projects within the programmes. The management of this archetype has strategic role in balancing overall uncertainty in the portfolio.

Figure 21.2 Screening process of portfolio components by operations management characteristics.

results in short-term, discontinuous interfirm relationships (Dainty et al., 2001; Briscoe & Dainty, 2005). In contrast, applying SCI to an engineering project portfolio formulates a supply chain best positioned to realise value in and between portfolio archetypes, aligned with their operational and management characteristics.

Supply chains on larger engineering projects typically involve hundreds of different companies supplying components, materials, and a wide range of services (Dainty et al., 2001; Briscoe & Dainty, 2005). Usually, the organisations involved in the supply chain are the PBO, as client, main contractor, and suppliers and subcontractors. Following the strategic planning approach of clustering projects into archetypes based on their operational and management characteristics requires integrating the supply chain in order to realise value from the portfolio management framework. Supply chain integration (SCI) is defined as "the extent to which an organisation manages its intra- and inter-organisational processes to achieve effective and efficient flows of products, services, information, money and decisions with the objective of providing maximum value to its customers" (Bakker et al., 2012). In addition, SCI is viewed as the enabler to a "movement towards a seamless supply chain, with integration from source to sink" and where "all actors think and act as one" (Childerhouse & Towill, 2011).

Against this context, the key roles supply chain integration (SCI) plays have been identified as overarching goal of SCM (Vrijhoef, 2011), antidote to fragmentation (Papadonikolaki et al., 2017), means of implementing sophisticated strategy (Wood & Ellis, 2005), and means of aggregating value (Broft et al., 2016). Although SCI has been recognised since 1989 (Stevens, 1989), its potential has not been fully realised in engineering project portfolios. The following section discusses in more detail the elements that constitute four SCI dimensions (strength, scope, duration, and depth) applicable to engineering projects. Through utilisation of the SCI dimensions, PBOs become equipped to understand, operationalise, analyse, and improve the extent of their SCI.

Dimensions of SCI

Following Leuschner et al. (2013) and Eriksson (2015), SCI in the project-based environment is described through four dimensions. These are the *strength*, *scope*, *duration*, and *depth* of SCI. Each dimension is discussed together with its relevant elements, drawing on supporting literature-based evidence, as appropriate for typical engineering projects.

Strength of integration

Leuschner et al. (2013) found that the strength of SCI linkages in project-based organisations depends on the extent of informational integration, operational integration, and relational integration, of which the first two involve activities and the third involves attitudes.

Informational integration

Informational integration is characterised by co-ordination of information transfer, use of appropriate information for the needs of integration-supporting technology, and collaborative communication (Leuschner et al., 2013; Eriksson, 2015).

The successful co-ordination of information transfer relates to systems and strategic collaboration of partners in the integrated SC. Systems collaboration strives for making partners ready for interfirm forecasting and planning (Sanders & Premus, 2005; Rai et al., 2006). This is in addition to routine electronic transactions and information exchange within the SC. Strategic collaboration, on the other hand, is an advanced level of interfirm interaction (e.g. Johnson, 1999; Hult et al., 2007), using coordination of information transfer with the purpose of developing greater insight and comprehension for making more informed interfirm long-term decisions (Richardson, 1990). It is defined as "*the extent to which supply chain partners actually forecast demand and plan business activities jointly while taking into account each other's long term success*" (Kim & Lee, 2010).

In order to integrate, organisations need supporting technologies that facilitate information exchange across firms' boundaries (Rodrigues et al., 2004). To enable this, certain IT attributes and functionality need to be present. In terms of attributes, SCI requires compatibility of information systems between construction partners (e.g. Xue et al., 2007), flexibility that supports backward integration in suppliers' value chains (Elliman & Orange, 2003), and allows for project-based SC efficiency (Titus & Bröchner, 2005). Regarding functionality, SCI requires IT that offers speed and quality of information exchanged and uses core building blocks, with linked IS, facilitating inter-organisational processes, consistent measures, aligned goals, and sharing of risk and reward (Näslund & Hulthen, 2012). The functionality of IT needs to also consider SCM as a cultural orientation and philosophy (Papadonikolaki et al., 2017), as "*IT-enablement causes change in work culture and nature of work of some of the employees*" (Kumar & Pugazhendhi, 2012).

In construction, "*communication refers to the level of exchange of information, knowledge and skills openly, timely and adequately among the owner, the designer, and the contractor*" (Mesa et al., 2016). In terms of information, this refers "*to the degree and breadth of exchanging information with supply chain partners*" (Turkulainen et al., 2017). Regarding exchange of knowledge, team members in an engineering project have not necessarily worked together before (Titus & Bröchner, 2005), and partners may not be familiar with the level of complexity underlying the integration of differentiated knowledge (Huang & Newell, 2003). Examples of such differentiation may include the possibility of building offsite a proportion of the assets or buildability of design ideas (Godsell et al., 2018). It is thus necessary for SCI to establish communication channels, enabling data and knowledge exchange. Lastly, communication also refers to exchange of skills. As pointed by Costa et al. (2019), "*multi-skilled groups could mitigate problems related to customization and variability, because they make it possible to overcome functional fragmentation and to cope better with every unpredictable situation*".

Operational integration

Leuschner et al. (2013) and Eriksson (2015) describe operational integration through coordinated decision-making, joint work processes, and development activities.

The demand for construction work can show considerable variation due to both the frequency (intermittence) and size (lumpiness) of projects in a pipeline (Godsell et al., 2018). This makes projects appear both unpredictable and non-repeatable, while in reality, high commonality in requirements can exist between them. Not accounting for the possible efficiencies locked in SCM, engineering contractors often create a new SC for each project, in contrast to SCI principles. As highlighted by Pillay and Mafini (2017), "*supply chain integration is a common approach for resolving supply chain coordination issues within and between supply chains*". Thus, coordinated decision-making "*refers to the redeployment of decision rights, work and resources to the best positioned supply chain member*" (Leuschner et al., 2013). In practice, coordinated decision-making in SCI can align the demand profile (different construction project characteristics) to the best-suited SC configuration, resulting in systemic production channels facilitating material, information, and finance flows (Xue et al., 2005; Godsell et al., 2018).

Pursuing better operational integration through joint work processes is associated with the "*intention of the firms within the supply chain to integrate their actions and interactively adjust their behaviours while pursuing opportunities over time*" (Leuschner et al., 2013). Such integrative actions can include both short-term actions, such as improving supplier scheduling, resource visibility and capacity planning, and long-term actions, such as developing joint flexibility and SC adaptability (e.g. Ireland & Webb, 2007).

Developmental activities in operational integration include product and process engineering, joint investment, use of knowledge, and capabilities within the strategic supply chain and supplier development activities. Product and process engineering concerns integration of products and processes across firms within the strategic supply chain. In practice, this is achieved by allowing suppliers to assume responsibility for product engineering and development activities, including suppliers' understanding of the complexity and scope of coordinated processes within work packages (Ireland & Webb, 2007; Koufteros et al., 2005). Joint investment is simply "*the extent to which supply chain members jointly invest in projects of mutual interest*" (Leuschner et al., 2013). Examples include capital and equipment investments, financial investment, partial ownership, or provision of resources (Modi & Mabert, 2007).

Use of knowledge and capabilities is indicated by the extent to which members of the integrated SC have developed joint knowledge-sharing routines and capabilities, applied to actual innovative practices, sharing of new ideas, and working together in identifying and implementing improvement initiatives (Saad et al., 2002; Saeed et al., 2005; Ataseven & Nair, 2017). Lastly, within the construction industry, suppliers are often classified via the use of preferred supplier arrangements, framework agreements, and approved lists (Thorpe et al., 2003; Gosling et al., 2010). Addressing operational integration requires focused supplier development (Gosling et al., 2015). In order to develop SCI, supplier development initiatives should not be seen as "one-size-fits-all", as many initiatives require significant investment. Instead, they should be deployed towards shaping the integrated supplier portfolio in accordance with the engineering SCI needs (Wagner & Johnson, 2004).

Relational integration

Relational integration refers to the strategic connection among partners based on attitudes of trust, commitment, and long-term orientation (Leuschner et al., 2013; Eriksson, 2015).

Commitment includes the contractual relations between partners, risk allocation practices, and objectives alignment. In engineering projects, SC contractual relations indicate the level of expected commitment from partners. In increasing order of commitment, engineering contracts are usually as follows: normal tendering contract, preferred partners, SC framework agreement, and uniform administrative conditions contract (translated from Dutch "Uniforme Administratieve Voorwaarden" UAV-GC). The UAV-GC is an integrated form of contract, which has a strong project-based orientation, provides reusable information across projects, could resonate with prior partnering commitments, and encourage future long-term relations (e.g. long-term goals, such as maintenance of assets) (Papadonikolaki et al., 2017).

Commitment also relates to risk allocation, which describes "*how the risk is allocated and the reward is given*" (Meng et al., 2011). In engineering and construction, this is usually executed through gain- and pain-sharing schemes, which define "*the level of sharing of profits or cost savings as well as losses or cost increases among the owner, the designer, and the constructor*" (Mesa et al., 2016). As SCI maturity improves, partners are expected to develop relational integration through commitment in risk sharing, allocation, and balance of risk and reward (Meng et al., 2011). Lastly, commitment in SCI also depends on "*the level of alignment of interest and objectives among the owner, the designer, and the constructor*" (Mesa et al., 2016). Uneven commitment among the project participants is often identified as a major problem to the success of partnering arrangements (Kim & Nguyen, 2018). As highlighted by Meng et al. (2011), the three areas of setting objectives in construction are alignment (towards long-term mutual objectives), benefits (towards win-win in the long-term), and continuity of work (towards guaranteed future work).

In SCI, "*trust has a significant influence on the relationship between the parties*" (Meng et al., 2011). The level of trust that exists between partners manifests through the type of trust exhibited, confidence in others' behaviour, monitoring of others' work, as well as situational trust-influencing factors. In increasing level, the type of trust shared can be contractual, competence-based, short-term goodwill, and long-term goodwill trust (Meng et al., 2011). Regarding confidence in others' behaviour, partners can exhibit from little to full confidence. Limited trust can also manifest through checking and monitoring others' work, while high levels of trust make checking almost unnecessary. Trust-influencing factors relate to situational expectations and views that influence trustworthiness and trustfulness attitudes. Examples include perception of future work opportunity, project-specific circumstances, economic climate, and payment practices, etc. (Manu et al., 2015).

Long-term orientation refers to supplier relationships based on recurring arrangements and supplier involvement, instead of competitive bidding and arm's length relationships

(Turkulainen et al., 2017). This can be established by perceiving and striving for suppliers as long-term partners. Developing long-term orientation relies on high levels of collaboration between partners, often based on close working relationship, no-blame culture, teamwork, and attitudes of mutual help (Mesa et al., 2016). In addition, long-term orientation requires procurement practices based not solely on price but multi-criteria, from a long-term perspective (Meng et al., 2011).

Scope of integration

The scope dimension is associated with the number and nature of supply chain partners and their interdependencies (Eriksson, 2015).

Number of supply chain partners

The number of supply chain partners in the integrated SC is a supplier portfolio concept related to the configuration of the supplier base. Configuring the supply base encompasses a number of sub-activities, including reducing the number of suppliers, segmenting the supplier base, and assessing and selecting suppliers (Wagner & Johnson, 2004). A supply base that is best positioned to realise value from SCI requires a healthy balance across partnerships categories (approved, preferred, strategic) to allow main contractors to effectively configure the supply chain for different project requirements (Gosling et al., 2015).

Nature of supply chain partners

The scope dimension of SCI also relates to the nature of partners within the SC. It is characterised by behaviour of actors involved, their power position in the SC, and the extent of integration of suppliers.

Van der Vaart and Van Donk (2008) outline that integration includes patterns of behaviour which are often ignored in potential interactions between different aspects of integration. According to Wagner and Johnson (2004), behaviours evident in SCI are joint responsibility, shared planning, and flexibility of arrangements. However, such behaviours are often displayed only at dyadic level in a buyer-supplier business context. In a project-based context, behavioural aspects can be guided by the role actors play in SCI (e.g. Titus & Bröchner, 2005) and, as suggested by Turkulainen et al. (2017), a set of common antecedents that can moderate their behaviour towards improved value.

The nature of actors also relates to their power position in the SC. Such position is characterised by:

> [The] extent to which the product or service is standardised or commoditised, number of alternative suppliers available to the buyer, number of alternative buyers available to the supplier, switching costs for both buyers and suppliers and the level of information asymmetry advantage that one party has over the other.
>
> (Manu et al., 2015)

Lastly, the nature of partners also relates to the extent of their supplier integration. This is characterised by "*the strategic integration of buyer resources with supplier resources and the extension and blending of relevant activities between the buyer and seller firms*" (Wagner & Johnson, 2004). Partners with high levels of supplier integration can affect prioritisation in allocation of resources in the integrated SC. Furthermore, it can foster value engineering but also create implications to maximising "*value and responsiveness with optimal number of SC actors to changing customer needs and market dynamics*" (Pillay & Mafini, 2017).

Interdependencies in the supply chain

The scope dimension also relates to the interdependencies between partners. This involves the types of SC interdependencies and the interdependent networks they constitute. The types of interdependencies between actors in the construction supply chain are important because "*difficulties in SCI might relate to how the temporary supply chains (for specific projects), meet with the permanent supply chains in production of raw material and components*" (Bankvall et al., 2010). A way to understand these challenges is through the different types of interdependencies (pooled, sequential, reciprocal, and synchronic). For example, distinguishing pooled interdependence between activities relates different supply chains to each other, as well as different engineering projects to one another. However, the types of interdependencies may give only a partial picture of the project execution processes involved. They do not account for interdependencies based on networks (of contractual relationships, performance incentives, and information exchange) that may exist between partners. Discrepancies in and between these network categories can shift the point of centrality for SCI and form coalitions that can lead to suboptimal results (Pryke, 2004).

Duration of integration

Few studies explicitly investigate the duration of integration as a distinct SCI dimension (e.g. Bagchi et al., 2005; Kaufmann & Carter, 2006). In engineering projects, the duration dimension involves the length of the relationship over a series of projects, as well as the timing of involvement in a single project (Eriksson, 2015).

Longer duration time spans over a series of projects are found to strengthen the integration, because the partners get familiar with each other, develop mutual trust, and enhance possibilities of future work as they develop collaboration rather than opportunism (e.g. Zheng et al., 2008). Low frequency and separation of projects into different stages, often executed by different actors, make the duration dimension critical for SCI (e.g. Crespin-Mazet & Portier, 2010). In practice, strategic arrangements spanning over a series of projects are unusual (Bygballe et al., 2010). While there is evidence in partnering ventures between main contractors and their clients, partnering agreements with production subcontractors and materials suppliers are less common (Dainty et al., 2001). This is largely due to the client (PBO) applying commercial pressure that translates into switching suppliers between partnering projects, regardless of actors' good performance (Alderman & Ivory, 2007). Such practices lead to abandonment of partnering, send shocks to the SC, inhibit effective and efficient flows (of information, materials, and finance), and exacerbate fragmentation, thus preventing SCI from aggregating value. In contrast, successful strategic partnering arrangements spanning over a series of projects and involving subcontractors strengthen integration over time and allow for continuous improvements (i.e. standardisation by project profiles) (Bresnen & Marshall, 2002; Caniëls et al., 2012).

Rönnberg-Sjödin et al. (2011) convey that the length of engineering projects also allows achieving strong integration within a single project, especially if partners collaborate over many project stages. The importance of timing relates to procuring contractors and suppliers early, in order to contribute in collaborative and customised design (Salvador & Villena, 2013). In addition, from initiation to later phases of an engineering project, actors are known to change their views in desired partnering characteristics (e.g. cost, cooperation, and teamwork) (Wood & Ellis, 2005). Thus, the timing of involvement in a single project can provide actors with more time to socialise and tune in to the partnering spirit (Eriksson, 2008).

Depth of integration

The depth of integration relates to customer involvement and personnel representation in integrative activities across the partnering organisations, thus also capturing the aspect of internal integration (Eriksson, 2015).

Customer involvement is characterised by communicating with and integrating the PBO's end users in engineering projects (Kleinsmann et al., 2010). This enables supply chain integration, as end users can contribute to the design work with valuable insights based on their high level of expertise and infrastructure network intelligence. Importantly, the client can commit to the end product before handover. This approach is minimising discrepancies between partners' different internal functions, involved at different stages of a project (Olson et al., 2001). Reciprocally, educating the PBO in how SCI realises value can enhance customer involvement and its practical adoption.

Partners' personnel representation concerns the number, hierarchical level, and function of personnel involved in integrative activities. Appropriate personnel representation can focus SCI efforts and facilitate capturing of value through the SC echelons. In the context of engineering projects, it is argued that top management commitment is critical for integration (e.g. Johnsen, 2009), while personnel at lower hierarchical levels can strengthen collaboration (Zheng et al., 2008), by increasing behavioural transparency and reducing information asymmetry (Dyer, 1996). In practice, this could mean that main contractors need to increase the depth and strategic importance of their relationships with subcontractors, especially where the majority of work efforts take place (Eom et al., 2008). Davis and Love (2011) point out that the right personnel representation builds commitment and is displayed by the way in which a firm organises patterns of contact with its partners, the frequency of contact, and the level of personnel involved.

Conclusion

This chapter has separated out the idea of integration within a single supply chain and the integration of multiple supply chains that feed into a portfolio of projects (and programs). In order to understand better the various characteristics of projects, four portfolio archetypes are discussed: single project, multiple projects, traditional program management, and the program management of repetitive projects. Recognising these archetypes allows SCI to be carried out more effectively, with specific approaches for the different archetypes. Supply chain integration is described through four dimensions in the chapter: strength, scope, duration, and depth. When supply chains are analysed in detail, using these four dimensions, a detailed understanding of the needs for integration can be determined and then implemented.

References

Alderman N. and Ivory C. (2007) Partnering in major contracts: Paradox and metaphor. *International Journal of Project Management* 25(4), 386–393.

Ataseven C. and Nair A. (2017) Assessment of supply chain integration and performance relationships: A meta-analytic investigation of the literature. *International Journal of Production Economics* 185, 252–265.

Bagchi P., Ha B. & Skjoett-Larsen T. Soerensen L. (2005) Supply chain integration: A European survey. *The International Journal of Logistics Management* 16(2), 275–294.

Bakker F., Tillmann B. & van Donk D. (2012) Identifying barriers to internal supply chain integration using systems thinking. 4th Production and Operations Management World Conference, 1–10.

Bankvall L., Bygballe L., Dubois A. & Jahre M. (2010) Interdependence in supply chains and projects in construction. *Supply Chain Management: An International Journal* 15(5), 385–393.

Bresnen M. and Marshall N. (2002) The engineering or evolution of co-operation? A tale of two partnering projects. *International Journal of Project Management* 20(7), 497–505.

Briscoe G. & Dainty A. (2005) Construction supply chain integration: An elusive goal? *Supply Chain Management: An International Journal* 10(4), 319–326.

Broft R., Badi S. & Pryke S. (2016) Towards supply chain maturity in construction. *Built Environment Project and Asset Management* 6(2), 187–204.

Bygballe L., Jahre M. & Sward A. (2010) Partnering relationships in construction: A literature review. *Journal of Purchasing and Supply Management* 16, 239–253.

Caniëls M., Gelderman C. & Vermeulen N. (2012) The interplay of governance mechanisms in complex procurement projects. *Journal of Purchasing and Supply Management* 18(2), 113–121.

Childerhouse P., Deakins E., Bohme T., Towill D., Disney S. & Banomyong R. (2011) Supply chain integration: An international comparison of maturity. *Asia Pacific Journal of Marketing and Logistics* 23(4), 531–552.

Costa F., Granja A., Fregola A. & Picchi F. (2019) Understanding relative importance of barriers to improving the customer-supplier relationship within construction supply chains using DEMATEL technique. *Journal of Management in Engineering* 35(3), 1–13.

Crespin-Mazet F. & Portier P. (2010) The reluctance of construction purchasers towards project partnering. *Journal of Purchasing and Supply Management* 16(4), 230–238.

Dainty A., Millett S. & Briscoe, G. H. (2001) 'New perspectives on construction supply chain integration. *Supply Chain Management: An International Journal* 6(4), 163–173.

Davies, A. & Brady, T. (2000) Organisational capabilities and learning in complex product systems: Towards repeatable solutions. *Research Policy* 29(7–8), 931–953.

Davies A. & Brady T. (2016) Explicating the dynamics of project capabilities. *International Journal of Project Management* 34(2), 314–327.

Davies A., MacAulay S., DeBarro T. & Thurston M. (2015) Making innovation happen in a megaproject: London's crossrail suburban railway system. *Project Management Journal* 45(6), 25–37.

Davis P. & Love P. (2011) 'Alliance contracting: Adding value through relationship development', Engineering. *Construction and Architectural Management* 18(5), 444–461.

Dyer J. (1996) Does governance matter? Keiretsu alliances and asset specificity as sources of Japanese competitive advantage. *Organization Science* 7(6), 593–682.

Elliman T. and Orange G. (2003) Developing distributed design capabilities in the construction supply chain. *Construction Innovation* 3(1), 15–26.

Eom C., Yun, S. & Paek, J. (2008) Subcontractor evaluation and management framework for strategic partnering. *Journal of Construction Engineering and Management* 134(11), 842–851.

Eriksson P. (2008) Achieving suitable coopetition in buyer-supplier relationships: The case of Astrazeneca. *Journal of Business-to-Business Marketing* 15(4), 425–454.

Eriksson P. (2015) Partnering in engineering projects: Four dimensions of supply chain integration. *Journal of Purchasing and Supply Management* 21(1), 38–50.

Godsell J., Masi D., Karatzas A. & Brady T. (2018) Using project demand profiling to improve the effectiveness and efficiency of infrastructure projects. *International Journal of Operations and Production Management* 38(6), 1422–1442.

Gosling J., Naim M., Towill D., Abouarghoub W. & Moone B. (2015) Supplier development initiatives and their impact on the consistency of project performance. *Construction Management and Economics* 33(5–6), 390–403.

Gosling J., Purvis L. & Naim, M. (2010) Supply chain flexibility as a determinant of supplier selection. *International Journal of Production Economics* 128(1), 11–21.

Hartmann A. & Caerteling J. (2010) Subcontractor procurement in construction: The interplay of price and trust. *Supply Chain Management: An International Journal* 15(5), 354–362.

Huang J. & Newell S. (2003) Knowledge integration processes and dynamics within the context of cross-functional projects. *International Journal of Project Management* 21(3), 167–176.

Hult T., Ketchen D. & Arrfelt M. (2007) Strategic supply chain management: Improving performance through a culture of competitiveness and knowledge development. *Strategic Management Journal* 28(10), 1035–1052.

Ireland P. (2004) Managing appropriately in construction power regimes: Understanding the impact of regularity in the project environment. *Supply Chain Management: An International Journal* 9(5), 372–382.

Ireland R. & Webb J. (2007) A multi-theoretic perspective on trust and power in strategic supply chains. *Journal of Operations Management* 25(2), 482–497.

Johnsen T. (2009) Supplier involvement in new product development and innovation: Taking stock and looking to the future. *Journal of Purchasing and Supply Management* 15(3), 187–197.

Johnson J. (1999) Strategic integration in industrial distribution channels: Managing the interfirm relationship as a strategic asset. *Journal of the Academy of Marketing Science* 27(1), 4–18.

Kaplan R. & Norton D. (2000) *Focusing Your Organization on Strategy – with the Balanced Scorecard*. Second Edition. Harvard Business Review Press.

Kaufmann L. and Carter C. (2006) International supply relationships and non-financial performance – A comparison of U.S. and German practices. *Journal of Operations Management* 24, 653–675.

Kim D. & Lee R. (2010) Systems Collaboration and strategic collaboration: Their impacts on supply chain responsiveness and market performance. *Decision Sciences* 41(4), 955–981.

Kim S. & Nguyen V. (2018) A structural model for the impact of supply chain relationship traits on project performance in construction. *Production Planning and Control* 29(2), 170–183.

Kleinsmann M., Buijs J. and Valkenburg R. (2010) Understanding the complexity of knowledge integration in collaborative new product development teams: A case study. *Journal of Engineering and Technology Management* 27(1–2), 20–32.

Koufteros X., Vonderembse M. & Jayaram J. (2005) Internal and external integration for product development: The contingency effects of uncertainty, equivocality, and platform strategy. *Decision Sciences* 36(1), 97–133.

Kumar R. & Pugazhendhi S. (2012) Information sharing in supply chains: An overview. *Procedia Engineering* 38, 2147–2154.

Leuschner R., Rogers, D. & Charvet, F. (2013) A meta-analysis of supply chain integration and firm performance. *Journal of Supply Chain Management* 49(2), 34–57.

Manu E., Ankrah N., Chinyio E. & Proverbs D. (2015) Trust influencing factors in main contractor and subcontractor relationships during projects. *International Journal of Project Management* 33(7), 1495–1508.

Meng X., Sun M. & Jones M. (2011) Maturity model for supply chain relationships in construction. *Journal of Management in Engineering* 27(2), 97–105.

Mesa H., Molenaar K. & Alarcón, L. (2016) Exploring performance of the integrated project delivery process on complex building projects. *International Journal of Project Management* 34(7), 1089–1101.

Modi S. & Mabert, V. (2007) Supplier development: Improving supplier performance through knowledge transfer. *Journal of Operations Management* 25(1), 42–64.

Näslund D. & Hulthen H. (2012) Supply chain management integration: A critical analysis. *Benchmarking* 19(4), 481–501.

Olawale Y. & Sun, M. (2010) Cost and time control of construction projects: Inhibiting factors and mitigating measures in practice. *International Journal of Project Management* 28(5), 509–526.

Olson E., Walker O., Ruekert R. & Bonner J. (2001) Patterns of cooperation during new product development among marketing, operations and R&D: Implications for project performance. *Journal of Product Innovation Management* 18(4), 258–271.

Papadonikolaki E., Verbraeck A. & Wamelink H. (2017) Formal and informal relations within BIM-enabled supply chain partnerships. *Construction Management and Economics* 35(8–9), 531–552.

Pillay P. & Mafini C. (2017) Supply chain bottlenecks in the South African construction industry: Qualitative insights. *Journal of Transport and Supply Chain Management* 11, 1–13.

PMI (2017) *The Standard for Portfolio Management*. Fourth Edition. Project Management Institute.

Polat G., Okay F. & Eray E. (2014) Factors affecting cost overruns in micro-scaled construction companies. *Procedia Engineering* 85, 428–435.

Pryke S. (2004) Analysing construction project coalitions: Exploring the application of social network analysis. *Construction Management and Economics* 22(8), 787–797.

Rai A., Patnayakuni R. & Seth N. (2006) Firm performance impacts of digitally enabled supply chain integration capabilities. *MIS Quarterly: Management Information Systems* 30(2), 225–246.

Richardson G. (1990) *Information and Investment: A Study in the Working of the Competitive Economy*. Second Edition. Oxford University Press.

Rodrigues A., Stank T. & Lynch D. (2004) Linking strategy, structure, process, and performance in integrated logistics. *Journal of Business Logistics* 25(2), 65–94.

Rönnberg-Sjödin D., Eriksson P. E. and Frishammar J. (2011) Open innovation in process industries: A lifecycle perspective on development of process equipment. *International Journal of Technology Management* 56, 225–240.

Saad M., Jones M. & James P. (2002) A review of the progress towards the adoption of supply chain management (SCM) relationships in construction. *European Journal of Purchasing & Supply Management* 8, 173–183.

Saeed K., Malhotra M. & Grover V. (2005) Examining the impact of interorganizational systems on process efficiency and sourcing leverage in buyer-supplier dyads. *Decision Sciences* 36(3), 365–396.

Salvador F. & Villena V. (2013) Supplier integration and NPD outcomes: Conditional moderation effects of modular design competence. *Journal of Supply Chain Management* 49(1), 87–113.

Sanders N. & Premus R. (2005) Modeling the relationship between firm it capability, collaboration, and performance. *Journal of Business Logistics* 26(1), 1–23.

Stevens G. (1989) Integrating the supply chain. *International Journal of Physical Distribution and Materials Management* 19(8), 3–8.

Syntetos A., Boylan J. & Croston J. (2005) On the categorization of demand patterns. *Journal of the Operational Research Society* 56(5), 495–503.

Thorpe A., Dainty A. & Hatfield H. (2003) The realities of being preferred: Specialist subcontractor perspectives on restricted tender list membership. *Journal of Construction Procurement* 9(1), 47–55.

Titus S. & Bröchner J. (2005) Managing information flow in construction supply chains. *Construction Innovation* 5(2), 71–82.

Turkulainen V., Kauppi K. & Nermes E. (2017) Institutional explanations: Missing link in operations management? Insights on supplier integration. *International Journal of Operations and Production Management* 37(8), 1117–1140.

Van der Vaart, T. & Van Donk, D. (2008) A critical review of survey-based research in supply chain integration'. *International Journal of Production Economics* 111(1), 42–55.

Venkataraman R. (2004) *Project Supply Chain Management: Optimizing value: The Way We Manage the Total Supply Chain*. Wiley.

Vrijhoef R. (2011) *Supply Chain Integration in the Building Industry: The Emergence of Integrated and Repetitive Strategies in a Fragmented and Project-driven Industry*. IOS Press.

Wagner S. & Johnson, J. (2004) Configuring and managing strategic supplier portfolios. *Industrial Marketing Management* 33(8), 717–730.

Wood G. & Ellis R. (2005) Main contractor experiences of partnering relationships on UK construction projects. *Construction Management and Economics* 23(3), 317–325.

Xue X., Li X., Shen Q. & Wang Y. (2005) An agent-based framework for supply chain coordination in construction. *Automation in Construction* 14(3), 413–430.

Xue X., Wang Y., Shen Q. & Yu X. (2007) Coordination mechanisms for construction supply chain management in the Internet environment. *International Journal of Project Management* 25(2), 150–157.

Zheng J., Roehrich J. & Lewis, M. (2008) The dynamics of contractual and relational governance: Evidence from long-term public-private procurement arrangements. *Journal of Purchasing and Supply Management* 14(1), 43–54.

22 Agile portfolio management

Steve Messenger and Katy Angliss

Introduction

This chapter focuses on agile portfolio management. To do this, the chapter firstly provides some context by briefly discussing the agile philosophy and the concept of the agile organisation. Less established within an academic and practical context, agile portfolio management is argued as underpinning the agile organisation as an enabler for business agility. Academic discussions, as in Chapter 10, sometimes refer to this as dynamic capabilities (Killen & Hunt, 2013) The chapter is not intended to advocate the use of agile or agile portfolio management, as there are varying perspectives on this area of portfolio management, with further reading including Krebs (2009) and Neilson (2021).

The chapter aims to present some current approaches and thinking in agile portfolio management to promote further discussion. The more practical elements within this chapter are aligned with the Agile Business Consortium's approach to agile portfolio management (Agile Business Consortium, 2021), adopting the VMOST (*vision, mission, objectives, strategy, and tactics*) technique for strategy definition.

The agile philosophy

Agile is a philosophy centred on people and their interactions, delivering benefits into an organisation. It includes fundamental ways of thinking, working, and interacting. In fact, agile is *foremost* a way of thinking and acting. The Agile Manifesto (Fowler & Highsmith, 2001) was created to explain this. Whilst the manifesto concentrates on software development, the agile approach is now used in all parts of organisations. Agile implementations may have many contexts and flavours, but underlying them all, there are some basic concepts:

- *It is better to give people capabilities they can benefit from as early and as often as possible.* Agile concentrates on the delivery of value early and often. Value comes when business processes and organisational structures are aligned to getting the most benefit from a solution. Work is prioritised based on what will give most value and can be delivered early, as some benefits may not be realisable immediately. Often, organisations lose the opportunity to benefit early from projects as nothing is delivered until towards the end of the project. Agile requires the design of projects so that they deliver capabilities incrementally as early and as often as possible. The organisation then reaps the benefits of early use and becomes more confident in the incrementally developing outputs.

DOI: 10.4324/9780367853129-25

- *Change will happen and should be taken as normal rather than as an exception that has to be avoided.* Scope change in projects has traditionally been hard to incorporate into projects and programs. It is often regarded as something to be avoided or assessed in detail and minimised. This results in projects and programs failing as they deliver something out of date that does not meet the requirements when delivered. Agile embraces change and treats it as normal whilst still needing to have a clear idea of where the customer or project deliverable ultimately wants to end up and whether it makes sense to do so. That is, the benefits will outweigh the potential costs, risks, and disruption of getting there. Therefore, there needs to be a vision and high-level plans on how to achieve it. However, there is no point in trying to predict and plan in too much detail too soon, so agile advocates planning enough to understand the problem and how to move forward, but no more. More detailed plans can be created as specific steps are started.
- *The best result emerges from iterative feedback.* Agile recognises that it is impossible to define up-front completely and in detail exactly what is required. It is necessary to define what the overall need is, but then to understand that the detail will emerge and evolve as more is known, and as inevitable changes in the business environment affect the requirements. This is achieved by constantly asking for, and acting on, feedback from those who will use the solution. It also implies that the customer is continuously and actively involved.
- *Small, motivated, empowered teams are more effective and produce better results.* In most agile approaches, small, multidisciplined teams are created that include those that will benefit from a solution, as well as those that will develop it. There is a specific goal and a common purpose that helps create a culture of collaboration. The teams are empowered to meet the goal – that is, they are generally left alone to deliver their goals, making their own decisions and evolving the solution. Empowerment is not limitless – it is restricted to the fulfilment of the goal and generally does not cover decisions that may impact others outside the team who have not empowered the team to speak for them.
- *Communication.* A small team, which can often be co-located, communicates naturally, and there is far less confusion or misunderstanding.
- *Fail fast.* Uncertainty is one of the drivers of agile. An agile approach encourages trying something early and getting feedback. If it is wrong, it can then be modified. This concept, called "fail fast", implies that no time is wasted following the wrong path and finding out it is wrong late in the process, when it becomes costly to put it right. Each failure eliminates wrong assumptions and helps create the right and best solution.

From Agile development to agile organisations

Although the Agile Manifesto wasn't created until 2001, agile concepts were being used in the early 1990s. Agile, as it's understood today, started because software developers saw the traditional ways of working were often not effective and produced the wrong results. Much of early agile was centred on software programming. Soon it was clear that, to solve complete business solutions, the agile approach needed to encompass and modify project management procedures – allowing the team empowerment and fast, iterative development whilst maintaining sufficient governance. In the mid-1990s, methods emerged to do this, notably DSDM (dynamic system development method) – now agile project management (Agile Business Consortium, 2021) – and SCRUM (an agile technique). Once these higher-level approaches to agile existed, it was relatively easy to use them for initiatives outside of software development and IT. The examples of this are many, including large-scale agile development within different sectors (Rautiainen et al., 2011; Laanti & Kangas, 2015; Cooper & Sommer, 2020).

The following three examples (Agile Business Consortium, 2021) show the different industries and areas that have benefited. Further case studies are available at the Agile Business Consortium (2021), ranging from companies like Moonpig (the online card and present business) through to universities. Examples include:

- Building equipment for use in the battlefield, where the DSDM approach was used to build and implement specialised communication equipment.
- Streamlining risk management at the ONS (UK Office for National Statistics), where agile project management and LEAN principles were used to improve procedures and reduce schedule and resource usage.
- Providing support for pain-related health problems in the pharmaceutical drug development industry.

More recently, the thrust for agile has been into programs, portfolios, and general business, creating the concept of the *agile organisation*. Holbeche (2015) shows how, from an organisational perspective, the agile philosophy has been used to change culture, recruitment, build strategy, and change business models. The use of agile portfolio management is one of the latest trends, as it has to underpin an agile organisation, helping to define and execute the projects needed to create value for an organisation.

Overview of agile portfolio management

Technology, expectations, and attitudes have all affected the speed of environmental and organisational change; organisations that cannot keep up will not survive. Consequently, organisations must ensure that they can react to change quickly and effectively. The approach to business improvement, organisational change, and transformation must reflect this and can be achieved by taking an agile approach to strategy, portfolio, and program management, as well as within projects and continuous improvement initiatives. Empowering teams to deliver value, reacting to change, and focusing on what delivers value are key. For this to work, it is important that the goals and strategy of the organisation are clear and well communicated. Scope changes in projects and programs can then be assessed against strategy, and the strategy amended if required. Business improvements, changes, and transformations can be managed within portfolios that reflect the strategy and ensure the creation of value for the organisation and its stakeholders. In this way, teams undertaking such initiatives will understand their end goal and can be self-directing within the limits of their empowerment.

This all implies that agile portfolio management must be underpinned by a good strategy, with the growing recognition of emergent strategy as part of managing agile portfolios (Kaufmann et al., 2020). This then comes with the added complexity of managing a portfolio of agile projects (Sweetman & Conboy, 2018). Some portfolios may need to manage both agile and non-agile (such as Waterfall) projects, adding a further dimension to the complexity and increasing the requirement for adaptiveness in managing emergent strategy, such that larger organisations have the "agility" to compete with other entrepreneurial enterprises (Stettina & Horz, 2015; Horlach et al., 2019; Imbrizi & Maccari, 2014).

Agile strategy

Often, strategy is defined by senior leaders in an organisation and expected to be implemented by others within the organisation who were not involved in its creation. It can also be hard to change. However, as previously stated, the ability to change quickly is essential in today's environment. Adopting an agile approach to strategy helps with this. Such an approach can be applied to many different levels, including defining the overall strategy for an organisation (which will then get delivered via agile portfolio management), through to the strategy for specific initiatives or portfolios. There are some key considerations (Lyngso, 2014):

- *Actively involve people.* When building a team to create strategy, people from all parts and all levels of the organisation should be included and involved. This will ensure all aspects are covered and that everyone understands the strategy and are willing and prepared to implement it. Involving customers and suppliers where possible and fostering a culture of collaboration within the strategy teams and to the wider community will ensure that the strategy makes sense in the marketplaces or communities served by an organisation. Having clear goals and creating a sense of purpose and urgency can often achieve this.
- *Communicate and welcome feedback.* As the strategy evolves, it should be communicated clearly and concisely to the organisation. The agreed strategy should be easy to understand and known by everyone in the organisation (and outside the organisation as much as that can be achieved). Communication is continuous: encouraging and listening to feedback on the strategy, evaluating the information seriously, then either changing the strategy or providing clear reasons why not.
- *Take small incremental steps.* Designing the strategy so that it can be implemented incrementally, early, and often. This enables the organisation to benefit as soon as possible (and hence get value) from the changes the strategy brings. It also gives an opportunity to test that the strategy is right and to change it if it is not.
- *Review frequently, change as required.* Build in reviews of the strategy to ensure it is still appropriate. However, be aware that too much change to the strategy may cause the organisation to lose faith in it.
- *Welcome change.* Internal or external changes to the environment in which the organisation operates may mean that the strategy must change. This is not seen as negative, but a natural occurrence, evaluating the change and amending the strategy as appropriate.
- *Pilot/iterate.* As early and often as possible, try out the parts of the strategy on specific areas of the organisation to get feedback and to check that the strategy is moving in the right direction. Again, review and change based on the feedback and experience.

It is important to say that the agile approach can be combined with existing, proven techniques for defining strategy. For instance, the VMOST technique shown in Figure 22.1.

This VMOST approach is inherently agile, with iterative development. From an initial vision and mission, considering the objectives and strategy will provide information to enhance the vision and mission. This can then flow back to alter the objectives and strategy that again feeds back into the vision and mission. At some point (often after three iterations), the model becomes stable, and tactics can be formulated. Using the tactics to implement the strategy will then also provide feedback to enhance

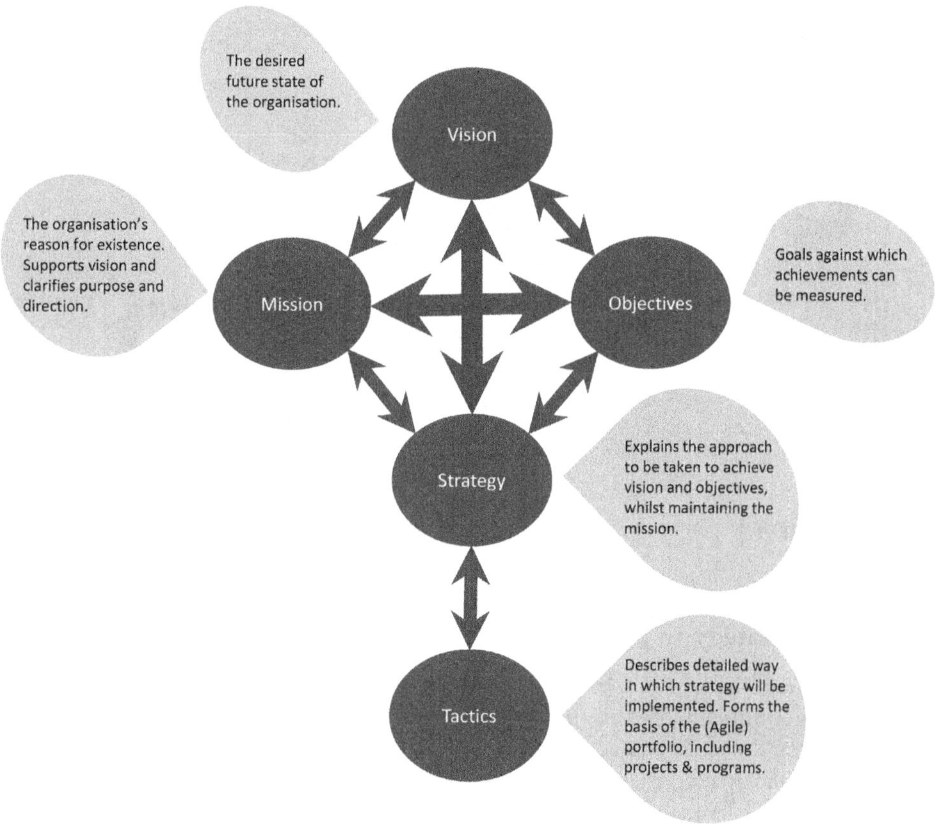

Figure 22.1 VMOST technique for defining strategy.

Source: Adapted from Rosasco and Dehlinger (2011).

the whole model. Business canvases (typically a one-page visualisation with a set of boxes representing the main elements of the business idea) are often used in agile approaches (Nidagundi & Novickis, 2017). Lean canvas models can typically include identifying:

1) The business problem.
2) Business outcomes (or changes in customer behaviour).
3) Users and customers.
4) User benefits.
5) Solution ideas.
6) Hypotheses (i.e. one hypothesis or user benefit obtained for each feature).
7) The riskiest assumption for each hypothesis (i.e. what is the greatest failure point).
8) The quickest actions (or experiments) to reduce or negate the riskiest assumptions.

Defining strategy in this way can also help define an effective agile portfolio management approach.

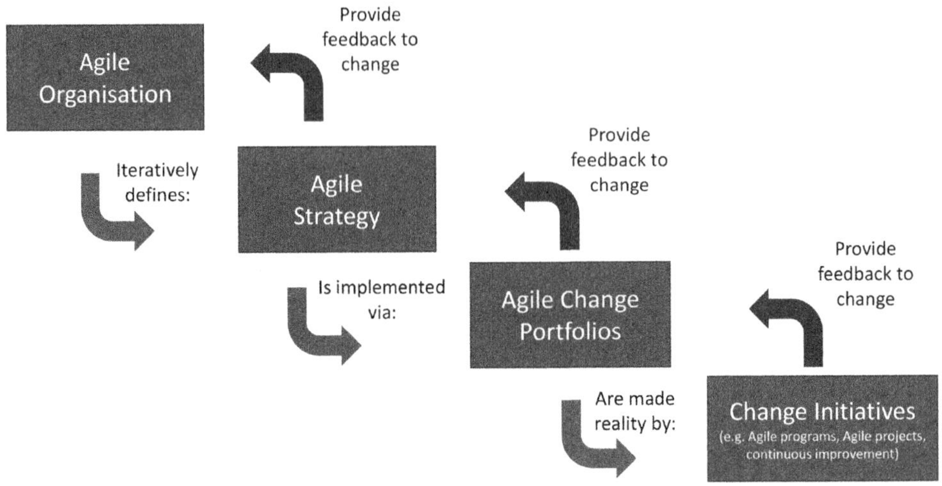

Figure 22.2 From agile strategy to agile change.

From agile strategy to agile change

Following one of the key themes in this book, an important question to ask is: How does the strategy get implemented in the agile environment? Figure 22.2 shows the potential steps in making the strategy a reality.

Agile portfolio management is used to examine the strategy and define a set of one or more portfolios to manage the implementation of the projects and programs required to implement the strategy (and thereby realise the vision). The agile portfolio management process will help define and subsequently manage the initiatives needed to deliver the strategy.

Agile portfolio management approach

This section will concentrate on the agile portfolio management step in the journey from strategy to reality. It is not the intention to reinvent the many useful concepts already defined for portfolio management, many of which will or can still apply in agile environments. The aim is to provide the right mindset to be successful as an agile organisation delivering portfolios of work. Thus, it is important to identify the key behaviours that will drive effective execution in agile environments. Many of these behaviours are centred on ensuring that everything an organisation does adds value, particularly for those whom the organisation provides products or services, and promotes a healthy and vibrant working environment. Based on the work done by the Agile Business Consortium in the area of agile portfolio management, these behaviours can be defined as follows (Agile Business Consortium, 2021).

All activity should create value for the organisation, its stakeholders, and its customers. From business strategy to small projects, as with continuous improvement, the aim is always to create value. In order to achieve this:

- The organisation's purpose, vision, strategy, and values must be clearly and simply defined, consistent with each other and understood by everyone.
- The required high-level outcomes should be defined, understood, and regularly reviewed.
- Strategy should evolve and have goals which reflect the vision.
- Any decisions should be consistent with the strategy and vision and lead to the creation of value.
- There should be effective measures and performance indicators that can show value is being achieved.
- There should be clear and transparent prioritisation criteria which are concentrated on the creation of value.
- Portfolios should be based around the value-driven strategy and cross-functional teams rather than aligned to individual business areas.

Continual review of the portfolio to ensure it reflects strategy and incorporates change. Strategy will evolve, and the business environment will change, based on internal and external events, and as previously discussed, the portfolio needs to reflect this. When reviewing or creating the portfolio, checks should ensure that:

- The portfolio is aligned to business strategy, therefore ensuring delivery of value.
- Items in the portfolio are reviewed and prioritised iteratively and frequently so that optimum value is created when the organisation requires it. This includes delivering related items together, because doing so creates more value for less effort. It is also important to consider the organisation's capacity to deal with change.
- The portfolio is planned to enable value to be delivered incrementally.
- Plans are for periods that are sensible and achievable and not based on an artificial annual or other long-term time period.
- Feedback is welcomed and reviewed frequently and may lead to updates to the portfolio.
- The amount of work in progress is limited to what is practicable given the availability of resources and the potential impacts on the organisation.
- Any capabilities or skills required to fulfil the portfolio which are currently not present in the organisation have been identified, and there are plans in place to bridge the gap (either through training or recruitment).

Delivering optimum value is the main purpose of portfolio management. It should always be possible to demonstrate that the portfolio is delivering optimum value to the organisation as and when it needs it. However, this does not imply rigid and bureaucratic procedures for capturing status information. Most information should come from that which is being created by the teams carrying out the changes. This is achieved by:

- Transparency and openness of progress and issues. The status of items in the portfolio should be clear and visible to all.
- A senior business owner taking responsibility for ensuring that the change is incorporated into the organisational processes and will deliver value.

Involving the right people to shape and manage and create the portfolio will produce more successful outcomes. It is important to consider the experience, capabilities, and aspirations of people when deciding on those who will be involved in the creation, management, and delivery of the portfolio. Look to:

- Ensure the right people will be available at the right time.
- Understand people's capabilities and aspirations. Giving people roles that use their skills and help them achieve their goals is very motivating and will lead to high-performing teams. Be aware that people may also have hidden skills not known to the organisation that could be useful in the portfolio work.
- Attract and retain the right people for the organisation.

Encouraging innovation and creativity builds a better strategy. New ideas can come from anywhere at any time. Many may be of great benefit to the organisation and its stakeholders. Thus, new ideas should be encouraged and taken seriously. Some key points to encourage this are to:

- Define a clear and simple process for introducing and evaluating new ideas, and make sure it is well communicated.
- Treat ideas respectfully and with an open mind.
- Recognise and reward organisational behaviours that encourage innovation.

Empowered and collaborative teams are more likely to be successful in delivering value. An organisation will be successful if people with clear goals, working together across the organisation, are empowered to deliver changes that add value. In order to achieve this, consider:

- Everyone must understand that anything they do must contribute towards the achievement of the business strategy and goals. This may imply that someone else's change is more valuable at this time than their own one.
- Build a culture of trust and ownership.
- Ensure commercial arrangements support and encourage agility.

Defining and running the portfolio

In order to be useful and effective, as is perhaps already obvious, the purpose of an agile portfolio must be clearly defined and structured to provide optimum value to the organisation. The Agile Business Consortium's agile portfolio management approach shows the flow for defining and running an agile portfolio, adapted in Figure 22.3. The first two steps (confirm drivers and confirm framework) deal with defining the purpose of the portfolio and how to choose change initiatives (including projects and programs) that should be contained within it. The second two deal with the selection and execution of change items to deliver the appropriate value to the organisation and to provide feedback to amend the portfolio parameters, or indeed, the strategy, based on experience.

Confirming drivers and framework

A portfolio may cover all initiatives the organisation is aiming to achieve (the corporate book of work), or it may be for a specific purpose. It is therefore important that the goals and boundaries of the portfolio are clearly defined and that they are aligned to the business strategy. This is particularly important in agile as the teams are self-directing and empowered and therefore need to be clear on the goals, expected outcomes, and

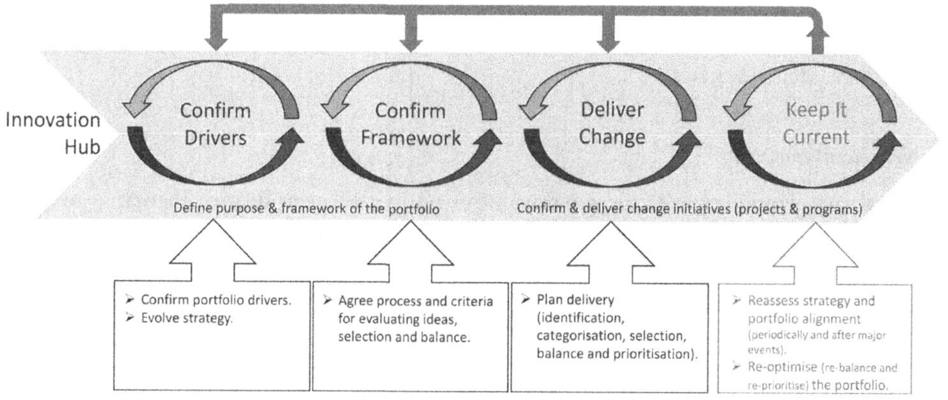

Figure 22.3 Agile portfolio management.

Source: Adapted from Agile Business Consortium (2021).

constraints of their empowerment. Based on the portfolio goals, a set of criteria can be created which are used for assessing ideas and initiatives to be included in the portfolio and how they will be prioritised. Such a set of criteria enables objective decision-making. Criteria may include elements such as risk, benefits realisation, costs, strategic alignment, innovation, ability to execute, capacity constraints, quality, change impact, short-term/long-term impact, etc. However, the key criteria must always be the creation of optimum value. Having clearly defined portfolio entry criteria ensures that:

- There is a clear and objective method for evaluating portfolio items.
- Continue/stop decisions for running initiatives are made using the same criteria.

Planning and selecting change initiatives (with projects and programs)

Whilst the parameters defined in "*Confirming drivers and framework*" will be used in the selection and prioritisation process, the key driver is still to produce optimum value now and as required. In agile portfolio management, prioritising and planning should be frequent and take into account changing circumstances. In fact, no initiative is really definite until it has started. This allows for changes in the business environment and/or the strategy and the incorporation of items of more value.

When selecting and prioritising, it is useful to think of two different fields of view, or horizons:

1 Longer-term horizon

To provide some higher-level plans and priorities for future work. This allows the organisation to see when longer-term initiatives may start and may be delivered. The majority of initiatives at this level typically will be immature, with a limited understanding of the size and shape of the solution to be evolved. Although there may be some view of when in the future the initiatives may start, they are not necessarily prioritised, and the plans are very volatile and subject to change. Some initiatives may be ready to execute but are not currently of a priority to start immediately. There may be dependencies between initiatives. These should be clearly stated, and any ordering or prioritisation done should reflect these dependencies.

2 Near-term horizon

Focused on planned work due to start now or in the near future. Prioritisation and dependency will determine the order within the horizon. Initiatives will typically be ready to execute or close to being ready, since these initiatives are seen as contributing most value in the immediate future (or required for future initiatives to deliver value). This horizon may also include some foundation work (analysis, etc.) on immature initiatives. This needs to be prioritised along with everything else. Whilst this plan is less volatile, as it is dealing with work that has already started, it still needs frequent review, especially to incorporate changing circumstances.

Planning

Agile portfolio prioritisation, balancing, blending, and subsequent planning should always be a collaborative activity and is often best done in a workshop environment. The process is iterative – continuing until a relatively stable plan is agreed. During this activity, a number of factors are considered:

- Current initiatives
- Ready initiatives (waiting to start)
- Current priorities
- Refined priorities – to make the most effective use of existing resources (blending and balancing)
- How to work with existing constraints
- Identifying any economies of scale
- Identifying alignment points where a combination of initiatives will deliver wider benefits, for example, a step change in the business as-is position
- The operational work being carried out that is not considered to be a project or a program (also known as business-as usual-work)

Budgeting

It is likely that a portfolio will be constrained by budgets. Budgets provide valuable information as to what is achievable and enable organisations to make big decisions about investment and strategy. However, many organisations attach detailed budgets to portfolios, often covering significant time periods and specific areas or initiatives, which are difficult to change. Often, not enough is known about future initiatives to make such informed budgetary decisions.

This often leads to bad behaviours or outcomes, such as:

- Potentially valuable initiatives being dismissed too early.
- Inability to introduce new, valuable initiatives.

- Reluctance to give up initiatives in the plans or stop running initiatives.
- Obsession with cost over value/benefit.
- Trying to fit initiatives into a fixed and often inappropriate timeframe because of budgets.
- False sense of future certainty.
- Budgets locked down after being based on insufficient detail.

There are two kinds of agile budgeting that can be applied, which provide the benefits of budgeting whilst helping avoid the pitfalls, often referred to as "beyond budgeting" (Hope & Fraser, 2003; Morlidge, 2017).

1. Fix money, resources, and time, and flex the initiatives (using prioritisation). This concentrates portfolio management on executing those initiatives that will provide optimum value.
2. Assign budget to the most valuable initiatives, which helps deliver optimum value early and incrementally. The initiatives will have been assessed (e.g. in a business case) for how much value they add to the organisation. These initiatives are then executed, as soon as the resources are available. The budget remains flexible and accumulates as initiatives are executed. The process can be stopped at any time if it is assessed that enough has been spent.

Often, organisations may choose to use both approaches. In either approach, budgets for initiatives are committed only when the initiative needs to start, in order to deliver its value at the right time. This will imply that there is sufficient evidence that the initiative will deliver value, and the value will normally outweigh the associated costs and risks – that is, there is an agreed business case.

Continuous improvement and small changes

Often in agile environments, there is a continuous improvement (CI) process, where value is added incrementally and often by a small amount of change. Teams are often dedicated to continuous improvement in specific areas. Whilst this is very effective, there are some considerations:

- Teams or team members are potentially not available for larger/more important initiatives.
- Teams can become too focused on a specific area and work on changes in that area that add little value.
- Teams are too focused to recognise that initiatives and changes outside their area are more important.

Incorporation into the portfolio of each of the items within all the CI initiatives may make the portfolio cluttered and hard to manage. It is important, though, that the overall CI initiatives are incorporated into the portfolio so that the resource usage (budget, people, etc.) and availability is clearly defined and agreed. There is also an opportunity to prioritise them against the wider portfolio (for instance, the team may be diverted for one period to work on a more important initiative). The teams should also refocus back to the business strategy and be aware of the overall organisational needs, highlighting when they believe their efforts may be more useful elsewhere (see Chapter 13 for further discussion on resource management).

Further considerations

When deciding about planning and prioritising the initiatives in the portfolio, it is useful to remember:

- Doing too much in parallel may deliver less value (see Chapter 13, discussing multi-tasking); therefore:
    - Run the most beneficial and most urgent initiatives to deliver value early.
    - Leave others for later consideration.
- Don't use the full portfolio budget without good reason:
    - "Good" reasons are decisions based around the business cases, which, as well as financial value, should demonstrate how initiatives support the strategy. Delivering value is always the driving force rather than simply spending the budget.

Delivering projects and programs in the portfolio to produce value

The delivering change step in Figure 22.3 can be seen as a funnel, along a four-stage portfolio horizon, from the *longer-term view*, with rough balancing and blending based on the organisational strategy, to the *near-term view*, with more accurate balancing and blending based on strategy and availability, to *today*, with fine-tuning based on strategy, progress, and availability, and finally, the *past, f*eeding the learning back into the earlier stages. The changes will be implemented via initiatives (or as part of continuous improvement). At the initiative level, the responsibility for delivery is with the team assigned to work on the change and will be managed using processes such as agile program management, agile project management, Scrum, etc.

The role of portfolio management is to entrust and empower the teams to deliver the projects and programs and to interfere as little as possible, understanding that there is a culture of collaboration, openness, and visibility. The portfolio team will use information already available within the delivery teams to ensure that value is being created and initiatives remain aligned to the organisation's strategy. They only need to intervene when there are indications that this isn't happening. Portfolio management will also have an oversight across initiatives: managing dependencies and ensuring dependent initiatives are kicked off at the right time.

Ensuring the portfolio is current and is delivering value

Continual review and refinement of the portfolio is important in ensuring that the changes it contains remain fully aligned to business strategy, and to check that the portfolio overall is delivering the value expected. There are several events or milestones, both internal and external, that provide a good opportunity to carry out portfolio reviews. For instance:

- Business strategy changes.
- Internal or external changes to the environment the organisation operates in.
- Delivery of key changes.

- The end of a planning period – some organisations may choose to revisit plans/re-plan on a regular basis.

Once a review is triggered, a series of activities should take place (see Chapter 14 for portfolio governance):

- A retrospective review to check that the portfolio process is working optimally and to identify improvements to it, to drive improvements (sometimes it may emerge that the selection/prioritisation parameters or the goals of the portfolio need to change).
- A review of the initiatives in the portfolio to ensure the right initiatives are being executed.
- A reassessment of the portfolio plans to ensure the right initiatives are planned in the right order to produce optimum value.

Conclusion

The aim of an agile approach, coupled with portfolio management, focuses on delivering value for the organisation, adapting to emergent strategy, advocating organisational agility, encompassing change management, including re-balancing and re-prioritising of the portfolio to maintain optimum performance in delivering value, and strategic objectives. Arguably, this can also be seen as the core principles of portfolio management and much of strategic portfolio management discussed throughout this book, focusing on the wider organisational environment comparable with the agile organisation.

References

Agile Business Consortium (2021) Agile portfolio management. www.agilebusiness.org.

Cooper R. & Sommer A. (2020) New-product portfolio management with agile: Challenges and solutions for manufacturers using agile development methods. *Research-Technology Management* 63(1), 29–38.

Fowler M. & Highsmith J. (2001) The agile manifesto. *Software Development.* http://users.jyu.fi/Agile-Manifesto.pdf.

Holbeche L. (2015) *The Agile Organization: How to Build an Innovative, Sustainable and Resilient Business.* Kogan Page.

Hope J. & Fraser R. (2003) *Beyond Budgeting: How Managers Can Break Free from the Annual Performance Trap.* Harvard Business Review Press.

Horlach B., Schirmer I. & Drews P. (2019) Agile portfolio management: Design goals and principles. *Proceedings of the 27th European Conference on Information Systems (ECIS).* June 2019. AIS Electronic Library (AISeL).

Imbrizi F. & Maccari E. (2014) Agile software development and project portfolio management in dynamic environments. *International Association for Management of Technology. IAMOT 2014 Proceedings.*

Kaufmann C., Kock A. & Gemünden H. (2020) Emerging strategy recognition in agile portfolios. *International Journal of Project Management* 38(7), 429–440.

Killen C. & Hunt R. (2013) Robust project portfolio management: Capability evolution and maturity. *International Journal of Managing Projects in Business* 6(1), 131–151.

Krebs J. (2009) *Agile Portfolio Management.* Microsoft Press.

Laanti M. & Kangas M. (2015) Is agile portfolio management following the principles of large-scale agile? Case study in Finnish broadcasting company Yle. Agile Conference, pp. 92–96.

Lyngso S. (2014) Agile Strategy Management: Techniques for Continuous Alignment and Improvement. Auerbach Publications.

Morlidge S. (2017) The Little Book of beyond Budgeting: A New Operating System for Organisations: What it is and Why it Works. Matador publishing.

Nidagundi P. & Novickis L. (2017) Introducing lean canvas model adaptation in the Scrum software testing. *Procedia Computer Science* 104, 97–103.

Neilson K. (2021) Agile Portfolio Management: A Guide to the Methodology and Its Successful Implementation "Knowledge That Sets You Apart". Productivity Press.

Rautiainen K., von Schantz J. and Vähäniitty J. (2011) "Supporting scaling agile with portfolio management: Case Paf.com. 44th Hawaii International Conference on System Sciences, pp. 1–10. Paf.com

Rosasco N. & Dehlinger J. (2011) Business architecture elicitation for enterprise architecture: VMOST versus conventional strategy capture. *Ninth International Conference on Software Engineering Research, Management and Applications*. pp. 153–157. IEEE.

Stettina C. & Horz J., (2015) Agile portfolio management: An empirical perspective on the practice in use. *International Journal of Project Management* 33, 140–152.

Sweetman R. & Conboy K. (2018) Portfolios of Agile projects: A complex adaptive systems agent perspective. *Project Management Journal* 49(6), 18–38.

Section IV

Portfolio management case studies

Introduction

This section of the book contains six case studies from different industrial contexts, organisational cultures, and company structures. Each of the authors have brought their huge experience and insight to the topic, bringing their own particular lens to help understand how strategic portfolio management is enacted in the real world.

Chapter 23 by Dave Yazdani begins with a case study looking at portfolio management used in a firm developing complex engineering systems. Dave Reggi follows in Chapter 24 with a detailed discussion of the design of a sophisticated portfolio decision support tool in a biopharmaceutical firm. Chapters 25 and 26, both by Paul Taylor, discuss firstly the use of SPM in the utilities sector for evaluating and managing a multi-billion-pound (£) construction portfolio, followed by a case study looking at how product standardisation and integrated delivery can be optimised within a construction portfolio.

The next, Chapter 27, focuses on organisational development, where Geoff Vincent discusses how to introduce portfolio management in organisations with a specific view on governance and leadership. The last case study, by Paul Clarke, Katy Angliss, and Pete Harpum, looks at portfolio management maturity, with an examination of the application of a maturity model to a business in the power sector.

Chapter questions

Katy Angliss

As before, following are some questions to consider when reading through the case study chapters in this section. Where appropriate, these are divided into material review questions and further discussion questions.

Chapter 23: Case study – engineering of complex systems with portfolio kanagement

Material review questions

23.1 How can organising for portfolio management in a complex engineering environment benefit the organisation?

Further discussion questions

23.2 Considering how relevant this case study may be to your organisation for engineering of complex systems, discuss how these portfolio management ways of working could be developed or improved.

Chapter 24: Case study – pharmaceutical portfolio decision tool

Further discussion questions

24.1 Considering the example portfolio tool examined in the case study for pharmaceutical and biotech, discuss how your organisation could develop, or improve, their portfolio assessment tool (with particular reference to portfolio reporting and data visualisation).

Chapter 25: Case study – delivering a multi-billion-pound portfolio

Material review questions

25.1 Critique the advantages and disadvantages of managing the AMP6 delivery work as a major program (programme) rather than a portfolio, considering aspects including business integration, strategic alignment and direction, systems thinking, duration, costs, culture, and organisational structure.
25.2 Following the previous question, consider the benefits of managing the AMP6 delivery work as a portfolio.
25.3 How do the ECI and the delivery stage of this portfolio map to other portfolio stages discussed in other chapters?
25.4 What are some of the key areas considered in the ECI design phase and throughout the case study in achieving a successful outcome for portfolio delivery?

Chapter 26: Case study – a utilities and construction portfolio

Material review questions

26.1 Compare and contrast the different contractual models, including DFMA, category management, and consolidation centres. Discuss how each affects, or can potentially improve, the management of the portfolio.
26.2 How can product standardisation and integrated digital delivery influence procurement management and the supply chain within the portfolio?

Chapter 27: Case study – portfolio governance and leadership

Material review questions

27.1 Critique the key aspects of the role of the portfolio manager as discussed in this chapter.
27.2 Establish how important effective governance is to the role of the portfolio manager.
27.3 Discuss the portfolio manager's responsibility for portfolio governance.

Further discussion questions

27.4 How could portfolio governance and leadership be improved within your organisation?

Chapter 28: Case study – portfolio management maturity model development

Further discussion questions

28.1 How could you set about assessing the current situation for portfolio management within your organisation or sector?

28.2 How could you address any improvement areas using portfolio management maturity for assessment of portfolio capabilities?

23 Case study – the engineering of complex systems with portfolio management

Dave Yazdani

Introduction

The challenges for this chapter are to explain what good product development looks like in the context of portfolio management. How does an organisation go about harnessing technology to deliver complex yet reliable products and services? How does it establish a reputation, seed and sustain a market, and design and deliver successfully whilst controlling the relevant intellectual property (IP) and knowledge base to be a technology leader? By achieving these goals, it generates a successful cycle of product and service innovation and delivery so that the business can grow and reinvent itself, to persist for the long haul. Yet of course, it all has to fit together as a multi-year jigsaw puzzle adapting to external events and internal discoveries – shocks like oil prices, wars or pandemics, disruptive world events like climate change, inventions and discoveries, and unexpected findings, good and bad.

The chapter will look at each of these in turn, from a Rolls-Royce case study perspective, delving into what good looks like and the possible reasons, and what pitfalls to avoid. Firstly, establishing a reputation for technology leadership, delivery, and the ability to take an idea to production. Here the route is simple; there is no shortcut: you have to deliver a success based upon your ideas, scale up, and delight customers, and then repeat in greater volumes.

The Rolls-Royce context for portfolio management

In the last 30 years, Rolls-Royce PLC has transformed from a UK-centric, traditional gas turbine design and manufacture organisation to a global group, spanning a range of power systems for air, land, and sea, still strong on gas turbines, but also reciprocating engines and nuclear plant. Design and delivery have evolved from drawing boards, with paper-based planning and scheduling, and capital-intensive, skill-based manufacture, assembly, and test, to an environment today that is wholly computer-based, through enterprise-wide product life cycle management (PLM) and enterprise resource planning (ERP) processes, and factories that operate on "Industry 4.0" principles – paperless, automated, and lightly staffed – and equally capable, focused suppliers and partners.

Even more fundamentally, the whole ethos has shifted from an original equipment manufacturer to a product and service provider, based on customer-centred design optimisation, robust delivery, and responsive through life support. This includes the industry-leading *Total Care* model that provides guaranteed "power by the hour" through regular payments driven by real-time operating data from every product. This transformation journey was not incidental or accidental; it was a conscious choice and has been essential

DOI: 10.4324/9780367853129-27

in growing the business – as much as mergers and acquisitions, product developments, and service innovations. The deliberate choice was made, with stakeholders, to invest in advancing the ability to operate and in acquiring advanced material, manufacturing, and design/analysis capability that has been instrumental in enabling advances in product performance and data-driven service innovation.

Without this engineering and operational foundation, it is inconceivable that we could have designed highly reliable and environmentally efficient engines, such as the *Trent XWB* for the latest Airbus A350 airliner, solved defence ambitions like routine vertical take-off, supersonic flight, and back to vertical landing on the JSF (*Joint Strike Fighter*), or delivered service innovation based on operating data through *Total Care* deals. This resulting advanced knowledge and experience base means that it is now possible to contemplate solving sustainability challenges with long-haul transport based on even higher efficiency from the *Ultrafan* next-generation aircraft engine; effective green energy sources, such as microgrids and small modular nuclear power plants; and supporting industry to supply sustainably synthesised aviation fuels and hydrogen in affordable volumes.

Organising for portfolio management

As Rolls-Royce transitioned over the last decades, it became clear that managing the work across the enterprise in a coordinated way was essential. How does the strategy translate through into programs sequenced in the right order? And how do leaders and teams respond to the inevitable changes and disruptions when things don't work out as initially envisaged? It was apparent that underpinning the individual elements, there was needed a system of strategy development, deployment, and portfolio management driving the right things to happen, in the right sequence. All this spanned multi-year thinking, sometimes decades ahead. Creating new materials or manufacturing processes can take 20 years, from elemental chemistry to production readiness. Some of this transition was structured, formalised, and managed as such, whilst some emerged organically as the strategy flow signalled to leaders a need, that they could in turn steer a portfolio to assist.

Why was this necessary? There are factors in play that drive the concept of shared knowledge, resources, and assets as the most cost-effective way of delivering products and services to customers. All complex power systems share the following capabilities (within the bounds of legalities to protect secrets and ensure fair competition):

- Research is universally applicable: materials science, thermodynamics, manufacturing technology all can find application in gas turbines, reciprocating engines and nuclear cores, electrical machines, and steam plants.
- Design knowledge and experience are transferable between engines: methods, tools, design styles, and databases.
- Integrated project teams need practice to be successful: a steady flow of work instead of disruption caused as one project ends and another starts in a different market. Knowledge grows instead of being lost.
- Capital assets, such as laboratories, test beds, and factories, are unaffordable if dedicated to just one product, and vulnerable to market changes. A common supply chain maximises productivity, smooths demand, and lowers schedule risk.

Coordination to steer the development of these capabilities and then their use in a cost-effective way, to deliver multiple products and services with overlapping life cycles, demands an embedded culture of portfolio management – not just a notional process and a regular portfolio board meeting, but a whole system of data, multi-level processes, management and change boards, and reporting measures.

Engineering talent is one of the most precious assets – recruitment and staff development, deployment to businesses and projects, talent pipelines for chief engineers and technology leaders (known internally as the RR engineering and technology fellowship) are all managed through portfolio processes across the group.

The organisation itself was shaped to enable portfolio decision-making within major supply chains as they organised into business units, each empowered to accept demand signals from multiple product teams for new designs and ongoing production. These business units and their supply chains develop their own plans for research and technology development, capital investment, and resource planning, including localised transformation to improve productivity. While they were accountable for delivering them, portfolio integration was used to ensure they were coordinated to deliver together to technical and commercial needs, for example, one unit leading for all, to ensure a new material and its supplier were capable of providing forgings for compressor, combustor, and turbine parts.

This has had the desired effect, as the product teams, alleviated of the burden of creating these things, can focus on creating a strong customer relationship, optimising the system level design, and delivering the development program. The supply chain is trusted to operate as a business within the group, steered by the long-term strategy deployment – a choice not without issues, which will be discussed later, but ultimately positive results are delivered.

This is not just confined to supply chains. Information technology and business process/productivity transformation work were also set up to self-direct to meet the strategy, forming their own portfolios of programs to transform from drawing boards to full CAD/CAM (computer-aided design/computer-aided manufacturing). This continues today as the organisation moves to exploit digital twins through "big enterprise data", massive computing power, and artificial intelligence.

Why is it complicated?

A common thread runs through all Rolls-Royce products. They are high-value capital assets, delivered in only several hundreds of units per year, and often operated by customers for extended periods to "sweat" the asset. It is not uncommon for a civil gas turbine to be operated for 20–30 years on wing, serviced regularly in situ, and periodically removed for a complete tear-down and reconditioning. These high-value products are operated in a highly regulated environment to ensure safety, with regular checks and oversight by third-party regulators. Their operation is under the supervision of highly skilled people, often licenced to operate. The parts used to make the engines are made in highly controlled factories, and any repairs or replacement parts have to have an equal provenance, being acquired either from the original source or from reputable reconditioned unit suppliers or (very rarely) from an approved vendor of a third-party designed and manufactured part that is proven to be safe and effective when installed in the engine. This last option is relatively rare, and this is a reflection of the reasons that drive *Total Care*–type models to be successful.

A gas turbine is a complex, closely coupled system and its performance is very much more than the simple sum of the performance of adding each part mathematically. To guarantee that the required thrust and power, contracted fuel consumption, ongoing compliance with noise and emission controls, and demonstration of safe, reliable operation throughout the varied flight conditions experience, is altogether no trivial technical task. It requires highly developed human skills, coupled to bespoke analysis models and decision-making criteria, to understand how the engine operates through life, and the impact of normal manufacturing and operational variation upon it. Fractional changes in material property, or clearances and gaps between static and rotating parts, can have dramatic effects on life, safety, and performance.

Consequently, altering the agreed list of part designs and the manufacturing and assembly definitions for an engine always requires deep understanding of the foreground design itself, but also legalised access to the legacy of background IP (intellectual property) upon which it is founded. New entrants to the gas turbine propulsion market are remarkably rare, and the leading technical competence is vested in the same few companies that were engaged during and after the Second World War, in finessing the ideas generated by Sir Frank Whittle, the inventor of operational gas turbines (Feilden & Hawthorne, 1998) and others, and turning them into a production product.

Within the product, the specialised cast alloy parts, such as combustors and turbine aerofoils, operate in a zone where temperatures exceed 2,000 degrees centigrade, at many times atmospheric pressure, creating the energy to drive turbines around at tens of thousands of RPM (revolutions per minute), within a "hair's width" of the much cooler external casings. All this is occurring at temperatures well above the melting point of the metals involved, and on an aircraft flying at high or even supersonic speed, typically manoeuvring at high G forces that can bend and distort the entire engine.

This description of the product development process shows that the complete set of technology needed to design, prove, and make these parts is limited to a few organisations in the world and has taken decades of heavy investment to perfect. This is the practical illustration of a barrier to entry – and if you want to sell a military or civil high-performance gas turbine, this is just one of the technologies to master amongst many. Although the product development description given here is predominantly for aviation gas turbines, the nuclear and power systems businesses have equally tough challenges guaranteeing reliable, safe reactor operation for decades, in highly ionised radiation fields, safely operating with megawatts of electricity in flight-worthy power systems or meeting the challenges of high fuel efficiency with increasingly strict emission control for land and sea power.

Getting the right reputation

Rolls-Royce, following its official foundation in 1904 (Botticelli, 1997), developed a preeminent reputation as a supplier of car chassis, coachwork, and power trains. From that, driven by the invention of powered flight and accelerated by the First World War, the business evolved from automotive piston engine technology to power aircraft. Increasingly, the aviation design requirements drove a divergence away from the "house-style" cars, ultimately pushed by driving more power from less weight, which is achieved by delivering better compression ratios, especially in thin, high-altitude air. More emphasis was placed on larger cylinders, lower structural weight, more efficient conversion from crankshaft power to propellor thrust, and "supercharging" by using some of the engine power to compress intake air before combustion in the cylinders, to further improve power-to-weight ratio. Compare a typical 1940s car engine side by side with the Merlin engine used extensively by the Allies in WW2 and you see the latter is much larger, is more complex, and has many more parts. It delivers exponentially more power to weight and does so at flight altitudes of tens of thousands of feet (if the reader is ever near the town of Derby, in the United Kingdom, please visit the *RR Heritage Trust* to see these amazing machines up close!). This reputation was further enhanced by the critical role products such as the Merlin engine and its successor, the Griffon, played during the

Second World War. This, in turn, created the relationship that meant that Rolls-Royce was the logical, trusted organisation to take up the work pioneered by Sir Frank Whittle to transform a successful flying gas turbine prototype into a mass-production engine, the Derwent. This engine was capable of operating at temperatures and pressures that would deliver usable power and range but that could be made from available materials and factories in time to enter service by 1945.

What underpinned this was a visible track record of delivering inventions at all scales: from microlevel material chemistry, characterising how metals and plastics perform under stress, how those material properties can be used to design effective component parts, how parts can be combined in effective architectures to act as systems delivering the performance the customer demands reliably, harnessing financial capital to build machine tools and factories, and having a skilled workforce and supply chain to deliver mass production–made products on time. Also important are vital ancillary processes, such as intellectual property management, to secure the rights to use inventions; people and talent development, to ensure that the workforce at all levels is able to perform and improve complex tasks; and the retention of skills and competencies, not lost to other industries.

So reputation? It comes from track record but also being able to show, by actions and by exposition, that the organisation is systemically capable of delivering high-technology results. It gives stakeholders confidence that a business is able to convert investment in patience, confidence, and sometimes capital, through agreement to a vision and key performance measures, into a successful delivery of product or service in the future that will allow them to achieve their goals. The need for more than track record is emphasised, especially as the costs and risks grow. A one-off success does not convince a major aerospace prime, or a defence ministry, to commit vast sums to a propulsion supplier and patiently wait in hope as the stakes grow bigger. Being able to show technical credibility to deliver is key to winning.

This will create two intriguing possibilities. Firstly, the incumbent, successful business that has delivered many times before – can it reinvent itself to move to new technology before the old, current one becomes obsolete? A glance at the personal computing and mobile phone world shows numerous examples to study: the disruption caused by Apple and its iPhone and Google and its smartphone operating system (Cusumano, 2010).

Secondly, the new innovator, the creator of new technology solutions: How do they get into a conservative market? The switch from petrol cars to electric, examples such as Tesla (Thomas & Maine, 2019), entering a car world dominated by mastery of mass production of a very proven and stable architecture. Interestingly, adjacent to the incumbent aviation providers, the impact of mass availability of image processing, autonomous control, weight-efficient batteries, and electrical motors on personal and short-haul flight? In both cases, one option to consider is repurposing knowledge and assets – can there be a move to adjacent technologies based on the elements of what is known today? And secondly, if you know what you don't know, can you find a partner, supplier, or hire expertise to accelerate your business through that gap?

Next is understanding the opportunity, shaping it to open a market, and sustaining that space to allow multiple generations of products and services to move from idea, through rising star, to cash generators.

Making choices to open up markets

In the 1970s, Rolls-Royce attempted to enter the emerging market for wide-body civil airlines, developing a new engine called the RB211, intended for the Lockheed Tristar aircraft. This attempt ended in painful and salutary failure, as the company found it impossible to deliver what it had promised on time without running out of cash. In effect, it became bankrupt through trying to create new technology solely with its own resources. This was a combination of trying to achieve a level of performance that was beyond the physics understood at that time – most notably the "Hyfil" composite (carbo fibre) fan blade (Marsh, 2012) – and as a result having an undeliverable plan to fulfil the commitments made to Lockheed. The net result was a period of nationalised ownership, the divestment of the automotive part of the group, and a technology reset for the RB211 itself that resulted in a viable product entering service on the Tristar and, in 1977, the Boeing 747.

The RB211, post its 1972 entry into service, was competitive with its US rivals, and so after a series of major wins, including launching a version onto the Boeing 747 with British Airways, a healthy market share, coupled with the company being returned to public ownership in the 1980s, led to a key strategic question: Should the company continue to operate as one of the big three aircraft engine manufacturers or drop the RB211 line and join forces with one of the major players?

The choice was made to continue as a full supplier, and the evolution of the RB211 into what became the *Trent* family began. So here is the first element: being able to see, understand, forecast, and evaluate risk to inform key strategic choices. In essence, without knowing exactly what a *Trent* engine would look like or what performance it would deliver or what sales would be achieved through winning a deal with Airbus or Boeing (and indeed others!). Senior leadership decided to go forwards and, in doing so, managed to take their stakeholders, the board, shareholders, and government with them to go on the journey that was clearly, in the short term, far riskier yet, in the long run, more rewarding.

This willingness to take a bold decision, with incomplete information, but underpinned by technical confidence, opened up the space for business development. It clearly stated that the company would compete on civil airliner engines with its unique RB211 architecture – which offered fundamental technical and operating advantages over its simpler US-based rivals but carried higher development and production cost risk.

In doing so, a family of engines was launched, developed in a sequence starting with the Trent 700/Airbus A330 combination, the Trent 800/Boeing 777, Trent 500/A340, Trent 900/A380, and then finally, the Trent 1000/Boeing 787 and Trent XWB/Airbus A350. Amongst these aviation offerings, industrial and marine power versions were also spun off that today are providing power to national grids (now supplied by our colleagues in Siemens PLC) and on naval vessels around the world.

This decision set in motion what has become a multi-billion-pound business, with product and service sales cover, contracted or implied over decades, and in practical terms powering hundreds of flights at any given moment every day, with these engines being mission-critical components to most of the world's major airlines. This is the outcome of the 1989 choice to remain independent and invest in Rolls-Royce's capabilities.

Sustaining the market once it's opened

Design and delivery successfully overlap with sustaining the market opportunity. The Trent family evolved as a series of solutions to the unique performance needs for each airliner. Each engine was tailored to meet the thrust and fuel burn needs of the airliner and matched physically to the space and weight available for it. When viewed, literally, side by side, each engine in the Trent series looks quite different, despite having the same basic three shaft architecture – length, weight, diameter, and external appearance. Each engine has a largely unique part level design and bill of materials. Some commonality is achieved by reusing low-level parts, but the majority of the "house style" lies in understanding and reusing proven functionality, system-level designs, and supply chains and manufacturing processes. Thus, sustainment comes firstly from close working with the airframe suppliers (Airbus, Boeing, etc.) to tailor the design within the established experience of design and manufacture.

However, simple geometric tailoring does not, in itself, deliver the performance. New technology is then inserted to provide the uplift through new materials, manufacturing processes, or design styles. These may be based on sound elemental physics and chemistry but are unproven in the complex environment of a jet engine. The Trent 900 internal aerodynamics marked the first use of "three-dimensional" aerodynamic design across the compressor, where each aerofoil was shaped to maximise the efficient flow of air over the surface in all directions. Prior to that, the knowledge base and toolset favoured simpler methods, where everything was optimised as a set of simpler two-dimensional slices, spaced radially outwards inside the engine (this is further developed later on).

This approach was, in theory, feasible but hadn't been applied in this way and at this scale before. As part of the relationship with the airframers and customers, extensive research and technology was undertaken to build the confidence that it would work when applied in a real multi-million-pound Trent design project. Joint work was conducted between the systems designers in-house and at Airbus and Boeing to not only optimise the design of airframe and engine as a system but to also demonstrate to peer and senior assurance reviewers that the architecture and resulting targets for component-level designs would be achievable in time for entry into service.

Finally, some elements such as the implications of three-dimensional aerodynamics on the fan system meant there would be fewer larger blades. These new fan blades were individually heavier and hence required a more robust casing to contain them in the event of one failing in flight (this being a key safety requirement). An innovative approach was used to design the fan case, exploiting known manufacturing and materials in a configuration that had never previously been used that way. Extensive computational simulation, coupled to experienced engineering decision-making, was used to de-risk the concept, and then a rapid sub-scale prototype was subjected to destructive testing to confirm that the simulation matched reality and could be scaled up to match the Trent 900 diameter.

Achieving these designs on time is in itself a massive organisational challenge, regardless of the technology challenge, and so sustainment is based upon a third vital strand – excellence in project and program delivery. This includes both the technocratic process skill – showing process, plans, risk registers, assurance models, professional project management certifications – and also soft skills in the leaders. Do they have the style, character, and team working competencies to succeed, leading a project team numbering hundreds of people spread across the globe? Is the team stable, skilled, and staffed fully? Can they make decisions, and can they convince the customer to trust their decisions? Can they cope when things go off plan?

Managing technology insertion requires three elements:

1. *Know if technology is ready*. Use a standardised scale to describe how ready design concepts are absolutely and compared to each other, and insist that the technology is properly captured in design rules, standards, and processes. Technology isn't developed by prototypes being tested and forgotten; it has to be published within the company to then consume it. Rolls-Royce uses the technology readiness level scale pioneered by NASA to understand if technology is ready to use.

2. *Know why, at the system level above the technology, you want to insert the new technology.* Prevent "gold plating" by understanding what target the new technology helps you meet and why before including it in the design and plans.
3. *Use configuration and change management.* Technology insertion is often affected by small part count changes. If the bill of material isn't controlled correctly, you risk not knowing how the system really will work and, if it doesn't work, why!

A significant reason for the Trent family's rolling success was the continuity of leadership across the generations. Visible growth of people, through proving delivery on one of the series engines, often led to being promoted for the next engine under development. There are numerous instances in the organisation's current and recently retired leaders where many started in hands-on design, analysis, and development roles on the RB211 family, rising via project manager, chief designer, or chief engineer, ultimately to direct programs or portfolios on behalf of the business or group.

Earning the right to do the next one

Delivery is crucial! And by this is not meant perfect delivery to a plan when the customer can plainly see it wasn't a challenge. It means showing the organisation can create, staff, and manage a project team and supply chain that, in turn, is seen to deliver complex technology, despite issues and problems on the way. This includes showing how they can diagnose and successfully manage design and project issues before they become late-stage (and so expensive) failures. They also need an exemplary tracking and reporting model to manage progress across a program involving tens or hundreds of people, covering the spectrum of technology acquisition, product, and production design and underpinning infrastructure investment. Thus, credible program management and portfolio optimisation becomes key, especially for multi-year, uncertain-outcome effort. Looking forwards, Rolls-Royce is positioning people, technology, and infrastructure now for the generation after the Trent XWB, based on technology and architectures researched under a demonstrator engine called *Ultrafan*.

Despite not having secured a launch platform yet, the organisation already knows what the configuration will likely be and that it will likely be far larger than the Trent family. This means needing to be able to manufacture new styles of parts and perform ground and flight testing. Hence, the organisation has invested in developing the people to form the program leadership through the demonstrator, materials technology to design and make composite fan blades and casings, factories capable of making advanced castings for the turbines against higher productivity and technology targets, test facilities on the ground in the USA and UK, and a flying test bed (converted from a Boeing 747). This will all be ready and proven to de-risk the production program when it arrives.

This up-front investment demonstrates a credible path to deliver when the launch comes, in effect building a barrier to entry compared to others who do not have the reputation, capital and funding access, and delivery productivity and reliability to get this infrastructure ready for a comparable sum. A new entrant would spend far more and/or take a far greater risk by delaying until the airframe was launched.

Design and deliver

Program management signals to the team what needs doing and by when, but an equally able functional approach is needed to explain to teams how to do the required tasks and why they are completed that way. Hence, a thoughtful approach to capability management is necessary. Some of the work required to be capable is individual – making sure every engineer is well trained and equipped with the right information technology and working environment to succeed. Some is cultural, setting the tone, behaviour, and ethical approach to the organisation's work.

Rolls-Royce achieves the required mix through a combination of approaches. This includes structured recruitment (including extensive apprentice and graduate schemes), focused all-hands training and communications, individually tailored technical and personal training managed through a regular cycle of performance and development review, and a clear, simple framework explaining company policies and standards. Rolls-Royce operates as an extended enterprise, so where appropriate, these standards are altered and flowed out across the group globally and, in some cases, onto key partners and suppliers.

The "how" is also explained and enabled through the enterprise architecture. This is a mix of process models, standards and specifications and design rules, and criteria supporting working-level tasks and reviews. Also, IT-based workflows control key high-volume/high-risk transactions, for example: use of a PLM (product life cycle management) software suite to manage design configuration, CAD (computer-aided design) models, and increasingly, simulation requests and results; use of an ERP (enterprise resource planning) system to schedule and manage orders for work and parts; use of common risk and project planning databases; and reports for each business to monitor and report progress against business plans.

Some of the "how" is technically challenging, carrying a high degree of uncertainty, for example, the two- and three-dimensional aerodynamics mentioned previously. These detailed working tasks are performed using all the controls just noted. Aerodynamic analysis is a recognised skill grouping, with dedicated recruitment and training pipelines to ensure engineers are skilled. Standards and specifications set out how the work should be done and are explained in sets of authorised guidebooks and decision-making criteria. These are given contextual explanation through a capability intranet that explains the history and expert information that underpins the guides and rules. Finally, dedicated analysis and design software is provided to enable the models to be constructed, analysed, and the findings shared for use downstream. This is a mix of bespoke software evolved over many years to capture gas turbine–specific IP and off-the-shelf software code for simpler models, processing, and data workflow/storage.

This approach of exploiting IT to create and flow the IP isn't confined to the high-end engineering analysis. A major transformation in engineering productivity was achieved alongside the Trent family and exploited elsewhere in the group, through a long-term portfolio of investment in developing and deploying the process landscape and IT systems to move product life cycle management from paper registers, drawing boards, and hand-drawn blueprints to today's fully computational design, configuration, and manufacturing execution system. At the start of those projects, as mentioned earlier, all designs were human-drawn, based on mainframe and hand-calculated analysis, and manually processed through change approval and distribution. Now, every part and assembly is modelled in CAD, simulated to the appropriate level computationally, ordered electronically through ERP, assembled in a digitally supported factory, and tested ultimately on test beds, such as the new fully *Digital Testbed 80*, commissioned in 2021 in Derby. The ambition is to stream multiple GB (gigabytes) of data from engine testing live, back to engineers' desktops, to support the design and development of the next generation of products, such as *Ultrafan*.

This transformation was, for the organisation, a multi-year high-risk portfolio in its own right. It started when the process and IT landscape was immature, in places non-existent. Now, much of the capability is available off the shelf, with enterprise design, planning, and project management tools available, especially for smaller-scale enterprises. The major lesson is that regardless of improved maturity of IT, the successful organisational approach to adoption requires a smart customer. If possible, encourage the employees to be deeply involved in the development and deployment; ideally, if the benefit outweighs cost, consideration should be given to dedicating team members to this work on behalf of the organisation, for its whole life cycle, including sustainment and continuous improvement once in place. While the individual tools and suites are quite mature, the integration between different vendor products can be challenging, and the out-of-box configuration almost never matches the established real-life business practice – a change project results to address culture, training, and compliance to changed process and/or to custom-configure the software.

Strategy into portfolio – managing the mix

All this work needs to be actively managed from inception, through execution, and controlled across the group-wide mix. This has been achieved by increasing program management capability and by maturing the portfolio process, metrics, and controls at product, business, and group levels.

The first, increasing PM (program/project management) capability, was addressed by means familiar to many with industry experience so will not be reviewed here – suffice it to say a consistent and ongoing journey is needed to embed standard good practice from bodies such as the APM (Association for Project Management), coupled to in-house training, development materials, and professional IT and process deployment.

The second, the culture and process of developing and deploying a complicated business strategy, evolving over many years, is a topic worth discussing. When it spans such a long period, external influences come into play: politics, economics, technology, and cultural shifts have to be considered, accommodated, and reacted to. Project life cycles sit within a multi-year portfolio, and even if a project is an individual success, it can, within that construct, become a wasted effort or, indeed, a hinderance through circumstances completely outside the control of the individual project manager.

The organisation must become adept at building up this jigsaw puzzle, understanding the evolution, change-controlling it, and pivoting to react to emerging events.

Firstly, product strategy shapes the choices on plans – what is required and what is feasible to deliver the business vision. The deliberate choice to remain as a full OEM (original equipment manufacturer) in the civil widebody aircraft market, through the Trent family of engines, set in train work both technical and commercial to identify and shape opportunities to deliver engines for more than the established Boeing base market (of 747/757/767 airliners). Work had to be undertaken to develop products for other airframes, build relationships with new customers, and establish new, higher-capacity supply chains.

The outcome of all that effort was highly uncertain, both in terms of technical difficulty and also financial success – what market share would be achieved, in what configuration, and how successful the products would be in service. A portfolio and governance model had to be developed that evaluated and managed technical investment alongside commercial development and production investments. For example, choices made in product architecture influenced sales campaigns, with certain customers in more challenging operating environments, and product development plans required risk mitigation options to be built in to mitigate the possible difficulties. Some of this depended on choices made years earlier to develop more capable materials or design styles that had no immediate application.

For example, the gas turbine industry has been working to develop metallic composite materials, akin to glass or carbon fibre but based on metal fibres and ceramic "resins", for over 40 years. It is only recently that this technology has matured to find a use in the turbines of the latest hottest engines, where the extra efficiency they bring finally justifies the cost. A more short-term-focused industry would have desisted years ago, yet now these materials may become a key part of delivering the high efficiency needed to deliver "net-zero" CO_2 in long-haul aviation, as they finally reach an affordable and mature readiness level.

Decision-making on starting and stopping the technology portfolio is based on a complex and experienced culture, looking beyond simpler economic or immediate technical status, and in some ways, applying "futurology" – if it works, is the benefit worth the risk? And what prospects to back? This is akin to pharmaceutical research, except the success rate must be much higher, as the technology development is driven by a much greater need for physical realisation and costly experimentation. On balance, many more end up being successful than not, the key being patience and a willingness to flex the definition of success (compare that to the 80 to 90% dropout rate for novel drug compounds).

To do this, the organisation and process must be set up to allow the balance of long- and short-term thinking and make sure those decisions are made in the right context. It is unwise for product development teams to have to make tough choices on immature technology; equally, a technology creation team can lack the delivery focus to bring a complex product system to market on time/budget.

The business organises research and technology projects differently to product development projects. In Rolls-Royce, technology projects are carried out using separate processes that are mutually supportive and are performed by engineers and project managers with specialised skills and an appropriate project management model culture – described as comparing navigating by compass to a stopwatch.

Research goes through a time-flexible set of readiness assessments and gates, where risk and technology achievement can be matched as the science is discovered, checking that it is in a position where it is mature, affordable, and characterised by data and design/manufacturing rules. Product development runs to a product quality planning timeline – product and production processes are checked to ensure delivery of volume, on the date committed to the customer, timescale is fixed, and risk and cost are flexed.

The outcome-flexible nature of the research and technology portfolio then, in turn, feeds back to the market-shaping and sales effort. It is quite common for the early system design of the airframe and engine to evolve together, moving from rough estimates of performance and cost to narrow down as the design and architecture is firmed up to a point of soft commitment, where customer and supplier both reserve the right to have some "wriggle room", simply because all understand that the real performance level will not be certain for a few more years. Progress shapes the product during its development, and all parties understand that where risk is taken, the outcome may be a mix of easing back on operational performance during early service, in exchange for insertion of revised designs and technologies later on that then exceed the original proposed level – in effect a mutually agreed deferred satisfaction.

Technology shapes what you can offer, not just purely along the product axis that is understood at that time, but also in seeding new offerings and businesses. These can be closely related spin-offs. The need to write and control safety-critical software drives expertise in engine health monitoring and hence underpins intelligently predicting life consumption and planning overhaul on an individual basis – the core of the *Total Care* service product. For example, expertise in core nuclear power plant design, when combined with gas turbine logistics, production planning, and control and program delivery, enables a lower risk approach when launching a whole new sector, such as for civil nuclear power provision (small modular reactors).

Practical steps

How is all this complex mixture of processes, technology, and culture managed? How do the technology strands emerge? How are they tracked? What ensures they are inserted into the right products and businesses for maximum effect?

There is a complex process landscape and organisation that has evolved over time to achieve this. It is a unique outcome of the culture and decisions so is not something that can be simply transplanted to other situations. Thankfully, the principles underneath are remarkably simple, scalable, and transferable.

1. Technology is, in itself, managed distinctly to products, production, and service. Technology development proceeds under its own budgets, with its own strategic imperatives, and executive leaders ensure alignment. It is incentivised at all levels, and a system is in place to promote thinking, encourage innovation, capture ideas, secure IP, and promote it to a readied position.
2. Technology development is fostered across an extended enterprise, not just inside the company. A diverse network of suppliers, partners, and universities makes up a technology ecosystem. Collaboration is the norm; virtually all work is performed in some form of multi-disciplinary team, and most are sufficiently small to be self-governing and agile.
3. From a governance and assurance perspective, leaders require teams to show how they are achieving against standard progress and delivery metrics. Independent experts frequently quality-assure work inside business units and to the executive. Teams always act flexibly towards risk/problem messages. The response to a problem is not simply to close the work down; instead, the need is understood, and resources flexed to where the cost benefit in the long run gives an advantage.
4. Only use a technology when it is ready, but *ready* doesn't mean finished; it just means mature enough to match the risk profile in the other parts of a product program. And think holistically, not just the science, but the design process, production method, supply chain, culture, etc.
5. Ensure leadership is both business-aware and technically excellent. Technology has no function if it cannot be used within a budget and delivered on time – engineering a product is about market success as well as functional excellence.
6. Finally, be persistent and treat technology development as a long-term portfolio composed of multi-year programs.

Conclusion (and final thoughts)

People use the analogy of flying at height to understand how things work, talking about the view from "60,000 feet" as simple and broad. As you go lower, to say 10,000–20,000 feet, the scenery gets clearer and rich local variation is visible. However, when you fly at 100 feet, everything is very real, very close, and sometimes terrifying!

Technology portfolio management is about understanding how to be comfortable flying at all heights. Able to sit high and look long-term across the horizon to see how some promising ideas could flourish, drop down to the detail to ensure the development and deployment is covering more than just the science, and survive a low fast trip in the detail, thinking and acting rapidly as problems emerge and decisions must be taken whilst trusting that the view above still makes sense.

The takeaway from 30 years immersed in transformation of technology development and organisational growth is that a long-cycle technology company, at its heart, must master this dilemma: how to decouple product development from technology, be comfortable and persistent to encourage the science, and think holistically about people, process, and supply chains so that an investment yields technology that is ready and that the working product development teams can successfully consume. It can only master this by investing in its people, developing deep pools of systems thinking, project leadership, and science/technology skills. Both broad engineering leaders with business and delivery acumen and world-class technical experts are necessary – but all must be united in one culture and behind one vision. These people will only succeed if they have access to the infrastructure and resources they need to succeed. This means not only physical assets but also an information technology and knowledge management environment to design, simulate, and share experiences to provoke further debate. And above all, patient financial capital, comfortable with longer-term risk for reward.

To provide that comfort, a robust enterprise architecture is necessary – an organisation and process that provides transparent, accountable leadership, so the "patient capitalists" and other stakeholders know who they are being asked to trust and can develop a relationship with them. This can evolve and change over time – indeed, it inevitably will – and so it must be professionally managed.

Also needed is a balance of conservative, stable culture and principles, tempered with the willingness to change style and shape as necessary to remain effective. Fundamentally, this transformation has been from drawing boards and hand calculation, deployed in departmental organisations, to today's agile, multi-disciplinary project teams, using computer-aided engineering, professional project, program, and portfolio management platforms, and production software suites. And there is more change to come as we exploit hyperscale computation, perhaps even quantum methods, and accompanying big-data science and artificial intelligence. This will transform the ability of an engineer to research and assess problems of high complexity. Individuals will then be able to do the work of teams, producing complex products, in small batches, for less cost than mass production. The future of our innovative portfolios is truly expansive.

References

Botticelli P. (1997) Rolls-Royce: How a legend was made. *The American Scholar 66*(4), 501–512.

Cusumano M. (2010) *Staying Power: Six Enduring Principles for Managing Strategy and Innovation in an Uncertain World (Lessons from Microsoft, Apple, Intel, Google, Toyota and more).* Oxford University Press.

Feilden G. & Sir Hawthorne W. (1998) Sir Frank Whittle, O.M., K.B.E. 1 June 1907–9 August 1996. *Royal Society* 44, 435–452.

Marsh G. (2012) Aero engines lose weight thanks to composites. *Reinforced Plastics* 56(6), 32–35.

Thomas V. and Maine E. (2019) Market entry strategies for electric vehicle start-ups in the automotive industry – Lessons from Tesla Motors. *Journal of Cleaner Production* 235, 653–663.

24 Case study – creating a portfolio management decision support tool for a medium-sized pharmaceutical company

Dave Reggi

Introduction

This case study chapter provides a detailed review of the creation of a portfolio tool for a pharmaceutical company based on the East Coast of America. The firm was transitioning from being almost wholly focused on early research (known as "discovery") to building significant capability to take drugs further down the development process and into the market. Operating a portfolio that included multiple stages of development and with rapidly increasing overall numbers of potential drug products required a step change in portfolio management sophistication and competence. The work described in this chapter to develop the portfolio tool – called in this organisation the *decision support asset review process and assessment tool* – demonstrates many aspects of the implementation of theory discussed in Sections I and II of this book. In particular, the chapter emphasises the centrality of understanding the company's strategic objectives and translating these into decision criteria to ensure portfolio management effectively delivers on strategic objectives.

The chapter starts with a review of the drug research and development process to orientate the reader to the context for the portfolio tool. It then goes on to describe the process used to develop the tool and finishes with a description of the tool itself. The primary aim of this case study is to present the work undertaken to design and implement a portfolio management decision support tool that brings significant competitive advantage to the pharmaceutical company. As such, commercially sensitive details of the decision process mechanics underlying the tool are not provided.

A glossary is provided at the end of the chapter in Annex 1. Terms, phrases, and other domain jargon that are in the glossary are identified by being in italics, with the signifier "G", for example: *pre-clinical*G.

It is also worthy of note that the tool and its associated processes had to reflect the *scientific method*G ethos of the firm. That is to say the portfolio tool had to meet expectations within the organisation for reliability and predictability of results, and as such, the methods employed to make and support a decision in one instance had to be replicable in subsequent instances, yielding the consistent result of optimising the portfolio, evidenced by an increasing portfolio valuation. This is, in fact, a high and challenging bar to reach, as this was intended as a decision support tool, not as a decision-making tool, and because decisions can also be influenced by intuition and other such factors (see Section III).

DOI: 10.4324/9780367853129-28

Background to pharmaceutical research and development

The complexities and details of the *pharmaceutical research and development*[G] (R&D) process, that is, how *small and large molecules*[G] progress through the various stages from *discovery*[G] to production and launch onto the global market, are well documented. For example, Dunson (2010) provides an expanded overview of the drug development process, and Elhassa and Alfarouk (2015) offer a more detailed exploration.

This case study focuses on two aspects of the development process:

1) A company that specialises in the earliest stage of research, that is, discovery.
2) The company's strategic and operational challenges as it faces the developmental prospect of organisational growth.

The pharmaceutical research and development process is a complex dynamic of higher-level decision-making or governance (i.e. management) and operational steps carried out by a cross-functional team representing multiple scientific, manufacturing, commercial, and marketing disciplines that execute the decisions made by the governance body. The overall process consists of multiple phases: discovery, preclinical, phase 1, phase 2a and 2b, phase 3, regulatory filing, and launch. The entire process can take up to 15 years and can cost a company up to $2.6 billion (Sullivan, 2019), based on data published before the COVID-19 pandemic. This cost does not include the expense of the compounds that failed to achieve market approval for that given indication, having been terminated in earlier phases for failing to achieve specific development requirements as defined by the *target product profile*[G]. Only 1 out of every 5,000 compounds in the *discovery* phase will make it to the development phase, and as of the time of this project, only 1 of 12 compounds entering *development* would make it to market. After the initial compound is *approved*[G], other forms of the drug may be developed, or it may be used for other indications. This is called *product line extension*[G] or, more commonly, *life cycle management*[G].

The operational part of the process is laid out to answer a staged and progressive series of questions that are determined by the *target product profile*[G] (i.e. a definition of what the product is expected to do in order to be marketable – its specifications). The content of which is guided by scientific, commercial, manufacturing, and regulatory goals and questions. The questions are associated with the phases mentioned previously. The answers are acquired through scientific work by the functional areas or operations and then processed to governance or management for decisions – that is, whether to proceed to the next step (go/no go) or, alternatively, put the research on hold, terminate further development, out-license, co-develop, etc. This is presented graphically in Figure 24.1.

The organisational context for the portfolio tool development

The client company (for whom the tool was developed), hereinafter referred to as *ClientCo*, was a biotech company that had a discovery platform technology that yielded a success rate for large molecules, higher than the industry average. The discovery process was subsidised by an outside large pharmaceutical company, herein referred to as *PhundoPharm*, that was given the right of first refusal of all molecules approaching transition to early development. ClientCo was faced with the following decision model shown in Figure 24.2:

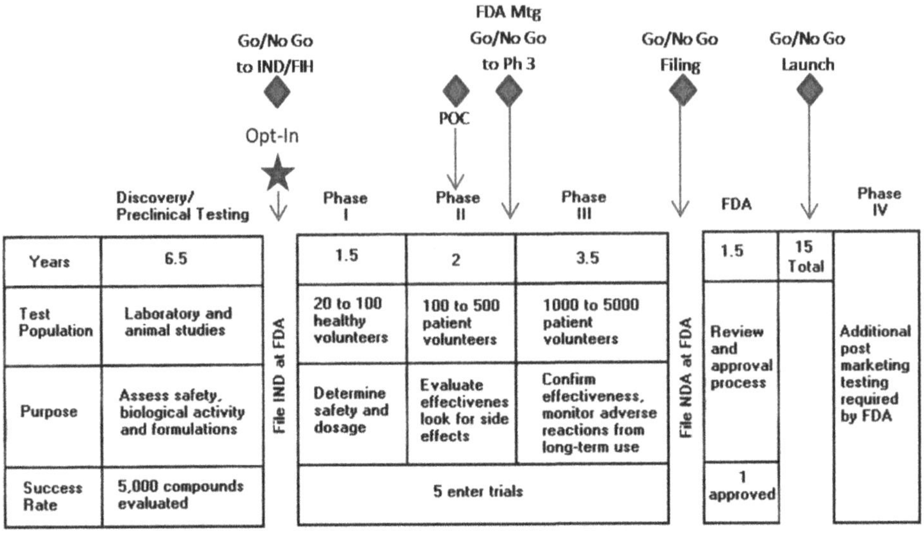

Figure 24.1 The drug research and development life cycle with governance decision points.
Source: Adapted from PhRMA (2021).

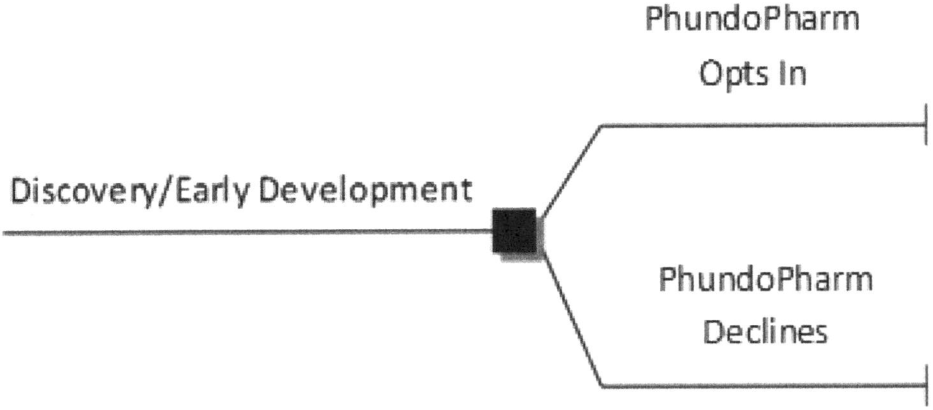

Figure 24.2 Single-arm decision process: discovery and opt-in.

Due to limited resources, PhundoPharm could only accept a limited number of molecules, leaving ClientCo with a large number of commercially viable assets in its discovery portfolio. The questions facing ClientCo were, firstly, how to characterise the attributes of these molecules; secondly, how to differentiate them; and thirdly, based on the relative profiles, to decide on what to do with them.

The view in ClientCo had been until this point in time that PhundoPharm was likely to take all viable compounds developed by ClientCo, as part of the "opt-in" arrangement. The organisation anticipated that this situation would soon change and PhundoPharm would begin declining viable candidates, due to resource constraints. This presented ClientCo with the opportunity to develop products in-house, using assets for which the discovery cost had essentially been borne by PhundoPharm. ClientCo would thus need a reliable decision-making approach to capitalise on this opportunity. The chosen approach had to reflect ClientCo's careful and moderated approach to growth.

At this stage, ClientCo was faced with a burgeoning discovery *pipeline*^{G}, together with projects moving from discovery and early development into late stage.[1] In addition, the characteristics of the overall pipeline were changing. The resource and financial demands of late-stage projects were significantly larger than those of early-stage projects, heavily dependent on cross-functional delivery capability and effective project team management. ClientCo's options for operational expansion included (1) *self-develop*^{G} (and grow internal operational capabilities), (2) *outsource*^{G}, (3) *out-license*^{G}, (4) *co-develop*^{G}, (5) *place on-hold*^{G}, and (6) *terminate*^{G}.

This change in the mix of the portfolio of projects led to an increase in the complexity of decision-making, and these decisions were predicated upon the overarching R&D and corporate strategy being translated into operational delivery. Resource and budgetary decisions for multiple smaller projects were fairly straightforward. Suboptimal decisions generally were countered by the sheer number of "options" being progressed (i.e. shots on goal). Decision-making for a few large projects was also fairly straightforward. The risk of poor decisions was greater (there were fewer options), but the certainty of success (i.e. progression to the next phase) was higher because well-run early-stage projects had been significantly de-risked, ensuring later-stage success. However, decision-making across a growing portfolio with multiple small and fewer large projects, in several *therapeutic areas*^{G}, would bring significant complexity.

ClientCo's management wanted to create an enhanced decision-making capability in anticipation of the complexity that would be generated from the changing characteristics of the pipeline. Hence, ClientCo was considering the following development decision model, shown in Figure 24.3.

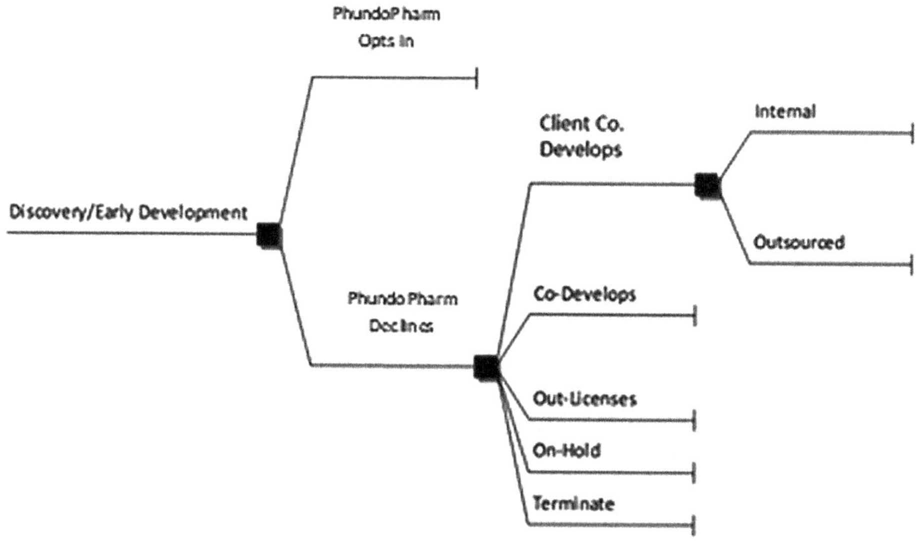

Figure 24.3 Expanded decision process – discovery and early development.

Gathering the data to build the decision support tool

In order to create a portfolio tool that would support decision-making effectively for ClientCo, a significant and wide-ranging data collection and analysis exercise was carried out. Three preliminary activities were required: (1) defining the parameters of the tool, (2) identifying the criteria that would be used to make decisions connected to strategic objectives, and (3) establishing the information needed to design the processes and reporting formats. Data was gathered in two stages: firstly, to outline the key parameters and expectations across the organisation and, secondly, to delve into more detail with the decision criteria and process for decision support.

Data gathering

The appropriate stakeholders included the members of the senior executive team, the project management community, functional area heads, and project heads. Each was interviewed using a tailored set of questions, derived from the issues noted previously (see this chapter's Annex 2 for the list of interview questions). The interviewees described current and future decision support needs with respect to:

- Strategic goals.
- Current decision-making approach.
- Prioritisation.
- Resourcing.
- Communication.
- Frequently voiced concerns around corporate culture and growth.
- Recommended data points for routine collection and suggested analytical views.
- Current and prior initiatives (and senior management's reactions to them).
- Corporate preferences and biases.

Once this data had been gathered and assimilated, the more detailed data gathering, based on individual assets, was carried out. This was achieved working primarily with several cross-functional focus groups. Each molecule undergoes careful scrutiny as it progresses through the stages of the development pipeline to eventually reach market. The research/science questions asked about early-stage compounds tend to be broad and generic and become more specific as the compound progresses through full development, as its intended use becomes more specialised and differentiated. This assessment is usually done in conjunction with the *Target Product Profiles*[G]. The earlier the stage of development, the greater the uncertainty and the more questions that need to be answered; as the molecule progresses, the inverse gradually becomes true – less uncertainty, fewer questions. The questions asked to ascertain or evaluate each molecule's merits for continuation fall into four broader categories of (1) commercialisation, (2) science and technology, (3) regulatory, and (4) risk.

Each asset in the portfolio was rated on these four attributes or dimensions. In this case, a "critical" question meant questions for which a POOR rating was a potential derailer to the asset value, which would result in the asset being put on development hold or terminated. Assets with favourable ratings on key attributes were more likely to proceed in development to the next key milestone. The course of action for assets with varied ratings would fall into the expanded development options, discussed later. Initially, the assessment group came up with hundreds of questions, which were distilled down to a critical handful, 10 to 20, for each attribute, eliminating the questions that were highly correlated.

Key information and findings

The main themes that were identified throughout the interviews, in understanding the key strategic drivers for the portfolio decision criteria, are discussed next. There were two clear findings from the data collection exercise that were expressed at every level interviewed. Firstly, the need to articulate and communicate a clear *strategic goal*, which was seen as an ongoing exercise, and secondly, there was a universally expressed desire to avoid becoming overly *bureaucratic*.

A need for well-defined strategic goals to guide decision-making and prioritisation

Some of the issues mentioned during the interviewing process, such as unclear priorities, sub-optimum communication, and changing processes in need of redefinition, were symptoms of the changing strategic goals of the organisation, as the operating environment was adapting to reflect the emerging pipeline challenges. The strategic goal for the portfolio tool, which required clear communication, was to continue to prepare molecules for PhundoPharm and to put a process in place to decide which molecules to move forward, self-develop, terminate, out-license or co-develop, etc. and, subsequently, to develop the functional capabilities to move forward on each of those decisions.

Avoiding bureaucracy

The sentiment that bureaucracy would not stand in the way of a good idea was echoed by all interviewees. ClientCo was not willing to sacrifice its key attributes of quality, accountability, and agility, by becoming bogged down in unnecessary procedures and processes. These attributes were considered crucial to maintaining and developing its competitive advantage, as the organisation continues to grow.

It is worth noting here that the term "bureaucracy" is often misunderstood to mean unnecessarily complicated business processes. This is not the original intention of bureaucracy: an alternative interpretation is that some processes are necessary for efficient operations and can be simple and standardised – but not at the expense of innovation. Similarly, efficient organisational functioning should be predicated upon managerial alignment, transparent communication, and accountability to ensure prompt and accurate decision-making and implementation. Hence, business sophistication and simplicity are not mutually exclusive.

Communication

Clear, prompt, decisive communication to governance, senior management, project teams, and operations to more efficiently execute, pursuant to a well-articulated strategic plan. In parallel, efforts were underway to develop the IT/knowledge management data warehousing infrastructure necessary to support this goal.

Managing the impact of PhundoPharm's culture on ClientCo

While PhundoPharm had played a prominent role in defining ClientCo's development, business practices, and priorities and would continue for the foreseeable future, the opportunity also existed to "go it alone" or find other development partners and become a "partner of choice". ClientCo was keen to create its own culture, avoiding the pitfalls of large pharma cultivating its own unique strengths.

Evaluation methods to support enhanced decision-making

ClientCo had specific requirements for the processes and tools to be developed. These were:

- *Balance quantitative vs. qualitative.* The final recommended template to facilitate decision-making would be a balance of *quantitative* and *qualitative* information and could be graphic and/or tabular but, in all cases, should be easy and quick to interpret, focusing on the key/pivotal information.
- *Validate/substantiate with data (QC).* The information provided had to be verifiable and point to the source data to establish its integrity, and hence its believability.
- *Ensure robustness.* While the decision points[G] and stage-gate review process were complex, the prepared analytics had to similarly capture the complexity distilled down to the essential asset attributes: scientific, technical, regulatory, and commercial dimensions. The support for each of these key dimensions would be traceable back to the wealth of source documents used to make the evaluation.
- *Prepare the PhundoPharm View and the ClientCo.* In the spirit of maintaining respect for a PhundoPharm view but developing a unique ClientCo view, alternate views/analyses were suggested. While many aspects could be similar, the use of the financial term NPV as an added dimension for the PhundoPharm view was suggested as the alternate – the caveat was added that this should not be an extensive exercise. It should be noted that as a valuation parameter for early assets, given all the enormous uncertainties, NPV and eNPV (expected NPV) are fairly meaningless, especially in discovery and early development phases (see Chapter 12 for a more detailed explanation of financial metrics used in portfolio management analysis).
- *Client stage-gate appropriateness.* Each review of the developing pipeline would be stage appropriate in order to ensure homogeneity of the pipeline asset sample being analysed, that is, for reviews at discovery, early exploratory (preclinical to phase IIa), late exploratory (phase IIb), and full development (phase IIb to phase III). The strategic criteria used for the evaluation would be relevant to what was known about that asset at that point in development.
- *Automated and quick to prepare and quality control (QC) for validation.* The final report(s) would be readily downloadable and quick and easy to prepare and QC. To accomplish this, the appropriate IT infrastructure would be put in place, which fortuitously was an ongoing organisational initiative. Most, if not all, of the scientific data supporting the attribute ratings required for the preparation of the proposed reports would be available within the system, and the data verifiable with the project directors, leads, and functional area heads, who are responsible for the data.

Identifying the pivotal data points that would facilitate enhanced decision-making capabilities

This work generated a list of 58 technical and commercial questions that were required to be answered. Most of the criteria proposed were rated on a three-point rating scale, with 1 representing the most favourable option and 3 representing the least favourable in most cases. These questions are fairly obviously commercially sensitive, as they are so critical to the portfolio decision process for ClientCo, and so are not presented here.

Better definition, understanding, and use of NPV

This was central to PhundoPharm's evaluations and decisions. The recent establishment of a commercial/marketing group acknowledged the need to develop this capability and, by extension, the need to better understand and use standard marketing methods and analytics. The most sensitive point of contention was the method and use of the NPV as a predictor variable, as it failed to withstand the scrutiny of senior management, who preferred to look at underlying market information, such as market size, potential for market penetration, competitive landscape, etc., and the ability to achieve "bestness".

Portfolio decisions

While eventually achieving a balanced distribution across therapeutic areas might have been a strategic goal, presently the goal was to achieve a balanced distribution across the phases (discovery, early, late, and full development), irrespective of the therapy area. A cross-functional review process, in alignment with this goal, evaluating targets excluded by PhundoPharm, was developed by the strategic and investor relations department within ClientCo. This focused solely on assets in discovery/early exploratory development and weighted in scientific, technical, commercial, regulatory, and risk factors.

Project and portfolio management

A project direction group setting standards to plan, track, manage, and communicate the status of projects in the portfolio was under development. The information, knowledge, and data generated from this effort would be captured in the IT project mentioned previously that was also under development.

The portfolio management tool (the decision support asset review process and assessment tool)

The portfolio tool was developed to address these research findings. The review process was developed as a routine, standardised asset valuation process, and the assessment tool was developed primarily as a project status report, providing a comparative visible "radar sweep" of the portfolio assets and related projects with their relative standing, including upcoming project deliverables. The process and the report were performed and issued on a predefined schedule appropriate to meet the business needs of the company. While the intended audience was senior management, functional area heads would find the report useful in determining workload, resource allocation, and project prioritisation. Typically, project teams would meet on a standardised schedule to address program and project status, strategy, operational tactics, risks, and risk mitigation, with a monthly or quarterly schedule recommended. The tool was built in Microsoft Excel, as the use of proprietary portfolio management software was discounted because these tools generally require the organisation to match its process to the tool rather than have the tool allow for a bespoke, organisation-specific decision process and criteria. This would defeat the objective of this work for ClientCo.

Worksheet 1: the client pipeline

The initial page of the report represented a static shot of all the projects within the pipeline, at their current stages of development, and a dynamic, tabular count or "progress towards goals" (PTG) assessment of all projects that have transitioned to discovery candidate, investigational new drug (*IND*[G]), *FIH*[G], full development (i.e. the drug has entered the late-stage portfolio, post-POC), or *filed*[G] and *approved*[G] for the current year. Each project could be colour-coded with respect to partner or therapeutic area (see Figure 24.4). This page illustrated exactly where the workload was building up over time. Clicking a link on any one of the assets would lead to the project status summary (PSS), providing further detail for that specific project.

Worksheet 2: portfolio scoring table

The second page of the report contained the portfolio scoring table for all assets under review (see Figure 24.5). The **d**ecision-making criteria would be used to evaluate each of the assets using the defined rating scale. Ratings would be derived for each attribute from a facilitated session, with a cross-functional project team. A single asset was presented in the final deliverable for the purpose of illustration. When generating this table and the accompanying graphic, assets would be grouped, analysed, and viewed by the same stage of development to ensure sample homogeneity and make decisions that would be uniquely applied to this subset of the pipeline. While the status reporting of each project could be updated on a monthly schedule, the more-intensive portfolio evaluation part of this report would more appropriately be performed every six months to a year, to monitor progress.

Risk assessment

The assessment of risk could range from quantitative and analytical to qualitative and subjective, with the mid-range representing some balance of the two. This balance is "user-defined". As the qualitative ratings are based on practical experience, they are given their due weight in the final valuation. The presented evaluation was a "broad stroke" assessment weighting in scientific, technical, and regulatory risks, given the asset's status in development, including the following attribute sub-categories:

- *Commercial dimension*. Sub-categories included: therapeutic candidate, unmet need, commercial opportunity, and competition.
- *Scientific and technical* dimension. Sub-categories included: target validation, POC (proof-of-concept), clinical trial (time and cost).
- *Regulatory* and *risk*. Sub-categories were unidimensional in this case and were not averaged.

A more detailed methodical approach was recommended, where the scientific/technical risk and regulatory or execution risk were assessed as high risk separately by the project team, on a scale from 1 to 3 (low, medium, high). The reasons for assessment were documented and recorded in the project strategy document in the risk section, with the overall risk being the average (weighted or unweighted). Industry data on probabilities of success of getting to market by molecule type, therapeutic area, indication, by phase or overall development could also be considered if available. Other methodologies and weightings

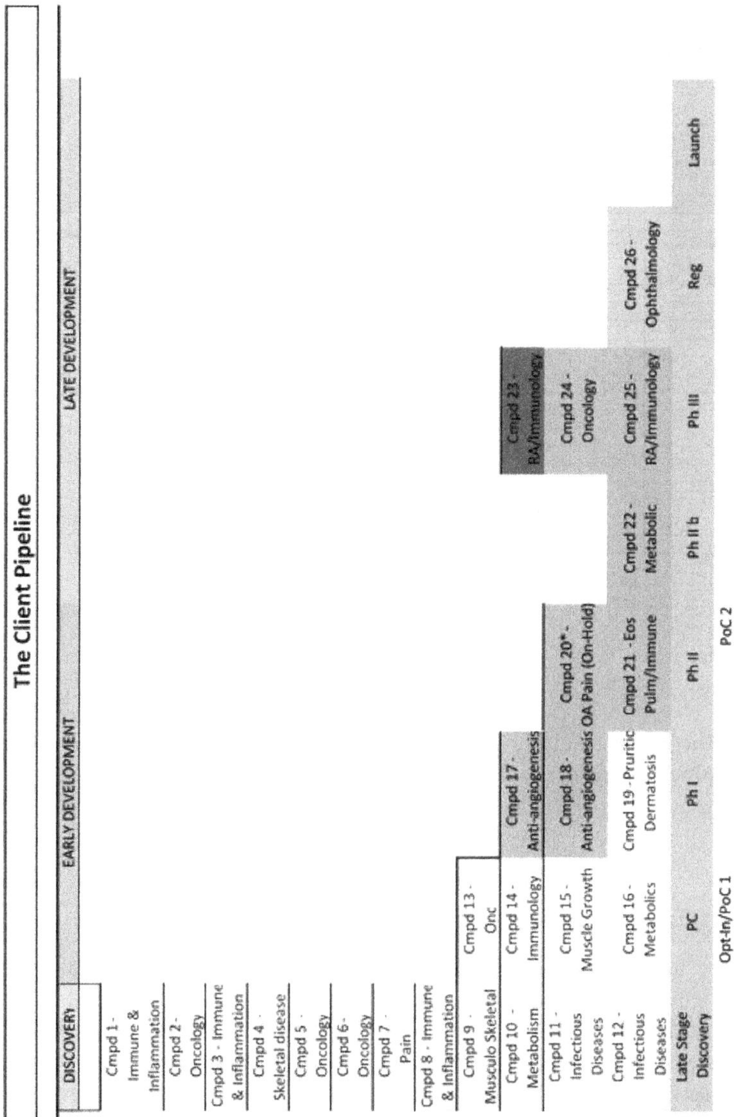

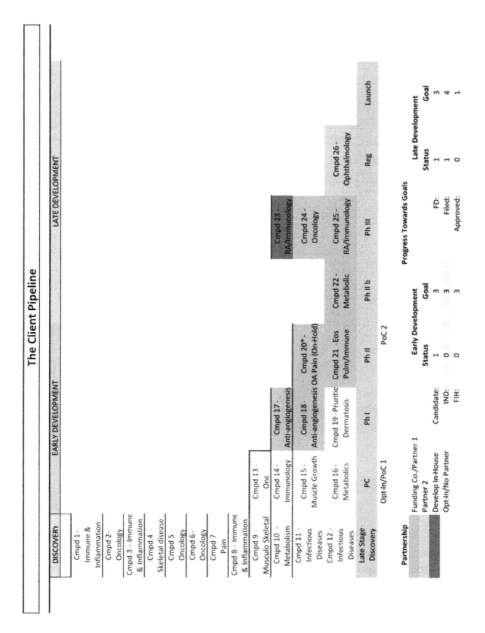

Figure 24.4 The client pipeline.

CRITERIA																	
NOTE: Click on compound to go to GRAPH		Commercial				Scientific & Technical				Reg	Tech & Reg Risk		Dimensions				
Compound/ Indication/ Formulation (Click on Compound to see Bubble Graph and Summary Documents)	Phase	1. Therapeutic Candidate	2. Unmet Need	3. Commercial Opportunity	4. Competition	5. Target Validation	6. Clinical Trial (Time & Cost)	7. POC - PC	8. POC - Clinical	Regulatory	Risk (Low, Med, High)	Overall Asset Criteria Rating	Commercial	Sci & Tech	Regulatory	Risk	Composite
Cmpd 26 - Ophthalmology	R							NA				#DIV/0!	#DIV/0!	#DIV/0!	0.0	0.0	#DIV/0!
Cmpd 23 -RA/Immun	III	2.0	2.0	3.0	2.0	1.0	2.0	NA	2.0	1.0	1.0	1.8	2.3	1.7	1.0	1.0	1.5
Cmpd 24 - Onco	III							NA				#DIV/0!	#DIV/0!	#DIV/0!	0.0	0.0	#DIV/0!
Cmpd 25 - RA/Immun	III	2.0	2.0	2.0	2.0	2.0		NA				2.0	2.0	2.0	0.0	0.0	1.0
Cmpd 22 - Metabolic	II b		2.0	2.0	2.0	2.0	2.0	NA				2.0	2.0	2.0	0.0	0.0	1.0
Cmpd 20 - OA Pain (On-Hold)	II		3.0	3.0	3.0	3.0		NA				3.0	3.0	3.0	0.0	0.0	1.5
Cmpd 21 - Pulm/Immune	II		3.0	3.0	3.0	3.0		NA				3.0	3.0	3.0	0.0	0.0	1.5
Cmpd 17 - Anti-angiogenesis	I							NA				#DIV/0!	#DIV/0!	#DIV/0!	0.0	0.0	#DIV/0!
Cmpd 18 - Anti-angiogenesis	I							NA				#DIV/0!	#DIV/0!	#DIV/0!	0.0	0.0	#DIV/0!
Cmpd 19 - Pruritic Dermatosis	I							NA				#DIV/0!	#DIV/0!	#DIV/0!	0.0	0.0	#DIV/0!
Cmpd 13 - Onc	PC							NA				#DIV/0!	#DIV/0!	#DIV/0!	0.0	0.0	#DIV/0!
Cmpd 14 Immunology	PC							NA				#DIV/0!	#DIV/0!	#DIV/0!	0.0	0.0	#DIV/0!
Cmpd 15 - Muscle Growth	PC							NA				#DIV/0!	#DIV/0!	#DIV/0!	0.0	0.0	#DIV/0!
Cmpd 16 - Metab	PC							NA				#DIV/0!	#DIV/0!	#DIV/0!	0.0	0.0	#DIV/0!
Cmpd 1 - Immun & Inflam	D								NA			#DIV/0!	#DIV/0!	#DIV/0!	0.0	0.0	#DIV/0!
Cmpd 2 - Onco	D								NA			#DIV/0!	#DIV/0!	#DIV/0!	0.0	0.0	#DIV/0!
Cmpd 3 - Immun & Inflam	D								NA			#DIV/0!	#DIV/0!	#DIV/0!	0.0	0.0	#DIV/0!
Cmpd 4 - Skeletal	D								NA			#DIV/0!	#DIV/0!	#DIV/0!	0.0	0.0	#DIV/0!
Cmpd 5 - Onco	D								NA			#DIV/0!	#DIV/0!	#DIV/0!	0.0	0.0	#DIV/0!
Cmpd 6 - Onc	D								NA			#DIV/0!	#DIV/0!	#DIV/0!	0.0	0.0	#DIV/0!
Cmpd 7 - Pain	D								NA			#DIV/0!	#DIV/0!	#DIV/0!	0.0	0.0	#DIV/0!
Cmpd 8 - Immun & Inflam	D								NA			#DIV/0!	#DIV/0!	#DIV/0!	0.0	0.0	#DIV/0!
Cmpd 9 - MusculoSkeletal	D								NA			#DIV/0!	#DIV/0!	#DIV/0!	0.0	0.0	#DIV/0!
Cmpd 10 - Metab	D								NA			#DIV/0!	#DIV/0!	#DIV/0!	0.0	0.0	#DIV/0!
Cmpd 11 - ID	D								NA			#DIV/0!	#DIV/0!	#DIV/0!	0.0	0.0	#DIV/0!
Cmpd 12 - Toxin B - ID	D								NA			#DIV/0!	#DIV/0!	#DIV/0!	0.0	0.0	#DIV/0!
Median Criteria Rating		2.0	2.0	3.0	2.0	2.0	2.0	#NUM!	2.0	1.0	1.0	#DIV/0!	#DIV/0!	#DIV/0!	0.0	0.0	#DIV/0!

Directions: For each criterion provide a rating from 1 to 3 to indicate the degree to which you believe that asset meets that criterion defined to the right. (Definitions below)

Figure 24.5 Portfolio scoring table.

could be used to view the results in either tabular or graphical format. See Figure 24.6 for an example of the graphical format, showing assets in full development. This additional flexibility allowed the reviewer to view the portfolio in several different ways for making decisions.

Worksheet 3: bubble graphic representation of the pipeline

This graphic was based on the arrangement of strategic criteria desired. In the example shown (Figure 24.6), the particular compound's ratings characterised it as an asset of moderate commercial, scientific, and technical value and low regulatory and overall risk for approval. Typically, this would be viewed in conjunction with evaluations for all the assets in this development phase to ascertain the asset's relative value for that phase of development. The valuation would be illustrated by the size, colour, and location of the bubble within the three-dimensional box.

Assets that PhundoPharm did not select or "opt in" to (i.e. excluded assets or targets[G]) were subsequently evaluated to decide their next step in development within ClientCo. A series of questions (not presented in this chapter) were discussed for each asset by the project teams and rated according to the predetermined scale. The ratings for commercial, science and technology, regulatory, and risk were weighted, averaged, and graphically presented according to the previous concept. The graphic for the excluded asset portfolio along with the development recommendations are shown in Figures 24.7a and b.

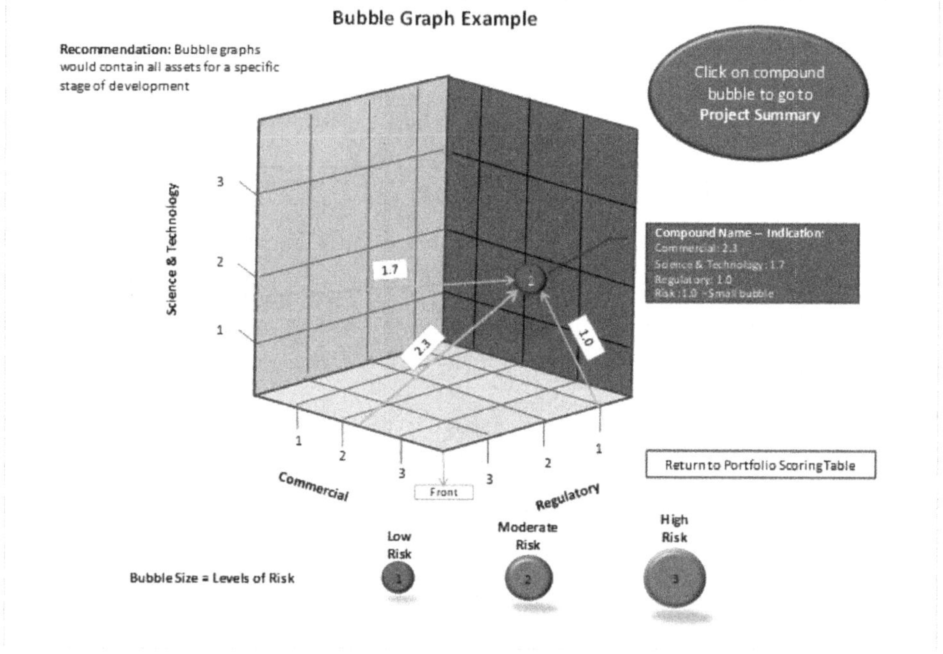

Figure 24.6 Bubble graph representation from rating scale.

Based on a very detailed set of company-specific technical questions (not presented in this chapter), those assets evaluated as warranting further development, compounds 1 through 4, can be characterised as moderate to mostly high risk, having a large predictable market with, perhaps, the need for some market development. They are also fairly inexpensive and quick to develop, with somewhat-predictive packaging, having a clear regulatory pathway with some guidance needed from the agency(ies). The assets not recommended for further development, compounds 5 through 8, had moderate to high developmental risk and were commercially viable but would require significant time and effort to adequately develop for the market. The scientific and technical challenges would only allow for a minimally acceptable label, and significant regulatory guidance would be required.

Heat map alternative

ClientCo expressed a preference for a heat map representation of the evaluation for each attribute of each asset. Additional attributes with sub-categories and a more sensitive rating scale (i.e. 1 to 5) was also requested to capture the depth of discussion and review, typical of their valuation process.

While the bubble graph (examples in Figures 24.6 and 24.7a) allowed for a visually global overall assessment of value, that is, the small red spheres clustered in the lower-left front of the three-dimensional space representing the best overall valuation, as opposed to the large green spheres in the upper-right back corner, the heat map allowed for each attribute category of an asset to be seen easily and discretely. In fact, quantitative values could be substituted in place of the qualitative colours. Colour allowed for quick visual interpretation of the portfolio assets, whilst the numerical values allowed for review of

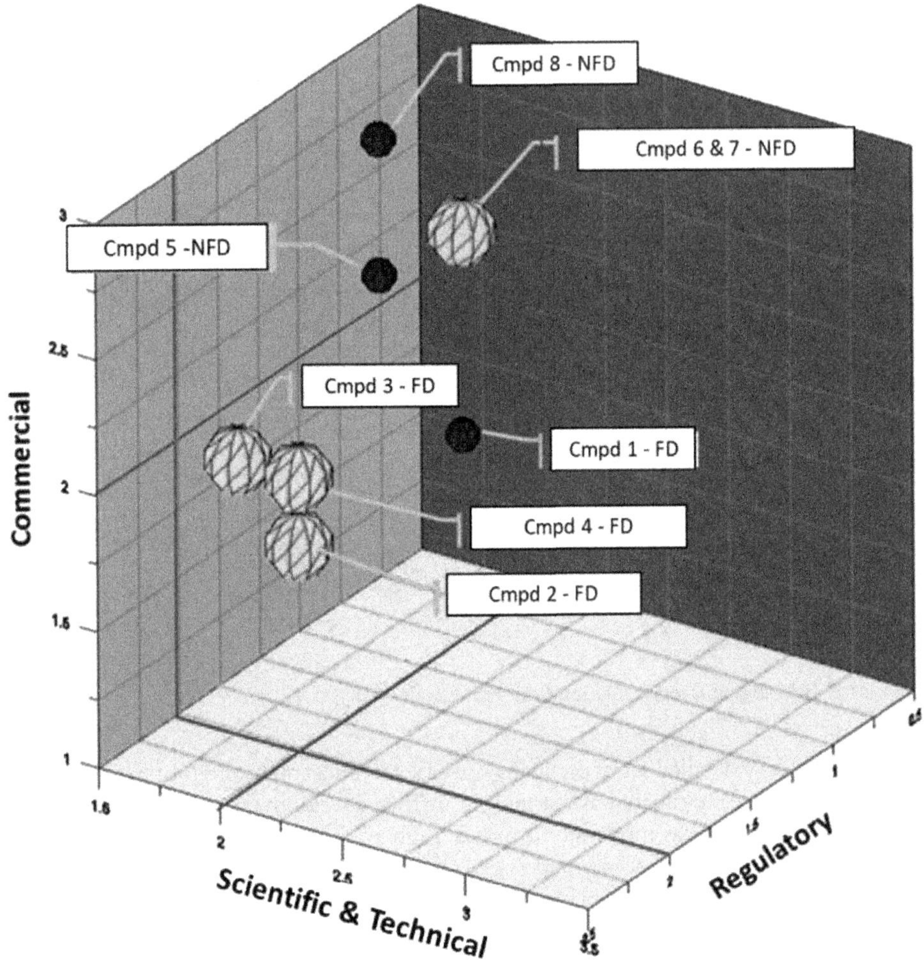

Figure 24.7a and b: Bubble graph representation for excluded asset portfolio.

(Key: FD: proceed to full development; NFD: no further development.)

the science and a validation of the final ratings. Each client tends to have a particular preference in how to view portfolio valuations (i.e. quantitative/analytical vs. qualitative/global) and in varying levels of granularity or detail.

In addition to the format of presentation, the heat map allowed *a greater level of sensitivity* to the overall assessment. This was achieved by having additional attributes, additional questions, and expanding the rating scale from 1 to 3 to 1 to 5, with 5 being optimal instead of 1 (as in the three-point rating scale). The categories and sub-categories for the heat map are shown in Table 24.1.

Each question was assigned an index number for reference. The colour assignment is a gradation, from RED (1) to YELLOW (3) to GREEN (5), similar to a traffic light analogy. Using the same basic method, ratings were weighted then averaged, first, for the sub-categories, then for the overall category or attribute. Finally, each asset received the

	Dimensions			
Asset	Commercial	Scientific & Technical	Regulatory	Risk
Cmpd 1	1.8	2.0	1.0	2.0
Cmpd 2	1.8	2.0	2.0	3.0
Cmpd 3	2.0	1.8	2.0	3.0
Cmpd 4	2.0	2.0	2.0	3.0
Cmpd 5	2.3	1.7	1.0	2.0
Cmpd 6*	2.5	2.0	1.0	3.0
Cmpd 7*	2.5	2.0	1.0	3.0
Cmpd 8	2.8	1.7	1.0	2.0
Cmpd 9†	1.5	3.0	n/a	3.0

Figure 24.7b (Continued)

Table 24.1 Heat map categories

Category	*Sub-category*	*Sub-category*
Scientific and Technical	1) Target validation	a) Target-specific b) Safety and toxicity
	2) Drug feasibility	
Clinical	1) Proof of concept	a) Cost b) Feasibility
	2) Full development	a) Cost b) Feasibility
Regulatory	1) Pathway 2) Safety factors 3) Study factors	
Commercial	1) Unmet need 2) Competitive environment 3) Pricing and reimbursement 4) Cost of sales	

STAGES of DEVELOPMENT						Targ Valid		Drg Feas	Clinical				Regulatory			Commercial			
									POC		Full								
	Drug Candidate	TA	PI/SF	Partner	Indication	Targ Spec	Saf & Tox	Drg Feas	Cost	Feas	Cost	Feas	Pathway	Safety	Study	Unmet Need	Compet Env	Price & Reimb	Cost of Sales
	Question Number					1.0-1.8	1.9-1.11	2.0-2.3	3.0	3.1-3.8	3.9	3.10-3.17	4.0	4.1-4.4	4.5-4.14	5.0-5.2	5.3-5.10	5.11-5.12	5.13
Launch	Cmpd 26	Oph	PI			2.6	3.0	4.0	2.0	3.6	5.0	3.8	3.0	4.5	2.2	2.7	2.9	5.0	3.0
	Cmpd 27	I&I	PI																
Full	Cmpd 26	Oph	SI																
	Cmpd 22	CVM	PI			3.2	3.7	4.0	5.0	4.5	3.0	4.5	3.0	2.0	3.7	4.7	3.5	4.0	5.0
	Cmpd 26	Oph	SI																
	Cmpd 25	I&I	PI																
	Cmpd 26	Oph	SI																
	Cmpd 23	I&I	SI																
	Cmpd 24	Onc	PI																
Early	Cmpd 21	I&I	PI																
	Cmpd 21	I&I	SI																
	Cmpd 21	I&I	SI																
	Cmpd 17	Onc	PI																
	Cmpd 18	Onc	PI																
	Cmpd 20	Pain	PI																
	Cmpd 15	CVM	PI																
	Cmpd 19	I&I	PI																
	Cmpd 21	I&I	PI																
Pre-Ind	Cmpd 16	CVM																	
	Cmpd 16	CVM																	
	Cmpd 13	Onc																	
	Cmpd 14	I&I				3.9	5.0	4.0	3.0	4.0	3.0	4.0	1.0	3.5	3.9	3.0	4.3	1.0	1.0
Discovery	Cmpd 9	I&I																	
	Cmpd 1	I&I																	
	Cmpd 8	I&I																	
	Cmpd 11	ID																	
	Cmpd 12	ID																	
	Cmpd 6	Onc																	
						Average: Attribute by Sub-Category													

Figure 24.8 Example heat map for portfolio valuation by question for each attribute.

averaged overall rating. In this method, the valuation of assessments could be validated by the supporting documentation related to each category. An example of a heat map grid for a portfolio valuation assessment for each of the attributes for each question by attribute category, averaged for each sub-category by attribute, then by each attribute, is presented next in Figure 24.8.

A completed heat map rolled up for actual assets, in the same stage of development, is provided in Figure 24.9. As a full development portfolio, the overall valuation for five assets is 3.6, trending GREEN (favourable); 14 of the 20 cells (70% – not including overall) were in the GREEN. With the exception of a few commercial (cmpds 4 and 5), regulatory (cmpds 2 and 3), and risk (cmpds 2 and 5) issues, the portfolio is fairly

	Drug Candidate	TA	PI/SF	Partner	Indication	Commercial	Sci & Tech	Reg	Risk	Overall
	Category					1	2	3	4	5
Full	Cmpd 1	CVM	SI	S	***	3.3	3.3	5.0	4.0	3.9
	Cmpd 2	ID	PI	S	***	3.3	4.0	3.0	3.0	3.3
	Cmpd 3	IM	SI	S	***	4.3	3.7	3.0	4.0	3.7
	Cmpd 4	CNS	PI	P	***	3.0	3.7	4.0	4.0	3.7
	Cmpd 5	OPH	SI	P	***	1.8	3.7	5.0	3.0	3.4
						3.1	3.7	4.0	3.6	3.6

Figure 24.9 Example heat map for full development asset valuation.

homogenous. By comparison, an earlier-stage portfolio analysis might yield a lower overall valuation and higher variability between the attribute cells. This view allows a quick visual evaluation of the overall portfolio (i.e. homogeneity/heterogeneity of colour) and enables further discussion and analysis cell by cell (attribute by attribute) for each asset. This engages the governance decision-making process and the determination of next steps. Also of note, ClientCo stated that market value is frequently not a driving factor in the valuation process. Therefore, a low commercial rating may not impede the development process for an asset, as it may have significant strategic value.

Worksheets 5 and 6: project status summary and the project strategy document

The project status summary was a single-page summarisation of *each* project graphically, indicating where the project stands in the development process, providing a brief description of the project, and identifying any issues of immediate concern that could cause deviation from the critical path (see Figure 24.10). A hyperlink on this page linked to the project strategy document (Figure 24.11) and a more detailed explanation of any items that have a YELLOW or RED stoplight, to provide details about overall strategies and rate-limiting concerns.

Conclusion

ClientCo was facing the imminent prospect of significant organisational growth. As a biotech company having a highly successful discovery technology yielding promising molecules for development, the company funding ClientCo's discovery process, PhundoPharm, was unable to integrate and manage all the viable assets into its portfolio due to financial and resource limitations. This left ClientCo with a burgeoning library of promising assets of significant medical and commercial value.

ClientCo was at the crossroads of organisational development. Where did it want to go? What did it want to become when fully grown? The need to articulate an organisational strategy was frequently expressed during the interview process as part of this case study. Interestingly, while ClientCo wanted to understand and respect the bureaucratic and more analytic nature of PhundoPharm, it was keen on remaining agile, both in its decision-making and operational capabilities, and also non-bureaucratic. Additionally, the company frequently emphasised that return on investment was not the driving factor

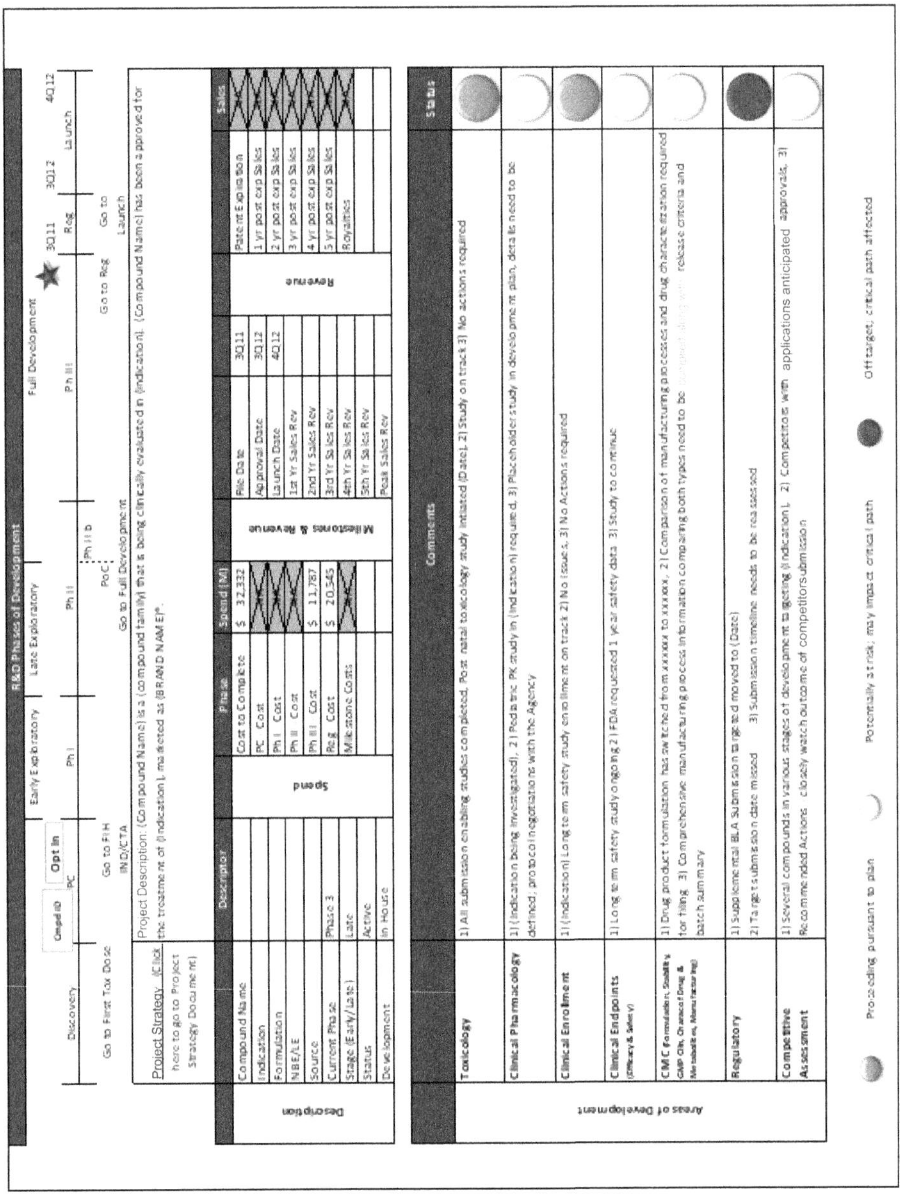

Figure 24.10 Example project status summary.

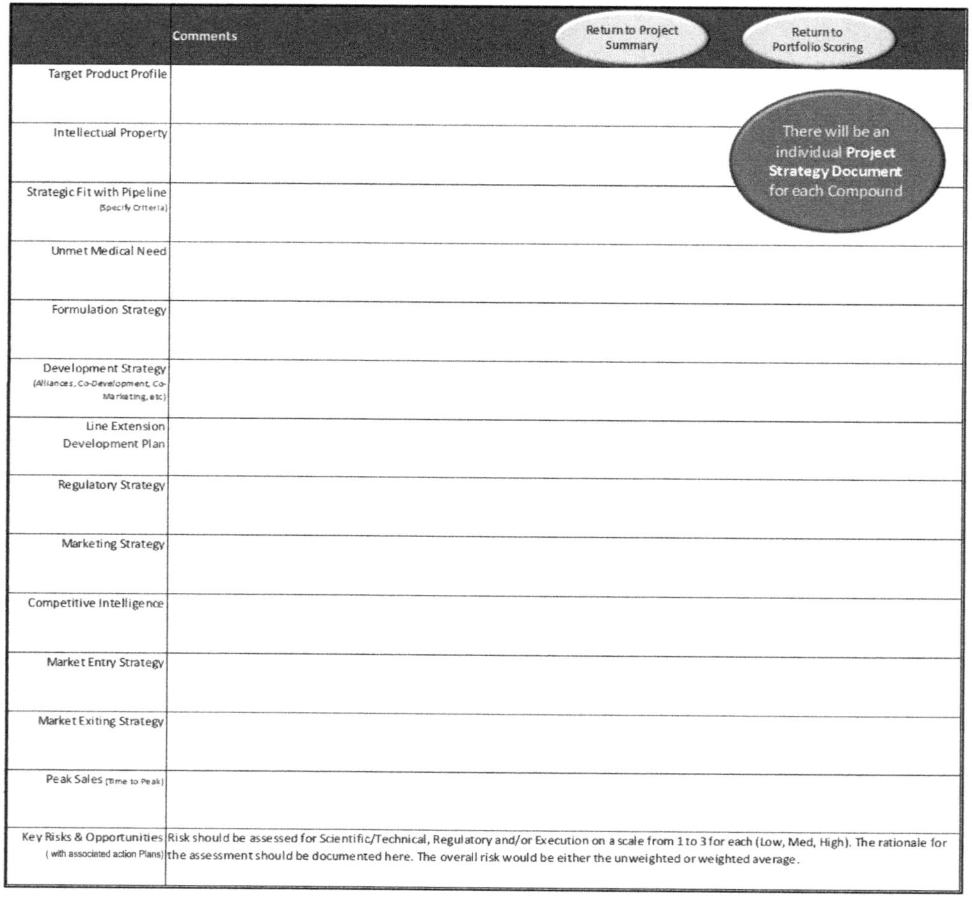
Comments
Return to Project Summary
Return to Portfolio Scoring
There will be an individual Project Strategy Document for each Compound
Target Product Profile
Intellectual Property
Strategic Fit with Pipeline (Specify Criteria)
Unmet Medical Need
Formulation Strategy
Development Strategy (Alliances, Co-Development, Co-Marketing, etc)
Line Extension Development Plan
Regulatory Strategy
Marketing Strategy
Competitive Intelligence
Market Entry Strategy
Market Exiting Strategy
Peak Sales (Time to Peak)
Key Risks & Opportunities (with associated action Plans)
Risk should be assessed for Scientific/Technical, Regulatory and/or Execution on a scale from 1 to 3 for each (Low, Med, High). The rationale for the assessment should be documented here. The overall risk would be either the unweighted or weighted average.

Figure 24.11 Example project strategy summary.

behind decisions to move forward with assets, but instead, medical need and intellectual gain were critical and often pivotal. That is, ClientCo viewed social and intellectual capital at least as equally important as commercial – a significant and interesting departure from other organisations in the industry.

The portfolio (decision support) tool enabled ClientCo to systematically articulate, categorise, rate, and weight all the essential questions, relevant to all the disciplines, and for the project teams involved, when evaluating each of the assets. The next step was to standardise the process to make it replicable and the assets comparable, and then to create a method of visualisation.

Some eight years after this tool was developed, it is still a critical component of their value optimisation process for the portfolio, even as the organisation has grown in terms of the portfolio size (number of compounds to be managed) and financial performance. This demonstrates that careful and thorough development of portfolio analytics to support decision-making, with decision criteria driven directly by strategic goals, and user-friendly and intuitive reporting interfaces and graphics, has lasting value for organisations.

Note

1 Late-stage projects are those that have passed the POC (*proof-of-concept*[G]) milestone in the drug research and development life cycle (see Figure 24.1). Early-stage projects are defined as those that have yet to reach POC.

References

Dunson, T. (2010) A Review of Project Management in Life Science Industry Sectors – Chapter in Harpum P. (2010) Portfolio, Program, and Project Management in the Pharmaceutical and Biotechnology Industries. Wiley, NY.

Elhassa G. & Alfarouk K. (2015) Drug Development: Stages of Drug Development. *Journal of Pharmacovigilance* 3(3).

PhRMA (Pharmaceuticals Research and Manufacturers of America) (2021) The drug development and approval process. Accessed at www.fdareview.org/issues/the-drug-development-and-approval-process.

Sullivan T. (2019) A tough road: Cost to develop one new drug is $2.6 Billion; Approval rate for drugs entering clinical development is less than 12%. *Policy and Medicine.* Accessed at www.policymed.com

Annex 1

Glossary of terms

In Table 24.2 that follows is a specific glossary of terms for this pharmaceutical portfolio tool case study.

Table 24.2 Glossary of terms

Term	*Definition*
Biologics License Application (BLA) Marketing Authorisation Application (MAA) in Europe	A formal request for permission from the relevant regulator to introduce or deliver for introduction a biologic product into the market.
Co-develop	Two or more companies sharing the operational and/or financial burden/risk of developing an asset for eventual sale, production, distribution, and marketing.
Decision Point	Any one of several key points in a development schedule where governance will choose to either advance, hold, or terminate the development of an asset based on its target and the data to date.
Discovery	Drug discovery is the process through which potential new medicines are identified. It involves a wide range of scientific disciplines, including biology, chemistry, and pharmacology (www.nature.com/subjects/drug-discovery).
Excluded Targets	Discovery assets that are opted out (i.e. not selected) by the funding company and available for further development by the discovery company.
First in Human (FIH)	The first dose administered to a human after an investigational new drug application approval which initiates phase I of the drug development process.
Governance	A management decision-making body and methods applied to supplying management with information/data to facilitate decision-making.
High-Throughput Screening	A drug discovery process that allows automated testing of large numbers of chemical or biological compounds for a specific biological target.
In Vitro	Tested in a test tube, culture dish, or outside of a living organism.
In Vivo	Tested in a living organism.
Investigational New Drug (IND)	A formal application submitted to the relevant regulator requesting permission to test a new drug for the treatment of a specific disease in humans.
Out-License	A legal arrangement with a partner who will collaborate in the development and marketing of a sponsor's compound.
Outsource	The reliance upon a vendor or third party through a contractual arrangement for the completion of specific functions.
New Drug Application (NDA) in USA Marketing Authorisation Application (MAA) in Europe	A formal request for permission from the relevant regulator to introduce, or deliver for introduction, a non-biologic product into the market.

Term	*Definition*
Pharmaceutical Research and Development (R&D)	The process of discovering and developing a compound for a specific medical use (e.g. treatment of a disease) designed to answer a series of focused, sequential, staged scientific and marketing questions to determine if a compound is medically and commercially viable and worth bringing to market.
Pharmacodynamics	A branch of pharmacology that studies the effects of a drug as it is processed through the body.
Pharmacokinetics	A branch of pharmacology that studies how a drug is processed through the body.
Pipeline	The entire portfolio of assets in the various stages/phases of development.
On Hold	Cessation of further development until further information/data are provided.
Proof-of-Concept (POC)	Scientific evidence that an asset has the properties and performs the actions intended as specified in the target product profile.
Safe and Efficacious	The evaluation that a molecule does what it is therapeutically designed to do with little to no untoward effects or toxicity.
Small and Large Molecules	Small molecule is a low-molecular-weight organic compound that may regulate a biological process; large molecules are proteins that have a therapeutic effect.
Target Product Profile (TPP)	A document that outlines the desired "profile" or characteristics of a target product that is aimed at a particular disease or diseases. TPPs state intended use, target populations, and other desired attributes of products, including safety and efficacy-related characteristics. (www.who.int)
Terminate	A decision to halt further development of an asset.
Therapy Areas	An area of medical practice that encompasses groupings of specific diseases and/or disorders generally treated by a specific medical specialty, such as oncology, cardiovascular, neurology, or haematology.

Annex 2

Interview questions

Questions for senior stakeholders

- What type of information is going to be most useful for you in supporting decision-making?
- How is strategy currently flowed down from the corporate level to the projects? (Thereby ensuring projects deliver outputs that will achieve the client company's strategic objectives.)
- What are the current and expected future company strategic objectives?
- What are the key markers of success for the client company as a company?
- What are the key factors influencing allocation of money and people between Dx/early work and post-POC later phase work (i.e. how do you believe the client company should weigh the resource allocation decision between many small early projects with low probability of success against fewer, high-resource-need, higher-probability-of-success projects?)
- What is the current governance structure, and how is it likely to change in the future?
- How much autonomy do project teams have to make decisions between stage gates/portfolio reviews? Is this likely to change in the future?
- A two-part approach is anticipated: firstly, qualitative project-centric data and, secondly, a quantitative scorecard: is this likely to meet your decision support needs?
- What are your immediate reactions to the draft we have put together already (as a starting point for these discussions)?
- What two or three key factors will indicate our work with you has been successful?

Questions for focus groups and other members of the project community (project teams, project support, etc.)

- Describe how the current governance decision-making process for projects works at the client company.
- What are the key parts of the process that need to be improved? Why?
- What will an ideal future decision-making process look like? What will be the inputs and outputs for that process?
- What is the most effective way to gather the data requested by senior stakeholders?
- What is the most effective way to present that data?
- Do projects articulate and document multiple alternative project strategies from which governance are able to select one or more for detailed planning? If not, would such an approach add value at the senior management and project levels?
- How are project risks and opportunities identified and managed and reported to senior management?
- What are your immediate reactions to the draft we have put together already (as a starting point for these discussions)?
- What two or three key factors will indicate our work with the client company has been successful?

Questions for functional managers

As previous for teams, plus:

- What are your preferences for data collection/data entry to feed information to governance to support their decision-making?
- To what extent can functions make use of the data collected for governance (function portfolio decision-making, function risk profile, function resource forecasting, function budget management, etc.)?

25 Case study – delivering a multi-billion-pound strategic portfolio

Paul Taylor

Introduction

Due to the scale of the Thames Water–regulated portfolio of works, worth circa £2bn for the 2015 to 2020 regulated cycle agreed with Ofwat (the UK government's water regulator, the Water Services Regulation Authority), known as the Asset Management Programme 6 (AMP6), Thames Water considered it needed a wide band of technical and professional capability. This, in turn, led to the creation of a leading special-purpose delivery alliance of firms in the industry that was fully aligned to the Thames Water imperatives. To provide a step change in delivery, the alliance had to be far less transactional than in previous contracting arrangements and more of a collaborative enterprise. To respect commercial sensitivities, throughout this chapter this alliance of multiple firms is referred to simply as the alliance, with the term *programme* applicable to this case study.

The Thames Water alliance structure consisted of eight delivery partners inside an overarching Thames Water framework. These included an overall portfolio manager who supported the overarching portfolio, and six defined program streams, a technology partner, and two delivery joint ventures (JVs), each consisting of engineering design consultants, infrastructure delivery organisations, and process delivery organisations. Thames Water personnel were seconded into key roles within all the organisations.

The work was in two clear stages (early contractor involvement) ECI and AMP6, the first being a transformation program, defining and setting out the regulated portfolio, the second enabling the delivery of the regulated portfolio.

This case study chapter discusses the development and delivery of this multi-billion-pound strategic portfolio. Firstly, the chapter defines the operating model around which the portfolio was developed, followed by a more detailed look at the processes and systems. How the portfolio was developed is covered with its expected outcomes and benefits. The case study then concludes with how the portfolio delivery was managed, including discussing the people aspects and knowledge management and, finally, listing the benefits achieved with a portfolio management approach for such a large strategic portfolio.

The operating model

Delivery structure

The alliance organisation was developed with the approach that it would run for a regulatory life cycle of five years, allowing it to grow and mature to deliver exemplar performance. The organisation was developed to be self-governing, but with clear separation between delivery and assurance.

DOI: 10.4324/9780367853129-29

Values and behaviours

One of the principal challenges faced was the assembly of the entities into a single cohesive alliance of this scale, with eight partners and an integrated overarching client, each with their own organisational and cultural idiosyncrasies. During the ECI stage, Thames Water and its alliance partners, through a series of facilitated workshops over a four-month window, developed an understanding of how all involved would be able to work together. These workshops flushed out the values of the differing organisations and enabled a common landing point. To support this process, behavioural management consultants were brought in as part of the team. From the workshops, an overarching alliance vision, blueprint, and target operating model were established that all the parties signed on to (see Figure 25.1, "AMP6 operating model"). During this stage, jointly developed, mutually assured contractual arrangements to mitigate organisational and cultural challenges were agreed. The approach could be summarised into five key points:

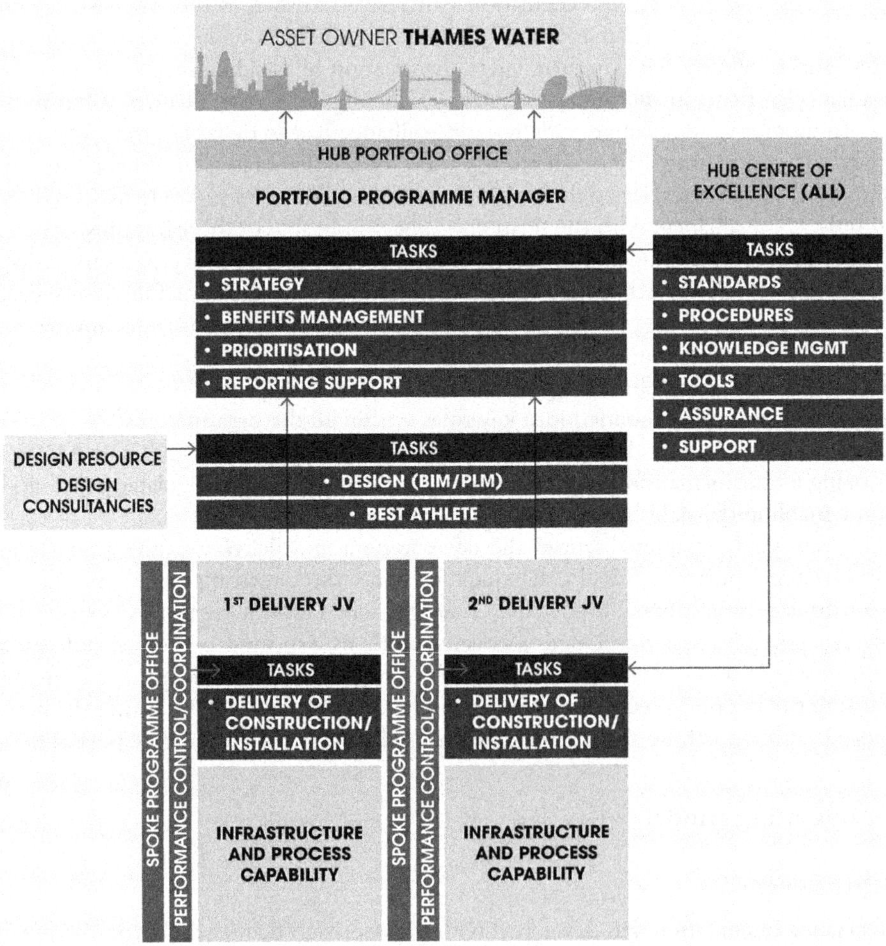

Figure 25.1 AMP6 operating model.

1. Incentives: that all partners were mutually incentivised to work together.
2. Collaboration: the partners should use their staff with collaborative working track records.
3. Integrated teams: the partners would work in fully integrated teams, including cross-JVs.
4. Portfolio visibility: forward visibility of workload to allow effective alliance investment.
5. Waste minimisation: that effort duplication, rework, material quantities were minimised.

Business transformation

The alliance organisation was set up two years before the start of the AMP6 delivery cycle to enable the individual companies to develop methodologies and protocols on how to collaborate effectively, removing interfaces and duplication by using hub-and-spoke techniques and appointing the right staff for the job on a "best athlete" basis. This basis was achieved by ensuring the individual had the right skills and was chosen on ability, regardless of which parent organisation (PO) the individual was employed by.

To ensure the overall working relationships between Thames Water, its alliance, and the supply chain was collaborative, efficient, and effective, an overall portfolio transformation strategy and implementation plan was developed. This strategy and transformation plan, which all parties contributed to, was known as *The Big Plan* (see Figure 25.2, "Transformation streams"). This was to develop a joint and common approach to the alliance operation and was split into ten workstreams. Each of the ten workstreams was assigned a responsible owner and had an 18-month transformation plan, with key deliverables, timescales, and resource requirements identified.

The processes and systems

Portfolio delivery system

The portfolio management team created an overarching delivery framework that complied with corporate governance and enabled the alliance to maximise its operational efficiency. This included the development of the business workflow and assurance system

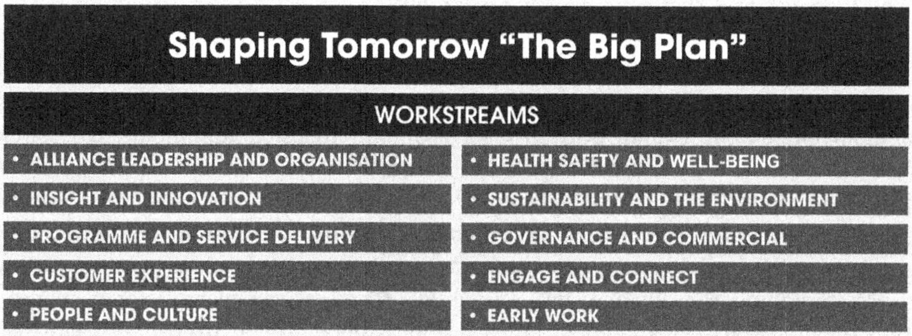

Figure 25.2 Transformation streams

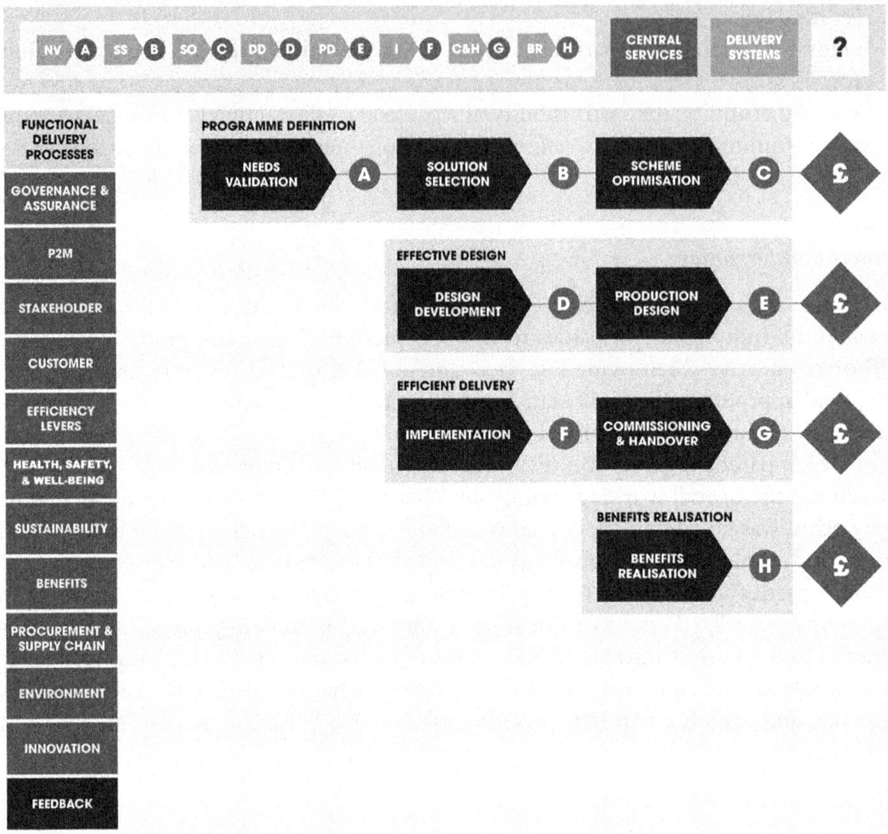

Figure 25.3 Portfolio delivery system level 1 for delivery life cycle.

known as a portfolio delivery system (PDS) that ensured common business processes and working practices for portfolios, programs, and projects. The upper level of the PDS is indicated in Figure 25.3, "Portfolio delivery system level 1".

The PDS ensured that outcomes were achieved in the timescales required, risks and opportunities were maximised from a technical design and commercial perspective, and all required stakeholders had been actively engaged throughout the life cycle. The PDS was referred to as the *Navigator*; it was a compendium of the alliance business processes that incorporated the overall portfolio, six program stream requirements, the standard project life cycle for the individual projects, and deliverable requirements for each stage. Figure 25.4 shows the portfolio delivery system level 2 for needs validation. The PDS defined technical and gateway reviews, including the lines of enquiry and questioning. This ensured the individual projects had reached the correct level of maturity to move forward, providing the alliance with the ability to assess the viability of each project within the portfolio. This enabled intervention as necessary to maximise performance against functional objectives and business outcomes of the six program streams and the overall portfolio.

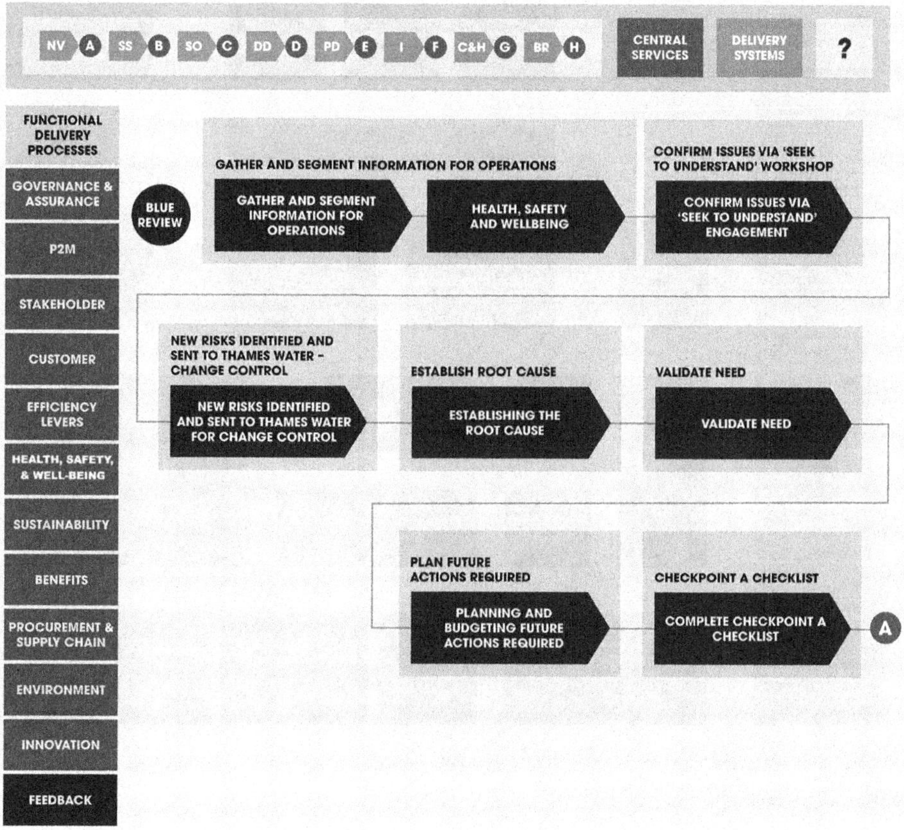

Figure 25.4 Portfolio delivery system level 2 for needs validation.

Development of enterprise program management applications

To align all the businesses, it was essential that projects and programs within the portfolio were held in a single environment (see Figure 25.5, "Thames IPMS architecture"). From a portfolio software platform perspective, the alliance deployed a UK government digital marketplace environment, called "*Programme Insight Manager*" (PIM), which was the integrated portfolio management system that enabled the alliance to link three financial systems (SAP, JD Edwards, and IFS), a common scheduling tool (P6), the risk registers (ARM), the health and safety systems, and timesheets system under a common framework.

The PDS was developed as a front-end graphics user interface linked to Thames Water's common data environment (business collaborator). The P6 scheduling software was also linked, via a simulation application (Synchro), to a 3D design model, enabling time-based digital rehearsals using virtual reality models to be carried out, together with challenges to method statements, schedule logic, and durations.

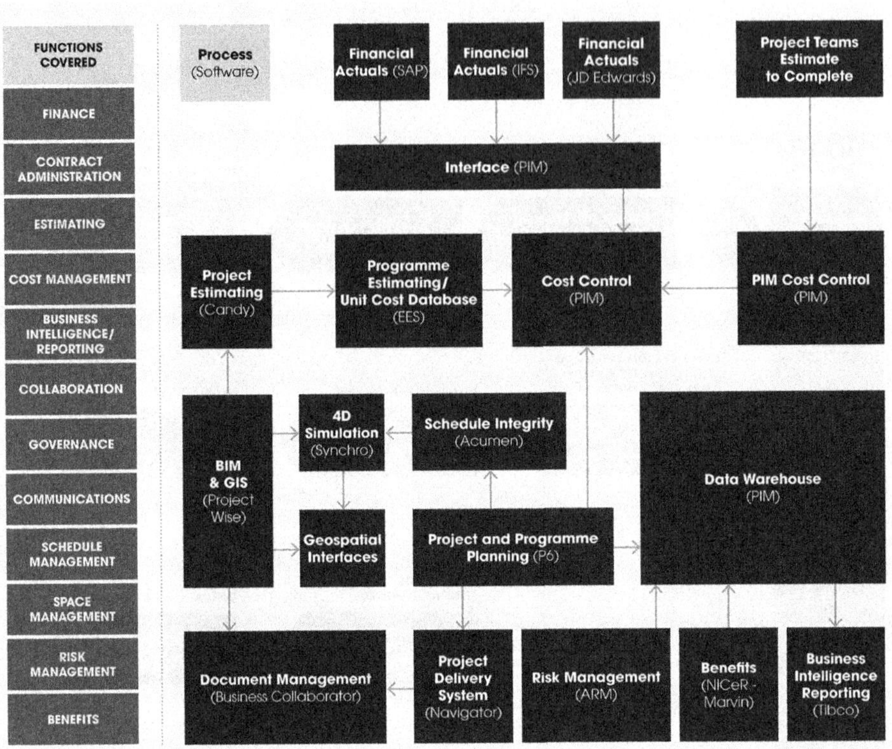

Figure 25.5 Thames IPMS Architecture.

Developing the portfolio

Capital planning

The alliance was specifically formed before the regulatory period to enable the partners to work with Thames Water to produce the regulatory submission. As all parties were responsible for developing the submission, it enabled these parts of regulatory submission to become shared objectives between Thames Water and its alliance partners; this then provided a clear step change from transactional management and CAPEX-only solutions.

As part of developing the portfolio between 2012 and 2014, the portfolio manager, working with Thames Water and all the alliance partners, agreed 6 major programs with 36 subprograms. Within these there were over 1,100 defined projects and 230 non-specific reactive maintenance financial allocations (see Figure 25.6, "AMP6 portfolio structure").

For reactive maintenance, monies using historic expenditure models were assigned to a group of operational assets, but the scope was not defined. These programs and projects were developed first for the Ofwat submission, ensuring all parties could buy into and agree on the defined outcomes and objectives.

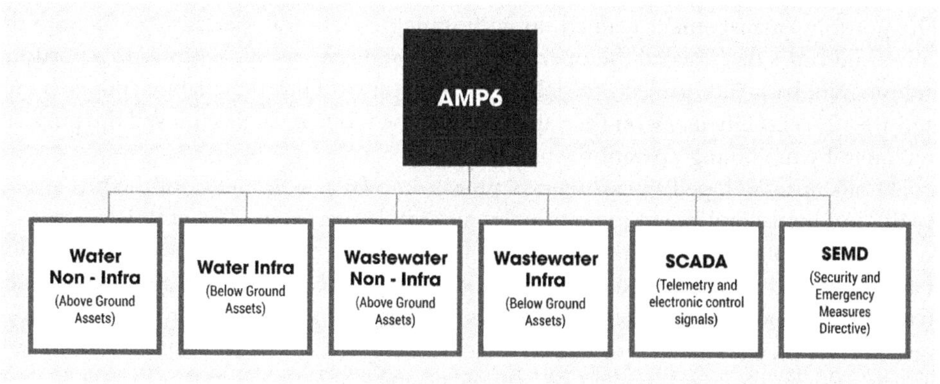

Figure 25.6 AMP6 portfolio structure.

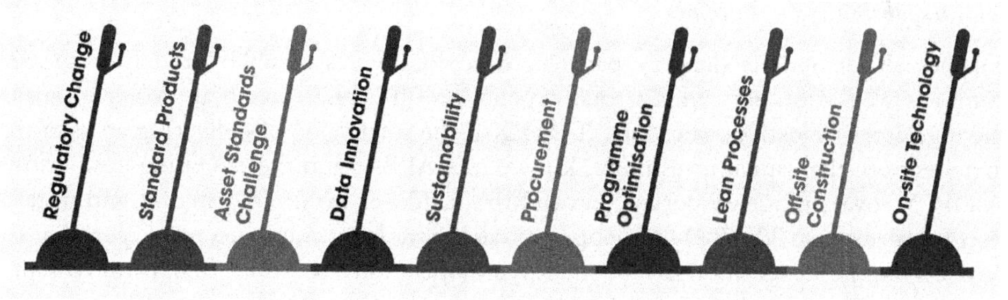

Figure 25.7 Efficiency levers for prioritisation and optimisation.

Portfolio prioritisation and optimisation

Ten prioritisation and optimisation efficiency levers (EL) formed the main driver of innovation on the contract to help deliver the multi-million pounds of savings across the portfolio of programs. The ELs were applied at the portfolio, program, and project level.

The portfolio management team worked with the alliance partners to develop a detailed process to guide the capture, assessment, prioritisation, and management of all ideas for efficiency and innovation. This comprised of five key phases: discover, assess and prioritise, develop initial business case, design solution, and embed.

Once the efficiency levers were identified and agreed (see Figure 25.7, "Efficiency levers for prioritisation and optimisation"), for each EL an efficiency lever management team was created. These teams comprised a project manager, a technical lead, and an EL lead, who developed and managed the potential efficiency through the five key phases outlined. Key to the approach was ensuring that all partners' expertise within the UK and globally was maximised for the benefit of the alliance, particularly across existing and developing frameworks within and outside the water sector.

Efficiency measurement

The portfolio/management teamed up with strategic technical specialists to identify the causes and issues that created the operational need and analysis of solutions on a portfolio and program basis (not project) to deliver the outcomes. This step change approach created 10–12% cost efficiency on the capital part of the scope but still achieved the program outcomes by modifying operational processes.

The alliance developed a prioritisation process known as a "*left shift*" for the first year of AMP6 to stimulate release of more projects into implementation. This approach was used to identify simple projects with low levels of design that could enable early construction starts. The reasoning and need were that once the alliance had been established, it had a management operating overhead that required a large construction throughput to support. Therefore, the *left shift* brought work forward to generate capital turnover in year 1, ensuring the ratio of management to construction was effective.

Outcomes and benefits

Joint responsibility for outcomes

Thames Water and its delivery partners were jointly responsible for delivering outcomes as well as outputs with a total expenditure (TOTEX) based approach to ensure the regulatory objectives were met. TOTEX is the total value of delivering an asset that includes both the capital investment, known as CAPEX, and the operating cost, known as OPEX, over an agreed period, beyond the handover from construction and installation to operations. The TOTEX approach also introduces the concept of resolving the business requirements and needs by identifying operational solutions first, prior to capital investment. The capital planning work helped clearly define and separate the operational solutions from the CAPEX scope.

Once the AMP6 cycle commenced, the design resource from the engineering consultants was provided to the individual integrated project teams within the programs (on a "*best athlete*" basis). The construction and installation stages of the projects were then carried out by the delivery entities within the two JVs, who constructed the individual asset output. The overarching PMO (portfolio management office), using the individual-spoke program office within the JVs, monitored performance of outputs towards the outcomes and benefits.

Benefits mapping

Benefits and outcomes measurement was introduced in the AMP6 Ofwat requirements, with a move away from financial spend and CAPEX-only deliverable outputs, seen in previous AMPs. To ensure the objectives and outcomes were met and complied with, the new TOTEX hierarchy was introduced to avoid the "*dash to concrete*" solutions. This phrase refers to the historical response of the sector to begin work on projects as soon as possible, usually driven by cash flow demands on the contractors and the (often incorrect) assumption by owners that moving to construction quickly will achieve the shortest construction schedule, and hence lowest cost. This has frequently, and at times disastrously, been proven to be a poor approach.

An end-to-end process covering needs, issues, causes, resolutions (NICeR) was designed (see Figure 25.8 for the NICeR root cause analysis model). This provided a clear line of sight of the required needs, the issues preventing implementation, the root causes of the issues, and the resolutions to the root causes. The process included all the supporting requirement management systems, enabling visibility from the Thames Water business objectives and defined benefits, through to the supporting outcomes and the deliverable solutions.

Measurement of outcomes and benefits – quantitative

Overall, from the hundreds of projects the alliance delivered, they rolled up into 36 capability and outcome streams, where qualitative and quantitative returns were measured. The benefits were initially tracked during their life cycle from project output to a program stream quantitative capability, in measures that were referred to as specific key factors (SKFs) (see Figure 25.9 for the specific key factors). Progress towards the SKF capabilities was continuously measured monthly and used by portfolio management for high-level status information.

Measurement of outcomes and benefits – qualitative

As well as measuring the delivery of outputs and each specific program capability, the program qualitative outcomes and benefits were part of the alliance's contractual obligations and measured as *outcome delivery incentives* (ODIs) towards the Thames Water overall portfolio objectives. Figure 25.10 shows typical benefits identified. (See also Chapter 7 for a more detailed review of benefits and benefit realisation.)

All work was monitored through the individual projects and specific programs' life cycles. Well after the individual project outputs and overall program capability were achieved, there was still an overall acceptance stage, which was up to a year into operational use after capability. This was to specifically confirm whether the Thames Water outcome had been achieved. All the benefit tracking information was continuously collated in an integrated program management system. This provided tracking using attributes that had been attached within each of the project schedules within the portfolio. These were collated and aggregated to the SKFs. This allowed a continuous status to be maintained of capability, outcomes, and benefits and had a financial value associated with the quantitative benefits. This was based at ODI level and were submitted to Ofwat as part of ongoing commercial monitoring, with penalties for underachieving and potential rewards for some of the ODIs if overachieved.

Managing delivery

Work allocation

The individual projects within the six programs were allocated to one of the two joint ventures, which had similar capabilities and geographical reach. The management of design was delegated down into one of the two joint ventures. Again, the two design companies inside the separate JVs worked together as a combined resource pool allowing the right team for the project, regardless of the parent organisation (PO) or JV. Therefore,

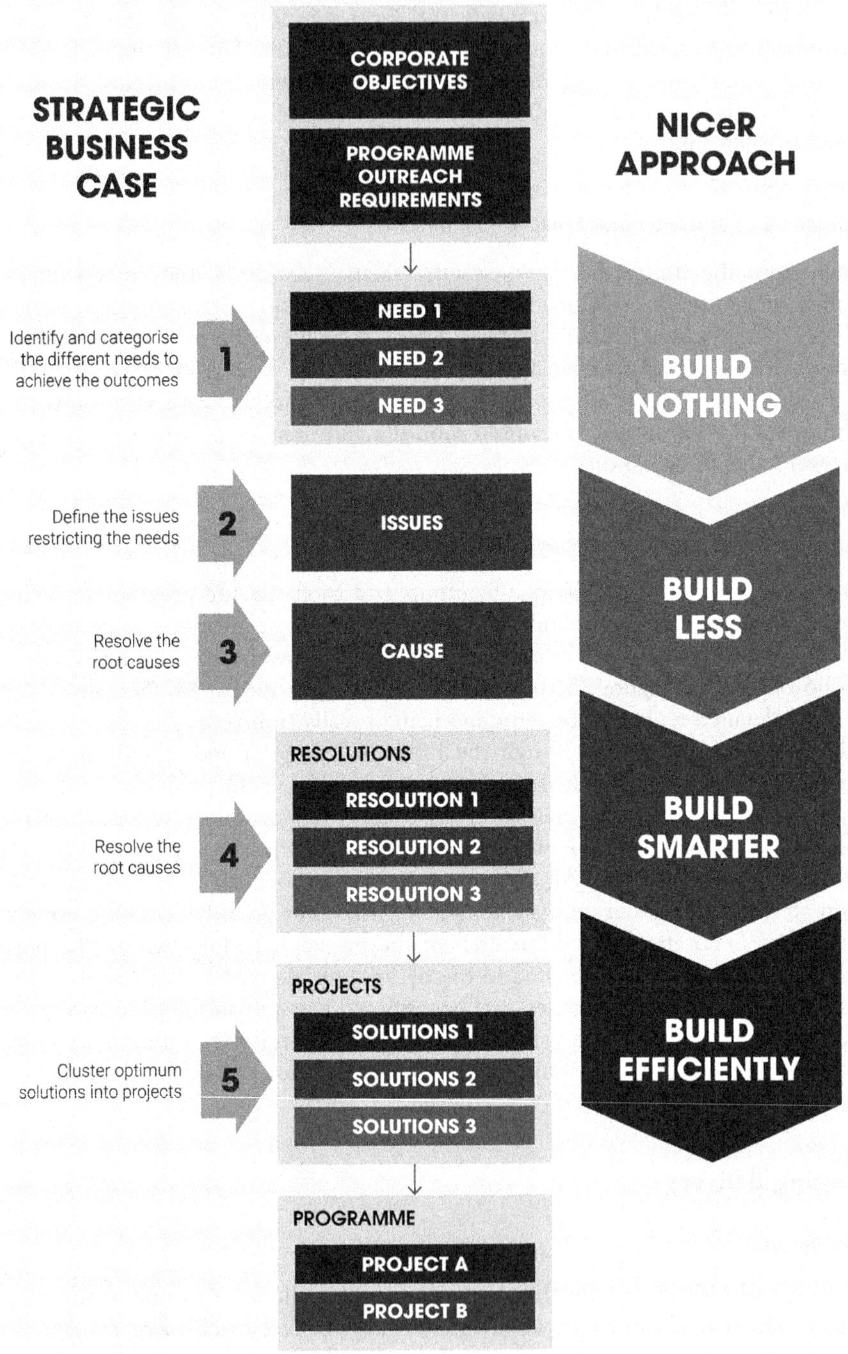

Figure 25.8 NICeR root cause analysis model.

Medium	Type	ID	Regulatory Objective Description	Detailed Description
Waste	Infra	SB2	Wastewater Asset Health	Sewer Crossing Railways - renovation Sewer Crossing Railways - surveys
		SB3	Properties protected from flooding due to rainfall	Catchment Drainage Studies Flooding Annualised benefit
		SB4	Number of Internal Flooding incidents, excluding those due to overloaded sewers	
		SB5	Contributing area disconnected from combined sewers by retrofitting sustainable drainage	Sustainable Drainage (SuDS)
		SC2	Pollution Incidents from Sewage related premises	
		SC8	Deliver 100% of agreed measures to meet new environmental regulations	National Environment Programme
	Non-Infra	SB1	Wastewater Asset Health	STW capacity added
		SB6	Compliance with SEMD (Security & Emergency Measures Directive) advise notes with or without derogation	SEMD - Advice notices complied
		SB7	PE of sites made resilient to future extreme rainfall events	Flooding Resilience
		SC1	Greenhouse gas emissions from operations	
		SC3	STWs discharge compliance	
		SC4	Waterbodies improved or protected from deterioration because of TW activities	
		SC5	Satisfactory Sludge disposal compliance	Sludge Treatment additional capacity / year (TDS)
		SC7	Modelled reduction in properties affected by odour	Odour - Modelled Properties
		SC8	Deliver 100% of agreed measures to meet new environmental regulations	National Environment Programme
		SC9	Reduced the amount of phosphorous entering rivers to help improve aquatic plant and wildlife	
		SD1	Energy imported less Energy exported	
Water	Infra	WA4	Reduce water consumption by issuing water efficiency devices to customers	
		WA5	Provide free repair service for customers with a customer side leak outside of the property	
		WB1	Water Asset Health	Mains Replacement Tunnels and Aqueducts Inspections
		WB4	Properties experiencing chronic low pressure	
		WB6	Security of Supply Index OFWAT KPI	
		WC2	Leakage	Mains Replacement Pressure Management Trunk Mains Leakage
		WC5	Deliver 100% of agreed measures to meet new environmental regulations	NEP Low Flow Alleviation Schemes
	Non-Infra	WB2	Water Asset Health	Water Sites Enhanced - SCADA
		WB3	Compliance with drinking water quality standards (OFWAT/DWI KPI)	DWI Undertakings
		WB7	Compliance with SEMD (Security & Emergency Measures Directive) advise notes with or without derogation	SEMD Outputs
		WB8	Ml/d of sites made resilient to future extreme rainfall events	Flooding Resilience
		WC1	Greenhouse gas emissions from water operations	
		WC5	Deliver 100% of agreed measures to meet new environmental regulations	National Environment Programme
		WD1	Energy imported less Energy exported	

Figure 25.9 Specific key factors.

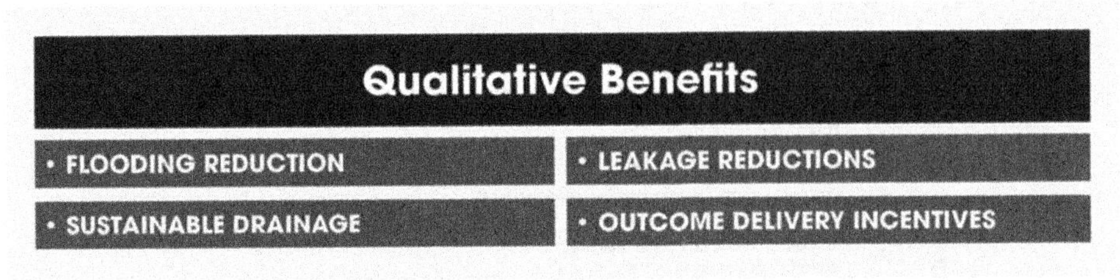

Figure 25.10 Typical benefits identified.

it was essential a common way of working was established to manage delivery, control consistency, and improve productivity.

Collaborative (pull) planning

Once the project solution had been selected and optimised within the program, the program and project teams implemented an approach known as *collaborative planning*. This involved all parties working out the most effective way to deliver the project whilst protecting the program and portfolio. This would include identifying all long lead items, key pinch points, stakeholder issues, and in general, the alliance working together, developing a far deeper understanding of the individual project and its relationship to the wider program and portfolio. The approach was to build more robust delivery schedules adopted by all. Once the schedule was redefined, it would work on a 12-week rolling-wave basis, with clear understanding of the tasks and actions for each week and assigned responsibilities.

Category management

Within the alliance, there was also a high degree of *category management* (a strategic approach for the procurement of equipment and services). This enabled centralised evaluation of the market for services and equipment availability, the capability of the supply chains, and threats and issues on specific goods (see Figure 25.11 for supply chain alignment). The approach minimised "fee-on-fee" issues, which are delivery partner mark-ups and profit for handling equipment; this is on top of the manufacturer or subcontractor profit. The approach also provided a consistency and control of products over the portfolio.

The centralised focus enabled strategic sourcing, increased design for manufacture and assembly (DFMA) with high levels of consistency and single source of supply information on a community hub, thus supporting performance management over the full supply chain and improvement in supply relationship management. The subsequent chapter, with the DFMA portfolio case study, discusses in more detail the strategic portfolio management approach adopted by Thames Water and the alliance in managing the supply chain.

Health and safety

An important aspect of the alliance objectives was in maintaining high levels of health and safety. The portfolio management approach, including governance and assurance, provided the ability to spot specific trends and help the alliance in the identification of portfolio- and

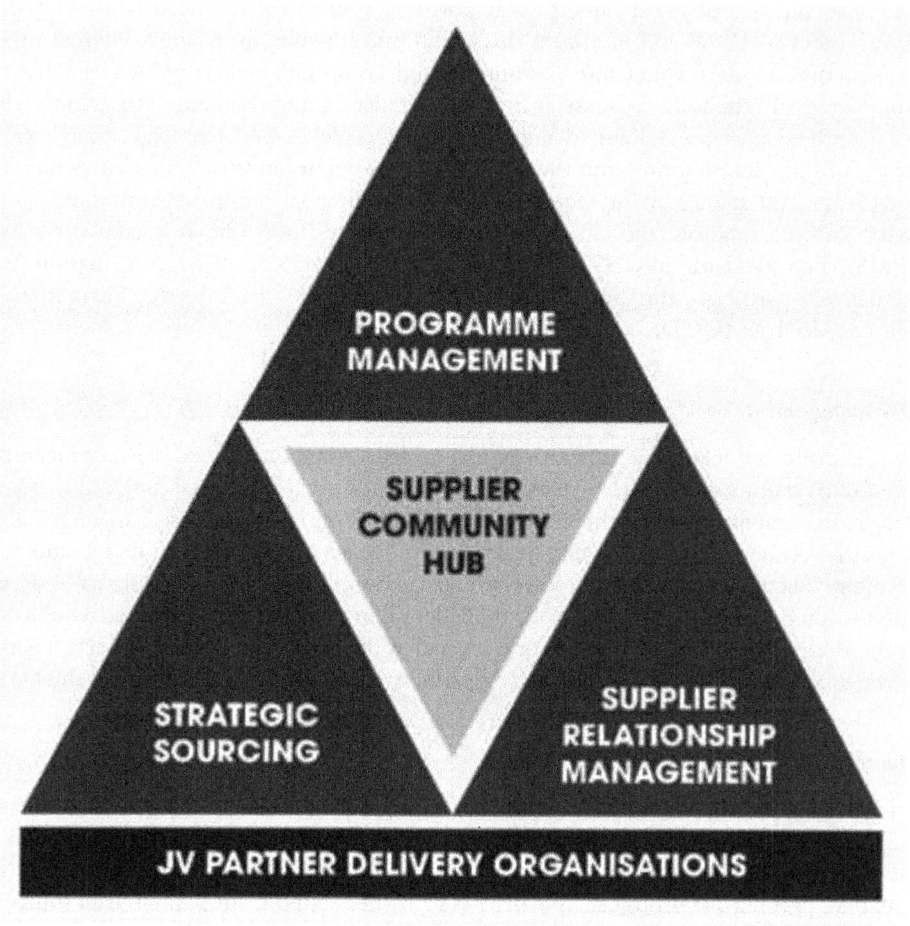

Figure 25.11 Supply chain alignment.

program-wide safety issues. For example, a spike in *high potential incidents* on health and safety performance was identified, resulting in the alliance taking the decision to stand down the workforce and communicate a resolution plan. The identification of this challenging issue and the decision to intervene helped drive a positive safety culture, as demonstrated through the accident frequency rate (AFR). The AFR is calculated by the number of accidents in a rolling year over the overall hours expended for that rolling year. The number is then multiplied by 100,000 hours to generate the AFR number. The alliance achieved a 0.06, rolling 12-month average, with a peak approaching five million hours per annum.

Enterprise planning and scheduling

Planning and scheduling were controlled centrally by a centralised scheduling database. This was managed and governance applied by the PMO, but facilitated access was available to all eight partners. This stopped double-handling of information, with each schedule updated monthly.

Enterprise cost management capability

The scale and size of the Thames Water portfolio resulted in the need to develop cost management processes and interfaces that could capture costs from three different financial systems and align them into a common and consistent format, which enabled the monitoring of schedule and cost against the regulatory requirements. To achieve this, a standardised cost breakdown structure (CBS) was developed that was applied to all projects in the six programs and the overall portfolio. This approach aligned estimating, day-to-day cost management requirements, and individual company requirements. To collate the information, the alliance used the integrated portfolio management system (IPMS). The standardised CBS ensured that at the life cycle gateways, information from the delivery partners estimating toolsets could be reconciled back to the Thames Water unit cost database (UCD).

Risk management

The portfolio and its programs primarily had to deliver outcome-based delivery incentives (the ODIs) that measured the regulated outcomes, and each individual project provided a mitigation capability towards the ODIs being achieved or, if service-based, maintained. At project level, there was a consistent approach to mitigate delivery risks in design and construction. These were managed in the risk management system, enabling risks to be aggregated to program and portfolio levels, thus identifying trends and issues that would then be incorporated into future projects or managed at the upper levels. Both aspects together provided a full, holistic picture of risks to portfolio, program, and project management.

Monthly reporting to all management levels

The IPMS collated information from the scheduling tool, the enterprise risk management application, and the separate cost management systems of Thames Water, including the two JVs. This was all then stored in a single data warehouse, which enabled all the portfolio, program, and project information to be generated from a single data source to reduce errors, mainly misalignment of data, during transposition processes, and information inconsistences due to process irregularities from partner systems (such as differing month-end financial closures). A standard suite of automated reports was developed and specifically tailored for user groups. The standard report suite was adopted by the senior leadership team for its periodic reviews and challenges. To augment the standard reports, an ad hoc compiler capability was part of the IPMS, which enabled the production of specialist information, again from the same data source. The primary way of viewing was through web-based interactive dashboards and then drilling down to the required reports. The information was stored for each monthly period to enable long-term reviews of performance and provide a fully auditable trail.

People

Recruitment and retention of staff

All employees within the alliance were employed by one of the partners and then seconded into the alliance. For the first two years of AMP6, this required an integrated resourcing approach to ramp up to approximately 2,700 full-time equivalents (FTEs)

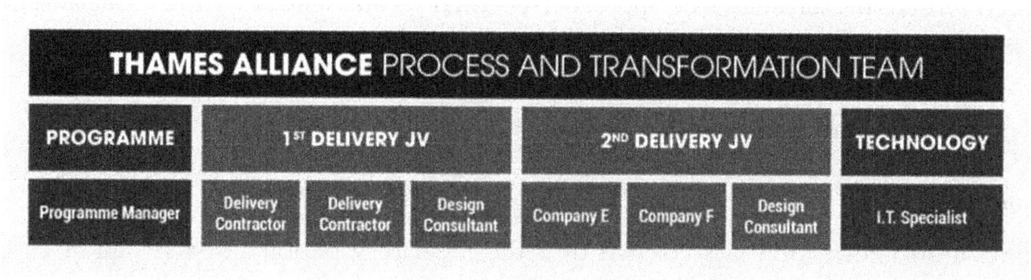

Figure 25.12 Process and transformation team structure.

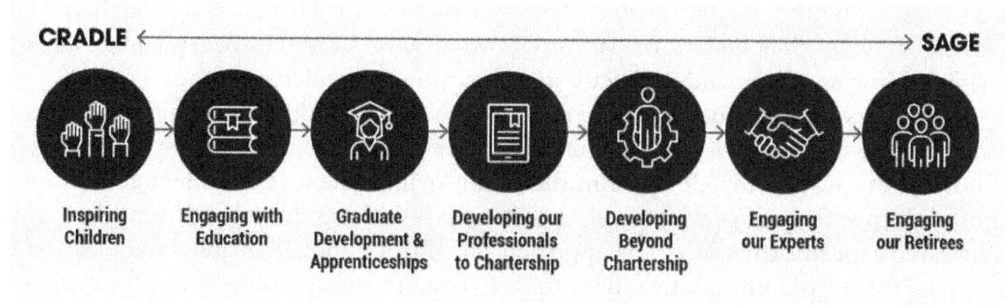

Figure 25.13 Career development with sustainability.

needed to deliver the portfolio and overcome resource shortages in the geographical region. Recruiting and retaining staff during this early period was the responsibility of the alliance's process and transformation (P&T) team (see Figure 25.12, "Organisational structure"), who had specific seconded HR and resource management personnel solely dedicated to the alliance; these individuals assessed demand requirements and highlighted issues that could affect retention.

The information was cascaded to the individual partners, who developed their own resource solutions and presented them back to the P&T team for acceptance. Once the alliance had transformed, to reach the desired operational capacity, the management of staff reverted to the alliance partners.

Retaining the best talent was essential to provide consistency for the alliance at the highest levels of performance. To support this, an understanding of the staff needs and wants was essential. This was partially achieved using two anonymous surveys, carried out within the alliance. The first one was a pulse survey carried out by the alliance across all staff, and partners then had their annual employee engagement surveys for their own staff. Both elements together were key drivers in shaping the business improvement plans for staff seconded to the alliance.

Training and development

A whole life talent development scheme was used to develop a skilled and experienced resource base for the alliance and enable the staff to fulfil their potential (see Figure 25.13, "Career development with sustainability"). The initiative helped select the best people and then provided a structured development process as they progressed throughout their careers inside the alliance. The approach was highly commended by the Association of Consulting and Engineering (ACE) in 2019.

Knowledge management

Innovation

Innovation information was collated over the regulatory period and was supported by the alliance, developing a dedicated innovation hub available to all the alliance staff and supply chain. This brought changes to design processes, construction, and provided a knowledge-based record, which enabled the ideas to become the future "business-as-usual". The innovation hub was built into the Thames Water alliance intranet site and was shared with other major initiatives being carried out by Thames Water, such as "The Thames Tideway Scheme", a megaproject which would also be incorporated into the Thames Water asset base and interact with projects in the wider portfolio.

It was also considered that to ensure innovation was adopted, multiple different ways to communicate were essential (see Figure 25.14 for types of communications and examples of innovation, such as top-down from the senior management team, direct communications with specific groups who would benefit, or pull using the intranet set when individuals look for information). The approach the alliance applied enabled the business to maximise the use of innovations and for these to become more readily "business-as-usual".

Knowledge sharing and continuous improvement

The ethos of the Thames Water alliance was to create an organisation that was sector leading in all aspects. Over the life of the portfolio, there was a culture of continuous improvement, including organisational approaches, individual business processes, and delivery improvements. There is a close link between innovation and knowledge sharing. The alliance created a team of *knowledge champions*, responsible for ensuring information on

Innovation Communication	Innovation Example	Innovation Type
KNOWLEDGE EXCHANGE	Use of resin instead of cementitious grout	IMPLEMENTATION
INNOVATION SHARES	Nitrate Removal software on existing plant instead of new ion exchange plant	PROCESS
INNOVATION VIDEOS	Safety cameras on dumpers	SAFETY
INNOVATION PRESENTATIONS	Use of canister pumps	PROCESS
ANALYTICS AND COGNITIVE	Vacuum excavation around services	SAFETY

Figure 25.14 Types of communications and examples of innovation

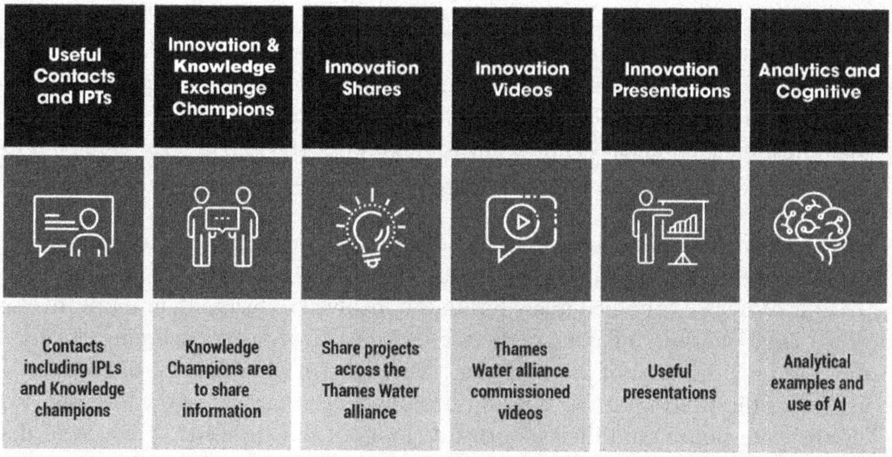

Figure 25.15 Knowledge capture.

improvements, or issues were shared throughout the alliance, including regular "knowledge share" briefings throughout the community. The knowledge share information was held on the Thames Water alliance common data environment (CDE).

To further stimulate knowledge transfer as much as possible, *subject matter experts* (SMEs) were identified within the alliance and in the parent body organisations, with contact details shared between the partners. It was important that teams and individuals did not have to reinvent solutions where the answers were already in existence somewhere within the organisations (see Figure 25.15 for knowledge capture).

Conclusion

The overall planned investment for the portfolio was circa £2.166bn, and the portfolio outturn cost was circa £2.143bn. The average annual expenditure projections within the last three years of the AMP6 had around 10% outturn variance, and all projects and programs within the portfolio were delivered in the five-year AMP6 cycle. Several important aspects of portfolio management, impacting the way in which the alliance delivered the work, are summarised here:

1. To deliver this level of investment whilst promoting a TOTEX model with partner organisations, who had CAPEX business models, required a step change in cooperation between all involved, plus an understanding by each party of how their own business objectives could be met, whilst still supporting the Thames Water portfolio.
2. The structure had to have contractual alignment between all parties to reduce transactional/adversarial positions between Thames Water and the alliance partners and between the partners themselves.
3. To make the operating model work, all roles and responsibilities had to be clearly defined. The individuals involved had to have the right collaborative behaviours as well as the technical and managerial skill sets for the role.

4. There had to be a clear line of site from the Thames Water business objectives at the portfolio level, flowing down to the separate programs, and then into the individual projects.
5. To enable common ways of working, a portfolio delivery system was required. This enabled all companies to operate within the same rules and parameters. The downstream impact was increased consistency over the entire portfolio.
6. Identification and pursuit of efficiency routes brought savings in some areas, but more importantly, it protected the overall portfolio due to unforeseen growth in other areas.
7. The overall business structure had to be able to react and accommodate change to maintain the overall portfolio objectives.
8. Thames Water's AMP6 had many businesses involved in bringing in innovative solutions, large amounts of construction/operational interfaces occurring at any one time, and the dispersal of projects over a wide area of the southeast of the UK. This generated the need for a vast amount of knowledge sharing, firstly, to ensure safety lessons were shared, and then also that techniques and common solutions in design and implementation were shared effectively.
9. The knowledge capture process ensured Thames Water kept its role and position as an intelligent client.

26 Case study – a utilities and construction portfolio (product standardisation and integrated digital delivery within a portfolio)

Paul Taylor

Introduction

Infrastructure and utility asset owners are striving to increase overall efficiencies within their portfolio investments, which in turn benefits their customers, shareholders, and key stakeholders (including regulators). The emergence of digital technologies, coupled with developments in logistics, has started to shape new thinking around the operational mechanics of portfolio, program, and project delivery models.

In these new delivery models, key elements are emerging that, when combined with existing practices, can introduce efficiencies to infrastructure delivery. Previously, these have only been seen in the manufacturing sector. Three of the major influencers for consideration are:

1. DFMA (designing for manufacture and assembly).
2. Use of category management and different contractual models.
3. Consolidation centres for off-site assembly and logistics control.

Combining aspects of these individual elements enables the infrastructure and utilities sectors to bring increased and sustainable efficiencies when creating new assets within their portfolios, programs, and projects.

This case study chapter centres on a utilities and construction portfolio in concluding that techniques within portfolio management, digital delivery, and logistics can bring major efficiencies to the delivery of portfolios within the infrastructure and utility sectors whilst recognising that these approaches will bring limited benefit to projects that continue to be delivered through current end-to-end delivery models. The chapter discusses DFMA (designing for manufacture and assembly) together with implementing category management, alternative contractual models, and consolidation centres as examples of having product standardisation and integrated delivery within a portfolio as the way forward to being the most effective way in which multiple product suppliers and multiple projects can be aligned and efficiencies ensured.

DFMA – design for manufacture and assembly

The move to DFMA

To maximise the benefits of DFMA in both the infrastructure and the utilities sectors requires careful transformational planning and a structured and measured approach to avoid just increasing the amount of work done off-site without achieving significant

DOI: 10.4324/9780367853129-30

opportunities and business gains. This needs a deep understanding of production management techniques and how these techniques can be effectively interfaced with program and project delivery. It must also consider the commercial contracts and current risk drivers that put major onus on the supply chain to manage effectively.

The current design and manufacture approach

Currently, the typical standard is that much construction sector manufacturing is managed on a project basis. This means each design is prepared in a 3D model with a mixture of bespoke elements and standard components. The standard components are taken from a product library and imported into the project model. This design model goes forward to implementation, where the standard and bespoke components are ordered, manufactured, and delivered to site for installation. Apart from standard products being held in a database, this approach has not changed from what was carried out 50 years ago, with the exception that the product catalogues are now digital, and we work in an electronic medium. Whilst this could generate some productivity improvement in design, overall, the benefits are limited, and this is not going to bring about major efficiencies in manufacturing, delivery, and installation.

Increasing effective use of DFMA

Infrastructure and utility client prioritisation of their portfolios and programs is usually based on regulatory compliance or other performance issues. Projects are then optimised for total expenditure (TOTEX) over a fixed time period, and the construction stage of the portfolios is usually optimised on a geographical basis. Overall, these optimisation mechanisms have not maximised the savings that could be made in the manufacture of the products for the assets. DFMA provides part of an approach to increase overall efficiencies in manufacturing of products for construction.

Defining the product demand

As part of the optimisation process, we need to look at the manufacturing equilibrium and volume of product throughput. In general, the benefits that can be created by DFMA need a volume of throughput to make the manufacturing process effective. For example, it would not be financially viable to invest and develop a mass production capability for phosphate dosing rigs, when the utility company's geographical footprint requirement is for a very small number. (A phosphate dosing rig is a process plant that introduces chemicals to a wastewater treatment facility to work as coagulants that bind to the phosphates in the water and allow them to settle in the tanks with the sludge.) For the regulated infrastructure and utility portfolios, large-scale packages of investment are developed, with either defined projects or blocks of budgets for reactive maintenance. What is currently lacking is the development of portfolios that clearly focus on the product, assemblies, and component demands.

The enterprise product breakdown structure

To balance the manufacturing volume throughput (i.e. supply), there is a need to look at this with a portfolio perspective (i.e. demand). Usually in projects, we refer to the

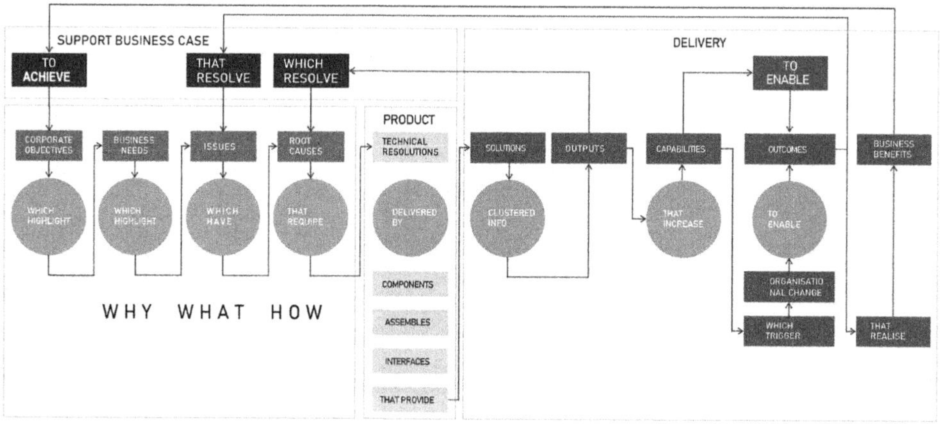

Figure 26.1 Initial product identification.

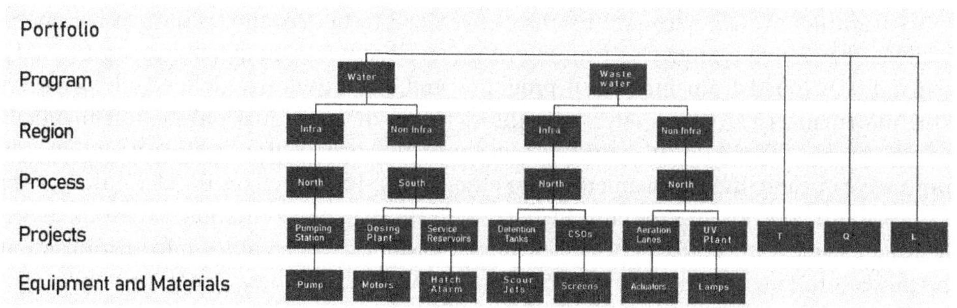

Figure 26.2 Typical enterprise product breakdown structure.

organisation, work, and cost breakdown structures and risk mitigation, but to take advantage of DFMA, there needs to be a clear understanding of the product requirements across the portfolio (see Figure 26.1, "Initial product identification"), whether that is an enterprise-wide portfolio or a lower-level portfolio (that may span supply chains).

To accommodate this information, the approach is to instigate an enterprise product breakdown structure. In general, most asset owners already use an asset data hierarchy; this enables the introduction of an aligned enterprise product breakdown structure that fits well within an asset management and operational model.

By incorporating the enterprise product breakdown structure over the full asset program (see Figure 26.2 for a typical enterprise product breakdown structure), we can quickly identify the high-level needs, the product assemblies, and as the portfolio, program, and projects mature, a continuous flow of the products and components themselves.

Mapping the program, project, products, assemblies, and components

We gain a fully integrated perspective when the product structure is aligned to the asset data hierarchy and the portfolio and programs. This enables downstream operations to fully understand the products and processes that are going to form part of asset operations and improves acceptance of major and minor changes.

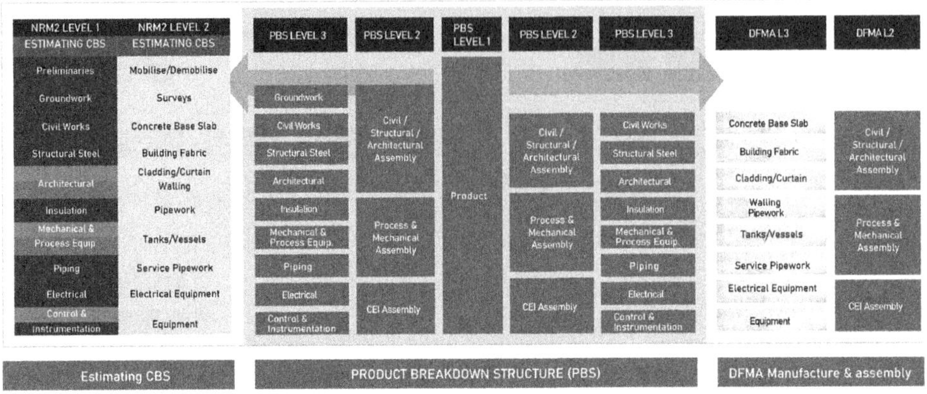

Figure 26.3 Linking the product breakdown structure (PBS) to the cost breakdown structure (CBS) and DFMA

To maximise overall delivery efficiencies, we need to understand, as soon as reasonably possible, the overall quantity and timing of the products that the portfolio requires. This demand is mapped from individual programs and, where clearly defined, the projects. This information can then determine the demand in individual production manufacturing streams. The more we understand about the overall product requirements, the more we can capitalise on manufacturing efficiencies. In general, as the definition of the portfolio and constituent programs matures with time, many commoditised products will become clear. More complex and customised products will require information about the projects to emerge on a continuous rolling wave basis. In these cases, the projects will first be identified, then as the individual project matures, the more complex products will emerge, followed by assemblies and finally components.

The increased move to DFMA will drive the standardisation of product designs that provide commoditised answers to the operational needs. This enables outline quantities of assemblies and components to be extracted early in the individual program and project life cycles; this, in turn, gives improved cost visibility and manufacturing demand. Clear mapping for effective tracking of component quantities, assemblies, and their costs is required. This information also supports manufacturing timescales and delivery to site (see Figure 26.3, "Linking the product breakdown structure (PBS) to the cost breakdown structure (CBS) and DFMA").

The detailed information will firm up as the program and projects progress, but in general terms, the commoditisation will give enough information to manage more effectively the supply and demand of products. This, in turn, supports the manufacturing supply chain to plan and balance workload more effectively.

Inside the factory

Once inside the factory, the introduction of DFMA is only one part of the portfolio management efficiency drive in off-site construction, other factors must also run with the DFMA. This includes the integration of lean processes similar to the Toyota Management System (TMS), which minimises all aspects of waste. (Additionally, the latest thinking on digital fabrication [Dfab] enabling rapid prototyping or simplified manufacture of complex components, using 3D laser printing, is developing at pace.) (See Figure 26.4, "Mapping and interaction between lean manufacturing, DFMA, and DFab".)

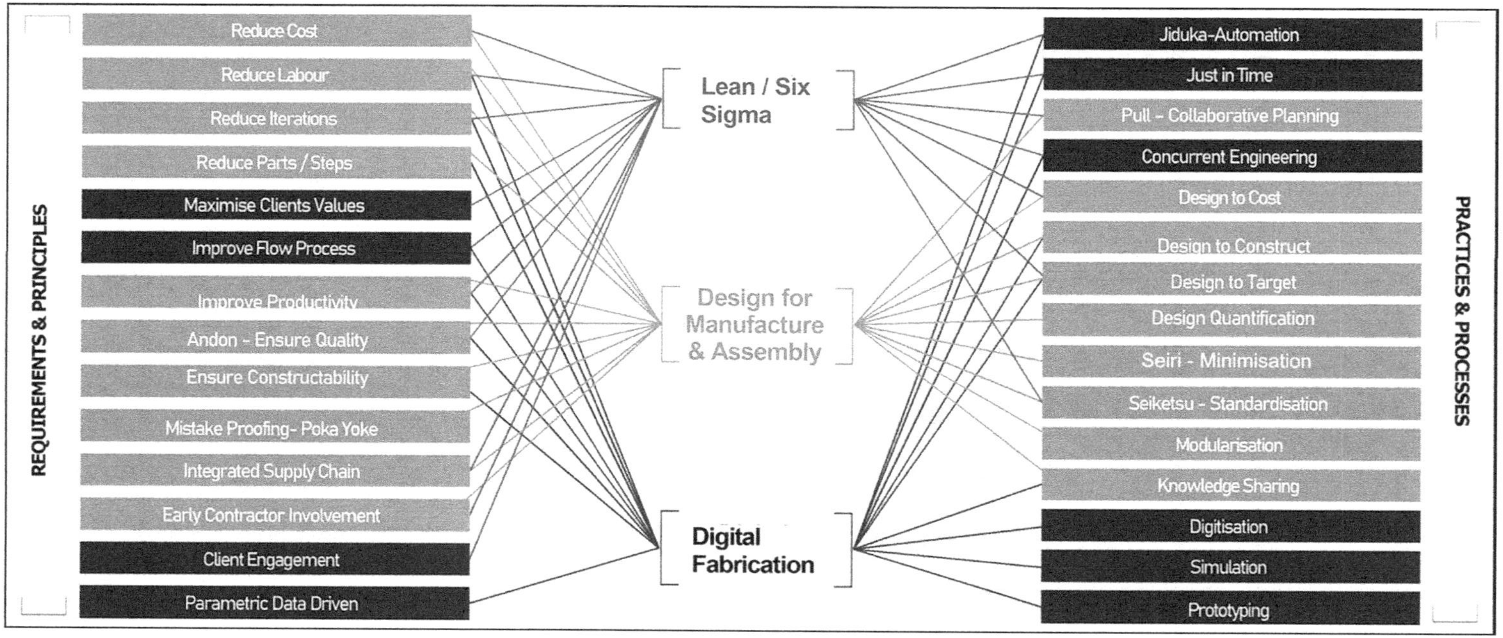

Figure 26.4 Mapping and interaction between lean manufacturing, DFMA, and dFab.

The overall approach that lends itself well to utility and infrastructure is, firstly, to standardise the design, thus increasing volume requirements; secondly, review and improve production processes for off-site manufacturing of components and assemblies; and finally, to simplify components using new printing technologies. Taking all these aspects into account provides, at the portfolio level, a huge potential of untapped optimisation efficiencies.

Use of category management and different contractual models

To maximise opportunities that new technologies and approaches bring to portfolio delivery, the supporting framework must be carefully considered. One component in that framework, which supports DFMA and is essential, is the introduction of effective procurement.

There are several routes to market that maximise the use of DFMA, with one of them being category management. This is an approach where equipment, materials, and services required by the projects within the portfolio are broken down into categories that support specific needs. The categories require careful definition, including:

1. Understand the overall business needs and develop an overall delivery strategy.
2. Devise a category management strategy that includes DFMA.
3. Clearly define the categories to understand what products are the most appropriate to them, for example, pressure vessels, process plant, cranage.
4. Set objectives and targets for the individual categories and appropriate manufacturing and delivery approach to the individual sites.
5. The project delivery entities must work with the asset owner's category managers around novation models to minimise fee on fee. (Note, fee on fee is where the contractor adds an on-cost/handling charge and profit to the subcontract or equipment supplier's price.)

Appointing a category program vendor

An emerging opportunity and aspect that must be taken into consideration to maximise manufacturing productivity and optimisation is that the manufacturing and assembly work can become a separate program or subprogram within the portfolio. This would enable a manufacturing program team to be responsible for all the off-site product manufacturing and its sequencing on standard packages. This work may well be done in advance of a delivery program. The delivery program/project team is then only responsible for taking the manufactured product to its on-site completion. In manufacturing terms, the manufacturing program consists of a group of products within the equipment categories that become the individual manufacturing projects. These take components and assemblies to the end of the off-site manufacturing cycle. From this point, the delivery project teams call off the components and assemblies when needed at site. This is the interface/transition point where the delivery program/project team take over the responsibility. This model is, however, always subject to contractual terms, though, and does change how risk is apportioned, with the manufacturing risks no longer the responsibility of the delivery program team.

Aligning contract strategies to maximise DFMA capability

There are several contractual models that can be used when introducing DFMA. The client should decide which model is preferred, influenced by whether a high degree of involvement is needed in the off-site manufacture. The decision needs to be made about whether the equipment selection process needs to be integrated in the selection of suppliers and scope of equipment or whether this should be delegated to the delivery organisations. There will be several factors that define this, such as if the project is building a facility that is standalone and has little interoperability elsewhere, or if it is a project within a program that, once accepted, fits into a wider business with a large number of interfaces.

Alliance model. This is a highly collaborative model where the client operates both in sponsor and delivery management roles. The client's delivery management role integrates with both the design consultant and the delivery contractor. This model uses an integrator to manage the interfaces between all parties and reduces the transactional issues between the various companies. In this model, it is the integrator's responsibility to manage the off-site manufacture, assembly, and logistics for site delivery.

Design and build framework. In this model, there are several variants, but in simplistic terms, the client usually defines the portfolio or program requirements, and the implementation of this is carried out by design and build delivery organisations. These usually consist of a design consultant, a delivery contractor, and a wider supply chain for goods and services. The wider supply chain is managed by the design and build delivery organisation and is either trusted subcontractors/suppliers or, in some cases, have been selected by the client and novated (this is where the original contract with the client is transferred with same terms and conditions) to the design and build delivery organisation. The design and build organisation in this instance manage the off-site manufacture, assembly, logistics for site delivery, and installation.

Traditional client, consultant, contractor model. This is where the client appoints a consultant to carry out the design and a contractor to deliver the project to the consultant's requirements. The contractor manages the supply chain, who are trusted parties to its organisation or have been selected by the design consultant due to specific skills or operational capability. The contractor in this instance manages the off-site manufacture, assembly, logistics for site delivery, and installation.

To bring in manufacturing optimisation, whichever model is used, the most important aspect that must be considered is the acquisition of the products within the contractual framework. This is to ensure the DFMA provides the necessary efficiency, which in turn relates to more business throughput, improved delivery times, and lower costs.

Traditional project-centric approach

Using a traditional project model, the equipment call-off, whilst optimising site work, does not optimise manufacture or off-site assembly (see Figure 26.5, "Project-centric procurement drawdown of products within the portfolio"). In general, it does not provide the most cost-effective production of equipment or material. In this traditional project

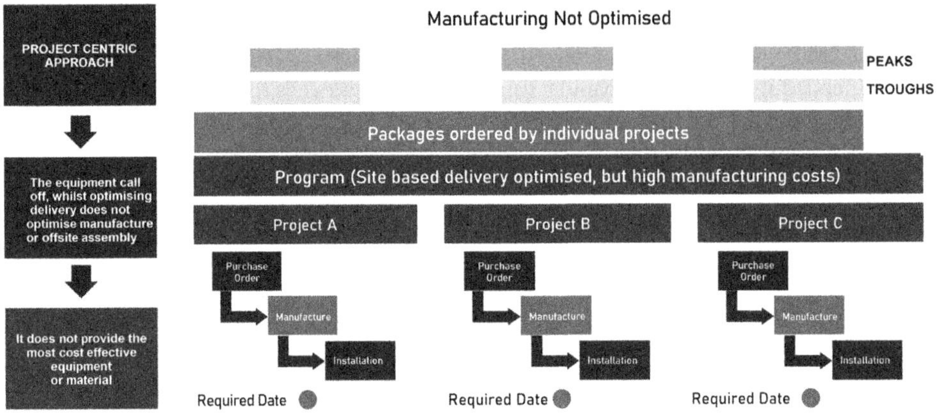

Figure 26.5 Project-centric procurement drawdown of products within the portfolio.

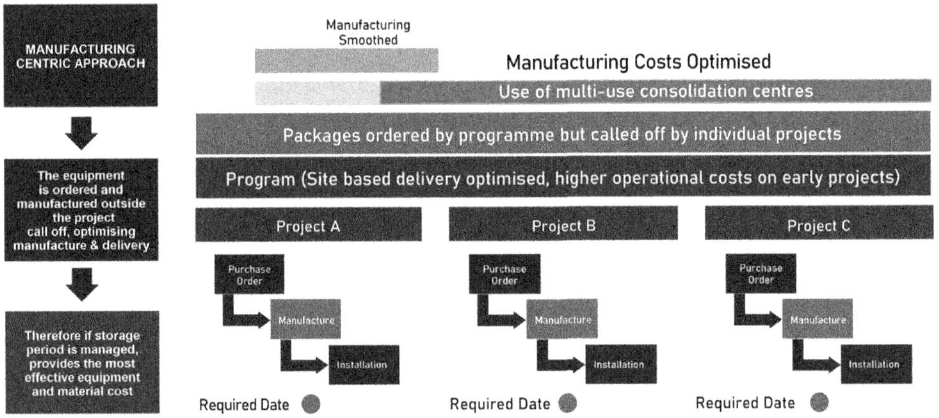

Figure 26.6 Manufacturing-centric procurement of products in the portfolio.

model, the use of DFMA will not bring in large amounts of efficiency. The day-to-day management, though, is proven, and a line of sight between goods, projects, and program is clearly visible.

Manufacturing-centric approach

In this model, the common equipment is identified, ordered, and manufactured outside of the project, at a portfolio or program level. A call-off approach at individual project level then occurs when the equipment is needed (see Figure 26.6, "Manufacturing-centric procurement of products in the portfolio"). This enables optimisation of manufacture, assembly, and delivery. Therefore, if the assembly and storage period is closely managed within a consolidation centre, it provides the most effective equipment and material cost. There is added complexity related to cost management, ownership of off-site products, and maintaining a line of sight between products, projects, and program. It also forward-profiles the expenditure, so overall the working of the model must be thoroughly mapped out.

This model works well in the alliance environment, where the integrator controls the category management. It provides major savings on the "fee-on-fee" costs charged in a design and build framework and works for traditional client, consultant, and contractor models that would be applicable, where effective novation clauses are in place that manage the uplifts charged.

Consolidation centres and containerised delivery

The next way of improving efficiency within portfolios where more construction products are manufactured off-site is through the management of logistics. Currently, most construction sites have deliveries from multiple manufacturing companies at differing times. This means that managing delivery, offload timing, site storage, and equipment handling is not efficient. In confined sites, there are also additional safety issues. It is good to learn from other industries (such as shipping) regarding dock consolidation facilities, loading sequencing, product containerisation, and movement of pre-assembled goods. In shipping, 98% of product handling time has been eliminated. It is also possible to evaluate business-to-consumer (B2C) distribution organisations, which act as routers for many of our home deliveries, where goods arrive from all over the world, are sorted, packaged, then dispatched from a single source as a consolidated order.

From a portfolio perspective, there is a need to capitalise on off-site manufacture by controlling product distribution. This then facilitates effective warehouse management of the product stock, enabling partial assembly, quality inspections, and functional testing (see Figure 26.7, "Controlling logistics flow from manufacturers to construction sites via centralised consolidation centres"). It also means we can introduce distribution resource planning, which will look at containerisation, packaging, inventory management, product tracking, and just-in-time delivery. Thus, having the potential to minimise vehicle movements to construction sites by central coordination with consolidation centres.

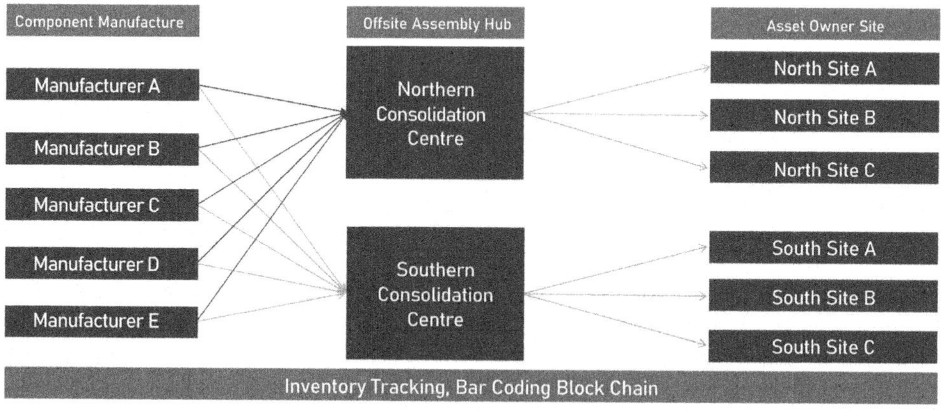

Figure 26.7 Controlling logistics flow from manufacturers to construction sites via centralised consolidation centres.

Issues to be aware of when increasing the use of DFMA

Patents, intellectual issues, and indemnity around products

As we move into a digital delivery and DFMA environment, care must be taken around intellectual property in an industry, where so much bespoke design and on-site work has previously occurred.

Manufacturers are used to development before sales commence and have established intellectual property rights and registered patents around their products and applications for years. The manufacturers have mainly invested their own finances at risk to create a market space advantage over their competition.

The infrastructure and utility sectors have previously used mainly bespoke design and on-site work. These bespoke packages will be replaced with commercial off-the-shelf (COTS) solutions and products, but the move to these prefabricated off-the-shelf packages will need far more rigorous management and contractual understanding around intellectual property (IP).

DFMA will see consultants and vendors moving to specific product design with standardised equipment, processes, and applications. Yet the consultants and vendors must be aware that what has been developed and paid for by one asset owner cannot be offered as vendor background IP to another asset owner without expressed contractual agreements.

The outline rule is, the IP is owned by the infrastructure or utility asset owner if the development is paid for by the asset owner. If the vendor does work financially at their own risk to develop a product that can be later sold to the client, then the vendor owns the IP.

Contractual models when service costs are reduced

One item that is rarely discussed is that as designs become standardised, available COTS, and commoditised, the fees earned by consultants are likely to reduce. This will result in changes to future charging models within the industry. The lower design costs may not accommodate the costs of professional indemnity and will create the need for an extra over-cost to be applied, similar to a product guarantee or warranty. One model being considered is a design cost that is no longer a service but a fixed price per product.

Sterilisation of competition within the portfolio

Depending on how DFMA is managed, moving to DFMA products and standard configurations can sterilise a market and restrict competition within the sector. This occurs if certain aspects have not been considered as part of a requirements management exercise. This can occur if there is more than one delivery entity within the portfolio and the product requirements are poorly defined by the asset owner, without interoperability considerations. Therefore, as well as performance specifications, constraints must be applied to the product interfaces as well. This ensures interoperability over the portfolio and prevents the asset owner owning orphaned or sterilised assets, meaning, the asset owner is only able to engage the same manufacturer if expansion of a facility is required.

The infrastructure and utilities sector can learn from other sectors using high levels of off-site manufacture. In 2010, the electricity sector commissioned a working group report into the use of gas-insulated switchgear (GIS), where it was noted that there were no international standards for design. This resulted in the equipment from differing manufacturers not being compatible with each other. The downstream impact was that to interface GIS between manufacturers was extremely costly, and therefore, once the initial GIS manufacturer had been chosen for a facility, the future procurement options for that facility became restricted.

Conclusion

Techniques within portfolio management, digital delivery, and logistics can bring major efficiencies to the delivery of portfolios within the infrastructure and utility sectors. However, it must be recognised that these approaches will bring very limited benefit to projects that continue to be delivered through current end-to-end delivery models. In summary:

- The sector needs to develop new procurement models that enable manufacturing and logistic efficiencies.
- The transition points where risk ownership moves between the client, the consultant, and the delivery organisations must be clearly mapped.
- The interoperability requirements of components must be clearly understood, which requires more in-depth upfront specifications.
- Intellectual property must be considered, and consultants will need to develop new charging models as an increasing number of off-the-shelf components and assemblies emerge.
- Use of consolidation and off-site assembly centres must be efficiently managed to avoid overhead inertia if products stay too long in storage.
- Mechanisms are needed to prevent assets being orphaned/stranded due to incompatibility with products supplied by a different company.
- Licence and intellectual property models need to be clearly agreed to prevent delivery organisations sterilising the market.
- There is a need for new monitoring techniques to measure both off-site and on-site work.

Once part of the construction process moves inside the factory, we will see an industry revitalised. As with all manufacturing, digital delivery approaches will bring in a large amount of standardisation. Thinking back in history to the UK's cotton and steel industries when they moved from looms in weavers' cottages and the blacksmiths hearths, we went through the Industrial Revolution. Now thinking ahead, if large amounts of construction effort is moved inside the factory, we will see exponential improvements in quality, productivity, and cost efficiency. This will only work if high-quality portfolio management approaches are adopted, as this is the most effective way in which multiple product suppliers and multiple projects can be aligned and efficiencies ensured.

27 Case study – portfolio management as governance and leadership

Geoff Vincent

Introduction

This case study discusses one approach to portfolio management based on both practical experience of working as a portfolio manager and from working with students from varying organisations in the project, program, and portfolio domain. The case study may help in considering how to approach or introduce portfolio management in an organisation, with a focus on governance and leadership. The case study relates both to Chapter 14 on portfolio governance and Chapter 18 on portfolio leadership. The view of portfolio management as governance is discussed initially, bringing this together by considering senior leadership when managing an organisational (or strategic) portfolio.

Portfolio management . . . or is it governance?

What does a portfolio manager do? The answer isn't obvious. Portfolio management is much less understood (and written about) than either project management or program management. It is sometimes considered a black art, or even a "Cinderella" subject, partly because it is so little understood.

Yet portfolio management, in many organisations, is where the rubber hits the road: where the theoretical discussions about strategy and objectives are turned into real resourcing decisions. What effort, attention, and resource are we going to actually put into activity X? What tolerance do we have for experimentation, innovation, and risk? How are we going to judge success?

If you want to know what an organisation's actual priorities are – as opposed to what it says, or intends, or thinks it is going to do – look at its portfolio management decisions.

This gives portfolio managers, in practice, quite a lot of power, even if much of this is less visible, unshowy, and under the radar. Portfolio management can include key strategic decisions affecting the direction of the organisation as a whole. It also involves a myriad of day-to-day resourcing decisions: which project or initiative to give resources to; who has first call on scarce skills, resources, and unique expertise; in a crisis, who gets help and attention and a sympathetic ear.

As the world becomes more dynamic and connected, organisations of all kinds – including some of today's most successful, such as Amazon, Google, Microsoft, and Apple – are constructed from a portfolio of initiatives at different stages of development. Speculative activities, research and development, and embryonic businesses sit alongside and interact with established operations. Arguably, this is what it now takes to survive.

DOI: 10.4324/9780367853129-31

The growth of agile and iterative methods complicates the picture still further. Agile may be best described as a different mindset, not just a set of techniques and approaches. Managing a portfolio often involves reconciling different mindsets, translating between people with different expectations, who see things in very different ways.

What's a portfolio?

Projects produce defined outputs – specific products. Programs are designed to achieve outcomes. What's a portfolio for? Basically, to hold and manage a set of different (often very different) activities that require investment of time, effort, and attention in a way that meets the overall objectives of the organisation – objectives that are sometimes ill-defined and ambiguous. While keeping everyone – at least the key stakeholders – reasonably happy. It's the job of the portfolio manager to manage competing demands, from multiple sources, and decide what actually gets done.

The most basic task of a portfolio manager is to distribute resources – time, attention, and money, together with people and equipment – between activities so as to achieve the optimum result. How do you determine what is "best"? That's rarely clear. Often, answering this is the first requirement of the job. In common parlance, the word "portfolio" is used to describe things as different as a set of investments, and the collected work of an artist. That's a useful clue: a good portfolio manager needs both analytic skills and an element of creative artistry. Portfolio management is less "hierarchical" and more "networked" than other management responsibilities. It's a tall order, but a skill set that is increasingly in demand and in tune with the way organisations are developing in a dynamic, connected world.

Management or governance?

In reality, portfolio managers rarely "manage" directly, in the traditional, hierarchical sense. What a portfolio manager actually does might be better described as "governance". Day-to-day management is carried out by those on the front line of individual activities, who may be in another part of the organisation, or in another organisation entirely. Portfolio managers often do not have line authority over the people they are – in theory – "managing". Yet they are responsible for the outcomes.

But portfolio managers can govern and can set up governance processes. They can also regulate, formally and informally. "Regulation" is often thought of as control and constraint. Yet it is much more subtle than that. The most effective regulation is not externally imposed but comes from shared expectations of "how things are done", communicated by observation and example. The best portfolio managers share examples, give visibility, and use praise to communicate "how things should be done", in ways that create a culture of expectations. Research and experience indicate this is much more effective than direct instruction, minimising the need for formal "management" and corrective actions.

A container for . . . anything?

At its most general, a portfolio is simply a "container" – a container that, depending on the context, might contain many different types of things. In modern life, and business, more and more things are "portfolio like" – that is, they are complex collections of things that, somehow, we have to manage together. A generation ago – even ten years ago – life was simpler. Tasks were neatly sorted into different categories (that is a project; this is business-as-usual operations). Businesses operated within clearly defined sector boundaries. (Now, what sector is Amazon in, for example? It seems to be everywhere. Or Google, which is developing driverless cars?) Professions were clearly delineated, and careers followed a linear track within professions, roles, sectors, and often companies. None of that is true now.

Managers at all levels, even individuals trying to manage their careers and personal lives, now sit on a complex powder keg of interacting activities and interests, any of which may blow up and require instant decisions at any moment. Organisations which used to have clear boundaries are increasingly "semi-permeable", with complex value chains that often cross previously rigid sector boundaries. With many functions contracted out, multiple partnerships, and cross-investments, the distinction between what is "inside" and "outside" the organisation is much less clear.

As a result, there is a resurgence of interest in how to manage collections of different things, i.e. portfolios. How do you manage, and govern, such a complex and changing collection of fundamentally different things, against an ambiguous set of goals, in an environment where the ground seems to be perpetually shifting? On what basis do you make decisions? How do you manage the complex sets of stakeholders involved, and the often-conflicting interests?

Perspective

Portfolio management needs a different perspective from either project management or operations. Rather than a single focused goal, portfolio managers need to balance multiple goals and objectives, which sometimes, inevitably, conflict. Portfolio managers have to juggle short- and long-term priorities, innovation and risk, consolidation and advancement. Always with less-than-complete information. Sometimes, it is worth investing time and effort in research and experimentation simply to gain knowledge and information that will lead to better decisions. New information may lead to different priorities.

There is much less overarching "theory" than is available to either project managers or program managers – although the techniques of stakeholder management, for example, translate effectively to portfolio management. More even than project and program managers, portfolio managers need excellent stakeholder knowledge and interaction. Portfolio managers have to get used to extracting information from a number of possibly ambiguous sources, sometimes simply from conversations rather than formal reports. Rather like real life, in fact.

People and priorities

Since the basis on which portfolio management decisions are made is frequently unclear, portfolio management decisions are often, inevitably, "political" to some degree. Which stakeholders' interests are given priority? How do you keep everyone – reasonably – happy? Clear evidence to support decisions may be hard to obtain though worth seeking wherever possible. A balanced scorecard can help, especially in justifying decisions, though to be effective the approach needs to be agreed with key stakeholders. People management is a key part of the job, even though portfolio managers may not have "teams" reporting directly to them.

Portfolio managers need to manage up, down, and across the organisation. To do this, they need a good understanding of people. Does project manager X ask for additional resources at the first sign of difficulty or only as a last resort? Does stakeholder Y cry wolf at the slightest provocation? Giving in to the loudest voice is not the best policy and likely to lead to problems when others hear of it, especially if they feel they have been short-changed for not speaking out. The job of the portfolio manager is to act in the best interests of the organisation as a whole. Sometimes, that may involve mobilising other stakeholders to help in dealing with "difficult" customers – internal and external.

All this requires a high degree of human judgement. Portfolio management decisions are difficult to automate. With AI (artificial intelligence) being applied to so many areas, this may be good news for portfolio managers. The complexity and the need for continuous relationship management mean that portfolio management is one of the least likely skills to be automated – a useful pointer when making career choices. When, inevitably, faced with difficult choices in ambiguous circumstances, it's worth remembering that this is what human beings are for.

Consequences

Portfolio management requires the ability to run "what if" scenarios – on a more or less continuous basis. If I take this decision, what will be the consequences for X, Y, or Z? How will stakeholder A respond if I action this request from stakeholder B? What might I need to do to resolve the situation – to reach a "best fit" decision and/or to deal with the consequences?

Portfolio managers need to be systems thinkers – aware that an action here will have an effect there, and that feedback, both positive and negative, can affect outcomes, either amplifying problems or acting to preserve the status quo despite strenuous attempts to change it. Sometimes, an action can provoke the opposite effect to what was intended, where the direct approach may not be the best. "Command and control" rarely works in a portfolio as the system has too many interacting parts. Similarly, attempts at micromanagement are usually counterproductive.

Portfolio management can be compared to the treasury function in government. The treasury has the power to make spending decisions and set the budget. But to avoid problems, this needs to be done in collaboration with the rest of government.

Managing complexity

Ultimately, portfolio management is about making decisions in complex and ambiguous situations, managing tensions when there is no obvious or "good" answer, and it is not possible to satisfy everybody. Where the information available is often limited or uncertain, missing, or in fundamentally different forms. It involves not just comparing apples with pears but evaluating the respective merits of apples, effort spent on the recruitment and motivation of apple pickers, spending on the marketing of apples, and investment improving the orchard. There is no simple way to compare these. The only test, ultimately, is whether it works.

It is not a job for the faint hearted. It needs both people skills and logical thinking. But it can be extremely satisfying. The way the world is going, more and more of the decisions that have to be taken in practice, in both work and life, are "portfolio like".

The future for portfolio management

Take this to the limit and everyone can be seen as a portfolio manager, with their own portfolio of interests, responsibilities, and accountabilities, collaborating where needed to achieve organisational goals. Some organisations – including some of the most successful – are already heading in this direction, with a high degree of individual autonomy and self-organisation and adaptive reorganisation in response to changing demands.

Start-ups tend to work in this much more fluid and dynamic way and are able to "pivot" as customer needs, competition, and technology evolve. Historically, organisations that grow beyond a certain size have had to switch to a much more rigidly structured, hierarchical, and "managed" approach. However, a number of organisations, including some of the most successful – organisations such as Amazon, Netflix, and Google – are finding ways to retain this much more flexible approach, even "at scale". Even on a global scale. The continued advance of digital technology – now affecting every sector, not just Silicon Valley companies – both demands and enables this more fluid approach.

Fortunately, human beings are natural portfolio managers. In our own lives, we all manage our "personal portfolios", distributing time, attention, and money between disparate activities to achieve multiple goals which change over time. And satisfy a diverse collection of stakeholders. But portfolio managers do it professionally.

In an increasingly digital, connected world, with boundaries that are much more fluid and a high degree of dynamic change, the ability to manage in this environment is a skill set that will be in high demand. An environment that seems ever more VUCA – volatile, uncertain, complex, and ambiguous – is very different to the hierarchical, highly compartmentalised world of twentieth-century industrial organisations, where there were rigid structures and clear boundaries. In today's world, organisations behave less like industrial machines and more like living systems, adapting and learning as circumstances change. But this is clearly the way of the future.

For those aspiring to senior leadership positions, the ability to manage a diverse portfolio in an uncertain environment is at least as important as the traditional focus on operating experience. Even the role of leadership is changing: Jeff Bezos, one of the most successful business leaders of modern times, operates more like a portfolio manager than a twentieth-century CEO, setting governance principles while delegating day-to-day management decisions throughout the organisation.

For everyone, developing the skills of portfolio management, with all the complexities and ambiguities this involves, is excellent preparation for this rapidly emerging world.

Conclusion

The increasingly uncertain and complex world we live in today is changing the way businesses are being managed and organisations are structured, suggesting a less-structured and more-adaptable environment that is capable of dynamic change. This considers a move to a more networked organisational design, advocating governance as a key part of this, and modern leadership skills that are able to manage diverse and complex portfolios.

28 Case study – portfolio management maturity model development

Paul Clarke, Katy Angliss, and Pete Harpum

Introduction

This chapter discusses the development of a portfolio management maturity model that was used in a large international power company. The starting point was an existing portfolio management maturity model developed by Pennypacker (2004) (Table 29.1). The research for the application in the specific context here developed this model, introducing three additional "hard factors", or "hardware elements", and a series of "soft factors" or "software elements". Both of these additional aspects influence the effectiveness of all managerialist approaches to organisational effectiveness when the maturity model is applied in other contexts.

Both these two sets of factors have been developed based on the specific context for the case study and are also influenced by the "collaborative relationship" (CR) model (UKNAO, 2006). This approach was adopted as other readily available models, such as the portfolio, program, and project management maturity model (P3M3) (Axelos, 2016), organisational project management maturity model (OPM3) (PMI, 2013), and Pennypacker's model, were seen to have insufficient focus on environmental factors, and particularly those present in the organisation in which this model was intended to be used. This is possibly due to a bias within the literature towards large projects and project-oriented environments, rather than the delivery of work within a more operational environment.

The chapter begins with a brief review of value drivers for portfolio management in large operationally dominated organisations, then describes the elements of the maturity model as defined for this extended model, before the full maturity model is presented. Finally, a brief overview of the approach for analysis of an organisation for portfolio management maturity using this model is presented.

Value drivers for portfolios

Value from an investment portfolio is primarily about return on investment. A company invests money in projects with the intent of generating value. Portfolio management can be seen as the value engine that ensures the best possible value is delivered.

By setting clear, consistent return/cost/benefit criteria for funding investments and only selecting projects that meet these criteria, all projects in the portfolio should deliver the required levels of value as defined by the business as a customer, which aligns to the premise of the "lean" philosophy (Murman et al., 2002), which by definition orientates an organisation to value that the business is willing to pay for. Also, by being aware of the timescales, risks, and resources associated with promised return, portfolio management

DOI: 10.4324/9780367853129-32

Table 28.1 Portfolio management maturity model

Level of Portfolio Maturity: / Portfolio Component:	**Level 1** Initial Process	**Level 2** Structured Process & Standards	**Level 3** Organisational Standards & Process	**Level 4** Managed & Embedded Process	**Level 5** Optimising Process
Portfolio Governance	Adhoc processes. Evaluation of projects doesn't consider organisational strategy alignment.	Basic process for creating division portfolio review boards. Strategic alignment of projects considered, but not systematically.	Process standard organisation wide. Divisional portfolio review boards consolidate & report to business review board. Projects /programs evaluated against strategic criteria.	Lessons learned used to improve decision making capability. Portfolio balanced for optimal business value. Organisational changes regularly reviewed for effect on portfolio(s).	Focus on continuous process improvement. Best practices benchmarked. Process metrics collected & analysed.
Project/Program Opportunity Assessment	Adhoc processes. List of opportunities unavailable. Business value of projects /programs not established.	Basic process. Roles/responsibilities for identifying opportunities defined. Near-term business needs designated for projects.	Process standard organisation wide & integrated with other business processes. Cost, benefit, schedule & risk are reviewed before funding.	Investment process lessons learned captured & evaluated. Opportunity information available organisational wide.	Focus on continuous process improvement. Best practices benchmarked. Process metrics collected & analysed.
Project/Program Prioritisation & Selection	Adhoc processes. Critical information missing for funded projects.	Basic process. Roles/responsibilities defined for establishing business value. Basic project/program prioritisation scheme used.	Process standard organisation wide. Portfolio prioritised at division level using standard criteria. Project/program strategy aligned with business strategy.	Processes validated by historic data. Active business portfolio review board. Projects/programs prioritised at all levels of organisation.	Focus on continuous process improvement. Best practices benchmarked. Process metrics collected & analysed.
Portfolio Communications Management	Adhoc processes. No list of approved projects/programs. Portfolio information not defined or readily available.	Basic process. Project data aggregated for divisional review. Portfolio information communicated across division.	Process standard organisation wide. Detailed information tracked for projects/programs. Portfolio information reviewed at organisational level to evaluate investment balance.	Portfolio information audited. Project investment information available on demand. Asset inventory maintained.	Focus on continuous process improvement. Best practices benchmarked. Process metrics collected & analysed.
Portfolio Performance Management	Adhoc processes. Organisation rarely evaluates project/program outcomes or identifies lessons learned.	Basic process. Portfolio information reviewed with sponsor organisation. Actual cost, schedule data compared to expectations.	Process standard organisation wide. Portfolio actively analysed & balanced. Benefit, value & risk management integral to control processes.	Common objectives & metrics defined. Performance measurement data collected & reviewed. Performance data used in prioritisation process.	Focus on continuous process improvement. Best practices benchmarked. Process metrics collected & analysed.
Portfolio Resource Management	Adhoc processes. Resources assigned to projects/programs when available.	Basic process. Resources identified by skill set & availability. Processes in place to collaboratively manage project/program priorities given limited resources.	Process standard organisation wide. Resource pool management process exists. Resources other than people considered.	Business & division resource analysis and reporting occurs on a scheduled basis.	Focus on continuous process improvement. Best practices benchmarked. Process metrics collected & analysed.

Source: Adapted from Pennypacker (2004).

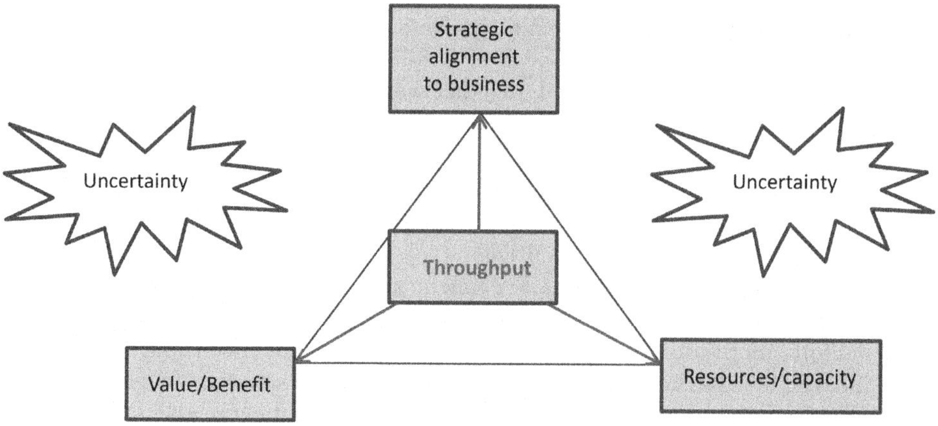

Figure 28.1 Portfolio throughput model.

can use schedule management to ensure that risk and return are balanced and actively managed across the portfolio. The application of portfolio management shifts investment delivery from spending the available investment funds to delivering a required level of return for the funds invested. This creates clearer criteria for when to stop a project, as for any business investment there must be a level of poor or underperformance that results in disinvestment. This approach is increasingly necessary as investment funds become more limited.

By acting at portfolio level, it is also possible to balance investments to align to the business requirements, thus ensuring the correct balance between investments for maintaining the assets and investments that generate revenue, such as between low-return versus low-risk investments and high-return versus high-risk investments. It also allows the WIP (work in progress) or "loading" to be aligned to the capacity of resources, particularly bottlenecks, so throughput can be maximised, cycle time minimised, and disruptions from emergent work reduced, within an uncertain environment (see Figure 29.1), with a theory of constraints approach (Goldratt, 1993) considered for portfolio management, where project delivery requirements are often in excess of available resources.

Portfolio management also allows feedback from completed projects to be used to adjust selection and performance management. In the model presented later (Table 29.2 and Table 29.3), this feedback information is assumed to be generated from the project/program management process but used by the portfolio management process.

Studies (De Reyck et al., 2005) have reported that benefits delivered from portfolio management are directly related to the level of portfolio management maturity. Various sources report large benefits from the application of portfolio management, which meet the intent of "more for less". Examples such as Kendall and Rollins (2003) and Perry and Hatcher (2008) state typical benefits as:

- 35% more projects completed.
- 10% less resource used.
- 37% lower cost.

The portfolio management maturity model development

A portfolio maturity model based on Pennypacker's model (Pennypacker, 2004), included as the benchmark for the context-specific "hardware factors" of the extended model, was shown in Table 29.1. This model, together with the collaborative relationship (CR) model (UKNAO, 2006), has been used as the basis for the "hardware" and "software" elements of the extended maturity model, described in the rest of this chapter. Other influences on the development of the extended model include lean principles (Liker, 2004; Womack et al., 2007) and theory of Constraints (TOC) (Goldratt, 1993; Levine, 2005; Kendall & Rollins, 2003; and NDA, 2013).

The hardware factors include the CR elements of processes, mission and strategy, and skills/resources, and the software factors include the CR elements of environment, leadership, culture, motivation, and behaviour, as seen in the extended model (Tables 29.2 and 29.3). The broad structure for the maturity levels in the extended model are based on the five levels of the Pennypacker model for portfolio management maturity (Table 29.1), adjusted to combine the three middle elements into two for simplification of the portfolio level and organisational level, with the four levels from low to high in the extended model including (1) initial process, (2) basic process, (3) organisational process, and (4) continuous optimisation. The six elements identified in Pennypacker's model have been modified, and three additional hardware elements have been added, these being mission and strategy (HI) relating to strategic delivery, project/program management maturity (H7), and skills and resources (H9). Opportunity assessment is also discussed as both strategic alignment and value alignment. Each hardware and software element for the extended model is described next.

Hardware elements of the extended portfolio maturity model

Portfolio mission and strategy (H1)

This element is essential to effective portfolio management, as the identification of the mission and strategy is implicit in defining portfolio management in the organisational context of a specific business. It is also key to ensuring that value can be defined, including non-financial factors, such as the regulatory dimension, which is key in many business domains. If portfolio is to be strategically focused, long-range targets and value need to be defined, both now and for future years.

Portfolio strategic alignment (H2)

The original Pennypacker element of opportunity assessment has been split into two separate elements, strategic alignment and value alignment, both being seen as key dimensions for portfolio management. The portfolio element has been split to test if there is a difference between the strategic and value alignment in large organisations. One of the key problems with portfolios is, vital capacity can be used up by non-strategically aligned projects slowing delivery. Therefore, a key measure of maturity is that work in the portfolio is aligned to the strategic requirements of the business and managed both at division level and business-wide, with the ability to learn and adapt being present.

Portfolio value alignment (H3)

This element expands the dimension by which value is defined to include financial and other elements, for example, non-financial, such as cash flow, risk, throughput, scheduling/phasing, and the balance between revenue and non-revenue-generating projects. With a mature position being established, investment return levels for different types of projects and different locations can also be analysed.

Project selection and prioritisation (H4)

Ensuring that the right projects are in the portfolio is key to any portfolio, and this was included in the original Pennypacker model. The original criteria has been adjusted to include prioritisation by independent force ranking, which is identified as a key component to ensure consistency in this area (Kendall & Rollins, 2003), and an explicit link to non-financial criteria has also been added as these are of significant importance in this type of operation.

Portfolio communications (H5)

This element has been modified to align to the best practice presented by the Nuclear Decommissioning Authority (NDA) of baseline management (NDA, 2013) using a work breakdown structure (WBS) and medium-term plan (MTP) and incorporating plan stability as a key performance indicator (KPI) that demonstrates maturity. The use of a visible MTP that extends into future years and ideally lifetime supports alignment of resources and comparison of performance, allowing additional value to be generated. It also allows emergent work and end-of-year adjustments to be accommodated more easily due to an increased definition of the work currently in the baseline. In a functional environment, a documented and detailed baseline provides a good cross-business information mechanism that mitigates the limited ability of functions to communicate with each other and enhances information available to the executive team, such as an executive dashboard. This enhanced visibility reduces or removes the "pet projects" syndrome, where function managers prioritise their own work rather than what is best value for the business.

Portfolio performance (H6)

The creation of value is the overall aim of portfolio management. Once the correct projects and prioritised are selected, then the portfolio needs to be managed in line with learning from the throughput approaches previously discussed. The Pennypacker model also linked to project management processes within this element, which has been separated out to element H7 so additional detail could be tested. The element has then been adjusted to incorporate the learning from other sources (Goldratt, 1993, Murman et al., 2002). Portfolio loading needs to be managed, and key to this is the control of project activation and linkages to critical (bottleneck) resources that determine the rate of the system.

Project maturity (H7)

Post-selection, mature project management processes and governance systems are needed to assure project delivery and provide the level of detail required to support portfolio-level actions. A gated project process linked to a progressive commitment for financial release is a key control mechanism that portfolio management requires. Therefore, mature portfolio management, which manages portfolio performance post–project selection, requires project and program management maturity.

Resource management (H8)

Resource management is a key issue for both projects and portfolios and is incorporated within the original Pennypacker model. The original model has been modified to recognise that throughput is controlled not by management of all resources but by the management of bottlenecks and that this is the area to gain control of first in order to improve performance. Further maturity is gained when full resource management is in place, giving additional, albeit smaller, benefits. As one of the prime dimensions of portfolio management in a mature organisation, it is expected that KPIs for resource management would be in place. Management of resources to maintain loading without overburden ensures a flow of projects can be maintained in line with lean principles. This also presents the means to improved alignment and improved work scheduling, with both delivery team support resources and suppliers where appropriate.

Portfolio skills and resources (H9)

The Pennypacker model does not directly consider skills and resources necessary to manage a portfolio; however, this is an element of the CR model. In a non-project organisation, the availability of these resources cannot be assumed, and their availability is a key element of maturity. Therefore, the capability, experience, and availability of portfolio management personnel is a key dimension of portfolio maturity.

Software elements of the extended portfolio maturity model

A maturity model for the "soft factors" considering the wider business environment is incorporated into the enhanced maturity model, with these elements drawn from the specific environment for which this model was developed. Nevertheless, there is no reason in principle that these software elements do not apply to, at the very least, organisations that run portfolios of large engineering-based projects. These elements are based on the categories of the collaborative relationship (CR) model (UKNAO, 2006), which are the environment, leadership, culture, motivation, and behaviours required to support successful investment delivery. The UKNAO research showed that the benefit of the CR approach was seen in the relative performance of oil and gas projects when measuring success through collaborative working relationships.

The portfolio maturity model presented by Pennypacker does not highlight software factors, possibly because these vary according to the environmental context, but the experience in large engineering organisations is that these factors are at least as important as the hardware elements. Therefore, adding these factors to the extended maturity model are seen as essential to fully understand the maturity of portfolio management within these organisational environments.

Organisation type is reflected in approaches (SI)

The organisational operational environment is strongly functional, unlike many other environments which have a matrix structure. In order for portfolio management to be effective, it must be aligned to the organisational environment, which is atypical. The criteria assumes that when good alignment is present, there will be an improved balance between operational and project demands and that decisions will be made on a prioritised basis, resulting in reduced operational impacts on planned investment. Alignment to the organisational type, in this case an operational and functional organisation, is seen as a key dimension of maturity.

Alignment of delivery organisation to work (S2)

This element is based both on observed behaviours and external examples, such as the NDA approaches (see hardware element H5). The alignment of delivery organisations to function, both in the current years and future years, is required in order to allow delivery resources to be optimised. The higher the degree of alignment and the further into the future the work is planned, the more mature portfolio management is and the more opportunities for economies of scale can be available.

Providing direction (S3)

Recent changes in the organisation on which this case study is based provided real benefit by improving clarity in roles within new processes, ensuring that no confusion is present and that key personnel understand their roles, with these roles delivered by trained and experienced personnel. A mature position in this context being when roles are clearly identified and executed by personnel with greater than, on average, five years' experience.

Management engagement (S4)

The implementation and adherence to any process such as portfolio management is enhanced by the engagement of senior managers who sponsor activities by directly involving themselves in the process, thus reinforcing its importance by their personal attention. This element is essential in order for a process to be implemented and sustained.

Balance in governance structures (S5)

Maintaining a balance of power in investment governance structures ensures that power in the process is shared and that no parties become frustrated or disenfranchised with the structures being used. This provides a mature structure that should be capable of being maintained and adapted, if necessary, in the longer term.

Structure of portfolio organisation (S6)

In this context, working with a decentralised organisation operating across the length and breadth of the country, in a distributed organisation structure, provides a mature solution to ensure that attention and focus are maintained at the right level and in the right areas. Allowing low-complexity work to be dealt with locally, with more complex work being dealt with centrally. This is a scalable solution that maximises engagement.

Project and portfolio value and cost drivers (S7)

In order to maximise value and minimise the cost of projects, and therefore maximise portfolio delivery, a common understanding of project cost and value drivers needs to be present throughout the key personnel engaged in portfolio management.

When understanding is present, mature behaviours follow, which allows delivery to be optimised.

Promotion of success (S8)

Business areas with high-performing investment delivery have been observed to have a high level of effective communications that reflect the good teamwork and promotion of success in delivering investments. Therefore, communications provide a good indicator of the maturity of the relations in the integrated team (such as within the investment delivery [ID] area, station personnel, and functional teams) that is needed to successfully deliver investments.

Need to collaborate is understood (S9)

In most projects, there is a need to collaborate, which the research into the CR model reinforces even where project resources are dedicated to the project. Projects are being delivered on operating stations and also within a functional organisation. Project delivery requires the integrated action of investment delivery (ID), station personnel, engineering and technical functions, and therefore, collaboration is essential. However, in a functional environment, partisan behaviours can conflict with this position; it is therefore seen as a key dimension of maturity that the need to collaborate is understood.

Extended portfolio management maturity model assessment

Following the previous descriptive sections of the portfolio maturity categories, the adapted and extended portfolio management maturity model matrix is presented for the hardware factors in Table 28.2 and for the software factors in Table 28.3, together with the four levels of maturity for assessment from low (1) to high (4).

Use of the model to analyse the organisation

To understand the maturity of the organisation's portfolio management maturity, a survey was carried out using the model, and three questions were asked as follows:

Question:	*Rationale:*
1 Please provide your assessment of the level of maturity for each element of the portfolio maturity model against the criteria shown in the model.	This provides a comparison of the organisation's position against the standard presented, showing the size of gap to the ideal position. Identifying any significant differences in view between functional areas.
2 Please quantify for each element of the maturity model what level that you consider is achievable within the next 36 months.	This indicates the perceived difficulty per element of potential improvement, identifying any significant differences in view between functional areas.
3 Please provide for each element of the maturity model any comments or suggestions, including if you believe any element is not needed/or adapted and why.	This will provide contextual information to refine the model and identify areas where elements are not needed, duplication is present, or further understanding is required.

Table 28.2 Hardware elements for the extended portfolio management maturity model

CR Element	*Portfolio maturity model "hardware" elements*					
	Hardware element					
	No.	*Description*	*Level 1 maturity (low)* *Initial development*	*Level 2 maturity* *Basic process*	*Level 3 maturity* *Organisational process*	*Level 4 maturity (high)* *Continuous optimisation*
Mission and Strategy	**H1**	**Portfolio mission and strategy** (Portfolio mission, strategy, and value is defined)	Mission for the portfolio is not clearly defined. The strategic requirements for the portfolio are not clear or misaligned to the current business (and regulatory) environment. Value for the organisation not fully defined.	Mission is only loosely defined. Strategic requirements are visible and aligned to current business (and regulatory) environment. Value for portfolio is defined in outline terms.	Mission is well defined. Strategic requirements are visible and quantified for all key dimensions, including regulatory. Value for portfolio is defined in quantifiable terms.	Mission provides clear targets for future years and informs the portfolio strategy. Strategic requirements are visible and quantified for all key dimensions, including regulatory. Value for the portfolio is defined in quantifiable terms with targets for now and future years.
Processes	**H2**	**Portfolio strategic alignment** (Sub-portfolios, programs, and projects within it are aligned to company strategy).	Evaluation of projects is ad hoc and does not confirm alignment to organisational strategy.	Basic processes for strategic alignment of projects and programs in place. Strategic alignment of projects and programs is considered, but not systematically. Function/location portfolio review boards present.	Process is standard organisation wide and covers all main project areas, including functional. The strategic alignment of all projects evaluated against criteria that cover all strategic requirements. Location/function portfolio review boards consolidate and report to a central portfolio board.	Lessons learned and project post-completion information used to inform future selection decisions. Level of alignment to strategic requirements optimised and reported at project, program, and portfolio level. Strategic criteria reviewed and adjusted yearly or when business requirements change.

(*Continued*)

Table 28.2 (Continued)

CR Element	*Portfolio maturity model "hardware" elements*					
	Hardware element					
	No.	*Description*	*Level 1 maturity (low)* *Initial development*	*Level 2 maturity* *Basic process*	*Level 3 maturity* *Organisational process*	*Level 4 maturity (high)* *Continuous optimisation*
	H3	**Portfolio value alignment** (Projects and programs in the portfolio are aligned to deliver a defined level of value against the benefits).	Ad hoc or no process to test project/program value. Business value of projects and programs not established. List of opportunities unavailable.	Basic processes for value analysis of existing projects. Roles and responsibilities for identifying opportunities and business value (£/time/other) defined. Short-term business return level/need established for projects.	Alignment processes standard organisation wide and integrated with other processes. Cost benefit, schedule, risk, and cash flow reviewed before funding. Value alignment looks at portfolio throughout and opportunities for phasing and aggregation to maximise value.	Investment processes lessons learned captured and evaluated. Opportunity information available organisation wide. Portfolio balanced between revenue and non-revenue projects. Return levels for different project types and locations reported to business quarterly.
	H4	**Project selection and prioritisation** (Projects/programs must meet selection criteria to be executed, and all projects prioritised against common criteria)	Ad hoc or no process. Projects funded with critical information absent or incomplete. Projects do not have a priority level.	Basic project prioritisation scheme (that balances both financial and other criteria). Roles and responsibility defined for determining business value. All projects have a priority based on a common assessment method.	Selection and prioritisation process is standard organisation wide. Projects prioritised (force ranked) by independents at function/location level using standard criteria. Projects aligned to business strategy and value. Priority linked to resource availability, including financial resources.	Process validated by historic data. Active business-level portfolio review board in place. Projects prioritised at all levels of the organisation. Prioritisation criteria adjusted based on portfolio performance feedback.

H5	**Portfolio communication management** (Portfolio, program, and project information is available business wide, and plans extend to lifetime)	Adhoc processes. No list of approved projects. Project information not defined or readily available.	Basic processes. Project data aggregated for function/location portfolio review. Portfolio information communicated across function/location. Partial baseline in place for next execution year, costed and planned 6 months in advance of execution. Standard WBS in use for all portfolios, which categorises work to common structure.	Standard organisation-wide processes. Detailed information tracked for projects. Portfolio information reviewed at org level to evaluate investment performance and balance. Work is a rolling plan and estimate for next two years with outline plans for execution year plus three-year strategic planning. Change control process in place. Standard WBS in place across portfolio.	Portfolio process information (no. of projects, resources used, value delivered) and is reported and (internally) audited. Project investment information available on demand. Executive dashboard in place and used. Full baseline plan in place: work is a rolling plan and estimated for next two years with outline plans for execution year plus five-year strategic planning and lifetime plan in place with basic costing and portfolio plans. Work under change control. Changes to plan, other than short-term phasing, are rare, and plan stability is a KPI.
H6	**Portfolio performance (monitoring and control)** (The portfolio is managed to maximise the throughput of projects/ programs)	Ad hoc processes. Organisation rarely evaluates project outcomes or identifies lessons learned. Number of projects is greater than available resources. Mission provides clear targets for future years which informs the portfolio strategy.	Basic processes. Portfolio information reviewed with sponsor organisation. Actual cost and schedule data compared to expectations. Number of projects and programs in portfolio is broadly aligned to resource capacity.	Standard organisation-wide process. Detailed information is tracked for projects and programs within the portfolio and any sub-portfolios. Benefit and risk management are integral to control processes. Projects which impact on critical resources are only activated when resource available. Project activation is phased and not just released annually.	Common objectives and metrics defined. Performance measurement data collected and reviewed. Portfolio and project performance data is used in prioritisation and selection process. Throughput of portfolio, portfolio loading, and cycle time of projects are actively managed to maximise performance.

(*Continued*)

Table 28.2 (Continued)

CR Element	*Portfolio maturity model "hardware" elements*					
	Hardware element					
	No.	*Description*	*Level 1 maturity (low)* *Initial development*	*Level 2 maturity* *Basic process*	*Level 3 maturity* *Organisational process*	*Level 4 maturity (high)* *Continuous optimisation*
	H7	**Project (and program) management maturity** (A mature and scalable project management process is in place and valued)	Basic project approach and basic PM practices in place. The organisation recognises differences between projects, programs, and BAU and runs them differently.	Structured project process in place. The organisation recognises that standard processes need to be defined and developed so that project and program success can be repeated. Each project and/or program runs its own process, and consistency between these processes is limited.	Standard project and program process used across organisation. The organisation defines a single methodology for project/program management in order to take advantage of the associated synergizing effect. Individual projects can flex the centrally controlled processes to suit their needs (processes are scalable).	Project and program process embedded and aligned to organisational characteristics. The organisation benchmarks project/program management practices and processes with others to maintain competitive advantage and performance data is readily available. Project/program performance data is used in prioritisation.

Resources and Skills	**H8**	**Portfolio resource management** (Resources are managed across the portfolio)	Ad hoc resource management processes. Resources are assigned to projects of portfolios when available. Resources frequently change. Resourcing decision-making is at project level.	Basic processes are in place to manage resource clashes, or resources are assigned to portfolios for a period of time. Resource availability by skills sets over time is known by the portfolio.	Standard organisation-wide resource management process is in place for the portfolio. Resources pool management process exists for critical resources (e.g. bottlenecks). Resources other than people considered.	Enterprise and function/location resource analysis and reporting occurs on a scheduled basis. Critical resource usage (e.g. bottleneck) is maximised. Resource management is a key management KPI.
	H9	**Portfolio management skills and resources** (Portfolio management is valued by the organisation and part of the core structures)	Portfolio management skills are not present or valued. None or little resources are devoted to portfolio management.	Portfolio management skills are present and utilised. Resources are devoted to portfolio management but operate largely in isolation.	Portfolio management is valued by the business and invested in. Training is available. All functions involved in portfolio management are coordinated.	Portfolio management is valued by the organisation as a strategic mechanism. Portfolio management resources are part of core organisational structures.

Table 28.3 Software elements for the extended portfolio management maturity model

CR Element	*Portfolio maturity model "software" elements*					
	Software element					
	No.	*Description*	*Level 1 maturity (low)* *Initial process*	*Level 2 maturity* *Basic process*	*Level 3 maturity* *Organisational process*	*Level 4 maturity (high)* *Continuous optimisation*
Environment	**S1**	**Organisation type is reflected in portfolio approaches** (Portfolio management structures reflect the functional organisation and minimise disruption to planned work)	Impact of organisation type on portfolio management is not identified or reflected in customisation of approaches applied. Key interfaces between portfolios and functions are not fully understood. Operational demands continuously impact project work delivery.	Portfolio management approach has been partial-customised to incorporate limited functional requirements, including production. Key interfaces between projects and functions are understood by all parties and documented. Operational demands frequently impact project delivery.	Portfolio management approach has been customised to incorporate all key functional requirements, including production. Key interfaces between project portfolio and functions are understood by all parties and reflected in plans. Impacts of operational demands on project delivery are managed jointly.	Key functions see portfolio management and their means to ensure key requirements are met by the investment portfolio. Adherence to processes enforced by all functions. Key interfaces between projects and functions are understood by all parties, reflected in plans, and joint resource management is in place. Impacts from operational demand on project work are rare.
	S2	**Alignment of delivery organisations to work** (Work is aligned to delivery team in advance)	Alignment of portfolio work to delivery by organisation is not present or ad hoc. Changes of delivery organisation work often occurs.	Portfolio work is partially aligned to delivery organisation. Changes of delivery organisation work rarely occurs.	Portfolio work is aligned to delivery organisations by type in advance of execution year. Continuity of delivery organisation is present.	Portfolio work is aligned to delivery organisation work for current and future years. Delivery organisations are involved in development plans to ensure optimum phasing of work.

Leadership	**S3**	**Providing direction** (Portfolio roles are understood and executed by trained and experienced staff)	Key roles for portfolio management are not understood.	Key roles for portfolio management are understood and documented. Portfolio roles are executed by untrained or inexperienced staff.	Key roles for portfolio management are understood and documented. Portfolio roles are executed by trained and experienced staff.	Key roles for portfolio management are understood, documented, and reviewed and updated yearly. Portfolio roles are executed by trained staff with > 5 years' experience.
	S4	**Management engagement and support** (Managers are engaged with portfolio management)	Senior management are not directly involved in portfolio governance structures and do not sponsor portfolio activities.	Senior management are not directly involved in portfolio governance structures but provide sponsorship for activities.	Senior managers are directly involved in some portfolio governance structures.	Senior managers directly involved in all portfolio governance structures.
	S5	**Portfolio governance is balanced** (Power balance in portfolio governance reflects organisation)	Governance mechanisms are operated by a single function.	Governance mechanisms include representation from key functional stakeholders.	Governance matches organisations balance, for example, station, centre, and functions.	Governance matches organisations balance, for example, station, centre, and functions. Personnel involved in governance roles are experienced.
Culture	**S6**	**Structure of portfolio organisation** (The portfolio organisation is distributed across locations and functions)	Portfolio management organisation is centralised as a single function.	Portfolio management organisation is distributed with elements at key locations or located with key stakeholders/ support capability.	Portfolio management organisation is distributed with elements at key locations or located with key stakeholders/ support capability and aligned to local cultures.	Portfolio management organisation is distributed with elements at key locations or located with key stakeholders/support capability and aligned to both local culture and central culture.

(Continued)

Table 28.3 (Continued)

CR Element	*Portfolio maturity model "software" elements*					
	Software element					
	No.	*Description*	*Level 1 maturity (low)* *Initial process*	*Level 2 maturity* *Basic process*	*Level 3 maturity* *Organisational process*	*Level 4 maturity (high)* *Continuous optimisation*
Motivation	**S7**	**Project and portfolio value and cost drivers** (Project/portfolio value and cost drivers are understood)	Project/portfolio value and cost drivers are not understood by sponsors and customers.	Project/portfolio value and cost drivers are partially understood by sponsors and customers.	Project/portfolio value and cost drivers are understood by sponsors and customers.	Project/portfolio value and cost drivers are understood by sponsors and customers and all work together to maximise value and reduce cost for the business.
	S8	**Promotion of success** (Success is communicated by the business)	Little communication of success or value from portfolio management. Performance measures are not in place.	Limited communication of success or value from portfolio management. Performance measures for portfolio management are identified and measured.	Frequent communication of success or value from portfolio management. Performance is continuously communicated to the business as a whole and to all key stakeholders.	The business promotes its portfolio management to others, and performance measures show high level of business value.
Behaviour	**S9**	**Need to collaborate is understood** (Collaborative relationships are in place and supported by leaders)	Collaborative relationships between functions and projects not established. Key leaders promote function, not portfolio.	The need to collaborate is understood, and relationships are developing. Some key leaders promote portfolio before function. Customer–supplier relationships are identified.	Collaboration visibly evidenced by actions, for example, resources shared. Most key leaders promote portfolio before function. Customer–supplier relationships are mature and collaborative, with forward planning in place.	Collaboration has been present for years, and relationship measurement is in place. The portfolio performance is more important than function. The organisation is adjusted to aid customer supply relationships between functions, and projects and teams are co-located.

By the application of these questions to each of the 18 maturity model elements (9 hardware and 9 software), the survey reflected an effective set of 54 questions. The survey returns, with the ratings of 1–4 for each element of the maturity model, provided a quantitative input. Simple descriptive statistical treatment of the survey results provided information about the level of maturity in the organisation, which could also be analysed for department, type of portfolio, business division, etc. The survey respondents were also asked to provide qualitative comments for each element of the model, as presented previously. This information provided a more detailed understanding of how the management of portfolios is carried out in the organisation, what leads to the scores given, and therefore, how the maturity of portfolio management can be improved.

For strengths and gaps, the comments returned by the survey were summarised to provide context and a qualitative view of the interdependency of the various elements. The overall strengths and gaps were then analysed. Strengths being those elements which are higher than the norm. Gaps being identified within three different categories as follows.

1. Elements where the current level presents a low absolute level of maturity.
2. Elements where there is a large difference between current and desired positions.
3. Elements which were at a low level compared to the external benchmark.

Although it is not intended here to provide a more comprehensive development or justification of the findings, the outcome of this research included the development of a portfolio management framework, implemented to provide a more robust decision-making process for project and program selection and prioritisation.

Conclusion

This chapter has discussed a portfolio management maturity model within a specific industrial context. The chapter began with how the extended model was developed from Pennypacker's original model and the collaborative relationship model and briefly shows how the model could be used for assessment and analysis of the portfolio management maturity for the organisation. The extended model is an example of the use of a portfolio management maturity matrix, which would need to be adapted for application within other organisational settings.

References

AXELOS (2016) *Portfolio, Programme & Project Management Maturity Model (P3M3).* Office of Government Commerce.

De Reyck B., Grushka-Cockayne Y., Lockett M., Calderini S., Moura M. & Sloper A. (2005) The impact of project portfolio management on information technology projects. *International Journal of Project Management* 23(7), 524-537.

Goldratt E. (1993) *The Goal: A Process of Ongoing Improvement.* Gower Publishing.

Kendall G. & Rollins, S. (2003) *Advanced Project Portfolio Management and the PMO: Multiplying ROI at Warp Speed.* J Ross Publishing.

Levine A. (2005) *Project Portfolio Management. A Practical Guide to Selecting Projects, Managing Portfolios and Maximizing Benefits.* Jossey-Bass.

Liker J. (2004) *The Toyota Way: 14 Management Principles from the World's Greatest Manufacturer.* McGraw-Hill.

Murman E., Allen T., Bozdogan K., Cutcher-Gershenfeld J., McManus H., Nightingale D., Rebentisch E., Shields T., Stahl F., Walton M., Warmkessel J., Weiss S. & Widnall S. (2002) *Lean Enterprise Value: Insights from MIT's Lean Aerospace Initiative*. Palgrave Macmillan.

NDA (2013) *Baseline Management System Programme Controls Procedures Doc.: Nuclear Decommissioning Authority (NDA)*. PCP-M.

Pennypacker J. (2004) *Project Portfolio Management Maturity Model*. Centre for Business Practices.

Perry R. & Hatcher E. (2008) *How Project and Portfolio Management Solutions are Delivering Value to Organizations*. Ca WhitePaper, IDC.

PMI (2013) *Organizational Project Management Maturity Model (OPM3)*. Third Edition. Project Management Institute.

UKNAO (2006) *Measuring Success through Collaborative Working Relationships*. HMSO: National Audit Office.

Womack J., Jones D. & Roos D. (2007) *The Machine that Changed the World: The Story of Lean Production – Toyota's Secret Weapon in the Global Car Wars that is Now Revolutionizing World Industry*. Simon and Schuster.

End note

The intention of this book has been to provide a fresh perspective on portfolio management, expanding on the currently held views of P3M (portfolios, programs, and projects) and PPM (project portfolio management), particularly from an organisational, rather than project management, perspective. In doing so, it is hoped to have shown a clearer focus on portfolio management, not as an extension of projects and programs or as an alternative to program management, but as an established and important element in its own right, fully integrated within the business, and delivering strategic intentions on an ongoing basis for the organisation.

In addition to the current text on portfolio management, within the project management sphere, and not to be confused with financial portfolio management, although the commonality is clear, this textbook has looked to provide a more stand-alone perspective of portfolio management within the organisational environment with strategic portfolio management (SPM), emphasising the importance on strategic portfolios being the link with the organisational strategy and strategic delivery.

To reiterate the preface, this book is not intended to provide a "how-to" guide for strategic portfolio management, recognising that the portfolio will be context-specific within every organisation. The book has presented alternative views and perspectives, both from an academic and practical perspective, discussing the current thinking from an academic viewpoint, and also advancing the thinking and providing "food for thought" to senior managers tasked with implementing or delivering strategic portfolio management.

The book began in Section I by setting the scene for strategic portfolio management within the organisational context, discussing the importance of integrating with the organisational strategy, and aligning organisational change. There is a focus on achieving organisational strategic value whilst recognising that benefits realisation from projects and programs is an essential part of portfolio management success. Section II introduces and defines the concept of the strategic portfolio, discussing portfolio integration and the external and internal environmental factors for consideration when developing or managing portfolio management capabilities and the strategic portfolio for effective portfolio management. Section III developed these portfolio capabilities in further depth, discussing asset and resource management, portfolio governance, including the portfolio office, portfolio reporting, and data analysis, with four chapters focusing on portfolio leadership, finishing with supply chain integration, and not forgetting the perhaps-contentious area of agile portfolio management. Section IV provided various case studies concerning the practical aspects of portfolio management.

Some key takeaways from the chapters, following the main themes introduced in the introduction in delivering strategic value and part of effective portfolio leadership, are:

- Deriving the correct set of projects and programs to deliver strategic objectives.
- Prioritising the set of projects and programs in the portfolio to maximise value creation.
- Linking strategic value to project and program business cases.
- Ensuring investment decisions are soundly based and consistently made.
- Correctly allocating resources within the portfolio to the projects and programs.
- Resolving conflict between projects and programs in the portfolio to maintain the strategic direction of travel.
- Properly and effectively deriving the benefits cases for programs and projects through portfolio mechanisms, aligned to value creation.
- Differentiating various types of projects and programs and ensuring the portfolio is balanced.
- Redefining, rebalancing, reclassifying, and reprioritising where necessary within the strategic planning and delivery process.
- Managing risk to the organisation and strategic delivery, through portfolio risk management, and the linkage to risk management in constituent projects and programs.

The future of strategic portfolio management

There is much more that can be achieved in recognising portfolio management within the organisational context and bridging the strategic connection to project and program management, firstly, perhaps, by further highlighting this change of mindset. Managing the strategic portfolio going forward for any business will be influenced by the external environment; developments including digital and artificial intelligence, sustainability, and corporate governance, to name a few, will have an influence on the future strategic direction of an organisation. Yet the principles of (strategic) portfolio management should not fundamentally alter as a result of future developments in this digital age, as managing change in an uncertain and complex or VUCA (volatile, uncertain, complex, and ambiguous) environment and continuously managing emergent strategy is expected to become the norm.

Glossary

ACE – Association of Consulting and Engineering
AHP – analytic hierarchy process
AI – artificial intelligence
AMP6 – Asset Management Program 6
APM – Association for Project Management
APP – approval
BAL – balancing
BI – business information
BIG – business integrated governance (a model developed by the Core P3M Club)
B2C – business to consumer
CAD/CAM – computer-aided design/computer-aided manufacturing
CAPEX – capital expenditure
CBS – cost breakdown structure
CDE – common data environment
CEO – chief executive officer
CEPI – coalition for epidemic preparedness innovations
CFO – chief financial officer
CI – continuous improvement
CIO – chief information officer
CL – classification
CM – capacity management
COGS – cost of goods sold
COTS – commercial off-the-shelf
CP – capacity planning
CR – collaborative relationship
CSO – chief strategy officer
CTO – chief transformation officer
DC – decision criteria
DCF – discounted cash flow
DEA – data envelopment analysis
Dfab – digital fabrication
DFMA – design for manufacture and assembly
DSS – decision support system
ECI – early contractor involvement
ERP – enterprise resource planning
EV – evaluation

E-NPV – expanded-net present value
FP – formalisation of portfolio
GIS – gas-insulated switchgear
GMP – good manufacturing practice
ID – investment delivery
IP – intellectual property
IPMS – integrated portfolio management system
IRR – internal rate of return
IT – information technology
IS – information system(s)
JIT – just in time
JV – joint venture
KPI – key performance indicator
KOC – knowledge about the organisational context
MHRA – Medicines and Healthcare products Regulatory Agency
MI – management information
MTP – medium-term plan
NDA – nuclear decommissioning authority
NPV – net present value
ODI – outcome-based delivery incentive
OEM – original equipment manufacturer
OFWAT – Water Services Regulation Authority
OI – opportunity identification
OPEX – operational expenditure
OPM3 – organisational project management maturity model
OTIG – opportunities, threats, imperatives, and goals
OTC – objectives, targets, and challenges
PBO – project-based organisation
PBS – product breakdown structure
PDG – portfolio definition group
PfM – portfolio management
PgM – program management
PjB – project (review) board
PjM – project management – an alternative term to PM
PLM – product life cycle management
PM –usually used to define project management
PPG – portfolio progress group
PgB – program (review) board
PMI – Project Management Institute
PMRP – program management of repetitive projects
PO – parent organisation
POTI – process, organisation, technology, and information
PPE – property, plant, and equipment
PPM – project portfolio management
PV – present value
P3M – portfolios, programs, and projects
P3M3 – portfolio, program, and project management maturity model
P4M – portfolio, program, project, and product

RA – resource allocation
RPM – revolutions/rotations per minute
RM – resource management
SC – supply chain
SCI – supply chain integration
SCM – supply chain management
SG&A – selling, general, and administrative
SMEs – subject matter experts
SP – strategic portfolio
SPM – strategic portfolio management (note SPM is also used in the context of single project management in Chapter 21)
SPMO – strategic portfolio management office
SPOS – selection, prioritisation, optimisation, and sequencing
TOC – theory of constraints
TOTEX – total expenditure
TMS – Toyota Management System
TQ – top quartile
TQM – total quality management
UCD – unit cost database
UKNAO – United Kingdom National Audit Office
USA – United States of America
VMOST – vision, mission, objectives, strategy, and tactics
VUCA – volatility, uncertainty, complexity, and ambiguity
WACC – weighted average cost of capital
WIP – work in progress
WBS – work breakdown structure
WEF – World Economic Forum

Index

Page numbers in *italics* indicate figures and page numbers in **bold** indicate tables.

Printed in the United States
by Baker & Taylor Publisher Services